THE AUTHORITATIVE HISTORIAN

In this volume an international group of scholars revisits the themes of John Marincola's groundbreaking *Authority and Tradition in Ancient Historiography*. The nineteen chapters offer a series of case studies that explore how ancient historians' approaches to their projects were informed both by the pull of tradition and by the ambition to innovate. The key themes explored are the relation of historiography to myth and poetry; the narrative authority exemplified by Herodotus, the 'father' of history; the use of 'fictional' literary devices in historiography; narratorial self-presentation; and self-conscious attempts to shape the historiographical tradition in new and bold ways. The volume presents a holistic vision of the development of Greco-Roman historiography and the historian's dynamic position within this practice.

K. SCARLETT KINGSLEY is an Assistant Professor of Classics at Agnes Scott College. Her research focuses on Greek historiography and philosophy, and she has published articles on Herodotus, Thucydides, and the Presocratics. She is finishing a monograph on Herodotus and intellectual culture, which was awarded a Loeb Classical Library Foundation Fellowship.

GIUSTINA MONTI is a Senior Lecturer in Classical Studies (Greek Culture) at the University of Lincoln. Her main research interests lie in Greek historiography, and she has published articles on Alexander the Great, Herodotus, and Polybius. She is the author of *Alexander the Great. Letters: A Selection* (2023).

TIM ROOD is a Professor of Greek Literature at the University of Oxford and Fellow and Tutor in Classics at St Hugh's College. He is the author of *Thucydides: Narrative and Explanation* (1998), *The Sea! The Sea!* (2004), *American Anabasis* (2010), and (with Carol Atack and Tom Phillips) *Anachronism and Antiquity* (2020). He is also the co-editor (with Luuk Huitink) of *Xenophon: Anabasis Book III* for the Cambridge Greek and Latin Classics series (2019).

THE AUTHORITATIVE HISTORIAN

Tradition and Innovation in Ancient Historiography

EDITED BY

K. SCARLETT KINGSLEY
Agnes Scott College

GIUSTINA MONTI
University of Lincoln

TIM ROOD
University of Oxford

Shaftesbury Road, Cambridge CB2 8EA, United Kingdom

One Liberty Plaza, 20th Floor, New York, NY 10006, USA

477 Williamstown Road, Port Melbourne, VIC 3207, Australia

314–321, 3rd Floor, Plot 3, Splendor Forum, Jasola District Centre, New Delhi – 110025, India

103 Penang Road, #05–06/07, Visioncrest Commercial, Singapore 238467

Cambridge University Press is part of Cambridge University Press & Assessment, a department of the University of Cambridge.

We share the University's mission to contribute to society through the pursuit of education, learning and research at the highest international levels of excellence.

www.cambridge.org
Information on this title: www.cambridge.org/9781009159456

DOI: 10.1017/9781009159463

© Cambridge University Press & Assessment 2022

This publication is in copyright. Subject to statutory exception and to the provisions of relevant collective licensing agreements, no reproduction of any part may take place without the written permission of Cambridge University Press & Assessment.

First published 2022

A catalogue record for this publication is available from the British Library.

Library of Congress Cataloging-in-Publication Data
NAMES: Kingsley, K. Scarlett, 1984- editor. | Monti, Giustina, 1981-editor. | Rood, Tim, 1969- editor.
TITLE: The authoritative historian : tradition and innovation in ancient historiography / edited by K. Scarlett Kingsley, Giustina Monti, Tim Rood.
DESCRIPTION: Cambridge, United Kingdom ; New York, NY : Cambridge University Press, [2022] | Includes bibliographical references and index.
IDENTIFIERS: LCCN 2022033168 (print) | LCCN 2022033169 (ebook) | ISBN 9781009159456 (hardback) | ISBN 9781009159449 (paperback) | ISBN 9781009159463 (epub)
SUBJECTS: LCSH: History, Ancient–Historiography.
CLASSIFICATION: LCC D56.A95 2022 (print) | LCC D56 (ebook) | DDC 930.1072/2–dc23/eng/20220720
LC record available at https://lccn.loc.gov/2022033168
LC ebook record available at https://lccn.loc.gov/2022033169

ISBN 978-1-009-15945-6 Hardback

Cambridge University Press & Assessment has no responsibility for the persistence or accuracy of URLs for external or third-party internet websites referred to in this publication and does not guarantee that any content on such websites is, or will remain, accurate or appropriate.

For John Marincola

Contents

List of Contributors	*page* x
Preface	xv
List of Abbreviations	xvi

Introduction: The Authoritative Historian   1
K. Scarlett Kingsley, Giustina Monti, and Tim Rood

PART I MYTH, FICTION, AND THE HISTORIAN'S AUTHORITY   17

1   Seven Types of Fiction in the Greek Historians   19
   Michael A. Flower

2   Folktale and Local Tradition in Charon of Lampsacus   41
   Nino Luraghi

3   Mythical and Historical Time in Herodotus: Scaliger, Jacoby,
   and the Chronographic Tradition   62
   Tim Rood

4   Myth and History in Livy's Preface   82
   A. J. Woodman

PART II DISLOCATING AUTHORITY IN HERODOTUS'
HISTORIES   99

5   Herodotus as Tour Guide: The Autopsy Motif   101
   Scott Scullion

6   Interpretive Uncertainty in Herodotus' *Histories*   121
   Carolyn Dewald

viii *Contents*

7 'It is no accident that . . .': Connectivity and Coincidence
in Herodotus 139
Richard Rutherford

8 Through Barbarian Eyes: Non-Greeks on Greeks
in Herodotus 157
Deborah Boedeker

PART III PERFORMING COLLECTIVE AND PERSONAL
AUTHORITY 177

9 Singing and Dancing Pindar's Authority 179
Lucia Athanassaki

10 Authority, Experience, and the Vicarious Traveller
in Herodotus' *Histories* 206
K. Scarlett Kingsley

11 *Veni, vidi, vici*: When Did Roman Politicians Use the
First-Person Singular? 224
Harriet I. Flower

12 Self-Praise and Self-Presentation in Plutarch 241
Frances B. Titchener

PART IV GENERIC TRANSFORMATIONS 259

13 Thucydides' Mytilenaean Debate: Political Philosophy
or Authoritative History? 261
Paul Cartledge

14 Tradition, Innovation, and Authority: Caesar's
Historical Ambitions 271
Kurt A. Raaflaub

15 Tradition and Authority in Philostratus' *Lives of the Sophists* 292
Ewen Bowie

PART V INNOVATION WITHIN TRADITION 313

16 'When one assumes the *ethos* of writing history': Polybius'
Historiographical Neologisms 315
Giustina Monti

Contents ix

17 How Tradition Is Formed: From the Fall of Caesar
to the Rise of Octavian 335
Mark Toher

18 Burn Baby Burn (*Disco* in Furneaux): Tacitean Authority,
Innovation, and the Neronian Fire (*Annals* 15.38–9) 353
Rhiannon Ash

19 The Authority to Be Untraditional 373
Christopher Pelling

Bibliography 392
Index Locorum 448
General Index 467

Contributors

RHIANNON ASH is Professor of Roman Historiography and Fellow and Tutor in Classics, Merton College, Oxford. She publishes widely on Latin prose narratives, especially Tacitus, including *Ordering Anarchy: Armies and Leaders in Tacitus' Histories* (1999) and two commentaries in the Cambridge 'green and yellow' series on Tacitus, *Histories* 2 (2007) and Tacitus, *Annals* 15 (2018). Her wider research interests embrace ancient epistles, Greek and Roman biography, battle narratives, paradoxography, Cicero, Sallust, Livy, Pliny the Elder (on whom she is currently writing a monograph), and Pliny the Younger.

LUCIA ATHANASSAKI is Professor of Classical Philology at the University of Crete. She has published extensively on Greek (and occasionally on Latin) lyric and Greek tragedy with emphasis on the dialogue of poetry with material culture. Lately she has been drawn to Imperial Greek literature, Plutarch in particular. She is the author of Ἀείδετο πᾶν τέμενος. Οι χορικές παραστάσεις και το κοινό τους στην αρχαϊκή και πρώιμη κλασική περίοδο (2009). She is co-editor of *Apolline Politics and Poetics* (with R. P. Martin and J. F. Miller, 2009); *Archaic and Classical Choral Song: Performance, Politics and Dissemination* (with E. L. Bowie, 2011); Ιδιωτικός βίος και δημόσιος λόγος στην ελληνική αρχαιότητα και τον διαφωτισμό (with A. Nikolaidis and D. Spatharas, 2014); *Gods and Mortals in Greek and Latin Poetry: Studies in Honor of J. Strauss Clay* (with C. Nappa and A. Vergados, 2018); and *Plutarch's Cities* (with F. B. Titchener, 2022). She is presently co-editing a volume titled *Lyric and the Sacred* (with A. Lardinois) and working on a book on Euripides.

DEBORAH BOEDEKER is Professor Emerita of Classics at Brown University; from 1992 to 2000, together with Kurt Raaflaub, she co-directed Harvard's Center for Hellenic Studies. Her publications include *Aphrodite's Entry into Greek Epic* (1973); *Herodotus and the Invention of History* (1987); *Democracy, Empire, and the Arts in Fifth-Century Athens*

List of Contributors xi

(co-edited with Kurt Raaflaub, 1998); *The New Simonides: Contexts of Praise and Desire* (co-edited with David Sider, 2001); and other monographs, articles, and edited volumes on Greek historiography, religion, and poetry (epic, lyric, elegy, tragedy). Her current work focuses on Herodotus and Hipponax.

EWEN BOWIE, an Emeritus Fellow of Corpus Christi College, Oxford, formerly was its Praelector in Classics from 1965 to 2007, and successively University Lecturer, Reader, and Professor of Classical Languages and Literature in Oxford University. He has written on early Greek elegiac, iambic, and melic poetry; Aristophanes; Herodotus; Hellenistic poetry; and many aspects of Greek literature and culture under the Roman Empire. He has published a commentary on Longus, *Daphnis and Chloe* (2019); edited a collection entitled *Herodotus: Narrator, Scientist, Historian* (2018); and co-edited collections entitled *Archaic and Classical Choral Song* (2011) and *Philostratus* (2009). His collected papers (three volumes) are being published by Cambridge University Press with the title *Essays in Ancient Greek Literature and Culture*; the first volume appeared in 2021.

PAUL CARTLEDGE is A. G. Leventis Senior Research Fellow, Clare College, Cambridge University, and A. G. Leventis Professor of Greek Culture emeritus, Cambridge University. He is the author, co-author, editor, or co-editor of some thirty books, most recently *Democracy: A Life* (2018) and *Thebes: Forgotten City of Ancient Greece* (2021). He is President of the Society for the Promotion of Hellenic Studies, UK. He is a Commander of the Order of Honour, Hellenic Republic, and an Honorary Citizen of Sparti, Greece.

CAROLYN DEWALD, currently retired, taught Classics for many years at the University of Southern California, and then Ancient History and Classics at Bard College. She is the author of *Thucydides' War Narrative: A Structural Study* (2005) and the Introduction and Notes to the Oxford World's Classics translation of Herodotus (1998). With John Marincola she co-edited the *Cambridge Companion to Herodotus* (2006), and she has written a variety of articles on the Greek historians.

HARRIET I. FLOWER, Andrew Fleming West Professor of Classics, Princeton University, has published on Roman social and cultural history, in both the republican and imperial periods. Her books include *Ancestor Masks and Aristocratic Power in Roman Culture* (1996), *The Art of Forgetting: Disgrace and Oblivion in Roman Political Culture* (2006), xii *List of Contributors*

Roman Republics (2010), and *The Dancing Lares and the Serpent in the Garden: Religion at the Roman Street Corner* (2017).

MICHAEL A. FLOWER is the David Magie '97 Class of 1897 Professor of Classics at Princeton University. He is the author of *Theopompus of Chios: History and Rhetoric in the Fourth Century BC* (1986), *The Seer in Ancient Greece* (2008), and *Xenophon's Anabasis, or The Expedition of Cyrus* (2012). He is the co-editor (with Mark Toher) of *Georgica: Greek Studies in Honour of George Cawkwell* (1991) and the editor of *The Cambridge Companion to Xenophon* (2017). With John Marincola he edited *Herodotus, Histories, Book IX* for the series Cambridge Greek and Latin Classics (2002).

K. SCARLETT KINGSLEY is an assistant professor of Classics at Agnes Scott College. Her research focuses upon fifth-century historiography and philosophy. She is currently finishing a monograph, *Herodotus and the Presocratics: Inquiry and Intellectual Culture in the Fifth Century*. Her upcoming book project (co-authored with Tim Rood), *The End of the Histories: Land, Wealth, and Empire in Herodotus*, explores the end of the *Histories* and its relation to contemporary debates on these themes and their reception.

NINO LURAGHI is the Wykeham Professor of Ancient (Greek) History at the University of Oxford. He specializes in Greek historiography, tyranny, ethnicity, and the history of the ancient Peloponnese. His publications include *Tirannidi arcaiche in Sicilia e Magna Grecia* (1994) and *The Ancient Messenians: Constructions of Ethnicity and Memory* (2008). He edited *The Historian's Craft in the Age of Herodotus* (2001), *Helots and Their Masters in Laconia and Messenia* (with S. Alcock, 2004), *The Politics of Ethnicity and the Crisis of the Peloponnesian League* (with P. Funke, 2009), and *The Splendors and Miseries of Ruling Alone* (2013).

GIUSTINA MONTI is Senior Lecturer in Classical Studies (Greek Culture) and Joint Programme Leader for the BA in Classical Studies at the University of Lincoln. Her main research interests lie in Greek historiography, and she has published articles on Alexander the Great, Herodotus, and Polybius. She is the author of *Alexander the Great. Letters: A Selection* (2023).

CHRISTOPHER PELLING is Emeritus Regius Professor of Greek at Oxford University. Among his books are *Literary Texts and the Greek Historian* (2000), *Plutarch and History* (2002), *Twelve Voices from Greece and Rome:*

List of Contributors

Ancient Ideas for Modern Times (with Maria Wyke, 2014), *Herodotus and the Question Why* (2019), and commentaries on Plutarch, *Lives of Antony* (1988) and *Caesar* (2011), Herodotus 6 (with Simon Hornblower, 2017), and Thucydides 6 and Thucydides 7 (2022).

KURT A. RAAFLAUB is David Herlihy University Professor and Professor of Classics and History emeritus at Brown University. From 1992 to 2000 he was co-director of the Center for Hellenic Studies in Washington, DC, and from 2005 to 2008 the Royce Family Professor for Teaching Excellence at Brown. He is the author of *Dignitatis contentio: Studien zur Motivation und politischen Taktik im Bürgerkrieg zwischen Caesar und Pompeius* (1974) and *The Discovery of Freedom in Ancient Greece* (rev. English ed., 2004), co-author of *Origins of Democracy in Ancient Greece* (2007), co-editor of *Democracy, Empire, and the Arts in Fifth-Century Athens* (1998) and *Between Republic and Empire: Interpretations of Augustus and His Principate* (1990), and editor of (among several other volumes) *Social Struggles in Archaic Rome: New Perspectives on the Conflict of the Orders* (expanded and updated ed., 2005), *War and Peace in the Ancient World* (2007), *Peace in the Ancient World: Concepts and Theories* (2016), and *The Adventure of the Human Intellect: Self, Society, and the Divine in Ancient World Cultures* (2016).

TIM ROOD is Professor of Greek Literature and Dorothea Gray Fellow and Tutor in Classics at St Hugh's College, Oxford. He is the author of *Thucydides: Narrative and Explanation* (1998); *The Sea! The Sea! The Shout of the Ten Thousand in the Modern Imagination* (2004); *American Anabasis: Xenophon and the Idea of America from the Mexican War to Iraq* (2010); and (with Carol Atack and Tom Phillips) *Anachronism and Antiquity* (2020). With Luuk Huitink he has edited *Xenophon: Anabasis Book III* (2019) for the Cambridge Greek and Latin Classics series.

RICHARD RUTHERFORD is Professor of Greek and Latin Literature at Oxford and Tutor in Classics at Christ Church, Oxford. Among his publications are commentaries on Homer, *Iliad* 18 (2019) and *Odyssey* 19 and 20 (1992), *The Art of Plato* (1995), and *Greek Tragic Style* (2012). He has a long-standing interest in ancient historiography and has published papers on Herodotus, Thucydides, and Tacitus.

SCOTT SCULLION is Fellow and Tutor in Classics, Worcester College, University of Oxford. He works primarily and has published widely on Greek religion; Greek literature, especially tragedy; and Greek textual criticism.

List of Contributors

FRANCES B. TITCHENER is Distinguished Professor of Classics and History and Director of the Classics Program at Utah State University. She was a Fulbright Research Fellow in Leuven Belgium (2003) as well as a Visiting Scholar at the University of Crete in Rethymno (2017) and is currently Secretary of the International Plutarch Society and co-editor of the journal *Ploutarchos*. She is the co-editor of numerous volumes on Plutarch or Plutarch scholars, and co-editor of the volumes *Plutarch's Cities* (2022) and *The Cambridge Companion to Plutarch* (2023).

MARK TOHER is Frank Bailey Professor of Classics (emeritus) at Union College. He is the author of *Nicolaus of Damascus: The Life of Augustus and the Autobiography* (2017) and of articles and essays on Greek and Roman history and historiography.

A. J. WOODMAN, BASIL L. GILDERSLEEVE Professor of Classics Emeritus at the University of Virginia and Emeritus Professor of Latin at Durham University, is currently Visiting Professor at Newcastle University. He is author or co-author of 'orange' commentaries on Velleius Paterculus (1977, 1983) and Tacitus, *Annals* Books 3 (1996), 4 (2018), and 5–6 (2016), and likewise of 'green and yellow' commentaries on Tacitus, *Annals* 4 (1989) and *Agricola* (2014), and Horace, *Odes* 3 (2021). He is author of *Rhetoric in Classical Historiography* (1988), *Tacitus Reviewed* (1998), *From Poetry to History: Selected Papers* (2012), and *Lost Histories: Selected Fragments of Roman Historical Writers* (2015), co-author of *Latin Historians* (1997), and translator of Tacitus' *Annals* (2004) and Sallust (2007). Currently, he is writing a commentary on Sallust's *Bellum Catilinae* for the series Cambridge Greek and Latin Classics, preparing a new edition and translation of Velleius Paterculus for the Loeb Classical Library, and working on a new edition of Tacitus' *Annals* for the series Oxford Classical Texts.

Preface

The contributors to this volume are all friends and colleagues of John Marincola, formerly Leon Golden Professor of Classics at Florida State University, who is widely seen as one of the most influential students of ancient historiography in our time. All but four of them were participants in *Revisiting Authority and Tradition in Ancient Historiography*, a conference held in Marincola's honour in Martina Franca, Puglia, Italy, in April 2019; another speaker, Christina Kraus, was prevented by other commitments from contributing. The brief for the conference participants was to return to the themes of Marincola's groundbreaking *Authority and Tradition in Ancient Historiography*, which was published by Cambridge University Press in 1997; our Introduction sets that monograph in some of its intellectual contexts and briefly explores how its themes have been pursued in subsequent scholarship, much of it indebted to the wide-ranging perspectives opened by Marincola.

We are extremely grateful to the late Nicola Leone (honorary president, founder, and former CEO of Carton Pack) for sponsoring the conference and so helping to create in a *masseria* in the hills above Bari a truly (and almost *trulli*) friendly and hospitable spirit in keeping with the character of the honorand. We were delighted to be joined, too, by John's wife, Laurel Fulkerson. All the participants would like to join one of the editors in thanking the other two, Giustina Monti and Scarlett Kingsley, both former students of John's at FSU, for their initiative in organizing the conference, and Giustina for her local expertise in Puglia. At Cambridge University Press we would like to thank Michael Sharp and his team for their willingness to take on a substantial edited volume of this kind and their efficiency in dealing with it, and also the press's readers for their helpful reports on the draft typescript. Moreover, we were greatly assisted by Flavio Santini at Berkeley in preparation of the indexes, and we are grateful to Agnes Scott College for providing the funding for this. But above all we join the other contributors in offering this small token of gratitude to John for his warmth, humour, and friendship.

K.S.K., G.M., T.C.B.R.
October 2021

Decatur, Lincoln, Oxford

Abbreviations

For ancient authors, we follow the abbreviations used by *The Oxford Classical Dictionary*. Abbreviations for journal titles follow *L'Année Philologique*.

CIL   *Corpus Inscriptionum Latinarum* (Berlin, 1893–).

DK   H. Diels (ed.), *Die Fragmente der Vorsokratiker*[6], 3 vols., rev. W. Kranz (Berlin, 1951–2).

FHG   C. Müller, *Fragmenta Historicorum Graecorum*, 5 vols. (Paris, 1841–70).

FRHist   T. J. Cornell, E. Bispham, J. W. Rich, and C. J. Smith (eds.), *The Fragments of the Roman Historians*, 3 vols. (Oxford, 2013).

GE   F. Montanari et al. (eds.), *The Brill Dictionary of Ancient Greek* (Leiden, 2015).

ILLRP   A. Degrassi (ed.), *Inscriptiones Latinae Liberae Rei Publicae*, vol. 1[2] (Berlin, 1965), vol. 2 (Florence, 1963).

ILS   H. Dessau, *Inscriptiones Latinae Selectae* (Berlin, 1892–1916).

LSJ   H. G. Liddell and R. Scott, *A Greek-English Lexicon*[9], revised and augmented by H. Stuart Jones, with the assistance of R. McKenzie (Oxford, 1996).

PMGF   M. Davies (ed.), *Poetarum Melicorum Graecorum Fragmenta* I (Oxford, 1991).

SEG   J. J. Hondius et al. (eds.), *Supplementum Epigraphicum Graecum*, 66 vols. to date (Leiden, 1923–).

Introduction
The Authoritative Historian

K. Scarlett Kingsley, Giustina Monti, and Tim Rood

> Historiography differs ... in that it also contains commentary on the narrative by the historian himself: here the narrator employs an 'artificial authority' by which he interprets the events in his work for the reader, and explicitly directs the reader to think in a certain manner.
>
> —John Marincola, *Authority and Tradition in Ancient Historiography*

I

The ancient historian's privileged discursive position within the text depends upon the creation of a circuit of consent with the audience, one that establishes the narrator's power and authority in detailing the unfolding of past events, their causes, and the agents animating them. The contract between the narrator and audience is brought about by the careful curation of the historian's agency in and out of the process of textual production. In antiquity, the stakes for this curation were even higher than in modernity because of the widespread association of literary production with individual character. The struggle for authority was uniquely pressing for Greek and Roman historians, as their texts could not call upon the inspiration of the Muse as the poets could. As a result, the self-positioning of the historian was highly self-aware and charged with meaning, constructed in relation to the authority of the poets, but with a degree of distancing from these figures and their Muse in the development of a new mode of narrative.

The modern study of the creation of authority within the genre of historiography has its roots in two strands of scholarship arising in the latter half of the twentieth century: first, in the critical methodologies pioneered on the effects that texts create for their readers and the importance of interaction of the text and audience in the process of interpretation; second, in the rise of the rhetorical school of historiography, according to which ancient history was, like poetry and oratory, a species of rhetoric.

The significance of the relation between the text and its readership was popularized beginning in the 1970s by the German literary scholar Wolfgang Iser, the father of reader response theory. According to Iser, the text/narrator alone cannot determine interpretation; this interpretation rests in the liminal space between the text/narrator and its reader. The way in which texts/narrators determine their own interpretative horizons was pushed further in 1984 by the narrative theorist Ross Chambers in *Story and Situation: Narrative Seduction and the Power of Fiction*. This work examines the intersection of the theory of narrative and of textual interpretation. In it, the storyteller and audience are connected in an underlying negotiation of power through the 'art' of seduction. The reliance on narrative manipulation through seduction is, for Chambers, a distinctive component of fiction itself, whose authority arises from the production of art rather the dissemination of information.[1] The focus on the negotiation of power between text/narrator and the reader in fiction provided a critical language to approach works of non-fiction, including those centred on the transmission of 'information', such as historiography.

A further intellectual movement contributing to the study of ancient historians' claims to authority rests in the alliance of rhetoric with historiography. From T. P. Wiseman's *Clio's Cosmetics* in 1979 to A. J. Woodman's *Rhetoric in Classical Historiography* in 1988, ancient historiography witnessed a seismic shift away the hunt for 'what actually happened' and toward its representation in narrative.[2] The literary techniques familiar from oratory and poetry quickened the study of historiography. Even with the subsequent recognition that ancient historians aimed at truth in a way that poets and orators did not have to, it has continued to be productive to attend to the narrative strategies they deployed to reproduce it.[3] It is the confluence of these two academic movements that gave rise to the study of the rhetorical strategies that Greek and Roman historians use to arouse readerly consent.

The title of this volume harks back to what is the gold standard of such research, John Marincola's 1997 *Authority and Tradition in Ancient Historiography*. That monograph reinforced the emerging consensus on the forms of persuasion that historians deployed in the literary

---

[1] Chambers (1984), 207.
[2] Brunt (1993), for the preceding tradition that these two scholars were building on.
[3] For the discussion of impartiality and truth, Marincola (1997), 158–74.

Introduction: The Authoritative Historian 3

composition of the past, even as it innovated by expanding literary criticism's concern for the distribution of the authority between the fictional text/narrator and audience to historical narrative. With the recognition that the ontological status of history as the past was not sufficient to 'seduce' (to use Chambers' language) the reader, this work looked to the generic conventions by which Greek and Roman historians cultivated consent: it canvassed the 'call to Clio', the use of contemporary and non-contemporary evidence, self-presentation as a historical agent, and self-positioning in the tradition as a continuator or innovator. Moreover, Greek and Roman historical writing was viewed as part of a single tradition.

In this respect, Marincola moved well beyond the conclusions of his advisor, Charles William Fornara, who had influentially argued for the importance of distinguishing the labour-intensive research undertaken by the Greek historians from their Roman counterparts, who were generally statesmen. The latter relied upon their own participation in politics and on the more circumscribed project of recording the history of Rome. Fornara held that it was the Roman historian for whom a specifically political and institutional *auctoritas* was essential. By contrast, he states of Herodotus, and Greek history by extension, 'the work was all and the writer little'.[4]

The success of *Authority and Tradition* can in part be measured by its continuing prominence in discussions on ancient historiography.[5] More recently, its impact has been felt by those investigating the construction of authority in non-historiographical genres, including the Hippocratic corpus and poetic verse.[6] Outside of classics, it has galvanized research in biblical and Byzantine studies.[7] The current volume also takes its cue from *Authority and Tradition* by surveying the effects of authority in the long arc of the Greek and Roman historiographical tradition, with historians ranging from the fifth century BC to the third century AD. Narrative histories form the central core of the contributions, but the contributors also examine related genres, such as mythography, local history, biography

---

[4] Fornara (1983), 54; for the discussion of the two traditions, 47–61.

[5] Cartledge and Greenwood (2002); Akujärvi (2005); Rood (2006b); Bradley (2010); Grethlein (2012); Roche (2016).

[6] On the Hippocratic corpus, Massar (2010). For its stimulation of a discussion of self-authorization in verse, J. Barrett (2002); Kahane (2005); Calame (2005); Mitsis and Tsagalis (2010); Morrison (2011); Bakker (2017).

[7] For authority in the New Testament, Moles (2011); Strelan (2013). In Byzantine studies, Armstrong (2013); Lilie (2014). For a broader survey of authority from antiquity to the Renaissance, Ceulemans and de Leemans (2015).

and autobiography, and the *commentarius*.[8] Individual chapters target the narrator's authority as *Authority and Tradition* did, but also the effects of the text as a whole in seducing the reader. At the same time, it embraces a broad set of critical approaches, including narratology, reader response theory, reception studies, and cognitive science. Further, it takes as essential to this project the productive tension maintained by ancient historians in their adherence to convention and their simultaneous innovation within it.

In the wake of post-structuralism's internment of the author, however, it may appear somewhat retrograde to return now to the figure of the historian as the producer of the text and a privileged site of authority. Yet in recent decades feminist narratology has productively re-examined the relation of the narrator to authority in the modern novel as a response to the gender-neutral analysis of traditional narratology. First, this research has complicated the strict separation of the author from the narrator, which has been taken to be foundational, on the grounds that the narrator's authorial voice is a performative commentary upon the kinds of authority espoused by the author.[9] The return to the narrating author in feminist narratology has stressed the fact that the narrator effects the 'structural and functional situation of authorship' for the audience, which has important implications for the negotiation of authority in narrative.[10] Second, it has emphasized the way in which discursive authority is shaped by a narrative's power relations in rhetorical and sociocultural terms. For feminist narratologists, this has presented an invitation to examine how marginalized voices respond to and challenge a patriarchal model of narrative authority. Such research has found that marginalized authors adopt, adapt, and subvert the dominant rhetoric of authority. As Susan Lanser has expressed it, this requires 'standing on the very ground one is attempting to deconstruct'.[11]

This critical methodology has been successfully applied to fiction, but the return to narrative authority may offer even greater advantages to historiography, where the narrator and implied author collapse into one another and where narrators are bidding for canonical status.[12] As has long been noted, the ancient historian's narratorial self-consciousness presents a crucial difference from the more anonymous narratorial voice of epic. In a

---

[8] For history's relationship to related genres, including geography and biography, Clarke (1999); Pigoń (2008); Hägg (2012).

[9] Lanser (1992); Nünning (2012); Birke (2015).   [10] Lanser (1992), 16.   [11] Lanser (1992), 7.

[12] For the return of the author, Lamarque (1990); Birriotti and Miller (1993); Woodmansee and Jaszi (1994); Simion (1996).

Introduction: The Authoritative Historian 5

sense, this urges a return to Fornara and his recognition of the importance of the extratextual, lived experience of the historian as an essential component to laying claim to authority. Beyond the *auctoritas* of the Roman statesman-historian, however, Greek historians were also appealing to their own autobiographical bona fides. Certainly, it is present in Polybius' near-unrivalled access to the levers of Roman political power, but doesn't Thucydides too give his reader a window in his post-exile activities for his own protreptic purpose (5.26)?

Positioning historiography within feminist narratology's return to the author will simultaneously enrich the modern discourse of self-authorization; as we shall see, even within the dominant paradigm of elite male authorship, authority is part of a continual and contested negotiation, often consisting of construction and deconstruction in turn.[13] Further, narratorial self-fashioning is internal to historical works and also part of a diachronic dialogue with predecessors and successors. In a different way, this dialogue extends into our present, as historical authority is dependent on and formulated in response to readerly expectations. For this reason, at stake in this volume is not an essentialist project dedicated to restoring authorial intention to historiography, but a set of readerly responses on the conditions of authorial self-fashioning and the power dynamics operating within historical texts.

II

The chapters that follow take as their point of departure *Authority and Tradition in Ancient Historiography* and the contexts in which ancient historians shored up authority and operated within and beyond their generic margins. The historical works range in time and space, but the chapters have been assembled based on the themes that they share. In Part I, 'Myth, Fiction, and the Historian's Authority', the volume begins by challenging the position that the ancient historian's establishment of authority places him in opposition to fiction, the folktale, and myth.

In Chapter 1, 'Seven Types of Fiction in the Greek Historians', Michael A. Flower examines the apparent paradox in historiography's rhetoric of truth and accuracy in its establishment of authority and its simultaneous use of 'fictional' devices familiar from the modern novel to narrate past events. These include the invention of speeches, exaggeration of

---

[13] Our own approach avoids the critique of the gender binary presumed by this movement, for which Page (2006).

methodological rigour, imaginative elaboration of gaps in the record, omissions, manipulation of chronology, attribution of motivation on the basis of likelihood, and the creation of patterns in events to explain historical change. The chapter investigates these aesthetic choices and the kinds of truth they produce and the authority they espouse.

If fiction cannot be disentangled from ancient historiography, neither can the folktale. Nino Luraghi analyzes the two in Chapter 2, 'Folktale and Local Tradition in Charon of Lampsacus'. The fifth-century historian's integration of the folktale presents a neglected avenue for gaining insight into the transformation of oral tradition into historical narrative. Luraghi offers evidence for rationalized folktales in the fragments of Charon's local history and uses this in support of the significance of oral storytelling culture in the writing of early Greek history. His conclusion turns to Herodotus and the attractions and drawbacks of his traditional 'splendid isolation'.

Tim Rood brings Herodotus to centre stage in Chapter 3, 'Mythical and Historical Time in Herodotus: Scaliger, Jacoby, and the Chronographic Tradition', which scrutinizes the opposition of myth and history in the *Histories*. Rood's argument complicates the temporal demarcations of 'myth' and 'history' by revealing the relative novelty of the *spatium mythicum* and *historicum*. After tracing the terms and their concepts in the scholarship of Felix Jacoby, Joseph Justus Scaliger, and ultimately Varro's tripartite division of time, Rood shows that Varro and ancient historians' use of the 'mythical' as a temporality is more nuanced than has been previously recognized. Significantly, Herodotus' own language of myth relies on its traditional associations with authoritative speech in order to reject it, but not on the grounds of its position in chronology.

How the opposition of myth and history develops in the Roman tradition of historiography is the subject of Chapter 4, A. J. Woodman's 'Myth and History in Livy's Preface'. Woodman approaches the apparent separation of *poeticae fabulae* (poetic fables prior to the founding of Rome) from *rerum gestarum monumenta* (hard historical facts after its founding). A close reading of Livy's preface, however, complicates this division. 'Before the founding' blurs into the more nebulous 'process of the founding' and both elicit narratorial neutrality, not rejection. Livy draws attention to the indulgence required of foundation narratives involving mortal-divine couplings, in an allusion to Romulus' divine paternity. Woodman determines that this reference undermines the common reading according to which Roman history proper begins only with the founding of the city; instead of a chronological qualification, Livy's is a thematic one

Introduction: The Authoritative Historian

based on divine-human interaction. This chapter concludes the section's theme of re-examining the temporal borders of historiography even as it references divine-human interaction, in a return to the opening discussion of history's relation to fiction.

As historians engage with fiction, oral tradition, and 'myth' to bolster their own authoritative stance in their narrative histories, likewise, the historical narrator plays a key role in the construction of persuasive history. Part II, 'Dislocating Authority in Herodotus' *Histories*', focuses on the narratorial persona of the first fully extant historian, Herodotus. As Marincola noted in *Authority and Tradition*, in comparison with epic Herodotus innovates by crafting a highly intrusive first-person narrator. In light of the historian's collapsing of the author/narrator distinction (for which, see Pelling, Chapter 19 in this volume), these chapters illustrate how Herodotus' authority-effects extend beyond first-person commentary and gesture to his establishment of a highly interactive and intersubjective authority, one that engages the audience in the creation of meaning through the use of ambiguity, irony, polyphony, and causal puzzles such as coincidence. The historian's credibility arises, then, from the seduction of the reader as symmetrical collaborator.

Chapter 5, Scott Scullion's 'Herodotus as Tour Guide: The Autopsy Motif' opens this part with an exploration of Herodotean ambiguity and irony in the historian's use of autopsy statements. Scullion examines the 'autopsy motif' in cases of apparent eyewitness accounting that beggar belief. Classic examples include Herodotus' viewing of thin Persian skulls on the battlefield or of skeletons of flying snakes, which have long inspired impassioned defence or critique from scholars of the *Histories*. To explain these episodes, Scullion revisits the infamous suggestion made by Detlev Fehling that Herodotus was willing to invent episodes wholesale. However, he departs from Fehling in his contention that Herodotus' language signals virtual tour-guiding, as it relies on oral sources rather than invention. As he argues, the autopsy motif enhances the immediacy of Herodotus' text and bolsters its authority. In line with the earlier contributions of Flower and Luraghi, this challenges modern, anachronistic expectations of the critical methodologies used by ancient historians.

Ambiguity and irony structure more than first-person claims to autopsy, as Carolyn Dewald shows in Chapter 6, 'Interpretive Uncertainty in Herodotus' *Histories*'. Ambiguity presents itself to Herodotus' audience in his use of irony and narrative glosses, and by paradoxical statements made by the narrator and the historical actors. Equally important in this regard are the interpretive circuits and intra-textual references generated by the unfolding narrative of the *Histories* itself. These circuits, Dewald maintains, at times disrupt apparently stable causal sequences. Dewald explains this interpretive indeterminacy by reflecting on the historian's considered understanding of time and human language. The instability inherent in change in time motivates Herodotus' introduction of ambiguity from the proem onward, where cities large and small enter his purview. Human language too has its limits in communicating reality and forms the second stimulus for Herodotus' embedding of ambiguity. The chorus of voices that populate the *Histories* works to resist any coherent, but ultimately illusory whole.

Chapter 7, Richard Rutherford's '"It is no accident that ...".: Connectivity and Coincidence in Herodotus', advances the discussion of causation in the *Histories* by considering the historian's combination of apparently unconnected events to produce coincidences. Rutherford follows Herodotus' interest in connections between space, peoples, customs, and beliefs. Coincidences call for explanation (Herodotus draws upon both human and divine causes), but they can also elicit the historian's suspension of judgement. Such uncertainty creates inconsistency in Herodotus' approach, as at times coincidence is attributed to the divine, while on other occasions the narrator keeps ostentatiously aloof from such extra-terrestrial causal paradigms. Discussion of chance and necessity were, significantly, prominent in fifth-century Presocratic circles, and they continued to preoccupy later philosophers, including Aristotle. In his conclusion, Rutherford calls attention to the difficulty of placing Herodotus either within this intellectual tradition or within the alternative tradition of traditional belief in the divine.

Chapter 8, 'Through Barbarian Eyes: Non-Greeks on Greeks in Herodotus', by Deborah Boedeker, turns to the polyphonic style of the *Histories* and the way in which the historian embeds foreign peoples' cultural commentary on the Greeks against the authoritative backdrop of his own narrative. Of course, negative judgements on Greek customs can prove highly tendentious, and instead illustrate the self-interestedness of some foreign appraisers of Greece. Yet, as Boedeker shows, ethnographic observation on the Greeks may be entirely justified; it may also reflect domestic critique in the voice of the 'Other'. Further, it can operate as a distorted mirror, showcasing Greece's exoticism to itself. Finally, Greece is revealed to itself by insider-outsiders, such as the exiled Spartan ruler Demaratus, and Artemisia, ruler of Halicarnassus and Persian subject. The measure of all such cultural commentary is, Boedeker finds, the authority of the narrative of the *Histories* itself.

Introduction: The Authoritative Historian   9

In the context of narrative authority, the polyphony of voices in the *Histories* serves as a valuable counterweight to the narrator's own first-person comments. Part III of this volume, 'Performing Collective and Personal Authority', delves into this negotiation of power through the manipulation of point-of-view in narrative by investigating choral, first-, and second-person speech.

Chapter 9, 'Singing and Dancing Pindar's Authority', by Lucia Athanassaki, visits the subject of poetic authority in Pindar's choral compositions. The plurality of the choral voice complicates the straightforward authority assured by the intimate relationship of the solo poet with the Muse. Athanassaki underscores the heightened prominence of the Graces in these compositions, in addition to the Muses, and argues for the authority of these songs as constituted by an audiovisual spectacle that embraces melody, movement, and lyrics. The shared authority in this model has important implications for early Greek historiography, which similarly relied upon a community of voices in the oral tradition.

The volumes shifts from the choral voice to that of the narratee in Chapter 10. K. Scarlett Kingsley's 'Authority, Experience, and the Vicarious Traveller in Herodotus' *Histories*' takes the reader as its subject and Herodotus' *Histories*' embedding of second-person virtual experience into the narrative as a strategy of producing interactive authority. Recent narratological and cognitive approaches to second-person narration have found that it generates uniquely vivid mental simulations of space and spatial relationships. This methodological background is then leveraged against the *Histories*, where the enfranchisement of the narratee leads to the virtual confirmation of the historian's conclusions. It is noteworthy that second-person narration creates readerly simulations in regions where Herodotus' first-person autopsy explicitly dries up; in these areas, hearsay is translated into second-person embodied, virtual travel. The narratee adds an additional layer to the prior section's exploration of the contractual nature of Herodotus' structuring of authority: the actual reader's role is not only implicitly present in the integration of ambiguity, irony, and causal puzzles; it is modelled in the explicit integration of the second-person narratee as well.

With Chapter 11, '*Veni, vidi, vici*: When Did Roman Politicians Use the First-Person Singular?', by Harriet Flower, the volume contextualizes the uses of the first person in experimental Roman memoirs. Of course, by Cicero's day, the former consul could affirm that a third-person account of his achievements would be more authoritative than a first-person one. Caesar seems to have had similar sentiments in light of his third-person dispatches. However, Flower argues that prescriptions against the first person were not always present in the Roman rhetorical imaginary: the first person had a brief but notable efflorescence in the autobiographical writings of several prominent senators in the early first century BC. The issue that animates Flower's contribution is thus the milieu that produces this phenomenon. Account books, legal documents, correspondence, epigrams, satire, epigraphy, and speeches all provide venues for first-person display. Indeed, it emerges as vital to the Roman politician's rhetorical arsenal, and experimentation with it as a politically advantageous gambit in the second century and beyond.

Chapter 12, Frances B. Titchener's 'Self-Praise and Self-Presentation in Plutarch', highlights another aspect of the centrality of the figure of the author and his desire to provide readers with a sort of *sphragis* that makes him recognizable. Titchener's essay draws inspiration from Marincola's categories for the techniques used by historians to build and advertise their own authority, but she applies them to the writings of the eclectic Plutarch. In doing so, Titchener goes beyond the classic Plutarchan work (*De se laudando*) that is typically used in scholarly discussions of self-praise. She highlights the way in which Plutarch, like many other historians, utilized self-presentation together with a deliberate and carefully managed self-praise to foster his authoritative voice.

The success of historiography's claims to authority are partially visible from its cross-fertilization with related genres. In Part IV, 'Generic Transformations', we transition to select genres adjacent to narrative history, including political philosophy, the *commentarius*, and biography. This part reflects on the interrelation of such categories and argues that their overlap validates the prospect of tracing historical authority in hybrid historical texts.

Chapter 13, Paul Cartledge's 'Thucydides' Mytilenaean Debate: Political Philosophy or Authoritative History?', surveys the vexed question of the relation of historical truth and embedded speeches by using the Mytilenaean debate in Athens in 427 BC as a case study. At stake in this scholarly debate is the status of Thucydides as historian (with a fundamental commitment to truth) or as a political philosopher (with a commitment to relating his own philosophy of political action). There are elements within the Mytilenaean debate that may hint at invention – for example, the shadowy figure of Diodotus; the neat political agenda recalling prior themes of fear, honour, and material interest; the speakers' dogged pragmatism; or the philosophical nature of the disquisition on the deterrence theory of punishment. Yet Cartledge counters such

Introduction: The Authoritative Historian 11

arguments by calling attention to the recent discovery of a *skyphos* with the name of a 'Diodotus' next to Pericles, and by revising the political circumstances that may have motivated Cleon's speech. Returning to Thucydides' rightful placement in either history or political philosophy, Cartledge demonstrates that, in important respects, he participates in both fields. A more nuanced view of tradition in historiography, then, pushes back against Thucydides as generically innovating away from history and toward what is more properly considered political philosophy, and instead indicates that it is modern conceptions of what his *History* is doing that will need to adapt to his project's intellectual dynamism.

Following Cartledge's assessment of the contact between political philosophy and Thucydidean historiography, Kurt A. Raaflaub considers the way in which narrative history enriches the *commentarius*. In Chapter 14, 'Tradition, Innovation, and Authority: Caesar's Historical Ambitions', he analyzes the military reports that constitute Caesar's *Gallic War* and outlines the ways in which the general co-opts characteristics from Greek narrative history – and Thucydidean historiography above all – to curate his authority and shape his reception in Rome.

What techniques, then, are taken from the historian's toolkit? Raaflaub discusses Caesar's choice of composing a third-person narrative rather than a first-person one to cultivate distance and objectivity. The *Gallic War* shows careful selectivity and omission in its structuring of events, which come to form self-contained sequences rather than strictly linear ones. Next, Caesar includes elaborate and at least partly fabricated direct and indirect speeches. Fiction has a hand in the reconstruction of events on the basis of probability too. Persistent themes running through the text bring a strong sense of unity and dramatic effect, which contribute to a gripping narrative experience. In Caesar's hands, the *commentarius* comes to be didactic, offering its audience exemplary models of his own making. In addition, his enemy is elevated and given a viewpoint, as events and decision-making play out on both sides of the field of war. Digressions, causality, and contingency all enter into the work. Time and distance are made imprecise, as Caesar largely avoids the day-to-day chronicle of events. Only the beginning of his war, Raaflaub argues, is given a precise date, much in the vein of Thucydides' *History*. The survey of historiographical praxis in the *Gallic War* is matched by the ways in which Caesar's *commentarius* remains distinct from historiography. It is best understood as an experimental, hybrid text. This finding sends us back, appropriately, to Cartledge's conclusions on Thucydides' own polygeneric *History*. For

Caesar, however, authority rests in the trappings of history's traditional narrative devices.

In Chapter 15, Ewen Bowie's 'Tradition and Authority in Philostratus' *Lives of the Sophists*', the rhetorical strategies that contribute to an authoritative narrator are central to understanding Philostratus' hybrid project, whether it is to be interpreted as history, biography, doxography, or a fusion of them all. According to Bowie, authority in the *Lives* is generated by a variety of tactics: the intrusive narrator claims knowledge; familiarity with the textual tradition (including quotations); eyewitness testimony; his own autopsy; and refers to hearsay. Additionally, Philostratus includes conflicting traditions, at times without comment or, more often, with an explicit denial of the validity of the information. He presents himself as a specialist on rhetoric and style and offers judgement on his contemporaries and predecessors on the basis of this knowledge. Contributing to this textual authority is the opening salvo in the introductory dedication to the proconsul, Antonius Gordianus. To clarify the role of the paratext, Bowie makes the case that the dedication lays claim to an even more influential brand of authority, one tied to Philostratus' sociopolitical standing in relation to Rome.

The preceding part relied on the concept of a stable rhetoric of historiography as a means of leveraging authority. However, as *Authority and Tradition* drew attention to in its investigation into the 'lonely historian', a strong current of innovation runs through historiography. With the concluding Part V, 'Innovation within Tradition', the contributors focus intentionally on departing from the shade of one's competitors to forge a place in the sun.

Chapter 16, Giustina Monti's '"When one assumes the *ethos* of writing history": Polybius' Historiographical Neologisms', examines historiographical digressions where Polybius comes up with words or expressions that he uses in a new way. Monti investigates how such expressions are reinvented and revisited by Polybius with the intention of establishing his own authority over his colleagues, and within the previous and well-populated historiographical tradition. Besides analyzing positive expressions, Monti explores how some of Polybius' historiographical neologisms are used to attack his predecessors and to flesh out a negative paradigm of the bad historian. She concludes that, in doing so, Polybius aims at forging his own philosophy of history and that he uses such neologisms to describe his new ideas on what historiography is about and how a historian should behave.

In Chapter 17, Mark Toher's 'How Tradition Is Formed: From the Fall of Caesar to the Rise of Octavian', he traces the creation of the tradition

Introduction: The Authoritative Historian 13

surrounding the year 44 BC through the descriptions of the death of Caesar and the early career of his successor, Octavian. The Ides of March and its aftermath is a case study in the way in which memorable events can be rhetorically embellished in light of the full view of their consequences. The evidence of Nicolaus of Damascus and Cicero is set alongside the later accounts of Appian and Dio, with the conclusion that the subsequent tradition departs from what preceded it in key aspects. This signals, Toher contends, the successful deformation of an earlier, more reliable narrative. He concludes that narratorial authority alone cannot produce a fixed historical tradition. Tradition consists, in this case, in underscoring the Roman imperial themes of *dignitas* and the liberation of the *res publica*.

The formation of historical tradition is also Rhiannon Ash's focus in Chapter 18, 'Burn Baby Burn (*Disco* in Furneaux): Tacitean Authority, Innovation, and the Neronian Fire (*Annals* 15.38–9)'. In this chapter, Ash looks to the way in which Tacitus' narrative artistry complicates the tradition on the infamous fire in AD 64. Narrating disaster has its own perils, including the need to elevate one's subject without falling prey to the temptations of 'tragic' history. While prior historians had relied upon emotional appeals and on fingering Nero as culprit, Tacitus emerges as a distinctive voice for his proliferation of factors contributing to the destruction of the city, including the importance of its topography and contingent weather phenomena. At the same time, through the historian's allusions to the paradigm case of a city devastated by fire, Troy, Tacitus subtly but effectively heightens the emotional appeal of the episode. By comparison with Suetonius and Cassius Dio, it is clear that Tacitus is shaping tradition on his own terms in one critical area, in his equivocal treatment of the role that Nero played in the catastrophe. Such treatment serves Tacitus' broader historiographical program of emphasizing the outsized influence of perception and rumour in directing Roman imperial history.

This part and the volume as a whole conclude, appropriately enough, with Christopher Pelling's Chapter 19, 'The Authority to Be Untraditional'. Pelling invites the reader into a consideration of what constitutes 'gamechanger' historians, those who move against tradition to set themselves apart. The gamechanger depends on engaging with tradition in order to transcend it. Thucydides' innovation on his predecessor, Herodotus, can be seen in his choice to compose contemporary history, with its expanded source materials. But while it is correct that Thucydides positions himself in opposition to Herodotus, Pelling carefully reveals how this interpretation masks a more nuanced picture. As examples,

Thucydides' narration of the tyrannicides is very much in keeping with Herodotus'. Stylistically as well as thematically, his first book returns again and again to the Halicarnassian. So, Pelling argues, innovation coexists with and is an outgrowth of successful emulation. Instead of rejecting Herodotus, Thucydides is more often concerned to 'out-Herodotus' him, as in his display piece in the *Archaeology* on how to do early Greek history.

Pelling uses Polybius as a second case study, charting three key innovations in his *Histories*. First, it showcases the way in which innovation in historiography is bound up with innovation in history. This interlinking is made exceptionally clear in Polybius' explanation of the unification of the inhabited world under Rome and its creation of a novel kind of historiography. Next, Polybius' work demonstrates the shifting sands of teleology in real time, as his work expands beyond the historian's initial plan to keep time with the changed political and moral condition. A third game change is Polybius' self-positioning within his history as historical actor in addition to his role as narrator.

These three Polybian themes set out the terms of the remainder of Pelling's chapter. He surveys a wide array of narrative historians, but settles ultimately on the biographies of Plutarch. As he observes, Plutarch is operating self-consciously within the tradition of historiography, although he ostentatiously rejects it for biography. His authority is best shored up by biography, rather than narrative history and its dangerous invitation to mime an anachronistic heroism.

III

At the close of *Authority and Tradition in Ancient Historiography*, John Marincola turned to consider the fourth-century AD *Res Gestae* of Ammianus Marcellinus and its 'homage and challenge' to the tradition of ancient Greek and Roman historiography of which it was a belated part.[14] Like Ammianus, this volume too aims at homage and is simultaneously a vehicle for the new questions that can be asked of authority and tradition in the wake of Marincola's seminal work. With *Authority and Tradition*, it canvasses a wide range of ancient historians and historical texts. It takes its place, however, alongside post-classical narratology's reimagination of the conceptual framework familiar from structuralist

---

[14] Marincola (1997), 257.

Introduction: The Authoritative Historian 15

theories of narrative.[15] The contributors offer a variety of approaches, which will contribute, we hope, to the continuing vitality of this subject matter.

How does the historian's authority emerge from this inquiry? First, ancient historiography is not straightforwardly opposed to fiction, myth, or orality. In key aspects, it is enriched by them. These conclusions deepen the rhetorical school of historiography's recognition of the need to go beyond the correspondence theory of truth in interpreting historical texts. Next, authority may be thought to imply a top-down model of persuasion, but in Herodotus' handling, the first extant history reveals a bilateral authority and the importance of the role that the audience is to play in creating meaning. In its emphasis on reader-response theory, this reaffirms the power of this methodological approach to authority.

Historians have often examined authority with a focus on first-person statements. The third part of this volume expands beyond this to consider the communal voice in poetic verse, the second person, and finally, the distinctive voiceprint that the first person offered Roman statesmen. An area that has suffered even greater neglect is the way in which historiography as a genre comes to enjoy discursive power. In the chapters devoted to generic transformations, elements found in historiography imbue 'political philosophy', the *commentarius*, and biography with authority. Finally, the volume concludes with a reversal of Marincola's emphasis on historiographical tradition by illustrating the ways in which historians innovate within their generic framework and deviate from tradition in their own right. As Pelling concludes, however, there is no innovation without tradition, and so scholars must integrate techniques with a view to assessing both.

---

[15] For post-classical narratology, which advances beyond narratology's origins in structuralist linguistics, see Prince (2008), 116: '[It asks] about the relation between narrative structure and semiotic form, about their interaction with knowledge of the real world, about the function and not only the functioning of narrative, about what this or that particular narrative means and not only about how all and only narratives mean, about narrative as process or production and not simply as product, about the influence of context and means of expression on the responses of the receiver, about the history of narratives as opposed to the system underlying them.'

PART I

Myth, Fiction, and the Historian's Authority

CHAPTER I

Seven Types of Fiction in the Greek Historians

Michael A. Flower

On the flyleaf of his personal copy of *The Red and the Black*, Stendhal wrote: 'I believe that the *truth* in small as in large things, is almost unattainable – at least a truth that is *somewhat circumstantial*. Monsieur de Tracy used to say to me: truth can be found only in novels.'[1] Ever since the emergence of 'scientific', evidence-based history during the second half of the nineteenth century,[2] the discipline of ancient history has set itself the task of establishing what actually happened in the past. In this day and age such positivism may well seem naïve to many, yet the ancient Greek and Roman historians themselves deserve much of the responsibility for giving the overall impression that their narratives correspond closely to events as they in fact happened. This is because they have the power to cast a spell over their readers by creating narratives that are so intensely vivid that the events seem to be taking place before our very eyes.[3] And that raises the question of what kind of truth they were attempting to reveal. Is it a truth that today can be found only in novels?

Let me say at the outset that I do not believe that the ancient Greeks and Romans had an ontologically different conception of truth than we do,[4] even if their ontological universe was significantly different from ours.[5] In other words, when we read the ancient historians we are not

---

*I would like to thank the editors for their extremely useful comments and suggestions, my colleagues Harriet Flower and Johannes Haubold for their advice and assistance, and, most of all, John Marincola, for several decades of friendship, encouragement, and collaboration.

[1] See Ginzburg (2012), 139.   [2] Tucker (2004), 44–5.

[3] For the importance of vividness (*enargeia*) in ancient historical writing, see Walker (1993) and Otto (2009), 31–134.

[4] Ruffell and Hau (2017), 8, raise the interesting possibility that the various literary concerns of the ancient historians acted as 'generators of plural truths within understandings of the past' and that the ancient Greeks and Romans might have been able 'to believe in more than one version of past events at the same time'. Nevertheless, I see no evidence that any ancient prose author believed that parallel versions of the past could simultaneously be true.

[5] For the ontological differences between their worldview and ours, see the provocative study of G. Anderson (2018).

coming face to face with radically different concepts of truth and fiction as much as with a different way of reconciling them.[6] Modern scholars tend to fall into two camps: those who see ancient historians as striving to represent the past as accurately as possible and those who believe that they were far more interested in constructing a rhetorically plausible account than a factually true one.[7] Indeed, it has often been pointed out, beginning with the provocative work of A. J. Woodman, that in the classical world historiography was generally seen as belonging to the genre of rhetoric. That would explain why ancient historians tended most often to oppose truth with bias, such that a truthful account is one that is probable in and of itself and unbiased in its evaluations. But the situation was not quite so simple. John Marincola has well observed: 'Truth, then, is opposed to partiality because one who is not impartial will think nothing of inventing deeds to make his portrait, his argument, greater or more persuasive or more plausible.' As long as one did not invent deeds that never took place at all, 'rhetorical amplification was acceptable to expand upon the "hard core" of historical information'.[8]

Yet even if a particular writer wished to adhere as closely as possible to what was explicitly reported to have taken place, a historical narrative is always much more than a self-explanatory collection of 'facts'. As Hayden White demonstrated long ago, facts alone constitute a chronicle, not a narrative.[9] In order to create a narrative one must also arrange the 'facts' into a story with a plot, characters, and themes, and one must do so in such a way that this particular story is a memorable one.[10] Of course, as soon as one does this, to a greater or lesser degree, one begins to fictionalize.[11] This is because real life does not usually conform to an artificially crafted and constructed narrative arc – the kind of arc that makes a story interesting and meaningful. A variety of narrative techniques serves to give

---

[6] The meaning of 'truth' (ἀλήθεια) and its cognates in the ancient historians is comprehensively surveyed by Marincola (2007a).

[7] For the former, note Rhodes (1994); Bosworth (2003); and Lendon (2009), and for the latter, see Woodman (1988); Luce (1989); and Bleckmann (2006).

[8] See Marincola (1997), 158–74 (quotations are from 161). For Woodman (1988), 87–94, the 'hard core' in the Roman historians could consist of a single factual statement upon which, using rhetorical elaboration, an elaborate superstructure could be built.

[9] White (1980).   [10] White (1978) is a fundamental statement of this point.

[11] It is important to stress that although White (1973, 1978, 1987) argues that historians and imaginative writers (poets, novelists, playwrights) use substantially the same techniques and strategies, he still acknowledges (in contrast to the more extreme forms of postmodernism) that in historical writing stable events lie beneath the various rhetorical versions of them. For critiques of White, note in particular Momigliano (1981) and Ricoeur (2004), 248–61; and, more recently, Wilson (2013) and (2014).

order to the chaotic and seemingly unconnected happenings of 'real life'. Eliminating events deemed to be extraneous makes the story easier to follow; postponing the disclosure of relevant information provides dramatic timing and can also bolster a particular interpretation of events. If nothing else, the very possibility of reproducing the past in all of its complexity is undermined by the constant tug of war between the ideal of comprehensiveness and the necessity for selectivity.

Herodotus, Thucydides, and Xenophon all utilized the techniques that I have just mentioned, as well as others, to great effect, and to a degree that would be unacceptable in a modern work of academic historical narrative. Of course, all historical narratives are artistic constructions. Nonetheless, the varieties and degrees of artfulness can vary considerably. To a much greater extent than the majority of their modern counterparts, the Greek and Roman historians were like research-oriented historical novelists, the ones who do not rewrite the public record, but who do freely invent thoughts, scenes, and dialogue in an attempt to convey the essential truth of a historical moment. As one modern critic has recently observed, 'standard historical fiction ... tends to consist of plausible stories that have been grafted onto enduring historical facts. The writer presents not so much "what might have happened instead" as "what could have happened as well".'[12] This particular species of historical fiction has astutely been called 'the documented historical novel', wherein 'the novelist is free, more so than the historian, to fill in with imagined details the gaps in recorded history'.[13]

The title of this essay is borrowed from that of T. P. Wiseman's well-known 1993 article 'Lying Historians: Seven Types of Mendacity'. I am consciously eschewing the words 'lying' and 'mendacious' since the ancient Greeks and Romans would not have considered the generic rules by which they wrote 'history' in such terms. By 'fiction' I emphatically do not mean the self-conscious invention or elaboration of facts in sharp contrast to an honest attempt to relate 'what actually happened', since that too would impose a modern conceptual framework. Rather, what we understand as 'fictionality' were simply the normative rules for writing narratives of contemporary and past events. The further back in time a narrative stretched, the greater degree of imaginative elaboration was necessarily employed. In what follows I will explore seven narrative devices that, if they appeared in a modern academic historical work, would most probably be considered 'fictional'.

[12] Mallon (2011), 117.   [13] Turner (1979), 344.

The types of narrative manipulation in which the ancient historians engaged were the following. (1) They filled in gaps in what they knew by creative elaboration. (2) They omitted relevant material in order to give the appearance of inevitability to a certain interpretation of what had happened and why it had happened. (3) They invented speeches and conversations, often whole cloth. (4) They transposed events in order to create a more dramatic or thematically satisfying narrative. (5) They made exaggerated claims about method, including claims of personal autopsy and consultation of sources. (6) They attributed motives simply on the basis of a priori assumptions of what most people would do in similar situations – or to put it differently, motives were inferred on the basis of assumptions about human nature. (7) On top of all of this, there was an overarching concern to find and articulate patterns in past events, patterns that can and will repeat themselves. Why do wars break out? Why do empires grow, overextend, and then contract? Thucydides and Herodotus were greatly concerned to isolate patterns of behaviour that explained historical change. But in order to do so effectively, all of the literary techniques that I have just mentioned needed to be mustered and combined. In theory, general truths and the historical patterns derived from them can be deduced from generally agreed-upon facts; but in practice one often needs to tweak the facts in order to make them fit the pattern that the historian either perceives or wishes to perceive.[14]

Herodotus, Thucydides, and Xenophon all utilized the techniques that I have just mentioned, as well as others, to a degree that would be unacceptable in a modern work of academic historical narrative. I cannot here discuss all seven of these devices in equal detail, but I am going to select some examples that encompass a number of them. Before looking at specific examples, there is one thing that I need to state clearly. Although I do not want to imply that the ancient historians collectively were guilty of malpractice, there is a caveat. The decision of what to include and what to omit in a historical narrative is never ethically neutral. As we shall see, some omissions, especially in histories that claim to offer guidance or insight for the future, can have serious unintended consequences.

---

[14] Raaflaub (2013) discusses the importance of patterns in both Herodotus and Thucydides, observing of the former: 'Using elaboration and even invention, he [Herodotus] shapes the past' (19), and of the latter, 'But patterning requires strong colors, sharp lines and contrasts, and simplification' (13). Raaflaub (2016) more explicitly speaks of their 'Übertreibung, Erfindung und Manipulation' ('exaggeration, invention and manipulation'). See further Hunter (1973), especially 123–48, 177–84 and Moles (1993b), 108–21.

Speeches and Deeds

Many contemporary historians will tell you that Greek and Roman historians made a sharp distinction between recording speeches and actions, that is to say, between 'words' and 'deeds'.[15] This idea goes back, of course, to Thucydides (1.22), who inadvertently set it in motion by making the simple distinction that he had to supplement what people had said but interviewed more than one eyewitness in order to establish precisely what they had done.[16] Yet this distinction can become blurred when the context for the making of speeches has been invented.

Herodotus' contemporary audience, as he himself twice tells us, objected to the 'constitutional debate' that he claims took place after the overthrow of the Magian pretender to the Persian throne in 522 BC. At this moment of crisis Herodotus claims the seven Persian conspirators who had killed the pretender held a debate as to which form of government to adopt – democracy, oligarchy, or monarchy. Herodotus twice tells us that some contemporary Greeks did not accept that these speeches were given, although he strongly insists that they were (3.80, 6.43). Apparently, the objection was not that Herodotus recorded speeches the content of which he could not possibly have known, but that the content he provided was not what they thought that Persians would have said under the circumstances. In particular, Herodotus' audiences, both contemporary and modern, do not accept that the Persian noble Otanes could have advocated the adoption of 'democracy' by the Persians in 522 BC.[17] Moreover, when Herodotus says that it seemed implausible to some Greeks that these speeches were given, this surely entails not only that they doubted their specific content but also that a debate was even held on this particular topic. A more plausible subject, even if a much more pedestrian one, would have been the respective qualifications of the seven nobles to become the next king – but Herodotus surely wanted to use this moment as an opportunity to stage an inquiry into the strengths and weaknesses of various forms of government.

Giving a debate on this topic a Persian setting rather than a Greek one lends it an impartiality detached from the political struggles of the Greek city states, much the same as Xenophon achieved in his *Cyropaedia* by

---

[15] For speeches in historical works, see Marincola (2007c).
[16] Rood (2006b), 236–7, succinctly discusses Thucydides' explanation of his method.
[17] Pelling (2002a) is a highly nuanced treatment. Munson (2019) posits a possible fifth-century Persian source.

24   MICHAEL A. FLOWER

using a Persian (rather than, say, a Spartan) as his model king.[18] But what seems to have worked for Xenophon failed for Herodotus because the various contemporary audiences of the Greek historians seem to have been content with plausible fictions, whether of speeches or deeds, but were much less accepting of implausible ones. Dionysius of Halicarnassus emphatically asserts that the arguments deployed by the Athenian speakers in the Melian dialogue were neither appropriate nor plausible (*On Thucydides* 37–41).[19]

Narratorial Claims and Statements of Method

Perhaps the most famous novel ever written is *Don Quixote de la Mancha* by Miguel de Cervantes, published in 1605. It begins with the narrator's claim that he found the story in the Archives of La Mancha and later on he also discusses other documentary sources that he consulted. At the end of Chapter 8 he must break off the story of a sword fight between a Basque squire and Don Quixote because the manuscript breaks off at that point. But then he starts the next chapter by telling his readers how he discovered an Arabic manuscript in a bazaar that continues the story, written by the historian Cid Hamet Ben Engeli. The narrator sounds all too much like a researcher who claims to take his account from sources that he carefully checks. Thus began a literary conceit that is fairly common in novels to this day, ranging from Daniel Defoe's *A Journal of the Plague Year* (1722) to Arthur Golden's *Memoirs of a Geisha* (1997). Most students of modern literature are unaware that Cervantes, whether he realized it or not, had predecessors in antiquity. In his now lost history of Persia, the Greek doctor Ctesias of Cnidus called Herodotus a liar and a writer of fables; he gave an account of events that was completely antithetical to Herodotus', and he claimed that his own account was based both on Persian oral testimony and on the Persian royal parchments.[20] Diodorus is our source for his alleged use of these parchments: 'Now Ctesias says that it was from the royal parchments, in which the Persians, in accordance with a certain law, kept a record of their ancient deeds, that he inquired closely into each

---

[18] See Tuplin (2013), 72–5.

[19] Dionysius even speculates that Thucydides, being angry because of his exile, wished to make his fellow Athenians hated by all mankind (41).

[20] Most modern scholars have characterized Ctesias as 'a poet-cum-novelist working within the framework of history' (Llewellyn-Jones (2010), 81). Meeus (2017), who gives a thorough survey of modern characterizations of Ctesias as a poet or romantic novelist, sees him as being 'a very Herodotean historian' (187).

Seven Types of Fiction in the Greek Historians

and every detail and, after having composed his history, he published it among the Greeks.' These parchments apparently were made of leather, since Diodorus calls them *basilikai diphtherai*.[21] To be sure, we know that the Persians kept financial and administrative records, and copies of king Darius' Behistun inscription, written on both clay and parchment, were circulated throughout the empire. Nevertheless, as Pierre Briant has pointed out, all of the attested archives were administrative, 'not a written record of the deeds and accomplishments of the Great Kings'.[22] Why then are there no other references to the 'royal parchments' that Ctesias refers to? It is surely because they did not actually exist.[23]

Generally speaking, statements of method and practice in the ancient historians do not necessarily reflect actual working methods. As John Marincola has brilliantly demonstrated, claims to truthfulness and accuracy, in particular, are rhetorical in nature and are intended to establish a writer's authority.[24] They are saying to the reader, 'This is the whole truth, this is what people told me, this is what I found out after careful inquiry, and you can believe me and put your trust in my version of events.' Thucydides claims that he listened to many speeches, which he adapted for inclusion in his history, and that he put together his narrative by cross-examining many eyewitnesses. I have no doubt that he did so, since he was a well-connected member of the international elite. But the first sentence of his history makes an assertion that, to me at least, sounds suspicious (1.1.1):

> Thucydides an Athenian composed the war (ξυνέγραψε τὸν πόλεμον) of the Peloponnesians and Athenians, how they fought against each other, having begun as soon as it started and expecting (ἀρξάμενος εὐθὺς καθισταμένου καὶ ἐλπίσας) that it would be great and more noteworthy than previous wars, taking as evidence that both sides went into the war at their peak in every respect of their preparation, and seeing that the rest of the Greek world was joining one side or the other, some right away, others intending to do so.

Should we take this statement at face value – was Thucydides really so prescient that he could tell that this war was going to be the big one and that he needed to start composing it immediately? Much later in his

---

[21] Diod. Sic. 2.32.4 (= *FGrHist* 688 T3, F 5). Diodorus (2.22.5 = *FGrHist* 688, F 1b.(22.5)) also refers to Ctesias' use of 'royal records' (*diphtherai anagraphai*). On the question of the historicity of the 'royal parchments', see Llewellyn-Jones (2010), 58–63; Stronk (2010), 15–25; Waters (2017), 16–19. For *diphtherai* as parchment books, see Hdt. 5.58.3.

[22] Briant (2002), 889.   [23] As was long ago concluded by Jacoby (1922), 2047.

[24] Note especially Marincola (1997), 3–12.

History, in Book 7 (28.3) he admits something that he might have told the reader at the start – that none of the Greeks believed that the Athenians would be able to hold out for more than two or three years at most. So, in effect, Thucydides is telling us that he knew better than everyone else.[25] Analogy is not proof, but let me make a comparison. Turning again to Stendhal, in the preface of his autobiography, *The Life of Henry Brulard*, he claims that he started to write it in Rome on 16 October 1832 when he was three months short of his fiftieth birthday. We know from his own correspondence that Stendhal was not even in Rome on that day and that he began his autobiography three years later in 1835 when he was the French consul in Civitavecchia. He surely realized that it was more impressive to have begun to write in Rome, inspired by the view from the Janiculum Hill, when he was nearly fifty, than in 1835, in a provincial town that he detested, when he was fifty-three. For his part, Thucydides was elected general in 424 BC and then exiled for twenty years on a charge of incompetence in his command. Would he have wanted to begin his history with a declaration that he had begun to write in exile, at a time when he had nothing better to do?[26]

Imaginative Elaboration and Invention

We will never know as much about Herodotus' working methods and sources of information as we would like. It is extremely probable that he drew both on oral traditions and on a rich tradition of popular storytelling when he came to compose his *Histories*.[27] It would be especially important to know whether Herodotus had direct access to Persian and Near Eastern oral traditions or whether he drew his information solely through Greek intermediaries.[28] But in a sense it does not matter. In the form in which he presents them, the stories that Herodotus tells are his own literary creations. The thematic unity of his history, the recurrence of motifs great and small, and the stylistic uniformity of the entire work guarantee as much. Like every accomplished storyteller, Herodotus surely made his own

---

[25] As Rood (2006b), 232–3 points out, he was claiming for himself a special foresight, the very type of foresight that he especially admired in Themistocles and Pericles.

[26] At least Thucydides' actual name was Thucydides, whereas Stendhal's real name was neither Stendhal nor Henri Brulard, but Marie-Henri Beyle.

[27] See especially Luraghi (2013).

[28] S. West (2011) and R. Thomas (2012) nicely articulate the problems involved.

Seven Types of Fiction in the Greek Historians   27

versions distinctive in ways that would have appealed to his various Greek audiences.[29]

One of Herodotus' main themes is the nature of empire. At the beginning of Book 7 Herodotus stages a lengthy debate between the Persian king Xerxes and his inner circle of advisors over whether or not to invade Greece. It is important to bear in mind when reading their speeches that Herodotus was writing some forty to fifty years later, by which time these men were long dead. He is, therefore, unlikely to have had an eyewitness source for what was actually said. The king's cousin Mardonius eggs Xerxes on, while his uncle Artabanus urges delay. Xerxes thinks that they should invade because they are too powerful to fail; it is their custom to conquer ever more countries; and the Athenians must be punished for their interference in the Ionian revolt and the defeat of Darius' forces at Marathon. Moreover, it is the will of god that the Persians expand their empire: 'Thus god guides us, and we, by following his guidance, prosper greatly.' Some of this may seem all too familiar to an American audience, whose government has justified imperialism in somewhat similar terms. But Xerxes goes a step further in the first of the speeches that Herodotus puts in his mouth (Hdt. 7.8γ1–3):

> If we shall subdue these Greeks (the Athenians) and their neighbours who inhabit the Peloponnese, we will reveal the land of Persia as having the same borders as Zeus's sky. For the sun will not look down upon any land that borders upon our own; but, with your aid, passing through Europe from one end to the other, I will make all of its lands one country.... In this way both the guilty and the innocent will put on the yoke of slavery.

Herodotus, in effect, ascribes to Xerxes a notion that we would call 'manifest destiny', to wit, that it was the will of god that the Persians conquer the entire inhabited world. The reference to the sun looking down on Persian territory (reminiscent of the later claim that the sun never set on the Spanish Empire of the sixteenth to eighteenth centuries or on the British Empire of the nineteenth and early twentieth centuries) is a common trope of imperial discourse from ancient to modern times. An inscription of the Neo-Assyrian King Sennacherib (reigned 705–681) boasts that 'From the upper sea of the setting sun, to the lower sea of the rising sun, all princes of the four quarters (of the world) he [the god Ashur] has brought in submission to my feet.'[30]

---

[29] For Herodotus' 'distilling' and adapting of Persian stories, see especially Pelling (2009a) and (2019), 129–45.
[30] Inscribed on a bull from the palace in Nineveh: see Luckenbill (1924), 66.

28   MICHAEL A. FLOWER

In general terms the sentiments expressed by Xerxes mesh quite nicely with the rhetoric of the royal inscriptions of Darius and Xerxes as well as with that of Sennacherib. They regularly begin with the same standard formula: 'Ahura Mazda is a great god, who created this earth, who created that sky, who created man, who created happiness for man, who made Xerxes king, one king of many, one lord of many. I am Xerxes, the Great King, king of kings, king of lands containing many men, king of this great earth far and wide, son of Darius, an Achaemenid.'[31] Such documents cannot be taken completely at face value, for Assyrian royal inscriptions express similar claims to world rule by divine dispensation. What they are is a rhetorical and ideological claim that very many different empires have employed. Johannes Haubold has brilliantly demonstrated how an originally Babylonian ideology of the all-conquering king who extends his power to the shore of the two seas, that is, the Mediterranean and Persian Gulf, or even across those seas, was taken over by Assyrians and Persians.[32] It may be the case that Herodotus had some indirect knowledge of Xerxes' propaganda to rule the seas and the lands beyond their shores, and it is even possible that traces of Assyrian ideology had entered common discourse on the nature of empire. Herodotus has taken whatever common knowledge he was exposed to and used it to create a vividly imaginative reconstruction of the interaction between an absolute monarch and his advisors. His account of this interaction is not history in our modern sense of the discipline; rather, it is akin to the work of a historical novelist who can build a plausible structure upon a few commonly attested facts.

In any case, it was probably too generous to call this a debate, since Xerxes ends his speech by saying that the expedition must be made, but if anyone has a different opinion, he should state it. His sycophantic cousin, the Persian general Mardonius, endorses the expedition, but everyone else is too afraid to push back. That is, everyone except for Xerxes' uncle Artabanus, who trusts in that relationship to urge caution. Not surprisingly, he has overestimated his freedom of speech, and Xerxes lashes out at his uncle with threats and a boast (Hdt. 7.11.2–3):

> I would not be born the son of Darius ... if I were not to avenge myself upon Athenians, knowing well that if we shall keep quiet, they shall not, but in very truth they shall attack our land, if it is right to judge from what they did first, they who both burnt Sardis and marched into Asia. Therefore, it is not possible for either of us to retreat, but the contest

---

[31] Brosius (2000) no. 47, with M. A. Flower (2006), 276–8.   [32] Haubold (2013), 98–117.

Seven Types of Fiction in the Greek Historians

before us is either to take the initiative or to suffer, in order that either all of Asia become subject to the Greeks, or all of Greece to the Persians. For there is no middle course in this enmity.

Herodotus is employing a common stereotype here, and one that seems to be universally true: how difficult, and dangerous, it is to speak truth to power in autocratic regimes. Yet there is an aspect of these words that is ethically troubling in our own time and place. It would be extremely surprising if any Persian ever said anything like this, because the sentiment is wholly Greek. It is part of an ideology that modern scholars label 'panhellenism', the notion that the warring and relatively poor Greek city-states could solve all of their economic and social problems by joining forces to attack the Middle East. This idea was especially prominent in the fourth century BC and, as is well known, was realized by Alexander the Great. But the idea was already being aired in the fifth century when Herodotus was writing. The innocent reader, however, might take these words to have actually been spoken by a Persian king, thus validating the notion that the clash of civilizations is something real, going all the way back to the first Iranian Empire. There is a terrible irony in this. Herodotus was actually not a chauvinistic author in the least and he eschews ethnic stereotyping. Yet he is here inadvertently confirming an orientalist view of the irreconcilable, inevitable, and timeless conflict between east and west. And that is one reason why it is dangerous not to understand his methods.

In my view, Herodotus was not a panhellenist – if anything, he subtly critiques such views.[33] Why, then, does he attribute these particular sentiments to a Persian king? Another major theme in his *History* is the notion that every offence inevitably and naturally leads to an act of retribution in an endless cycle of reciprocal acts of violence. But Herodotus also believed that the gods humble those who exalt themselves and that arrogant over-expansion inevitably leads to a fall. But what if Herodotus has imposed this theme on the Persians without real evidence? If the speeches in the debate are fictitious, are not the motives that they express fictitious as well?[34]

Herodotus' own account reveals that the Persians realized that the world was much bigger than just the countries bordering Greece. They certainly knew about the Greek and Phoenician cities in the Western

---

[33] See M. A. Flower (2000), 69–76.

[34] Tuplin (2009) expresses similar concerns about Herodotus' narrative of Darius' Scythian expedition in Book 4.

Mediterranean. Moreover, around 600 BC some Phoenician ships circumnavigated Africa and it had taken them two years to do so. Xerxes himself dispatched a member of the Persian elite on a similar voyage, but he was unable to complete it (Hdt. 4.42–3). Nor do I find it very likely that Xerxes intended to turn Central and Southern Greece into an official Persian satrapy (or province), which would have demanded a huge military presence. One should not be tempted to think that the huge number of fighting men in Xerxes' army would have been sufficient to conquer and garrison the whole of mainland Greece just because Herodotus calculated (7.184–7) its size as 1,700,000 infantry, 80,000 cavalry, and 20,000 camel riders and charioteers. Those numbers are logistically impossible.[35]

So what was Xerxes hoping to accomplish? This may seem perverse, but one could make a plausible case that Persian strategy was limited to punishing Athens for supporting the rebellion of the Greek cities that dotted the coast of Turkey in the unsuccessful Ionian revolt of 499–494 BC. This strategy would include placing a tyrant in Athens and forming an alliance with Argos, who was Sparta's traditional rival in the Peloponnese. Such measures, what we might call imperialism on the cheap, would insure that the mainland Greeks never again interfered in the affairs of Asia. And, as a result, Xerxes could more fairly claim to rule over the two seas and the lands beyond their shores. In a sense, if that was the strategy, it was successful insofar as Athens was destroyed, Greek forces were defeated at Thermopylae and Artemisium, and the Argives remained neutral.[36] But in real terms Persian strategy backfired. Flushed with victory at the battles of Salamis and Plataea, the Greeks went on to liberate the Aegean islands and Greek cities on the coast of Turkey from Persian rule. The end result, therefore, was not the destruction of the Persian Empire, but its curtailment or pruning. And in Herodotus' world view that was the god's way of cutting them down to size. But my strong suspicion is that the whole account of Persian motives and strategy is basically a fiction, and it does not really matter if Herodotus is merely giving form to what most Greeks thought was the case.[37] The point is that the narrative in all its literary texture and complexity is his own.

It may not surprise most modern readers that Herodotus needed to take liberties in reconstructing the actions, speeches, and motives of non-Greek actors who were no longer alive at the time of his writing. But surely we

[35] See M. A. Flower (2007) for modern estimates.   [36] So Waters (2014), 132.
[37] Wallinga (2005), 1–6, following Will (1964), maintains that the Greeks could not have had reliable first-hand information about Persian objective in 490 and 480, but were reduced to speculation.

Seven Types of Fiction in the Greek Historians

can trust Thucydides, whose self-advertised passion for strict accuracy is usually taken as a given?[38]

One of the most discussed episodes in Thucydides is the Melian Dialogue (5.84–116). In 416 BC the Athenians made an expedition against the small island of Melos. Although Melos was a colony of Sparta, Thucydides insists that it had remained neutral throughout the war, being an ally of neither side. Their continuing state of neutrality is stressed by Thucydides himself (2.9.4; 5.84.2), as well as by the Melian (5.94, 98, 112.3) and Athenian participants in the dialogue (5.89). Yet there is evidence external to the text that renders these assertions highly questionable, despite Thucydides' self-proclaimed passion for accuracy.

The Athenian general Nicias unsuccessfully attacked Melos in 426 (Thuc. 3.91.1–3). Thucydides does not record a motive, but Diodorus (12.65.1–2) claims that they were attacked precisely because they were allies of Sparta: 'for Melos alone among the islands of the Cyclades was preserving its alliance with the Lacedaemonians, being a colony of Sparta'.[39] This information almost certainly derives from Ephorus of Cyme, who was Diodorus' primary source for the period. As has recently been demonstrated, Ephorus' alternative versions, even when they conflict with Thucydides, always need to be given serious consideration.[40] In any case, if the Melians were not already Spartan allies at the time of Nicias' assault, it certainly would have been prudent for them to become allies in anticipation of future Athenian expeditions. In any case, most probably between 427 and 416 the Melians made two contributions to the Spartan war fund, one for twenty minas of silver and another for an amount that is not preserved on the stone.[41] Athens, however, was never easily thwarted. The Tribute Reassessment Decree of 425 BC assessed the Melians the

---

[38] But not always: see note 14 above, as well as Woodman (1988), 1–69. Badian (1993) accuses Thucydides of engaging in systematic disinformation in his account of the origins of the Peloponnesian War (see below) and H. I. Flower (1992) demonstrates that the omissions in his account of the Pylos debate (4.27–29) are intentionally misleading.

[39] Diodorus' assertion of an alliance is rejected by Kierdorf (1962) and Seaman (1997), 407, n. 83, on insufficient grounds. Green (2010), vii–x, 1–8, maintains that Diodorus' version of events should never be dismissed out of hand.

[40] Ephorus' seriousness as a researcher has been amply demonstrated by Parmeggiani (2011). The orthodox view (restated by Parker (2011), biographical essay, section 2.F) that Books 11–15 of Diodorus (apart from the Sicilian narrative) are essentially an epitome, or 'long fragment', of Ephorus has come under sustained criticism (see, in particular, Parmeggiani (2011), 357–73).

[41] The inscription is Osborne and Rhodes (2017), no. 151, whose dating (pp. 299–300) I accept (see also Loomis (1992), 56–76) as well as their contention that the Melians must have been added to the list before 416, since they are not listed as exiles as are the Ephesian and Chian donors. Others, however, have argued in favour of a later date: e.g. Piérart (1995), who concludes that the entire list was compiled in c. 409 BC.

large sum of fifteen talents.[42] As far as we know, this was never paid either in whole or in part, but the very fact of being included in the reassessment indicates that the Melians were officially considered 'allies' of Athens.[43] An entry in the Suda, under 'Melian famine', specifically claims that 'Nicias besieged Melos and brought the city to terms because it had revolted from the Athenians, although recently having become tributary'.[44] The name of the commander may be incorrect, but that does not by itself invalidate the other information.[45]

If Melos was indeed considered to be a tributary 'ally', the true justification for the Athenian expedition of 416 was not to force a neutral party into the empire, as Thucydides would have it, but rather to subdue an ally in rebellion, one that had given tangible support to the Spartan war effort. That would explain the harsh punishment meted out to the Melians after they had unconditionally surrendered: the Athenian forces killed all of the adult males and sold the women into slavery (Thuc. 5.116). The other known recipients of this treatment were all allies who had rebelled: Mytilene in 427 (Thuc. 3.36, although it was not fully carried out) and Scione in 421 (Thuc. 5.32.1).

Finally, if Melos was indeed caught between two alliances in 416, being affiliated by choice with Sparta but unwillingly with Athens, this would also serve to explain a purposefully ambiguous statement of Thucydides (5.84.2): he claims that at first the Melians kept quiet, being allied to neither side, 'but later, when the Athenians tried to coerce them by ravaging their land, they entered into open war (ἐς πόλεμον φανερὸν κατέστησαν)'. The context makes it clear that this 'open war' must predate the Athenian expedition of 416 (since the dialogue precedes any Athenian devastation: 5.84.3).[46] It is left to readers to figure out for themselves what it can mean to be at war and to be neutral at the same time.

For his part, Thucydides has sacrificed specific truths in his uncompromising quest to articulate general truths (e.g. 'hope is an expensive commodity' (5.103) and 'Of the gods we believe and of humans we know, that

---

[42] Osborne and Rhodes (2017), no. 153, column I, line 65.

[43] As argued by Treu (1954) and followed by Raubitschek (1963); but rejected by Eberhardt (1959), and also by Seaman (1997), who vigorously defends the historical accuracy of Thucydides' account of Athenian relations with Melos.

[44] Adler number = lambda 557.

[45] Contra Seaman (1997), 404–8. Raubitschek (1963) argues for an alternative tradition, originating in Ephorus, that put Nicias in command in 416 and depicted Melos as an ally in rebellion (Diod. Sic. 12.80.5 implies that Nicias was in command of Athenian forces).

[46] See Gomme, Andrewes, and Dover (1945–81), iv. 156–8, and Hornblower (1991–2008), i.228–9, commenting on 5.84.2.

Seven Types of Fiction in the Greek Historians 33

by a necessity of their nature, wherever they have the power to do so, they always rule' (5.105)). His desire to stage a philosophical debate on the nature of power has overridden the historical context of that debate. Moreover, his manipulation of the status of Melos serves to create the calculated parallels with the Sicilian expedition that we find in Books 6 and 7 – on Thucydides' arrangement of the evidence, both were unprovoked attacks driven by hubristic expansionism, during which the Athenians ended up making the very same mistakes that the Melians did, bringing on their own destruction by trusting in false hopes and divine assistance. One naturally thinks of the Melians' own debating points when Nicias says to his troops in their pathetic flight from Syracuse in 413 that 'even in our present circumstances it is necessary to have hope' (7.77.3 with 5.102) and that 'it is now reasonable for us to hope that the gods will be kinder to us (for we are now more worthy of their pity than of their jealousy)' (7.77.4 with 5.104).[47]

Gaps and Omissions

It should not be at all controversial to state that all works of literature include gaps, whether they be fiction, non-fiction, or inhabit the grey area in between. Long before this was stated in theoretical terms by Wolfgang Iser, who posited that readers create a work's meaning by filling in the gaps left by the text itself, writers knew this, and not just intuitively.[48] Lord Byron, it has recently been observed, 'filled his work with tantalizing omissions to fire the imagination'.[49] As Byron himself made explicit in the sixth canto (lines 97–8) to *Don Juan*, 'An outline is the best – a lively reader's fancy does the rest.'[50] Purposeful narrative gaps, of course, are much older than Byron. Indeed, they can be found as far back as Homer.

The important question is how modern readers of ancient texts can determine the difference between narrative gaps that for reasons of economy or thematic effect exist in any work of literature, and omissions that are calculated to promote certain ways of interpreting a text while closing down others. How do we navigate between the extremes of either reading too much or too little significance into gaps and omissions? The subjective element in our interpretation of texts is never arbitrary, since (as Iser argues) it is guided, as well as limited, by the structures that the text contains.

[47] See Macleod (1983a [1974]), 52–67, and Connor (1984), 201–2.   [48] Iser (1978).
[49] Throsby (2016).   [50] See Howe (2013), 113.

34 MICHAEL A. FLOWER

When a gap in a work of narrative fiction is serious enough, critics call it a crux. A crux is a gap where there is an insufficiency of cues, or where the cues are sufficiently ambiguous, to create a major disagreement over the intentions of the narrator. Thucydides devotes a whole book to explaining the causes of the Peloponnesian War. Nonetheless, scholars cannot come to any consensus about the reasons for the outbreak, not least of all because of a major gap in Thucydides' narrative.

In 432 BC the assembly of Spartan citizens voted that the Thirty Years' Peace between Athens and Sparta had been broken and that the Athenians were acting unjustly (Thuc. 1.87–8). Despite Thucydides' assertion to the contrary, the Spartan resolution was not a declaration of war per se, but merely a statement of record.[51] This is fake news, ancient Greek style. This vote was followed by vote of Sparta's allies, undoubtedly on the same resolution as voted on by the Spartan Assembly, during a meeting of the Peloponnesian League (1.119, 125).[52] Immediately after their allies had voted, the Spartans sent at least three separate embassies to Athens (1.126, 139) in the hope of reaching a resolution of their allies' complaints against Athens. And now comes a major interpretative crux. Thucydides does not take these embassies seriously, and he says that their purpose was 'to have the greatest excuse for going to war, if the Athenians did not make any concessions'.[53]

The first embassy was a demand to expel the Athenian statesman Pericles, since his family was under a curse for an impious act that had been committed several generations earlier. More demands followed:

> On the occasion of their first embassy the Spartans had made these demands, and had received counter demands concerning the expulsion of those who were under a curse. On later visits to the Athenians they ordered them to withdraw from Potidaea and to leave Aegina autonomous, and most of all, and in the plainest possible terms, they declared that they could avoid war by rescinding the decree about the Megarians, in which it was specified that the Megarians were not to use any of the harbours in the Athenian Empire or even the market place in Athens. The Athenians,

---

[51] As astutely argued by Badian (1993), 145–52 (first published in 1990 and then reprinted with revisions in 1993). His interpretation has been almost universally rejected – for example, by Cawkwell (1997), 34–7; E. A. Meyer (1997), 35–9; and E. Robinson (2017) – but is accepted by Hornblower (1991–2008), i.132, 201–2.

[52] So Badian (1993), 150–1; also accepted by Hornblower (1991–2008), i.196, 201–2.

[53] To my mind, the most convincing account of the purpose of these embassies is Badian (1993), 150–8. Parmeggiani (2018) argues, on the basis of Diodorus 12.41.1, that after the rejection of the Spartan embassies there was a third vote (not mentioned by Thucydides), in which the Peloponnesians finally decided to go to war.

Seven Types of Fiction in the Greek Historians

however, were neither heeding the other demands nor did they rescind the decree, but they accused the Megarians of encroachment upon the sacred land and upon the borderland not marked by boundaries, and also of harbouring runaway slaves. Finally, one last set of ambassadors came from Sparta, consisting of Ramphias, Melesippus, and Agesander, who said nothing of what they had previously been accustomed to say, but only this: 'The Spartans want there to be peace, and there would be, if you let the Greeks be autonomous.' The Athenians called an assembly and debated amongst themselves; and it was resolved to give their answer once and for all after considering the entire issue. Many others came forward and spoke in support of both sides of the question, some saying that war was necessary, others that the decree should not stand in the way of peace, but should be rescinded; and Pericles the son of Xanthippus also came forward, the leading man of the Athenians at that time, being most capable both in speaking and in action, and he advised them as follows.

Pericles, we are told, convinced the Athenians not to make any concessions to the Spartans, because as soon as they gave in to one demand, others would follow. They did offer arbitration, as was stipulated in the terms of the Thirty Years' Peace (Thuc. 1.145), but that left open the awkward question of what people or polis would have been neutral enough to act as arbitrators. The Spartans may later have regretted their refusal, even if arbitration, attractive in theory, was unmanageable in practice.[54] What is truly striking is that although the Athenians rebuffed the Spartan ambassadors and sent them home empty-handed, a state of war still did not exist. The Spartans and Athenians continued to visit each other 'without a herald', and that can only mean that the Thirty Years' Peace was still in force. Actual fighting broke out only in the spring of 431 BC, when the Thebans made a surprise attack on Plataea. The decisive piece of evidence that neither Sparta nor the Peloponnesian League had ever formally voted for war and that the peace was still in force at the time of the attack on Plataea is later provided by Thucydides (7.18.2) himself in a passage in which he is discussing the Spartan resumption of war against Athens in winter 414/413: 'In the former war, they considered, the offence had been more on their own side, both on account of the entrance of Thebans into Plataea in time of peace, and also of their own refusal to

---

[54] So Ager (1993), 11: 'Perhaps the most glaringly obvious problem with the arbitration clause in the Thirty Years' Peace Treaty is the simple question of "who?" Who would have been a suitable arbitrator between Sparta and Athens in fifth-century Greece? The Greek world in 431 was largely divided into two opposed camps. Who would have had the required characteristics of prestige, neutrality and good will?'

36   MICHAEL A. FLOWER

listen to the Athenian offer of arbitration ...'[55] And yet even after the
Theban attack, when a huge Spartan-led army assembled for the invasion
of Athenian territory, the Spartan king Archidamus dispatched an ambassador in the hope of getting a last-minute concession from the Athenians
(Thuc. 2.12). But Pericles would not allow this Spartan to address the
people or even to enter the city.

Thucydides' narrative of these Spartan embassies is problematic for at
least three reasons. First of all, he records only one speech in response to
these various Spartan demands, that of Pericles, and Pericles addresses only
the question of rescinding the Megarian decree. Thucydides tells us that
many other speakers came forward, some arguing for and others against
revoking the decree. But he chooses not to record the detailed arguments
for revoking it, in a speech that could have been paired with Pericles'. Nor
does he record any debate about the other demands, and the narrative gives
the distinct impression that those demands were not worth debating.
Second, although he tells us that most Spartans voted for war during a
meeting of the Spartan Assembly, he does not tell us how close the vote
was at Athens. Note that his account of the Mytilenian debate includes the
information that the votes of the Athenians were nearly equal
(Thuc. 3.49.1). Third, and much more seriously, he gives no date for
the Megarian decree nor any indication of its effects on the Megarians.[56]
One of Plutarch's sources for his life of Pericles (30) attempted to fill this
narrative gap by inserting into the story the murder of the Athenian herald
Anthemocritus by the Megarians and the subsequent passage of a very
harsh punitive decree by an Athenian named Charinus. Unfortunately, the
date, significance, and authenticity of this supplementary information is
uncertain.[57]

Now I suppose that we can live without hearing the arguments of those
Athenians who were willing to lift the siege of Potidaea or give autonomy
to the island of Aegina. And perhaps no one even bothered to debate the
ultimatum delivered by the final embassy, which in effect demanded that

---

[55] This decisive piece of evidence is not cited by Badian (1993).

[56] The date, purpose, and effects of the Megarian decree have been endlessly debated. Most scholars
assume a date in 432 (or perhaps in 433) and estimate its economic impact on Megara to have been
severe (e.g. Cawkwell (1997), 27–9, 31–4). Brunt (1993), however, argues for a much earlier date,
perhaps in the 440s, and both he and Ste. Croix (1972), 225–89 see its economic effects as
negligible. Yet one gets the impression from Dicaeopolis' speech in Aristophanes' *Acharnians*
515–39 (our only evidence on this point) that, even accounting for comic exaggeration, the
Megarians were experiencing a food shortage.

[57] See Stadter (1989), 274–6, and Cawkwell (1997), 111–14. Connor (1962) argues that Plutarch has erred
and that the Charinus decree actually belonged to another dispute with Megara in the 350s.

Seven Types of Fiction in the Greek Historians

the Athenians disband their empire. But the narrative's failure to contextualize the Megarian decree makes it extremely difficult to measure how justified the Spartans were for fearing the growth of Athenian power, as Thucydides emphatically claims that they were in several key passages (1.23, 88, 118).[58] Perhaps the most famous sentence in the whole of his *History*, and one of the most problematic, is this one (1.23.6): 'The truest cause of the war was the one least spoken about; I believe that the growth of Athenian power and the fear that this instilled in Sparta made war inevitable' (τὴν μὲν γὰρ ἀληθεστάτην πρόφασιν, ἀφανεστάτην δὲ λόγῳ, τοὺς Ἀθηναίους ἡγοῦμαι μεγάλους γιγνομένους καὶ φόβον παρέχοντας τοῖς Λακεδαιμονίοις ἀναγκάσαι ἐς τὸ πολεμεῖν).[59]

Why do I find this statement, in conjunction with Thucydides' particular narrative choices, so troubling? Why does all of this matter? Would our understanding of the situation be significantly altered if Thucydides had recorded the speeches that advocated for making concessions to Spartan demands and gave us more information about the Athenian decree against Megara and its economic implications? Now if one assumes that the Spartans were not making these demands seriously and were merely looking to score propaganda points on the eve of a war that they very much desired, then Thucydides' abbreviated treatment seems reasonable. And this way of underreading the text is in harmony with Thucydides' own interpretation of Spartan motives. If, on the other hand, the Spartans were genuinely looking for a face-saving way to avoid a full-scale conflict and that Pericles' aggressive policies had pushed them into a corner, then Thucydides' gaps and omissions look a bit different and his claim that the Spartans very much wanted the war is untenable. So a great deal of historical reconstruction hinges on whether one over-reads or under-reads Thucydides' narrative of these failed negotiations.

The art of the deft omission can be a very potent tool for controlling reader response and interpretation, even if the gaps thus opened up sometimes allow us to read against the grain of the narrative. Gaps, however, are not morally neutral – if they mislead future readers, they can have serious unforeseen consequences. When I used to teach Greek history before the breakup of the Soviet Union, just when my students had finished reading Thucydides, I was accustomed to ask the class how many

---

[58] As Ed. Meyer (1899), 302–3, perceptively concluded, 'Thucydides does not give the Megarian Decree sufficient motivation, or rather, he does not give it any motivation at all.'

[59] There are competing translations of this sentence, but I here accept the authoritative analysis of Ostwald (1988), especially 1–5. As he demonstrates, ἀναγκάσαι lacks a direct object and by not providing one Thucydides instead emphasizes the compulsion itself.

38   MICHAEL A. FLOWER

of them believed that a war between the United States and Russia was inevitable. They all raised their hands that it was. Such is the power of historical narrative.[60]

Chronology

Briefly, I want to conclude with the least flashy of all narratological topics, that is, with chronology. Xenophon is the probably the ancient historian whose sense of chronology, as well as his notion of what it was permissible to omit, is the most notorious.[61] The strengths and weaknesses of his historical method are well brought out in his account of the Thirty oligarchs (later known as the 'Thirty Tyrants') who ruled Athens for roughly eight months after the end of the Peloponnesian War. This is the longest and most detailed account of any single episode in the *Hellenica,* covering a single year in twenty pages of the Oxford classical text (2.3.11–2.4.43).[62] Even so, it is beyond doubt that Xenophon has simplified events in order to present an account that focuses on the Thirty's escalating use of violence and terror to achieve their ends.[63] At the same time, the story of their rise and fall has a very novelistic quality to it. Extraneous details are omitted and the story focuses on three characters: the brutal and extreme Critias, the moderate oligarch Theramenes, and the exiled democratic leader Thrasybulus. What is disturbing to the modern historian is the possibility (and for some the *probability*) that Xenophon not only has omitted a great deal of information, but even has rearranged the sequence of events for greater dramatic effect.[64] The following is one particularly striking example.

According to Aristotle, the deposing of the Thirty in 403 BC was accompanied by a reconciliation and an amnesty.[65] Xenophon indeed places the initial reconciliation in this context (*HG* 2.4.38), but he

---

[60] Schwartz (1929), 133, well observed that in Book 1 'historical presentation has turned into apology'. Kagan (1969), 370–1, and (2009), 23–74, maintains that the war was not inevitable and could have been avoided if the Athenians had been willing to compromise.

[61] For chronological problems in the *Hellenica*, see Tuplin (1993), 169–71, 201–5, 207–9 and D. Thomas (2009), 331–9. For omissions, see M. A. Flower (2017).

[62] Dillery (1995), 139, 146.

[63] Other sources contain details omitted by Xenophon: Arist. *Ath. Pol.* 34–41; Lysias, speeches 12 and 13; Diod. Sic. 14.3–6, 32–3.

[64] For lists of the omissions, see Tuplin (1993), 43 n. 1 and Krentz (1995), 122; and for the arrangement of material, see Wolpert (2002), 15–24 and Shear (2011), 180–5.

[65] *Ath. Pol.* 39.

Seven Types of Fiction in the Greek Historians   39

mentions an amnesty only after the subsequent reconciliation in 401 BC with those oligarchs who had taken refuge in Eleusis:

> Later, hearing that those in Eleusis were hiring mercenaries, they made an expedition against them with their entire army. They slew their generals during a parley, but by sending to the others their friends and relatives, they persuaded them to be reconciled. And they swore oaths that they would not remember past wrongs, and still even now they live together as citizens and the people abide by their oaths. (*HG* 2.4.43)

Xenophon's displacement of the amnesty to the very last sentence of the story of the Thirty may have a purely literary function, allowing him to end his account of this brutal episode in Athenian history on a positive note.[66]

This type of temporal displacement happens all the time in historical novels, as well as in films, and most of us do not get too upset about this, unless, of course, we are expecting the novel or film to do the educational work of narrative history proper. Let me give just one example of the type of purposeful chronological inaccuracy that is permissible in historical fiction, this time turning to an American writer. In Willa Cather's 1927 novel, *Death Comes for the Archbishop*, the main character is a bishop, Jean Marie Latour, who leaves France with his childhood friend, the priest Joseph Vaillant, in order to become missionary priests in the United States. The novel is closely based on the life of Jean-Baptiste Lamy (1814–88), who would become the first bishop, and then archbishop, of the Diocese of Santa Fe in New Mexico Territory. In order to create a more dramatic arc to the narrative, Cather reverses the order of a central event; she has Archbishop Latour's close friend, Joseph Vaillant (whose real name was Joseph Machebeuf), predecease him (whereas the historical Lamy died nearly seventeen months earlier). This temporal manipulation serves a dramatic purpose. It allows Latour to travel to Colorado to attend his friend's funeral and it adds poignancy to Latour's final deathbed thoughts that bring the novel to its close – his attempt to persuade the young Vaillant to board the coach for Paris, the first stage of their long and arduous journey to America.

In conclusion, let me circle round to the question that I asked at the beginning of this essay. Can a truth that is at all circumstantial be found only in novels? If we are speaking of a kind philosophical and poetic truth, then, yes, it can be found in novels; but it can also be found in many of the

---

[66] Note Krentz (1995), 155–6, and see further M. A. Flower (2017), 310–11.

Greek and Roman historians, and not least of all in Herodotus, Thucydides, and Xenophon. As Kurt Raaflaub has so eloquently expressed it, they wanted to impart to their readers a truth deeper and more profound than a mere surface truth.[67] Yet we should not think that the motive behind their manipulations and elaborations was always, or even primarily, altruistic. And in this they share something with their modern counterparts, whose narratives can be imbued with partisan ideology and whose motives may include the desire for fame, wealth, and, occasionally at least, the wish to settle scores. Stendhal also says of Comp de Tracy that his manners were perfect except when he was in one of his nasty dark moods because the French had not appreciated his *Logic* and *Idéologie*.[68]

---

[67] Raaflaub (2016), 619–20.

[68] That is, his *Logique* (1805) and his five-volume *Éléments d'idéologie* (1817–18). The complaint would be valid today as well. See Stendhal's *Memoirs of an Egotist* (*Souvenirs d'égotisme*), ch. 4.

CHAPTER 2

Folktale and Local Tradition in Charon of Lampsacus

Nino Luraghi

The study of traditional narrative originated largely as a result of the combined influence of two of the most momentous historical phenomena of the nineteenth century, namely, romanticism and the rise of the nation-state. The first modern collection of folktales, the *Kinder- und Hausmärchen*, edited by the brothers Jacob and Wilhelm Grimm, started coming out at the beginning of 1813, months before the *Völkerschlacht* in Leipzig in October 1813, which marked the end of Napoleon's Empire. It is more than a mere coincidence that the 'battle of the nations' received its nickname from the German romantic literate Achim von Arnim, who was also one of the original sponsors of the Grimm enterprise.[1] The ultimate goal of the collection was transparent in the very technique adopted by the brothers: by gathering stories directly from the voice of oral informants whenever possible and including data on the informant and on the time and place of the recording, they intended to document with philological accuracy the spirit of the German people in the most pristine and least adulterated form possible. Here, however, comes a striking paradox, for soon the Grimm brothers themselves realized that many of the stories they had collected found close parallels far away in time and space – so much for the German spirit. Their response to this finding, in extreme simplification, consisted in connecting folktales to an original corpus of Indo-European myths that had devolved into folktales over time and spread all over Indo-European cultural areas. This theory, however, dissolved

---

[1] On Achim von Arnim, one of the most influential intellectuals of early romanticism in Germany (technically, the 'Heidelberg romanticism' in German scholarship, where the definition 'early romanticism' is reserved for the Jena circle, some ten years earlier; from a European perspective, though, von Arnim, like his close associate Clemens Brentano, would definitely count as an early romantic), see T. J. Ziolkowski (2009); on his connection to the Grimm brothers, Rölleke (1977), 815–18 and Uther (2013), 459 and 468–9.

quickly, as soon as sufficient evidence was compiled from non-Indo-European cultures.[2]

The Indo-European theory was then replaced at the turn of the century by the historic-geographic method, as it was called, also known as the Finnish method, consisting in analysing each folktale in order to identify a fundamental narrative structure, composed of a number of recurrent motifs, and then plotting its diffusion in time and space in order to find out where the story originally came from. In order to facilitate the application of this method, in 1910 the Finnish folklorist Antti Aarne compiled a repertoire of story-types, the *Verzeichnis der Märchentypen*, which was later updated and expanded by the American folklorist Stith Thompson in 1928 and then again in 1961, under the title *The Types of the Folktale*.[3] Meanwhile, even this version has been supplanted in 2011 by *The Types of the International Folktales*, in three volumes, edited by the German folklorist and editor in chief of the *Enzyklopädie des Märchens*, Hans-Jörg Uther.[4] Behind the slight change in title from Aarne's original book to Uther's volumes lies a sea-change in the approach to traditional narrative, something we might broadly characterize as a transition from historical diffusionism to typology. Already Stith Thompson, with his invaluable index of motifs, had facilitated the approach to folktales as complex products made of simple parts that could be assembled in different ways by way of a process similar to formulaic composition.[5] Vladimir Propp's formalist approach pointed in the same direction.[6] After World War II, the notion that the historical origin of a story could be traced systematically has been essentially set aside, and the study of what is now known as international folktales has turned largely typological, while acquiring a stronger interest in audiences and performance, without, however, entirely giving up the notion that stories do travel, and their movements across cultural boundaries may in certain cases be traced.[7]

---

[2] On the methods and concerns of the Grimm brothers, see Uther (2013), 459–95. For a concise and authoritative overview of the early stages in the study of folktales, see W. Hansen (2002), 1–12.

[3] On the origins and early development of the Finnish method, see Thompson (1946), 395–8 and 415–27.

[4] Uther (2011); references to ATU, for Aarne-Thompson-Uther, indicate types from Uther's collection.

[5] Thompson (1955–58); in the following, references to single motifs collected in this work will follow the conventional format composed of a capital letter followed by digits (such as D1415, quoted below).

[6] Propp (1928). On Propp and his influence, see Voigt (2000) with further references. For a brief introduction to Propp's method, with practical examples, see Burkert (1979), 5–22.

[7] It is intriguing to observe how the results produced by large collections of folktales regularly refuted the assumptions they were meant to prove.

Folktale and Local Tradition in Charon of Lampsacus   43

The study of early Greek historiography has paid intermittent attention to the concerns, methods and results of folklore studies. Long ago, the work of Wolf Aly had alerted ancient historians to the presence in the writings of early Greek historians, especially of Herodotus, of a good number of stories that more or less closely followed known folktale types.[8] Aly approached the problem within what was still an essentially romantic paradigm, attempting to tease out from early Greek prose the real voice of the Greek people, and both the implicit political agenda of his approach and his explicit commitment to National Socialism have contributed to marginalizing his work in research after World War II – as well they ought to, one might say.[9] While the cultural framework in which Aly placed his empirical observations is dubious at best, however, the empirical observations themselves still stand and pose a challenge to our understanding of the work of the first Greek historians and of the nature of oral historical tradition in classical Greece. That challenge is at the same time an opportunity, and points to specific avenues of research. If we believe, as we presumably do in the wake of Felix Jacoby, Arnaldo Momigliano and Oswyn Murray, that early Greek historiography largely relied on pre-existing oral narratives, the study of traditional narrative in general and of folktale types and motifs in particular provides one of the few ways of gaining insight into the dynamics of Greek oral historical tradition.[10] While Herodotus' *Histories* obviously offers the best corpus for trying out this set of methods and ideas, a close look at the few early historians whose work is preserved in more than just one-line references may offer a chance to broaden our horizon and counteract to some extent the negative consequences of Herodotus' splendid isolation, arguably one of the more serious obstacles in the way of a historical understanding of his work. The present contribution will focus on selected fragments of the fifth-century historian Charon of Lampsacus, analysing them with the methods of folklore studies. It will then conclude with some remarks on the style evidenced by such fragments in comparison with Herodotus' style.[11]

---

[8] Aly (1969), originally published in 1921. On Aly's methodology and outlook, see Luraghi (2013), 90–2.

[9] On Aly's political ideas and the way they interacted with his career and scholarship, see Malitz (2006), 307, with references to documents and evidence.

[10] See, in particular, Murray (2001) and the development of scholarship outlined in Luraghi (2001a), 4–10. I have attempted to test the usefulness of folktale studies for this purpose in Luraghi (2013).

[11] For an introduction to Charon, see especially Ceccarelli (2016), providing a thorough discussion of every aspect and a comprehensive bibliography.

In 1977, in his survey of Charon's fragments related to Persia, Mauro Moggi concluded: 'Charon's image remains rather opaque and subtracts itself to any attempt at a more precise and detailed understanding.' Paola Ceccarelli's recent survey strikes a similar note. It is certainly true that the little we know about Charon interacts in perverse ways with all that we do not know, making it truly prohibitive to form a general picture of his work.[12] The Suda has a detailed list of works, including ten different titles, and in moments of despair one is visited by the thought that we would be better off without it. The list of the Suda includes *Aithiopika*, *Persika* in two books, *Hellenika* in four books, *On Lampsakos* in two books, *Libyka*, *Annals of the Lampsakenes* in four books, a chronographic work called *Prytaneis of the Lakedaimonians*, *Foundations of Cities* in two books, *Kretika* in three books (where the laws of Minos were discussed) and a *Periplous of the Lands beyond the Pillars of Herakles*. None of these titles would be absolutely impossible for the interests of early Greek historians, although some seem rather unlikely, and more importantly, it is hard to see how they all belong together. In such a situation, naturally scholars have been busy pruning the list, suggesting conflations of titles and pointing to possible duplications.[13] Felix Jacoby famously took the opposite approach, accepting the list almost in full and making Charon into a pro-Spartan historian active in the late fifth century and into the years of the Spartan hegemony in the early fourth, possibly connected to Lysander. The two cornerstones of Jacoby's reconstruction were the titles *Prytaneis of the Lakedaimonians* and *Hellenika*, the latter pointing to a genre that is not attested as such until after Thucydides. Jacoby's typically robust and imaginative reconstruction, however, cannot mask the fact that he was skating over very thin ice. After all, the word *Hellenika* is used to refer to the early history of the Greeks already by Thucydides, which strongly discourages one from using its appearance as what became the title of works on that topic as a chronological parameter.[14] In any case, in spite of the usual fascination of Jacoby's vision, it is fair to say that nowadays scholars have essentially returned to the chronology indicated by Dionysios

---

[12] Moggi (1977), 26; similar remarks in Jacoby (1956), 183, and Ceccarelli (2016).

[13] Jacoby (1956), 184–5, provides a list of attempts up to his time and criticizes them radically; see also the discussion of Moggi (1977), 2–6, and Ceccarelli (2016), commentary to 262 T 1.

[14] Thuc. 1.97.2, where *ta Hellenika* appears in a clearly historiographical sense; cf. the comments of Jacoby (1956), 196–7. It is a revealing detail that, while Jacoby wrote that correcting *Prytaneis of the Lakedaimonians* into *Prytaneis of the Lampsakenes* was out of the question, presumably on philological grounds, Robert Fowler (2013), 642, recently called this 'a very attractive emendation'.

Folktale and Local Tradition in Charon of Lampsacus   45

of Halikarnassos, putting Charon before Thucydides and probably also before Herodotus, and occasionally expressing puzzlement at the variety of his works.[15]

Such a variety, it has to be said, has only rare parallels among the early prose writers, the group to which Charon is supposed to belong. Only Dionysios of Miletos comes close to Charon, with a list of six titles, and this is really not terribly encouraging, given the uncertainties that surround Dionysios.[16] We come on somewhat firmer ground with Hellanikos, whose many works overtaxed even the patience of the lexicographers. Jacoby thought there was a close relation between the two, and recently Paola Ceccarelli has pointed in the same direction.[17] Parallels between the works of Hellanikos and those of Charon are more suggestive than informative, however, and this is due in part to the shape of their respective fragments. While the titles attributed to Charon may suggest antiquarian and chronographic interests on his part, nothing of the sort is actually evidenced by the fragments. On the other hand, unlike Hellanikos' very many fragments, which are normally references of detail of the sort of 'Hellanikos said X about topic Y,' Charon's very few fragments are occasionally rather substantial, as fragments go, including passages that read very much like verbatim excerpts. It is for this reason, in my opinion, that the remains of Charon's work may deserve a second look.

The three major fragments this contribution will focus on – 1, 7, and 17 in Jacoby's numbering – share an interest in local history. Two of them, fragments 7 and 17, deal directly with Lampsacus, in fact with crucial moments in the early history of the city, while fragment 1 talks about the city of Kardia, a neighbour of Lampsacus on the western side of the Thracian Chersonesos, which appears to have been in close and often hostile relations with Lampsacus itself. Only the latter fragment is attributed to a specific work of Charon's: according to Athenaios, who quotes it, it comes from the second of the supposedly four books of the *Annals of Lampsakos*. As for the other two fragments, there is little doubt that they, too, derive from one of the two works on Lampsacus attributed to Charon, which many scholars think are one and the same work anyway.

Fragment 1 opens with a sentence that reads almost like a title ('The Bisaltai attacked Kardia and won'), then continues with the story of Naris,

---

[15] See Dion. Hal. *Th.* 5 and *Pomp.* 3.7 (= Charon 262 T 3a and 3b) and the commentary to 262 T 1 by Ceccarelli (2016).
[16] On the shadowy Dionysios of Miletos, see Moggi (1972), 434–8 and Zambrini (2006), 192–200.
[17] Ceccarelli (2016), commentary to 262 T 1.

a Thracian of the tribe of the Bisaltai, who had been sold as a slave to a man of Kardia when he was a boy. His master turned him into a barber, and it so happened that in the barber shop Naris overheard local customers discussing an oracle according to which the Bisaltai would attack Kardia.[18] Thereupon Naris fled and rejoined his people, became their leader and led them against Kardia. Knowing that the people of Kardia had taught their horses to dance to the sound of *auloi* during their *symposia*, Naris got hold of a female *aulos* player from Kardia and had her teach many Bisaltai the tunes the horses were used to. When they came to battle, Naris ordered the *aulos* players to play the tunes and, lo and behold, the horses stood up on their hind legs and started to dance, whereupon the Kardians were defeated, since the cavalry was their main strength. Overall, the narrative is quite laconic. We are not told, for example, why Naris was chosen by the Bisaltai as their leader; we must assume either that he came originally from a prominent family, as Aly thought,[19] or that he persuaded his compatriots to put him in charge because he had found an infallible way to defeat the enemy, as in one version of the corresponding Sybaris story to which we will come in a moment. The dancing horses are presented with the minimum possible amount of detail, and the crucial information that they reacted to specific tunes is provided only in the context of the battle. We will return to these observations in connection with Charon's style later on.

It is difficult to connect this episode in a meaningful way to the little that we know about the history of the two parties involved during the archaic period. According to the geographical works that go under the names of Pseudo-Skymnos and Pseudo-Skylax and to Strabon, Kardia had originally been founded by Milesians and Klazomenians, an indefinite amount of time before the arrival of Miltiades the Elder in the Thracian Chersonesos, itself tentatively dated to the 540s BC.[20] From that moment onwards, the history of the area is documented in some detail by Herodotus, and there seems to be no space in which to insert the battle between Kardians and Bisaltai, which suggests that the episode narrated by Charon should be situated in the earlier phase of the life of the city, that is,

---

[18] *Pace* Hepperle (1956), 75, the topos of the barber shop as a place where one could eavesdrop on conversations is not Hellenistic; it goes back to the fifth century, as shown by Nicolson (1891), 42, with references to Old Comedy.

[19] Aly (1969), 219; see also Hepperle (1956), 74.

[20] Hdt. 6.34–5. On the Milesian and Klazomenian foundation, see Ps.Skyl. 67; Ps.Skym. 698–703; Str. 7 fr. 51 and Loukopoulou (2004), 907. For the date of Miltiades' arrival to Kardia, see the discussion in Isaac (1986), 163–4 and 170–1.

during the first half of the sixth century at the latest.[21] In terms of geography, the Bisaltai, it must be said, were not the most obvious enemy for Kardia. Assimilated into the Macedonian kingdom under Alexander the First according to Thucydides, they are known to us thanks to a handful of references in Greek authors and to the silver coins minted with their name and that of their kings between the sixth and fifth centuries. Clearly, in this period they had access to the precious metals mined in the Dysoron mines in the lower valley of the Strymon, which is the area in which they appear to have been located, in the hinterland of what would later be Amphipolis.[22] We cannot exclude that in earlier times they had lived further to the east, but it may be more reasonable to assume that the attack on Kardia was a raid and that even then the Bisaltai were not the immediate neighbours of Kardia. This would be consistent with the impression, conveyed by the story, that the Bisaltai did not know an awful lot about Kardia and its inhabitants before Naris enlightened them.

Before turning to the narrative side of the story, two more points related to the historical background may be made explicit. First of all, in the way Herodotus depicts the mission of the Thracian Dolonkoi to Greece searching for help, one does not have the impression that there were already Greek settlements in their area. This is mildly puzzling, and one may speculate whether this silence regarding the existence of a Greek colony at Kardia is innocent or replicates a bias in the Athenian or Philaid tradition. Alternatively, it is possible that the actual outcome of Charon's story, left out by Athenaios, was the abandonment of Kardia by its original Greek colonists. The second point has to do with the metropolis of Kardia, Miletos. By the late fifth century, the Milesians had somehow acquired a reputation for excessive sophistication, causing a loss of military efficiency.[23] Again, one may wonder whether the Kardians might have inherited a similar reputation from their Milesian forefathers. It scarcely needs to be recalled that the other city that had a reputation for excessive luxury that compares to that of the Milesians, and in fact is very

---

[21] See the comprehensive discussion of the Greek settlements in the Chersonese until the Persian conquest in Isaac (1986), 159–75. Conceivably, the clash between Kardians and Bisaltai may have been inserted by Charon in his *Annals of Lampsakos* as a retrospective excursus prompted by the war between Miltiades and Lampsacus at the time of Kroisos, mentioned by Herodotus (6.37).

[22] Thuc. 2.99.6. On the territory of the Bisaltai, see Hammond (1972), 192–9 and Archibald (1998), 106 and the map at 108. The coinage of the Bisaltai appears to continue until around the middle of the fifth century BC; see Kraay and Moorey (1981).

[23] See Gorman (2001), 13 and 103–4. The reputation is attested as early as Ar. *Pl.* 1003, but at that point the Milesians' loss of martial virtues was already proverbial. It may well have originated from attempts at explaining a posteriori the failure of the Ionian revolt; see Murray (1988), 471–2.

48   NINO LURAGHI

often mentioned in connection with the Milesians, is Sybaris, whose cavalry supposedly had the same misadventure as that of Kardia.[24] We will come back to this.

Whatever its actual historical value, the story told by Charon is striking for the abundance of folktale motifs embedded in it, often with a thin rationalizing veneer. Stith Thompson's motif index makes it relatively easy to isolate them. The most obvious motif is the dance of the horses, which is clearly a variation on the pattern of the Zaubertanz. Documented in narrative traditions ranging from India to the British Isles, the motif most often involves a magic musical instrument, such as a lute, a flute or a violin, that compels to dance those who listen to its music.[25] In another variant, it is a specific tune that has magic qualities and compels the listeners to dance, and in some cases the dancing listeners are animals.[26] In the story of Kardia and the Bisaltai, as in the parallel version that involves Sybaris and Kroton for that matter, the motif is rationalized in that the horses, we are told, had been specifically taught by their owners to dance, and the magic quality of the music can thereby be dispensed with: the horses just reacted as they had been trained to. This detail makes it possible to embed in the story further meanings with what looks like a cross-cultural relevance and also more specifically Greek aspects. For the latter, note that the horses were supposed to perform as entertainers in the most typically Greek framework for sophisticated entertainment, namely, the *symposion*.[27] Thinking for a second of the practicalities of bringing a horse into an *andrōn* is enough to realize that even in this version the story remains very close to the genre of the folktale. The punishment for excessive refinement, which ends up damaging the very people who practice it, is a cross-culturally common notion, even though here declined according to specifically Greek cultural codes such as the concept of *tryphē*.[28] On a more general level, one could say that the people of Sybaris and Kardia got punished for perverting nature by teaching animals to behave like humans, thereby creating automata they could not fully

---

[24] On the connection between Miletos and Sybaris, see Hdt. 6.21.1.

[25] Thompson (1955–58) D1415.2.

[26] See the various motifs collected under Thompson (1955–58) D1440; magic tunes: D1275 with its several variants, and cf. D1441.1.4 and D1444.4.

[27] Murray (2018), esp. 282–309.

[28] See Lubtchansky (2005), 51–5, with further references, showing, among other things, that *pace* Gorman and Gorman (2007) in Greek literature the historiographical topos of luxury causing disaster is much older than Athenaios of Naukratis.

Folktale and Local Tradition in Charon of Lampsacus 49

control; famous variations of this motif include the legend of the Golem and the story of Frankenstein.

Already Bolte and Polívka, followed by Aly, recognized in the story elements of a very popular folktale, listed in the collection of the Grimm brothers under the title 'Der Jud im Dorn', but they did not provide a close comparison.[29] The task is made much easier for us by the typology of folktales originally developed by Antti Aarne and then revised by Stith Thompson and finally by Hans-Jörg Uther. Under the title 'The Dance among Thorns', the story appears to belong to a larger group of stories that focus on magical objects.[30] The summary of the type provided by Uther goes as follows. The first phase of the story deals with the acquisition of the magical object or objects. A boy, driven from home by an evil stepmother or dismissed from service with an unfairly inadequate reward after years of labour, gives his money or any part of his meagre possessions to a poor man, who turns out to be a friendly spirit who grants the boy three wishes. The boy asks for a magic fiddle or other musical instrument that compels people to dance, a never-failing crossbow and the power of having his wishes obeyed or some other magic object or power (typically, the third wish varies and appears to be less important in the development of the narrative; one has the impression that it enters the story only because of the traditional force of the motif of the 'three wishes'). In the second phase, the hero is confronted by an antagonist whom he challenges to some sort of duel and then defeats with the help of the magic object. In the 'Jew in Thorns' version, the boy shoots a bird on a wager with his magical crossbow, so the Jew is compelled to fetch the bird from a thorn bush, and when he is there the boy plays the violin and compels the Jew to dance among the thorns. In other variants, the boy defeats a giant by compelling him to dance. In the final phase, the boy is brought to court for his misdeeds and condemned to be hanged, so he asks to be allowed to play his fiddle one last time and compels the judge and the guards to dance until he is released. Variants of the story are documented from the fifteenth century onwards in Germany, all over Scandinavia and the Baltic area, but also in Greece and among enslaved Africans in Jamaica.

The comparison between the folktale and the story of Naris is illuminating in various ways. Clearly, in the first phase of the story the basic mechanism is the compensation for injustice suffered, which in the case of Naris consists in being sold into slavery as a child. As a reward, thanks to his position he acquires privileged knowledge that will benefit his people.

---

[29] Bolte-Polívka (1915), 490–503.   [30] Uther (2011), vol. 1, 349–50 (ATU 592).

For the theme of the competitive advantage derived from awareness of an oracle given to the enemy, one just needs to recall the story of Alyattes, Thrasyboulos and Periander in Herodotus.[31] Even though Charon is not explicit on this, the oracle the Kardians were talking about must have involved their being defeated at the hands of the Bisaltai, and it is of relevance for the logic of the story that the Bisaltai were not the next-door neighbours of the Kardians and accordingly not their most obvious enemies. As is often typical when comparing a type realized in the genres of the folktale and of the novella, in Charon's story the magical elements are elided. Naris relies only on his own wits and receives no supernatural help, but the result is the same. When he returns to the Bisaltai with the promise of leading them to certain victory, he is chosen as their leader, receiving the first part of his reward, which in some sense reinstates him in the position he had lost at the beginning of the story. He then acquires a magical object, of whose existence he was already aware, in the form of an *aulos* player, herself a slave, who can teach the right tune to get the horses of the Kardians to dance. The trial of the battle ends well for Naris and the Bisaltai, and their victory corresponds to the final reward of the protagonist of the folktale.

Interestingly, the repertories of folktales do not seem to offer close parallels for the motif of the Zaubertanz in the context of a battle. Closer to home, as it were, Jacoby pointed to Herodotus' story of the stratagem of Harpagos that allowed king Cyrus to rout the Lydian cavalry, by exploiting the alleged terror of the horses for the camels, but this parallel is very loose at best.[32] The motif of horses, or elephants for that matter, that panic and turn against their own army is itself fairly widespread, and Herodotus' story is an example of this motif, which is different in fundamental ways from the dancing horses of Kardia. A very close parallel does exist, however, and has been long since recognized. The Achaian colony of Sybaris in Southern Italy, famous for the wealth and refinement of its inhabitants, was fatally defeated in battle by the neighbouring Krotoniates in the same way as the Kardians by the Bisaltai. Like the Kardians, the hyper-sophisticated Sybarites had taught their horses to dance at their banquets. When the two armies were drawn up for battle, the Krotoniates stroke the appropriate tune and the whole cavalry of the Sybarites went over to their side.[33]

---

[31] Hdt. 1.19–20. [32] Jacoby (1943), 6–7, referring to Hdt. 1.80.
[33] The most detailed analysis of the various versions of the episode, and by far the most robust argument in favour of a historical kernel for the dancing horses of Sybaris, is found in Lubtchansky

Given the rarity and the specificity of the dancing horses motif, it is almost inevitable to wonder whether Sybaris or Kardia featured in the original version of this story. Athenaios reports the story told from the Aristotelian *Constitution of Sybaris* in a somewhat summary fashion that makes comparisons difficult.[34] The question of how the Krotoniates knew which tune to play is not even brought up, although given the closeness of the two cities, it may not have appeared to be a question in the first place. The only other version of the story, however, explains that the necessary know-how had been provided by an *aulos* player who had escaped from Sybaris after having been maltreated. He persuaded the Krotoniates to put him in command of their army and instructed a unit of *aulos* players, the ones who, according to Aristotle, were disguised as soldiers in the ranks of the army of Kroton deployed for battle. This version is transmitted in the *Kestoi* of Sextus Julius Africanus, a younger contemporary of Athenaios.[35] Clearly, in it the disgruntled *aulos* player has the role that is played by Naris in Charon's story, or, more precisely, his character conflates the role of Naris and that of the female *aulos* player, herself a slave acquired by Naris from Kardia. This detail may be of importance in making up our mind as to which version is the original one. Female *aulos* players were stock characters at Greek *symposia*, notoriously performing multiple roles.[36] Adult male *aulos* players, on the contrary, do not seem to belong there. On the other hand, the *aulos* player from Sybaris had to be male because he had to play double duty, music teacher and leader of the army, but this was possible only at the cost of some cultural inconsistency. Naris, on the contrary, is perfect for the role of the 'enemy within' that the imagination of slaveholders liked to attribute to slaves with cross-cultural consistency.[37]

(1993), reworked and extended in Lubtchansky (2005), 45–69. On Sybaris and its image in Greek literature, see Ampolo (1994).

[34] Fr. 533 Rose quoted by Athenaios, *Deipn.* 12.520c–d. Ael. *NA* 16.23 has a version of the story that resembles Aristotle's (see Lubtchansky (2005), 63–4); a shorter reference to the dancing cavalry of Sybaris occurs in Plin. *Nat.* 8.157.

[35] Julius Africanus *Cesti* F 12, 11 Wallraff et al. For a brief sketch of Africanus' intriguing figure, see Chadwick (2001), 130–1. On the *Cesti* and their cultural environment, Adler (2009).

[36] See Davidson (1997), 81 and 92–3. Goldman (2015) provides a nuanced assessment of the role of the female flute-players, questioning their role as sex workers (but not as potential sexual objects).

[37] The story of the dancing horses appealed to the fantasy of Renaissance poets: it was picked up from Africanus by Angelo Poliziano, *Miscellaneorum centuria prima*, ch. 15 of the Aldine edition of 1498 (Wallraff et al. (2016), lxxxiv); this must be the direct source of Francesco Cieco da Ferrara, *Mambriano* 3.61–6, where the motif of the dancing horses was noticed by Bolte and Polívka (1915), 503 (on this little-known chivalric romance of the late fifteenth century, see Everson (2011) and Martini (2016)).

This conclusion regarding the relation between the story of Kardia and that of Sybaris does not amount to a demonstration, because after all we cannot tell exactly how close the older Aristotelian version was to what we read in Africanus, but certainly in terms of originality the Sybarite cavalry faces an uphill battle. Now it has to be said that the presence of *Wandermotive* in the stories about the luxury of the Sybarites would come as no surprise and finds easy parallels, to say nothing of the obvious applicability of the *lectio difficilior* principle to the question of priority between Kardia and Sybaris.[38] Still, if one thinks of what has been built, in terms of historical interpretation, on the dance of the Sybarite horses, it does not seem trivial to recognize that the original dancing horses are probably those of Kardia rather than those of Sybaris. This of course does not yet tell us how the story migrated from the East to the West of the Greek world. A further study of the development of the ancient tradition on Sybaris would be necessary to define chronological parameters, and this is clearly not the venue for such a study. Suffice it to say that it is not inevitable to believe that Charon's work itself was the source of the Sybarite version or versions, although certainly such a working hypothesis could have striking implications for the circulation of Charon's local historical work.

In the case of fragment 17, as anticipated, we are at least one more step removed from Charon's original text, and possibly even more. In the absence of other works of local historiography devoted to Lampsacus and considering that Polyainos also has a version of fragment 7, attributing to Charon the passage at hand seems reasonable enough but, of course, far from certain.[39] The story deals with a border controversy between Parion and Lampsacus, a common occurrence in relations between neighbouring poleis. An agreement having been reached according to which two parties would leave on the same day from Parion and Lampsacus, respectively, as soon as the birds sung at dawn, the Lampsacenes persuaded certain fishermen along the coast, as soon as they saw the Parians arriving, to start frying large amounts of fish and offering libations to Poseidon, inviting the Parians to join them. The latter duly fell into the trap, forgetting the seriousness of their mission, and the Lampsakene walkers arrived undisturbed to a place called Hermaion, only 70 stades away from Parion but 200 stades from Lampsacus. On the face of it, the story probably

---

[38] Ceccarelli (2016), commentary to F 1, is also inclined to think that the story about Kardia is more likely the original (because 'Sybaris seems to offer a better context for an adaptation').

[39] Jacoby (1943), 23–4, is more sanguine than Ceccarelli (2016), commentary to F 17.

Folktale and Local Tradition in Charon of Lampsacus 53

performed an aetiological function in explaining why the border between the two poleis was so much closer to Parion than to Lampsacus. The motif of the clever hero distracting the adversary from an important task by offering an immediate and enticing reward has many parallels in folklore, from Jacob and Esau to the Master thief.[40] But there might be more to this story.

The race to determine the boundaries between two cities appears several times in Greek colonial narratives. The most famous case is that of the Phileni brothers and the border between Carthage and Cyrene, but Jacoby points to a less-known example, 'aus heller historischer Zeit' as he says, involving Kymai and Klazomenai and providing the closest parallel to the story from Charon. Here, the two poleis were disputing the possession of a place called Leuke, and the Pythia ordered that the place should belong to the polis whose citizens would be the first to sacrifice there, whereupon it was agreed that two parties should leave from either polis at sunrise. In all three cases, victory is achieved by cheating of some sort: the simplest expedient was adopted by the Phileni, who with true *Punica fides* left earlier than agreed in the version of Valerius Maximus; the version of Sallust exculpates them, thereby dissolving the possible connection between their cheating and their final sacrifice. The Klazomenians founded a new polis ad hoc so as to have a closer starting point. The Lampsakenes, let it be noted, are the only ones who are innocent of fraud, or almost: in their story, it is the stupidity of the antagonist that determines the result, and the folktale motif is preserved in its purest form, free from specifically Greek or imputed Carthaginian cultural elements such as the foundation of a new colony or human sacrifice.[41]

Compared to the story of Naris and the Kardians, in the race to the border folklore motifs are built into a story that makes sense only in specific political contexts. Accordingly, the race to the border does not feature as a type in the repertoires of international tales.[42] This is not to say that there are no parallels to the story in modern folklore – far from it. Here, however, the underlying motif of the lack of a definite border between communities appears to have migrated from the colonial situation

---

[40] See W. Hansen (2002), 357–70.

[41] Kyme and Klazomenai: Diod. Sic. 15.18.204 and Jacoby (1943), 23. Phileni brothers: Sal. *Iug.* 79 and V. Max. 5.6 *ext.*4 and Malkin (1990); on the relation between the version of Sallust and Valerius Maximus, see Oniga (1990), 57–61.

[42] It does, however, bear a clear relationship to the many stories of races between animals won by deception of some sort: see, for instance, ATU 200D 'Why Cat Is Indoors and Dog Outside in Cold'.

54   NINO LURAGHI

to marginal borderlands in mountainous areas. Renato Oniga's remarkable
investigation of this story pattern offers two parallels from modern alpine
folklore, both involving the establishment of the border between two
communities by a converging competitive race of champions.[43] In both
cases, the crowing of the rooster at dawn was a key factor, and more or less
successful stratagems that are intended to ensure that the roosters involved
would wake up as early as possible have the function discharged by various
tricks in the Greek versions. One of the two stories involves the cantons of
Uri and Glarus in central Switzerland; the other one, the towns of Auronzo
in Veneto and Toblach in Südtyrol. In the Swiss case, documented from
the early nineteenth century, the champions were two mountaineers, and
the one from Glarus, who had started later because his canton fellows had
fed their rooster too rich a fare, managed to gain a little portion of territory
for his canton by accepting to continue the race transporting his opponent
attached to his neck. As a result, the Glarus man died, sacrificing his life for
his community, which kept perpetual grateful memory of his sacrifice. In
the example from Auronzo, collected from oral narrators in 1951, the
champions who decide the ownership of the rich pasture lands of Misurina
and Rinbianco are the two oldest women of the two towns, and it turns
out that the boundary they established was also the border of the
Repubblica Serenissima.

   The story of the *Grenzlauf* between Glarus and Uri shares with the story
of the Phileni brothers the motive of the sacrifice of the runner. This detail
invites some further reflection. In myth as well as in ritual, sacrifice is an
effective way of inscribing meaning in the landscape, and Oniga provides
rich evidence for the use of sacrifice in order to establish a border.[44] Once
one starts looking at the story from this angle, one cannot but notice that
sacrifice is precisely the confirming action that the winners are meant to
perform in the story of Leuke. One also wonders whether the fact that the
citizens of Klazomenai who were sent to found the new colony were
selected by lot, as we are told by Diodoros, might not be a slight
transformation of the motif, the lottery pointing to the expulsion that is
frequently associated with the selection of colonists.[45] This would perhaps
bring us one step closer to understanding why in the case of Auronzo and
Toblach the two oldest women of the villages were chosen, as if potential

---

[43] Oniga (1990), 77–85. On the complex history of the Swiss version, which was included in the
   Deutsche Sagen of the Grimm brothers, see Röhrich (1949/50), 352–6.
[44] See Oniga (1990), 87–109 and Malkin (1990). On the relation of rituals and foundation stories,
   Burkert (1979) and the contributions collected in Burkert (1991).
[45] On the motive of expulsion in Greek colonial narratives, see Dougherty (1993), 31–44.

pharmakoi.[46] At this point, one may start to look with different eyes at the fact that the fishermen who delayed the party from Parion did so by organizing a sacrifice. Might these all be permutations of the same motif, one wonders? At the very least, what we might at this point call the pattern of the *Grenzlauf* turns out potentially to involve a deeper cultural symbolism, which the story of Lampsacus and Parion deploys in a rather more light-hearted way than the other ones, possibly replacing the dramatic motif of sacrifice with the merry story of the fishermen frying fish and drinking in honour of the god of the sea.

Finally, let us now turn to fragment 7a, the foundation of Lampsacus as narrated in Plutarch's *Bravery of Women*.[47] Of the fragments of Charon, this is by far the one that has received most attention, especially in recent years. Attracted by the similarities with stories connected to the foundation of Massalia and reported via the Aristotelian *Constitution of Massalia* and Justin's *Epitome* of Pompeius Trogus, scholars have focused on aspects that seemed liable to being historicized, in an attempt at defining specific characteristics of Phokaian colonization, that supposedly developed organically out of pre-existing trading connections.[48] With all due caution, elements such as military cooperation with the locals and the offer by a local ruler of land on which to settle seem indeed to belong to a specific pattern, whose association with the Phokaians is all the more plausible if we think of the case of Argantonios, the king of the Tartessians, where the invitation was not accepted, as pointed out in a recent contribution by Pier Giovanni Guzzo;[49] the actual historical meaning of this narrative pattern would still require a precise assessment.

The story tells of two twin brothers of royal blood, Phobos and Blepsos. The former had the distinction of being the first on record to commit suicide by jumping in the sea from the Leukadian Rocks. Previously, he had travelled to the Propontic area for trading purposes and there befriended Mandron, the king of the Bebrykoi of Pytoessa, to whom he lent military support against aggressive neighbours. Mandron suggested to Phobos that he come back with colonists, promising him a portion of the city and of the territory. Phobos went back to Phokaia and sent thence his twin brother, Blepsos, with colonists. Mandron kept his word; the Phokaians settled down and further prospered thanks to their martial

---

[46] On the *pharmakos* between ritual, myth and folklore, see Burkert (1979), 59–78.

[47] The version collected by Jacoby as 262 F 7b comes, without reference to Charon, from Polyaenus, 8.37; see Jacoby (1943), 11–12; on Plutarch as Polyainos' direct source, see Stadter (1965), 10–17.

[48] Arist. fr. 549 Rose and Iust. 43.3.4–11 with Brugnone (1995) and Guzzo (2010), 201–5.

[49] Hdt. 1.163.2–4 with Guzzo (2010), 203.

skills, which brought in booty taken from the neighbours. This caused concern among the Pytoessans, who decided to get rid of the Greeks. King Mandron could not be persuaded to assent to the plot, and so the treacherous barbarians waited until he was out of the way. His daughter Lampsake, though, no less loyal to the Greeks, did her best to prevent the Bebrykoi from committing a crime and, as her attempts failed, decided to betray them to the Phokaians. The latter employed a stratagem of which we have many examples in Greek authors: they organized a religious festival outside the city, invited the Bebrykoi to participate, and as the Bebrykoi were outside the city walls the Phokaians occupied the city and massacred their former fellow citizens. They then invited back the loyal Mandron and proceeded to rename the city after Lampsake, who died apparently soon thereafter. Mandron, however, decided to lead away the children and wives of the slaughtered Bebrykoi, in order to avoid the suspicion of treason – which I take to mean the suspicion that he had betrayed his fellow Bebrykoi to the Greeks. Finally, Lampsake was upgraded and received divine cult instead of the heroic cult she had previously been granted.[50]

Walking, consciously or not, in the footsteps of Wolf Aly, many scholars have been captivated by the fact that the story appears to adumbrate a marriage or romantic connection between the Greek founding hero and the daughter of the local ruler, a variation of which famously appears in the story of Odysseus and Nausicaa.[51] The story of Lampsake, on the other hand, has clear resemblances to a different narrative pattern, which we might call the treason of the local woman, or the Tarpeia pattern – and notice that the reference to the potential suspicion of treason for Mandron implicitly characterizes as such his daughter's actions.[52] Jacoby, whose commentary on the fragments of Charon missed no occasion to criticize Aly with characteristic harshness, insisted that the differences between stories are more important than the resemblances, and pointed out that anyway in the case of Phobos, the suicide by jumping from the Leukadian Cliff could hardly indicate unreciprocated love for Lampsake, since it was Blepsos, not Phobos, who led the colonial contingent, and Lampsake had died of an illness, quite unromantically.[53] We have to recognize, however,

---

[50] Considering that the story narrated the foundation of Lampsacus, the suggestion, often advanced, that only the suicide of Phobos was actually attributed to Charon by Plutarch seems rather unconvincing; see the comments of Ceccarelli (2016) on 262 F 7.

[51] Aly (1969), 218.   [52] On the myth of Tarpeia, see Burkert (1979), 76–7.

[53] Jacoby (1943), 12–13.

that the form in which the story of Lampsake has come down to us is such that the meaning of some of its elements, which must have had narrative relevance, escapes us. In the twin brothers, Phobos and Blepsos, for instance, we recognize a folktale motif, and it is clear, it seems to me, that Phobos sent his brother as a substitute for himself, that is, that Blepsos was meant to be taken as Phobos and function as his Doppelgänger. Doppelgängers most often have to do with the success or failure of the beloved one, spouse or lover, in recognizing them – a classicist will immediately think of the *Menaechmi*, but the motif is omnipresent in narrative traditions all over the world.[54] Accordingly, the presence of an erotic element in the original form of the story of Phobos, Blepsos and Lampsake is quite likely. If this is the case, again a well-known story type may lurk below the surface, the type catalogued by Uther as 'The Twin or Blood-Brothers' (ATU 303), in which the protagonist is one of two twin brothers who embarks on a journey to foreign lands, where he performs some extraordinary deed and thereby wins the hand of the king's daughter. The protagonist is then temporarily (or finally) eliminated by an antagonist, and his twin brother replaces him, is not recognized by his brother's bride, and successfully confronts the antagonist and, depending on the variant, brings his brother back to life or replaces him for good. This appears to be one of the most widely attested among international folktales, with over 2,000 occurrences in many different variants. As William Hansen summarizes it, the plot basically consists of a protagonist performing certain tasks with initial success followed by failure, and a second protagonist, identical to the first, performing the same tasks with complete success.[55] If we knew more about Phobos' dive from the cliff, we might be in a position to add the foundation story of Lampsacus to the over 2,000 variants mentioned above.

The fact remains, in any case, that the story on the whole is built around a double opposition, male/female and colonist/indigenous, and in the way these two oppositions operate in the narrative mechanism it is impossible not to recognize a recurrent motif of the colonial imagination. The indigenous female becomes a correlate of the land, and by defending the Greeks against the indigenous males she implicitly establishes the colonists' right to the land above that of the locals. The marvellous possessions

---

[54] See Pape (1981).

[55] W. Hansen (2002), 450–3, on the type, which he shows has a parallel of sorts in the *Menaechmi* story.

investigated years ago by Steven Greenblatt offer instructive parallels, showing that in the colonial situation the two oppositions operate very much in the same way across cultures.[56]

Nobody would object, I presume, to defining the three longer fragments of Charon as local tradition, and especially the two that deal with Lampsacus can easily be taken to provide foundational narratives for important aspects in the lives of the Lampsakenes as a community. This local tradition comes to us in the form of highly sophisticated narratives, in which folktale motifs and story types are deployed and manipulated for aesthetic as well as broadly political purposes alongside narrative patterns that reflect religious notions and mimic rituals. In his book *Homo narrans*, John Niles writes: 'I find it helpful to think of oral narrative as satisfying six main functions: the *ludic*, the *sapiential*, the *normative*, the *constitutive*, the *socially cohesive*, and the *adaptive*. Not all these functions need be satisfied simultaneously, but most of them are likely to be.'[57] The short narratives we have been looking at correspond well to this checklist, reinforcing the impression that they indeed derive, however remotely, from oral narratives. Two of them deal with foundational moments in the history of Lampsacus, at the same time conveying aetiological information and interpreting events according to shared social norms. The story of Kardia is rather a cautionary tale, weaving in different ways the motifs of deviation and retribution and of injustice and reparation. Two aspects that I would like to stress are, on the one hand, the literary skill displayed in these narratives and, on the other, the very generic continuum between the folktale patterns one sees in the background and in the historical narratives of Charon: in terms of William Bascom's widely used typology of traditional narratives, Charon's fragments provide examples of legends that borrow narrative building blocks and even whole plots from folktales.[58]

In a previous contribution I formulated similar observations in the case of several narratives embedded in Herodotus' *Histories*.[59] The fact that an author like Charon, early but very poorly preserved, provides evidence for these dynamics, too, seems to me to support my previous conclusions. Like Herodotus, these scanty remains of Charon's work shed some light on the operation of a rich storytelling culture of which very few traces have

---

[56] Greenblatt (1991), 52–79; more specifically, Snyder (2015), 159–61. [57] Niles (1999), 70.
[58] See Bascom (1975). [59] Luraghi (2013).

Folktale and Local Tradition in Charon of Lampsacus   59

survived. It is from this culture that the historical narratives preserved by Herodotus and his contemporaries originated. The recognizably different texture of the vast majority of historical narratives from Thucydides onwards in all likelihood points to the progressive marginalization of this oral genre, which is after all the expected result of the increasing role and prestige of writing in Greek culture at the turn of the century.[60] The narratives I have been trying to trace and analyse in the present contribution belonged in a world in which the separation between story and history would not have made sense, and folktales, legends and myths easily shared and traded narrative tropes, patterns and motifs. This is why the powerful and increasingly fine-tuned instruments of *Märchenforschung* are such a precious tool when we try to approach what we tend to call early Greek historiography.

From another point of view, however, there may be interesting differences between Charon and Herodotus. The availability of verbatim quotations makes it possible for the reader to form an impression of Charon's style, an impression that corresponds broadly to what the remarks of Dionysios of Halikarnassos on the early Greek historians would have led us to expect.[61] Of particular interest are the two fragments quoted by Plutarch in his wholesale attack on Herodotus' mean-spiritedness. The first gives a streamlined account of the fate of the Lydian Paktyes, whom Cyrus had left in charge of Kroisos' treasury according to Herodotus. The second mentions the participation of the Athenians in the Ionian revolt, and more specifically in the conquest of Sardis. In both cases, Herodotus provided a much more detailed narrative. Charon's passages read almost like a *prographe*, and the enormous disproportion between them and the corresponding passages of Herodotus is striking.[62] Beyond this, both fragments display a distinctive style, characterized by the juxtaposition of sentences with a modest amount of subordination and extensive use of the conjunction καί in order to connect periods.[63] Noticeable also is the change of subject between the first and the second sentence of fragment 10. Clearly, it was not the Athenians alone who attacked and conquered

---

[60] On the marginalization of oral narratives in the transition from mostly oral to mostly literate stages, see Niles (1999), 14.

[61] Dion. Hal. *Th.* 5; see Schick (1955), 94.

[62] Charon 262 F 9 and 10. On the proportion between the two fragments of Charon and the corresponding chapters of Herodotus (1.157–61 for F 9 and 5. 97.3 and 100 for F 10), see Hepperle (1956), 72–3 and Moggi (1977), 13–16.

[63] On Charon's narrative style, see the remarks of Schick (1955), 98–100.

60   NINO LURAGHI

Sardis, so the subject of ἐστραεύσαντο and εἷλον is not οἱ Ἀθηναῖοι but the
rebels as a whole. We meet precisely the same phenomenon in the
narrative of the foundation of Taras quoted verbatim from Antiochos of
Syracuse by Strabon.[64]

As we turn to the longer fragments, we notice immediately that the
same stylistic features are displayed prominently in fragment 1, the famous
story of the dancing horses of Kardia reported by Athenaios. Fragments 7a,
12 and 17, on the other hand, read much more like later Greek prose,
which may suggest either that the authors who quote them did not bother
to preserve the original style or that they are not first-hand quotations,
which in the case of fragments 12 and 17 is uncontroversial anyway.
Compared to Herodotus, the story of the dancing horses, too, like the
two passages from Charon's *Persika*, displays, mildly put, a very low level
of redundancy. There is no trace of the tendency to ring composition on a
smaller or larger scale that is endemic in Herodotus' prose, nor of the
repetition used to tie sentences together.[65] Actually, nothing is repeated
twice in the story told by Charon. This very distinctive narrative style,
concise to the extreme and with no redundancy whatsoever, is shared
among the very few longer fragments of the early historians, from
Hekataios to Antiochos: it is the style identified by Robert Fowler, which
will remain typical of mythography well after the fifth century BC.[66] This
observation confirms and fleshes out the remarks of Dionysios of
Halikarnassos, suggesting that among his contemporaries Herodotus was
the outlier, in terms of style as well as in terms of scope and structure. For
all its rootedness in the tradition of oral prose narratives, Charon's
narrative reads more like a script that an oral storyteller would need to
expand upon in a major way in order to turn the written text into a
successful oral performance.[67] Turning to Herodotus, instead, one is
reminded of the observations of the late Simon Slings on the way the

---

[64] See Schick (1955), 100. On the change of subject between two propositions joined by *kai* as typical
of popular narrative, see Aly (1969), 220 n. 1. For a parallel example, see Antiochus of Syracuse 555
F 13 lines 12–13.

[65] On these narrative devices and their function in Herodotus' prose, see de Jong (2002), 259–63 and
Slings (2002), 60–3 and 71–3. Compare the analysis of Charon's F 1 in Hurst (1975): the narrative
structure he identifies is supported purely by the repetition of themes, without any verbal clue.

[66] See R. Fowler (2006b).

[67] Charon's narrative displays the features of what scholars sometimes call a 'transitional text'; see S. A.
Mitchell (1987), 414–15, who provides an example of Icelandic saga and describes it as 'a written
work which bore a peculiar stylistic trait of its origins in oral performance and composition, namely
a notable disregard for the sort of detail which could be best composed during oral presentation'.

prose style of the father of history endemically adopts strategies characteristic of oral communication; perhaps what set him apart from his peers, in
terms of style, was the attempt at replicating in writing the style of the oral
storytelling tradition – but more than a conclusion, this is a starting point
for further reflections.[68]

[68] Note that the famous passage of Dionysios' *On Thucydides* does remark on the fact that Herodotus'
style had all the *aretai* that his predecessors were lacking (*Th.* 5). Contrary to Sling's conclusion,
however, this choice was by no means natural, as shown by the fact that, as far as we can tell, it was
not shared by any of the other early historians; cf. Slings (2002), 76–7.

CHAPTER 3

Mythical and Historical Time in Herodotus
Scaliger, Jacoby, and the Chronographic Tradition

Tim Rood

'At the very beginning of non-contemporary history there was myth.'[1] Thus wrote John Marincola, in a much-cited section of *Authority and Tradition in Ancient Historiography* devoted to history and myth or, more precisely, the ways in which historians established authority by their exclusion, and occasional inclusion, of myth. One of the attractions of Marincola's discussion is that he stresses not just the reaction against the 'mythical' that was one of the hallmarks of the historiographic tradition at least from Thucydides onwards, but also the continuing importance of myth for writers such as Diodorus Siculus and Dionysius of Halicarnassus. 'The charms of myth, like those of the Sirens', he concludes, 'were simply too great to resist.'[2]

This chapter explores the opposition of history and myth in Thucydides' great predecessor, Herodotus, as well as the concepts through which this topic has been explored in scholarship, in particular, the *spatium mythicum* and *historicum* (mythical and historical time). While this topic has attracted a great deal of attention,[3] two passages have dominated scholarly debate. The first (1.1–5) comes near the beginning of the *Histories*, after Herodotus has related the explanation of conflict between Greeks and barbarians supposedly presented by 'the Persians' learned men' (Περσέων ... οἱ λόγιοι). Herodotus reports that these Persians attribute the start of hostilities to the Phoenicians' seizure of the

---

[1] Marincola (1997), 117. Translations are my own unless otherwise stated. Research for this chapter was funded by the Leverhulme Trust ('Anachronism and Antiquity' Research Project Grant). I am grateful to Carol Atack, Mathura Umachandran, and my co-editors for comments on a draft of this chapter, as well as to the participants at the conference for John Marincola for comments on the oral version.

[2] Marincola (1997), 127.

[3] Recent discussions include Harrison (2000), 197–207; Cobet (2002); Williams (2002), 149–71; Feeney (2007), 68–76; Irwin (2007), 171, 214; R. Fowler (2010), 327, (2011), 62; Wesselmann (2011); Baragwanath and de Bakker (2012b), 23–9. For helpful guidance on earlier bibliography, see Harrison (2000), 198 n. 61; Baragwanath and de Bakker (2012b), 24 n. 95.

Mythical and Historical Time in Herodotus 63

Argive princess Io, but suggest that the Greeks subsequently escalated the conflict by going to war over Paris' seizure of Helen. He adds a Phoenician variant on the story of Io, before himself continuing: 'I am not proceeding with any intention to say that these things happened in this way or any other way; I shall indicate the man who I myself know (οἶδα αὐτός) began unjust deeds against the Greeks, and then go forward to the rest of my narrative' (1.5.3). He then names the Lydian king Croesus as the man responsible for the first acts of injustice against the Greeks. The second passage occurs towards the end of Herodotus' account of the reign of the Samian tyrant Polycrates. Herodotus describes how the Persian satrap Oroetes tricks Polycrates into coming to Sardis in the hope of gaining Persian support for his ambitions:

> For Polycrates is first of the Greeks of whom we know (πρῶτος τῶν ἡμεῖς ἴδμεν Ἑλλήνων) to have conceived the plan of controlling the sea, excepting Minos the Cnossian and anyone earlier than Minos who ruled the sea; but Polycrates is first of what is called the human generation (τῆς ... ἀνθρωπηίης λεγομένης γενεῆς), having great hopes of ruling Ionia and islands. (3.122.2)

The first two sections of this chapter seek to throw some light on the scholarly debate over these passages by considering the history of the terms through which it has been conducted. The third section will briefly suggest that these terms have distorted Herodotus' thought in important ways. The chapter as a whole supports the position that it makes no sense to apply the opposition of myth and history to Herodotus.

In Search of *Spatium Mythicum* and *Historicum*

Scholars of ancient historiography frequently speak of *spatium historicum* and *spatium mythicum*, but rarely reflect on the terms themselves.[4] Within Anglophone scholarship, they were popularized by W. M. von Leyden in a 1949 article, '*Spatium historicum*'. By *spatium historicum*, von Leyden understood the continuous span of human past that was open to historical enquiry. He attributed the creation of this sense of time to Hecataeus and other genealogists in the fifth century BC. It was not that Hecataeus had any new evidence for the distant past but that he removed some of the

---

[4] Exceptions include Pelling (2002b), 188, who overtly comments on the spatial metaphor (in discussing a spatial metaphor for the distant past at the start of Plutarch's *Theseus*), and Dewald (2002), 287, who, in a discussion of Herodotus' proem, suggests redefining the *spatium historicum* as 'the presence of his own alert and critical authorial consciousness'.

64   TIM ROOD

fabulous elements contained in Greek traditions: in von Leyden's words, 'their assumption that the history of the mythical period could be recovered by the help of rational principles implied the notion of a *spatium historicum* stretching from olden times to the present'.[5] He proceeded to suggest that the difference between the genealogists' writings and those of Herodotus and Thucydides lay in the later historians' more sophisticated treatment of the problem of gaining knowledge about the distant past. Thus it is in terms of knowledge that von Leyden glosses Herodotus' treatment of Polycrates and Minos in the second of the passages cited above: he thinks that 'a special kind of knowledge' applies to a period of roughly 200 years prior to Herodotus' own time, and opposes this 'so-called historical age' to the time of Minos, 'a fabulous period different in kind from the age of Polycrates'. Nonetheless, von Leyden argues that this special knowledge was 'subordinated to Herodotus' general scheme of telling what he has heard of the history of all times'.[6] Thucydides, by contrast, developed more 'advanced' principles for dealing with the distant past – though his adherence to universal categories means that it is still questionable whether Thucydides had a 'genuinely historical conception'.[7]

While von Leyden makes a clear argument for the creation of a *spatium historicum*, he introduces the term *spatium mythicum* only once, in a footnote attached to his treatment of Herodotus. In this note he mentions the 'systematic arrangement of the *spatium historicum*, *spatium mythicum*, etc.' by the first-century BC Roman antiquarian Varro, 'to my knowledge the first of this kind in Antiquity', with periods whose character is 'outlined according to the nature and extent of our knowledge of them'.[8] Von Leyden here refers to a passage cited by Censorinus (*De die natali* 21) in which Varro defines three 'distinctions of times' (*discrimina temporum*): the first interval, 'from the beginning of humans to the earlier flood', was 'called "unclear" (*adelon*) because of our ignorance', and was of uncertain length (perhaps even infinite); the second, 'from the earlier flood to the first Olympiad', was 'called "mythical" (*muthicon*) because many fabulous things are reported in it', and was believed to be around 1,600 years; the third, 'from the first Olympiad to us', was 'called "historical" (*historicon*), because the events done in it are contained in true histories'. Tellingly, von Leyden glosses over Varro's *spatium adelon* with a bare 'etc.', thereby

---

[5] Von Leyden (1949–50), 91.   [6] Von Leyden (1949–50), 95.
[7] Von Leyden (1949–50), 103. Collingwood (1946) lies behind the final claim.
[8] Von Leyden (1949–50), 95 n. 32. Scholars debate the scheme's origins in Hellenistic chronology: Jacoby (commentary on *FGrHist* 241 F 1c) attributed it to Eratosthenes, but Möller (2005), 255–6, thinks Castor of Rhodes more likely.

Mythical and Historical Time in Herodotus

encouraging a bipartite division of myth and history (even though in his own discussion of the fifth-century historians he deals only with the *spatium historicum*).

In scholarship on Herodotus, an overt opposition between *spatium mythicum* and *historicum* was introduced by Max Pohlenz in his 1937 monograph *Herodot.*[9] Pohlenz used this opposition in discussing Herodotus' allocation to Croesus of responsibility for conflict between Greeks and barbarians. While acknowledging that 'essential features' of the Greek tradition such as the rape of Helen and the expedition against Troy 'remained "historical facts"' for Herodotus, he stressed that, unlike Hecataeus, Herodotus refrained from making 'this "mythical" time the actual object of his work', thereby completing 'the separation of *spatium mythicum* and *historicum*'.[10] Like von Leyden, Pohlenz insisted that Herodotus used the sort of knowledge available as his criterion for differentiating periods; he differed in using the term 'mythical time' for the less securely attested period.

The term *spatium historicum* by itself seems first to have been applied to Herodotus' work by the foremost twentieth-century scholar of Greek historiography, Felix Jacoby, in the famous 1909 *Klio* article in which he set out the principles of his edition of the fragments of the Greek historians.[11] Jacoby introduced the term in discussing the difference between fifth-century BC local historians such as Hellanicus of Lesbos and the tradition of historiography inaugurated by Herodotus: 'For the so-called *spatium historicum*, which entered into the literature only with Herodotus and was coherently treated for the first time after the publication of most of the ὧροι [chronicles] by Ephoros, Hellanikos could only prepare, in his chronicles of the various leading cities, the unifying systematic order.'[12] With the teleology typical of his reconstruction of the history of Greek historiography, Jacoby thought that local histories covering what we would see as both mythical and historical time paved the way for the universal historian Ephorus of Cyme, who, according to Diodorus, 'passed over the old mythologies (τὰς . . . παλαιὰς μυθολογίας) and commenced his history with a narration of the events which took place after the Return of the Heraclidae' (4.1.3 = *FGrHist* 70 T 8). As for Herodotus' introduction of

---

[9] Hunter (1982), 86 n. 50.   [10] Pohlenz (1937), 7. Pohlenz further refers in a note to 3.122.

[11] Canfora (1991), 5; Parmeggiani (1999), 107.

[12] Jacoby (2015), 13 = (1909), 87. Cf. already Jacoby (2015), 11 n. 19 = (1909), 86 n. 1: 'The feeling of opposition between the narrator of the *spatium historicum*, who considers himself the true historian, and the genealogist, is already present in Herodotus. In Ephoros, however, this feeling has become distinctly sharper.'

66   TIM ROOD

historical time, that is set by Jacoby against the temporal conceptualization
of genealogical writers such as Hecataeus: 'the stream of contemporary
history ... arises as the expansion and continuation of the Γενεαλογίαι
[Genealogies] for the *spatium historicum*, a concept that we find worked
out as early as Herodotus. Herodotus – for he and not Thucydides here
plays the decisive role – apparently ties in with the genealogical literature
and feels himself as its continuator.' Jacoby further suggests that
Herodotus' refusal to treat this period comes 'not out of clearly formed
critical suspicion about the truth and the historical accuracy of the tradition about this period' but because it had been treated already by genealogists.[13] This suggestion points also to the reason why Jacoby refrained
from using the concept *spatium mythicum* in relation either to the genealogists or to Herodotus: he referred to genealogists down to the beginning
of the fourth century BC as composing 'the "history" of the mythical
period – because for both author and reader this is accepted as history',[14]
and he wrote that Herodotus' proem marks a shift to the 'historical' only
in our sense of the word.[15]

Jacoby's usage, then, both resembles and contrasts with the way the
concepts were later used by von Leyden and Pohlenz. Like Jacoby, von
Leyden does not suggest that Herodotus had a conception of *spatium
mythicum*; unlike Jacoby, he suggests that Hecataeus did have a conception
of *spatium historicum*. Pohlenz, on the other hand, does identify *spatium
mythicum* in Herodotus, in large part because he employs the term in a
different sense from Jacoby.

To understand Pohlenz's introduction of the opposition of myth and
history, we need to look beyond Jacoby's treatment of Herodotus in his
1909 article on Greek historiography to his earlier writings on Greek
chronography. Jacoby used both *spatium historicum* and *spatium mythicum*
in his 1902 edition of the second-century BC chronographer Apollodorus
of Athens. In his introductory essay, he cited Ps.-Scymnus 22 and
Diodorus 1.5.1 as evidence that Apollodorus began his work with the
destruction of Troy, and described this choice as the 'circumscription' of a
'*spatium historicum*'. He suggested that Apollodorus was following the
example of the third-century BC chronographer Eratosthenes 'in this
cautious exclusion of the mythical time', while again pointing to the

---

[13] Jacoby (2015), 32–3 = (1909), 99.
[14] Jacoby (2015), 10 = (1909), 85. The 2015 translation misleadingly adds a gloss to Jacoby's uses of
spatium historicum to explain that the term implies an opposition to mythical time; similarly, e.g.
Canfora (1991), 6; Baragwanath and de Bakker (2012a), 85.
[15] Jacoby (1913), 335.

Mythical and Historical Time in Herodotus

precedent of Ephorus in the genre of universal history.[16] He argued, too, that Apollodorus took over from Eratosthenes the divisions within this *spatium historicum* prior to the first Olympiad, namely, the fall of Troy, the return of the Heraclidae, the Ionian migration, and Lycurgus' legislation.[17] As for *spatium mythicum*, that term appears in the commentary section of the edition of Apollodorus. Commenting on the evidence for Apollodorus' pre-Olympiad chronology preserved by Clement, Eusebius, and Diodorus, Jacoby notes again that Apollodorus' source was Eratosthenes and points out that Eratosthenes must have worked out his intervals by counting back from 'the first secure year in his table, Olympiad 1.1, from which *graeca de temporibus historia vera creditur* [Jerome *Chronicle* 86a.16–17 Helm: 'Greek history is believed true in its dates']'. He then concludes that 'the *spatium mythicum* ..., as Varro says, ends with the year 777/6, which Eratosthenes signals as τὸ προηγούμενον ἔτος τῶν πρώτων Ὀλυμπίων ['the first year of the first Olympics']'.[18]

Jacoby's use of *spatium mythicum* in his work on Apollodorus produces an immediate problem. His claim in the introduction that Apollodorus' *spatium historicum* starts with the fall of Troy is contradicted by his claim in the commentary that his *spatium mythicum* ends with the first Olympiad. Jacoby later tackled this conflict in his introduction to the section on *Zeittafeln* (Chronological Tables) in his *Fragmente der grieschishe Historiker*: 'The consequence of the Timaean–Eratosthenian chronography should have been that one let the *spatium historicum* begin with Olympiad 1, and, as in our Christian year-calculation, dated consistently by Olympiads and years before Olympiad 1', but 'the power of tradition was too strong, and forced even Eratosthenes and his successor Apollodorus, the most influential chronographers, to go back to the dividing-line between heroic and historical time, the Trojan War'.[19] While Jacoby is right to stress the role played by Trojan War traditions in the Greek chronographic imagination, the contradiction in his earlier usage might be thought to reveal the arbitrariness of making one or the other of these dates a firm chronological boundary; even Varro, on whose authority Jacoby drew for the end of the *spatium mythicum*, cited year intervals between epochal points within the mythical interval.

---

[16] Jacoby (1902), 11.   [17] Jacoby (1902), 36.

[18] Jacoby (1902), 76. Laqueur (1907), 527, similarly writes that 'the end of the *spatium mythicum* falls in 777/6'.

[19] *FGrHist* II.C 663.

68   TIM ROOD

We have seen, then, that while Jacoby introduced *spatium historicum* as well as *spatium mythicum* in writing about chronographers who defined temporal intervals over a long and continuous time span, it was Pohlenz who extended the terms beyond chronography to a historian who did not offer a continuous chronological list. But from where did Jacoby himself draw these terms? He surrounds *spatium historicum* with quotation marks in the two 1902 uses and adds so-called once in the 1909 *Klio* article, but he does not explain the origins of the terms beyond hinting at a connection with Varro's *intervallum historicon* and *mythicon*.

An explanation of the phrase *spatium historicum* has been offered by Denis Feeney in an important study of Roman chronological consciousness. Feeney proposes that the term was 'taken over from Jerome [the fourth-century AD theologian and historian, and translator of the third-century AD *Chronicle* of Eusebius], who has a "historical space" for recording events between his columns'.[20] As he explains, Jerome (following Eusebius' model) used columns down the page for the various dating systems used in the course of the *Chronicle*; one of these columns was a year count starting from the birth of Abraham, while the others changed with the rise and fall of different powers. In the centre of the page, between the columns of dates, Jerome offered a short summary of events attached to a particular year, and it is this space that Feeney suggests Jerome called the *spatium historicum*.

Feeney is right to link *spatium historicum* with Jerome's *Chronicle*, but mistaken in his claim that Jerome himself coined the term. The phrase was in fact taken over from a discussion of Jerome by the scholar who is often seen as the founder of modern chronology: the French Protestant Joseph Justus Scaliger (1540–1609), inventor of the Julian Period, a cycle of 7,980 years based on 28-year solar, 19-year lunar and 15-year indiction cycles, with a starting date equivalent to 4713 BC (year 1 in each of the three cycles).[21] Scaliger included a detailed chronological commentary on Jerome/Eusebius in his 1606 work *Thesaurus temporum*, and it is in his reconstruction of the physical layout of the pages of Eusebius that he uses the term *spatium historicum* (as well as the Greek χωρίον ἱστορικόν).[22]

Jacoby, then, took the term *spatium historicum* from Scaliger (or from later scholarship on Eusebius or Jerome inspired by Scaliger), but

---

[20] Feeney (2007), 242 n. 15.
[21] Indiction cycles were used for administrative purposes from late antiquity to the early modern period.
[22] Scaliger (1606a), 5.

Mythical and Historical Time in Herodotus

transformed it in the process. Scaliger's *spatium historicum* is a space on the pages of Eusebius and Jerome between the parallel columns that indicate the progression of the years and extending back to the birth of Abraham. Jacoby introduced two changes: he turned Scaliger's two-dimensional space on the page into a conceptual timeline and (seemingly through the influence of Varro's *intervallum mythicon* and *historicon*) divided the timeline into *spatium mythicum* and *historicum* – the division that Pohlenz subsequently found in Herodotus.

That the modern use of *spatium historicum* entirely distorts Scaliger's use of the term does not in itself undermine the conceptual opposition between mythical and historical time that many scholars have found in Herodotus. Jacoby could, after all, have followed Varro by using *intervallum* (itself originally a spatial metaphor) instead of *spatium*, or else used purely temporal expressions such as *aevum/tempus/saeculum mythicum/historicum*. One advantage of the spatial metaphor might seem to be that it avoids the associations with a qualitatively different, 'primitive' mentality that 'mythical time' acquired in the wake of the writings of Christian Gottlieb Heyne (1729–1812). But in fact Jacoby did use the phrases *historische/mythische zeit* and 'historical/mythical time' (indeed, he speaks of the Parian Marble's inclusion of *mythische zeit* on the same page on which he first uses *spatium historicum*).[23] Perhaps, then, Jacoby sought to draw authority from the technical aura of the Latin phrase; his usage in turn established a tradition for later scholars such as Pohlenz to follow.

The idea that Herodotus distinguished between mythical and historical times can be traced beyond Pohlenz' use of the Latin terms. Bernard Williams notes that the phrase Herodotus applies to Polycrates at 3.122.2 – that he was first 'of what is called the human generation' (τῆς ... ἀνθρωπηίης λεγομένης γενεῆς) to attempt to rule the sea – is often, and misleadingly, translated in terms of a contrast between human or historical and divine or mythical time – a translation whose history he traces back to Legrand's 1932 Budé edition.[24] As we shall see, the trail can in fact be extended more than 300 years further, to Joseph Scaliger's *Thesaurus temporum* – and, as with the distinction of *spatium mythicum* and *historicum*, Varro's schematic division of time lies behind this usage.

---

[23] Jacoby (1902), 11; for the English usage, e.g. Jacoby (1949), 112–13.
[24] Williams (2002), 155 with n. 9, 158 with n. 19.

Herodotus and Mythical Time

Joseph Scaliger was repeatedly drawn to Varro's tripartite temporal model. Its interest for him lay initially in Varro's use of the first Olympiad as the basis for reckoning time.[25] Varro's distinctions subsequently helped Scaliger to confront historical traditions from Egypt and China that went back beyond the biblical date for the world's creation. Sceptical that other nations could have preserved knowledge from before the flood, he thought that the long pasts they attributed to themselves were a sign of ignorance and affectation. What Varro's chronology seemed to provide was positive evidence to support the biblical chronology: working back from the first Olympiad, Scaliger calculated that Varro's transition from the 'unclear' to the 'mythical' period began eighty years after the biblical date for the flood – a sign that 'the beginnings of things were not unknown to the old writers of Greece or to Varro himself, most learned of the *togati* [Romans]'.[26]

Scaliger's engagement with Varro took a new turn in *Thesaurus temporum* (1606). The discovery of Syncellus' *Chronography* provided him with detailed and authentic-seeming Egyptian king lists from a third-century BC Egyptian writer, Manetho, that seemed to prove that the historical record in Egypt did stretch beyond the biblical creation date.[27] This new evidence led Scaliger to combine Varro's 'unclear' and 'mythical' periods into a single period (though he acknowledged that 'many times are ἄδηλα [unclear] which however are not μυθικά [mythical], and in contrast there are many mythical things which are referred to ἱστορικὸν time'). For this single period – which would include all events recorded 'before the epoch determined by Moses, as befits a Christian' (i.e. before the birth of Adam) – Scaliger initially chose the term 'mythical', but later preferred 'proleptic' (*prolepticon*).[28] That word was commonly applied to the use of a term or noun before it came into use; thus Scaliger explained that 'by prolepsis' he used Julian years for chronological purposes for periods before Caesar's calendrical reforms (a use of 'proleptic' that survives in modern English).[29] The 'proleptic time' necessitated by the Egyptian king lists, however, was a much bolder concept – a time seemingly before time itself

---

[25] Scaliger (1583), 208.   [26] Scaliger (1598), 345.

[27] The length of Egyptian history was familiar from Herodotus and Diodorus, but they were not native traditions and were less detailed and authentic-seeming.

[28] Scaliger (1606b), 273; see Grafton (1983–93), 2.717–18 for Scaliger's draft (images of the manuscript are available at https://digitalcollections.universiteitleiden.nl/view/item/991171#page/1/mode/1up, accessed 22 July 2021).

[29] Scaliger (1606b), 174.

Mythical and Historical Time in Herodotus

(an 'ὀξύμωρον' (oxymoron), as Scaliger himself acknowledged), stretching not just beyond the biblical creation date but also beyond Scaliger's own Julian period (which started in 4713 BC). Hence the need for another new concept: Scaliger supplemented the current Julian period – now termed an 'ordinary' period – with an 'earlier Julian Period of proleptic time' or a 'postulatitious Julian Period', and noted the possibility of adding, if necessary, an infinity of earlier periods.[30]

While Scaliger's modification of Varro effectively brought out the greater antiquity of the biblical tradition (the 'historical' period began with Adam, not, as for Varro, with the first Olympiad), he at once confused the picture by mapping his new division of 'proleptic' and 'historical' time onto a different distinction, Herodotus' contrast between Polycrates and Minos: 'What we call historic time ['tempus historicum'], Herodotus in book 3 calls ἀνθρωπηίην γενεήν [human generation].... Therefore ἀνθρωπεία γενεά [human generation] is opposed by Herodotus to τῇ μυθικῇ, καὶ τῇ προληπτικῇ [the mythical, and the proleptic]).'[31] Here, then, we have the origins of the temporal interpretation of Herodotus 3.122 to which Bernard Williams objected. In a context where he has just defined the birth of the first human in the biblical account as the beginning of 'historical time', Scaliger manipulates Herodotus to create a distinction between historic time (linked with Polycrates as the first aspiring thalassocrat 'of what is called the human generation') and myth-ical/proleptic time. He thereby suggests an analogy between Herodotus' position on Minos and his own position on Manetho's Egyptian history.

While on the surface designed to assert the authority of biblical chro-nology, Scaliger's use of Herodotus and Varro raises disturbing questions about that chronology. Scaliger rightly stressed that the 'mythical' period of Varro contained both non-fabulous and fabulous elements. The char-acter of the periods Varro separated is defined in broad terms: that 'many fabulous things are reported' in the mythical period implies that non-fabulous things are reported too; that is, unlike in the 'unclear' period,

---

[30] Scaliger (1606b), 117 ('Vocetur *prior Periodus Iuliana temporis proleptici*: vel *Periodus Iuliana postulatitia*'). The terms 'ordinary' and 'postulatitious' were taken from gladiatorial contests (Seneca *Epistles* 7.4): 'postulatitious' matches were those held 'on demand' after 'ordinary' ones. I have altered Grafton's translation 'postulated period'; 'postulatitious' (not found in the *Oxford English Dictionary*) is used in this context by Strauch (1699), 134 (a translation of a chronological work written in Latin).

[31] Scaliger (1606b), 273.

72   TIM ROOD

there are genuine historical traditions preserved for the mythical period.[32] Following Varro's model, and like almost all scholars prior to the nineteenth century, Scaliger saw no reason to doubt the existence of figures such as Minos.[33] Indeed, he more than once suggested that 'heroic' was a better label than 'mythical' for Varro's middle period: as he put it, he preferred 'heroic' because Hercules had existed, while Varro had chosen 'mythical' because the Hydra had not.[34] In developing the notion of 'proleptic time', Scaliger reverted to the vaguer term 'mythical'. But for anyone worried by the threat posed by Manetho to biblical authority, Scaliger did not provide much comfort. His use of terminology from Varro and Herodotus hints by analogy at the possibility of genuine historical traditions in Egypt prior to the biblical creation date.

Scaliger's temporal understanding of Herodotus' Polycrates passage was quoted by Wesseling in his 1763 commentary and subsequently (doubtless via Wesseling) cited by the eighteenth-century French translator Larcher and by some early nineteenth-century commentators.[35] In the process, Scaliger's scholarly context was forgotten (Wesseling quietly dropped 'proleptic' time from his quotation of Scaliger). What endured was his reduction of Varro's tripartite model to a dichotomy of 'mythical' and 'historical' time in relation to Herodotus. As we shall now see, the underlying Varronian model has been further distorted by changes in the understanding of myth since Scaliger.

Beyond the Myth/History Boundary

Our last section showed that Varro's tripartite temporal model (refracted through Scaliger and Jacoby) lies behind the use of the terms *spatium mythicum* and *historicum*, and mythical and historical time, in scholarship on Herodotus. One problem with this use of Varro's terms is that modern scholars tend to use them in a rather different sense. Varro, as we have seen, uses the 'mythical' to denote a temporal period. This usage is paralleled in his near-contemporary Dionysius of Halicarnassus, who

---

[32] Grote – who took the then radical step of questioning the reliability of all pre-776 BC traditions – rightly noted that he was introducing a 'wider gap' than Varro would have admitted (1904–7: 1.436).
[33] See Scaliger (1606a), 37, where he cites testimonies of Tatian and Clement for Minos' date.
[34] Scaliger (1607), 80–1.
[35] Wesseling (1763), 258; Larcher (1786), 3.98 (translating 'ce que l'on appelle les Temps Historiques'). Scaliger is referenced, too, in Veegens' study of Polycrates (1839), 56 n. 1.

Mythical and Historical Time in Herodotus

speaks of the Assyrian Empire as 'old and led back to mythical times' (*Ant. Rom.* 1.2.2: παλαιά τις οὖσα καὶ εἰς τοὺς μυθικοὺς ἀναγομένη χρόνους),[36] and a similar notion is expressed by another first-century BC historian, Diodorus, when he observes that Ephorus and other writers passed over 'the old mythologies' (4.1.3). For none of these authors, however, does the concept of myth imply that the events of the period cannot be subjected to historical analysis. Varro, as we noted, allows for non-mythical elements within the mythical period; Dionysius in the early books of the *Roman Antiquities* uses his discretion in separating 'more mythical' and 'truer' variants (e.g. 1.39.1 on Heracles); and Diodorus proclaims his own willingness to deal with the most ancient traditions and faults Ephorus for not putting in the hard work required by conflicts in the 'old mythologies' (a phrase he uses as equivalent to 'archaeology', i.e. for an account of ancient times).[37] When Diodorus contrasts bare 'mythology' with 'history' (1.2.2), moreover, it is the mythology of current beliefs about the underworld that he rejects as less useful than the lessons to be learned from history; history itself includes the 'old mythology', which Diodorus presents in a rationalized, Euhemeristic form from which lessons can be drawn.[38]

By the time of Varro, then, the 'mythical' was used in historical writing partly as a qualitative term for the fabulous, partly to cover a traditional body of stories set in the distant past; it did not imply that the human or heroic figures of 'myth' are themselves fictional. The association with the fabulous was maintained in ancient theories of narration from the Hellenistic period onwards, which introduced divisions between the 'true', the 'verisimilar' and the 'mythical'.[39] The 'mythical' and 'mythology' continued to be used in these senses, moreover, throughout late antiquity and into the Renaissance: fabulous elements were often allegorized, but there was no doubt that the 'old mythology' could preserve genuine historical traditions;[40] early Greek king lists were indeed taken seriously

---

[36] Seemingly a unique combination of a 'myth' adjective with χρόνος in extant Greek. Contrast the use (in keeping with Scaliger's preference) of the phrase 'heroic times' at e.g. Arist. *Pol.* 1285b4, 21; Diod. Sic. 15.50.6, 79.5, 33.10.1; Str. 10.5.2.

[37] E.g. 2.47.1, 3.66.5 (Hecataeus and Dionysius Scytobrachion as writers of), 4.8.1 (τοῖς ἱστοροῦσι τὰς παλαιὰς μυθολογίας); for the link with ἀρχαιολογία, e.g. 4.1.3, 4.44.5. Luraghi (2014) questions whether Ephorus himself defined the starting point of his work in terms of a rejection of 'myth'.

[38] Sulimani (2011).   [39] Meijering (1987), 75–90; Feeney (1991), 42–4.

[40] Thus the 1567 *Mythologiae* of Natale Conti (Natalis Comes), one of the standard Renaissance mythographic handbooks, accepts the historicity of Minos (Conti (2006), 1.177–8).

74   TIM ROOD

in chronological writings such as Isaac Newton's 1728 *The Chronology of Ancient Kingdoms Amended* as well as in histories of Greece before Grote.[41] Modern usages of *spatium mythicum* and *historicum*, by contrast, draw on an Enlightenment sense of 'mythical time' as qualitatively different and on Grote's rigid sense of myth as unhistorical.[42]

This modern usage is even less appropriate for Herodotus than it is for Varro and his contemporaries. Robert Fowler has traced a shift in the meaning of μῦθος over the fifth and fourth centuries BC from the epic usage, where it is applied to assertive public speech, to the realm of the fabulous.[43] The latter sense is first clearly found in Thucydides, who rejects stories that 'through time untrustworthily have won through to the mythodic' (1.21.1: ὑπὸ χρόνου αὐτῶν ἀπίστως ἐπὶ τὸ μυθῶδες ἐκνενικηκότα), and boasts of the 'non-mythodic' (τὸ μὴ μυθῶδες) character of his own contemporary history (1.22.4); it then becomes more common over the course of the fourth century, recurring, for instance, in Demosthenes' comment that Athens' great deeds against the Persians 'have not yet been mythologized' owing to their being relatively recent in time (60.9). While Thucydides and Demosthenes point to a connection between the mythical and time (reports about distant periods are implied to be less reliable), the association with the fabulous remained strong: when Herodotus is called a 'mythologist' (μυθολόγος) and 'mythographer' (μυθογράφος) in the Aristotelian corpus,[44] it is presumably on account of his treatment of the natural world and of his tall stories, many of which fall within the bounds of what scholars see as the *spatium historicum*.

What of Herodotus' own use of 'myth' words? He uses the noun μῦθος twice in the *Histories*, once in a geographical context, once in relation to a story from the distant past. First, he argues that poets who have spoken of an encircling river Ocean 'cannot be refuted' (οὐκ ἔχει ἔλεγχον) because they have 'referred their story to the unseen' (2.23.1: ἐς ἀφανὲς τὸν μῦθον ἀνενείκας). Second, he calls the 'story' (μῦθος) that Heracles overcame a crowd of Egyptians who were about to sacrifice him 'silly' (εὐήθης) (2.45.1). Nickau has plausibly suggested that Herodotus used μῦθος in these two passages because he was polemicizing against Hecataeus, who used a cognate word at the start of his *Genealogies* (*FGrHist* 1 F 1: Ἑκαταῖος Μιλήσιος ὧδε μυθεῖται). Herodotus does, then, reject both

---

[41] On Minos, see Newton (1728), 115 (synchronism with Solomon), 149–52.

[42] Significantly, it is only in the nineteenth century that the singular 'myth' (spelt 'mythe' by Grote) enters English, on the model of Heyne's *mythus*.

[43] R. Fowler (2011). See also Detienne (1986) and Calame (2003), 12–27.   [44] R. Fowler (2000).

Mythical and Historical Time in Herodotus

stories, but it is the accompanying terms (οὐκ ἔχει ἔλεγχον, ἐς ἀφανές, εὐήθης) rather than μῦθος itself that signal the rejection.[45]

'History' is as problematic a term as 'myth' in the opposition of *spatium historicum* and *mythicum*. In general Greek and Latin usage, ἱστορία and *historia* rarely overlap straightforwardly with 'history' (at least with the English use of 'history' as opposed to 'myth'). As titles, they are applied to works with what we would see as fabulous elements (enquiries into the gods and heroes, for instance).[46] Frequently, they mean no more than 'story',[47] and grammarians apply them to matters of fact pertaining to a text under study (including what we would see as mythical data).[48] As for Herodotus himself, while, as often noted, he uses ἱστορίη in the sense of 'enquiry' in describing his work at the outset (1.proem), within the work itself he uses words related to ἱστορίη more often in relation to geographical enquiry (2.19.3, 29.1, 34.1, 99.1, 4.192.3) than to the distant (2.113.1) or more recent (7.96.1) past.

To probe the opposition of history and myth properly, we need to look beyond the lexical realm. Herodotus includes within the display of his enquiry many stories that fall within 'myth' as understood temporally (see the Appendix below for an annotated list). Supporters of a myth/history divide in Herodotus often point out that he introduces many 'mythical' stories through indirect discourse.[49] But, as the Appendix shows, Herodotus alludes to many such events without any distancing, and he often offers an opinion of his own (with varying degrees of uncertainty) about the 'mythical' period.[50] Herodotus' different modes of treatment point to an implicit understanding of mythologization (the stories told without distancing tend to lack fabulous elements), and in discussing Trojan War traditions he points to the potential distortions of genre (2.116.1: Helen's presence at Troy is more suitable for epic poetry). The process of mythologization can be found, however, in the more recent past too. Herodotus comments on distortions in accounts of the birth of Cyrus

---

[45] Rightly e.g. Calame (2003), 16; contrast e.g. R. Thomas (2019), 75 n. 1.

[46] E.g. *FGrHist* 466 T 1.

[47] Artemidorus 4.43, for instance, distinguishes between more and less credible ἱστορίαι, grouping the Trojan and Persian Wars among the former.

[48] Cameron (2004), 90–3; Schironi (2018), 96.

[49] E.g. Feeney (2007), 74, objecting to Harrison's claim (2000), 205, that Herodotus treats Minos 'straightforwardly as a historical figure' at 7.170–1; he could have added that the story attributes to Minos posthumous powers of vengeance against the Cretans. But see below on 1.170.2–3.

[50] Besides the passages in the Appendix below, Herodotus' account of Psammetichus' experiment (though he does not explicitly approve its methodology or conclusions) suggests that the temporal limits of historical enquiry stretch in theory back to the origins of humankind (2.1).

(1.95.1; cf. 1.122.3); he uses indirect discourse frequently for events during or after the lifetimes of Croesus and Polycrates, with attributions that typically highlight how particular peoples present versions that cast themselves in a good light;[51] and his presentation of patriotic rhetoric in direct speech in the later stages of the work shows how events that Herodotus has himself narrated come to be distorted.[52]

How do the two passages cited at the start of this chapter bear on this analysis? In the proem, there is an emphatic shift in time and tone from the Persian stories about Io, Europa, Medea and Helen to Herodotus' assertion that Croesus began unjust deeds against the Greeks.[53] The temporal division relates, however, solely to the question of who started the conflict between Greeks and barbarians, and it is in any case one that is problematized later in the *Histories*.[54] Herodotus is manipulating the rhetoric of knowledge to highlight the role of Croesus, who becomes in the ensuing narrative a paradigm of human fragility.

Herodotus' discussion of Polycrates and Minos at 3.122 raises different questions from the proem. As we saw, Herodotus calls Polycrates 'first of the Greeks of whom we know' to have planned to control the sea 'excepting (πάρεξ) Minos the Cnossian and anyone earlier than Minos who ruled the sea'; he then asserts that Polycrates was 'first of what is called the human generation'. Bernard Williams rightly notes that Herodotus must mean 'of whom we know, if we do not count' rather than 'of whom we know, that is to say, not counting' and that the qualification 'of the human race' makes no sense if Herodotus has 'already excluded anyone earlier than Polycrates from the comparison'. That is, Herodotus is not denying Minos' thalassocracy outright. Williams further suggests that some modern scholars, in trying to understand Herodotus' reasoning, have mixed two categories: status (Minos was legendary) and knowledge (Minos lived too long ago to be certain what he did). He then provocatively argues that Herodotus himself did not make this muddle 'because it was not yet possible for him to do so'. It was Thucydides' discovery of 'historical time', according to Williams, that made the distinction between status and knowledge possible: 'Thucydides imposed a new conception of the past, by insisting that people should extend to the remoter past a practice they already had in relation to the immediate past, of treating what was said

---

[51] Luraghi (2001b).   [52] Rood (2010), 67.

[53] See Rood (2010), with 65–7 on the issue of myth and history.

[54] At 2.120 Herodotus accepts that Paris wronged his Greek host; the difference between this transgression and Croesus' may lie in the scale (Croesus imposed tribute on whole Greek cities). See also M. Lloyd (1984) on the immediate aftermath of 1.5.

Mythical and Historical Time in Herodotus 77

about it as, seriously, true or false.' Thucydides, that is, was aware that the past was someone else's present and that 'our today will be someone else's distant past'.[55]

One problem with Williams' discussion is that the elements of historical time that he attributes to Thucydides can be found in Herodotus. When Herodotus concludes his proem with the reflection that 'what was great of old has mostly become small, and what was great in my time was formerly small' (1.5.4), his use of an imperfect tense for his own present implies a future audience — and it is for the sake of this future audience, living at a time when human prosperity will have shifted again, that he promises to treat both the small and the great in his work.[56] Herodotus applies, too, a serious categorization of truth and falsehood to the remote past when he disputes (as we have seen) the story that Heracles was able by himself to overpower a large number of Egyptians (2.45). And again when he supports the view that Helen was in Egypt rather than Troy throughout the Trojan War, since otherwise the Trojans would have given her back rather than persevering with the war just so that Paris could sleep with Helen (2.120). His reasoning here is similar to the argumentation from probability used in fifth-century law courts in reconstructing the recent past. Elsewhere, too, Herodotus extrapolates from the recent past both to the more distant past and to the future, notably in his discussion of the steady increase in the size of Egypt owing to the silting of the Nile (2.11, 13–14).[57]

What, then, does exclude Minos? Many scholars have followed Scaliger's lead and suggested that Herodotus was drawing a contrast between myth and history: Michael Lloyd, for instance, writes that Herodotus 'explicitly excludes Minos and any predecessors that he may have had, and reiterates that Polycrates was the first historical figure [to have a thalassocracy]'. But if Herodotus is dismissing Minos as unhistorical (and so as a figure invented by the poetic tradition), it is hard to see why he allows for the possibility that Minos had predecessors (i.e. figures unknown to the poetic tradition). Earlier in the *Histories*, moreover, Herodotus reports Minos' exercise of his naval power without implying

---

[55] Williams (2002), 298 n. 18, 161, 163, 167. Williams' claim that Thucydides discovered 'historical time' may be compared with von Leyden's discovery of a *spatium historicum* in Hecataeus (above); there is similarly no opposition to 'mythical time'.

[56] Herodotus elsewhere uses the imperfect in describing the state of physical monuments in his own time; Naiden (1999).

[57] It is in fact much less clear that Thucydides' construction of historical time is based on the move Williams posits from the more recent to the more distant past.

doubts about his historical status; at most he expresses some uncertainty about his claim that Minos did not exact tribute from his subjects (1.171.2: 'as far as I can reach by hearsay').

A different approach (attested already in Stephanus' 1566 edition[58]) is to suggest that Herodotus makes an exception of Minos because of the tradition that he was a son of Zeus – and hence according to some ancient categorizations a ἡμίθεος (demi-god) or ἥρως (hero). A problem with this solution, as Williams notes, lies in the chronology. Minos, according to Herodotus, lived in the third generation before the Trojan War. But in his account of Egypt Herodotus reports that Egyptian priests dismissed Hecataeus' claim of a genealogical link with a god sixteen generations back. According to these priests, Herodotus continues, it is more than 10,000 years since the gods ruled on earth, and there is no record of any human born of a god during the intervening time. Beyond this chronological problem, a further difficulty with this solution is that Herodotus is elsewhere extremely wary about *all* stories of sexual union between gods and mortals.[59] It is not just that Minos was born too late to be the son of a god; it is that the category of 'demi-god' is one that Herodotus seems hesitant to accept.

Williams, then, is justified in claiming that Herodotus has not made it clear what excludes Minos, but he ignores the more complex ways in which Herodotus deals with questions of historical time in his work as a whole. Given his attitudes elsewhere, it is tempting to speculate that Herodotus would, if asked, have responded that there was nothing wrong with Minos himself (even if temporal distance precluded clear knowledge about many of his doings). The claim that Polycrates was the first of 'what is called the human generation' to achieve naval power may be based on a purely conventional opposition between humans and heroes or demi-gods; if so, the reason Herodotus gestured towards this opposition at this point in his narrative was to highlight the reversal to Polycrates' aspirations that immediately attended his visit to Oroetes' court.

Whatever the explanation for Herodotus' exclusion of Minos, the analysis of this chapter has suggested that it is misleading to frame the debate in terms of an opposition between *spatium mythicum* and *historicum*, or mythical and historical time. To use those terms is to frame the question in the wrong way from the start. The dichotomy of mythical and historical time retrojects a structure that Jacoby applied to later

[58] Marginal note *ad loc.*: 'Id est, Primus inter homines. Hoc addit quod Minos haberetur Iouis filius.'
[59] Harrison (2000), 89.

Mythical and Historical Time in Herodotus 79

chronographic writing, thereby encouraging possibly misleading comparisons between Herodotus and chronography.[60] In addition, it retrojects later developments in the sense of 'myth', leading to some of the confusions that Williams highlights while closing off other, potentially more fruitful, approaches to the development of Greek traditions about the past.[61] Finally, the opposition between *spatium mythicum* and *historicum* panders to progressivist accounts of historiography's liberation from myth, accounts that tend to ignore the possibility that the poetic and local traditions received by Herodotus were themselves areas for the exercise of rational thought, just as they continued to be for the likes of Scaliger and Newton.

Appendix: 'Mythical' Material In Herodotus

This appendix includes most of the material included by Herodotus that can be dated prior to the return of the Heraclidae, to use the temporal boundary adopted by Robert Fowler in the standard modern work on Greek mythography (2000–13: vol. 1, p. xxx).

1. Personal opinions: 1.57–8 (Pelasgian migrations); 1.172 (Caunian origins); 2.42–5 (two Heracleses); 2.51–2 (early Pelasgian and Athenian cults: note esp. 2.52.1 'as I know from hearing in Dodona' (ὡς ἐγὼ ἐν Δωδώνῃ οἶδα ἀκούσας)); 2.56–7 (the origin of the oracle at Dodona); 2.98.2 (Archandropolis named after the son-in-law of Danaus); 2.104 (the Egyptian settlement of Colchis); 2.116–20 (Helen in Egypt in Trojan War); 2.145–6 (the Greek adoption of the gods Dionysus and Pan); 5.57 (origins of the Gephyraei); 5.58 (the Greek adoption of the alphabet and early Ionian writing technology); 5.76 ('correct' date of the first Dorian invasion of Attica in the reign of Codrus); 9.43 (oracle referring to an assault on Delphi by the Encheleis, evidently the same as the attack with Cadmus predicted at Euripides *Bacchae* 1336–8: note οἶδα, 'I know').

2. Reported without any distancing: 1.7 (Heraclid ancestry of Mermnad kings); 1.52 (Amphiaraus' 'courage and suffering': as discovered by Croesus, but presupposed); 1.56.2–3 (Dorian migration, early

---

[60] E.g. Baragwanath and de Bakker (2012b), 27 (on the fluidity of Herodotus' notion of chronological demarcation).
[61] For instance, the comparative study of oral traditions, for which see e.g. Murray (2001); R. Thomas (2001) (on the 'floating gap').

Athens); 1.143.2 (?) (Ionian migration); 1.171.2 (Minos' control over Carians); 1.173 (sons of Europa); 2.171.3 (daughters of Danaus spreading a rite: contrast deliberate silence on the religious rite itself); 3.91.1 (foundation of Poseideum by Amphilochus); 4.45 (Europa); 5.59–61 (inscriptions set up in the times of Laius, Oedipus and Eteocles); 5.65.3–4 (Neleid descent); 5.67.3–4 (Adrastos, Melanippus); 6.35.1 (Philaus son of Ajax first in the family to move to Athens); 6.47.1 (Thasos son of Phoenix: eponym); 6.137.1 (expulsion of Pelasgians); 7.20.2 (Trojan War and the pre-Trojan War Mysian/Teucrian expedition, included among στόλων ... τῶν ἡμεῖς ἴδμεν ('the expeditions of which we know') even if the magnitude of the Trojan War is qualified by κατὰ τὰ λεγόμενα ('according to reports'); 7.59.2 (Cicones: evidently mentioned because of their appearance in the *Odyssey*); 7.61.3 (Perseus: eponym); 7.62.1 (Medea: eponym); 7.90 (settlement of Cyprus from Salamis: i.e. by Teucer brother of Ajax); 7.91 (Cilix son of Agenor: eponym; Pamphylians descended from those scattered after the sack of Troy with Amphilochus and Calchas); 7.92 (Lycus son of Pandion: eponym); 7.94 (Ionians in Achaea); 7.95.1 (Pelasgians); 7.134.1 (Talthybius: descendants still in Sparta); 7.204 (Heraclid ancestry of Spartan kings: so too 7.208.1, 8.131.2); 8.43 (Dorian migration; Heracles' expulsion of Dryopians); 8.44.2 (early Athens, Erechtheus); 8.134.2 (Amphiaraus: rules for oracle); 9.34 (Melampus).

3. Reported with distancing (indirect discourse etc.): 1.1–5 (Persian stories on abducted women, Phoenician variant on Io); 1.67–8 (bones of Orestes: note esp. 1.68.3 for greater size); 1.171.2–6 (Carians); 2.63 (Ares' upbringing); 2.91 (Perseus); 2.122 (Rhampsanitus' descent to Hades and back); 2.144 (gods in Egypt); 2.156.4–6 (Leto); 3.5.3 (Typhos); 3.111.1 (Dionysus' upbringing); 4.5–12 (Scythian origins); 4.32–5 (Hyperborean visitors at Delos); 4.45 (Libya); 4.82 (Heracles' large footprint); 4.85.1 (clashing rocks); 4.127.4 (ancestry from Zeus); 4.145–9 (Argonauts' descendants: revealed at 4.150.1 to be agreed story of Spartans and Therans); 4.179 (Jason at Lake Tritonis); 5.7 (Thracian kings claim descent from Hermes); 5.43 (Heracles in Sicily); 5.80.1 (Aegina and Thebe); 5.94.2 (Trojan War); 6.53–5 (Spartan kingship); 6.137–8 (variants on Pelasgians); 6.138.4 (Lemnian women); 7.8g, 11 (Pelops); 7.150.2 (Perseus); 7.161 (Athens at Troy, autochthony); 7.170–1 (Minos, Cretans in Trojan War); 7.189.1–2 (Boreas and Orithyia); 7.193.2

Mythical and Historical Time in Herodotus 81

(Heracles and Argonauts); 7.197 (Phrixus), 7.198.2 (Heracles on pyre); 7.221 (descent from Melampus); 8.55 (earth-born Erechtheus, Athena and Poseidon competing for Attica); 9.27–7 (Tegean and Athenian appeals); 9.51.2, 4 (daughter of Asopus); 9.73 (Theseus), 9.120 (Protesilaus)

4. Cult of heroes: 5.66.2 (eponymous tribal heroes); 5.82.3 (Erechtheus); 5.89 (Aeacus); 7.43.2 (heroes at Troy); 8.64.2 (Aeacids); 8.121.1 (dedication of trireme to Ajax); 9.116.1–2 (Protesilaus).

CHAPTER 4

Myth and History in Livy's Preface

A. J. Woodman

I

If a scholar proposes to write on the subject of authority and tradition in ancient historiography, it is inevitable that he will pay particular attention to the prefaces of historical texts. Almost every ancient historian began his work with a preface in which he sought to establish his literary authority by deploying those elements of the tradition that were appropriate to his forthcoming narrative.[1]

In his famous book, John Marincola begins his section 'Myth and History' with the preface to Thucydides, before moving on to Diodorus and Dionysius of Halicarnassus. He then turns to the Latin historians:[2]

> The Latin historians also show themselves aware of the inappropriateness of *fabula* to history, but since it is not really a Roman characteristic to comment on the quality of the material they relate, there are only a few 'methodological' references among the Latins to the fantastic element which is or is not included in their histories. Perhaps the best known is Livy's in his preface, where he distinguishes between the events to be narrated before the city was founded and those of later times. The former he considers more in the way of 'poetic myths' (*poeticae fabulae*) than 'reliable remnants of historical deeds' (*incorrupta rerum gestarum monumenta*).

The passage of Livy's preface to which Marincola is referring is indeed well known (6–8):

---

*I am extremely grateful to Giustina Monti and Scarlett Kingsley not only for inviting me to their wonderful conference in honour of John Marincola, whose friendship and support I have enjoyed for almost three decades, but also for their impeccable arrangements. I am grateful too to the other participants in the conference, and to the late J. N. Adams, D. S. Levene and the editors for commenting on an earlier draft of this chapter; on no account should it be assumed that they agree with it.

[1] See the invaluable work of Herkommer (1968).   [2] Marincola (1997), 123–4.

82

Myth and History in Livy's Preface

> Quae ante conditam condendamue urbem poeticis magis decora fabulis quam incorruptis rerum gestarum monumentis traduntur, ea nec adfirmare nec refellere in animo est. [7] Datur haec uenia antiquitati ut miscendo humana diuinis primordia urbium augustiora faciat; et, si cui populo licere oportet consecrare origines suas et ad deos referre auctores, ea belli gloria est populo Romano ut cum suum conditorisque sui parentem Martem potissimum ferat, tam et hoc gentes humanae patiantur aequo animo quam imperium patiuntur. [8] Sed haec et his similia, utcumque animaduersa aut existimata erunt, haud in magno equidem ponam discrimine.

Despite its familiarity, however, the passage has not been well served by commentators. Ogilvie in his great commentary, for example, says almost nothing. He refers to the very beginning of Thucydides' preface (1.1.3) and to a passage of Cicero's *De inuentione* (1.23), but there is no comment either on Livy's Latin or on Livy's argument, both of which Ogilvie seems to regard as self-explanatory.[3] Yet that is far from being the case, as we are about to discover.[4]

II

For the purposes of comparison, the following are four different translations of the passage:

> Such traditions as belong to the time before the city was founded, or rather was presently to be founded, and are rather adorned with poetic legends than based upon trustworthy historical proofs, I purpose neither to affirm nor to refute. It is the privilege of antiquity to mingle divine things with human, and so add dignity to the beginnings of cities; and if any people ought to be allowed to consecrate their origins and refer them to a divine source, so great is the military glory of the Roman People that when they profess that their Father and the Father of their Founder was none other than Mars, the nations of the earth may well submit to this also with as good a grace as they submit to Rome's dominion. But to such legends as these, however they shall be regarded and judged, I shall, for my own part, attach no great importance. (Foster (1919))

> Those tales which are handed down, dating from the period before the city was founded, or indeed before its foundation was planned – tales glorified

---

[3] Ogilvie (1965), 26–7.
[4] Livy's Latin will be treated in Sections II–IV, his argument in Section V. The classic discussion of the preface as a whole is by John Moles (1993a), whose presence at the 'Authority and Tradition' conference was greatly missed. When his discussion was reprinted, it was accompanied by a brief editorial update (Chaplin and Kraus (2009), 86–7), and of course there have been various more recent contributions from other scholars too, e.g. Delarue (1998); Wiseman (2002); Burton (2008).

more in the fictions of poets than in the unadulterated records of history – it is not my intention either to support or reject. To antiquity this licence is conceded, that, by mingling with human affairs touches of the supernatural, it makes the origins of cities more imposing. And if any people should be permitted to claim divinity for its origins and to attribute them to the work of gods, such military glory belongs to the Roman people that when they put forward no less a god than Mars as their own and their founder's father, the races of mankind resignedly acquiesce in this claim too, as they do in their supremacy. But these tales and others like them, however they are considered and assessed, I shall not for my own part regard as of great importance. (Gould and Whiteley (1952))[5]

Events before Rome was born or thought of have come to us in old tales with more of the charm of poetry than of a sound historical record, and such traditions I propose neither to affirm nor refute. There is no reason, I feel, to object when antiquity draws no hard line between the human and the supernatural: it adds dignity to the past, and, if any nation deserves the privilege of claiming a divine ancestry, that nation is our own; and so great is the glory won by the Roman people in their wars that, when they declare that Mars himself was their first parent and father of the man who founded their city, all the nations of the world might well allow the claim as readily as they accept Rome's imperial dominion. These, however, are relatively trivial matters and I set little store by them. (de Sélincourt (1960))

Events before the city was founded or planned, which have been handed down more as pleasing poetic fictions than as reliable records of historical events, I intend neither to affirm nor to refute. To antiquity we grant the indulgence of making the origins of cities more impressive by commingling the human with the divine, and if any people should be permitted to sanctify its inception and reckon the gods as its founders, surely the glory of the Roman people in war is such that, when it boasts Mars in particular as its parent and the parent of its founder, the nations of the world would as easily acquiesce in this claim as they do in our rule. Yet I attach no great importance to how these and similar traditions will be criticized or valued. (Luce (1998))

Each of these translations has some claim to authority; how do they measure up to Livy's Latin?

III

We may begin *in mediis rebus* by considering the phrase *ante conditam condendamue urbem*. If for the moment we exclude *condendamue*, we are

---

[5] Gould and Whiteley unfortunately provide no commentary on the preface, offering only a translation instead.

Myth and History in Livy's Preface

left with a familiar construction in which 'the noun together with the predicative participle forms an abstract noun-phrase wherein the leading idea is conveyed by the participle'.[6] In Cicero, for example, *quid autem me iuuat quod ante initum tribunatum ueni* (*Att.* 11.9.1) means 'And why should I be glad to have come before the start of the Tribunate' (Shackleton Bailey).[7] Livy's phrase, paralleled word for word in Cicero (*Tusc. Disp.* 5.7 *ante hanc urbem conditam*) as well as in some late authors (Fest. p. 134, Solin. 40.16, Serv. *A.* 8.343), thus means 'before the founding of the city' and refers back to the title by which Livy's history was headed: *Ab urbe condita*, 'From the Founding of the City'.[8] Since Rome's foundation is not mentioned in the main narrative until *condita urbs* at 1.7.3, *Quae ante conditam urbem* would be equivalent to saying, 'As for the things *before* the starting point that was advertised in my title just above' (the emphasis would be on *ante*). But our phrase displays the extra *condendamue*; what does this addition mean?

When Pinkster quotes our passage in his recent study of Latin syntax, rather surprisingly he does no more than repeat Foster's Loeb translation:[9] 'Such traditions as belong to the time before the city was founded, or rather was presently to be founded, I purpose neither to affirm nor to refute.' Neither scholar seems to have realized, however, that this translation says the same thing twice: 'presently to be founded' merely repeats the idea of futurity in 'before the city was founded'. What we need is an interpretation of *condendamue* that does justice to its difference from *conditam* – and here we encounter a major difficulty: *ante* + gerundive is a construction without parallel in the whole of classical Latin literature: it is therefore exceptionally difficult to determine what the words *ante . . . condendam . . . urbem* might mean. Weissenborn and Müller, who are reduced to comparing a passage from Virgil's *Georgics* where *ante* is constructed with a gerund (3.206 *iam domitis . . . ante domandum*),[10] suggest that Livy is referring to the fated foundation of Rome and that the meaning of *condendamue* is 'or rather before it was due to be founded' ('oder vielmehr ehe sie gegründet werden sollte'). But although this

---

[6] Woodcock (1959), 75–6 §95.

[7] For other examples of *ante* + past passive participle, cf. *TLL* 2.134.24–65.

[8] The title is presented in this form by the MSS and 'is confirmed' by the opening words of Book 6 (*Quae ab condita urbe . . .*): so Horsfall (1981), 112 n. 50. Oakley (1997) on 6.1.1–2 states more cautiously that '*ab urbe condita* glances back to the probable title of the work as a whole'. Only Foster of our four translators offers a translation of Livy's title; his wording is the same as that adopted here.

[9] Pinkster (2015), 1.550. Leumann, Hofmann and Szantyr (1972: 2.377) are unhelpful.

[10] Weissenborn and Müller (1908) *ad loc*. So too Kühner and Stegmann (1962), 1.751. Unfortunately, there is no mention of either the Virgilian or the Livian passage in Wills (1996).

86   A. J. WOODMAN

interpretation is echoed by Heurgon,[11] a gerundive need not express necessity; ancient commentators and grammarians generally discuss the form in terms of a future passive participle: thus Probus writes *praeteritum scriptus, futurum scribendus, raptus . . . rapiendus, nutritus . . . nutriendus* (*GL* 4.171.2–3, 174.20–1, 177.42–178.1).[12] Given the uniqueness of Livy's construction, it may be worth exploring possibilities other than necessity.

When Livy in the very first chapter of narrative uses the expression *condendae . . . urbi locum quaerere* (1.1.8), he means 'were seeking a place for a to-be-founded city': here *condendae* does indeed seem equivalent to a future passive participle. A little later in Book 1, however, Livy writes *Romulus . . . urbe condenda regnum adeptus est* (1.18.6), which is a trickier sentence. Kühner and Stegmann in their discussion of the ablative gerundive stress that the construction is to be differentiated from that involving a past participle:[13] *dux urbe defensa magnam sibi peperit gloriam* is not the same as *dux urbe defendenda magnam gloriam sibi parere studuit*, although both expressions can be translated as 'by defending the city' in English. How does this rule apply to *urbe condenda* in Livy's sentence at 1.18.6? Kühner and Stegmann regard the phrase as 'peculiar' and say that one would have expected *condita*, but in fact it is very similar to 8.36.7 *ita dextere egit ut medendis corporibus animi . . . militum imperatori reconciliarentur* ('he acted so adroitly that the soldiers' hearts were won over to their commander because their bodies were being treated'): in this case, as Pinkster remarks, the gerundive is equivalent to a present passive participle,[14] an equivalence that seems appropriate not only at 1.18.6 but also in an even more interesting passage at 26.48.2 *quippe qui et acie dimicassent et capienda urbe tantum laboris periculique adissent et capta cum iis qui in arcem confugerant . . . pugnassent* ('since they had struggled in the line of battle and had encountered so much toil and danger in the process of the city being taken and, on its having been taken, had fought with those who had fled to the citadel').[15]

Is this evidence relevant to *condendamue* in the preface? Since the gerundives at 1.18.6, 8.36.7, and 26.48.2 seem equivalent to present passive participles and denote a process, perhaps that is also the case in the preface: 'before the city's founding, or rather the process of its being founded'. Now the process of founding Rome is inextricably bound up

---

[11] Heurgon (1970) *ad loc.*   [12] I owe this information to the kindness of R. Maltby.
[13] Kühner and Stegmann (1962), 1.755.   [14] Pinkster (2015), 1.294.
[15] This passage is quoted by Aalto (1949), 137, alongside that from the preface.

Myth and History in Livy's Preface

with the earlier life of Romulus and is first mentioned at 1.6.3 (*cupido . . . urbis condendae*).[16] Had Livy said merely *ante conditam urbem*, the relative clause *Quae . . . traduntur* would have had the potential of being applicable to the entire narrative between 1.1.1 and the actual foundation of Rome at 1.7.3; but this possibility is excluded on the present interpretation of the added *condendamue*, where *-ue* seems to have the corrective sense of 'or rather' which is adopted by Weissenborn and Müller in their commentary and by Foster and Pinkster in their translation.[17] Thus, if *condendamue* denotes a process, its construction with *ante* serves to narrow down the potential reference of *Quae . . . traduntur* from 1.1.1–7.3 to 1.1.1–6.2; we shall see later, in Section V, that the actual reference of *Quae . . . traduntur* is narrower still.[18]

If, however, it is regarded as unsatisfactory to think of *condendam* either as expressing necessity or as equivalent to a present passive participle, one might consider, as a last resort, whether the gerundive results from interpolation: a scribe, worried by the seeming incongruity of anteriority (*ante*) coupled with a past participle (*conditam*), wrote *condendam* ('to be founded') as a marginal gloss, which, with the addition of *-ue*, eventually found its way into the main text. The hypothesis, though radical, is not as far-fetched as it may seem at first sight: in just the same way a modern scholar, worried by a similar incongruity that he detected at Tac. *Ann.* 4.6.1 *quoniam Tiberio mutati in deterius principatus initium ille annus attulit* ('because that year brought the start of the change for the worse in Tiberius' principate'), proposed to change *mutati* to the gerundive *mutandi*.[19] The fact that *ante* + gerundive is unparalleled in the whole of Latin inevitably casts some doubt on the transmitted text, and an editor of Livy's preface might reasonably be tempted to write '*an* condendamue *secludendum?*' in the apparatus.

---

[16] Cf. also *qui conditam imperio regeret* at 1.6.4. For the notion of a process perhaps compare the strange sentence that Cicero puts into the mouth of Scipio at *Rep.* 2.4 *Quod habemus . . . institutae rei publicae tam clarum ac tam omnibus notum exordium quam huius urbis condendae principium profectum a Romulo? Qui patre Marte natus . . .* ('What origin of an established state do we know that is as distinguished and as universally familiar as the beginning of the founding of this city that started from Romulus? He was born with Mars as his father . . .'). It has been argued recently that Livy was influenced by Cicero's *De Republica* (Vasaly (2015), 9–21), though no mention is made of the two passages under consideration here.

[17] It should be acknowledged that such a sense is not recognized in *OLD* s.v. *-ue*, but it is very hard to see what else the enclitic could mean in the present context.

[18] Since the process of founding precedes the actual foundation, it may be asked why Livy did not simply write *Quae ante condendam urbem . . .*; but that form of words would not have provided the reference back to his title, which he evidently required.

[19] Lund (1989), 126–7.

88 A. J. WOODMAN

Yet these are not the only problems raised by the words *ante conditam condendamue urbem*. Since the words constitute an adverbial phrase, one might expect them to be taken with the verb, which is *traduntur*; but *traduntur* is present tense and refers to the time of Livy and his readers: it makes no sense to say 'the things that are being handed down before the founding of the city'. One has only to look at the various translations to see the scholarly contortions that are required to get the clause to make sense. The likelihood is that this is one of those places where the passive of *trado* should be followed by an infinitive (*OLD trado* 10). Livy has several examples, such as 7.28.9 *iudicia eo anno populi tristia in feneratores facta . . . traduntur* ('in that year grim judgements by the people are related as having been made against usurers'); the difference is that in our passage the infinitive – such as *accidisse* or *acta esse* – has to be understood. There is admittedly no parallel in Livy for such an ellipse with the passive of *trado*, although he will use the active in this way (e.g. 9.36.2, 10.41.5 *Octauium Maecium quidam eum tradunt* (sc. *fuisse*), 'some relate that it was Octavius Maecius'). If the lack of a precise parallel is deemed to be fatal to this interpretation, the only alternative is to assume that *Quae ante conditam condendamue urbem . . . traduntur* is condensed for *Ea ante conditam condendamue urbem quae . . . traduntur* ('Those events before the founding . . . that are handed down . . .'); but this would scarcely be a straightforward example of an adnominal prepositional phrase.[20]

Before we finish with this sentence, it remains to contextualize the contrast between poetic fables and the unadulterated records of history. The terms *fabulis* and *rerum gestarum* make it clear that Livy is dealing with the well-established division of narrative into *fabula* and *historia* as found in Cicero's *De inuentione* (1.27 *fabula est in qua nec uerae nec ueri similes res continentur . . . Historia est gesta res, ab aetatis nostrae memoria remota*, '*fabula* is that which comprises things neither real nor realistic . . . *Historia* is something done, remote from the time of our own age') and the *Rhetorica ad Herennium* (1.13 *fabula est quae neque ueras neque ueri similes continet res . . . Historia est gesta res, sed ab aetatis nostrae memoria remota*). Nevertheless, Livy has (as it were) suppressed the term *historia* and instead has used the phrase *rerum gestarum monumenta*. This is a surprisingly uncommon phrase in Latin literature, being found before Livy only in Cicero, in whose works it occurs five times.[21] In the speeches it refers to literal monuments such as statues or sculptures (*Ver.* 4.82, 4.88, *Font.* 41),

---

[20] For such phrases, see Wharton (2009).
[21] After Cicero it is found again at Liv. 6.29.9, Plin. *Nat.* 35.7, Gel. 13.4.1.

Myth and History in Livy's Preface

but in the *De oratore* it refers to written records and is so used in the famous passage where Cicero is discussing the early Roman historians (2.53): *qui sine ullis ornamentis **monumenta** solum temporum, hominum, locorum **gestarum**que **rerum** reliquerunt*, 'who without any elaboration have left only markers of dates, persons, places and events'. These 'markers' or *monumenta* are what I have called the 'hard core facts' of history,[22] and it seems very likely that Livy is alluding to this passage of the *De oratore* in order to emphasize the contrast between 'real' history and fable.

What, finally, is the meaning of the adjective *decora*? Weissenborn and Müller tell us that in Livy *decorus* usually means 'appropriate' but that on this occasion it means 'adorned' or 'decorated'. The commentators seem to have persuaded the *Thesaurus* (5.1.216.45–72), where very many examples of the meaning 'appropriate' are listed from Cicero through to Apuleius and beyond, including several from Livy – but not our passage. Weissenborn and Müller seem certainly to have persuaded our four translators, none of whom translates *decora* as 'appropriate'; on the other hand, none of the four translations seems to me to bear the slightest resemblance to Livy's Latin. In my opinion it is quite obvious that *decora* is here constructed with the dative and means 'appropriate to', and if I were to venture a translation of the sentence as a whole, it would go something like this (substituting singular for plural, since it is easier that way in English): 'With reference to what is handed down <as having happened> *before* the founding or rather the process of founding the city, more appropriate as it is to poetic fables than to the unadulterated records of history, I intend neither to affirm it nor to rebut it.' The contrast strongly resembles that in the so-called chapter on method in Thucydides' preface (1.21.1), although there are no verbal similarities.

IV

There follow two sentences joined by *et* (§7); the first of them, which refers to cities in the plural, is the foil for the second, which refers to Rome, and the relationship between the two is articulated linguistically. On the one hand, the gerund *miscendo* in the first sentence is a not-so-oblique reference to sexual coupling and hence anticipates the rape of Rhea Silvia by Mars to which Livy will allude in the second sentence.[23] On the other hand, there is an etymological link via *augeo/auctus* between *augustiora* and

---

[22] Woodman (1988), 88–93.   [23] Cf. e.g. Verg. *A.* 7.661 *mixta deo mulier; OLD misceo* 4c.

90   A. J. WOODMAN

auctores:[24] it is because the *auctores* of cities are gods that the cities enjoy origins that are *augustiora*. Despite this articulation, however, the nature of the relationship between the two sentences has remained obscure, and the reason for the obscurity resides in the word *antiquitati*. What does this word mean?

Although each of our translators retains the abstract noun, it seems clear from their translations that they regard it as an example of metonymy: *antiquitas* stands for the personal noun *antiqui*. This is certainly how our passage is classified in the *Thesaurus* (2.174.81–2) and in the *Oxford Latin Dictionary* (4); if these authorities are right, we should be able to substitute *antiquis* for *antiquitati* and the sentence will still make sense: 'this *uenia* is given to the ancients, that by the coupling of divine and human they make the origins of cities more numinous'. If that seems acceptable, it remains to be asked who these *antiqui* are. We should remember that, although the sentence is a generalization, its function as a foil for the second sentence means that it has to be applicable to Rome; with that proviso, there seem to be four theoretical possibilities for the identity of the *antiqui*.

The first is Romulus and those associated with him in founding Rome. But this is extremely unlikely, since in Livy's narrative of the foundation of Rome there is no reference to Mars or to Romulus' divine ancestry. Livy treats the rape (1.4.1–2) and the foundation (1.7.3) as independent stories; Romulus is nowhere made to capitalize on the fact that his father was a god. The second possibility is the Vestal Virgin, Rhea Silvia, who was raped by Mars. The sense in which 'by the coupling of divine and human she made the origin of the city more numinous' is self-evident, but it needs to be pointed out that, when she gave birth to her twins, she had no idea that they would be involved in founding a city. Her role in the founding of Rome was completely unconscious, and, since that is so, it makes no sense for her to be given *uenia*: she had done nothing for which *uenia* was needed. The third possibility is that *antiqui* means ancient writers: 'this *uenia* is given to ancient writers, that by the coupling of divine and human they make the origins of cities more numinous'. This appears to make good sense, and it is true that Fabius Pictor, the first Roman historian, told the story of the Vestal's rape by Mars (F4C/5P). But there are two difficulties. If Livy in the preface is giving prominence to early historians, we might expect there to be some reference to Fabius and similar writers when Livy comes to tell the story of the rape in his narrative; but there is no such reference: the first time Fabius is mentioned is two-thirds of the

---

[24] Cf. Maltby (1991), 64, 66.

Myth and History in Livy's Preface 91

way through Book 1 (1.44.2). The second difficulty with this interpretation is that it does not align, as it should, with what Livy says in the following sentence. If by *antiqui* he means that it is ancient writers in general who make the origins of cities more sublime, logic dictates that in the second sentence he specifies Roman writers as responsible for the story of Mars; but this is not at all what happens. In the second sentence those responsible for the story of Mars are the Roman people at large, whom he mentions twice: they are an entirely different entity from the small and specific group of early Roman historians. This leads to the fourth and final possibility, namely, that *antiquitas* is a reference to the Romans' earliest ancestors, those who lived between the time of Romulus and that of Fabius Pictor and who had handed down an oral tradition of the Vestal's rape by Mars. Once again, however, there is no reference (as might have been expected) to *fama* or an equivalent in Livy's brief narrative of the rape, where the intervention of Mars is attributed either to the Vestal's own conviction or to her attempt at covering up her act of intercourse (1.4.2). Since, therefore, none of the possible interpretations has proved to be entirely satisfactory, it is perhaps worthwhile to consider a different approach.

If it is to be inferred from our second sentence that it cannot be 'antiquity' that 'makes the origins of cities more numinous', as I have just argued, it follows that we need an alternative subject for the verb *faciat*, and the only other singular noun in the sentence is *uenia*. That *uenia* is the subject of *faciat* is not as surprising as it may seem at first sight. *uenia* is not only the subject of the main verb but is regularly constructed with a defining *ut*-clause, which here is additionally signposted by *haec*: from this perspective *uenia* is the natural subject of *faciat*, and the usage of the verb is almost identical to that found in a passage of the younger Seneca, where *uenia* is again the subject of *facere* and the verb is again followed by an accusative and predicate: *De ira* 2.34.2 *Illud quoque occurrat, . . . quam multos uenia amicos utiles fecerit* ('Let this too be remembered, . . . how many individuals *uenia* has made useful friends'). If this is right, our troublesome sentence will mean something like this: 'Antiquity is given a particular indulgence that makes the origins of cities more numinous by coupling the human with the divine.' *antiquitas* is a true abstract noun but is compressed for 'the concept of antiquity' or 'the notion of antiquity'; the 'indulgence' is given by us in the present day; and the sentence as a whole expresses the idea that we in the modern world go along with such stories as that of Mars and Rhea Silvia because that is the way in which we

92 A. J. WOODMAN

indulge antiquity. A similar idea appears in the opening of Tacitus' *Germania* (2.3–4):

> Celebrant carminibus antiquis ... Tuistonem deum terra editum.... Quidam, ut in licentia uetustatis, plures deo ortos pluresque gentis appellationes ... adfirmant.

> In ancient songs they record ... that god Tuisto was born from the earth.... Some of them, *ut in licentia uetustatis*, affirm that there were more offspring born from the god and more national names.

Rives in his edition renders the untranslated phrase as 'inasmuch as antiquity gives free reign (*sic*) to speculation',[25] which is simply a rewording of the translation given by Anderson in his commentary sixty years earlier ('as is natural in view of the scope allowed by antiquity to conjecture').[26] But Tacitus was thinking of Livy's preface, as the presence of *licentia* and *adfirmant* shows (~ *adfirmare ... licere*); the phrase means 'as you would expect, given the licence allowed to antiquity'.

The sentence of Livy that we have been considering, surely one of the most elegant he ever wrote, consists principally of a conditional clause, a consecutive clause and a comparative clause in that order; and, as each unfolds into the next, the reader is presented with a surprise. When we read 'If any people should be allowed ...', we expect him to conclude 'that people is the Roman people'; but instead 'the Roman people' is relegated to an oblique case and he says 'such is the glory of the Roman people in war ...'; and, when he continues 'such is the glory of the Roman people in war that ...', we expect him to conclude with something like '... that they rightly claim Mars as their ancestor'; but instead that point is relegated to a *cum*-clause and he in fact concludes with the most remarkable surprise of all: the nations of the world accept the Romans' descent from Mars as equably as they accept their Empire – as if other nations found the Romans' claim to divine ancestry potentially more intolerable than the fact of their imperialism. The nearest parallel I have found to the idea expressed by *imperium patiuntur* is in an imaginary speech in the *Rhetorica ad Herennium*, perhaps dating from the early first century BC (4.13):

> imperium orbis terrae, cui imperio omnes gentes, reges, nationes partim ui, partim uoluntate consenserunt, cum aut armis aut liberalitate a populo Romano superati essent

---

[25] Rives (1999), 77.   [26] J. G. C. Anderson (1938), 41.

Myth and History in Livy's Preface

dominion over the globe, in which dominion all peoples, kings and nations have acquiesced, partly through force, partly willingly, after they had been overcome by the arms or generosity of the Roman people.

It is unfortunate that Richardson in his discussion of the term *imperium* does not classify the Livy example as 'the *imperium* of Rome over the *orbis terrarum*' and has not realized that Livy's preface was written before the Battle of Actium, perhaps in the mid-30s BC.[27]

Since Livy is here contrasting the Romans with other peoples, his description of the latter as *gentes humanae* is pointed. It is relatively common in Latin to use *gens humana* in the singular to express the notion of 'the human race', but the plural is decidedly unusual and in fact before Livy is to be found only in Lucretius, in whom it occurs four times (1.727, 2.595, 5.161, 5.1306). Livy's *gentes humanae* will have even more point if he is alluding to the passage near the beginning of Lucretius' Book 5, where Lucretius is arguing that the gods played no part in the creation of the world (5.156–65):

> Dicere porro hominum causa uoluisse parare
> praeclaram mundi naturam proptereaque
> adlaudabile opus diuom laudare decere
> aeternumque putare atque inmortale futurum,
> nec fas esse, deum quod sit ratione uetusta   160
> *gentibus humanis* fundatum perpetuo aeuo,
> sollicitare suis ulla ui ex sedibus umquam
> nec uerbis uexare et ab imo euertere summa,
> cetera de genere hoc adfingere et addere, Memmi,
> desiperest.

To say further that for men's sake they [the gods] had the will to prepare the glorious structure of the world, and that therefore it is fitting to praise it as an admirable work of the gods; and to think that it will be everlasting and immortal, and that a thing which has by ancient contrivance of the gods been established for the races of mankind to all eternity may not ever lawfully be shaken from its foundations by any force, nor assailed by argument and overthrown from top to bottom; to feign this and other conceits, one upon another, Memmius, is the act of a fool.   (trans. M. F. Smith)

If the gods played no part in the creation of the world, a fortiori they will have played no part in the founding of a people. That Livy has Lucretius in mind is perhaps suggested by his use of *primordia* to describe the origins of

---

[27] J. Richardson (2008), 129. For Livy's date, see Woodman (1988), 132–4; it is suggested by Burton (2008) that the preface was written around early 32 BC.

94   A. J. WOODMAN

cities: the noun is exceptionally common in Lucretius, and, unless we accept Priscian's rather than Servius' wording of the preface to Sallust's *Histories*,[28] its combination with *urbis* or *urbium* occurs in no other Latin author until Tacitus (*H.* 5.2.1 *Sed quoniam famosae urbis supremum diem tradituri sumus, congruens uidetur primordia eius aperire*, 'But, because we are about to record the last day of the famous city (Jerusalem), it seems appropriate to explain its origins').

V

Livy's discussion of myth and history is brought to an end in §8, where only Luce of our four translators has realized that *animaduersa* and *existimata* are antonyms rather than synonyms: the tense of the verbs is future perfect and, as in a future vivid condition, indicates that Livy is referring to verdicts that his contemporaries have yet to make (the sense is 'whatever other individuals may think').[29]

The passage as whole may now be translated as follows:

> With reference to what is handed down <as having happened> *before* the founding or rather the process of founding the city, more appropriate as it is to poetic fables than to the unadulterated records of history, I intend neither to affirm it nor to rebut it. [7] Antiquity is given a particular indulgence that makes the origins of cities more numinous by coupling the human with the divine; and, if any people should be allowed to sanctify its own origins and trace back its progenitors to the gods, such is the glory of the Roman people in war that, when it claims none other than Mars as its own and its founder's parent, human races tolerate this with as equable a mind as they tolerate its Empire. [8] But, however much these and similar matters will be criticized or valued, I for my part will not make a big issue of them.

The argument of the passage proceeds by a series of foils. The events of the first sentence are described so generally (6 *Quae . . . traduntur*) that it is quite unclear to what Livy is referring, whether it is to a selection of the events or to the totality; all we are told is that they occurred 'before the founding or rather the process of founding the city' (*ante . . . urbem*), that they are more appropriate to poetic fables than to proper history, and that Livy's attitude towards them will be one of neutrality. The second sentence

---

[28] Cf. Sal. *Hist.* 1.8.M/1.2R *Nam a primordio urbis* (*primordio* Priscian: *principio* Servius).

[29] The implied subject of *utcumque animaduersa aut existimata erunt* is picked up by *quisque* in the next sentence.

Myth and History in Livy's Preface

is more specific: here we are given to believe that the events involved the mingling of divine and human elements (7 *miscendo humana diuinis*). It is only in the third and longest sentence that Livy reveals at last what he is referring to: *Quae . . . traduntur* is a reference to the siring of Romulus by Mars (*et si cui . . . imperium patiuntur*). The passage then concludes with a final sentence (8) in which these various elements are repeated chiastically. *haec* refers back to Romulus' divine paternity; *his similia* refers back to the divine paternity claimed by other cities (7 *Datur . . . faciat*);[30] and finally the authorial indifference of *utcumque . . . discrimine* refers back in detail to the authorial neutrality of §6 (*animaduersa - refellere, existimata - adfirmare, haud in magno equidem ponam discrimine - nec . . . nec . . . in animo est*). The ring composition testifies to the self-contained nature of the passage,[31] while the interconnectedness of the argument underlines the homogeneity of its topic. Moreover, although in Section III I suggested on the basis of parallels that *condendam* be understood as denoting a process (as translated above), the argument of §§6–8 of the preface would be unaffected if the gerundive were thought to denote necessity, as Weissenborn and Müller suggested, or even if it were deleted altogether.

The above analysis makes it clear that *Quae . . . traduntur* must involve 'the mingling of divine and human elements' and is in fact a specific (albeit oblique) reference to Romulus' allegedly divine conception: it therefore follows that the reference of *Quae . . . traduntur* can be narrowed down to the passage at 1.4.1–2, where Romulus' conception is described.[32] There is no other event in the relevant narrative to which the phrase *miscendo humana diuinis* is applicable. If this conclusion is correct, it allows us to challenge some of the widely held beliefs that depend upon extracting *Quae . . . traduntur* from its context and thereby misinterpreting it.

'The author's preface', writes G. B. Miles, 'has led us to believe that the entire tradition "before the city was founded or planned" was unreliable'; and in the course of a long, dense and influential discussion he uses this

---

[30] Kajanto (1957), 23–4, 29–30, believed that the importance of *his similia* had been overlooked and that Livy was referring to 'the irrational factors' of history and to 'legends' in general; but the articulation of Livy's argument is entirely against this.

[31] Naturally, I am not saying that the passage plays no part in the larger argument of the preface. The adverbial phrase *ante . . . urbem* (6) looks back to the temporal markers *nostra . . . aetas* and *prisca illa* in §5, while *haec et his similia* (8) looks forward to the contrasting *ad illa* in §9. In fact §§6–8 as a whole act as a foil for §§9–10.

[32] It may be asked why Livy devoted a significant portion of his preface to an event that is treated in so brief a passage of narrative, but Romulus and his role as founder featured prominently in the late Republic, especially under Julius Caesar, a descendant who had planned to build a temple to Mars (Weinstock (1971), 175–84, esp. 183). The suggestion that Octavian should be called Romulus (Suet. *Aug.* 7.2) arose after Livy had written his preface (above, note 27).

96 A. J. WOODMAN

statement to argue that this alleged unreliability does not manifest itself in the pre-foundation narrative, an apparent mismatch between theory and practice that he then deploys to problematize the later narrative as well.[33] Yet Miles' whole discussion is based on a false premise. Livy's words *Quae ... traduntur* do *not* refer to 'the entire tradition "before the city was founded or planned"'; as we have just seen, they refer only to that element of the tradition where there is interaction between the divine and the human, and in particular to the allegedly divine conception of Romulus (1.4.1–2). There are no grounds for a mismatch at all.

A different belief is illustrated by Heurgon in his commentary on §6:[34]

> T.-L. paraît croire que ce qui suit la fondation de Rome est fondé sur des sources sûres. Mais encore au livre V, 21, 8 (siège de Véies) il devra, dans les mêmes termes, répéter la même réserve. C'est seulement au début de VI qu'il se sentira sur un terrain solide.

> Livy appears to believe that what follows the foundation of Rome is based on secure sources. But again in book VI, 21, 8 (siege of Veii) he will be obliged to repeat, in the same terms, the same reservation. It is only at the start of VI that he will feel himself on solid ground.

Like many other scholars, Heurgon mistakenly interprets §6 as meaning, first, that Livy is dividing his narrative into pre-foundation and post-foundation sections and, second, that Livy is expressing agnosticism about the pre-foundation section (1.1.1–7.2); but, unable to believe that Livy's agnosticism about the evidence for the earliest Roman history extends only to the first ten pages of Book 1 and that in Livy's opinion the rest of the first pentad, amounting to 380 pages of Oxford text, is 'true history', Heurgon misrepresents Livy's explicit statement ('paraît croire', 'appears to believe') and, with an appeal to a passage in Book 5, explains what he thinks Livy ought to have said instead. The passage in Book 5 runs as follows (5.21.8–9):

> Inseritur huic loco fabula immolante rege Veientium uocem haruspicis dicentis qui eius hostiae exta prosecuisset, ei uictoriam dari, exauditam in cuniculo mouisse Romanos milites ut adaperto cuniculo exta raperent et ad dictatorem ferrent. Sed in rebus tam antiquis si quae similia ueri sint pro ueris accipiantur, satis habeam; haec ad ostentationem scaenae gaudentis miraculis aptiora quam ad fidem neque adfirmare neque refellere est operae pretium.

> At this point there is inserted the story that, while the king of the Veientines was sacrificing, the soothsayer's voice was heard in the tunnel saying that victory would be given to whoever cut the victim's entrails, and it prompted

---

[33] Miles (1995), 8–74 (quotation from p. 30). [34] Heurgon (1970) *ad loc.*

Myth and History in Livy's Preface

the Romans to open up the tunnel, seize the entrails and take them to the dictator. But, while in matters of such antiquity I would be satisfied if the realistic were accepted as real, these things, being more suitable to a stage display delighting in wonders than to credibility, it is worthwhile neither to affirm nor to rebut.

Yet Livy here explicitly states that he is perfectly content to regard the post-foundation narrative (*rebus tam antiquis*) as generally true (*pro ueris*) and deserving of credence (*fidem*); but occasionally there will be an exceptional episode (*haec*) that is to be categorized differently from *historia*: this passage of Book 5 complements rather than questions the sentence in the preface. The nature of the complementarity is revealing. In Book 5 Livy sees the difference from *historia* in terms of spectacles on the stage (*scaenae gaudentis miraculis*), whereas in the preface the difference is seen in terms of poetic fables (*poeticis . . . fabulis*): this is exactly what we should expect for episodes that involve 'the mingling of divine and human elements' (*miscendo humana diuinis*), since poetry itself could be defined as that which 'contains an imitation of things divine and human' (Posid. fr. 44E–K μίμησιν περιέχον θείων καὶ ἀνθρωπείων).[35]

VI

The younger Pliny, who would not be distracted from reading Livy even by the eruption of Mt Vesuvius (*Ep.* 6.20.5; cf. 2.3.8),[36] was well aware of the difficulties that beset the translator of a text (*Ep.* 7.9.2 *quae legentem fefellissent transferentem fugere non possunt*, 'whatever might have been overlooked by the reader cannot escape the translator'). These four sentences from the preface of a favourite author have shown how right he was.[37]

---

[35] It is interesting that Luce (1977), 176, crucially omits *poeticis* when translating §6, which he interprets in much the same way as Heurgon. At 6.1.1–3, to which Heurgon also refers, there is a comparable complementarity. Livy there offers three reasons why the matters treated in Books 1–5 were 'obscure' (the extreme distance of antiquity, the scarcity of contemporary literature, the destruction of documents in the Gallic Sack), but none of them has anything to do with 'the mingling of divine and human elements', which constitute the grounds for his stated attitude in the preface. The opening of Book 6 suggests a rhetorical pose typical of so-called second prefaces, since 'there is absolutely no qualitative difference in narrative mode between, let us say, Book 3 and Book 23. It is all "history"' (Feeney (1991), 257).

[36] For a gripping account, see R. Gibson (2020), 56–72.

[37] Regardless of whether or not my discussion here is found acceptable, it reaffirms the inadequacy of relying solely on vernacular translation when one is trying to understand the Latin historians (see Woodman (2012), 322–38, originally in Marincola (2007e), 133–44).

PART II

Dislocating Authority in Herodotus' Histories

CHAPTER 5

Herodotus as Tour Guide
The Autopsy Motif

Scott Scullion

I put forward a new suggestion here about what John Marincola in an important paper called 'the narrator's presence' in Herodotus' *Histories*.[1] I reconsider, in particular, a number of claims of autopsy and suggest on that basis that it is sometimes illuminating to think of Herodotus as adopting the role of tour guide or, rather, virtual tour guide. My arguments involve a view about Herodotus' 'good faith' or 'trustworthiness' that will not be agreeable to those who receive with (sometimes exasperated) indignation any suggestion that Herodotus knowingly said untrue things in the *Histories*. I hope, however, that what I have to say makes a coherent and convincing case, with a more persuasive explanation than has been offered by others,[2] that false statements some scholars would condemn as mere lies make in their context in the *Histories* an effective and readily comprehensible contribution to Herodotus' narrative aims, and that he would have seen them as harmless or, in our contemporary term, 'victimless' untruths.

Narrative Techniques in the *Histories*

I approach the motif of autopsy by way of general observations on a range of sophisticated, sometimes ironic narrative techniques employed in the *Histories*.[3] I have discussed elsewhere Herodotus' technique of roundabout

---

[1] Marincola (1987); see also the important discussion of Marincola (2007b), 51–66. I am very grateful to the editors for helpful bibliographical advice, to Giustina Monti and Scarlett Kingsley for conceiving and organizing a splendid conference, to many of the participants in it for encouraging and helpful questions and comments, and above all to John Marincola, its honorand, for more than thirty years of wonderfully life-enhancing friendship.

[2] Especially Fehling in his indispensable study (1989) and Armayor (1985).

[3] In our contributions to this volume Scarlett Kingsley and I have come independently to some comparable conclusions about aspects of Herodotus' narrative technique. See Kingsley's discussion in Chapter 10 of the role of the narratee in second-person and impersonal 'one' passages and of the

criticism of aspects of Greek culture and religion.[4] He says, for example, that the Persians do not employ statues, temples, and altars and 'accuse those who do so of being fools, I suppose because they have not established the convention, as the Greeks have, that the gods are of human form' (1.131.1), and this reflects a discomfort with Greek anthropomorphism detectable throughout the *Histories*.[5]

Herodotus' style of communication prompts an alert response alive to various kinds of ambiguity and irony, and he is ironic in a variety of ways, from pointed expression of a different but potentially illuminating way of looking at things, as in the comment I have just quoted, to what one might call the 'wink of mutual understanding'[6] that accompanies at least some of his many statements of the sort 'I am bound to record what has been said' (7.152) or 'Let anyone who finds such things credible make what he will of these Egyptian stories, but the basis of my whole work is to write down as I heard them the things I have been told by everyone' (2.123).[7] Other readers must have found such statements ironic, but it does not seem to be normal to do so. David Asheri, for example, says that 'Herodotus feels under a moral obligation to report all the versions collected, even if they are not trustworthy',[8] but I cannot understand – whether on general grounds or because the stories this motif accompanies are often compellingly strange or marvellous, always entertaining, and never dull – how such statements can be accepted at face value as Herodotus' assurance that he operates with no filtering principle whatsoever in his use of such information as he has gathered, and that the *Histories* therefore include every account he has ever heard. Surely, the sense is often ironic: 'Fascinating stuff! May be dubious, but I have to pass on what they tell me!'

---

embedding in the text of virtual experience, including virtual or vicarious travel (see note 12 below); further references to specific parallels are given below.

[4] Scullion (2006), 201–2, picking up on Burkert (1990), 20–1; cf. D. Boedeker's Chapter 8 in this volume.

[5] He resists claims of divine epiphany or human contact with or descent from a god; has a very marked tendency, when speaking of the divine in his own person, to speak of ὁ θεός, 'god', τὸ θεῖον, 'the divine/divinity', or, for example, τὰ θεῖα τῶν πρηγμάτων (9.100), 'the divine element in things', rather than of Greek gods under their traditional names; and explicitly claims (again rather diplomatically, while discussing Egyptian religion) that the 'provenance, genealogy, appearance, epithets, privileges, and competencies' of the Greek gods were invented 'yesterday or the day before' (πρώην τε καὶ χθές) by Homer and Hesiod (2.53.1–2). See on all this Scullion (2006).

[6] This is a variant of the type of irony Carolyn Dewald referred to in her paper at the conference as Herodotus' 'narrative smirk'.

[7] Cf. Lateiner (1989), 79.   [8] Asheri, Lloyd, and Corcella (2007), 20.

Herodotus as Tour Guide: The Autopsy Motif   103

Another striking example is the introduction of the 'constitutional debate' in Book 3: καὶ ἐλέχθησαν λόγοι ἄπιστοι μὲν ἐνίοισι Ἑλλήνων, ἐλέχθησαν δ᾽ ὦν, 'and speeches were delivered, speeches beyond credibility to some Greeks, but delivered they were' (3.80). There will certainly have been – and Herodotus will have known there were – ancient readers as well aware as he and we that no such constitutional debate took place, and I assume that such readers would take Herodotus' statement, as I do, ironically – as an amusing acknowledgement, as it were with a wink, that such a debate never happened, not as a poker-faced assertion to anyone reading the words that it did really happen just as narrated. For all readers, however, the debate has the same function. Darius' accession to the throne is the one break in hereditary succession during the period of Persian history Herodotus covers, and so is the point at which the Persians could have done otherwise but as it were opted to carry on with monarchy as their system of government; it is therefore the natural point in the *Histories* at which to reflect – in Greek terms, for a Greek audience – on *why* the Persians preferred monarchy, that is, on the combination of social and cultural assumptions and personal qualities that led to Darius' accession and the persistence of monarchical rule in Persia.[9] By vividly dramatizing the debate and the events leading up to it, Herodotus highlights and emphasizes the significance of the persistence of Persian monarchy under Darius. It is surely incredible that some Greek pre-Herodotus – in a vacuum, as it were, rather than with the explanatory motive appropriate to this point of the *Histories* – concocted a tale of a debate that Herodotus believed, and that was also precisely what was needed at this point in his narrative. In this and similar cases it is far simpler to attribute responsibility to Herodotus the master of many narrative techniques than to dream up another of the contingent of pre-Herodoti we require in order to attribute responsibility for any falsehood to someone – anyone – other than a Herodotus we insist must be honest on pain of revocation of his historian's licence.

This may all seem highly subjective, but I hope that it is not difficult to accept that Herodotus employs many different techniques – irony in many forms, vivid simplification, and a variety of narrative roles, including keeper of a richly stocked cabinet of curiosities – to keep all his readers

---

[9] For the clear connections between the views taken by individual conspirators in the debate and their personal character as manifested in the surrounding narrative, see e.g. Pelling (2002a), esp. 129–31.

involved and satisfied.[10] In what follows I explore another of the ways in which he seems to me to do so, that is, in his role as virtual tour guide, and through careful management of what one might call the 'autopsy motif'.[11]

The phrase 'tour guide' in my title is of course in part a nod to James Redfield's well-known paper 'Herodotus the Tourist', but Herodotus as narrator is virtual tour guide as well as tourist.[12] I confess immediately that what I have to say about the ethos of tour guiding is based not on any scholarly study of the subject but on my own experience of hearing or overhearing tour guides at work. I would be surprised, however, if any reader had not had similar experiences. I remember especially vividly a guide in Heraklion in Crete who was asked by someone in a tour group what the Minoan frescoes meant. I cannot now recall the details of what the guide said in reply, but it was a wildly eccentric, probably entirely personal theory about how to interpret them. What I do recall clearly is how happily the group took in the guide's eccentric interpretation, and that it began with the words 'We think that . . .'. This is very effective guidecraft: of course the group like to think that they will take away from their direct encounter with the original site or object a correspondingly authoritative account of its meaning, and that this should come directly from the 'we' voice of expertise is much more satisfying than any mediation of what 'they' – sources external to the immediate encounter – say about it. Nor can we regard narrative artifice of this general sort as shocking dishonesty repellent to all decent people. Experience suggests that people not seldom make a story of some event more effective by streamlining its content, enhancing its liveliness, or reducing the stages of mediation by which it reached them, perhaps even saying or implying that they were present at the original event, and that they may do so simply to make the story more vivid, to lend it greater authority, or to cast themselves in a more central role. Awareness of such communicative dynamics may help us to understand some controversial passages in the *Histories*.

---

[10] On the rich variety of Herodotus' narrative techniques, including 'novelistic devices, meant to encourage wonder', see Marincola (2007b), 51–66 (quotation at 57).

[11] For collections of Herodotus' references to autopsy, see Schepens (1980), 47–51 and Marincola (1987), 122–3 with n. 5, 137. On the importance of autopsy in Greek historiography and its background in the *Odyssey*, see Marincola (2007b), 5–20.

[12] Redfield (1985). Kingsley in this volume says of ἰδόντι, 'one seeing' at 2.5.1, that it 'opens up a vicarious tour' (p. 213), and of the second-person verbs in the same passage that 'the *Histories* invites a second-person virtual travelling experience' (213–14); cf. Kingsley on 'simulated travel' and on 'mental tours' and rhetorical techniques leading to 'more immersive depiction of geography' (217).

Egyptian and Persian Skulls

Let us start with the skulls, which Herodotus tells us he saw at Pelusium in Egypt:

> θῶμα δὲ μέγα εἶδον πυθόμενος παρὰ τῶν ἐπιχωρίων· τῶν γὰρ ὀστέων κεχυμένων χωρὶς ἑκατέρων τῶν ἐν τῇ μάχῃ ταύτῃ πεσόντων (χωρὶς μὲν γὰρ τῶν Περσέων ἔκειτο τὰ ὀστέα, ὡς ἐχωρίσθη κατ᾽ ἀρχάς, ἑτέρωθι δὲ τῶν Αἰγυπτίων), αἱ μὲν τῶν Περσέων κεφαλαί εἰσι ἀσθενέες οὕτω ὥστε, εἰ θέλοις ψήφῳ μούνῃ βαλεῖν, διατετρανέεις, αἱ δὲ τῶν Αἰγυπτίων οὕτω δή τι ἰσχυραί, μόγις ἂν λίθῳ παίσας διαρρήξειας. [2] αἴτιον δὲ τούτου τόδε ἔλεγον, καὶ ἐμέ γε εὐπετέως ἔπειθον, ὅτι Αἰγύπτιοι μὲν αὐτίκα ἀπὸ παιδίων ἀρξάμενοι ξυρῶνται τὰς κεφαλὰς καὶ πρὸς τὸν ἥλιον παχύνεται τὸ ὀστέον. [3] τὠυτὸ δὲ τοῦτο καὶ τοῦ μὴ φαλακροῦσθαι αἴτιόν ἐστι· Αἰγυπτίων γὰρ ἄν τις ἐλαχίστους ἴδοιτο φαλακροὺς πάντων ἀνθρώπων. [4] τούτοισι μὲν δὴ τοῦτό ἐστι αἴτιον ἰσχυρὰς φορέειν τὰς κεφαλάς, τοῖσι δὲ Πέρσῃσι, ὅτι ἀσθενέας φορέουσι τὰς κεφαλάς, αἴτιον τόδε· σκιητροφέουσι ἐξ ἀρχῆς πίλους τιάρας φορέοντες. ταῦτα μέν νυν τοιαῦτα [ἐόντα εἶδον]· εἶδον δὲ καὶ ἄλλα ὅμοια τούτοισι ἐν Παπρήμι τῶν ἅμα Ἀχαιμένει τῷ Δαρείου διαφθαρέντων ὑπὸ Ἰνάρω τοῦ Λίβυος. (3.12)

> Here I saw an amazing thing, informed about it by the local people. The bones of those who fell in the battle were heaped up in distinct areas, for the bones of the Persians lay separately, as they originally fell, and those of the Egyptians on the other side. The skulls of the Persians are so fragile that if you were inclined to tap at them with nothing but a pebble you would pierce through them, but those of the Egyptians are so tough that you could scarcely break them if you struck them with a rock. [2] They told me, and easily persuaded me, that the cause of this is that the Egyptians, starting straightaway when they are children, shave their heads, and the bone is thickened by exposure to the sun. [3] This is the same reason that they do not go bald; for among the Egyptians, by comparison with all mankind, one sees the fewest bald people. [4] This, then, is the reason they have tough skulls, but as for the Persians having fragile skulls, the reason is this: from the outset they shade themselves, wearing felt caps. So much for this matter, but I saw the same sort of thing at Papremis among those led by Achaemenes the son of Darius who were destroyed by Inarus the Libyan.

Detlev Fehling, in his analysis of this chapter, regards it as a prime example of wholesale Herodotean invention.[13] He thinks that Herodotus knew the Hippocratic theory that the bodies of Scythian nomads are moist (Hp. *Aer.* 20–2), but the notion that this theory is relevant to what

[13] Fehling (1989), 28–30.

Herodotus says needs challenging.[14] The Hippocratic treatise attributes this bodily moistness and 'softness' (μαλακίη) or 'slackness' (ἀτονία) – not 'fragility' (Asheri) – to their specifically nomadic habits of spending their time sitting in wagons as children and riding horses as adults. I see no basis here for a Greek assumption, such as Fehling posits, that Persian skulls should be thinner and more fragile than Egyptian, and so Fehling's theory of the genesis of the story seems to me impossibly arbitrary. But other analyses of the passage are equally improbable.

Very minor ethnic differences in skull thickness are possible, but no such stark contrast as Herodotus says he observed between Egyptian thickness and hardness and Persian thinness and fragility is credible. What then are we to make of the passage? 'The fallen soldiers, left unburied on the battlefield', Asheri notes, 'would probably have been mostly Carian and Greek mercenaries of both armies; Persians and Egyptians were probably buried or embalmed, according to their customs.'[15] Herodotus has just mentioned these mercenaries (3.11), whose remains must at least have constituted a considerable admixture. The heaps of skulls in distinct locations are also bizarre: the ancients did not shoot one another down at opposite ends of the battlefield with guns, so distinct groups of Egyptian and Persian remains – never mind the Carians and Greeks – seem incredible. 'It is also probable', claims Asheri, by way of vindicating Herodotus' honesty, 'that the two heaps of bones had been prepared by the guides for the spectacle.' As for the putative differences in thickness, Asheri says that 'In fact the skulls of the ancient Egyptians are of normal hardness; in the case of the Persians it is possible only to say that the fragility of the skull and of the bones in general is a typical symptom of rickets, a disease more common in northern countries than in tropical ones, due to malnutrition and Vitamin D deficiency.'[16]

I will not take a stand on the broader question of where in Egypt Herodotus actually went,[17] but I am confident that he did not go to this battlefield and see what he says he saw. Neither, however, do I think he dreamt the whole thing up himself in the way Fehling rather recklessly imagines. It is simplest to suppose that Herodotus as virtual tour guide has enhanced with the 'autopsy motif' a story he was told. His account is

---

[14] Fehling (1989), 28; cf. Asheri, Lloyd, and Corcella (2007), 409–10 on 3.12.2.

[15] Asheri, Lloyd, and Corcella (2007), 409 on 3.12.2.

[16] Asheri, Lloyd, and Corcella (2007), 410 on 3.12.2. Pritchett (1993), 29–32 offers an even less cogent defence of Herodotus' trustworthiness in this passage.

[17] On which question, see, in addition to the commentators, Armayor (1978b) and (1985) and S. West (1991), 149–50, all with references to earlier studies.

Herodotus as Tour Guide: The Autopsy Motif   107

highly implausible, and the likelihood is vanishingly small that most of the Persians killed at Pelusium were suffering from advanced rickets. Asheri tries to vindicate Herodotus' honesty by suggesting that the skulls were separated by local guides, but unless we accept the rickets hypothesis they must have not only separated the skulls but ground half of them down until they looked like they would shatter at the touch of a pebble. That would be a very demanding and very curious undertaking: it is one thing to retail the false story, quite another to fake physical evidence by the heap. Above all, we would have to imagine guides busily grinding down skulls not only at Pelusium but also, many years later, at Papremis, where Achaemenes and many Persian troops had fallen in battle against the rebel Inarus and his Athenian allies circa 462/1 BC,[18] and where Herodotus says he 'saw the same sort of thing'.

Far the simplest conclusion is that Herodotus is enhancing his description of something he had merely heard about by saying that he saw it.[19] It was easier to believe that he invented the constitutional debate than that some pre-Herodotus invented a story that just happened to fit perfectly where Herodotus needed it, and it is simpler to attribute the skulls story to Herodotus the one virtual tour guide than to two actual local guides – two further pre-Herodoti – at Pelusium and Papremis, both of whom mocked up a display of unusual skulls on a battlefield.

The parallel at Papremis, however, needs more thought than it has been given. If we were game enough to postulate a *single* spectacle-creating guide, it is far more likely that Herodotus encountered him at the site of the battle of Papremis during a trip to Egypt in the 440s,[20] fifteen or so years after the battle, than that he ran into a third- or fourth-generation guide still profiting from showing faked skulls where the battle at Pelusium had been fought in 525 BC. It is far more probable still, however, Papremis being a battle in which Athenian troops were involved and from which they doubtless brought back stories, that it was some Athenian veteran(s) of the battle who told Herodotus about the difference between Persian and Egyptian skulls and claimed that you could see it on the battlefield. Herodotus found such things fascinating: at 9.83 he reports that the Plataeans, following the battle there, found a skull made of a single bone, a jaw in which the teeth were all joined together as part of a single

---

[18] On the battle, see e.g. Asheri, Lloyd and Corcella (2007), 410 on 3.12.4 with further references.
[19] Kingsley in this volume (p. 215) describes Herodotus' use of impersonal forms in this passage as creating a 'visualization of the scene that the narrator and the narratee share'.
[20] A. B. Lloyd (1975–88), i.61–2, very plausibly suggests that Herodotus will have visited Egypt sometime after 449/8 BC.

bone, and a skeleton five cubits (7.5 feet) long. Very likely the 'comparandum' of Papremis in fact prompted and was the basis of Herodotus' description: the confirmatory 'parallel' from a period later than that covered by the *Histories* is an excellent clue to the single source of Herodotus' bizarre story. Having heard from Athenian veterans of Papremis a fascinating tale about Persian and Egyptian skulls, which he had no reason to doubt, Herodotus worked it up as a fascinating stop on the tour when he came to recount the greatest battle between Egyptians and Persians that fell within the chronological scope of the *Histories*. This is obviously not a certain conclusion, but it seems an infinitely more plausible account of the genesis of Herodotus' story than the trustworthiness-preserving notion that one person at Pelusium in 525 and a second at Papremis in 460 took it into their heads to fake up the same kind of minor tourist attraction and that not only the second but the first of these attractions was still a going concern when Herodotus visited Egypt in the 440s.

Flying Snakes

A second clear case of enhancement by a claim of autopsy is Herodotus' account of the skeletons of flying snakes at Bouto in the eastern Nile delta:

> Ἔστι δὲ χῶρος τῆς Ἀραβίης κατὰ Βουτοῦν πόλιν μάλιστά κη κείμενος, καὶ ἐς τοῦτο τὸ χωρίον ἦλθον πυνθανόμενος περὶ τῶν πτερωτῶν ὀφίων. ἀπικόμενος δὲ εἶδον ὀστέα ὀφίων καὶ ἀκάνθας πλήθει μὲν ἀδύνατα ἀπηγήσασθαι, σωροὶ δὲ ἦσαν τῶν ἀκανθέων καὶ μεγάλοι καὶ ὑποδεέστεροι καὶ ἐλάσσονες ἔτι τούτων, πολλοὶ δὲ ἦσαν οὗτοι. (2.75.1)

> There is a place in Arabia in the vicinity of the city of Bouto, and I went to this place to learn about the winged serpents. When I arrived there, I saw bones and spines of serpents in quantities impossible to express. Some among the heaps of spines were large, some smaller, others smaller still, and there were many of these heaps.

Herodotus says that the winged serpents try to enter Egypt through a mountain pass but are killed there by ibis birds, which the Egyptians therefore highly esteem.

For Fehling this story too is wholly the product of speculative invention. Herodotus, he says, 'might well have wondered why [the ibis] was so especially revered. From there it would be a short step to supposing that it destroyed some particularly serious pest' – but that 'short step' is no more than Fehling's arbitrary conjecture. 'Herodotus' final step', Fehling continues, 'was to cast a suitable creature in that role, and the winged serpents

Herodotus as Tour Guide: The Autopsy Motif 109

of Arabia happened to be available' (27), but this further stage of arbitrary conjecture renders Fehling's explanation altogether forced and unpersuasive.

One defence of Herodotus' trustworthiness here, which was still made by W. K. Pritchett, is that the 'winged serpents' are really locusts, which ibises do eat.[21] There are, however, two good Greek terms for locust: ἀκρίς, which can also mean 'grasshopper', and ἀττέλαβος, which means specifically 'locust' and is used by Herodotus himself (4.172) as well as by Aristotle and others.[22] Pritchett claims that the Greek vocabulary for insects was imprecise and fails to mention that Herodotus uses the word ἀττέλαβος, but he does use it, and he would clearly also have been able to distinguish the *exuviae* or outer shells of locusts from sloughed snake skins or snake bones. This is an especially good example of the sort of case where, in Stephanie West's memorable line, 'Herodotus' reputation for good faith can only be maintained at the cost of his intelligence.'[23]

Alan Lloyd says in his commentary that 'H[erodotus] clearly saw something which could be mistaken for snake skeletons but what it was is a complete mystery.'[24] The imaginative notion of winged snakes certainly existed, as did depictions of them,[25] and Herodotus describes them carefully, comparing them to water snakes and saying that they have wing-like membranes without feathers, like bats (2.76.3). The skeletons of such creatures, like those of bats, would be unmistakably distinctive, and far the simplest conclusion, as in the case of the skulls, is therefore that someone told Herodotus about the winged snakes and the heaps of their skeletons; he saw no reason to disbelieve what he heard; and in his role as virtual tour guide he took it from there. The autopsy motif is developed so as to bring the hearer or reader close to the site, that is, the site with heaps of skeletons that Herodotus imagined. So far as I know, no one has suggested in this case that some pre-Herodotus or team of pre-Herodoti carefully glued wing bones of bats onto skeletons of snakes in large quantities and disposed them in large, small, and even smaller heaps in the mountain pass. Was Herodotus doing his job as virtual tour guide with creative panache, or was he taken in by very busy fakers of very many heaps of skeletons?

---

[21] Pritchett (1993), 27–9; this view goes back at least as far as Rawlinson (1858–60), ii.124 n. 5.

[22] Ἀκρίς: Hom. *Il.* 21.12; Ar. *Ach.* 1116; Arist. *HA* 555[b]18, where it means 'grasshopper'; LXX *Ex.* 10:4; ἀττέλαβος: Arist. *HA* 550b32; 556a8, where it means 'locust' by contrast with 'grasshopper'.

[23] S. West (1985), 279, cf. 294: 'the attempt to maintain the literal truth of his words here seems to entail the sacrifice of his common sense'.

[24] A. B. Lloyd (1975–88), ii.327 on 2.75.   [25] A. B. Lloyd (1975–88), ii.326–7 on 2.75.

110   SCOTT SCULLION

A List of the Kings of Egypt at Memphis and Statues of Archpriests at Thebes

I turn now to a more elaborate use of the autopsy motif, Herodotus' representation of how information about the number of Egyptian kings and archpriests was conveyed to him.[26] The priests of Memphis tell him about the first king, Min (2.99), and then read aloud to him from a papyrus roll the names of Min's 330 successors; of 328 of these they could offer no 'demonstration of accomplishments' (ἔργων ἀπόδεξις, 2.101.1), but added remarks on the two, Nitocris the queen and the last of the 330, Moeris, who had achieved anything worthy of note (2.100–1). There follows a long account of ten further kings, again attributed to the priests of Memphis (2.102–42),[27] and after discussing the tenth, Sethos, Herodotus tells us that the priests demonstrated (ἀποδεικνύντες) to him that in these 341 generations there were equal numbers of kings and archpriests (2.142.1).

Herodotus does not say that the papyrus roll was translated for him nor that he studied the document itself, but simply conjures up a picture of priests reciting names from it in his presence. 'When we try to visualise the scene', says Fehling, 'it becomes frankly hilarious: a priest droning an endless succession of names and Herodotus listening intently and trying to keep count, often desperately wondering whether a particular sequence of outlandish syllables counted as one name or two.'[28] A Memphite list or oral tradition of something like 330 kings may well have existed (even if 330 is a suspiciously round number),[29] but it is overwhelmingly unlikely that it was communicated to Herodotus in the way he describes.

The recitation from the papyrus roll is the vivid focus of Herodotus' story but also, and not coincidentally, the basis of his emphatic claim for the great antiquity of Egyptian civilization, which is lent striking salience by the reading aloud of a single sequence of 330 regnal names (equivalent by Herodotus' reckoning to 330 generations, at a rate of three per century). Numbers as such are unexciting, but this one is important, and Herodotus employs a version of the autopsy motif to highlight it.

---

[26] Fehling (1989), 71–86, discusses these passages acutely, and much of what I have to say about them is consonant with his analysis, but I approach them from a distinct point of view and stress different aspects of Herodotus' motivations and techniques.

[27] See Fehling (1989), 72–4.   [28] Fehling (1989), 76.

[29] A. B. Lloyd (1975–88), i.93–111; A. B. Lloyd (1988), 25–8, 33–8; Pritchett (1993), 75–8; Moyer (2002), 75–82, esp. 75–8. On the round number, see Fehling (1989), 78, 216–17.

Herodotus as Tour Guide: The Autopsy Motif

The passage set at Memphis is closely connected with Herodotus' subsequent story of the statues of archpriests in the great hall of the Karnak temple at Thebes:

Πρότερον δὲ Ἑκαταίῳ τῷ λογοποιῷ ἐν Θήβῃσι γενεηλογήσαντι ἑωυτὸν καὶ ἀναδήσαντι τὴν πατριὴν ἐς ἑκκαιδέκατον θεὸν ἐποίησαν οἱ ἱρέες τοῦ Διὸς οἷόν τι καὶ ἐμοὶ οὐ γενεηλογήσαντι ἐμεωυτόν· [2] ἐσαγαγόντες ἐς τὸ μέγαρον ἔσω ἐὸν μέγα ἐξηρίθμεον δεικνύντες κολοσσοὺς ξυλίνους τοσούτους ὅσους περ εἶπον· ἀρχιερεὺς γὰρ ἕκαστος αὐτόθι ἱστᾷ ἐπὶ τῆς ἑωυτοῦ ζόης εἰκόνα ἑωυτοῦ· [3] ἀριθμέοντες ὦν καὶ δεικνύντες οἱ ἱρέες ἐμοὶ ἀπεδείκνυσαν παῖδα πατρὸς ἑωυτῶν ἕκαστον ἐόντα, ἐκ τοῦ ἄγχιστα ἀποθανόντος τῆς εἰκόνος διεξιόντες διὰ πασέων, ἐς οὗ ἀπέδεξαν ἁπάσας αὐτάς. [4] Ἑκαταίῳ δὲ γενεηλογήσαντι ἑωυτὸν καὶ ἀναδήσαντι ἐς ἑκκαιδέκατον θεὸν ἀντεγενεηλόγησαν ἐπὶ τῇ ἀριθμήσι, οὐ δεκόμενοι παρ' αὐτοῦ ἀπὸ θεοῦ γενέσθαι ἄνθρωπον. (2.143.1–4)

Previously, in Thebes, the priests of Zeus had given the writer Hecataeus, who had connected himself genealogically with a god in the sixteenth generation, the same experience as they gave me, who had not traced my genealogy. [2] Having led me into the interior of the hall, which was large, they pointed to the colossal wooden statues there and counted out precisely as many of them as I have just stated [viz. 341, the number of kings attested by the priests of Memphis]; for each archpriest, during his lifetime, erects a statue of himself here. [3] As, then, they counted and pointed to the statues, the priests indicated to me that each was a son who succeeded his father, and they went through all of them, beginning with the image of the most recently deceased, until they had pointed out absolutely all of them. [4] To Hecataeus' genealogical claim of descent from a god in the sixteenth generation they responded with a genealogy on the basis of their own count, not accepting his notion that a human being could be descended from a god.

For Herodotus, as previously for Hecataeus, the priests counted out 341 statues – or rather 345, the number he gives further on (2.143.4), which is presumably meant to include four Saite kings between Sethos and the time of Hecataeus' visit. 'This passage', says Lloyd, 'has rightly excited considerable misgivings.... It is a most remarkable coincidence that the total of generations derived from oral and written sources ... should fit that of the statues and we may well ask whether the narrative does not contain considerable, if unconscious, confusion.'[30]

The passage does not strike me as confused, but it is certainly heavy with coincidence. We should note first that Egyptian king lists varied

---

[30] A. B. Lloyd (1975–88), iii.107–8 on 2.143.

considerably; there was no single, authoritative list and there is therefore no reason to think that a Theban list would have precisely or even closely resembled a Memphite.[31] Nor does Herodotus take any thought for a Theban king list, but simply claims that, unbeknownst to the Thebans, he could predict the number of their statues because he had learnt at Memphis how many reigns there had been. Now the Memphites not only had evidence for 341 reigns but also asserted that the number of kings corresponded precisely to that of archpriests, who must of course be *Memphite* archpriests. Herodotus then tells us that the statues of *Theban* archpriests confirm the number of generations in Egyptian history. The linchpin here is the Memphites' assertion, in itself a gratuitous sidenote to their recital of kings' names, that their archpriests corresponded in number to the kings: Herodotus implicitly and arbitrarily transposes such a correspondence to Thebes as the sole basis of the notion that the Theban statues of archpriests confirm the Memphite count of kings' reigns.

The Memphite priests' assertion, however, is less gratuitous sidenote than gratuitous *end*note. It comes at the very end of the forty-four chapters Herodotus devotes to the Memphite list of kings (2.99–142), to which it is strictly irrelevant, and immediately before the chapter in which he turns to the Theban priests' count of archpriestly statues (2.143), to which Herodotus implicitly makes it highly relevant, indeed fundamental. Has Herodotus downplayed the unlikelihood of the same numerical correspondence of archpriest and kings coincidentally occurring both at Memphis and at Thebes by slipping the Memphite claim in at the very end of the Memphite chapters to condition, as an implicit assumption, our reading of the Theban story? Or is it that Herodotus expects – or finds it convenient to assume – that the traditions of the priests of Memphis and Thebes (and Heliopolis) will converge (2.3–4), and that in a version of his habit of 'dovetailing' mutually supporting material and sources he therefore simply attributes a claim of corresponding numbers of archpriests and kings over 341 generations to the Memphite priests in close narrative proximity to a count of 341 statues of archpriests by the Thebans?[32] Either way, there is narrative artifice at work here.

Chronology, Divine Descent, and the Autopsy Motif

Herodotus tells us many things that are manifestly false but may be 'honest errors'. Neither at Memphis nor at Thebes did the temple and sequence of

---

[31] See the discussions cited in n. 29 above.   [32] On dovetailing, see Fehling (1989), 112–18.

archpriests go back anywhere close to the beginnings of Egyptian dynastic history, which Herodotus' calculation puts at about 11,800 rather than 3,100 BC. Nor is the claim that son consistently succeeded father as archpriest plausible: the hereditary principle was not firmly established until the Ramesside period (twelfth century BC), and on grounds of general probability sons cannot have succeeded fathers for more than a few generations at a time.[33] Theban priests may have claimed, however, that they did so consistently,[34] even if, as we shall see, *Herodotus'* motivation for wanting things that way is much more obvious. It is nevertheless clear, every allowance having been made, that a count of statues confirming Herodotus' prior expectation cannot have happened as he claims it did.

Egyptian temples were full of statues of local worthies of various statuses and dates, in no general chronological sequence. Many such statues have been found at Karnak itself, most of them of stone rather than (as Herodotus says) wood, including many of priests, only some of whom were archpriests.[35] As Lloyd notes, 'there could not possibly have been anything like 345 statues of *different* High Priests', Herodotus' span of Egyptian history being more than four times longer than the reality.[36] 'If [Herodotus'] informants', Lloyd says, 'were not downright rogues, they must have assumed from one or two statues of High Priests that the entire group belonged to the same category with a blissful disregard for the chronological consequences.'[37] Dim local misinformants, however, are no more than a scholarly hypothesis designed to save Herodotus' 'good faith', their dimness meeting the potential objection that a local's *conscious* misrepresentation of the statues to a Greek visitor would be motiveless, whereas a Herodotean motive for misrepresenting them is obvious. The fundamental 'roguery' must be Herodotus' baseless implication that the number of Theban archpriests should correspond to the count of kings' reigns he attributes to the priests of Memphis.

Most scholars do not believe that Theban priests counted off the Memphite number of 341 (+ 4) statues for Herodotus, and an incredible story only becomes more incredible if one is meant to believe that many years before they had done the same for Hecataeus (whom we are to imagine boasting of divine descent to Egyptians both able and moved to refute him and whose refutation persisted in local memory and was

---

[33] A. B. Lloyd (1975–88), ii.170–1 on 2.37, iii.109 on 2.143; S. West (1991), 149 n. 29.
[34] A. B. Lloyd (1975–88), iii.109–10; Moyer (2002), 76–8.
[35] A. B. Lloyd (1975–88), iii.109 on 2.143.   [36] A. B. Lloyd (1975–88), iii.109 on 2.143.
[37] A. B. Lloyd (1975–88), iii.109 on 2.143.

recounted to a later Greek visitor). Herodotus, however, paints a vivid picture of precisely such a protracted, all-inclusive count, accompanied by a running genealogical commentary as the priests explained to him how each statue, from that of the most recently deceased backward through the generations, represented a son who succeeded his father.

Lloyd constructs a scenario designed to preserve Herodotus' truthfulness as far as possible. The priests, he suggests, had demonstrated to Hecataeus that he was wrong by showing him 'several hundred statues allegedly of high priests', but without specifying a total number or counting them off precisely. Herodotus arrived decades later, expecting there to be 341 generations of kings. 'He presented the figure to the priests', says Lloyd, 'and the latter, under persistent badgering and faced with the prospect of being forced to count the statues one by one, may have been perfectly willing to accept it.'[38] This is a version of the classic 'leading questions' defence of Herodotus' ('essential', that is, not complete) truthfulness. 'Subsequently', Lloyd goes on, 'perhaps over a period of years, H[erodotus] subconsciously grafted elements of his own experience onto his conception of what had happened to Hec[ataeus].'[39] On Lloyd's own hypothesis, however, there was never a precise count of statues, so we are left with a subconsciously concocted *past* event, which Herodotus presents, in full and vivid detail, as though he had himself experienced it. Thus, though Lloyd is a defender of Herodotus' trustworthiness, his scenario still involves knowing untruthfulness on Herodotus' part. Perhaps for Lloyd the claim to 'autopsy' and therefore to ('essential'?) trustworthiness is satisfied simply by Herodotus' presence in a hall with many statues in it, but that would be a very strained claim, and would leave the precise description of the count to be accounted for in some other way – and most readily and obviously as the narrative technique I am calling the autopsy motif.

In this passage as in that on the king list (2.100), Herodotus seems to be employing the autopsy motif in a rather different way than when he uses it to enhance the story of a marvel. The effect is not unlike the use of appearances of gods in Homeric epic to emphasize the special significance of a scene: the description of priests reading documents aloud or counting off statues in the presence of Herodotus – and, by narrative mediation, of his readers – brings the scene into tight visual focus, makes it very

---

[38] Like many other readers, A. B. Lloyd elides the distinction between number of royal reigns and number of statues of Theban archpriests.

[39] A. B. Lloyd (1975–88), iii.108 on 2.143.

Herodotus as Tour Guide: The Autopsy Motif 115

immediate, and highlights as authoritative both the source and the nature of the information conveyed.

When he makes the priests at Memphis read their papyrus roll, Herodotus is stressing the great span of Egyptian history, but the story about Hecataeus emphasizes, in particular, Herodotus' consistent view that human beings cannot claim descent from gods.[40] His insistence on an unbroken series through millennia of human sons immediately succeeding human fathers has the advantage of producing a tight, gapless body of evidence confirming his span of 341 generations, but is primarily aimed at thoroughly confuting Hecataeus' claim by excluding any possibility of divine descent. In this respect, a sequence of anonymous archpriests makes safer and more effective 'evidence' of his central point than would the sequence of kings with its known breaks in father-son inheritance (e.g. in the sequence of the 'pyramid-builders' Cheops, Chephren, and Mycerinus, 2.124–9) and with the semi-divine status of pharaohs in the background. The passage, then, is also a further example of the ironic technique of roundabout criticism of Greek ideas I mentioned at the beginning of the chapter, demonstrating the absurdity of Greek notions of divine descent just as the recitation of the names of the 330 monarchs at Memphis demonstrates the inadequacy of Greek notions of chronology.

It is, then, highly probable that the matching numbers of archpriests and kings, at any rate at Thebes, is Herodotus' own conjecture, designed and positioned in the narrative to produce a unified sequence associating a (perhaps freshly invented) story about Hecataeus with vividly 'objective' exemplification of the hugely long and exclusively human span of Egyptian history. That the number of reigns and statues would be mutually confirming, anyway roughly so, and certainly sufficiently so as to refute Hecataeus, is surely nothing more than Herodotus' hunch, but he is confident in its cogency and realizes it prominently – and imaginatively – in his narrative.

Ἀπόδεξις: Demonstration by Narrators and Guides

It might be said that what Herodotus is doing with the king list and statues, for a special polemical purpose, is extending the chain of tour guidance, such that he is not here our primary guide but mediates the authoritative guidance and information of the priests, who recite the kings'

---

[40] See 4.5.1 (Targitaus), and against epiphanies 1.182.1 (cf. 1.60), 2.91.3, 4.5.1, 5.86; cf. also 2.122–3, 6.105.

names and count the statues in his presence. Herodotus frequently applies to the Theban priests the verb δείκνυμι, 'show/point out', and its compound ἀποδείκνυμι, 'show/demonstrate', and in the previous chapter he had used the compound form of the Memphite priests 'demonstrating' that over 341 reigns there was an equal number of kings and archpriests (ἀποδεικνύντες, 2.142.1). The chapters in which the Memphite priests name the 341 kings and talk about the accomplishments of thirteen of them begin with the statement that of the other 328 they offered no 'demonstration of accomplishments' (ἔργων ἀπόδεξις, 2.101.1), which indicates that the discussion of the thirteen is such a 'demonstration'. The demonstrative exposition of tour guides is, of course, well within the semantic range of these verbs and noun. Herodotus presents the whole of his work as a ἱστορίης ἀπόδεξις (1.proem), and the priests' account at Memphis is an embedded ἀπόδεξις. It begins with a vivid picture of the priests reading aloud to Herodotus from their papyrus roll, but the parallel ἀπόδεξις of the Theban priests' count of statues is much more elaborately vivid. The narrative technique is essentially the same in both cases, but the more striking visualization of the Theban count corresponds to its special importance for Herodotus as polemic against both Hecataeus and the notion that human beings may be descended from gods.

Other Possible Uses of the Autopsy Motif

These tales of ἀπόδεξις, 'demonstration', in the temples at Memphis and Thebes, like the skull and skeleton passages, are most readily explicable in terms of the narrative techniques of autopsy and virtual tour, and this increases the plausibility of the same explanation in some other controversial cases. Take, for example, the triumphal pillars of King Sesostris that Herodotus says he saw (αὐτὸς ὥρων) in 'Palestinian Syria' and claims featured the image of female genitalia he says Sesostris added to pillars in the territory of opponents who were 'lacking in courage' (2.106.1, cf. 2.102.5). The prevailing view is that Herodotus did not see any such pillars.[41] Mockery of opponents through depiction of female genitalia finds no parallel in Egyptian tradition,[42] and the best that defenders of Herodotus'

---

[41] Fehling (1989), 132, 134–6; Armayor (1980), 56–7, 62, and esp. 65–73 with many references to previous discussions (including those of a number of earlier scholars who knew the territory very well and concluded that Herodotus had never toured inland Asia Minor); Pritchett (1993), 267–81; A. B. Lloyd (1975–88), iii.20–1 on 2.102, iii.26–8 on 2.106; S. West (1985), 298–302; S. West (1992).

[42] See A. B. Lloyd (1975–88), iii.20 on 2.102.

Herodotus as Tour Guide: The Autopsy Motif

trustworthiness can do is suggest that he mistook hieroglyphic or Hittite symbols for such a depiction.[43] That is not completely impossible, but it seems more likely that Herodotus heard tell of such mockery, found the story not incredible and too fascinating to omit, and added a fillip to our virtual visit to a pillar of Sesostris by including the obscene taunt.

Another much-discussed passage is Herodotus' description of an enormous bronze cauldron – 600 amphorae (more than 5,000 gallons) in capacity and six fingers in thickness – which he says he saw in Exampaios in Scythia (4.81). Despite Pritchett's collection of evidence for quite large vessels (of all kinds, and not only or primarily of cast bronze),[44] there is no persuasive parallel or argument for Scythians in the archaic period having been able to make (or acquire) such a vessel.[45] The usual thing to say is that, like many other numbers in Herodotus, this is an exaggerated estimate. There are, however, reasons to doubt that Herodotus ever visited the Black Sea region,[46] and even if he did, he describes a specific object as many times the size it can have been, and the magnitude of his exaggeration indicates that, if he really saw the cauldron rather than passing on (or enhancing) something he had heard, he either had a seriously dysfunctional visual memory or lacked all reliable sense for relative size, despite giving more or less accurate measurements of the base-lengths of pyramids (2.124.5, 127.3, 134.1).[47] If, on the other hand, we detect here another good example of the autopsy motif, no such conclusions need be drawn.

So likewise in the case of Herodotus' description of what we now know as the 'Biahmu colossi' at the Lake of Moeris in the Fayûm, which is so wildly wrong that genuine autopsy again seems very unlikely.[48] He describes two 'pyramids' that emerge fifty fathoms or about 300 feet above the surface of the lake, and says that 'on top of each of these is a colossus of stone sitting on a throne' (2.149.2); he does not specify the height of the colossi, but the total height above the surface of the water reached by the monuments, on his estimation – and in the following sentence of the

---

[43] Pritchett (1993), 268 with n. 87; A. B. Lloyd (1975–88), iii.20–1 on 2.102.

[44] Pritchett (1993), 245–55.

[45] See Armayor (1978a), 49–57; Fehling (1989), 223, who puts the measurements of the cauldron in the context of the frequent occurrence in Herodotus of 6/60/600 (sometimes halved to 3/30/300) in connection with the number, weight, and capacity of vessels.

[46] Armayor (1978a).

[47] See A. B. Lloyd (1975–88), 66, 74, 83 ad locc.; cf. A. B. Lloyd (1995), 274–83.

[48] On this passage and Herodotus' general treatment of the Lake of Moeris, see A. B. Lloyd (1975–88), iii.124–30 on 2.149–50 and Evans (1987), an important corrective to the discussion of Armayor (1985), 15–39.

118   SCOTT SCULLION

passage he gives a series of precise equivalences between fathoms, stades, plethra, feet, cubits, and palms – must have been well above 300 feet. We know that the monuments he is talking about were in fact not pyramids but statues about 40 feet high standing on pedestals about 20 feet high – and were built on land, even if the level of the lake had risen in Herodotus' day to surround the monuments and so make it seem that they had been constructed within a manmade lake. Hence Herodotus both falsely describes the form of the monuments and wildly overstates their height. Some scholars have doubted that Herodotus ever made it up the Nile as far as the Fayûm,[49] but in any case his description of the monuments as not (say) twice but more than five times their actual height again suggests that we are dealing either with the autopsy motif or – surely much less plausibly – with seriously defective visual memory or sense of proportion. The monuments were not far out in the midst of the lake, which would make such wild misjudgement of their size more comprehensible, but near its edge.

Herodotus tells us that the 'pyramids' were in fact 100 fathoms in height because they extended the same length below the surface of the water as they rose above it (2.149.2). He does not tell us how he knows this, but it must be something he was told, which suggests, in turn, that his hugely inaccurate account is the result of turning hearsay into the autopsy motif rather than of any testing or confirming of what he had been told through direct visual experience of the monuments themselves.

Conclusions

It seems uncontroversial to say that many passages and some long stretches of the *Histories* consist of virtual tour-guiding, and of course the tours are often of places and things Herodotus did in fact see or that we are in no position to doubt he saw. Herodotus is keen to stimulate his readers' visual imagination. 'More than any other historian of Greco-Roman antiquity', says Schepens, 'he gives his reader the opportunity to follow him – sometimes step-by-step – in his inquiry,' and there is often a strong visual dimension to that 'step-by-step' investigation.[50] It is striking that the particular things that Herodotus specifically mentions *not* seeing – while

---

[49] See esp. the discussions cited in n. 17 above, especially Armayor (1985).
[50] Schepens (1980), 46: 'Plus qu'aucun autre historien de l'antiquité gréco-romaine il donne au lecteur l'occasion de le suivre – parfois pas à pas – dans son enquête'. Cf. Kingsley in this volume (p. 217) on Herodotus 'walking the reader through his own journey in Egypt'.

prompting us to imagine them all the same – are things he *could* not have seen: a twelve-cubit statue of solid gold at Babylon, which Xerxes had looted before Herodotus' visit (1.183), and the Phoenix, which appears only every 500 years (2.73). We have seen how Herodotus 'pulls in' his readers – engaging them with marvellous sights, highlighting specially important information – as a good tour guide does, and recognition that the autopsy motif is not always based on actual, extra-narrative autopsy is easy and straightforward by contrast with the complicated and improbable scenarios generated by those resisting any suggestion of 'dishonesty'.

When it comes to the facts about skulls, winged serpents, Egyptian kings, and so on, scholars regularly come to the same conclusions on the same grounds; it is in our reaction to narrative presentation that we differ. Some are untroubled by the notion that Herodotus occasionally employs for narrative effect what from his point of view was harmless falsehood. The opposite response often amounts to anxious defence of Herodotus' character reflecting the defender's personal notions of honesty rather than dispassionate assessment of evidence. Angry accusations that other scholars turn Herodotus into a '*Schwindler*' or '(barefaced) liar' are obvious man-ifestations of a strong emotional predisposition to construct a trustworthy Herodotus,[51] and so are contemptuous dismissals of prudent doubt as attacks on Herodotus.[52] The standard method of defence is to attribute some of the endless false information in the *Histories* to (sometimes very wildly) faulty observation or recollection by Herodotus himself, but to blame most of it on someone else: dodgy tour guides and informants telling him false and sometimes absurd stories, some of which he 'con-firms' by prompting people who would be expected to know better to nod assent to his leading questions. Where commitment to Herodotus' trustworthiness encounters obvious falsehood Ockham's razor is conspic-uous by its absence.[53]

In the paper I referred to at the outset, John Marincola persuasively suggests that Herodotus' use of 'his own experience' – autopsy and

---

[51] Jacoby (1913), 251; A.B. Lloyd (1975–88), i.94 n.26; Pritchett (1993), title. An especially clear manifestation of such emotional predisposition is A.B. Lloyd (1975–88), i.75: 'It is surely incredible that such a man would tell a series of bare-faced lies. If he said he went to Upper Egypt, he went!'.

[52] See e.g. Jacoby (1913), 251, dismissing the doubts of Sayce (1883) as 'hardly worthy of mention' ('kaum der Erwähnung wert'), and 403 on the work of Panofsky (1885), which 'in fact does not deserve the mention that it still sometimes gets' ('. . . verdient die ihm immer noch zu teil werdende Erwähnung eigentlich nicht'); for comparable damnations in more recent work see e.g. Pritchett (1993) *passim*.

[53] Cf. Marincola (2007b), 54–5 with n.155 on scholars' complicated (and inconsistent) attempts to avoid the simplest explanation.

meetings with sources – is especially prominent in Book 2 and was aimed in part at 'bettering or contradicting Hecataeus' reports' of Egypt. He notes that Herodotus typically employs this technique 'to validate or repudiate oral report' or, particularly outside Book 2, 'for the unusual and the marvelous and ... frequently in tacit polemic with, or improvement upon, a previous (or contemporary?) writer'.[54] The approach to autopsy and meetings with sources I take here is consonant with Marincola's, but I stress the distinction between genuine, extra-narrative personal experience, on the one hand, and description of experiences as narrative function, on the other, and argue that for Herodotus the latter is not contingent on and need not correspond to the former. In the passages we have considered, Herodotus uses the motif of autopsy to enhance his readers' encounter with marvellous things in faraway places or to dramatize authoritative communication of information that is unexciting in itself but has fundamentally important implications. Unlike Fehling, I see no reason to think that Herodotus randomly engages in complete invention. He represents things that he takes to be true, or has no reason to think are not true, in the way best suited to their context, role, and significance in his great narration of the results of his inquiries rather than in the way appropriate to a legal deposition. What I regard as readily comprehensible and successful technique, however, may seem, to those anxious to deny that Herodotus uses it, a gross outrage on History and Truth. I have tried here to strengthen the argument that in order to communicate his results most effectively, Herodotus sometimes employs what he will have seen as minor and harmless untruths, and I hope in the process to have weakened confidence in the assumption (unconscious, implicit, or otherwise) that Herodotus' modes of engagement with his readers ought to correspond to and can be defined and judged by modern canons. The single, simple explanation of narrative artifice is also to be preferred to the needlessly multiplied and elaborated ad hoc explanations – often terribly implausible, but not seldom angrily defended – that have been generated by modern scholars in order to conform Herodotus to their own values and expectations.

---

[54] Marincola (1987), 135, to be read alongside the important reflections on 'truth', 'accuracy', and narrative art in Marincola (2007b), 51–66.

CHAPTER 6

Interpretive Uncertainty in Herodotus' Histories

Carolyn Dewald

In the treatise conventionally entitled *De malignitate Herodoti*, Plutarch charges Herodotus with systematic malevolence, claiming that his intent as an author was to tarnish the reputation of the great cities and individual heroes featured in his *Histories*. Plutarch lists eight different ways in which he thinks Herodotus deliberately presented information that would diminish reputations: that he used the harshest of descriptive adjectives, when softer ones were possible; emphasized personally discreditable gossip; omitted mention of noble deeds; sided with the worst version when two or more versions of events were available; attributed base and self-serving motives whenever possible; claimed the desire for money as a motive when it was unnecessary; used disreputable reports while claiming that he did not personally believe them; and, finally, used some weak words of praise in order to make his much stronger criticisms more convincing.[1]

For many years I thought Plutarch's essay was only ostensibly purporting to be an attack directed against Herodotus' depiction of prominent characters. In reality it seemed to me instead to be a bravura *paignion*, a bumptious showpiece designed both to display how well Plutarch knew Herodotus' work and to allow him to present himself as a loyal Boeotian patriot. But in several important articles on the *De malignitate* and more generally in chapter 3 of *Authority and Tradition*, John Marincola has made it clear that Plutarch's hostility to the Herodotean project was real and, moreover, quite understandable; yes, Plutarch was showing off his knowledge of Herodotus' text, as well as defending Boeotians and Corinthians, in particular, from what he saw as Herodotus' malicious slanders, but more importantly, he was criticizing Herodotus using the

---

[1] Plut. *Mor.* 854e–856d. I have paraphrased Marincola (2017), 296–9, for the summary of Plutarch's eight charges. I would like here to thank John Marincola for many years of friendship, much wonderful learned conversation, historiographic and otherwise, and also to honour his many and essential scholarly contributions to the field of ancient historiography.

CAROLYN DEWALD

historiographical standards that largely prevailed throughout the Hellenistic and Imperial periods of Greco-Roman culture.[2]

By the first century AD, history had become closely associated with, if not seen as an actual part of, epideictic rhetoric. The historian was expected to distribute judicious blame but also well-thought-out praise to the characters in his history; the historian's prose was assumed to reflect the quality of his own character. Herodotus' apparent systematic refusal to depict patriotic, high-minded goals and effective, brilliantly executed action on the part of many of the protagonists of his *Histories* created for Plutarch as a Greek reader in the Roman Empire the reasonable conclusion that Herodotus' own character was a deeply faulty and malicious one. His intent, to malign as many of the great heroes of the past as possible, made him a thoroughly mean-spirited fellow in Plutarch's eyes. As one reads through the *De malignitate* one can feel Plutarch's exasperation and even frustration.[3]

Today the charge of malice does not look plausible, although the work of Marincola and others has made it historically understandable. One answer to Plutarch is historiographic: Herodotus was the contemporary of the early sophists and the great Athenian dramatists, and the conventions for the genre that later became part of Greco-Roman history writing did not yet apply.[4] He saw his task principally as that of collecting, critiquing, and recording *logoi* drawn from a variety of informants in the Greek city-states and elsewhere; each community possessed its own set of traditional stories and anecdotes, old and new, preserved by competing and very likely mutually envious aristocratic families.[5] It was inevitable that the stories Herodotus collected, not only about the fallen heroes Themistocles and Pausanias but about many other individuals and cities that played a

[2] Marincola (1994), 192–3; (1997), 128–74; (2003), 302–15; (2015a), 41–83; (2015b), 92–5. Cf. Woodman (1988), 40–7 (principally considering Thucydides). Pelling (2007b), 146–8, points out that the habit of glorification of the Greek role in the Persian Wars had its roots in lyric poetry, fourth-century oratory, art, tragedy, and philosophy. Cf. Grethlein (2010), 9–145, in particular discussing the 'commemorative' response to the past.

[3] Pelling (2002b), 150–2, surveys the extent to which in his *Lives* Plutarch generally follows the principles laid down in the *De malignitate*; cf. the useful addendum of Pelling (2007b), 150–62.

[4] For Herodotus as a contemporary of the sophists, see R. Thomas (2000), passim. For tragedy, see Pelling (2000), 164–88; Saïd (2002); and Griffin (2006). For other contemporary prose writers, see R. Fowler (2013 [1996]). More generally, see Raaflaub (2002), 149–86 and Pelling (2019), 40–93. For Herodotus' use of Homer and Homeric tropes, see Boedeker (2002) and Marincola (2013 [2007]); on his prose and poetic predecessors more generally, see R. Fowler (2006a) and Marincola (2006).

[5] For Herodotus' use of oral traditions and their storytelling techniques, see Momigliano (2013 [1966]); Evans (2013 [1980]); Gould (1989), 19–41; Murray (2001); Slings (2002); Luraghi (2013 [2005]) and (2006); Dewald (2006a); Pelling (2019), 59–61 with nn. 16–31.

Interpretive Uncertainty in Herodotus' Histories   123

part in the Persian Wars, would have been told in competing versions, both by their supporters and by their political enemies, at home and abroad.

Sixth- and fifth-century Greeks and, no doubt, Greek-speaking foreigners were not generally in the business of making each other appear noble or even respectable.[6] In his frequently repeated desire to λέγειν τὰ λεγόμενα (7.152.3),[7] Herodotus collected many hundreds of *logoi* that reported for the individuals under narration a variety of different and sometimes conflicting motives and assessments of their achievements.[8] So one obvious answer to Plutarch's charge is that Herodotus was concerned to report what his sources had to say rather than to depict a version of events that would glorify the Greek heroes of the distant or recent past. Ancient historiographers have made it increasingly clear in the last several decades that Herodotus is to be read carefully as a historian, interested in the meticulous (and often subtle) assessment of historical causation. Using Homer and contemporary writers, including the sophists and Hippocratic doctors, as intellectual models, he applied all his considerable skills as a fifth-century thinker and prose writer to the task of tracing the causal processes in the human realm that might help explain for his readers why the Persian Wars turned out as they did. His narrative throughout uses a variety of techniques that ferret out and carefully display a wide variety of *aitiai*, the many causes and complex resulting consequences leading to yet further consequences, that make as understandable as possible for his Greek audience the defeat of the Persians in Greece in 479 BC.[9]

And yet ... even though Plutarch's attack on Herodotus' bona fides does not convince, nonetheless, his patent exasperation points to an

---

[6] Fisher (2002), 209–24; Harrison (2003); generally, Sanders (2014). For the aggressive, mocking uses of humour in Greek culture, see Halliwell (1991). In Herodotus one thinks of the bitter rivalry between Cleomenes and Demaratus (6.65–6), Xanthippus and Miltiades (6.136), Themistocles and Aristides (8.79), and the Philaids and Pisistratids (6.35, 103–4). Pelling (2019), 206–10, surveys of some of the most egregious stories of competitive Greek elites collected by Herodotus. Cf. the competitive rivalries in the Persian court throughout Books 7–9 that severely impact the Persian war effort.

[7] E.g. 2.123.1, 130.2; 3.9.2; 4.173, 195.2; 6.137.1; 7.152.3, 189.1–3; Rösler (2002), 90–1. This does not make him undiscriminating in assessing them (note 9 below).

[8] Baragwanath (2008) and Pelling (2019), with their generous bibliographies, should be consulted for a full discussion of specific characters and the complexities of their motives, including the paradoxes and ambiguities their individual narratives contain.

[9] Pelling (2019), 68, pertinently quotes R. Fowler (2013 [1996]), 81: 'He discovered the *problem* of sources.' See Immerwahr (2013 [1956]); Gould (1989), 63–85, on Herodotus' explanatory mode and emphasis on chains of reciprocity; Pelling (2019), passim and esp. 163–89. As is often pointed out, the *Histories* open with the promise that the *aitiai* of the wars between Greeks and *barbaroi* will be explored (as well as many other things).

124   CAROLYN DEWALD

interesting problem, one with which we, as twenty-first-century audiences, continue to struggle. Using Plutarch as a beginning focus, we might restate it more generally as follows: what does the choice of critical or at least highly ambiguous and conflicting accounts of many characters' motives, abilities, and achievements mean, if it does not reflect an authorial desire to defame?

Herodotus makes it clear in the *Histories* that he has put thought into selecting the *logoi* that constitute his text.[10] As many scholars have noted, the main focus of Herodotus' narrative is war, and the *logoi* in his main account describe individuals, cities, and cultures in crisis and trauma, situations that do not contain many successful people behaving well and content with their lot.[11] But Plutarch's essay focuses on a particular aspect of those traumatic conditions: the degree to which a wide variety of characters in the *Histories* are depicted as misunderstanding, mismanaging, and misbehaving in important aspects of their lives. What does Herodotus mean to be saying about τὰ ἀνθρωπήια πρήγματα (2.4.1) by choosing to present actors and events in the *Histories* as critically or at least ambivalently as he often does? Especially since he claims at the outset of his text to be rescuing from oblivion the ἔργα μεγάλα τε καὶ θωμαστά (1.proem) of the Greek and barbarian human past? Even if wrong-headed, Plutarch's essay suggestively points toward some features in Herodotus' text that leave us as readers puzzled about some of its basic interpretive assumptions.

It is useful to begin by describing a feature of the *Histories* often known as 'Herodotean irony', the subject of a recent challenging survey by Richard Rutherford.[12] Rutherford describes three different ways in which Herodotus definitely uses irony (saying one thing but meaning another) as a basic narrative move.[13] What I want to focus on here is that, different as they are in presentation, the three kinds of irony prominently discussed by Rutherford call into question the understanding or control over events exerted by a given character or group. What Rutherford labels 'irony' is one of the essential tools Herodotus uses to convey the kinds of

---

[10] Dewald (1987) and (2002); Marincola (1987) and (2001), 25–42; Lateiner (1989), 55–75; Brock (2003); Branscome (2013), 3–21. For other bibliography on aspects of Herodotus' authorial persona, see Dewald (2015), 67 n. 1 and Dewald and Kitzinger (2015), 86 n.1.

[11] Stahl (1975); cf. Shapiro (1994); Boedeker (2006); Lateiner (2012); Stahl (2012) and (2015), are important additions to the bibliography cited in Dewald (2011), 19 nn. 3–4.

[12] R. B. Rutherford (2018). This long essay on many different kinds of Herodotean ambiguity has helped clarify my own interest in highlighting the structural and stylistic features considered here.

[13] R. B. Rutherford (2018), 5–18.

Interpretive Uncertainty in Herodotus' Histories   125

uncertainty and misunderstanding that many important actors in the *Histories* experience.

The first ironic context, that Rutherford calls 'dramatic irony', involves an individual misunderstanding the meaning of his situation, often, in particular, something that has been spoken; the true meaning of the context or misunderstood statement is revealed to great effect later in the story, often to the individual who has acted on his incorrect definition of his situation, always to us as readers, as the text unfolds. Croesus' narrative begins the *Histories*, and his misinterpretations of the Delphic oracle are a striking example of dramatic irony (1.53–56); they lead him to serious misjudgements that become clear only after his defeat by Cyrus. He does not understand the truth lying behind what he has been told or the nature of his own errors until he himself sends the manacles that are the marks of his defeat to Delphi, where the Pythia, speaking for Apollo, explains the situation fully to him (1.90–1).[14]

Later in Book 1, Harpagus does not know that the sacrifice to which he is invited by Astyages will be his own son, whom he will be forced inadvertently to eat for supper (1.118). He understands the true meaning of Astyages' words only when the severed head, hands, and feet of his son are delivered to him, after he has eaten (1.119). Sometimes a speaker is unaware of the ironic import of his own words. In Book 8, Xerxes tells the Spartans that Mardonius will give them recompense for the murder of their king, Leonidas, at Thermopylae (8.114.2). Xerxes intends sarcasm but speaks more truly than he knows, because the story goes on to show that Mardonius himself is slain at Plataea, a recompense indeed for the murder of Leonidas (9.63–4, 84). In each of these instances, and many others as well, it is the undesirable outcome of the narrative that reveals the nature of the individual's initial misunderstanding or misjudgement; we, the readers, at the end of the episode are left in no doubt about the nature of the irony involved. Like Oedipus, many powerful individuals in Herodotus' account do not know what they do not know – until it is too late, and then they are sometimes depicted as haplessly confronting the consequences of their faulty decisions.[15]

---

[14] R. B. Rutherford (2018), 6–9 and 38–40 (endnotes 1–2, 4) discusses 'oracular irony' (including dreams and portents) as a very prominent subset of dramatic irony. The prominence of these phenomena in Book 1 goes a long way in setting the tone of interpretive uncertainty for the *Histories* as a whole (Harrison (2000), 122–57, esp. 156 n. 121).

[15] It is perhaps worth noting that Herodotus does not focalize Xerxes' thoughts, on his retreat after the defeat at Salamis, or include awareness on Xerxes' part here of misjudgement or mismanagement. Instead, he makes a sarcastic authorial comment at Xerxes' expense (see discussion of 7.187 and

Whereas the truths underlying 'dramatic irony' are revealed within the narrative, often to the individual involved (in 1.91, Croesus admits his own previous errors), the truths in situations of 'historical irony' become clear not within the parameters of Herodotus' text but to people living afterward, including, of course, us, Herodotus' much later readers. We know of later consequences, not made explicit in Herodotus' narrative, that cast a number of narrative passages in the *Histories* in an ironic light. Three of the most blatant examples of such historical irony involve Herodotus' narratives of Themistocles, Pausanias, and Xerxes; Herodotus as narrator does not describe these men's painful later ends, but his reading or listening audiences would have known them, and he would have expected that knowledge to influence their reading of these men's actions.[16] Contemporary scholarship has in this one sense often ironized the whole of the *Histories*, since we now almost universally suspect that the story of Persia's defeat in 479 BC serves as a well-timed but ironic reflection on the behaviour of the Athenian Empire of Herodotus' own day.[17]

A third type of irony occurs when ethnically distinct participants in the events narrated remain ignorant of their ignorance about each other, making faulty assumptions that Herodotus as author intends us, his audience, to see.[18] Cross-cultural misunderstandings arise from their mutual failure to understand each other's most basic ideas of how human beings normally behave and should behave. In Book 4, Darius' Persians have chased their Scythian opponents all over the place, without getting them to stand and fight, until the Persians suddenly realize how badly their

---

8.103 below); Xerxes seems not to have learned very much (Grethlein (2009)). Very close to the end of the work as a whole (9.108–113) comes the story of Xerxes' later abuse of his brother's family. One implication might be that the war was not prosecuted by the Persians after 479, at least in part, because of Xerxes' need to stamp out the revolt brought about by his own failures to understand basic things about the exercise of power (Pelling (2019), 32–4; cf. Baragwanath (2008), 278–80 for a less critical view of 'the *eros* of Xerxes and the death of Masistes' (9.113.2)).

[16] R. B. Rutherford (2018), 10–13. See Pelling (2019), 213–31, for a careful discussion of how the dating of Herodotus' *Histories* influences and complicates the question of historical irony.

[17] For Herodotus' treatment of Athens, see Fornara (2013 [1971]); Moles (1996); Dewald and Marincola (2006), 3–4; Strasburger (2013 [trans. from 1955]); Grethlein (2018), 223–8.

[18] R. B. Rutherford (2018), 14–18; he calls them 'ironies of incomprehension'. Most blatant is the ignorance of Greece that pervades the Persian ruling class (e.g. 7.9, 101–5, 135, 209–10), which Artabanus tries to warn Xerxes of (7.10, 49). To the cultural incomprehension that Rutherford discusses can be added the frequent inability of men to see women as actors with goals of their own (Dewald (2013 [1981]), 157–61, 165–71; Boedeker (2011), 231; Pelling (2019), 108), and the general inability of powerful people to see the desires and actions of less powerful people as important factors in their own right (Candaules and his wife, Astyages and Harpagus, Harpagus and Mitradates/Cyno, Darius with Democedes and Histiaeus, Xerxes and Artaynte/Amestris). For the seriousness of Herodotus' own attempt to understand the Persians, see Munson (2013/2009).

Interpretive Uncertainty in Herodotus' Histories   127

battle plans have worked; they have misunderstood the Scythian strategy (4.126–32). They have potentially been trapped, very far from their own territory; lacking an enemy whose towns they can capture, they give up and retreat back to Persian territory as fast as possible (4.134–6, 141–3). But the irony does not end with Persian misunderstanding of Scythians. The Scythians proceed to sneer at the Ionians as the 'most servile of men' for letting Darius escape back over the Hellespont on his bridge made of boats; the Scythians, however, do not realize that they have not, strictly speaking, been negotiating with Ionians, but rather with Ionian tyrants, whose personal fiefdoms will be hard to maintain without Persian support (4.136–40, 142).[19] Again, as in instances of historical irony, often the individuals involved do not understand the nature of their errors; Herodotus intends us as readers to be the recipients of the text's ironic depiction of cultural misunderstanding.[20]

As Rutherford goes on to observe, the prevalence of these three kinds of irony leads to a major interpretive difficulty for us as readers. Given the obvious pervasiveness of irony in contexts where we as readers are in no doubt that a character is acting in ignorance of the true nature of their situation, what are we to do with many, many other equally ambiguous situations narrated in the *Histories* that are not as clearly intended by Herodotus to be ironic? Once the possibility of an ironic reading, particularly of the latter two types mentioned above, is understood in our readerly experience as an acknowledged and recurring feature of Herodotus' text, we become progressively more uncertain about how to know when irony *is* in play – and whether, in the many instances of potential irony of the same sort that might arise, Herodotus as narrator wants to do more than 'provoke and intrigue the reader'.[21]

For instance, are we meant at the beginning of Book 7 to read ironically Demaratus' posture as an adviser to the Persian king about which son to choose as legitimate heir, when his own past history has been so thoroughly compromised around this very issue (6.61–70; 7.3)? Herodotus does not tell us, and this is only one of a number of puzzles that cluster

---

[19] Dewald (2003), 39. The Ionians in power in their cities are not themselves innocent of such misunderstandings. Hecataeus the Milesian tries to bring the rest of the Ionians to their senses, regarding the enormity of the undertaking they are planning to make against Darius, by lecturing them on the extent of the king's holdings and his vast wealth and power, but his advice is ignored (5.36).

[20] See the discussion of 9.82 below and Pelling (2019), 210.

[21] See R. B. Rutherford (2018), 23, 34–6, and note 39 below; see Dewald (2011) for comparable kinds of indeterminacy concerning the interpretation of many significant objects in the *Histories*.

128   CAROLYN DEWALD

around Demaratus' story.[22] Even if we resist interpreting such ironic or proto-ironic passages, as Plutarch often does, as attempts to defame, we certainly become accustomed to Herodotus' predilection for showing us the spectacle of many important individuals in the *Histories* who have no idea how little understanding or control they have over the events of their own lives.

The curious fact, however, is that as readers of Herodotus we in turn often experience an interpretive uncertainty that in certain respects mirrors that of the characters within the *Histories*, in a move that in literary criticism is sometimes called a *mise en abîme*. Our lives and our fortunes are hopefully not at risk, but our readerly certitudes are put at risk, as Herodotus uses a variety of literary techniques that lead to difficulties in knowing what judgement we are to make about what is transpiring in the text. The problem we confront in knowing where Herodotean irony begins and ends is only the first of these.

Sometimes more subtle in their destabilizing effect than full-fledged irony are Herodotus' many 'glosses', interjections or interruptions in the narrative of events that can come with or without an explicit first-person authorial component. They add what in current scholarly writing would be a footnote, often either of historical analepsis or geographical and ethnographic information.[23] These can be of considerable length; they do not often confuse or change the meaning of the individual account as irony does, but they can set up expectations for the reader – for example, truth-telling as an important quality emphasized within the Persian ethnography (1.138.1) – that the narrative later sometimes does not bear out. Are we meant, observing Darius' flagrant ability to bend the truth in Book 3, to criticize him, as a result of the information in the earlier ethnography?[24] The information given in short glosses can also complicate our response to a given narrative. The statement that barbarians do not like to be seen naked perhaps serves as a mitigating factor in our assessment of Candaules' queen's over-vigorous response to Gyges' and Candaules' voyeurism (1.10–12). Herodotus, however, does not intrude as narrator to help clarify what we are to think.

---

[22] Baragwanath (2008), 173–6; Hornblower and Pelling (2017), 174–83 (on 6.66–71); R. B. Rutherford (2018), 18, 21–3.

[23] Munson (2001), 298–9, lists other kinds of glosses as well as those discussed here; see also Dewald (2002), 283–6.

[24] Darius enthusiastically embraces lying (3.72; Baragwanath (2008), 85–7 with n. 23). Cf. his use of tricks and misdirection: 3.85–7, 127–8, 154–8; 5.23–5.

Interpretive Uncertainty in Herodotus' Histories 129

Herodotus can also insert apparently random judgemental comments that are not, strictly speaking, informative glosses or formal authorial first-person observations but, rather, critical or paradoxical statements that complicate our understanding of what is under narration. They provide a sudden, unexpected turn, an intrusive almost-editorial element that momentarily changes the narrative's tone. At the end of the long series of narratives about Croesus, the genial but misguided Lydian king, Herodotus suddenly and offhandedly remarks that some temple dedications Croesus made had been the property of a political enemy he had had tortured to death (1.92.4). This is startling information, quite at variance with the Croesus we apparently already know: what does Herodotus intend it to mean for our more general understanding of Croesus?[25] Sometimes the unexpected or destabilizing element within a given narrative is subtler still. Martin Ostwald loved the comment that Herodotus makes toward the conclusion of the Candaules and Gyges episode that comes with a sudden change to the present tense, αἱρέεται αὐτὸς περιεῖναι (1.11.4), 'Gyges chooses to live.' For the alert reader, this suggestively hints both at the curse on Gyges' family that is to come and at elements in the Croesus story that remain mostly unelaborated in the Gyges account.[26] But at the point where it appears, Herodotus' interjection on Gyges merely interrupts the narrative flow and makes one wonder what, if anything, Herodotus intends by it.[27]

Toward the end of Book 7, Herodotus describes the enormous number of humans, pack animals, and dogs that made up the Persian fighting force in Greece as well as the difficulty of provisioning all of them, so that it was no surprise to him, Herodotus the narrator, that they drank many Greek rivers dry. But he ends 7.187 with a surprising statement: 'among all those thousands upon thousands of men, not one of them on account of his looks and his height was more worthy to deserve the position of authority than Xerxes himself'. What do Xerxes' looks have to do with anything in the immediate context?[28] Are we meant to intuit a certain dubious theatrical or ekphrastic quality inherent in the elaborate and lengthy

---

[25] Pelling (2019), 113.

[26] When Croesus chooses that others he cares about survive, but at some cost to their reputation – isolating his son and, at least in the youth's eyes, unmanning him in the eyes of his new bride (1.37), or later rendering the Lydians less warlike so that Cyrus will not destroy them (1.155.4–156.1) – is he following the significant choice of his ancestor Gyges?

[27] See Baragwanath (2008), 73–4 and Pelling (2019), 108–10, for more on the interpretive problems of the Gyges episode.

[28] Boedeker (2002), 105; cf. R. B. Rutherford (2018), 35 nn. 89–90.

display of Persian might that has just concluded, or is this merely a piece of simple praise, by a historian who does like noting good-looking and tall people (e.g. 1.60.4; 9.25.1)? These questions recur for the reader in full force with Herodotus' comment in 8.103 after the Persian defeat at Salamis, when Xerxes has just decided on a rapid retreat from Greece. A first-person authorial assertion adds emphasis: 'for not even if all the men and all the women had counselled him to remain would he have stayed, I think – he was that terrified'. A similarly unexpected comment occurs in 3.143.2, summing up a confusing political situation after the death of Polycrates: apparently the Samians 'did not at all want to be free'. What does Herodotus intend this to tell us about the preceding complex account of treachery and counter-treachery on the part of Samian aristocrats, Maiandrius, and Maiandrius' family? Is he dismissively damning all the characters in the Samian account, or does it mean something more complex and subtle than that?[29] Again, he does not explain.

One of the most notorious such statements is the addendum, at the end of the long episode on the Battle of Marathon, that the Alcmaeonidae were tyrant haters, but that nevertheless a shield was shown that was a sign to the Persians (6.121–4). Given the degree of interpretive ambiguity the reader is accustomed by this point to tolerate in the narrative, we are not at all sure what overall judgement on the Alcmaeonidae Herodotus means to give.[30] Is the declaration of their innocence here to be given great weight, as an important concluding judgement? Is it meant by reminding us of the shield, rather, to re-instil doubt? Or is it merely a wry postscript, rounding out an episode? In any case, it is difficult not to see some irony in the contrast between the defence of the famous Athenian family mounted here and the very different valence of other anecdotes about them and their political aspirations.[31]

Sometimes it is not a disruptive statement but a plot turn of the narrative that takes an episode in a surprising or paradoxical direction. After Cyrus' victory, Croesus makes a remarkably speedy adjustment to his new subordinate status, giving Cyrus advice about how to save his recent Lydian acquisitions from plunder by his Persian troops (1.88). Certainly, reliance on money has figured before in the Croesus narrative, but

---

[29] For Herodotus' very complex presentation of the ambiguities inherent in the nature of freedom, see Dewald (2003), 35–49; Baragwanath (2008), 100–7; Pelling (2019), 174–89, esp. 179–80.

[30] See Hornblower and Pelling (2017), 266–71, for the many controversies engendered by 6.121–4. For the larger issues raised by Herodotus' depiction of 'democracy', see Pelling (2019), 190–8.

[31] Hornblower and Pelling (2017), 271–87 on 6.125–131; see also 1.60–61 (which Plutarch mocks, *De malig.* 858c).

Interpretive Uncertainty in Herodotus' Histories 131

Croesus' willingness to become a courtier, advising his new master how to save his new wealth gained from Croesus' own defeat, is an unexpected outcome of events.[32] In a similar vein, the response by Pausanias, victor of Plataea, faced with the opulence of the Persian dinner left by Xerxes' troops in Central Greece, is not only astonishing but almost comical (9.82). As Chris Pelling well observes, Pausanias' response is not the expected one – 'this is precisely the sort of luxury that has contributed to the Persians' undoing' – but, rather, 'why on earth did they take the trouble to come here, if at home they could already eat like this?' A portent of things to come, or a hint at some underlying weaknesses in Pausanias?[33] Herodotus does not say.

Also to be noted are the unexpectedly clever and even sometimes gnomic observations made by people in the narrative to interrogation, causing us as readers at least momentarily to reassess the dynamics of the situation at hand. In the Cyrus half of Book 1, the villainous Median king, Astyages, is standing in chains after being defeated by Cyrus, when his earlier victim, Harpagus, comes up to gloat (1.129). So far our sympathy as readers has been entirely with Harpagus, given the cannibalism of his son inflicted on him earlier as punishment by Astyages. But when taunted by Harpagus, Astyages rebukes him, pointing out that his, Astyages', actions had been intended for the good of the Medes, while Harpagus, driven by his desire for private vengeance, has handed Median sovereignty over to the Persians! We are not meant suddenly to admire Astyages (Herodotus shortly thereafter blames the Median loss on Astyages' own *pikrotes*, harshness, as a leader, 1.130.1) – but Astyages is not wrong in his judgement of Harpagus, either.

Many other unexpected moments of paradoxical response are delivered to powerful people demanding some sort of subservience, which cause an ironic recalibration in the reader's mind about who is in control of or understands a given situation. These include several delivered to Cambyses: his royal sister's response to seeing the puppies (3.31–2), Psammetichus' reactions to the captives paraded before him (3.14), even the Ethiopian king's assessment of Persian 'gifts' (3.21). Similar responses are made to Darius, by Intaphrenes' clever wife (3.119) and the captive physician Democedes (3.130).[34] The Andrians make an unexpectedly

---

[32] This note is struck again in 3.34.5 and 36, where Croesus is a hapless Polonius-like courtier, subject to Cambyses' mad wrath. Herodotus is the only historian to describe this end for Croesus' career.

[33] Pelling (2019), 170, 209–10.

[34] Democedes' cleverness becomes very significant in Persian affairs a bit later (3.133–7). Cf. Rutherford's 'ironies of incomprehension', note 18 above.

valiant and pertinent response to Themistocles' demand for money (8.111). Sometimes the status differential is more ambiguous. Hermotimus the eunuch makes a horrifying but pertinent observation to his former castrator Panionius (8.106), while Themistocles himself is the master of a clever response to the jealous Athenian Timodemus (8.125). We shall revisit at the end of this essay Themistocles' brilliantly cynical and self-serving speech in the debate over whether to pursue Xerxes making his way back to Persia (8.109–10); it simultaneously gives the credit for the Greek victory at Salamis to 'the gods and heroes' and also provides clever preparation for the feathering of Themistocles' own nest, should he need ever to find refuge in Persia.

These various ways that within a given narrative Herodotus, so to speak, pulls the reader up short were partly inherited from the oral anecdotes out of which he fashioned the *Histories*, perhaps also honed and polished as Herodotus delivered parts of his *Histories* orally to different Greek audiences.[35] Certainly, they add point and zest to the ongoing narrative, but they do not help us gain a clear notion of Herodotus' considered judgement on many prominent individuals whose deeds he has narrated. Plutarch's comment begins to seem disconcertingly pertinent: 'it seems to me that just like Hippocleides gesticulating with his legs on the table, one could say that Herodotus has "danced away" the truth and that "Herodotus doesn't care"' (*De malig.* 867b).[36]

A more general kind of interpretive ambiguity is created by the paratactic nature of Herodotus' ongoing narrative structure. It occurs when a new episode begins, replete with its formal introductory sentence, that apparently derails the ongoing course of events, sending the account temporarily off its tracks and into an entirely different direction. It places Herodotus the narrator front and centre, reminding us that he is in charge of the λόγων ὁδός (1.95.1) and that he can take the narrative in whatever direction he wants. The story of Arion in 1.23–4 is a famous example; Arion's adventure on the dolphin has only a very tenuous connection to the wars between Lydians and Ionians that has been the point of the immediately preceding narrative sequence. Herodotus leaves it to us, his readers, to make sense of Arion's miraculous marine salvation, finding thematic resonances of our own to explain its appearance.[37] Variant

---

[35] Dewald (2002), 277–8. See note 5 above, on orality.

[36] Marincola (2017), 316, at the end translating Plutarch's adaptation of Herodotus (6.129.4), οὐ φροντὶς Ἡροδότῳ.

[37] Munson (2001), 252–3.

Interpretive Uncertainty in Herodotus' Histories   133

versions of *logoi* scattered throughout the text also produce a milder form of such destabilization, reminding the reader that there is rarely a clear indication in Herodotus' *logoi* of the past that he has vouched for them as containing 'the truth'.[38]

Finally, different episodes, sometimes close together and sometimes far apart, seem to go in quite different interpretive directions, leaving the reader confused about what the overall point seems to be. There might be a tacit irony in the suggestive succession of stories early in Book 1, in the first of which an Ionian wise man (Herodotus is not sure whether it was Bias or Pittacus, 1.27) indirectly and very successfully warns Croesus not to try to conquer the Ionian islanders by building boats; Croesus gets the subtly delivered message and acts accordingly. This stands in sharp contrast to the failure of Solon's subsequent elaborate conversation with Croesus, where the long-winded and somewhat portentous advice of the Athenian speechmaker, though certainly correct, entirely fails of its object (1.30–3). Reading this sequence, are we to doubt Solon's effectiveness? Is Herodotus obliquely reflecting on the inadequacy of long speeches, even when delivered by famous Athenian savants, and even when their content becomes one of the great themes followed throughout the *Histories*? The most challenging and far-reaching of these narrative disjunctures comes in the way that Cyrus' advice about hard lands producing hard men, given at the very end of the *Histories* (9.122), does not send the same message as the story in 1.125–6 of how Cyrus persuaded the Persians to go to war, pointing out that a day of fun-filled eating and drinking is more pleasurable than one spent in arduously clearing an uncultivated field.

So how are we to understand these various phenomena?[39] It is clear that Herodotus expects his readers to exercise their readerly judgement about

---

[38] See Lateiner (1989), 76–90; Pelling (2019), 101–5. One of my favourite variant versions is the alternate account of Xerxes' return to Anatolia, not by his bridge of boats but by sea (8.118–19). In this variant, a sea storm occurs and the captain of the boat is given a gold crown for saving Xerxes' life but then is beheaded because Xerxes' courtiers have all had to jump overboard to lighten the ship's load. This is the point at which, straight-faced, Herodotus adds that he actually thinks this to be a false report, οὐδαμῶς ἔμοιγε πιστός (8.119.1), because if it had really happened, Xerxes would have had the crew jump overboard and would have seated his courtiers at the oars. Herodotus is reflecting obliquely, but very cogently, on the way Xerxes has run his expedition to Greece – in effect seating at the oars of the ship of state courtiers of his who are incapable of managing it effectively. The variant version may have been a genuine one, but Herodotus includes it for the chance it gives him to criticize Xerxes' management of the war, by means of a mock-serious subsequent objection that turns the whole variant version into a significant, if subtle, metaphor.

[39] R. B. Rutherford lists several serious reasons why Herodotus might have chosen to use so many 'destabilizing techniques' (2018), 27–30, 36–7: challenging us as readers to use our own judgement, to be sceptical about mythological stories from the distant past, to understand his own critical

how individuals in the narrative have thought and acted. His own use of variant versions of events, authorial interventions occasionally expressing his own opinion, and frequent depiction of significant moments of decision-making on the part of individuals in the *Histories* point to the fact that exercising judgement is an important and basic human function that he exercises himself and expects his readers to utilize also.[40] But by constructing a narrative that seems frequently to realign our developing understanding or refuse a clear interpretive direction, how are we as readers to exercise that critical function? What are we to learn from him about what makes an effective leader, military or political, or even about how the world works, other than that it often does not work as people in the narrative, or we as readers, expect it to?

These are real questions, and as a long-time reader of Herodotus I am much clearer on them as questions than I am on their correct answers. But one answer might have to do with Herodotus' understanding of the nature of time and the nature of language itself. Time is what the *Histories* are made of; their nine books trace about a century of Median and Persian imperial growth and its eventual check in Greece in 479 BC.[41] The overall picture of Persian defeat at the end is clear, and Herodotus has demonstrated in the course of his narrative many of the reasons for it. But how are the many events comprising this process to be understood? Or the individual moments of success or failure that make up such a span of time to be judged? Even the final meaning of the Persian defeat in 479 is difficult to puzzle out.[42]

A wonderful anecdote from Book 2 about Amasis, king of Egypt, might be instructive here. First, Herodotus tells us that Amasis had been a commoner and felt he was not sufficiently respected as king, so he took a gold basin in which he and others had vomited, urinated, and washed their feet, and turned it into a statue of a god, to be honoured. Amasis then pointed out to the Egyptians that times have changed, that like the gold

---

approach to his material, and also intending to entertain us with material he clearly doesn't believe. Or, perhaps, he works out of a romantic or even postmodern desire that we, his readers, remain aware that the text is a text 'under construction'. Rutherford ends his piece with a convincing comparison of Herodotus to contemporary sophists like Socrates and Protagoras, delighting in all the ambiguities of their arguments, exemplifying the term 'Socratic irony'.

[40] In the past I have perhaps over-emphasized this point (e.g. Dewald (1985); (2006b), 160; (2007), 94–101). Cf. Lateiner (1989), 221. Baragwanath (2013) convincingly argues that Herodotus depicts Athenian civic intelligence, properly exercised, as a crucial element making possible the Greek victory in 480–79.

[41] Marincola (2001), 25–31; Cobet (2002); de Jong (2013 [1999]), 267–81, on the 'anachronical structure' of the *Histories*.

[42] Dewald (2013 [1997]).

Interpretive Uncertainty in Herodotus' Histories   135

pisspot he himself has now changed his identity and consequently requires their respect and honour (2.172). In the narrative present, Amasis really now is a king, whatever his identity had been before, or what it becomes later.[43] But that is not the end of the Amasis story in the *Histories*. The indignities suffered by Amasis' son and other members of his family are recounted later, in 3.14–16, and the shameful outrages suffered by his corpse are described (as true, in Herodotus' judgement) in 3.16. Where exactly does Herodotus want us to put our weight, in thinking about the meaning of Amasis' reign?

With the episode of the golden pisspot, we are not in the issue of irony *per se*, saying one thing but meaning another, but in a stranger and more ambiguous world, one that Herodotus has set out to negotiate for us. Interpretation and understanding seem to be phenomena that are malleable and transient over time, very much depending on the immediate context in the narrative but also on the point of view and the changed and always changing circumstances of the recipient of the narrative. Both Herodotus' use of irony and the pervasive interpretive indeterminacy found in some of the *Histories'* basic narrative structures imply as much.[44]

In the very beginning of the *Histories* (1.5.3), Herodotus famously announces, 'I will proceed to the rest of the *logos*, going alike through small and large human communities. For the things that were earlier great have many of them become small, while the ones great in my time were earlier small. Knowing then that human prosperity never remains in the same place, I will record both alike.' Herodotus does not know what, from our vantage point as later readers, we will consider important or interesting, so his own approach to his material is intentionally a catholic one. Some of the systemic interpretive difficulties we encounter when we try to evaluate the meaning of the individual *logoi* and the characters within them stem from the fact that Herodotus seems to believe that meaning itself is highly fluid, depending both on the context under narration and on the context and condition of the person who is encountering the narrative; interpretation is not something that is definite, fixed for all time. Herodotus knows that we readers of the future will read his *Histories* – and, no doubt, interpret the thoughts and actions of people therein – in ways that he, Herodotus, cannot guess at the time of writing, because

---

[43] See Vannicelli (2001) for the more general and extensive role that Egyptian history plays in Herodotus' idea of historical time.

[44] Grethlein (2018) develops ironies entailed in Herodotus' understanding of himself as a historian within his own historical context.

136 CAROLYN DEWALD

things change their meaning over time.[45] In 2.172, Amasis' point is that his meaning changes; at the moment of his discussion with his courtiers, he is really, right now, a king. But his dynasty will come to a tragic end, and Amasis' own corpse will be treated shamefully. What is the 'reality' of Amasis' place in the *Histories*?[46]

Herodotus' assumptions about the nature of human language itself are also important here. If one looks at how people within the text communicate with each other, the picture is fairly bleak. Throughout the *Histories*, people generally use language not for clear and honest communication, but to achieve their own (and often unexpressed) ends.[47] This is a point made right at the outset by the self-serving and odd little excursus into the Greek mythic past made by otherwise unidentified Persian *logioi* and Phoenicians, each carefully exonerating their own people from blame for starting the hostilities between East and West and happily of one accord in blaming the Greeks (1.1–1.5.2). Many of Herodotus' authorial interruptions into the text make it clear that the *logoi* he must use to tell his story of the past are similarly fallible; one of his jobs as their investigator and recorder is to leave us, his readers, engaged with him in extracting as much accurate information as he can get out of *logoi* that did not originate, and were not saved by others, with that intent in mind. When Herodotus strings them all together, along with his own editorial additions, we have a genuine case of Bakhtin's heteroglossia – in which, if we are fortunate, the individual idiosyncratic interpretive valences of the *logoi* resonate with each other in a variety of ways and a larger, more complex pattern not dominated by any one focalization begins to emerge. But it is a messy process, composed of many voices, from many times, and many points of view, which Herodotus as author does not choose to weld together into a single clear and coherent interpretive whole.

In Herodotus' eyes, even if one intends to communicate real knowledge, the recipient often does not understand it correctly. Herodotus puts into the mouth of an anonymous Persian in Book 9 a despairing recognition of the difficulty of conveying truth through language. When an Orchomenan

---

[45] Cf. changes in the twentieth-century assumptions about Herodotus' treatment of Athens (note 17 above). For his use of *es eme*, distinguishing his own time from the time narrated, see Rösler (1991); (2002), 91–3 and Dewald (2002), 283.

[46] An additional level of irony is achieved if one adds to the overall Amasis story the anecdote told later in Book 3 of how Amasis unsuccessfully tried to advise Polycrates of Samos on how to avert a terrible end (3.39–43). But as observed already, Herodotus does not tell us whether this is a move we are meant to make.

[47] Pelling (2006c), 116; Dewald (2015), 67–82.

Interpretive Uncertainty in Herodotus' Histories 137

at dinner with a Persian ally before the battle of Plataea asks his Persian dinner-mate why he is not telling Mardonius about his conviction that the coming battle will end in Persian defeat (9.16.4–5), the Persian replies: 'Friend, whatever must come from the divine is impossible for a human being to avert, since no one is willing to trust even those saying trustworthy things.... But the most hateful sorrow of those among human beings is this, understanding many things, to control none of them.'

If we keep these two points in mind – that meaning is temporally contextual and that language seems to be a highly slippery and imperfect way to communicate reality – many of the difficult passages described above can be reframed. We can encounter them not as paradoxes created principally to tease, amuse, or challenge us as readers (though they frequently do all three), but as aspects of the narrative that reflect a reality found both in the medium with which Herodotus has to work and in the world in which he believes we as human beings do things that matter historically, without a complete understanding of what we are doing.

So the answer I would make to Plutarch is this: briefly put, the deeds of the past that Herodotus wants to retell were indeed μεγάλα τε καὶ θωμαστά, but both the stories that Herodotus has collected about them and, probably, the real people involved in those events were often as confused about the direction and significance of events at hand as we ourselves are about the conditions that confront us today, in real time. It appears that Herodotus wanted to record as much as he could and as accurately as he could the great variety of things that he was told happened in the past that led to and might explain the Persian defeat in Greece. It is arguably one of the great *thomata* of the *Histories* that, despite the jealousies, confusions, and failures of many Greek human beings, the Greeks really did win the Persian Wars.

As readers, we can use Herodotus' narrative to reflect on the remarkable fact that, on the one hand, when we look back to the past we *can* see a pattern, a story line, with meanings emerging; on the other, given the nature of both time and human language as human beings generally employ it, it is much less clear that Herodotus thinks that those meanings will be stable or that we will be able to use the information we glean for our own benefit or to communicate clearly and honestly with others.[48] There are many good things about human beings that Herodotus celebrates in the *Histories*: the love of freedom, the loyalty that family members or army

---

[48] This interpretation would separate Herodotus rather sharply from Thucydides' Pericles and his sense of the usefulness of Athenian political deliberations (Thuc. 2.40.2–3).

comrades often have for one another, and the courage to face an overwhelmingly powerful enemy, to found a new city when conditions at home become intolerable, and to act ethically or boldly when circumstances make it difficult to do so. But as Herodotus presents them, people also often seem destined to resemble Croesus, one of the first individuals encountered in the *Histories*. They understand and control far less of events at hand than they think they do, in their various quests for security, freedom, and power.

It is left to the clever and clearly self-seeking Athenian politician Themistocles in Book 8, after the very important Greek victory at sea, to enunciate an ambiguously uncomfortable truth: 'These things we did not achieve ourselves, but the god and heroes, who begrudged that one man, both impious and presumptuous, would reign over both Asia and Europe' (8.109.3).[49] This point of view is more deeply embedded in both the form and the content of Herodotus' text than we sometimes acknowledge. Perhaps Plutarch was not wrong to highlight Herodotus' repeated refusal to glorify (or even clarify his own judgement about) the many individuals' thoughts and actions that drove forward the great events he set out to narrate.

---

[49] See Pelling (2019), 156–62, for the role of the gods in creating the Greek victory; it also seems at the end of the day as though the Persian mistakes were more serious than (the many) Greek ones (Dewald (2013) [1997]), 383–8). For the vexed question of divine *phthonos* or envy as part of Herodotus' explanation of human failure, see Eidinow (2016), 223–4, 227–8, 231–2 and Pelling (2019), 161–2.

CHAPTER 7

'It is no accident that . . .'
Connectivity and Coincidence in Herodotus

Richard Rutherford

> A certain man . . . once lost a diamond cuff-link in the wide blue sea, and twenty years later, on the exact day, a Friday apparently, he was eating a large fish – but there was no diamond inside. That's what I like about coincidence.
> —Vladimir Nabokov, *Laughter in the Dark* (English translation, 1938, ch. 17)

> Even chance events seem more marvellous when they look as if they were meant to happen – take the case of the statue of Mitys in Argos killing Mitys's murderer by falling on him as he looked at it; for people do not think that things like this are merely random (εἰκῇ).[1]
> —Aristotle, *Poetics* 9.1452a6–10

The quirkiness of the comment made by a character in Nabokov (quoted above) makes an apt beginning for an essay that will have much to say about meaningful coincidences. A reader who encounters Nabokov's novel without knowing Herodotus' story about Polycrates may be momentarily puzzled, though amused. Those who do catch the allusion will note the modernizing variant (a cuff-link, not a ring), and the added detail of its being the anniversary of the loss, a point that reinforces the unlikelihood of a parallel outcome; but above all such a reader will recognize that the climax has become an anti-climax: nothing happens, and the fish is just a fish. In a sense there is no story. Or rather, the story becomes effective here only through the contrast, because in Herodotus Polycrates *did* recover his ring from the belly of a fish. Nabokov's outcome is, of course, overwhelmingly more plausible, but accustomed as we are to narratives in which loose ends are tied up, we feel that something is missing. In Herodotus, however, the general tendency is for items and episodes to connect, for

---

[1] It is common to translate the last part of this quotation as 'we do not think . . .', as in the translation by Bywater for the Oxford Aristotle (reprinted in Barnes (1984), vol. ii.2323), Hubbard in Russell-Winterbottom (1972), 104, and (*mea culpa*) R. B. Rutherford (2012), 347, but the original Greek has the third person, and the comment is thus distanced from Aristotle's own view.

139

140 RICHARD RUTHERFORD

links to be made, and for meaning to emerge from these connections. The following pages will explore how far that tendency extends, and the final section is intended to place Herodotean practice in a larger context.

I

Ever since I was asked by Cambridge University Press to read the draft of his indispensable 1997 book, John Marincola's work has been a constant source of stimulation and pleasure. His productiveness and fertility of ideas make it difficult to think of an appropriate topic on which he has not already given us a standard article. This is especially true with Herodotus,[2] but I hope that he may find something fresh in what follows.

When the news of the usurpation of the Persian throne by Smerdis the Magus reaches King Cambyses, he is at first convinced that Prexaspes has failed to carry out his orders by killing the real Smerdis, his brother. Once he realizes that he has been displaced by an impostor, he rushes to his horse, but in his haste he injures himself with his own sword, an injury that eventually results in his death (3.64).

The episode is dramatic; it is also characterized by a positive rash of coincidences. First there is the fact that Cambyses' dream (3.30.2) warned him of danger from Smerdis, but he failed to realize that the Magus not only resembled his brother closely but bore the same name.[3] Second is the location of Cambyses' death: he had previously been told by an oracle that he would die in Ecbatana (though this is the first we hear of it), and assumed this meant he would die in his bed, in the imperial capital; but it turns out that the town in Syria where he currently lies injured actually shares that name. Third is the injury itself – his sword strikes home in the very part of his anatomy in which he had earlier struck the sacred bull Apis, an act of sacrilegious madness (28–9). The event is markedly overdetermined: the addition of the prophecy about Ecbatana seems superfluous as well as unheralded and improbable. The homonymity may even have been added to increase the parallelism between Cambyses and Cleomenes, two

---

[2] Most obviously in his commentary (with Michael Flower) on Book 9 and his work on the *Cambridge Companion*, but I have also derived much benefit, in my own studies and in teaching, from his *Greece & Rome* survey on Greek historians, and from his skilful upgrading of the Penguin translation.

[3] One unhistorical detail among many: the Bisitun inscription names the Magus as Gaumata, and the man he impersonates Bardiya (DB 11–14, Brosius (2000), no. 35).

Connectivity and Coincidence in Herodotus

crazed tyrannical figures who meet with unexpected reversal.[4] In addition there is a linguistic doubling: the truth about the usurpation 'struck him' (64.1 ἔτυψε), and the same verb is then used to refer to the self-wounding (64.3 τετύφθαι): the fatal recognition leads to a fatal blow.

Coincidences of this kind are not rare in Herodotus. Others will be mentioned in due course, but one oddity about the present case is that he makes no comment on this extraordinary cluster of parallels that accompany Cambyses' disastrous demise. The dream and the oracle reach their fulfilment, but this is not spelt out. Nor is it ever made explicit, even as the view of the Egyptians, that Cambyses was being punished for his attack on the sacred bull Apis.[5] Perhaps for this reason, the passage has been less prominent in discussions of Herodotus and causation than other cases such as Polycrates' ring or the sons of the Spartan heralds.[6]

John Gould in his last published essay wrote that 'for Herodotus, there is no such thing as "coincidence" *tout court*'.[7] I am not sure I agree, though it may be that we understand slightly different things by the term. A definition will be helpful: one interesting proposal is that of Dannenberg, in what I have found the most useful general survey: 'Coincidence is a constellation of two or more apparently random events in space and time with an uncanny or striking connection.'[8] That seems to be over-precise and to be leading the reader to presuppose something abnormal or even supernatural ('uncanny'). I propose a more moderate formulation: 'Coincidence is a combination of two or more events in space and time that though apparently unconnected can be seen as significant when considered together.' This may not cover everything I refer to below, but part of my object is to suggest that the borderline between coincidence and other phenomena is hazy.

Earlier discussions have been concerned to illuminate Herodotus' own beliefs and religious outlook, or that of his sources or contemporaries; they have shed abundant light on his narrative techniques and drawn effective parallels with the epic and tragic genres with which he shares many themes

---

[4] The detailed parallelism between these two figures was demonstrated by Griffiths (1989); see also Hornblower and Pelling (2017) on 6.61–4, 75.1, 80.

[5] It is suggested at an earlier stage that he might have been driven mad because of this action (3.33), but this is given as an alternative to an account that stresses Cambyses' affliction with the 'sacred disease' from birth; cf. Pelling (2019), 159.

[6] Brock (2003), 14, remarks that the passage might repay closer attention. It does not figure in the exemplary discussion by Eidinow (2011), 93–118, no doubt because her analysis focuses on the occurrence of key terms such as *tuche* and *daimon*. That is not to say that the passage has been ignored: see e.g. Gould (1989), 74–5; Harrison (2000) (see index).

[7] Gould (2003), 299.   [8] Dannenberg (2008), 93.

and motifs (divine foreknowledge revealed through oracles, the wise adviser, retribution delayed but inevitable, and so forth).[9] This has perhaps resulted in something of a gap opening up between the narrator concentrating on a tragic moral and the historian seeking an explanation of events. Without wanting to play down the importance of these ideas, I shall try in what follows to relate the 'coincidences' to Herodotus' historical project, and at the end I shall say a little about the continued importance of coincidence in the later tradition.

Closely analogous with the case of Cambyses is that of Cleomenes in his campaign against Argos. Here only one coincidence is involved, the discovery that the grove Cleomenes has burned down is called Argos. He therefore concludes that he has already fulfilled the oracle and has no chance of taking the city of Argos itself (6.76 and 80).[10] Here, differently from the Cambyses example, the oracle in question is referred to at a slightly earlier stage; but here again, as with the Apis bull, sacrilege is in question, since the grove appears to be sacred ground (6.75.3). The reasons for Cleomenes' hideous death are disputed by Herodotus' authorities, but his actions at the grove of Argos are mooted as one possible explanation. Here then the homonym plays a part in a narrative of retribution – for something, even if not for this precise act of the Spartan king.

Homonymity figures elsewhere in Herodotus, but in a rather different way. Cleisthenes of Athens at his first appearance in the *Histories* is said to have undertaken his tribal reforms in imitation of his grandfather, Cleisthenes of Sicyon (5.67.1, 69.1). Here there is nothing odd about the nomenclature, since Greek males often bore the name of a male grandparent, but the inheritance extends to his constitutional and political strategy, and is said to have been deliberate 'imitation' (67.1, ἐμιμέετο). Here the family connection is used to *explain* how Cleisthenes went about his reforms.[11]

To take the topic further means broadening the discussion. In what follows I shall consider how coincidence-spotting fits into the larger scheme of the *Histories*.

---

[9] The parallels with Sophocles are especially clear, whatever we think about specific borrowings and whether or not we accept the testimony that Sophocles wrote a poem in honour of Herodotus. See further S. West (1999).

[10] Fontenrose (1978), 58–62, on the 'Jerusalem chamber' pattern, so called after the example in Shakespeare, *II Henry IV*, Act IV sc. 5.

[11] For a modern discussion of what the younger Cleisthenes may have owed to his grandfather, see Salmon (2003).

II

Every reader of Herodotus is perplexed by the structure and sequence of his work upon first reading, and often on successive encounters. Why does one thing lead to another, what has X to do with Y, how does the whole thing hang together? Much has been done to clarify the overall plan of the *Histories*, and it is obvious that the later parts, especially from Marathon onwards, follow a more linear plan. In earlier parts the links are often genealogical: Alyattes was the father of Croesus, and what he did was . . .; sometimes horizontal relationships are relevant (Dorieus the brother of Cleomenes, and his career in the West). A marital alliance, exchange of favours, the origins of exceptional wealth or fame may need to be explained; elsewhere there is a past offence that needs to be avenged, either by an individual concerned or (since many of the agents are rulers) by the community or polis as a whole.[12]

Transitions between episodes or *logoi* are often achieved by the movement of a person, a social group or a military force into other territory (most obviously with Persian aggression, e.g. 2.1, 4.1).

Besides these linking elements, which figure predominantly in the narrative sections, we also find many comments that are basically comparative. Scythians, like Egyptians, are hostile to Greek ways (4.76); the Nasamones, like the Massagetae, share their wives in common (4.172). These similarities are not meaningful, and the comparisons do not explain, but they provide perspective and offer parallels between societies or social groups. Analogy offers a way to put extraordinary things in context. Comparison also allows things to be set on a scale. A single building or animal cannot be called unusually large in itself, because such judgements rest on comparison. Thus the tomb of Alyattes is extraordinary but not on the same scale as the great monuments of Egypt and Babylonia (1.93).

Elsewhere the historian pursues the parallel and draws a connection. In general the Persians are extremely receptive to foreign ways, and specifically, they wear Median costume 'because they think it handsomer than their own'; they favour Egyptian corselets as armour; and they practice pederasty, which they have learned from the Greeks (1.135). The mechanisms of transmission in the first two cases are easy to discern: Persia was formerly subject to the Medes' rule and went on to conquer Egypt as Herodotus describes in Book 3. How exactly pederasty is supposed to have

---

[12] Immerwahr (2013 [1956]); De Romilly (1971); Gould (1989), 63–85 (revenge and reciprocity); and many others.

RICHARD RUTHERFORD

become fashionable stretches the imagination slightly, but the *History* provides plenty of evidence for Persian contact with Greek culture. Elsewhere we are told that the sundial and the divisions of the day came to Greece from Babylon (2.109) and that the erection of ithyphallic herms is a practice Greeks borrowed from the Pelasgians (2.51).[13] Above all, numerous Greek customs and beliefs, including a range of cults, are said to be derived from Egypt (2.49, 51, 81, 123, 171).[14] In discussing the worship of Dionysus (whom he equates with Osiris), Herodotus is particularly emphatic that 'I will never admit that the similar ceremonies performed in Greece and Egypt are the result of mere coincidence (οὐ γὰρ δὴ συμπεσεῖν γε φήσω ...) ... Nor will I allow that the Egyptians ever took over from Greece either this custom or any other' (49.2–3). We shall have further occasion to note the use of the verb συμπίπτω below.

When Herodotus observes parallels of this kind, his normal assumption is that this is a matter of direct influence. Both shields and helmets, he asserts, were introduced into Greece from Egypt (4.180). The clothing and style of the aegis that Greeks include in representations of Athena are said to derive from Libya, and Greeks also learned from the Libyans how to harness four horses to a chariot (4.189). Circumcision, he maintains, was transmitted from Egypt through Syria to the Phoenicians (and Colchians) (2.104). He is a fanatical diffusionist. Independent development is something he never asserts explicitly, though his formulations are sometimes neutral: the Chaldaeans and the people of Egyptian Thebes share a belief that the god comes in person to rest in his temple (1.182); the marriage-market found in Babylon is 'a custom which, I understand, they share with the Eneti in Illyria' (1.190).[15] There is perhaps a counter-case in the Scythian ethnography, when he is describing the Getae, 'who believe they will never die' (4.93.1). After describing their practices, he refers to a different account that he has been told, which ascribes their beliefs about the afterlife to Pythagorean teachings that Salmoxis had brought to the Getae after a sojourn in Samos. Herodotus is evidently not tempted by this particular case of cultural transference and concludes with the dismissive comment that in his view Salmoxis lived long before Pythagoras (4.94–6).[16]

---

[13] Cf. Burkert (2013 [1985]), 201.   [14] See further A. B. Lloyd (1975–88), i.147–9.

[15] See also 1.199.5; 2.79 (raising but not answering the question where Egypt derived the Linus song); 2.80 (Egypt and Sparta); 2.167.

[16] Cf. my remarks in R. B. Rutherford (2018), 31–3.

Connectivity and Coincidence in Herodotus

For influence of this kind to occur, there must, of course, be contact between the cultures, and this argument is carried even to improbable lengths by Herodotus. An elaborate argument in Book 2 (102–5) sets out his case for the Colchians at the river Phasis being of Egyptian descent, which he explains as the result of extensive campaigning by the Egyptian king Sesostris. Either Sesostris left a detachment of settlers behind or some of his force deserted: Herodotus is not prepared to decide between these explanations, but he is convinced that the resemblances he describes between Colchians and Egyptians cannot be accidental. Moderns would regard both the supposed resemblance and the proposed line of descent as fantastic.

Influence can be seen at work in nomenclature as well. The Persians are said to believe they derive their name from Perseus, who was an Assyrian who adopted Greek nationality, and his ancestors were in fact Egyptian (6.54, 2.91); Media gets its name from Medea (7.61–2), and some other ethnic names are similarly explained by cross-cultural links (7.92, 94). Herodotus does not linger to explain why there should have been a town called Ecbatana in Syria, and we can only speculate as to whether he would have hypothesized a connection with the Median/Persian capital (3.64, see above).

Although we may dismiss extreme and improbable cases such as the Colchis-Egypt connection, nobody will doubt that in the archaic period there was extensive mobility in the Mediterranean and beyond.[17] Quantifying it is impossible, but estimates currently operate at the high end of the spectrum.[18] That people moved around, individually and en masse, is not in itself noteworthy. Our concern is not so much with the real archaic world as with the mechanisms of the Herodotean text. We are considering cases where activity, including travel from place to place, has an impact on events and generates a narrative turning point.

(1) At 3.4 Phanes the Halicarnassian arrives just at the right time to advise Cambyses on the best means of crossing the desert and embarking on his conquest of Egypt.

(2) At 4.146–8 the Minyae arrive in the territory of Lacedaemon just in time for Theras of Sparta to enlist them as part of the band of settlers which he leads to Callista (to be renamed Thera).

---

[17] Purcell (1990); cf. Horden and Purcell (2000), emphasizing 'connectivity' throughout; Malkin (2011) treats the subject in terms of 'networks'. For another approach using topology and hodography, see Barker et al. (2016).

[18] I use the language of Purcell (1990).

146   RICHARD RUTHERFORD

(3) At 2.152.4 bronze-clad raiders arrive in Egypt in time to assist Psammetichus, and so fulfil an oracle that no one had understood or credited.

(4) At 3.129 it so happens (συνήνεικε)[19] that Democedes the doctor has been brought to Susa shortly before Darius damages his foot in a riding accident, which the medic is called upon to cure; and since he also shows his value by curing Queen Atossa, he finds high favour and soon brings about an expedition by the Persians to western waters – an episode marked as a significant 'first' by the narrator (3.138.4).

(5) At 3.139 we are told how Syloson of Samos gave Darius a cloak he admired, long before Darius was monarch – a happy chance,[20] as it seems, which enables him to visit the king's court and claim a favour in return. The favour does not work out as well as both men expect (the result is a Persian attack and extensive slaughter on Samos), but this is a paradigm case of Herodotus' repeated emphasis on the power of individuals to direct events down unexpected paths.

(6) At 7.3 Darius is pondering the choice of his successor and just at the right time Demaratus arrives to give him some advice based on Spartan practice (though whatever Demaratus' value as a 'wise adviser' figure later on, he does not have a brilliant record at handling matters to do with succession planning: see 6.61–6). Darius takes his advice, though in this case the historian remarks that he would most likely have taken that course anyway of his own accord.

(7) Shortly after the last passage, at 7.6, Mardonius' desire to convince Xerxes to undertake the punishment of the Greeks is aided by the timely arrival of the Aleuadae from Thessaly; the Pisistratids and Onomacritus add their exhortation to the same end. This time Herodotus is explicit that the combined pressure of all this unanimous advice is decisive in persuading Xerxes.

Other unpredicted but apt arrivals are less fully developed; in certain cases they may seem superfluous. When Pisistratus is told by the Acarnanian seer that 'the net is cast', the verse-prophecy seems to be confirming him in a plan already adopted rather than making a difference to events; yet it presumably strengthens his resolve, in the conviction that the gods favour his intent (1.62.4, Amphilytus). Some other timely visitors turn out to

---

[19] Powell s.v. συμφέρω 3: impersonal use, seventeen examples, including 3.4.1 cited above, and also 3.42.1 (introducing the fisherman who made the remarkable catch).

[20] 3.139.2 εὐτυχίη ... θείη τύχῃ χρεώμενος. On these and related expressions, see Eidinow (2011).

Connectivity and Coincidence in Herodotus 147

have appeared in vain, as the sage advice they offer goes unheeded, such as Chilon of Sparta to Pisistratus' father (1.59), Bias and Thales at the Panionium (1.170), and, of course, Solon to Croesus (1.29–33).

Perhaps especially telling is the account the historian gives of the inception of the Ionian Revolt (5.35). Aristagoras is already in difficulties with the Persian governor Artaphernes and is therefore contemplating stirring up a revolt; at that very moment 'something else occurred (συνέπιπτε) to confirm his purpose', the arrival of the message from Histiaeus on the slave's tattooed head. The point is reinforced shortly after, with the emphatic statement that 'Aristagoras found himself faced with a combination of circumstances, all of which urged him in the same direction' (5.36.1).[21] The verb here, συνέπιπτε, repeats the one used in the previous chapter with reference to the same occurrence; it closely corresponds to the English 'coincide' (*co + incidere*). In this and other cases, it invites the question: did this really 'just happen'? Was there more to it than chance? Does coincidence hide some kind of design? But despite the repeated emphasis, in this case Herodotus makes no suggestion that we should be seeking any explanation beyond the human motivations of the agents involved.

The opposite is the case in two other passages in which the same verb figures: 7.137.2 and 9.101.1.[22] In the first he marvels at the way that the wrath of Talthybius seemed to have found its victim and taken suitable revenge on heralds and that these men should have been the sons of the two original offenders: 'this, to me at least, is clear evidence of divine intervention'. In the second he begins with the declaration of faith: 'many things make it plain to me that the hand of God is active in human affairs', and cites first the way that a rumour spread among the army at Mycale as they confronted the Persian force, a rumour that the other Persian army in mainland Greece had been defeated that day at Plataea (τότε τῆς αὐτῆς ἡμέρης συμπιπτούσης), thus raising morale and arousing their spirit for the fray; and second that 'it was another odd coincidence' (τόδε ἕτερον συνέπεσε) that both conflicts took place near a precinct of Demeter of Eleusis. In both these passages we have a kind of credo – coincidences can be so remarkable that they can be explained only by the hypothesis of divine involvement.

My argument has been that Herodotus is constantly on the watch for resemblances of many kinds and that where he sees resemblances he is

---

[21] Pelling (2007a), 185.
[22] Other cases cited by Powell's *Lexicon* are 1.82.1, 139, 8.15.1, 132.2, 141.2.

keen to find connections, ways of linking different places and peoples, customs and beliefs. The most obvious cases cross space, but there are also links across time (and generations), as between Cleisthenes and his grandfather, or the two Spartan heralds and their sons. Connections need or call out for explanations, which may be supplied by simply assuming imitation or instruction. Often explanations can be given in terms of human action, but at times the historian feels the need to cast his net further. It might be argued that he appeals to the gods when human explanations are not available or seem insufficient,[23] but there seems also to be a certain reluctance to make that appeal even when we might expect it (as with the case of Cambyses).

Yet at times he is willing to suspend judgement: readers have rightly emphasized the intriguing comment at 5.9, where he reports that the Sigynnae, far to the north of Thrace, call themselves settlers (ἀποίκους) from Media and remarks, 'How they can be this I myself cannot understand, but anything may come about in the long age of time.' We may be reminded of Protagoras, for whom the brevity of human life was one of the obstacles inhibiting knowledge of the divine (DK 80 B4). Protagoras is not the only Greek thinker to assert a version of the uncertainty principle, that there are topics on which precise knowledge is impossible to achieve.[24]

By bringing in Protagoras I have implied that there is an intellectual, even a philosophical dimension to this topic. Another well-known passage about Protagoras refers to the discussion he and Pericles had on where the responsibility lay for the death of a boy during an athletic contest (Plut. *Per.* 36.5): was it the javelin itself, the thrower, or the *agonothetai*? Everyday idiom would term this an accident, however regrettable, but we can see that there is potential for ingenuity of argument in such a case, as also shown by the parallel in Antiphon's *Tetralogies*.[25] But concerns about the nature of accident or coincidence are more widespread.

We know that the Presocratics discussed chance and necessity: Empedocles was criticized for having first posited six ultimate principles but then adding in *Tyche* and *Ananke*.[26] For him organic bodies were

---

[23] Pelling (2019), ch. 10, is a typically acute and stimulating discussion of this thorny issue.

[24] Gould's statement of the 'uncertainty principle' in Greek religion has been influential: see Gould (1985), 8–16 = (2001), 211–16, (1994), 94 = (2001), 362. Burkert (1985 [2013]) and (1990), followed by Scullion (2006), presents a picture of a more modern, less pious Herodotus; Harrison (2000) and Mikalson (2003) are closer to Gould's account.

[25] Pelling (2019), 69–70, discusses the case.

[26] Guthrie (1965–81), 2.159–63, 200–11. On Empedocles and accident, see more recently Sedley (2007), 60–2.

Connectivity and Coincidence in Herodotus

produced by chance combinations: earth 'happened upon' equal quantities of the other elements (DK 31 B98), fire 'chanced to meet' a little earth in the making of the eye (B85). Closer to Herodotean concerns is Empedocles' account of the survival and evolution of animals through the possession of certain biological characteristics (B59), a topic that naturally reminds us of Herodotus' analysis in 3.108–9 and of Protagoras' main *rhesis* in Plato's dialogue (*Prt.* 320d–21b). Herodotus noted that more vulnerable species breed abundantly, whereas more powerful predators are less fertile. He ascribed this to divine providence (3.108.1), but according to Aristotle Empedocles made it a matter of chance.[27] Aristotle himself discusses chance as part of his treatment of causes, subdivided into various types (*Ph.* 2.4–6).[28] As usual he is conscious of his predecessors, drawing out the germs of truth in a variety of views, though the references are brief and cryptic. For our purposes we may note that he refers to 'some people' who claim that nothing occurs by chance, whereas some say that the heavens and all the worlds, or the vortex, came into being spontaneously, and some allow chance to be a cause but argue that it is 'inscrutable to human intelligence, as being a divine thing and full of mystery' (*Ph.* 2.4.196b5–6, ἄδηλος δὲ ἀνθρωπίνῃ διανοίᾳ ὡς θεῖόν τι οὖσα καὶ δαιμονιώτερον). The anonymity of this attribution is frustrating, but its relevance to our theme is obvious.

Aristotle's account of coincidence is to be found in a variety of passages in the *Metaphysics*: the regular verb he employs is συμβαίνω (e.g. Δ.30.1025a4, 25).[29] It is not my intention to offer any contribution to Aristotelian scholarship, which would be an act of hubris rivalling any of those found in the *History*, but I would like to cite some of the instances he gives.[30] There are complications in that his terminology is not used in the same way as modern 'coincidence', but seems often to be closer to 'accident'.[31] He is partly concerned to distinguish different attributes that

---

[27] B59.2 ταῦτα τε συμπίπτεσκον ὅπῃ συνέκυρσεν ἕκαστα, with Aristotle's comment at *Ph.* 2.8 198b29 (B 61 in DK).

[28] For detailed discussion, see Judson (1991).

[29] Kirwan (1993) is the standard commentary on the relevant books; see also Sorabji (1980), ch. 1.

[30] In this section, I am very grateful to Lindsay Judson for advice and for drawing my attention to his own articles cited in notes 28 and 35, but he is emphatically not to blame for any blunders I may commit here.

[31] Kirwan (1993), 76, notes that older versions often prefer the rendering 'accident' or 'accidental', but he prefers the translation 'coincide' and so on, partly because 'accident' lacks a cognate verb. On the terminology, see also his p. 217: 'Throughout it is important to remember that (i) some commentators on Aristotle, notably Sorabji ... use "coincidence" *not* to translate "*sumbebekos*" but in its modern English sense, and (ii) many use other words to translate "*sumbebekos*", e.g. "accident", "concurrence", "concomitant".'

coincide in the same individual (e.g. the same man can be pale and also artistic, but neither attribute accounts for the other). More interesting is the observation in *Metaph.* Δ.30 that it would be a coincidence if a trench-digger engaged in digging in order to plant something were to find buried treasure (since this is not the aim of his efforts): we may be reminded of various people who 'get lucky' in Herodotus.[32] Another case is: 'It was a coincidence for someone to visit Aegina if he went there not in order to visit but having been forced off course by a storm or captured by pirates.' This may strike us as a slightly odd example, since it would seem that something ought to happen in Aegina to make the mishap worthy of note: possibly some version of Plato's allegedly being sold into slavery in Aegina may underlie this passage.[33] But the idea that a traveller's intentions may be derailed and that the cause of arrival has nothing to do with his intentions is certainly familiar – and a valuable narrative motif.[34] The third example is very abbreviated and forms part of a more complicated argument about causation, but involves a man who will die by violence if he leaves his house.[35] He is obliged to do so because he has made himself terribly thirsty through spicy food (and presumably has no water on the premises). Much has to be supplied to make sense of the story (later commentators make explicit that the man needs to go to a well to get water), but it seems reasonable to assume that Aristotle is implying he will meet violent men if he leaves his house. What is the cause of his death? Not the enmity of his killers, if it is purely accidental that they meet him: it is not suggested that they are looking for him or are personal enemies. Is it his leaving his house, or the tormenting thirst, or the spicy food that caused it? Or is there in fact no cause, only an intersection of two chains of events? Although dyspepsia is not a historical driver in Herodotus' narrative, it is easy enough to think of cases where a disastrous meeting might so easily have been avoided – above all, perhaps, the chance encounter in

---

[32] For discovery of treasure, cf. 7.190, 9.83. More loosely comparable is 1.68, where the Spartan spy is looking for the bones of Orestes and is intrigued by the work of the blacksmith, whose conversation puts him on the right track.

[33] See Riginos (1976), 86–92. Pirates are mentioned in two late sources (Riginos 91). Kirwan (1993), 220, seems to have this story in mind when he refers to Plato in his further comment on this passage.

[34] For storms diverting travellers in Herodotus, see 7.168, 170.2; piracy, e.g. 3.47 (cf. 1.1). See further Ormerod (1924); Horden and Purcell (2000), 387–8.

[35] See Judson (1998) for detailed discussion of this chapter, esp. pp. 196 and 200, in which he develops the idea that there is no single process that accounts for the man's death, but simply the intersection of 'two independent (sets of) processes – the chain of events which takes the man to the well and the one which takes the ruffians there' (196).

Atarneus of Hermotimos with the man who once castrated him, Panionios, with horrific consequences for the latter (8.105–6).[36]

There is, of course, no question of Herodotus delving into causation theory in anything like this way; and setting Protagoras aside, there is no reason to connect the historian directly with any of the thinkers mentioned. Nor does Aristotle have Herodotus in mind in these passages (though he cites his work occasionally elsewhere). Rather, these examples suggest that the relation of cause, coincidence and explanation was the subject of active debate well before Aristotle's time.

If we revert to the Cambyses example with which we began, some of the same issues arise. Why did Cambyses die? The common-sense answer is because his self-inflicted wound proved fatal. The fact (if it is one) that he inflicted it in that particular spot on his body is accidental, we might say; likewise, the 'fact' that this took place in a township that happened to bear the name of Ecbatana. These coincidences seemed significant facts to Cambyses and the bystanders, but perhaps they were mistaken. But this, of course, is to ignore the narrative emphasis on the recklessness of Cambyses' conduct, especially his outrageous assault on the Apis bull. Yet Herodotus refrains from asserting that his death was punishment for that atrocity. We are left with the oracle, which does imply a supernatural dimension to the king's demise; yet here too Herodotus uses the motif without commenting on it, and the warning is referred to only by Cambyses (and only here), without the historian's endorsement. It seems that the death of Cambyses is from one point of view overdetermined but from another a simple accident.

These questions take us to the heart of a central issue of Herodotean scholarship: how far was he a traditional believer, how far in step with more 'modern' sophistic or scientific thinking?[37] Some have argued that he minimizes the use of the gods as explanation for events, restricting his enquiries to what can be known, the human sphere. The counter-arguments emphasize the way in which the influence of the gods on events is frequently referred to (even if they may often act indirectly through oracles and dreams) and can be deduced or discerned as underlying human events. Some possibly divine activity is ambiguous; other speculations are couched in cautious terms or distanced as the views of others. But when

---

[36] See the outstanding discussion by Hornblower (2003). The verb εὑρίσκει in 8.106.1 suggests that he comes upon Panionios by chance, and indeed we have just been told that he was dispatched to Atarneus on some specific errand. Yet at the end of the chapter we are told that 'retribution (τίσις) and Hermotimos had caught up with Panionios' (106.4).

[37] See esp. A. B. Lloyd (1975–88), i.141–70; R. Thomas (2000).

nothing is said about the role of the gods, should we assume they are active nevertheless or allow that some events may be regarded as merely random? Although much of the most influential recent scholarship has favoured Herodotus the up-to-date thinker, and found the same sophistication in their author as they have brought to his interpretation, we may have to end in aporia on this crucial point. It takes a Momigliano to be happy with this situation, but we might remember one of his light-hearted aperçus: '[Herodotus] would not have been disturbed [by a modern scholar's observations].... He liked a certain amount of confusion.'[38]

Causation and explanation are of the essence of historical writing. If history is not to be just a congeries of events ('one damn thing after another'), meaningful connections must be made between events or contingencies. Within that framework coincidence has an ambiguous status. The effect is clear but there seems no obvious cause. Hence the need to supply it – or imply it.

III

Herodotus includes three synchronisms of battles: Salamis and Himera (7.166, introduced by 'the Sicilians maintain ...'), Thermopylae and Artemisium (8.15.1) and the climactic case of Plataea and Mycale, which receives greater emphasis, including the comment quoted above (9.100–1). The Salamis-Himera coincidence was the one that received greatest attention in later writers: the temptation to make stronger links between the battle for freedom in the East against Persia and in the West against Carthage was too strong to resist. The analogy had already been drawn by Pindar (*P.* 1.71–80), but a further step was to introduce a direct connection, by the suggestion that Persia and Carthage were in alliance. This elaboration appeared in Ephorus (who seems to have made the synchronism between Himera and Thermopylae), and has been treated seriously by some modern scholars.[39] Herodotus makes no reference to such an alliance and it was probably invented after his time.

An eye-opening passage in Plutarch shows how far-reaching the craze to detect coincidence could be.

---

[38] Momigliano (1978), 131.

[39] Ephorus, *FGrHist* 70 F 186, Diod. Sic. 11.1.4, 20.1. Rejected by Asheri (1988), 773–4. See further Feeney (2007), 43–52, 231; Marincola (2007d), esp. 112–14; Rood (2018). Contrast Arist. *Poet.* 23.1459a24–9, whose 'tough-mindedness' is praised by Feeney (2007), 43.

Connectivity and Coincidence in Herodotus

When we reflect that time is infinite and Fortune for ever changing her course, it can hardly surprise us that certain events should often repeat themselves quite spontaneously. For if the number of those elements which combine to produce a historical event is unlimited, then Fortune possesses an ample store of coincidences in the very abundance of her material; if, on the other hand, their number is fixed, then the same pattern of events seems bound to recur, since the same forces combine to operate upon them. Now, there are some people who take pleasure in collecting by hearsay or from their reading examples of accidental occurrences which look like the result of calculation and forethought. They notice, for instance, that two men named Attis have become celebrated in legend, the one a Syrian and the other an Arcadian, and that both were killed by a wild boar; that there were two Actaeons, one of whom was torn to pieces by his dogs and the other by his lovers; that there were two Scipios, one of whom conquered Carthage in the Second Punic War, while the other destroyed it utterly in the Third; that the city of Troy was originally captured by Heracles on account of the horses of Laomedon, then by Agamemnon through the so-called 'Wooden Horse', and finally by Charidemus, because a horse fell in the gateway and prevented the Trojans from closing the gates quickly enough.... Let us therefore add our own contribution to this collection ... [Plutarch goes on to point out that three eminent generals were all one-eyed men.] (Plut. *Sert.* 1)[40]

Coincidences (including synchronisms of the Plataea-Mycale type) became a seductive feature in the work of later historians (and in other genres too: the synchronism of the founding of Rome and Carthage, perhaps first proposed by Timaeus, remains important in modified form in the *Aeneid*).[41] The many parallels between Greek and Roman historical events listed by Ogilvie in his commentary on Livy include the conspicuous synchronism of the liberation of Athens from the Pisistratid tyranny and the liberation of Rome from the rule of the Tarquins; it is difficult to believe that Roman chronology coincided so obligingly.[42]

Yet there were always sceptics. Tacitus sneered at people who are impressed by trivia of this kind, specifying those who marvelled at the fact that Augustus died on the same day of the year in which he had originally accepted imperial office; and that he passed away in the same house and

---

[40] Trans. Scott-Kilvert and Pelling (2010). See further *Quaest. conv.* 717c–d.

[41] Timaeus, *FGrHist* 566 F 60; Horsfall (1974); Feeney (2007), 88, 93–7.

[42] Ogilvie (1965), 195 on 1.49–60, who notes that the 'coincidence' was already observed by Gel. 17.21.4; cf. his index, p. 765, s.v. 'Greek: episodes adapted from Greek mythology and history'.

154   RICHARD RUTHERFORD

room as his father Octavius (*Ann.* 1.9.1: *vana mirantibus*). Similar marvels are provided by Suetonius (*Aug.* 100.1).[43]

In some cases, we can witness the same writer acclaiming a coincidence as meaningful and deriding it as insignificant, depending on context. Thus, Cicero in addressing the Roman people emphasizes the significance of the fact that the newly enlarged and repositioned statue of Jupiter Stator has been put finally in place on the very day that the captive conspirators were led under armed escort to imprisonment, to the salvation of the city (*Cat.* 3.18–22). Yet in sceptical mode in the *De divinatione* he mocks any suggestion that this accidental combination of events should be seen as indicating a divine hand at work (*Div.* 2.21). Modern scholars have gone further and seen Cicero himself as engineering the coincidence by fixing the timetable for the statue – a type of argument also found in readings of some of the Herodotean cases.[44]

Obviously, this does not exhaust the field, and it would be easy to extend the survey to later periods and still further genres (many of them still retaining links with the ancient tradition: thus Euripidean recognition scenes feed into New Comedy, and Roman comedy into Shakespeare). Coincidences are notorious for their presence in the Victorian novel.[45] Thus in *Great Expectations* Estella turns out to be the daughter of Magwitch, and Magwitch's arch-enemy Compeyson proves to be the same man who jilted Miss Havisham.

There is a long tradition of despising those who overuse or overvalue coincidence, in real life and in textual plots.[46] But this is not only a matter of plausibility and plot construction. It is plausibly argued that the Victorian fondness for plots of this kind is closely related to the belief in Providence. Chance is not mere chance, and accidents can lead to momentous consequences; an improbable coincidence may actually be evidence of

---

[43] A writer in the *Catholic Herald* for 23 April 2014 opines, 'Apart from the astonishing coincidence that Shakespeare died on his own birthday, it is also singularly appropriate that England's greatest poet should have been born and should have died on the feast day of her patron saint' (https://catholicherald.co.uk/commentandblogs/2014/04/23/why-is-shakespeare-so-mysterious, accessed on 14 January 2020). I refrain from citing still wilder remarks on the significance of Psalm 46 (23 + 23) for 'Shakespeare and the Bible Code'.

[44] I refer to Hegesistratus in 9.91–2. At 91.1 Herodotus remarks that Leutychidas may have asked the envoy his name 'because he was looking for an omen, or it might even have been just a lucky question, prompted by some god'. Religious motivation is present in either option, but the first suggests a rather more calculated approach. See Diod. Sic. 11.35 and Polyaen. 1.33 for the rationalizing interpretation that Leutychidas circulated the rumour at Mycale to boost morale.

[45] Goldknopf (1972), 159–76; Dannenberg (2004) and (2008).

[46] Julian Barnes, *Flaubert's Parrot* (1984), 66–73, has an extended disquisition on this topic.

Connectivity and Coincidence in Herodotus

a benevolent higher power at work. Negatively, cruel coincidences may suggest that mortals are mere playthings of a malicious deity, as in Hardy. A valuable treatment of the subject by Vargish detects development in the handling of this theme. According to his account, Bronte and Dickens in their early novels provide illustrations of the providential worldview as a structuring principle, but in their later work present 'increasingly radical and brilliant defences against what proved in the end to be its "extirpation" as a general cultural and aesthetic premise'.[47] George Eliot, he maintains, is concerned to adapt the fictional representation of providence to secular imperatives; when Eliot makes use of coincidence, it arises from human ignorance and error and lacks a providential aspect.

It would clearly be unwise to draw any close parallels between the nineteenth century AD and the fifth century BC. Students of Victorian literature and society could certainly find weaknesses in the developmental picture of Dickens' oeuvre and outlook that Vargish offers.[48] And the notion of tracing development in Herodotus is rightly out of fashion, and one hopes will remain so.[49] But I am less sure that we should dismiss out of hand the idea that his work may contain some inconsistency of attitude, perhaps not least in areas where, to cite Gould again, the uncertainty principle prevails. Coincidence is sometimes explicitly marked as significant and as showing the gods at work. When this is not the case, perhaps we can simply say that the historian suspends judgement.

There is arguably another dimension to this whole issue, a metatextual aspect. The web of connections and structurally interwoven threads is the work of a controlling mind, the historian himself, whose design represents a kind of sub-creation,[50] the execution of a master plan. Like the epic poet,[51] the chronicler is analogous to the divine power overseeing the

---

[47] Vargish (1985), 1–35, at 5. The term 'extirpation' is drawn from Trilling (1972), 116, who writes of the loss of the assumption that there was purpose in the universe and calls the extirpation of that conviction 'a psychic catastrophe.'

[48] Thus Dannenberg (2008), 102–3, cautions against the assumption of a general worldview and stresses the plurality of perspectives to be found even in an individual author, let alone a culture or a period.

[49] This has been emphatically asserted, for example, by Dewald and Marincola (2006), 1–4; Munson (2013), 1.3–4.

[50] I use this word in the sense popularized by J. R. R. Tolkien, who saw the imaginative work of an author as analogous to the creation of our world by a divine power (see Tolkien (1964), 1–83).

[51] Cf. R. B. Rutherford (2013), 51, citing *Iliad* 16.644–55, where the analogy between Zeus and the poet is especially plain. The point is not a new one: see e.g. Fränkel (1975), 75; M. L. West (2011), 211.

unfolding of history, for whom perhaps there are no coincidences. But that approach would involve seeing Herodotus as an author highly self-conscious about his own creative contribution to his material – more so, I think, than either I or John Marincola would be altogether happy with. In any case it would be a subject for a different essay, and this one has gone on long enough.

CHAPTER 8

Through Barbarian Eyes
Non-Greeks on Greeks in Herodotus

Deborah Boedeker

Recognized as 'father of ethnography' as well as history, Herodotus is famous for his keen attention to human cultures and their diverse ways of life; accordingly, discussion of cultural differences has a long history in Herodotean studies.[1] In his translation of the *Histories*, for example, George Rawlinson shares his impression of the Persians in that work (more recent scholars, needless to say, have discussed Herodotean ethnography from quite different points of view[2]):

> Brave, lively, and spirited, capable of sharp sayings and repartees, but vain, weak, impulsive, and hopelessly servile toward their lords ... Clearly marked out from other barbarous races by a lightness and sprightliness of character, which brought them near to the Hellenic type, yet vividly contrasted with the Greeks by their passionate *abandon* and slavish submission to the caprices of despotic power ...[3]

Ethnographic observations in Herodotus typically consist of the narrator's descriptions of other cultures, occasionally offering positive or negative comments on them.[4] What especially interests me here, however,

---

*This chapter has profited from conversations with participants during and after the colloquium, particularly Kurt Raaflaub and Carolyn Dewald, and the excellent editors have saved it from various infelicities. To these generous Herodoteans for their fellowship, stimulation, and helpful feedback, I offer great appreciation and gratitude.

[1] See Marincola (1997), 83 n. 100. It is a pleasure to acknowledge with this chapter the creative scholarship of John Marincola, whose illuminating work in *Authority and Tradition in Ancient Historiography* so fruitfully blends the roles of philologist and historian.

[2] E.g. Hartog (1988); Redfield (1985); Konstan (1987); Lateiner (1989), 145–62; Nenci (1990); R. Thomas (1997), (2000), and (2011); Flower and Marincola (2002), 37–9; Kartunnen (2002); Rood (2006a); Skinner (2012); especially relevant to this chapter are Pelling (1997b) and Munson (2001), who demonstrate in different ways that cultural difference, for example, between Greeks and Persians, is far from a simple contrast in the *Histories*.

[3] Rawlinson (1858–60), i.130; the passage is cited in Konstan (1987), 50–1. Rawlinson opines that similar traits were still to be found in those who occupied the Persians' territory in his own time.

[4] E.g. he praises the elaborate marriage auctions previously held at Babylon as their 'wisest' (σοφώτατος) and 'fairest' (κάλλιστος) *nomos* (1.196.1, 5), and castigates as the 'most shameful'

157

158   DEBORAH BOEDEKER

follows from John Marincola's central insight on how ancient historians, Herodotus not least among them, seek to give their work authority and credibility by using a panoply of literary strategies.[5] Instead of discussing cultural characteristics per se as presented in the *Histories*, I will focus on a number of passages where Herodotus foregrounds the *rhetorical* dimension of cultural differentiation by having characters in the narrative express their judgement of another group, a technique that has received relatively little attention in studies of Herodotean ethnology. I will look primarily at the comments of non-Greeks ('barbarians' or 'others') concerning Hellenic ways; these judgements are mostly negative,[6] in contrast to the narrator's own generally neutral stance toward the ways of non-Greek cultures. Naturally, the historian does not present his Greek audience with a primer on the habits of Hellenes.[7] But at times he has 'others' point out something about Hellenic culture or disposition, such as their food, battle tactics, festivals, valour, and lack of unity, from (purportedly) the speakers' point of view, rather than doing so in his own voice. It is characteristic of Herodotus that the contents of his (more authoritative) narrative sometimes call such judgements into question.

We first encounter the device of 'Barbarians Looking at Greeks' in the prologue, at the end of the famous series of ancient bride-stealing adventures between East and West: Phoenicians capture Io, certain Greeks then steal Europa and later Medea, and, finally, Trojan Paris takes Helen (1.1–3).[8]

According to Herodotus, the Persians consider this event to mark the beginning of long-standing East/West hostilities:

> Up to this point, [the Persians say] it was only seizures [of women] by both sides, but afterwards, the Greeks were quite guilty, for they waged war against Asia before the Persians attacked Europe. They say they considered the seizing of women to be the work of unjust men, but that only foolish men hasten to avenge such seizures, and the wise pay no heed to women

---

(αἴσχιστος) the requirement that before marriage every woman must once offer herself for prostitution at the temple of Aphrodite/Mylitta (1.199.1).

[5] Marincola (1997).

[6] As pointed out by Munson (2001), 145–6, who notes (n. 32) that two exceptions occur 'in the highly celebrated narrative of Thermopylae': at 7.208.1–3 (Xerxes' scout 'marvels when he sees' (θεώμενος ἐθώμαζε) the Spartans calmly exercising and combing their hair in preparation for the battle) and at 8.26.3 (discussed below, pp. 172–3).

[7] Herodotus makes an exception for Sparta, known for many practices that diverged from those of other Greek poleis (see esp. 6.56–60).

[8] Among many perceptive treatments of this passage I draw attention to Dewald (1999), 221–9, and passim, emphasizing the different voices involved in addressing the question of blame.

Non-Greeks on Greeks in Herodotus

who have been carried off – for it is clear that if they weren't willing they wouldn't have been taken. The Persians say that they, men of Asia, took no account of the women who were seized, but that because of a Lacedaemonian woman, the Greeks gathered a large expedition, went to Asia, and destroyed the power of Priam. From that time on, they say, they have always considered the Greek world hostile to them (ἀπὸ τούτου αἰεὶ ἡγήσασθαι τὸ Ἑλληνικὸν σφίσι εἶναι πολέμιον). (1.4.1–4)

So much then for the Persians' attitude toward the Trojan War and the East/West animosity that followed: they blame the Hellenes for a naïve and destructive over-reaction to the mere kidnapping of a woman.[9] Herodotus further reports that the Phoenicians took issue with the Persians' view in one respect: they said that the Phoenicians did not *seize* Io (as reported in 1.1.2–4, the version attributed to Persian *logioi*), but that she willingly sailed with them from her home in Argos, because she did not want to tell her parents that she had become pregnant by the ship's captain (1.5.2).[10]

At a later point, however, Herodotus emphatically puts forth his own judgement. Helen was not even in Troy to be returned when the Greeks demanded her, for she was being kept safe for Menelaus by Proteus, the Egyptian king (as the Egyptian priests told Herodotus, 2.113–15); nevertheless, the gods still allowed the destruction of Troy as an object lesson, to show that 'great offenses [such as Paris' theft of Helen from Menelaus] meet with great punishments' (2.120). With this judgement the narrator calls into question the Persian assessment he had reported earlier, namely, that Greeks were responsible for the long-standing East/West hostility, thus allowing his audience to question that version as self-serving propaganda.

Much later and in a very different context, Herodotus as narrator enumerates a series of East/West conflicts prior to the expedition of Xerxes. The earliest of these attacks was initiated by Asians against Europe: 'Mysians and Teucrians [Trojans] crossed into Europe at the Bosporus before the Trojan War, subjugated all the Thracians, advanced down to the Ionian Sea, and drove southward as far as the Peneus river'

---

[9] On the complications of the 'blame game' in this section, see esp. Pelling (2019), 25–31. Here, two different sets of focalizers/speakers, Persians and Phoenicians, give varying accounts of the 'same' story, each clearly informed by self-interest. Herodotus also notes (1.2.1) that the Greeks have a different account of how Io came to Egypt (presumably an allusion to the myth that Hera envied and harassed Io for becoming Zeus' paramour).

[10] See Dewald (1999), 225; Dewald (1987), 149–50 and passim, discusses the significance of introducing such a multiplicity of focalizers at the very beginning of the *Histories*.

160   DEBORAH BOEDEKER

(7.20). Here too, without comment, we are shown that Asians attacked Europe first: again, the narrator implicitly contradicts what the Persians said at 1.4.1–4 (quoted above).

Later in Book 1, we hear again – this time very differently – what certain non-Greeks think about an aspect of Hellenic culture. In the midst of his excursus on Persian customs in Book 1, Herodotus briefly changes perspective to report what Persians say about the Greek diet:

> They [the Persians] have sparse main courses but many side dishes, not served all at once. For this reason the Persians say (φασὶ Πέρσαι) that Greeks stop eating while they are still hungry, since nothing worth mentioning is served to them after the main meal; but [they say] if something else were served, the Greeks wouldn't stop eating (εἰ δέ τι παραφέροιτο, ἐσθίοντας ἂν οὐ παύεσθαι). (1.133.2)

Why does Herodotus tell us here what 'the Persians say' about Greeks, instead of stating in his own voice that Persian food is richer and more elaborate? In the ethnographies he often reports what members of a group eat and drink: consider the three Babylonian tribes that eat only food made of dried fish meal (1.200), or the Egyptians, whose dietary regimes, including regular monthly purges, are among the healthiest in the world (2.77). Practices characteristic of barbarians are focalized from a Greek perspective, in the neutral, credible voice of the narrator.[11] Calling attention to Hellenic cultural characteristics by showing them through the eyes and voice of the Other, as happens here, allows the description to be more laden with judgement from the less 'neutral' speakers. Here, for example, Persians see Greek meals not just as different, but also as *deficient* in comparison with their own.[12]

Greek poverty in contrast with Persian wealth and luxury is an obvious and important theme in the *Histories*, to which the passage quoted above seems a rather trivial introduction. Along with 'factual' appraisal of the Hellenic diet, however, the Persians' attitude expressed here not only implies pity or disdain for the poor Greeks, but also suggests that they would be more voracious if but given the chance. That brief assessment of the difference in eating styles is recalled, I believe, at an important turning point much later in the narrative.

---

[11] For a magisterial discussion of credibility as an important goal of early historians, see Marincola (1997), 158–74 and passim. Dewald (1999), 222–3 with n. 4, offers a succinct explanation of the distinction between focalizer and narrator.

[12] On Greek attitudes about Persian excess with food and alcohol, see R. Thomas (2011), 245–6.

Non-Greeks on Greeks in Herodotus   161

After the Greek victory at Plataea (9.82), the Spartan commander Pausanias visits the quarters that had belonged to the Persian commander Mardonius – and before him, to Xerxes himself. He orders Mardonius' servants to prepare the kind of meal they made for their master. Thunderstruck by the luxurious food and furnishings set before him (9.82: ἐκπλαγέντα τὰ προκείμενα ἀγαθὰ), he then, as a joke, has his own staff cook up a Laconian meal. The contrast between the two dinners is too much for Pausanias to enjoy alone:

> When that [Persian] feast was ready, very different [from the Spartan meal], Pausanias laughed and sent for the generals of the Greeks. When they had assembled, pointing to the way each dinner was prepared, Pausanias said: 'Men of Hellas, I brought you here because I wanted to show you the foolishness of the leader of the Medes who, having a lifestyle such as this, came to us with our pitiable substance to take it away from us' (ὃς τοιήνδε δίαιταν ἔχων ἦλθε ἐς ἡμέας οὕτω ὀϊζυρὴν ἔχοντας ἀπαιρησόμενος). (9.82.2–3)

While Pausanias' culinary cultural comparison is framed as a joke, the scene in Xerxes' tent suggests that the generic Persians in Book 1 had a point: Greeks are poor, but they would eat more and better if they could! At this point, the narrative of Pausanias' behaviour after Plataea appears to corroborate the Persian attitude that pointed to potential Greek envy of Persian wealth and luxury.[13]

The culinary contrast so clearly on display here is hinted at elsewhere as well, also with disparaging cultural comparisons. A few generations earlier, the Lydian sage Sandanis advised Croesus that he would be foolish to cross the Halys River and invade the Persian land of Cappadocia: the Persians are so poor and primitive that they drink water instead of wine, and have no figs or other delicacies (1.71.1–3) – a situation that the narrator also verifies for Persia at that time (1.71.4).[14]

In 1.207.6 Croesus himself uses a similar argument when advising Cyrus how to overcome the Massagetae, a hardy tribe who enjoy no luxuries; rather than attacking them directly, he should pretend to withdraw from the Persian camp in their territory, but leave behind large stores of wine and rich food for the Massagetan troops to find, thus luring them into drunkenness and lethargy. This tactic succeeds: the Persians return and kill or capture many of the Massagetae, overcome by these unfamiliar

---

[13] See the extended commentary on this passage in Flower and Marincola (2002), 251–3.
[14] After being delayed by the omen of an eclipse (1.74), the Lydians fight a fierce but inconclusive battle against the Persian army (1.76).

162   DEBORAH BOEDEKER

and dangerous luxuries – but that attack will ultimately prove to be the end of Cyrus.[15]

As readers of Herodotus have noted,[16] the same Pausanias who marvelled at the Persian feast set in the quarters of Xerxes and Mardonius is also shown elsewhere to be developing a taste for Persian luxury and power. In an earlier passage, Herodotus tells his audience that after the war, the Spartan commander desired to marry a Persian princess, the daughter of Darius' cousin Megabates, because he 'fell in love with becoming ruler of Greece' (5.32: ἔρωτα σχὼν τῆς Ἑλλάδος τύραννος γενέσθαι).[17] This theme is picked up by Thucydides in his excursus on Pausanias' sojourn in Byzantium after the battle of Plataea (1.128–30). Thucydides declares that the Spartan commander asked to marry a daughter of Xerxes himself (1.128.7) and that he started to dress and behave like an aristocratic Persian (1.130). He even notes that the Spartan general 'had a Persian table set before him' (1.130.1: τράπεζάν τε Περσικὴν παρετίθετο), upsetting his fellow citizens to the extent that they summoned him back to Sparta. After being charged with other offenses related to self-aggrandisement, Pausanias ultimately sought asylum in a temple of Athena, where he was kept imprisoned until he starved (Thuc. 1.131–4).[18] In all these examples, we observe that the historical narrative favours the simpler diet and lifestyle, disparaged though it is by speakers in cross-cultural comparisons.

A few negative views of Hellenic practices that Herodotus attributes to non-Greeks might have sounded familiar to some in his audience. One example comes just after the Persian ethnography in Book 1. After defeating Croesus' ill-starred attempt to destroy his empire, Cyrus turns his attention to establishing control over the Greek cities of Ionia and Aeolia, which had refused his request to revolt against Croesus when he attacked Cyrus' realm, and now were seeking to establish favourable terms with the new regime. Cyrus turns down those terms – offered too late, he explains – so the Ionians send an embassy to Sparta to ask for help against Cyrus (1.141). The Spartans provide no military assistance to the Ionians, but they do send an envoy to inform Cyrus that they have proclaimed in a *rhesis* that

---

[15] Among its victims was Spargapises, son of the Massagetan queen, Tomyris, who took his own life in shame when he awoke in Persian custody. The queen leads her troops to victory in the ensuing battle; when she finds the corpse of Cyrus on the battlefield, in vengeful rage over his perfidy and bloodthirstiness, she stuffs the Persian king's head into a sack of blood (1.207, 211–14).

[16] E.g. Pelling (2019), 117.

[17] Hornblower (1991–2008), i.211–19, discusses the ambitions of the post-Herodotean Pausanias; Munson (2001), 68–70, emphasizes Pausanias' ambivalence in the *Histories*. On *eros* in Herodotus, see Boedeker (2011), 231–2 and passim.

[18] For discussion of the political-historical background of Pausanias' fate, see again Hornblower (1991–2008), i.217–19, with references.

Non-Greeks on Greeks in Herodotus

he must not harm any city in Greek territory, or the Lacedaemonians would punish him (1.152). Cyrus asked who these Lacedaemonians were; when his question was answered he replied to the envoy:

> I have never been afraid of the kind of men who set aside a place in the middle of their city where they gather to swear oaths and then deceive each other (συλλεγόμενοι ἀλλήλους ὀμνύντες ἐξαπατῶσι).... He cast this word against all Greeks, because they have set up markets where they practice buying and selling (ὅτι ἀγορὰς στησάμενοι ὠνῇ τε καὶ πρήσι χρέωνται). The Persians themselves are not at all accustomed to using *agorai*; they have no *agora* at all. (1.153.2)[19]

What Herodotus' Cyrus says here is framed as a condemnation not so much of retail trade per se but of the lying and cheating that he considers endemic to it. The king's denunciation of deceit conforms to Persian *nomoi* as described in the ethnography: elite Persians teach their sons only three things – to ride horses, shoot the bow, and tell the truth (1.136.2: ἰχνεύειν καὶ τοξεύειν καὶ ἀληθίζεσθαι) – and Persians consider lying (τὸ ψεύδεσθαι) to be the most disgraceful action (1.138.1).

Cyrus roundly rebukes the Greek institution where buying and selling is linked to deception. But as Leslie Kurke and other scholars have pointed out, his rebuke resembles an opinion voiced by *Greek* sources, most notably a passage where the Megarian elegist Theognis bewails the mores of his non-noble fellow-citizens:[20]

> Kyrnus, this city is still a city, but the people are different,
>> people who formerly knew neither justice nor laws,
> but wore tattered goatskins about their sides
>> and lived outside the city like deer.
> And now they are noble, Polypaïdes, while those who were noble before
>> are now base. Who can endure the sight of this?
> They deceive (ἀπατῶσιν) one another, mock (γελῶντες) each other...
>> [*6 lines omitted here*]
>> there is no trust (πίστις) to be placed in their actions,
> but they love treachery, deceit, and craftiness
>> (δόλους ἀπάτας τε πολυπλοκίας τ')
>
> just like men beyond salvation (μηκέτι σωιζόμενοι).
> Theognis 53–9, 66–8 (trans. Gerber, adapted)[21]

---

[19] How and Wells on 1.125 note that this passage points to the 'contrast between the town life of the Greeks and the village life, feudal in its arrangement, of the Persians'.

[20] Kurke (1989), cited with approval in Asheri, Lloyd, and Corcella (2007), 180.

[21] Cf. Thgn. 1109–14 for similar language and sentiment.

164 DEBORAH BOEDEKER

Cyrus' dictum thus reflects sentiments expressed by an archaic Greek poet, one who decidedly identifies with an elite perspective (here and elsewhere framed as *agathoi* vs. *kakoi*). For Theognis, the newcomers make his city almost unrecognizable, not only by their rustic dress and manners, but especially by their untrustworthy, deceptive, and tricky dealings. For King Cyrus, such banausic cheaters evidently lack the character and training that would make them good warriors; hence, one supposes, he has no fear of them.

Cyrus' characterization of (Hellenic) agora-based deception is slightly complicated by the ensuing narrative: immediately after he voices this opinion, he appoints Tabalus, a Persian, to rule Sardis and a Lydian, Pactyes, to be in charge of all its gold (1.153.3). But as soon as the king departs from the city, Pactyes leads a revolt against him, using the wealth of Sardis to pay for his mercenaries (1.154). Cyrus has misjudged the trustworthiness of his *own* (non-Greek) appointee. We should bear in mind, however, that Pactyes is a Lydian, and that the agora, that hotbed of deceit, is a prominent feature of the Lydian city where Cyrus proclaims his antipathy to this institution: it is mentioned no fewer than three times in the later dramatic description of the burning of that city (5.101.2).

Another opinion about Greek customs, this one attributed not to an individual such as Cyrus but to Persians in general, also recalls thoughts voiced by an early Greek poet. In the ethnography, Herodotus reports that it is not Persian custom to have statues, temples, or altars of gods[22] – 'and those who do they charge with foolishness (μωρίην ἐπιφέρουσι), because it seems to me [says Herodotus], they do not consider the gods to be of the same nature as men (οὐκ ἀνθρωποφυέας ἐνόμισαν τοὺς θεούς), as the Greeks do' (1.131.1).[23]

This sentiment resonates strongly with several fragments of Xenophanes, which also suggest that humans (not Greeks specifically) are foolish in the anthropomorphic way they imagine and depict gods:

> But mortals imagine that the gods were born (γεννᾶσθαι)
> And have their own clothing and voice and body (DK 21 B 14)

---

[22] David Asheri, in Asheri, Lloyd, and Corcella (2007), 166 on 1.131.1, reports that the lack of anthropomorphic images of deities reflects actual Persian religious practice. How and Wells i.111–12 on 1.131.1 note that this *nomos* was somewhat inconsistently carried out.

[23] The resemblance between Xenophanes and the non-anthropomorphic gods of Herodotus' Persians is not often discussed, but see R. Thomas (2011), 242, and especially Raaflaub (2002), 157: 'Xenophanes' critique of Homer's and Hesiod's stories about all too human gods and of the concept of anthropomorphic deities (DK 21 B 11–16) is incorporated into the description of Persian customs (1.131, cf. 2.53).'

Ethiopians say their gods are flat-nosed and dark-skinned,
And Thracians that theirs are blue-eyed and red-haired' (DK B 16)

But if cattle and horses or lions had hands
And could draw with their hands and make works of art as men do,
They would each make images of the gods (θεῶν ἰδέας)
with bodies like themselves,
horses like horses and cattle like cattle. (DK B 15)

Here, as throughout his work, Herodotus is respectful of sacred rites and beliefs. But it seems likely that in attributing to Persians the idea, also expressed by the Greek Xenophanes, that anthropomorphic gods are at best a questionable concept, he is encouraging his audience to consider critically some of their own cultural assumptions.

Occasionally, Herodotus attributes blanket opinions about 'others' (not only Greeks) to entire ethnic or cultural groups.[24] His Persians, for example, are highly chauvinistic: 'They honour (τιμῶσι) most of all those who live closest to them, and next those who are second-closest, and so on ... thinking that they are themselves in every way by far the best of human beings' (1.134.2: νομίζοντες ἑωυτοὺς εἶναι ἀνθρώπων μακρῷ τὰ πάντα ἀρίστους). Yet paradoxically, just after ascribing to the Persians this sense of cultural superiority, Herodotus asserts that of all peoples, they are 'most eager to learn about and adopt foreign customs' (ξεινικὰ δὲ νόμαια Πέρσαι προσίενται ἀνδρῶν μάλιστα) – for example, they dress in Median style, wear Egyptian breastplates into battle, and practise pederasty learned from the Greeks (1.135). These juxtaposed statements allow the audience to conclude that Persians are inconsistent in their attitudes toward other cultures: ideologically, they deem foreigners to be less worthy of honour, but in practice they show themselves eager to take up foreign ways.

In contrast, we are told that Egyptians 'refrain from using Greek and in general *all* foreign customs' (2.91.1: ἑλληνικοῖσι δὲ νομαίοισι φεύγουσι χρᾶσθαι, τὸ δὲ σύμπαν εἰπεῖν, μηδ' ἄλλων μηδαμὰ μηδαμῶν ἀνθρώπων νομαίοισι).[25] In keeping with this binary 'us versus them' distinction, Egyptians (like Greeks) categorize as *barbaroi* all who do not speak their language (2.158.5: βαρβάρους δὲ πάντας οἱ Αἰγύπτιοι καλέουσι τοὺς μὴ σφίσι ὁμογλώσσους).[26]

---

[24] See Munson (2001), 118 with n. 220, who labels such statements 'universal cultural chauvinism'.

[25] Herodotus then describes the anomalous worship in the city of Chemmis of a figure he calls 'Perseus'; see Alan Lloyd's discussion in Asheri, Lloyd, and Corcella (2007), 203–4 on 2.91.2–6.

[26] Rood (2006a), 298, argues that this Egyptian resemblance to the Greek view of foreigners could encourage Herodotus' audience to take a more relativistic view of their own assumptions about cultural superiority: they are foreigners to Egyptians just as Egyptians are to them.

166   DEBORAH BOEDEKER

The Scythians also avoid adopting foreign, particularly Greek, ways, as is demonstrated by the dramatic narratives of Scyles and Anacharsis (4.76.2).[27] Anacharsis travelled widely and gained wisdom, including knowledge of the mystery rites of the Mother of the Gods, which he observed in the Milesian colony of Cyzicus. When he returned home safely, he fulfilled a vow to the goddess, by practising her rites privately in a deep forest. Unfortunately, he was seen doing this by a Scythian who reported it to the king, Saulius. The king came, personally observed Anacharsis, and killed him with a shot from his bow (4.76.5); Herodotus adds that he learned this king was Anacharsis' own brother (4.76.6). Anacharsis even suffered *damnatio memoriae* as a result: 'And now if anyone asks about Anacharsis, the Scythians say they know nothing about him; this is because he left his homeland for Greece and took up the customs of foreigners' (4.76.6).[28]

An even more colourful example of Scythian animosity toward Greek customs is the story of their king Scyles. Scyles' father was the Scythian king Areiapeithes, but his mother was a Greek woman from Istia, who taught him to speak and write her language. King Areiapeithes was assassinated, and Scyles was expected to take his father's Scythian wife as his own. Instead, dissatisfied with the Scythian lifestyle, he became more and more Hellenized (4.78.3: πολλὸν πρὸς τὰ Ἑλληνικὰ μᾶλλον τετραμμένος ἦν). He spent extended periods as a private citizen, living in the Greek city of Borysthenes (better known as Olbia) on the Black Sea, with a Greek wife. The king's Scythian subjects were to know nothing about this, of course (4.78).

Then 'since he had to come to a bad end' (ἐπείτε δὲ ἔδεέ οἱ κακῶς γενέσθαι), Scyles set his heart on being initiated in the rites of Bacchic Dionysus (4.79.1: ἐπεθύμησε Διονύσῳ Βακχείῳ τελεσθῆναι). At that point the god struck Scyles' grand house in Olbia with lightning and burned it to the ground; the king did not heed the warning, however, but went ahead with his sacred revels (4.79.1–2). An Olbian Greek told a group of Scythians that their own king was involved in the very Bacchic frenzy that they criticized the Greeks for, 'for they [the Scythians] say it is not seemly to seek out a god who leads people to go mad' (4.79.3: οὐ γὰρ φασὶ οἰκὸς εἶναι θεὸν ἐξευρίσκειν τοῦτον ὅστις μαίνεσθαι ἐνάγει ἀνθρώπους). The Olbian then brought the Scythians to observe their Bacchic king; they in

---

[27] Hartog (1988), 61–83, provides a multi-sided analysis of Anacharsis and Scyles, with special attention to their connection with ecstatic rites.
[28] On the 'legend' of Anacharsis, see Asheri, Lloyd, and Corcella (2007), on 4.76–7.

Non-Greeks on Greeks in Herodotus

turn told the Scythian army what they had seen. This disclosure led to the pursuit and capture of Scyles by an army led by his brother Octamasades, who was involved in a coup against him,[29] and soon to the king's decapitation by his own brother (4.80.1–4).[30]

Herodotus concludes the Scyles episode with a recapitulation: 'In this way the Scythians hold tight to their own customs, and they give punishments like these to those who supplement them with foreign practices' (4.80.5: οὕτω μὲν περιστέλλουσι τὰ σφέτερα νόμαια Σκύθαι, τοῖσι δὲ παρακτωμένοισι ξεινικοὺς νόμους τοιαῦτα ἐπιτίμια διδοῦσι). The power of the Scythian rejection of Greek customs is reinforced by the fact that both these royal Scythians were killed by their own brothers, a detail that Herodotus mentions pointedly in each case, but without calling attention to the parallel.

Each of these stories presents aspects of Greek culture, mystery cults in particular, as practices that degrade even Scythian kings through their exotic and extravagant rites. In his ethnographies, Herodotus normally focalizes through the lens of Greeks looking at exotic 'others',[31] but in the stories of Anacharsis and Scyles[32] he switches perspective to give his Greek audience a taste of how they appear to barbarians.

Comments on cultures such as Egypt and Scythia that reject foreign practices, so memorably illustrated by the tales of Anacharsis and Scyles, do not make explicit how the narrator himself evaluates wholesale rejection or disdain of foreign ways. Elsewhere, however, Herodotus emphatically and in his own person disagrees with gross disrespect for the customs of other groups (an attitude attributed only to non-Greeks). The clearest example of such disrespect comes in the description of Cambyses' contempt for Egyptian religious practices, which extended to his personally killing the divine Apis bull calf (3.27–9).[33] Herodotus declares that such actions prove the king was quite insane (ἐμάνη μεγάλως): since every human group considers its own customs to be by far the best (νομίζουσι

---

[29] In Asheri, Lloyd, and Corcella (2007), 638–40, Aldo Corcella attempts with due caution to reconstruct the historical background of the Scythian power struggle underlying the events of Hdt. 4.80.

[30] As often recognized, the parallel is unmistakable to the *Greek* story of Pentheus, maddened by Dionysus and torn apart by his mother Agave and other Maenads, as memorably dramatized in Euripides' *Bacchae* a decade or so after the death of Herodotus.

[31] See François Hartog's influential structuralist interpretation of how Herodotus uses 'the imaginary Scythians' as 'others' vis-à-vis the Greeks: Hartog (1988), 61–192. Rosaria Munson's balanced approach incorporates many of Hartog's insights: Munson (2001), 107–23 and passim.

[32] On Anacharsis and Scyles, see Hartog (1988), 62–84 and Munson (2001), 115–23.

[33] Not insignificantly, in 3.64.3, Cambyses dies when he accidentally stabs himself in the thigh, the very place where he had stabbed Apis.

πολλόν τι καλλίστους τοὺς ἑωυτῶν νόμους ἕκαστοι εἶναι), only a madman would laugh at a people's deep-seated traditions (3.38.1–2).[34]

He illustrates this truth with the subsequent passage (3.38.3): Cambyses' successor Darius summoned two groups of Persian subjects – certain unspecified Greeks and the Callatiae of India – and asked them how much money it would take to get them to change the way they treat the bodies of their dead parents (the Greeks, by burning; the Callatiae, by eating them). Each group refused to commit such an abomination at any price. Speaking in the first person, Herodotus concludes (3.38.4), 'So these things have become customary practices (νενόμισται), and it seems to me that Pindar was correct to have said in a poem that custom is king of all' (νόμον πάντων βασιλέα ... εἶναι).[35] This seems consistent with Herodotus' practice of describing at length, with interest but not mockery, the *nomoi* of many peoples, as he recounts the growth of the Persian Empire.

Herodotus' practice of mirroring to a Greek audience what their customs look like to others, as with the Scythians observing ecstatic Hellenic mystery cults, might call to mind Robert Burns' famous prayer 'O wad some Power the Giftie gie us / to see oursels as ithers see us, / it wad frae mony a blunder free us, / An' foolish notion' ('To a Louse', lines 43–8). The speaker voices this prayer for self-knowledge as he watches a louse creep around on the bonnet of a vain lady while she sits in church, oblivious to the unseemly intruder that is attracting an unwanted kind of attention from others in the congregation who are winking and pointing at her (lines 41–2: 'Thae winks and finger-ends, I dread / Are notice takin!'). Twenty-two centuries before Burns, was Herodotus interested in showing members of his Greek audience their flaws by describing how 'others' viewed them?

In some cases, pointing out Hellenic imperfections may indeed be a goal, or an effect, of having non-Greeks comment on Greek practices, as with the highly critical assessment of Greek hoplite warfare offered by Xerxes' cousin Mardonius.[36] This comes as the king is planning to launch an invasion against Greece to exact vengeance on the Athenians for the destruction of Sardis[37] and the subsequent defeat of Persian forces at Marathon. Xerxes calls an assembly of the noblest Persian to solicit their

---

[34] On this incident, see further Munson (1991); Christ (1994), 187–9; Rood (2006a), 298–300.

[35] See the succinct remarks of Asheri in Asheri, Lloyd, and Corcella (2007), 224.

[36] For general discussion of this passage, see Pelling (2006c), 108–10.

[37] According to Herodotus, the burning of the Lydian capital was unintentional: see 5.99–101.

opinions, making it clear that it is his intention to invade (7.8β). In terms perhaps flattering to Herodotus' audience, Xerxes declares that once Greece has been subdued, there will be no limit to the Persian realm: no *polis* or *ethnos* would dare to challenge it (7.8γ).

Mardonius is the first to respond, with effusive praise for the king and support for his plan. He declares that there is nothing to fear from the Greeks: they are few, poor, and weak in battle (7.9α). Then he proceeds to criticize their battle strategy:

> And further, as I hear, the Greeks are accustomed to wage wars very foolishly through stupidity and lack of sense. When they declare war against each other, after finding the best, most even ground they go down and fight there, with the result that the winners depart with great harm; I won't even begin to tell about the losers, for they are totally destroyed. [2] Since they speak the same language, they ought to use heralds or messengers to overcome their difference, or any means besides fighting. But if they simply *must* make war against each other, both sides should figure out where they would be hardest to defeat and make their attempt there. (Hdt. 7.9β)

Despite his sensible observations about Greek hoplite battle tactics (and, by extension, about the senselessness of 'optional' warfare), Mardonius' advice to Xerxes is compromised by his motivation. Herodotus previously reported that earlier, before Xerxes was inclined to attack Greece, Mardonius was encouraging such an invasion 'because he was eager for new undertakings and wanted to rule Greece himself' (7.6.1: νεωτέρων ἔργων ἐπιθυμητὴς ἐὼν καὶ θέλων αὐτὸς τῆς Ἑλλάδος ὕπαρχος εἶναι).

Mardonius' rash speech at the council is followed by a counterargument from Xerxes' uncle Artabanus, who speaks at length against going to war with Hellas, drawing on examples from Persian experiences, including his own, in foreign campaigns. His argument could have been further supported by something very relevant that conspicuously is not mentioned here: the fairly recent Persian defeat at Marathon, described by Herodotus in a detailed narrative (esp. 6.111–17), and certainly familiar to many in his audience. In this battle the Athenians with a few allies had fought bravely, cleverly, and victoriously (using their hoplite formation!) against a Persian invasion.[38] Later, Herodotus' stirring narrative will show how a few Spartans would battle to their deaths against the massive Persian forces

---

[38] In 7.8β.3, Xerxes refers to this sequence of events as a crime to be punished. Significantly, he too does not explicitly mention Marathon, but refers obliquely to 'what they did to us when Datis and Artaphrenes led an expedition that disembarked in their land'. As with Artabanus' later speech, here too a Persian speaks only very allusively about the Greek victory.

at Thermopylae (7.210–12, 219–25), and how the Persians were defeated by allied Greek armies at Plataea (9.58–70) and Mycale (9.97–104). Artabanus then points out many dangers for the proposed invasion, ending with 'but if they attack you with their ships and defeat you in a sea battle, and then sail to the Hellespont and destroy the bridges there, that is a dire thing for the king' (7.10β.1–2: τοῦτο δὴ βασιλεῦ γίνεται δεινόν). Here too Artabanus' warning proves strikingly accurate: following the Persian defeat by sea at Salamis (8.83–96), the Athenians will indeed dismantle the Hellespont bridges (already destroyed by a storm: 8.117) at the end of the *Histories* (9.121). What comes to pass later in the narrative therefore proves Mardonius' assessment of the Greeks to be dreadfully wrong. Artabanus now turns to Mardonius, criticizing what he has said about the Hellenes: 'But you, Mardonius son of Gobryas, stop saying foolish things about the Greeks, who do not deserve to be spoken of disparagingly (παῦσαι λέγων λόγους ματαίους περὶ Ἑλλήνων οὐκ ἐόντων ἀξίων φλαύρως ἀκούειν). By slandering (διαβάλλων) the Greeks you urge the king to go to war; for that purpose, I think, you are unfurling all your zeal' (7.10η.1).

We see here that when he has a non-Greek point out Greek weaknesses, Herodotus is not interested simply in showing his audience how they might do things better, even if some of those disadvantages (e.g. their poverty and comparatively small population) are verified by his historical narrative. He also illustrates that the way an 'outsider' describes the Greeks, or anticipates their behaviour, is largely subjective. Thus, Xerxes' assessment of the Greeks differs from Mardonius': according to the king they are so formidable that no other force could stop Persia if he defeats them; Mardonius instead emphasizes how *easy* it will be to defeat them. Even if (as here) what 'others' say about Greeks is not an outright falsehood, in its incomplete truth it may be used to mislead the internal audience.

Several times non-Greeks comment on the Olympics, the iconic Greek cultural phenomenon. In two very different contexts, unlike most passages we have seen, Greeks are not just spoken about; they converse with 'others' about the greatest panhellenic festival. First, in Herodotus' lengthy ethnography of Egypt, a delegation of the Olympic game-hosters from Elea visits the wise Egyptians:

> While Psammis was ruler of Egypt messengers came from Elis, boasting, that of all people they had established the most fair and just contest at Olympia, maintaining that not even the Egyptians, the wisest of all men, could improve it.... [T]hereupon the king called together those Egyptians

Non-Greeks on Greeks in Herodotus

said to be the wisest. The Egyptians came together and learned from the Eleans everything they did pertaining to the contest; after explaining this, the Eleans said that they had come to learn whether the Egyptians could discover anything more just. They, after taking counsel, asked the Eleans whether their fellow citizens participated in the contest. The Eleans answered that they did, and that any Greek who wished to was allowed to compete, from their own and other cities alike. But the Egyptians said that in setting it up this way they fell short of total fairness, for there was no way that they would not prefer a fellow-citizen who was competing, treating the outsider unjustly. If they truly wanted to set it up fairly and they had come to Egypt for this purpose, they told them to admit only outsiders as contestants, and none of the Eleans. That is what the Egyptians suggested to the Eleans. (2.160.1–4)[39]

Herodotus characterizes these Eleans as boasting (αὐχέοντες), a primarily poetic verb that appears only one other time in the *Histories*, as we shall see shortly.

This anecdote allows Herodotus to show a subset of Hellenes (the Eleans, organizers of the Olympics) how they appear to non-Greeks – or perhaps how any group too confident in its virtue might appear. His narrative highlights and undercuts Elean pride, showing their defeat by the Egyptians' superior wisdom. At the same time, Herodotus reports that the king took the trouble of assembling the wisest Egyptians – whose reputation for superior wisdom has been acknowledged but challenged here. They did not simply reply to the question, but first deliberated (βουλευσάμενοι) and then asked a follow-up question, in order to discover a flaw in Elean judging procedures. A frisson of jealous pride in cultural achievements on both sides makes the encounter especially engaging, but the Egyptians win the contest of wisdom and fairness by making a valid point,[40] while the Eleans silently disappear from the narrative.[41]

In a more familiar example, Herodotus has us look at the Olympic games through non-Greek eyes in a scene that focuses on the ideology behind the famous olive-branch crown. After their victory at Thermopylae and the indecisive sea battle of Artemisium, Xerxes and his entourage are visited by some informants who tell them about the great festival that is now going on:

---

[39] For background on this passage, see the commentary of A. B. Lloyd (1975–88), 165–7.
[40] As Munson (2001), 145–6 with n. 33, rightly points out.
[41] Discussing this embassy from the perspective of the history of athletics, Kyle (2008), 149–51, is dubious about its plausibility, and notes (149 n. 2) that the same story is applied to a different pharaoh, Amasis, in Diodorus Siculus 1.95.2; in that version the king answers the question himself.

172   DEBORAH BOEDEKER

> There came to them some deserters, a few men from Arcadia, who needed a
> source of livelihood and were looking for work. Bringing them into the
> king's presence, the Persians asked them about what the Greeks were doing
> (one man said this to them, speaking for all). They told them that the
> Greeks were celebrating the Olympic festival, and were watching an athletic
> and an equestrian competition. He asked what the prize was for which they
> competed, and they told him about the olive wreath that was awarded.
> Then Tritantaichmes the son of Artabanus uttered a very noble thought,
> which got him charged with cowardice by the king: when he learned that
> the prize was a wreath and not money, he could not stay silent but said in
> front of everyone there, 'Ah Mardonius (παπαῖ Μαρδόνιε), what kind of
> men have you led us here to fight? They compete not for worldly goods but
> for the sake of excellence' (οὐ περὶ χρημάτων τὸν ἀγῶνα ποιεῦνται ἀλλὰ
> περὶ ἀρετῆς). That is what he said. (8.26)[42]

Tritantaichmes' exclamation παπαῖ, a *hapax legomenon* in Herodotus, is a
poetic word attested often in tragedy and comedy, but never before in extant
prose. This striking diction, together with the narrator's unique and arresting
description of the remark as a 'very noble thought' (γνώμην γενναιοτάτην),
gives the Persian's outburst an emotional intensity, underscoring the noble
ideology that he attributes to one of the Greeks' most cherished national
traditions. We may contrast it with the Egyptians' undercutting the boastful
Eleans about another aspect of the same tradition. It stands in contrast also
with what many in Herodotus' audience knew about the additional privileges
Olympic victors enjoyed: for some, supplemental gifts from their local
communities such as free dinners for life at public expense; for all, lasting
prestige with its social and political consequences.[43]

These Arcadian informers, while Greeks, are not idealized as are the elite
Olympian competitors they describe. Rather, they are deserters and medizers,
looking for work from the Persians, presumably as mercenaries. They resemble
in a way the deposed king Demaratus, another insider-outsider whose situation
in life has been lowered, who now as Xerxes' advisor provides him with accurate
cultural commentary on Spartan mores before and during battle.

Xerxes, for example, is incredulous when he sees the small number of
Spartans who will oppose his huge army at Thermopylae; he asks
Demaratus how they will behave in the face of such a mighty threat.
Demaratus promises him that, whatever the odds, the Spartans will fight to

---

[42] See Konstan (1987), 61–2, for a cogent analysis of the contrast between περὶ χρημάτων and περὶ
    ἀρετῆς in this passage.
[43] Kyle (2008), 157: 'The passage cleverly misrepresents the general practice of Greek athletics overall,
    for Herodotus knew that most games were chrematitic and had material prizes.'

Non-Greeks on Greeks in Herodotus

the death, in obedience to their *nomos*. Hearing this, Xerxes laughed (γελάσας)[44] and said,

> Demaratus, what kind of word have you have spoken, that a thousand men will fight with such a great army! ... But if you men who boast (αὐχέετε) like that[45] are similar to yourself and the other Greeks who come to speak with me, and are about the same size, then see to it that what you say is not just empty noise (ὅρα μὴ μάτην κόμπος ὁ λόγος οὗτος εἰρημένος ἦ). (7.103.1–2)

Xerxes' sceptical attitude is proved wrong, needless to say, by the subsequent course of events: Leonidas and the Three Hundred fall fighting bravely, in one of the *Histories'* most compelling narratives.[46]

Herodotus' Greeks, however, are by no means *only* brave and freedom-loving and motivated by ἀρετή. As their Persian adversaries suspect, they are also susceptible to other motivations. Greek disunity – personal or individual *polis* interests gaining priority over the fragile (and only partial) alliance of Greek states, always a possibility and a recurring theme in the account – becomes an increasingly urgent theme as the war moves on.[47] And the advantages of this tendency do not go unnoticed by the Persians.

After Thermopylae, Xerxes' counsellors disagree on exactly how he should deploy his land and sea forces, but all agree that he should seek to foment Greek disunity. At a staff meeting following the indecisive sea battle at Artemisium, Artemisia, the brilliant Greek queen of Persian-ruled Halicarnassus, advises Xerxes not to hasten into another sea battle as he planned to do (this would be the forthcoming Battle of Salamis, which turned out to be disastrous for Xerxes). She says:

> I will tell you how I think your enemies' fortunes will turn out. If you do not rush to undertake a sea battle, but keep your ships here, staying near land, or even advancing into the Peloponnese, then, master, you will easily accomplish what you intended when you came here. The Greeks are not able to hold out against you for long, but you will scatter them, and each of them will flee to their own cities. For I hear that they have no food on this island, and if you march your troops to the Peloponnese, it is not likely that the men who came from there will stay in place here, nor will they care about fighting at sea for the sake of Athens. (8.68β)

---

[44] On laughter as an ominous reaction, see Lateiner (1977).

[45] This is the second and final appearance of the verb αὐχέω in the *Histories* (see 2.160 for the first: discussed above p. XXX); both times the charge of boasting is applied to Greeks by non-Greeks.

[46] On Demaratus' declining influence as an advisor to Xerxes, see Boedeker (1987), 195–6.

[47] Harrison (2002), 566–7, provides a succinct discussion of Greek disunity during the war.

174 DEBORAH BOEDEKER

Xerxes appreciates Artemisia's advice, but does not act on it (8.69.2). Yet the ensuing narrative will show how shaky the alliance was:[48] the queen's perspective was realistic.

Finally, the two general categories of Hellenic poverty and questionable unity combine in the belief expressed by non-Greeks that bribery will convince Greeks to separate from their fragile alliance against the Persian forces. Before battle was joined at Plataea, with Xerxes having returned to Persia, his commanders Artabazus and Mardonius debated what to do. Artabazus advised that the Persians retreat within the walls of their ally Thebes, where 'they could sit at their ease' and send bribes of Persian gold and silver to the leading men in all Greek poleis:

> [If they do this, he said] the Greeks would quickly give up their freedom; but do not let the Persians risk again joining battle.... Mardonius' argument, however, was more forceful and reckless and completely uncompromising (ἰσχυροτέρη τε καὶ ἀγνωμονεστέρη καὶ οὐδαμῶς συγγινωσκομένη). He said that he thought that their army was much stronger than that of the Greeks, and that they should engage in battle as soon as possible so that they would not just watch more Greeks assemble than had done so already. (9.41.2–3a)

Mardonius' comment about Hellenic battle strength recalls what he said to Xerxes when he was urging the king to invade mainland Greece (7.9).[49] Here again, he is confident of victory against Greeks in open warfare, despite Persian experiences of defeats at Marathon in the past and the recent sea battle at Salamis, as well as the mighty resistance displayed at Thermopylae – despite omens (mentioned at 9.41.4) warning against the plan to attack at this point. Mardonius prevails in the current debate, however, and soon he will be killed in the Hellenes' great victory at Plataea (9.63), followed by the Persians' departure from mainland Greece.

Evidently, however, Artabazus' advice about how to defeat the Greeks was more realistic than Mardonius': the historical narrative here as often reveals the 'truth' to both internal and external audiences. Not only will it soon show that Mardonius' advice to rush to battle at Plataea was faulty, but even before the conference between Mardonius and Artabazus, the narrative has *already* indicated (to us, the external audience) that Greeks were susceptible to bribery, the tactic preferred by Artabazus.

---

[48] Examples include 7.206, 8.57, 8.72. On Herodotus' view of medizing Greeks, see Pelling (2019), 178.

[49] Quoted and discussed above, pp. 169–170.

Non-Greeks on Greeks in Herodotus   175

Bribery played an important role, for example, at the beginning of Book 8, when the Persian and Greek navies were gathering for battle at Artemisium, opposite the island of Euboea. The Euboean islanders rightly feared that the Greek alliance would split apart and abandon them. They bribed Themistocles with thirty talents to keep that from happening. Themistocles gave five talents to the Spartan commander Eurybiades and three to the Corinthian Adeimantus, with which he convinced them to stay and fight, while he kept for himself the twenty-two talents that remained.[50]

Here as elsewhere, then, the attitudes expressed by Persians toward Greeks can be checked against the 'facts' of the historical narrative. Accurate observations point to useful ways of dealing with their Greek foes. We see this in Artabanus' advice (the voice of wisdom and experience) to Xerxes *not* to cross the Hellespont and invade Hellas, in Artemisia's shrewd but unheeded advice to march into the Peloponnese and cause Greek cities there to desert the alliance,[51] and in the suggestion of Artabazus to send bribes to the leading men of Greek cities so that they would capitulate to Xerxes. Herodotus indicates the likely success of these strategies, but they are not accepted by the Persian commanders.

The malleable trope of 'non-Greeks speaking about Greeks' functions in the *Histories* in other ways as well, as we have seen. This device subtly reveals how mistakes in judgement may arise from cross-cultural perceptions and prejudices, as with Mardonius' repeated arguments (echoed at times by Xerxes) that the Greeks, few and poor and scarcely unified as they are, will not fight well and can be readily defeated by attacks from superior Persian forces. Such opinions may arise also from the speaker's selfish motivation, as made explicit by the narrator in the case of Mardonius, who describes the Greeks as weak and foolish because he wants Xerxes to invade their land and ultimately make him its ruler.

Moreover, as we have seen, some negative views of Hellenic practices that Herodotus attributes to non-Greeks are also found in *Greek* poets earlier than Herodotus. This occurs, for example, when Herodotus attributes to Persians the idea, also expressed by the Greek Xenophanes, that anthropomorphic gods are a highly questionable concept, or to Cyrus the complaint about deception and cheating of fellow-citizens in the agora, which echoes sentiments stressed by Theognis. Such echoes might

---

[50] For another Themistoclean bribe, see 8.112.2–3.

[51] Like the equally knowledgeable Demaratus, Artemisia is an 'insider/outsider', a Greek advisor of Xerxes, and thus better positioned to predict Greek behaviour.

encourage members of Herodotus' (Greek) audience to see aspects of their culture in a wider context; the criticism comes not just from 'outsiders', but it resonates with what they have heard from Greek voices as well. This is not to say, of course, that criticism from non-Greeks (e.g. Mardonius' criticism of internecine Greek warfare) could not be taken to heart as well.

Cultural prejudice can also mark groups or individuals in the *Histories* as unreasonable or inconsistent (the Persians who see themselves as best of all, but are most eager to adopt foreign practices), or overly savage (Cambyses brutally kills the Apis bull sacred to Egyptians, Scythians murder Anacharsis and Scyles because they were found ecstatically worshipping foreign gods). In contrast, Herodotus' carefully articulated position of cultural relativism, acknowledging every group's traditions (3.38) is made to seem a reasonable alternative.

The piquant stories where Herodotus shows the Greeks as 'others' by looking at them through the eyes of non-Greeks ultimately have the effect of pointing out cultural differences in *both* directions: the audience learns about how Greeks (i.e. they themselves) may appear to outsiders and also about the perspective from which these 'others' (non-Greeks) see the world. Cross-cultural descriptions of Greeks by non-Greeks is an aspect of the multifocal or dialogic technique Herodotus has developed: it seems that anyone in the *Histories* can become a speaker, whether accurately and truthfully or not. Along with the voice of the narrator, a kaleidoscope of perspectives come into play. We see in how many ways they can be used for the purposes of the one recounting them.[52] This technique, I submit, is not only an effective device for enlivening the narrative; it also raises unsettling questions.

---

[52] On dialogism or 'heteroglossia' in Herodotus, see Dewald (1999), esp. 247; Boedeker (2003), esp. 30–1; for fundamental groundwork in this approach, Bakhtin (1981), esp. 11–21.

PART III

Performing Collective and Personal Authority

CHAPTER 9

Singing and Dancing Pindar's Authority

Lucia Athanassaki

This chapter revisits the issue of poetic authority, focusing on a selection of Pindar's song-dances, mainly epinicians, paeans, dithyrambs, and hyporchemes. It responds to John Marincola's introductory discussion of the background to historiographical authority in his *Authority and Tradition in Greek Historiography*:

> In archaic lyric poetry, the invocation of the Muses remains common, although one can also see traces of new validations interspersed amongst the traditional ones: Theognis invokes the gods at the outset of his poems, yet speaks of some of the content of his poem as derived from 'the experience of my elders'; Mimnermus appeals to eyewitnesses as validators for his description of a fighter's prowess in battle; Solon calls the Earth to witness for his political actions.[1]

Marincola's point is well taken: although Theognis, Mimnermus, and Solon keep the poet's privileged relationship with the Muse, they broaden the model of authority to include other factors such as collective human experience and eyewitness accounts. Moreover, Marincola chose poets who composed for the solo voice to illustrate his point – a wise choice, because the relationship of monodic poets with the Muse is fairly straightforward, as is the authority they claim for authoritative composition. As is the case with the historians too, the audience or the reader is invited to attribute the claimed authority to the author/speaker.

In this chapter I shall explore the question of authority focusing on the choral compositions of Pindar, who also broadens the traditional epic model of authority, in order to account for aspects of composition and performance for which the model of a one-to-one relationship with the

---

[1] Marincola (1997), 4. For helpful comments and suggestions on this chapter and earlier versions I wish to thank Peter Agócs, Myrto Aloumpi, Ewen L. Bowie, Stelios Chronopoulos, K. Scarlett Kingsley, Gregory Nagy, and Anastasia-Erasmia Peponi.

179

180   LUCIA ATHANASSAKI

Muse is inadequate. It is inadequate because a collective body of choreuts claims authority by invoking the Muse(s) and other deities. Despite the shift of scholarly attention to the performative aspects of archaic poetry in the 1980s, choral authority has not received the attention it deserves.[2] My focus on Pindar is dictated by considerations of space, but some of my observations are also valid for other choral poets.

Choral lyric was an audio-spectacle that required coordinated singing and dancing by smaller or larger groups of performers.[3] Moreover, the choral poets were responsible not only for composing the lyrics and the music but for training the choruses to sing and dance in unison. We do not know if they made decisions on costumes, but they might have chosen or advised on costumes on occasion. This multitask is very different from modern lyric experience. Verdi, for instance, was inspired by Victor Hugo and Alexandre Dumas' novels when he composed his amazing music for *Rigoletto* and *La Traviata*, but it was Francesco Maria Piave who wrote the libretti. Any contemporary re-performance of opera involves an increasingly intimidating number of experts in addition to the maestro, such as the chorus teacher, the ballet teacher, the stage director, and the costume-designer. I shall come back to opera after looking at the ancient song-dances because the paradigm of opera can offer valuable insight into lyric composers' ideas, sensibilities, and expectations, despite the fact that the ancient Greek audio spectacle cannot have been as complex as modern opera and that the ancient masters were as a rule responsible for the whole show.

The professed wisdom of the inscribed persona has been studied especially in the epinicians.[4] In revisiting the issue of authority I shall ask if Pindar's representations of his relationship with the gods and goddesses of music restrict divine inspiration only to the words (ἔπεα) or if they include his melodies and the movement of the chorus, that is, μουσική as a whole.[5]

---

[2] A notable exception is Nagy's wide-ranging discussion of the authority of the poet as chorus leader; see Nagy (1990), 341–82 (especially §27, §71, §75, and §78–81). See also below note 4.

[3] For *choreia* as synchronized singing and dancing, see Naerebout (2017) with references to earlier literature. Other scholars opt for more open models. See e.g. Lardinois (1996) and Nagy (2013).

[4] Recent discussions include Maslov (2015), who focuses on ἔπεα but takes into account the social and religious context; Kuhn-Treichel (2020–1) focuses on the inscribed relationship of the poetic 'I' with the Muses whom he considers metaphors. Earlier studies include Duchemin (1955); Athanassaki (1990); Lefkowitz (1991). Cf. Hornblower (2004), who explores the overlaps in the worlds and individuals presented by Pindar and Thucydides.

[5] For the traditional melodic patterns used by Pindar and other lyric poets, see Nagy (1990), 82–115.

The answer is not straightforward for a number of reasons, not least because only the words survive, and these frequently in fragmentary form. But despite the limitations of our evidence, the question is worth asking because, as we shall see, there are textual indications showing Pindar's holistic take on authority, that is, authoritative content, melody, and dance, an authority modelled after divine *choreia*.[6]

In what follows I shall argue that, in order to stress the divine quality and allure of the choral performance as an authoritative audio spectacle, Pindar gives the Graces a role equally prominent to that of the Muses in the artistic process, thus bringing to the surface the collaborative nature of the choral event and the social dimension of poetic authority:[7] Pindar's divine model of authority features the Muse(s), the Graces, and sometimes other gods associated with music, in their composite role as composers of words and melodies, singers, and *chorodidaskaloi*;[8] following this divine paradigm the human speaker/performer is depicted in a variety of divinely inspired musical activities, sometimes in the presence of the Muses, the Graces, and other gods. The Graces (*Charites*), divine person-ifications of reciprocal activities, values, and pleasures, were an ideal complement to the Muses to represent the complexities of poetic authority in choral composition and performance, a collaborative artistic project and event.

Before turning to the discussion of Pindar's holistic take on the divine authority of his medium, I wish to look briefly at two examples of his remarkable range of variations on this theme. The first example displays the traditional focus on words. It comes from the conclusion of the *Fourth Pythian*, where the speaker extols a spring of divine words that Damophilus found in Thebes (*P.* 4.299: παγὰν ἀμβροσίων ἐπέων).[9] The second comes from the *Third Olympian* and catches a glimpse of

---

[6] My take is similar to Gregory Nagy's broad conception of authorship and authority, which encompasses words, melodic patterns and traditions, and dance. Nagy, however, looks at archaic and classical choral lyric at large and deploys different evidence and argumentation: Nagy (1990) 82–115, 339–81, and passim.

[7] For the role of *Charis*, see Duchemin (1955), 54–94, who takes account of the performative aspect. See also MacLachlan (1993), 41–55 and 87–123, with a very useful discussion of the importance of *charis* in Bacchylides. For *charis* in the epinician economy of gift-exchange, see Kurke (1991); Day (2010) focuses on *charis* in dedicatory epigrams without losing sight of their affinities with hymnic poetry.

[8] For the divine chorus as model of human choruses, see Nagy (1996), 56, who draws attention to Plato's formulation (θείου χοροῦ) in *Phaedrus* 247a.

[9] Cf. *N.* 9.7 where the song is designated as divine (θεσπεσία . . . ἀοιδά).

182 LUCIA ATHANASSAKI

the composer/performer in the course of the creative process. Our speaker relates how he came up with his divinely inspired innovative composition in the presence of the Muse:

> κλεινὰν Ἀκράγαντα γεραίρων εὔχομαι,
> Θήρωνος Ὀλυμπιονίκαν
>   ὕμνον ὀρθώσαις, ἀκαμαντοπόδων
> ἵππων ἄωτον. Μοῖσα δ᾽ οὕτω ποι παρέ-
> στα μοι νεοσίγαλον εὑρόντι τρόπον
> Δωρίῳ φωνὰν ἐναρμόξαι πεδίλῳ   5
> ἀγλαόκωμον· ἐπεὶ χαίταισι μὲν
>   ζευχθέντες ἔπι στέφανοι
> πράσσοντί με τοῦτο θεόδματον χρέος,
> φόρμιγγά τε ποικιλόγαρυν
>   καὶ βοὰν αὐλῶν ἐπέων τε θέσιν
> Αἰνησιδάμου παιδὶ συμμεῖξαι πρεπόν-
> τως, ἅ τε Πίσα με γεγωνεῖν· τᾶς ἄπο
> θεόμοροι νίσοντ᾽ ἐπ᾽ ἀνθρώπους ἀοιδαί[10] (O. 3.2–10)   10

Honouring famous Acragas I pray, having raised up Theron's Olympic victory hymn, for the finest reward for horses with untiring feet. With this in view the Muse stood beside me somehow as I found a shining new way to join to Dorian sandal a voice of splendid celebration, because crowns bound fast upon his hair exact from me this divinely inspired debt: to mix fittingly the varied voices of the lyre, the cry of pipes, and the composition of words for Aenesidamus' son; and Pisa too bids me lift up my voice, from which [sc. Pisa] divinely allotted songs come to men.

The image of the spring of divine words in the *Fourth Pythian* indicates the constant supply of fresh authoritative compositions in terms of content. The representation of the composer in the creative process at a moment of a splendid innovative musical achievement in the *Third Olympian* broadens the image so as to include melody, rhythm, and dance. Pindar's choice of denoting rhythm by using the term for something material, πέδιλον, suggests that he was thinking of the dance step, something that one of the ancient commentators also proposed (Σ *Ol.* 3.9b: τὴν βάσιν οὖν εἶπε). The image here shares important differences and similarities with the famous invocation of the lyre in the *First Pythian*:

---

[10] Pindaric quotations are taken from Snell-Maehler and Maehler's editions. Translations are mine, unless otherwise noted.

Singing and Dancing Pindar's Authority

Χρυσέα φόρμιγξ, Ἀπόλλωνος καὶ ἰοπλοκάμων
σύνδικον Μοισᾶν κτέανον· τᾶς ἀκούει
  μὲν βάσις ἀγλαΐας ἀρχά,
πείθονται δ' ἀοιδοὶ σάμασιν
ἀγησιχόρων ὁπόταν προοιμίων
  ἀμβολὰς τεύχῃς ἐλελιζομένα.   (*P.* 1.1–4)

Golden Lyre, rightful possession of Apollo and the Muses with the violet-locks; to you the step listens, the beginning of splendid festivity, and the singers heed your notes, when with vibrating strings you strike up the chorus-leading preludes.

Both descriptions draw attention to the divine origin and quality of the musical event, but whereas the *Third Olympian* offers a rare glimpse of the creative process, the *First Pythian* focuses on the lyre and represents choral performance as an incipient event. It is also worth noting the strong emphasis on the divine origin of the song in the *Third Olympian*: it is called a divinely inspired debt (θεόδματον χρέος), and divinely allotted (θεόμοροι ἀοιδαί), while the composer's innovative endeavour takes place in the Muse's imagined presence. Diction, literal and metaphorical, suggests that Pindar was thinking of all components of *choreia* (Δωρίῳ φωνὰν ἐναρμόξαι πεδίλῳ ἀγλαόκωμον, φόρμιγγά τε ποικιλόγαρυν καὶ βοὰν αὐλῶν ἐπέων τε θέσιν ... συμμεῖξαι πρεπόντως).

Pindar as a Choral Composer

Although the intended mode of performance of the epinicians, solo versus choral, has been intensely debated, Pindar's production shows that his formation was that of a choral poet. The Alexandrian scholars classified Pindar's poetry in seventeen books according to genre: hymns (one book), paeans (one book), dithyrambs (two books), *prosodia* (two books), *partheneia* (three books), hyporchemes (two books), *encomia* (one book), epinicians (four books), and *threnoi* (one book).[11] Clearly, the bulk of the poet's production indicates that he composed for choruses far more often than for the solo voice.

It is reasonable to assume that Pindar trained choruses for festivals in Thebes, Delphi, Athens, and elsewhere. The evidence about choral poets as *chorodidaskaloi* is scant and late but extremely valuable. Athenaeus, for instance, offers precious testimony, which he attributes to Aristocles,

---

[11] See Pfeiffer (1968), 183–4; Race (1987).

184 LUCIA ATHANASSAKI

Aristoxenus, and Chamaeleon. The majority in Athenaeus' list are dramatists, but it is significant that he concludes with a reference to Pindar:

Καὶ Αἰσχύλος δὲ οὐ μόνον ἐξεῦρε τὴν τῆς στολῆς εὐπρέπειαν καὶ σεμνότητα, ἣν ζηλώσαντες οἱ ἱεροφάνται καὶ δᾳδοῦχοι ἀμφιέννυνται, ἀλλὰ καὶ πολλὰ σχήματα ὀρχηστικὰ αὐτὸς ἐξευρίσκων ἀνεδίδου τοῖς χορευταῖς. Χαμαιλέων γοῦν πρῶτον αὐτόν φησι σχηματίσαι τοὺς χοροὺς ὀρχηστοδιδασκάλοις οὐ χρησάμενον, ἀλλὰ καὶ αὐτὸν τοῖς χοροῖς τὰ σχήματα ποιοῦντα τῶν ὀρχήσεων, καὶ ὅλως πᾶσαν τὴν τῆς τραγῳδίας οἰκονομίαν εἰς ἑαυτὸν περιιστᾶν. ὑπεκρίνετο οὖν μετὰ τοῦ εἰκότος τὰ δράματα ... Φίλλις ὁ Δήλιος μουσικὸς τοὺς ἀρχαίους φησὶ κιθαρῳδοὺς κινήσεις ἀπὸ μὲν τοῦ προσώπου μικρὰς φέρειν, ἀπὸ ποδῶν δὲ πλείους, ἐμβατηρίους καὶ χορευτικάς. Ἀριστοκλῆς γοῦν φησιν ὅτι Τελέστης ὁ Αἰσχύλου ὀρχηστὴς οὕτως ἦν τεχνίτης ὥστε ἐν τῷ ὀρχεῖσθαι τοὺς Ἑπτὰ Ἐπὶ Θήβας φανερὰ ποιῆσαι τὰ πράγματα δι' ὀρχήσεως. φασὶ δὲ καὶ ὅτι οἱ ἀρχαῖοι ποιηταί, Θέσπις, Πρατίνας, Κρατῖνος, Φρύνιχος, ὀρχησταὶ ἐκαλοῦντο διὰ τὸ μὴ μόνον τὰ ἑαυτῶν δράματα ἀναφέρειν εἰς ὄρχησιν τοῦ χοροῦ, ἀλλὰ καὶ ἔξω τῶν ἰδίων ποιημάτων διδάσκειν τοὺς βουλομένους ὀρχεῖσθαι ... Ὀρχήσεις δὲ ἐθνικαὶ αἵδε· Λακωνικαί, Τροιζήνιαι, Ἐπιζεφύριοι, Κρητικαί, Ἰωνικαί, Μαντινικαί, ἃς προκρίνει Ἀριστόξενος διὰ τὴν τῶν χειρῶν κίνησιν. οὕτως δ' ἦν ἔνδοξον καὶ σοφὸν ἡ ὄρχησις ὥστε Πίνδαρος τὸν Ἀπόλλωνα ὀρχηστὴν καλεῖ·

ὀρχήστ' ἀγλαΐας ἀνάσσων, εὐρυφάρετρ' Ἄπολλον. (Ath. 1.21e–22b)[12]

Aeschylus as well not only invented the elegance and dignity of costume that the hierophants and torchbearers imitate when they dress themselves, but also created many dance-steps himself and passed them on to the members of his choruses. Chamaeleon (fr. 41 Wehrli = A. test. 103), at any rate, says that he was the first to arrange the dances, and that he did not use special trainers, but worked out the dance-steps for his choruses himself and generally took on the entire management of the tragedy. Most likely, therefore, he acted in his own plays.... The musician Phillis of Delos (fr. 3, FHG iv.476) says that in the old days citharodes did not make many facial expressions, but they moved their feet more, producing marching-steps and dance-steps. Aristocles (fr. 11, FHG iv.332 = A. test. 81), for example, says that Aeschylus' dancer Telestes was so skilful that when he danced the *Seven Against Thebes* he could make the action apparent simply by his dancing. They also say that the ancient poets – Thespis, Pratinus, Cratinus, and Phrynichus – were called 'dancers' because not only did they integrate their own dramas with choral dancing, but, quite apart from their own compositions, they taught anyone who wanted to learn to dance.... The following dances are associated with particular peoples: the Spartan, Troezenian,

---

[12] The Greek quotation and the English translation is taken from Olson's Loeb edition. In the last section of this chapter I offer my own translation of the Pindaric quotation: see below, p. 197.

Singing and Dancing Pindar's Authority 185

Epizephyrian, Cretan, Ionian, and Mantinean, which Aristoxenus (fr. 112 Wehrli) prefers because of the hand-gestures. Dancing was so respected and involved so much skill that Pindar (fr. 148) refers to Apollo as a dancer:

Dancer, lord of brilliance, Apollo of the broad quiver!

It is worth noting that Athenaeus represents Aeschylus not only as a poet but also as a costume designer, a choreographer, a *chorodidaskalos*, and an actor. Athenaeus does not inform us of Pindar's range, but the Pindaric passage he quotes constitutes precious testimony, because it is the only surviving image of Apollo as dancer and leader of festival choruses in the Pindaric corpus. As we shall see, Athenaeus' reminder of the importance of dance in the archaic and classical period chimes with Plutarch's testimony.

The χάρις of Human *Choreia* and Its Divine Authority

The *First Isthmian Ode* offers a precious image of the speaker/poet as choreut on two different occasions, at the Isthmus celebrating the chariot victory of Theban Herodotus and on Delos leading a Cean chorus. Before discussing this image, however, I wish to turn first to a contradictory piece of evidence, namely, a scholiast's claim that Pindar had a weak voice and could not therefore train his choruses:

> For this Aeneas was the *chorodidaskalos*, whom Pindar used because he was weak-voiced and could not lead the choruses by himself in public, which most of the poets and especially those who had strong voices used to do when they participated in contests, teaching the choruses themselves. (Σ *ad Olymp.* 6.148a)[13]

This is a gloss on *Olympian* 6.91, where Pindar compliments Aeneas, a *chorodidaskalos*, as a sweet mixing bowl of loudly ringing songs:

> ... ὄτρυνον νῦν ἑταίρους,
> Αἰνέα, πρῶτον μὲν ῞Ηραν
>   Παρθενίαν κελαδῆσαι,
> γνῶναί τ᾽ ἔπειτ᾽, ἀρχαῖον ὄνειδος ἀλαθέσιν
> λόγοις εἰ φεύγομεν, Βοιωτίαν ὗν.
>   ἐσσὶ γὰρ ἄγγελος ὀρθός,
> ἠϋκόμων σκυτάλα Μοι-
>   σᾶν, γλυκὺς κρατὴρ ἀγαφθέγκτων ἀοιδᾶν· (*O.* 6.87–91)   90

---

[13] The same claim is repeated in *scholium* 149a.

Now, Aeneas, urge your companions first to celebrate Hera the Maiden, and then to know if by our truthful words we escape the age-old taunt of 'Boeotian pig', for you are a true messenger, a message stick of the fair-haired Muses, a sweet mixing bowl of loudly ringing songs.

The scholiast's claim has no external authority and seems to be deduced from Pindar's compliment to Aeneas.[14] This impression is reinforced by the speaker's declared intention to sing and dance at Isthmus and Ceos in the *First Isthmian*, which we shall consider in a moment. Moreover, if the scholiast's contention had any weight, we would expect Pindar to address the *chorodidaskaloi* he used more often. As it happens, his request to Aeneas may be unique. The only other instance, the request to a certain Nicasippus in *Isthmian* 2.47 to deliver the poet's message/song to Thrasybulus, does not necessarily make Nicasippus a *chorodidaskalos*. But even if, like Aeneas, Nikasippus was also a *chorodidaskalos*, Pindar's requests to them do not indicate that he had a weak voice and could not train his choruses.[15] There are more plausible explanations.

The simplest explanation for such requests is that poets of Panhellenic stature and in high demand could not train all choruses in all cities that had commissioned song-dances. In cases of conflict poets had to make choices and delegate the task to a local *chorodidaskalos*. There is no way of knowing if Pindar had met Aeneas or simply had heard about him from the honorand. As I have suggested elsewhere, his lavish praise of Aeneas' musical abilities, turned on its head, points to the anxiety these poets must have felt once they sent their compositions to be performed by others.[16]

We may now turn to the *First Isthmian*, which exemplifies Pindar's response to pressing commitments, the Isthmian song for the chariot victory of his fellow-citizen Herodotus and a paean for the Ceans, usually thought to be the *Fourth Paean*. Despite the pressure, the poet expresses his optimism concerning the timely delivery of both song-dances. It is worth noting that in this instance the envisaged completion is not that of a script but of the choral performance. I offer a literal translation in order to keep the text's emphasis on *choreia*:

---

[14] See also Adorjáni (2014), 48 n. 64.
[15] I have suggested elsewhere that Nicasippus may be a nickname or a pun on the name of the charioteer, Nicomachus: Athanassaki (2014), 217–18.
[16] Athanassaki (2022), 3–18.

Singing and Dancing Pindar's Authority

Μᾶτερ ἐμά, τὸ τεόν, χρύσασπι Θήβα,
πρᾶγμα καὶ ἀσχολίας ὑπέρτερον
θήσομαι. μή μοι κραναὰ νεμεσάσαι
Δᾶλος, ἐν ᾇ κέχυμαι.
τί φίλτερον κεδνῶν τοκέων ἀγαθοῖς;   5
εἶξον, ὦ Ἀπολλωνιάς· ἀμφοτερᾶν
   τοι χαρίτων σὺν θεοῖς ζεύξω τέλος,
καὶ τὸν ἀκερσεκόμαν Φοῖβον χορεύων
ἐν Κέῳ ἀμφιρύτᾳ σὺν ποντίοις
ἀνδράσιν, καὶ τὰν ἁλιερκέα, Ἰσθμοῦ
δειράδ'...   (I. 1.1–10)   10

My mother, golden-shielded Thebes, I shall put the undertaking that concerns you above my lack of leisure. Let rocky Delos, for whom I have been pouring myself out not be angry with me. What is dearer to good men than their cherished parents? Yield, island of Apollo: for with the help of gods I shall indeed yoke the end of both graces, singing and dancing in honour of unshorn Phoebus on sea-girt Ceos with her sea-men, and the sea-flanked ridge of the Isthmus.

Insofar as the performance of the Isthmian ode is concerned, Pindar opens with a well-known trope, the representation of the performance underway as a future event.[17] If we take the poetic assertion concerning the priority of Thebes at face value, we must assume that the Cean song-dance for Apollo is a future event. Far more interesting than timing, however, is Pindar's envisaged involvement in the event.

Pindar's apostrophe to Delos (6) indicates that the performance will take place on Apollo's sacred island. Immediately afterwards, however, the poet envisages himself singing and dancing with the Ceans on Ceos. The explanation offered by the ancient scholiasts is that the song-dance had to be available to the chorus ahead of time so as to allow them time for study and rehearsal.[18] As is clear from the first-person participle χορεύων, our speaker has his eyes on the performance on Ceos, that is, at a time when all elements of *mousike*, including words, melody, and orchestic movement, have come together and are actualized by the Cean chorus under the leadership of Pindar, the poet of the two χάριτες, the epinician and the paean.[19] The metaphorical designation of the

---

[17] See Bundy (1962), 21, who labels it 'encomiastic' future.
[18] Σ I. 1.6d. See also I. C. Rutherford (2001), 284 and 292.
[19] This is an instance of the chorus impersonating the poet. On the impersonation of the poet by the chorus when there are markers indicating the poet's persona, see Nagy (1990), 379–80.

188   LUCIA ATHANASSAKI

two song-dances as τέλος χαρίτων enhances the emphasis on the audio spectacle as a finished piece of *mousike*. The word χάρις captures at once the grace of the choral show and the reciprocity that the musical offering is expected to activate. The graceful performances that the poet hopes to 'yoke' (ζεύξω) in time are the celebration underway and the Ceans' gift to Apollo, whose grace their *choreia* seeks to secure.[20] The verb ζεύξω evokes another famous Pindaric poetic chariot, the chariot of the Muses.

In Pindar's odes the role of Graces (Χάριτες) in musical activities on earth and heaven is distinct from that of the Muses, despite occasional overlaps. The *Fourteenth Olympian*, composed probably for an epinician celebration in the course of the *Charitesia*, the ancient festival of the Graces at Orchomenos, features such an overlap. Here Pindar represents them as performers and stewards of all choruses and banquets on Olympus (8–12), a role that elsewhere they share with the Muses.[21] In the same ode he depicts them as the source of every sort of pleasure and sweetness, thanks to whom a mortal can acquire wisdom/poetic talent (σοφός), beauty (καλός), or splendour (ἀγλαός). The role of the Graces as a source of pleasure and sweetness complements the role of the Muses who are traditionally depicted as a source of wisdom.[22] In a fragment preserved by the Christian writer Didymus the Blind, χάρις denotes a property of song:

> θεὸς ὁ πάντα τεύχων βροτοῖς
> καὶ χάριν ἀοιδᾷ φυτεύει (fr. 141)

god who provides everything for mortals also plants grace in song

In what follows I shall discuss a number of odes where Pindar uses χάρις with reference to the end product, the choral performance, with special emphasis on its appeal and divine authority.

As already mentioned, many scholars have thought that in the opening of the *First Isthmian* Pindar refers to the *Fourth Paean*, to which we may now turn. Again, I offer a literal translation:

---

[20] Cf. Kurke (1988), who takes the yoking metaphor as a reference to the *First Isthmian* and to the variety of genres that Pindar has managed to yoke, that is, a paean, a *kallinikos* song, a Castoreion, didactic poetry, and a home-coming invocation, a poetic pentathlon (Kurke (1988), 112).

[21] Cf. *h.Ap.* 182–205 where the Muses play a more prominent role than the Graces.

[22] See further Duchemin (1955), 93.

Singing and Dancing Pindar's Authority

ἤτοι καὶ ἐγὼ σ[κόπ]ελον ναίων δια-
γινώσκομαι μὲν ἀρεταῖς ἀέθλων
Ἑλλανίσιν, γινώσκ[ο]μα[ι] δὲ καὶ
μοῖσαν παρέχων ἅλις· *Pae.* 4.21–4

Truly, I too, who dwell on a rock am renowned for Hellenic excellence in games on the one hand and on the other I am also known for providing the Muse in plenty.

The phrase μοῖσαν παρέχων ἅλις merits scrutiny. For this phrase I have adopted Ian Rutherford's literal translation.[23] William Race, who translates μοῖσαν as 'poetry', thinks that the 'reference can be to the amount of poetry their [i.e. Cean athletes'] victories have occasioned or to the Cean poets Simonides and Bacchylides (whose first two odes celebrate Cean victors)'.[24] Whereas the expression is general enough to include the inspiration that Cean athletic victories offered to Simonides and Bacchylides, textual and contextual indications suggest that the reference cannot be so restrictive.

The most obvious difficulty is that it is hard to see why the present composer, Pindar, would not like to include himself in the group of those who contribute to the abundant musical production. Would the poet who made explicit reference to his Cean fellow-dancers in an ode for a Theban fail to mention them in the song-dance that he composed for their city and that they danced? Probably not. This is a choral self-referential statement in which they stress their contribution, which is their beautiful singing and dancing. This is certainly the contribution of the present chorus in a statement that has a general reference. The μέν ... δέ construction indicates that the chorus boasts of the athletic excellence and abundant musical production of the Ceans in general. The Cean Muse includes Simonides and Bacchylides and their choreuts, but it also includes all those poets and performers who built and sustained the rich musical tradition, but remained anonymous.

Pindar has not supplied an indirect object of the participle παρέχων, but it is not hard to imagine the recipients: first and foremost, the chorus sing and dance for Apollo. They also sing and dance for the human audience of the paean. An important beneficiary of their musical talents is the composer of the paean, Pindar, who envisaged himself as the *chorodidaskalos* of the Ceans and associated χορεία (<χορεύων) with χάρις in the *First Isthmian*.

This is not the first time that a choral master thought of the chorus as his Muse for, as Anastasia-Erasmia Peponi has shown, the idea is already

---

[23] I. C. Rutherford (2001), 282.   [24] Race (1997), 261.

present in Alcman. In fragment 30 *PMGF* Alcman identifies the Muse with the Siren (ἁ Μῶσα κέκλαγ' ἁ λίγηα Σηρήν, 'the Muse cries out, that clear-voiced Siren'). Peponi, drawing attention to Aelius Aristides' reception of the identification, offers a very attractive interpretation:

> The identification of the Muses with the Sirens is not random from the leading figure's point of view. If he imagines the voice of the chorus as that of Sirens and in turn identifies these with the Muses, he can be considered as both attracted to and inspired by the chorus that he leads. Or, to put this another way, the poet/choral leader acts out a position that is at once active and passive. He is made to yearn for the voices he hears while drawing from them the power to compose and sing.[25]

I suggest that a similar image emerges if we correlate the self-referential statements of the *Fourth Paean* and the *First Isthmian*, even if the *Fourth Paean* is not one of the two χάριτες: the chorus provides plenty of graceful singing and dancing (μοῖσαν παρέχων ἅλις) and the poet yokes the graces of *choreia*. What emerges from the composite image is that Pindar thinks of choruses as his Muse and of himself as a recipient of the grace they emanate. The advantage of terming a song-dance χάρις are evident. The word denotes at once the collaborative graceful audio spectacle and the reciprocity between performers, trainers, and their audiences, human and divine.

We may now turn to the *Twelfth Paean* Pindar composed for a Naxian *theoria* to Delos, which features the Graces in the midst of sacrifices:

[ ]με[. . . . . .]ωνιο[
. . .]. οισιν ἐννέ[α Μοί]ϲαις
.]αλαδαρτεμι. [..]. ωϊονασ[
..]χος ἀμφέπο[ισ' ἄν]θεα τοια[ύτας
.]ὑμνήσιος δρέπη· θαμὰ δ' ἔρ[χεται   5
Να]ξόθεν λιπαροτρόφων θυσί[ᾳ
μή]λων Χαρίτεσσι μίγδαν
Κύ]νθιον παρὰ κρημνόν, ἔνθα [
                 (*Pae.* 12.1–8)

> With the nine Muses
> Artemis (?)
> (you) in attendance cull the flowers of such
> hymnic song. Often there comes
> from Naxos for the sacrifice
> of richly-fed sheep, mixed with the Graces,
> to the slopes of Cynthus, where

---

[25] Peponi (2012), 87.

Singing and Dancing Pindar's Authority

The subject of ἔρ[χεται is not preserved, but the reference must be to the *theoroi* who come for the sacrifice. By the same token Χαρίτεσσι μίγδαν must refer to some aspect of the Naxian *choreia*, in all likelihood the songs accompanying sacrifices, a reference that gains support from the earlier mention of the Muses (2).[26] The image is similar to the one of sacrifices and dithyrambic performances in the *Thirteenth Olympian*, which we shall discuss later.

In the odes we have seen so far the X/χάριτες broadly designate the divine, and therefore authoritative, quality of choral performance and its appeal, but there are instances in which individual components of *mousike* are also listed, as in the *Ninth Paean*, composed for a ceremonial supplication at the Theban Ismenion. The opening invocation of the hidden rays of the sun is an indication that the total eclipse of 463 is the occasion for the composition. In the second triad the chorus turns from the hidden rays of the sun to Apollo, who remains the addressee of their supplication throughout the preserved part:

> ἐκράνθην ὑπὸ δαιμονίῳ τινί 35
> λέχει πέλας ἀμβροσίῳ Μελίας
> ἀγαυὸν καλάμῳ συνάγεν θρόον
> μήδεσί τε φρενὸς ὑμ[ε]τέραν χάριν.
> λιτανεύω, ἑκαβόλε,
> Μοισαίαις ἀν[α]τιθεὶς τέχνα[ι]σι 40
> χρηστήριον. [.]πῳλοντ[..(.)]ι
>
> ———
>
> ἐν ᾧ Τήνερον εὐρυβίαν θεμίτ[ων υ- 41
> ἐξαίρετον προφάταν ἔτεκ[εν λέχει
> κόρα μιγεῖσ᾿ Ὠκεανοῦ Μελία σέο, Πύθι[ε. τ] Κάδμου (*Pae.* 9.35–43)

I have been ordained by some divine (portent?) near the immortal bed of Melia to link illustrious voices to the *aulos* and your *charis* to the counsels of my mind. I beseech you, far-shooter, dedicating your oracle to the arts of the Muses, ... in which Oceanus' daughter Melia bore to you, Pythian god, Tenerus, an outstanding prophet of *themites*

The chorus comments here on the quality of its performance.[27] It mentions in one breath the combination of (a) illustrious voices (ἀγαυὸν ...

---

[26] For the close association of the Naxian choral performance with the ritual performance context, see Nagy (2013), 254–5 and Kowalzig (2007), 60 and 66–7, for the close association of the Naxian performance with the performance of the Deliades.
[27] See I. C. Rutherford (2001), 196.

θρόον) with the melody of the pipe (καλάμῳ) and (b) his counsels (μήδεσί τε φρενός) with the grace of Apollo – and possibly other gods or even the honorands Tenerus and Melia, if the pronoun ὑμετέραν has a plural reference.[28] I construe line 38 as μήδεσί τε φρενός (*sc.* συνάγεν) ὑμ[ε]τέραν χάριν. Linking the god's grace to the speaker's thoughts in this instance denotes the gift of the paean and the divine favour it is expected to elicit.[29] The circulation of reciprocity is the purpose of hymns and other dedicatory gifts, as Joseph Day has shown:

> [T]he *charis* offered and requested refers to the gift itself, but also to the occasion of utterance in reading or performance and sometimes its repetition in the future. The parallelism, however, goes beyond semantics into pragmatics or verbal efficacy, which consisted partly in persuasiveness. Epigrams and hymns presenting themselves as dedications, as well as prayers that accompany (or promise or recall) an offering, all betray a ritually central concern to persuade the god to consider the gift and respond favorably.[30]

There is no question that the credit for linking together melody, voices, words, and all other elements of *choreia* goes first and foremost to the poet. In the course of the performance, however, the chorus can equally take the credit for the combination (συνάγεν), because it is the choreuts who actualize the poetic creation by singing beautifully and thus mediate the circulation of *charis*. Given the Theban context, it is possible that Pindar was the leader of the chorus who sang and danced for Apollo at the Ismenion. In such a scenario, the poet-musician-teacher and the singer-dancer-pupil would join forces for the synchronization and success of the audio spectacle. But the *charis* of the performance depended heavily on the performers, the virtuosity of the pipe player, and the chorus' beautiful and harmonious singing and dancing, which contributed greatly to the authority of the audio spectacle.

In comparison to graceful singing, references to choral movement in the surviving corpus are fewer, but I wish to look at a couple of fragments that show the importance Pindar attributed to dance, something that impressed Athenaeus and, as we shall see, Plutarch. Fragment 140b features a chorus that compares its response to music to that of a dancing dolphin:

---

[28] The pronoun ὑμετέραν can have a singular reference; see I. C. Rutherford (2001), 196 with the references in n. 20.

[29] Slater (1969) *ad loc.* 1β also seems to take χάριν as a direct object on the analogy of *P.* 8.86. Cf. I. C. Rutherford (2001), 196, who takes ὑμετέραν χάριν as an adverbial phrase.

[30] Day (2010), 251.

Singing and Dancing Pindar's Authority

⊗} Ἴων[
ἀοιδ[ὰν κ]αὶ ἁρμονίαν
αὐλ[οῖς ἐ]πεφράσ[ατο
τῶ[ν τε Λο]κρῶν τις, ⌊οἵ τ᾽ ἀργίλοφον⌋
πιὰρ Ζεφυρί⌊ου κολώⸯναν⌋   5
ν[. . . ὑπὲ]ρ Αὐσονία[ς ἁλός
λι[. . ...]ις ἀνθ.[
οἷον [ὄ]χημα λιγ[υ
        κες ὁ[.]όν παιηρ[ν
Ἀπόλλωνί τε καὶ [10
ἄρμενον. ἐγὼ μ[
παῦρα μελ[ι]ζομεν[
[γλώ]σσαργον ἀμφέπω[ν ⸱ερε-
        θίζⸯομαι πρὸς ἀϋτα[ν
⌊ἁλίοⸯυ δελφῖνος ὑπόκρισιν⌋,   15
⌊τὸν μὲν ἀκύμονος ἐν πόντου πελάγει
αὐλῶν ἐκίνησ᾽ ἐρατὸν μέλος.⌋

(Ionian?)
one of the Locrians, who (dwell?) by the white-topped hill of Zephyrion above the Ausonian sea, devised the song and musical mode for pipes . . . . . . such a chariot . . . (high-pitched?) word . . . paean(s) . . . fitting for Apollo and I . . . singing a few songs, cherishing the garrulous . . . am incited to . . . playing the part of a dolphin of the sea, which the lovely melody of pipes excited in the expanse of the waveless deep. (trans. W. H. Race, adapted)

The common denominator between the speaker and the dolphin is their graceful movement,[31] as is clear from Plutarch's assessment, who preserves lines 15–17 and probably had the whole ode in front of his eyes:

> ὁρῶμεν γὰρ ὅτι καὶ μουσικῇ πολλὰ κηλεῖται τῶν ἀλόγων, ὥσπερ ἔλαφοι σύριγξιν, ἵπποις δὲ μιγνυμέναις ἐπαυλεῖται νόμος, ὃν ἱππόθορον ὀνομάζουσιν· ὁ δὲ Πίνδαρός φησι κεκινῆσθαι πρὸς ᾠδὴν ἁλίου δελφῖνος ὑπόκρισιν·
> τὸν μὲν ἀκύμονος ἐν πόντου πελάγει
> αὐλῶν ἐκίνησ᾽ ἐρατὸν μέλος·

---

[31] The comparison is between the movement of the chorus and the dolphin. See Henderson (1992), 154 with n. 34, for references to earlier literature. Henderson (1992), 156, sees the following advantages in the image of the dolphin: 'natural beauty, spontaneity, gracefulness, vitality, an intelligence of its own, and freedom from human control'. For the Dionysiac/dithyrambic imagery, see Steiner (2016).

ὀρχούμενοι δὲ τοὺς ὤτους αἱροῦσι, χαίροντας τῇ ὄψει καὶ μιμητικῶς ἅμα δεῦρο κἀκεῖσε τοὺς ὤμους συνδιαφέροντας. (*Quaestiones convivales* 7.5.2, 704f–705a)

We observe that many nonrational creatures are bewitched by music, for example stags by flutes; and a tune, which is called 'Hippothoros' ('The Stallion's Leap'), is played to mares while they are being covered. Pindar speaks of himself as stirred towards song,

playing the part of a dolphin of the sea, whom on the main of the waveless deep the lovely strain of pipes has set a-dancing.

And by dancing they capture horned owls, which take pleasure in the spectacle and in an imitative way move their shoulders rhythmically this way and that.[32]

Plutarch has preserved another excerpt, fragment 107ab, which also shows the importance choral masters attributed to *orchesis*. Attribution is not certain, because Plutarch assigns it to the best poet of hyporchemes. Who was the best poet of hyporchemes? Athenaeus names two, Pindar and Xenodamus (Ath. 1.15d). Modern scholars have attributed it to Pindar, Simonides, Bacchylides, or Pratinas.[33] Although the question of authorship cannot be settled, it is worth looking at this fragment and Plutarch's assessment, because it expresses concerns that all choral practitioners must have shared:

δηλοῖ δ' ὁ μάλιστα κατωρθωκέναι δόξας ἐν ὑπορχήμασι καὶ γεγονέναι πιθανώτατος ἑαυτοῦ τὸ δεῖσθαι τὴν ἑτέραν τῆς ἑτέρας· τὸ γὰρ

Πελασγὸν ἵππον ἢ κύνα
Ἀμυκλαίαν ἀγωνίῳ
ἐλελιζόμενος ποδὶ μίμεο καμπύλον μέλος διώκων,
οἳ ἀνὰ Δώτιον ἀνθεμόεν πεδί-
ον πέτεται θάνατον κεροέσσᾳ
εὑρέμεν ματεῖσ' ἐλάφῳ
τὰν δ' ἐπ' αὐχένι στρέφοι-
σαν κάρα πάντ' ἐπ'οῖμον

καὶ τὰ ἑξῆς μόνον οὐ . . . † λειόθεν τὴν ἐν ὀρχήσει διάθεσιν τὰ ποιήματα καὶ παρακαλεῖν τὼ χεῖρε καὶ τὼ πόδε, μᾶλλον δ' ὅλον ὥσπερ τισὶ μηρίνθοις ἕλκειν τὸ σῶμα τοῖς μέλεσι καὶ ἐντείνειν, τούτων λεγομένων καὶ ᾀδομένων ἡσυχίαν ἄγειν μὴ δυνάμενον. αὐτὸς γοῦν ἑαυτὸν οὐκ αἰσχύνεται περὶ τὴν ὄρχησιν οὐχ ἧττον ἢ τὴν ποίησιν ἐγκωμιάζων, ὅταν λέγῃ,

---

[32] The Greek quotation and the English translation, slightly adapted, are taken from Minar, Sandbach, and Helmbold's Loeb edition.
[33] For the question of attribution, see D'Alessio (2020).

Singing and Dancing Pindar's Authority

ἐλαφρὸν ὄρχημ᾽ οἶδα ποδῶν μειγνύμεν·
Κρῆτα μὲν καλέουσι τρόπον.

ἀλλ᾽ οὐδὲν οὕτως τὸ νῦν ἀπολέλαυκε τῆς κακομουσίας ὡς ἡ ὄρχησις. διὸ
καὶ πέπονθεν ὃ φοβηθεὶς Ἴβυκος ἐποίησε,

δέδοικα μή τι παρὰ θεοῖς
ἀμπλακὼν τιμὰν πρὸς ἀνθρώπων ἀμείψω. (Plutarch
Quaestiones convivales 9.15.2, 748bc)

And that each art needs the other is made plain by the writer who has been considered to be most successful in the composition of hyporchemata, and nowhere to have carried more conviction. Take this passage:

> Pelasgian horse or Amyclaean hound
> Make your model as you whirl
> On competitive toe,
> Chasing the melody's twists;
> As along the flowery plain of Dotion he flies
> Seeking to find a way of death
> For the horned hind, who turns her head
> Back on her shoulder, trying every track ...

and so on. Shall we not say that these lines almost dictate representation in dancing, summoning our hands and feet, or rather twitching and bracing our whole body to the tunes, as if on strings, so that when these words are spoken or sung it cannot keep still? It is evidence of the author's views that he is not ashamed to praise himself for his dancing as much as for his poetry, when he says,

> I know how to mix my steps in light-foot dance;
> They call it the Cretan style.

But to-day nothing enjoys the benefits of bad taste so much as dancing. As a result it has really suffered what Ibycus feared when he wrote,

> I dread that for some sin against the gods
> I may be honoured at the hands of men.

Like Athenaeus in the case of Pindar, Plutarch feels the need to comment on this choral poet's mention of dance. The poet, Plutarch tells us, is not ashamed to praise dance as much as poetry, because dance in those days had nothing in common with contemporary dance, which has nothing musical about it. The word Plutarch uses is κακομουσία. In contrast, the hyporcheme recommends the agility and speed of a Pelasgian horse and a hunting dog. Moreover, the Cretan style is a light-footed dance (ἐλαφρὸν ὄρχημ᾽ ... ποδῶν).

196 LUCIA ATHANASSAKI

The light-footed nature of the dance is precisely one of the qualities that the choreuts dancing Pindar's *Fourteenth Olympian* in the presence of the Orchomenian Graces single out for mention (*O.* 14.17: κοῦφα βιβῶντα). The choreuts, designating themselves as κῶμος, also tell the Graces that they are singing in the Lydian mode and that they have come prepared for their performance (18: ἐν μελέταις τ' ἀείδων ἔμολον). The *Fourteenth Olympian* offers yet another example of Pindar's holistic take on a song-dance that conjures up the sanctuary of the Graces as the setting of its performance. In this instance the Graces are ubiquitous; they are simultaneously imagined as performers and stewards of choral performances and banquets on Olympus and as the music-loving audience of the epinician performance underway.[34]

Dionysiac contexts yield a similar image. In the *Thirteenth Olympian*, for instance, the speaker asks rhetorically:

> Ταί Διωνύσου πόθεν ἐξέφανεν
> σὺν βοηλάτᾳ χάριτες διθυράμβῳ; (*O.* 13.18–19)

Wherefrom appeared Dionysus' graces with the ox-driving dithyramb?

The scholiasts unanimously gloss the periphrasis in line 2 as χάριτες διθυράμβων, that is, dithyrambs. Dionysus was closely associated with the Graces in both poetry and cult. Despite the brevity of the rhetorical question, the diction conjures up the image of Dionysiac celebrations with ox sacrifices accompanied by the *charis* of dithyrambic performances.[35] In the next section we shall see another instance where χάρις is used with reference to dithyrambic performance and celebration in its totality. The designation of one aspect of choral performance (words, melody, movement) or the entire audio spectacle as *C/charis* points up its complex and collaborative nature, links it to its divine model, and enhances its authority.

Divine *Choreia* as Pindar's Model of Authority

Whether the poet of fragment 107ab was Pindar or one of his contemporaries, Plutarch's assessment chimes with Athenaeus' later report concerning Pindar's representation of Apollo as a dancer as proof of the widely

---

[34] For human and divine performances in this ode, see further Athanassaki (2003) and (2009), 103–7.
[35] The image is a variant of the combination of song and sacrifice in the *Twelfth Paean*, lines 5–7, discussed above.

Singing and Dancing Pindar's Authority

held view that dancing was a respectable and sophisticated art (εὔδοξον καὶ σοφόν): ὀρχήστ' ἀγλαΐας ἀνάσσων, εὐρυφάρετρ' Ἄπολλον (fr. 148: 'Dancer, who rule over the celebration, Apollo with the broad quiver'). As already mentioned, this is the only surviving reference to Apollo as a dancer and king of celebrations, presumably including choral performances, in the Pindaric corpus.

We are a little luckier with Dionysus. Although there is no surviving depiction of Dionysus as dancer in Pindar's odes, Aelius Aristides reports that Pindar said in a hymn that Dionysus was given Pan because he was the most perfect choreut (χορευτὴν τελεώτατον) amongst gods.[36] Pausanias (3.25.2) preserves another excerpt from another Pindaric song depicting Silenus, the husband of a Naid, dancing (ὁ ζαμενὴς δ' ὁ χοροιτύπος,/ ..., Ναΐδος ἀκοίτας/ Σιληνός, 156 Maehler).

The most elaborate example of a divine performance, however, features a Dionysiac celebration staged by the gods on Olympus. It comes from the famous dithyramb that Pindar composed for a Theban festival in honour of Dionysus, which exemplifies a different poetic strategy, the close parallelism of the human performance underway with the divine performance that is presented as the ideal paradigm.[37] The performers begin their song-dance with a reference to asigmatic dithyrambs and proceed to relate the divine choral performance in the festival in honour of Dionysus:

Π̣ρὶν μὲν ἕρπε σχοινοτένειά τ' ἀοιδὰ δι̣θι̣υράμβων	(1)
καὶ τὸ σạ̀ν κίβδηλον ἀνθρώποισιν ἀπὸ στομάτων, διαπέπ[τ]ạ[νται ......]...[	
κλοισι νέạι [... ε]ἰδότες	(5)
οἵαν Βρομίọυ [τελε]τάν	
καὶ παρὰ σκᾶ[πτ]ον Διὸς Οὐρανίδαι	
ἐν μεγάροις ἵ̣στạι̣ντι. σεμνᾶ μὲν κατάρχει	
Ματέρι πὰρ μι̣εγ̣ιάλạ ῥόμβοι τυπάνων,	
ἐν δὲ κέχλαδ[εν] κρόταλ' αἰθομένα τε δαῒς ὑπὸ ξαν̣ιθαῖ̣σι πεύκαις·	(10)
ἐν δὲ Ναΐδων̣ ẹ̓ρίγδουποι στοναχαί	
μανίαι τ' ἀλαλιαί̣ι̣ τ' ὀρίνεται ῥιψαύχενι	
σὺν κλόνῳ.	
ἐν δ' ὁ παγκρατὴς κεραυνὸς ἀμπνέων	(15)
πῦρ κεκίνη̣[ται τό τ'] Ἐγυαλίου	

---

[36] *Or.* 41.6 Keil = Pindar fr. 99: διδόασι δ' αὐτῷ καὶ τὸν Πᾶνα χορευτὴν τελεώτατον θεῶν ὄντα, ὡς Πίνδαρός τε ὑμνεῖ καὶ οἱ κατ' Αἴγυπτον ἱερεῖς κατέμαθον.

[37] For the view that the human performance may have a highly mimetic character, see Duchemin (1955), 83.

ἔγχος, ἀλκάεσσά [τ]ε Παλλάδο[ς] αἰγίς
_μυρίων φθογγάζεται κλαγγαῖς δρακόντων.
ῥίμφα δ' εἶσιν Ἄρτεμις οἰοπολὰς ζεύ-
ξαισ' ἐν ὀργαῖς   (20)
Βακχίαις φῦλον λεόντων α[‿‿—‿‿—
ὁ δὲ κηλεῖται χορευοίσαισι κα[ὶ θη-
ρῶν ἀγέλαις. ἐμὲ δ' ἐξαίρετο[ν
κάρυκα σοφῶν ἐπέων
Μοῖσ' ἀνέστασ' Ἑλλάδι κα[λ]λ[ιχόρῳ   (25)
εὐχόμενον βρισαρμάτοις ρ[‿ Θήβαις,
ἔνθα ποθ' Ἁρμονίαν [φ]αμα γα[μετάν
Κάδ'μον ὑψη[λαῖ]ς πραπίδεσ[σι λαχεῖν κεδ-
νάν· Δ[ιὸ]ς δ' ἄκ[ουσεν ὀ]μφάν,
καὶ τέκ' εὔδοξο[ν παρ'] ἀνθρώπο[ις γενεάν.   (30)
Διόνυσ[.]' θ.[. . . . .]' τ[.]γ[
ματέ[ρ
πει.[(fr. 70b)

In the past the song of dithyrambs moved stretched out like a rope and from people's mouth the san came out counterfeit [missing words] are thrown open [missing letters] new/young (?) knowing well what sort of rite for Bromius the Heavenly gods set up beside the sceptre of Zeus in his palace. Beside the august Mother the circling movement of drums, there the castanets ring out and the burning torch under the blond pine-trees; there the Naiads' resounding groans and their bouts of frenzy and their wild cries are roused with the neck-tossing confusion. There also the all-powerful fire-breathing thunderbolt is set in motion and Enyalius' spear too, and the valiant aegis of Pallas sounds loudly with the hissing of innumerable snakes. Swiftly comes solitary Artemis, having yoked in Bacchic mood the race of lions. And he is enchanted by the dancing herds too. And the Muse has set me up as her chosen herald of wise words to Hellas with the beautiful dancing-spaces, as I pray for Thebes, powerful in chariots, where the story goes that once Cadmus was allotted Harmonia as his wife thanks to his lofty mind; and he/she (?) heard Zeus' voice and begot a glorious generation of men. Dionysus . . . mother

The opening of this dithyramb and in particular the meaning of σὰν κίβδηλον has puzzled Pindar's readers, ancient and modern. No consensus has been reached, but I find Armand D'Angour's line of interpretation particularly productive.[38] D'Angour argues for a contrast between the straight line and the cyclical formation of the choreuts, a transition that improved the -s-acoustics. Both the choice of metaphor (σχοινοτένειά τ' ἀοιδὰ διθυράμβων)

---

[38] D'Angour (1997).

Singing and Dancing Pindar's Authority 199

and diction (ἕρπε, διαπέπ[τ]ᾳ[νται, κλοισι) favour D'Angour's correlation of shape and sound.

The close association of the human with the divine performance is particularly significant for the present argument. In the opening Pindar makes a distinction between the human performances of the past and the present. Although several words are missing it is clear that the present formation, probably cyclical, was chosen by those who knew well (ε]ἰδότες) what sort of performance the gods set up for Dionysus. Unfortunately, the identity of these experts remains unknown, but the transition from the divine to the human performance is made by the choral assertion that they have been the Muse's chosen herald of wise words. The σοφά ἔπεα that our chorus is broadcasting to Hellas include the story of the birth of Dionysus that follows and, more importantly from our point of view, the details of divine performance in honour of Dionysus. For this reason, Pindar and his dithyrambic chorus must be counted among the experts.

It is worth noting that Pindar's emphasis is on the sonic and orchestic aspect of the divine and animal dance. In addition to the sound of musical instruments (drums, castanets) there is special mention of other sounds: the sound of burning fire and the sounds produced by the cries and rhythmical movement of choruses, that is, the Naiads and the hissing snakes. In terms of movement Pindar captures the Naiads tossing their necks, which is the most characteristic Dionysiac movement. Do the hundreds of snakes dance too on Athena's shield? It is possible, but not certain. The only animal group that is represented as dancing is a pride of lions. Unlike the other animal dances we have seen, Pindar does not comment on their movement, but lions are of course at home in Dionysiac contexts, and, like all felines, they move speedily and gracefully despite their size. The heavily metaphoric diction (19–21) makes it hard to assess Artemis' role, but the participle ζεύξαισ' suggests that Pindar probably imagined her as the chorus-leader of the pride.

This dithyramb is an instance of a feature that Albert Henrichs identified in tragedy and labelled 'choral projection', namely, the choruses' tendency to merge their own performance in the orchestra with divine or other imaginary performances. Henrichs reached the following conclusion: 'Far from "breaking the dramatic illusion" outright and unconditionally, as some scholars have suggested, such choruses invite the audience to participate in a more integrated experience, one in which the choral performance in the orchestra merges with the more imaginary performance of the rituals of polytheism that take place in the action of each play.'[39]

The Pindaric corpus offers several instances of choral projection that enhances the authority and the appeal of the human performance. We have seen that the chorus performing fragment 70b asserts their privileged access to the details of the divine Dionysiac performance thanks to the favour of the Muse and takes on the role of the herald of wise words. The male choreuts singing and dancing the *Sixth Paean* evoke the choruses of the Delphides performing in the sanctuary of Pythian Apollo (15–18), where in another paean, the *Eighth*, Pindar depicts the chorus of Keledones in action until the earth swallowed them up.[40] The male choreuts of the *Second Paean* also evoke female choruses honouring Pythian Apollo (96–103); that part of the text is very lacunose, but the purpose of choral projection must be to enhance the authority of the chorus of Abderitans.[41] I have argued elsewhere that these representations show that, like poets, choruses were believed to be in close contact with the gods who taught them music and ritual expertise in *illo tempore*.[42] Pindar was not, of course, the only one who held such a belief. To stay with only literary representations, the *Homeric Hymn to Apollo*, for instance, depicts Apollo giving detailed ritual instructions to his Cretan priests who form the archetypal chorus led by the god.[43] In the *Bacchae* Euripides shows Dionysus singing, dancing, and celebrating with his Maenads. In the *Laws* Plato theorizes this belief and depicts gods and mortals as fellow-dancers and celebrants (653e–654b: συγχορευταί and συνεορτασταί). These depictions shed light on the great esteem dance enjoyed in archaic and classical thought and explain why Pindar and other poets were not ashamed to single it out for special mention, a choice that both Plutarch and Athenaeus felt the need to justify.

My last Pindaric example comes from another famous dithyramb, fragment 75 for the Athenians, and exemplifies choral interaction of mortals and immortals and the importance of divinely sent χάρις, which the chorus pray to the Olympians to bestow on their performance:

---

[39] Henrichs (1994/5), 59.

[40] For the analogies between the chorus of Keledones and the Delphides, see Power (2011), 98.

[41] See also *N*. 5.28ff. where the song of the Muses becomes imperceptibly the song of the epinician singer.

[42] Athanassaki (2018). [43] *h.Ap.* 490–501 and 513–23.

Singing and Dancing Pindar's Authority

⊗ Δεῦτ' ἐν χορόν, Ὀλύμπιοι,
ἐπί τε κλυτὰν πέμπετε χάριν, θεοί,
πολύβατον οἵ τ' ἄστεος ὀμφαλὸν θυόεντ'
  ἐν ταῖς ἱεραῖς Ἀθάναις
οἰχνεῖτε πανδαίδαλόν τ' εὐκλέ' ἀγοράν·   5
ἰοδέτων λάχετε στεφάνων τᾶν τ' ἐαρι-
  δρόπων ἀοιδᾶν,
Διόθεν τέ με σὺν ἀγλαΐᾳ
ἴδετε πορευθέντ' ἀοιδᾶν δεύτερον
ἐπὶ τὸν κισσοδαῆ θεόν,
τὸν Βρόμιον, τὸν Ἐριβόαν τε βροτοὶ καλέομεν,   10
γόνον ὑπάτων μὲν πατέρων μελπόμεν<οι>
γυναικῶν τε Καδμεϊᾶν Σεμέλην.
ἐναργέα τ' ἔμ' ὥτε μάντιν οὐ λανθάνει.
φοινικοεάνων ὁπότ' οἰχθέντος Ὡρᾶν θαλάμου
εὔοδμον ἐπάγοισιν ἔαρ φυτὰ νεκτάρεα.   15
τότε βάλλεται, τότ' ἐπ' ἀμβρόταν χθόν' ἐραταί
ἴων φόβαι, ῥόδα τε κόμαισι μείγνυται,
ἀχεῖ τ' ὀμφαὶ μελέων σὺν αὐλοῖς,
οἰχνεῖ τε Σεμέλαν ἑλικάμπυκα χοροί. (trans. W. Race)

Come to the chorus, Olympians, and send over it glorious grace, you gods who are coming to the city's crowded, incense-rich navel in holy Athens and to the glorious, richly adorned agora. Receive wreaths of plaited violets and the songs plucked in springtime, and look upon me with favour as I proceed from Zeus with splendour of songs secondly to that ivy-knowing god, whom we mortals call Bromios and Eriboas as we sing of the offspring of the highest of fathers and of Cadmeian women. Like a seer, I do not fail to notice the clear signs, when, as the chamber of the purple-robed Horai is opened, the nectar-bearing flowers bring in the sweet-smelling spring. Then, then, upon the immortal earth are cast the lovely tresses of violets, and roses are fitted to hair and voices of songs echo to the accompaniment of pipes and choruses come to Semele of the circling headband.

The male dancers invite the gods to come to the Agora and be fellow-celebrants, as is clear from their invitation to the gods to wreath themselves with violet garlands. There is a broad consensus that Pindar composed this dithyramb for the Dionysia, but various reconstructions have been offered concerning the timing of this performance within the festival and its locale in Athens.[44] Moreover, the invitation δεῦτ' ἐν χορόν, as well as the use of

---

[44] Following John Papadopoulos' (2003) finds and definitive arguments, an increasing number of scholars believe that the ancient Agora was located to the east of the Acropolis before the Persian wars. Neer and Kurke (2014) follow Papadopoulos, read the Pindaric ode against buildings in that part of the city, and locate the performance of the dithyramb there some time before the Persian wars. Sourvinou-Inwood (2003) seems to have thought of the Agora north of the Acropolis as the

202   LUCIA ATHANASSAKI

the same verb, οἰχνεῖτε and οἰχνεῖ, to describe both the movement of the gods and human choral dances in honour of Semele at lines 5 and 19, respectively, suggests that the chorus imagine the gods as their fellow choreuts. To use Plato's formulation, gods and mortals are here envisaged as συγχορευταί and συνεορτασταί.

The dithyrambic chorus also prays for glorious grace (κλυτὰν χάριν), which refers to the allure of the whole audio spectacle, as is evident in lines 16–18 where they mention in one breath their rose crowns, their singing voices, the pipes, and their dancing step. There are remarkable similarities between this song-dance and the *Fourteenth Olympian*, which the Orchomenian chorus sings and dances in the presence of the Graces. Yet the Athenian chorus goes a step further, for they imagine their graceful performance not only in the presence of gods, but with the gods as fellow-dancers in graceful interaction. In Joseph Day's words,

> The gods are asked to bestow on both song and occasion the *charis* that makes them beautiful and delightful, and in return to accept that delight as a dedication from the performers and, with the open deictics, the audience.[45]

I would not be surprised if this delightful and idyllic image informed Plato's account in the *Laws*.

Perennial Artistic Concerns

Only Pindar's ἔπεα have survived through the centuries, but his popularity during his lifetime was due to his talent and expertise in combining words, music, and dance. On the basis of several odes I have argued that (a) all three components of *mousike* are singled out for mention in different combinations; (b) in addition to the Muse(s), he attributed an equally important role to the Graces in order to broaden the traditional model of poetic authority to account for the needs of his multifaceted artistic medium and to enhance the wisdom of the Muses with the dancing virtuosity and irresistible appeal of the Graces; and (c) Pindar's model of authority is to be found not in a relation of the poet alone to the Muse(s)

---

locus of performance. She proposed the rite of Dionysus' *xenismos* in the Academy as the performance context (Paus. 1.29.2; Philostr. *VS* 2.1.549 (note that her study was published the same year as that of Papadopoulos)). Since Dionysus was thought to be present in Athens throughout his festival, Pindar, who frequently telescopes events and venues, could have conceived of the interaction of mortals and immortals on both occasions.

[45] Day (2010), 250.

Singing and Dancing Pindar's Authority

but in the complex model of divine *choreia* that involves composition of song, melody, and dance.

Does Pindar's beautiful, inspired, and bold diction and imagery suggest that ἔπεα reigned sovereign over tunes and dance in his mind? It is not impossible, but I would not be surprised if he hesitated to give a definitive answer if asked.[46] I conclude my discussion by bringing into the picture Richard Strauss' swan song, which poses the question of the relative merits of music, words, and drama. *Capriccio*, an opera about opera, was first performed in Munich in 1942. For the libretto, Richard Strauss, who had initially planned to collaborate with Stefan Zweig, in the end collaborated with Clemens Krauss.

Capriccio, subtitled *A Conversation Piece for Music*, is set in a luxurious chateau near Paris a few years before the French Revolution. The chateau belongs to the beautiful and cultured countess Madeleine, a widow, and her brother. The opera opens with two rivals, the composer Flamand and the poet Olivier, who debate the supremacy of music over words and are competing for the love of Madeleine. The debate becomes more complex when the theatre director La Roche wakes up and starts advertising the merits of theatre-staging by bringing in ballet dancers, tenors and sopranos specializing in Italian opera, and the gifted actress Clairon, who charms the count, Madeleine's brother. In scene 7 Flamand confronts Madeleine with the double dilemma: 'Decide, decide now: music . . . or poetry? Flamand, Olivier . . . who wins the prize?' After a parade of arguments and artists, Madeleine decides to commission an opera and make the most of the talents of all three:

> *To Flamand.* To the sweet impulse Apollo has endowed upon you, may the poet give his noble thoughts!
> *To Olivier.* What the genius of poetry has so splendidly begun, be glorified through the power of music!
> *Pointing to La Roche.* May it take shape on his stage, to move hearts with its dignity and grace.[47]

Madeleine's decision offers a solution to the artistic impasse that runs through the opera but not to her personal dilemma between poetry and music, the poet and the composer. At the end of the opera, however,

---

[46] For recent emphasis on Pindar's words, see Sigelmann (2016) and Spelman (2018).
[47] The quotation is taken from the Pacific Opera Victoria's English libretto based on the Surtitle Text created by Teresa Turgeon.

Madeleine, who admits to being in love, looks at the mirror and then leaves, gracefully humming the melody of a sonnet.

Strauss' choice to dedicate a whole opera to the question of the importance of the components of his complex medium shows that he did not have a straightforward answer, although, if *Capriccio* had not survived, one might be tempted to think that he would not hesitate for a moment about the supremacy of music. *Capriccio* in turn echoes the debate of an earlier opera composed by Antonio Salieri to a libretto by Giovanni Battista Casti, entitled *Prima la musica e poi le parole* and performed in Vienna 1786.

There are differences between modern and ancient composers, but *mutatis mutandis* some of their concerns are perennial. In addition to the relative importance of the various components of an audio spectacle, another perennial concern that ancients and moderns share is its appeal to the audience. *Capriccio* is a good *comparandum*, because Madeleine, the centre of the competitors' attention, is not only the most important member of their audience, but their sponsor as well. The fact that she falls in love in the end indicates that the artists' hope to charm their audience was realized. In Pindar's universe the irresistible appeal of *choreia* belongs to the realm of the Graces.

The Social Dimension of Choral Authority

The variety of choral performances that I have discussed show that Pindar was deeply aware of the challenges of his multifaceted and collaborative artistic medium. The collaborative nature of this medium is the reason for moulding an elaborate divine model that is also cooperative. In addition to the Muses and the Graces, divine performances feature Apollo and other deities in several combinations as composers, performers, chorus leaders, and audiences. The range of variants of divine choral performances on which the Pindar's authority rests is remarkable indeed, and it may have been fostered by the variety of genres in which he tried his hand.

Pindar's awareness of the collaborative nature of his art offers an important corrective to the image of a male genius working in isolation, which emerges if we look at his songs only as texts, a time-honoured approach fostered by both the nature of its transmission and centuries of male-centred print culture.[48] This is not to deny Pindar's status as an elite

---

[48] For the implications of male-centred print-culture on female authority, see Lanser (1992), cited also by the editors of this volume in their Introduction.

Singing and Dancing Pindar's Authority

male poet but to draw attention to his awareness and appreciation of the important contribution of all those with whom he worked closely, men and women alike, who sang and danced his songs or trained his choruses.[49]

It is a pity that only a tiny fraction of Pindar's song-dances for young women survive, but it is appropriate to close this reading, whose aim has been to revisit Pindar's conception of his authority, with a quick look at his precious snapshot of the choral pursuits of two Theban women in the daphnephoric song-dance he composed for the family of Aeoladas: he captures one of them, either Damaina or a female relative, as she is dancing in the *hic et nunc*: the phrase πεδίλοις βαίνοισα (walking on sandals, 70) is evocative of the metaphorical use of πέδιλον in Olympian 3.5 and draws attention to the rhythm she keeps with her feet. This choreut is said to have been trained by Andaisistrota (Ἀνδαισιστρότα ἃν ἐπά-/σκησε μήδεσ[ι, 71–72). The text is too fragmentary to allow certainty regarding the kind of training Andaisistrota offered, but the following reference to countless roads (?), to yoking (ζευξα[, 75), and to nectar (76) in a first-person statement argue in favour of the arts of song and dance. Despite the uncertainties, this passage together with the heavily self-referential opening make clear that Pindar enabled his female choreuts to draw attention to their choral excellence and allude to the rich local tradition of which their present performance was an instantiation. He was not the only one. The similarities of this song with Alcman's *partheneia* leave no doubt that the choral masters were not simply aware of, but happy to acknowledge, the collaborative nature of their art.

If we view Pindar as a team player who valued the contribution of those with whom he cooperated, first-person authoritative statements such as 'I wish . . . to sing with the Graces' (*Pyth.* 9.1–3: ἐθέλω . . . σὺν . . . Χαρίτεσσι γεγωνεῖν) should be interpreted as references not only to the divine origin of his songs but to the rich nexus of the poet's reciprocal relations with his performers and chorus trainers that were indispensable for the success of his performances all over the Greek world. This social dimension extends of course to Pindar's relations with his audiences and, of course, with the gods, whose goodwill and favour choruses sought to obtain.

---

[49] For the collaborative aspect of *choreia* and the importance of *C/charis* for social cohesion, see Fisher (2003) and (2010).

CHAPTER 10

Authority, Experience, and the Vicarious Traveller in Herodotus' Histories

K. Scarlett Kingsley

John Marincola's research has thoughtfully explored the negotiation of authority in Herodotus' *Histories*, revealing the extent to which the narrator is a highly intrusive one who organizes and steers the reader's progression through the text.[1] In *Authority and Tradition in Ancient Historiography*, he demonstrated how Herodotus' first-person verbs mediate historical memory for his audience and in doing so draw upon the authority of performers of wisdom evident in fifth-century intellectual culture.[2] This work also gestured toward the alternative means by which the *Histories* could generate expertise effects but did not have the scope to go beyond the narrator's self-representation. This chapter will contribute to this project by surveying the rhetorical function of the narratee through the second person and impersonal 'one', and I will argue that its embedding of virtual experience into the text contributes to the work's construction of authority.

Ancient critics identified the second person as characteristic of highly engaging, experiential narrative, and the *Histories* was singled out for its handling of this rhetorical strategy. In a discussion in *On the Sublime* on the abrupt change of address to the second person, Herodotus is seen to produce the sublime in the following terms:[3]

---

*Thanks are owed first and foremost to John Marincola, who fired my imagination as an undergraduate classicist and who has since been an exemplary mentor and critical reader, and the dearest of friends. Versions of this chapter were delivered orally at the 'Revisiting Authority and Tradition in Ancient Historiography' conference in honour of John Marincola, at Heidelberg University in the Gräzistisches Forschungskolloquium, and at Corpus Christi, Oxford, in the Classics Centre. All three audiences raised rich questions and comments for which I am grateful. Finally, I am indebted to my co-editors for their helpful suggestions.

[1] Marincola (1997), 6–7, in the context of distinguishing between the historian and the epic poet's more effaced narratorial persona. On Herodotus' narratorial voice, Marincola (1987), (2007b), 34–7, 51–66.

[2] Marincola (1997), 8.

[3] See Russell (1964) *ad loc.*: 'The imaginary second person (i.e. "you" = French *on*, German *man*, Greek τις) is much less common in Greek than in Latin (where all styles welcome it) or in English

Authority, Experience, and the Vicarious Traveller

Change of person is similarly actively engaging (ἐγαγώνιος), and often makes the audience feel themselves set in the midst of the danger: 'You would say that unworn and with temper undaunted / Each met the other in war, so headlong the rush of their battle' (*Il.* 15.697–8)... Herodotus does much the same: 'You will sail up from the city of Elephantine and there arrive at a smooth plain. And when you have passed through that place you will board again another ship and sail two days and then you will come to a great city, the name of which is Meroe.' Do you see, friend, how he takes your soul along through these places and makes hearing sight (ὁρᾷς, ὦ ἑταῖρε, ὡς παραλαβών σου τὴν ψυχὴν διὰ τῶν τόπων ἄγει τὴν ἀκοὴν ὄψιν ποιῶν)? All such things when directed to actual persons put the hearer in the presence of the action itself (ἐπ' αὐτῶν ἵστησι τὸν ἀκροατὴν τῶν ἐνεργουμένων) ... you will make him more impassioned and more trans-fixed and full of the struggle as one roused by the appeals to him in person (ἐμπαθέστερόν τε αὐτὸν ἅμα καὶ προσεκτικώτερον καὶ ἀγῶνος ἔμπλεων ἀποτελέσεις, ταῖς εἰς ἑαυτὸν προσφωνήσεσιν ἐξεγειρόμενον). ((Longin.) 26, trans. Fyfe-Russell, adapted)

For Herodotus, the second person effectively dislocates the reader, transporting him in time and space.[4] The historian's trip from Elephantine leads to mental simulations, as hearing becomes sight.[5] Ps.-Longinus playfully expresses the power of this technique with his own switch to address the narratee's vision, asking, 'Do you *see*, friend?' Yet this cognitive engagement includes embodied action too, as is clear from Herodotus' future-tense verbs and participles of movement (you will 'sail up', 'arrive at', 'pass through', 'embark', and 'come').[6] These verb forms destabilize the

---

(where it has a strongly colloquial flavour) but it is not exactly rare. It seems to be confined to potentials (past or present) and futures.' For this passage, I have found the commentary of Mazzucchi (1992) *ad loc.*, useful. Cf. the discussions of Too (1998), 199–200; de Jonge (2015), 1008–9; Allan, de Jong, and de Jonge (2017), 42. De Jonge (2020), 163, 166, touches on the second person in the context of Ps.-Longinus, where he treats it as immersive.

[4] For studies on apostrophe and the second person, see Parry (1972a); Gilmartin (1975); Block (1982); Byre (1991); de Jong (2014a), 23–5; Caterine (2015). More recently, Cowan (2018), 270, argues that 'This narrative must be distinguished from first- and third-person narratives which include the occasional apostrophe of the "dear reader", but where that reader plays no other role in the narrative itself.' On Plato and Isocrates' enfranchisement of the reader, Collins (2012). In the *Histories*, such deixis almost always requires the actual reader to position himself within the historian's narrated world rather than to reposition imagined items into his own context; for such 'imagination-oriented deixis', Bühler (1982), 27–30. Cf. de Jong (2014b), for the anonymous – and often only hypothetical – traveller in the European tradition; at 317, she too draws attention to this passage of Ps.-Longinus.

[5] De Jonge (2015), 1009. Further emphasized by the term ἐγαγώνιος, on which Ooms and de Jonge (2013), 98: '"Vivid", "energetic", or "passionate" can all be correct translations of the term, if we understand them to point to one underlying meaning, that is, "involving" or "engaging".'

[6] On the future tense in the second person, B. Richardson (2006), 28–30, where it most closely falls under the rubric of the 'hypothetical form' (also called the 'subjunctive form'), though these categorizations can shift in the same text. Sanford and Emmott (2012), 178–9, describe how

distance between the narratee and the actual reader's act of reading, inviting a virtual experience of travel to Meroe.[7] That is, the second person is seen to position the reader inside the action of the text as an active participant. *On the Sublime* hints at the authority effect generated in noting that this figure, 'after receiving your soul, leads it'; the metaphor puns on the proximity of ψυχή and ἄγω, which together form the word ψυχαγωγία, 'persuasion'.[8]

Ps.-Longinus' account of the powerful effect of the second person is in accord with the findings of rhetorical narratologists and cognitive scientists. Working on modern literature, narratologists have shown that second-person narration refers to an 'empty' linguistic sign; it creates a communicative circuit that can be identified as a form of self-address (a covert first person), appeal to a character (a covert third person), or an invitation for the actual reader to identify with it.[9] Readers can also fully identify with 'you' as an extratextual narratee and later attribute 'you' to an intratextual protagonist or self-address in a more distanced reading experience. Some texts constantly renegotiate the status of you, with the reader positioning and repositioning themself in and out of the same narrative world.[10] A related phenomenon is the so-called double-deixis where the same utterance blurs 'you' into an extra- and intratextual narratee.[11] In double-deixis the reader fails to fully identify with the narratee, but the narratee is not wholly immersed in the narrative world of the text. In sum, this research has shown that the second person is highly unstable and ambiguous. It requires a unique kind of readerly involvement to make sense of it.[12]

---

neuroscientific studies have demonstrated that the second person leads to a different kind of embodiment and experientiality.

[7] Allan, de Jong, and de Jonge (2017), 37, 'this formulation comes quite close to saying that the narratee is "immersed" into the story world'. For geography as a space for haptic exploration, Purves (2013).

[8] On *psychagogia*, see Asmis (1986); Chandler (2006), 147–68; Halliwell (2012), 223–7.

[9] For studies on second-person narrative, Morrissette (1965); Bonheim (1983); McHale (1992), 89–104; Kacandes (1990); B. Richardson (1991), (2006), 17–36; Fludernik (1993), (1994); Margolin (1993); Phelan (1996), 135–53; Bell and Ensslin (2011). Fludernik (1996), 172: '[G]eneric *you* cannot usually be upheld for very long without referentially attaching itself either to the real reader or to a protagonist. In the first case the real reader is swallowed up in the hypothetical situation and consents to the text's implications about herself.... In the second case, the reference is ultimately aligned with a fictional protagonist, leaving the reader to withdraw from the referential circuit.'

[10] B. Richardson (1991), 320–2, of the 'autotelic' second person. For this phenomenon, McHale (1992), 87–114; Fludernik (1993); Kacandes (1993); Phelan (1994).

[11] Herman (1994); Mildorf (2006); Bell and Ensslin (2011).

[12] Nor will all readers respond in the same way; see note 26.

Authority, Experience, and the Vicarious Traveller 209

More recently, psychological and cognitive approaches to the second person have confirmed and expanded upon these findings.[13] Working from the premise that reading can produce a mental simulation of narrative action, this work has demonstrated that when presented with short texts that variably use the first, second, or third person, readers are consistently found to internally identify with the second-person addressee. That is, readers of second-person narrative adopt the positionality of the narratee.[14] A more surprising finding in this line of inquiry is that these readers have been shown to create more vivid and affectively stimulating story worlds. It is noteworthy that this perspective enhances mental representations of space. As Brunyé et al. conclude,[15]

> [D]irectly addressing readers as protagonists may be a reliable method for promoting the tracking and representation of space because such information is needed for developing perceptually and motorically rich mental simulations that subserve inference generation.

Related experiments have established that second-person narratives containing information on spatial relationships, such as action toward or away from 'you', affect the motor system of test subjects.[16] Additionally, action statements that use 'you' enter into short- and long-term memory more successfully than first- and third-person examples.[17] We can infer from the active nature of the actual reader's engagement with such language that greater sensory and motor cognition is present, which leads to its integration in memory. Readers of second-person narration mentally recreate the events of the text from their own viewpoint, which corroborates the deictic circuit that rhetorical narratologists have argued exists between the actual reader and the narratee. This indicates that pronouns help to determine readerly engagement and that the second person can be used to induce particularly vivid mental simulations.

In line with this finding and as Ps.-Longinus affirmed, the Herodotean second person transports the audience and renders the narrative more affecting. Modern scholars, by contrast, have interpreted it either as a

---

[13] For the cognitive turn in ancient Mediterranean studies, see above all Grethlein (2017); Grethlein and Huitink (2017); Anderson, Cairns, and Sprevak (2019); Meineck, Short, and Devereaux (2019); Grethlein, Huitink, and Tagliabue (2020). This work has yet to grapple in detail with the potential for immersion and experiential narrative that the second person presents.

[14] Brunyé et al. (2009), where the third person prompted an external perspective and the first person either external or internal. For embodiment and first-, second-, and third-person narrative, Sanford and Emmott (2012), 161–90. This aligns nicely with Ryan (2001), who has popularized concept of 'immersion', wherein the reader is a witness to the textual world.

[15] Brunyé et al. (2011), 663.   [16] Glenberg and Kaschak (2002).   [17] Ditman et al. (2010).

mark of the orality of the *Histories* or as a borrowing born of the text's interaction with geographic writings. Donald Lateiner, for example, identifies it as conversational, considering that it suggests 'sometimes the intimacy of personal observation and sometimes the truculent tone of someone who has met disagreement ... Herodotus thus appears to permit his reader to believe differently by reifying the possibility of another point of view, a form of presentation rarely found in other historians.'[18] In this way, the reader continues the inquiry of the historian but with an important shift in authority, as first-person verbs recede into the background. It is a 'rhetoric of familiarity and uncertainty rather than of authority and omniscience'.[19] This interpretation has its roots in the interpretation of the *Histories* as an oral text, with Herodotus embracing the techniques of the raconteur.

Alternatively, scholars have suggested that this rhetorical technique arises when the historian goes 'geographic'.[20] In this vein, Tim Rood draws a persuasive parallel between Herodotus' account of the Royal Road and the style of the geographers, arguing that Herodotus' use of second-person verbs and the dative of the reference participle meaning 'one' in this passage mimics what we see in the *periplus* and *periegesis* genres.[21] This can be supported by the fragments of Hecataeus; for example, he locates the city of Kabessos 'as one crosses (ὑπερβάντι) the Thracian Haimon' (*FGrHist* 1 F 169). In much the same way Herodotus' reader discovers fantastic figures who populate Scythia: 'as one crosses (ὑπερβάντι) the mountains are other men who spend nights lasting six months out of the year' (4.25.1). Rood contends that such expressions in Herodotus above all are used to indicate distance and to explain unfamiliar geography to the audience.[22]

---

[18] Lateiner (1989), 30–1. See also Brock (2003), 11, who comments briefly on the second person and rightly notes that it appears when Herodotus is at his 'most combative'. He continues (12): 'Many of the features of Herodotus' narrative presentation to which I have drawn attention appear oral in nature ... but that is not to say that his narratorial personality is a feature of oral style, an unmediated consequence of the character of his material, still less that it is something "archaic".'

[19] Lateiner (1989), 25. Lately followed by Wiater (2017), 243–6.

[20] See Hornblower (1994), 149; Nenci (1994), s.v. 5.52.8; Rood (2006a), 295, (2012a); Branscome (2010); Akujärvi (2012). Note that these scholars at times focus on the dative of reference particles at the expense of the second-person verbs they travel with in the *Histories*. On the dative of reference participle, Smyth (1956), 345 [1497]; de Jong (2004), 110; Akujärvi (2012), passim.

[21] Rood (2006a), 295–6, (2012a), 127–31. Cf. also 2.97.2.

[22] Rood (2012a), 128, observes that they fall out of use for the most part after Xerxes advances beyond Asia into the more recognizable landscape of Europe. Akujärvi (2012) compares Pausanias' use of the dative singular participle as traveller-effect to the *periplus* genre, establishing that Pausanias uses this to specify a location's object in relation to a traveller's gaze, and she too points to Herodotus as

Authority, Experience, and the Vicarious Traveller

These interpretations have much to recommend them, explaining Herodotus' formulation as they do through his compositional style and literary predecessors. Yet neither accounts for the effect that this figure has in its new context in Herodotus' experimental prose work nor the response that it elicited from Ps.-Longinus. Herodotus is not elsewhere bound to a colloquial style, and his text does not require the structural framework of the impersonal narrator that the geographers in the *periplus* genre do. In fact, its use in the *Histories* is very circumscribed; it has no wider structural role at all. So too, Herodotus seldom otherwise assumes the critical distance that this mode offers; given the usual prominence of his first-person narrator, the introduction of these verb forms is all the more surprising.

Lateiner's discussion directs us to a further issue that this narrative strategy raises, that of the historian's authority. Important work has been done on the way in which Herodotus opens up his 'workshop' to his audience, creating a dialogic narrative that enfranchises the reader.[23] The bilateral character of this textual authority indicates that Herodotus' first-person narrator is seldom the final arbiter. Does the shift to second-person verbs (and attendant dative of reference participles, 'one') function as a parallel enfranchisement of readerly competence?[24]

Herodotus first moves the deictic centre of the narrative to the narratee in his discussion of Persian *nomoi*, a section that ends in his findings on the significance of their names. He argues that Persian names map onto Persian bodies and magnificence and that, despite their ignorance of it, all these names (meaning all Persian male names) end in the letter 'san' or 'sigma', translated for Dorians and Ionians, respectively. To support his argument, there is a change of person: 'in seeking, you will find that the names of the Persians end in this letter' (1.139: ἐς τοῦτο διζήμενος

---

operating in the same tradition; quite different from Herodotus' practice is the relatively rare first-person in Pausanias; for this reason the traveller persona in Pausanias might be interpreted as a veiled 'I'.

[23] Cf. Baragwanath (2008), passim. The dialogic nature of the *Histories* has been explored by Bakker (2002), 18; Dewald (2002), 276 (2006b); Boedeker (2003), 17–36; Zali (2015), 305–10. See Wiater (2017), 244, on Herodotus' alternative versions as giving significant authority to the reader, with 'both equally entitled to their respective opinion'.

[24] Fludernik (1996), 173, 'The same tendencies can be observed to recur with the use of *one- (on, man)* narrative. Not only are these indefinite pronouns frequently replaceable with second-person forms (*you; tu* or *vous; du* or *Sie*); inversely, the indefinite pronoun is also frequently used in lieu of first- or second-person forms.' By contrast, de Jong (2014b), 317, distinguishes 'you might have seen' and 'someone might have seen' in narratological terms as closely related but distinct. For the purposes of this chapter I will confine my passages to those that include a second-person verb, though, as we shall see, the dative of reference 'one' is an alternative to this.

εὑρήσεις τελευτῶντα τῶν Περσέων τὰ οὐνόματα). Who is 'you'? It is not self-address, nor a call to a historical actor in the *Histories*;[25] rather, it is an appeal to the audience.[26] It is extratextual, inasmuch as 'you' are invited to continue the historian's inquiry. If the seduction of the reader is complete, then the ontological boundary of the text is violated in a form of metalepsis. At the same time, those readers who will do no 'seeking' may nonetheless feel themselves implicated in the request. The result is not a rhetoric of hesitation; the future tense 'you will find' admits of no other alternative.[27] Herodotus both forecasts and records.[28] Nor is it a bid to familiarize distant geography; the appeal of the communicative circuit between the narratee and the actual reader works to bolster the conclusions of the historian, who has already modelled his own successful inquiry. It is significant that Herodotus does so by inviting one to step into the represented world through a cognitive process of 'seeking and finding' that is elsewhere aligned with didacticism.[29] The historian's philological chops are confirmed by the ensuing narrative, as Hellenized masculine Persian names do all end with the sound.[30]

At times, Herodotus' second person reveals a self-consciousness of its immersive sensory potential. In the historian's explanation of the sedimentation of Egypt, for example, after interviewing Egyptian priests and finding that they agree with one another, he asserts:

[25] Cf. de Jong (2009), 95, on the immersive nature of the Homeric narrator's address to characters: 'the sum effect of the apostrophe is to add to that vital characteristic of Homeric epic, *enargeia*: the events are presented in such a way that they seem to take place before the eyes of the narratees ... Moreover, the metaleptic apostrophe also adds to the authority of the Homeric narrator's story: his characters are real, since they can be addressed.'

[26] Brunyé et al. (2016) demonstrate that not all readers mentally simulate language comprehension in an empathetic reading experience. I, for example, do not identify with the Herodotean narratee's masculine participles. However, no reader response model will expect *all* to respond in the same way.

[27] Del Conte (2003), 214: 'Moreover, the hypothetical and shifting nature of the narratee-protagonist suggests a sense of inevitability of events: regardless of exactly who is experiencing these events (i.e. acting as the narratee), the outcome will be the same.'

[28] See the discussion of Phelan (1996), 150.

[29] The invitation to contemplate does not rupture the experiential effect of the verb; for the compatibility of immersion and reflection, Grethlein (2020). For the joining of these verbs with the second person, Hes. *Op.* 427–8; Thgn. 1.82.

[30] The rule, however, fails with Old Persian, and Herodotus may have meant to discuss only their Hellenized counterparts. As Schmitt (2015), 255, 'For it is well imaginable that Herodotus did intend with his "rule" nothing else than to emphasize the contrast to the Greek situation', whose names end also in -ην, -ων, and -ωρ. See too Chamberlain (1999), 298–300. By contrast, How-Wells, 'H. is at his weakest as a linguist'; more balanced are Asheri, Lloyd, and Corcella (2007), where the rule is 'not entirely wrong'.

Authority, Experience, and the Vicarious Traveller 213

> Even if one has not heard it before, he can readily see, if he has sense (μὴ προακούσαντι ἰδόντι δέ, ὅστις γε σύνεσιν ἔχει), that that Egypt to which the Greeks sail is a land deposited for the Egyptians, the river's gift.... For this is the nature of the land of Egypt: in the first place, approaching it from the sea (προσπλέων) and being still a day distant (ἀπέχων) from land, if you let down a sounding line you will bring up mud and you will be in a depth of eleven fathoms (κατεὶς καταπειρητηρίην πηλόν τε ἀνοίσεις καὶ ἐν ἕνδεκα ὀργυιῆσι ἔσεαι). This shows that the deposit from the land reaches this far (τοῦτο μὲν ἐπὶ τοσοῦτο δηλοῖ πρόχυσιν τῆς γῆς ἐοῦσαν). (2.5)

Herodotus' proof of the truth of the priests' reasoning takes the form of a future experiment involving the release of a rope lead to measure alluvial deposits. Often, as here, second-person verb forms are introduced by a dative of reference participle, 'one'.[31] Silting is proved by seeing; prior hearing is not necessary or even preferable to verify the historian's conclusions. 'One seeing' that the coast is silting opens up a vicarious tour. Nominative masculine participles of movement follow as someone 'approaches by sea', 'is distant from', and 'lets down a line'. These might initially be thought to be identified with the first-person narrator, as Herodotus has so far been our guide. This assumption has to be revised in stride, however, on reaching the concluding second-person verbs: 'you will bring up mud' and 'you will be at a depth of eleven fathoms'. The vibrancy of the narration is commented upon by Asheri, Lloyd, and Corcella: 'both tense and person are designed to create a sense of immediacy by involving the reader imaginatively in the action'.[32] Beginning from the dative of reference, the actual reader is invited to identify with the narratee's movements in Egyptian space.

What stands out is that a technique used structurally by the geographers takes on a strong protreptic role in its adaptation in the *Histories*. The narratee authenticates the narrator's conclusions, proving the silting of Egypt, a highly debated issue in the fifth century.[33] The emphasis on sight is significant; though the audience is connected to the narrative via sound, hearing is demoted and instead the *Histories* invites a second-person virtual

---

[31] Cf. 1.199.4, where the historian gives an account of the shameful *nomos* of temple prostitution in Babylon. The narrator explains that all women perform this ritual act at some point. Rejecting 'the one first throwing' (τῷ δὲ πρώτῳ ἐμβαλόντι) a coin is impossible, even for the aristocratic woman. But after copulating 'you will not give her any gift great enough to win her' (καὶ τὠπὸ τούτου οὐκ οὕτω μέγα τί οἱ δώσεις ὥς μιν λάμψεαι). For 'one' as impersonal you, McHale (1985), 100–1.

[32] Asheri, Lloyd, and Corcella (2007), on 2.5.2.

[33] Christ (1994), 183, finds that Herodotus 'speaks of hypothetical experiments that one might carry out to prove a particular point' and he places this passage alongside 2.11.4 and 2.26, where the appeal to the reader is not made. For this thought experiment in Herodotus, Gera (2000), 28–9.

travelling experience. Herodotus blurs vicarious sailing into verified proof in the finale of the episode: 'this *shows* to what extent there is a silting of the land'. And this effect is borne out by the reception of Herodotus' appeal. Arrian, for example, mentions that Hecataeus had reached similar conclusions on the silting of the Nile valley, but that Herodotus 'has given a display of this with no uncertain proofs' (καὶ οὐκ ἀμαυροῖς τεκμηρίοις ὅτι ταύτῃ ἔχει Ἡροδότῳ ἐπιδέδεικται).[34] Arrian's reception of the passage may point to the powerful effect of the combination of the hypothetical experiment and the appeal to the second person, both of which combine here to result in his comment that the proof is literally 'not unseen' or 'not without light'.[35] The experiential language is presented as a visual demonstration of the validity of the historian's deductive reasoning. As in the previous passage, the dialogic enfranchisement of readerly competence is simultaneously predetermined.[36]

We can see a similar use of the second person in a moment of high protreptic discourse in Herodotus' description of the battle between the Persians and the Egyptians at Pelusium.[37] There are several first-person indications of autopsy in this passage. Herodotus' account of the skulls on the battlefield opens with 'I saw a great marvel' and closes with 'now I saw things such as these; I saw similar things on the battlefield at Papremis' (3.12).[38] His eyewitness account records that the skulls of the Persians and Egyptians were separated after the battle and that the Persian skulls were weaker because of their custom of covering their heads from childhood, whereas the Egyptians' were stronger, a result of the sun's thickening their

---

[34] *FGrHist* 1 F 301 = *Anab.* 5.6.5, where Hecataeus is said to have also called Egypt the 'gift of the river'. Elsewhere, the Halicarnassian is willing to single out a specific individual for such proofs, as when the Egyptian king Psammetichus is said to test the depths of the source of the Nile and release a sounding line into the water that never found an end, 2.28.

[35] Chantraine (1968) s.v. ἀμαυρός: 'attesté pour la première fois *Od.* 4.824 et 835 comme épithète d'un fantôme "sombre, difficile à distinguer", épithète des morts chez Sapho. Se dit d'une trace difficile à distinguer . . . de la nuit, de la vue' ('attested for the first time in *Od.* 4.824 and 835 as an epithet of a shade "dark, hard to make out", as an epithet of the dead in Sappho. It is said to be a track that is hard to make out . . . of the night, of sight').

[36] Asheri, Lloyd, and Corcella (2007), on 2.5.1: 'the major source is ὄψις', which perhaps suggests they interpret the second person as a masked first person, e.g. 2.12.1. Cf. Hp. *Aer.* 8.44, 13.8, 16.27, 20.2, 24.29, 24.32, 24.47 (Littré), for εὑρήσεις; Hp. *VM* 18: ἢν δὲ τὴν χεῖρα προσφέρῃς ('if you put your hand on it'); 22: τῷ στόματι κεχηνὼς ὑγρὸν οὐδὲν ἀνασπάσαις· προμυλλήνας δὲ καὶ συστείλας, πιέσας τε τὰ χείλεα, ἔτι τε αὐλὸν προσθέμενος, ῥηϊδίως ἀνασπάσαις ἂν ὅ τι θέλοις ('if you were to have your mouth gape open you would not suck up any fluid; but if you made a pout and drew them in, pursing your lips, and adding also a hollow tube, you could easily suck up whatever you want').

[37] See Scullion, Chapter 5 in this volume (pp. 105–8), for a discussion of the skulls as part of the 'autopsy motif' in Herodotus' role as virtual tour guide.

[38] R. Thomas (2000), 30–2.

Authority, Experience, and the Vicarious Traveller 215

skulls as a result of their habit of shaving the head. The experiment itself, however, is placed in the second person: 'the skulls of the Persians are so weak that if you should be willing (θέλοις) to strike them with a single pebble, you will break them (διατετρανέεις), while the skulls of the Egyptians are so strong that if you struck them (παίσας) with a stone you could break them (διαρρήξειας) only with difficulty' (3.12.1). The conditional underscores the autonomy of the actual reader, who may generate an immersive simulation with the battlefield through the experiment. The appeal to the reader continues in the explanation that this custom in the Egyptians eliminates baldness, 'for one would see (ἄν τις ... ἴδοιτο) that of all men the fewest Egyptians go bald' (3.12.3). The visualization of the scene that the narrator and the narratee share offers up a particularly vivid authentication of the marvel that the historian has witnessed. The addressee is involved as an inspector on the battlefield, virtually cracking Persian and Egyptian skulls. The spatial, visual, and embodied immersive features of this passage have often led commentators to fold it into Herodotus' own account of his autopsy. As Dawson reconstructs: 'In his thirst for knowledge, Herodotus, when visiting the battlefield of Pelusium, threw stones at the skulls of the Persians and Egyptians that lay scattered about, in order to ascertain their relative hardness.'[39] While this interpretation rightly gets at the persuasive power of the narratee's verification of the conclusions of Herodotus, naturalizing the second person as a covert first person should be resisted precisely because of its ability to establish a circuit of consent between the narrator, the narratee, and the actual reader.

This effect can be sustained in longer narrative sections as well. This is clear if we return to the description of the trip to Meroe that Ps.-Longinus drew attention to. *On the Sublime* severely compresses the journey and elides or changes the more varied dative singular participle and impersonal verb forms into the second person. An even more intrusive narratee emerges from the unadapted text, following the historian's introduction of the journey:

> But for the rest I learned so much as here follows by the most diligent inquiry; for I went myself as an eyewitness (αὐτόπτης ἐλθών) as far as the city of Elephantine and from that point onwards I gathered knowledge by report (ἀκοῇ ἤδη ἱστορέων). (2.29.1)

[39] Dawson (1986), 93. More recent is Purves (2013), 33, 'Herodotus also stresses his physical presence at the scene. He tells us that he was close enough not only to see these bones of the Egyptians and Persians, but even to feel them for himself. But in addition, by his use of the second-person singular, Herodotus also asks us to imagine performing these actions in an embodied way'.

Emphasis begins on the sensory value of the report that the historian is about to offer, one guaranteed not by autopsy but by hearing (ἀκοῇ).[40] With the historian's absent eyes, so too first-person verbs and nominative participles recede after the explanation of the limits of his eyewitness research. The narratee takes over this experiential gap, as the journey up the Nile takes place through the dative of reference participles and second-person verbs: 'as one goes up from Elephantine', 'you will arrive at', 'sailing past', 'you will come to', 'disembarking', 'you will make a land journey', 'passing', 'you will embark', 'you will sail', and finally 'you will arrive' at Meroe. The sheer number of verbal forms contributes to the immersive effect of the travel narrative.[41] Spatial deictic markers perform a similar function: 'on this spot' (ταύτῃ) one has to affix ropes to both sides of the boat; 'on this spot' the Nile is just like the Maeander river; it takes four days on the boat to journey through 'this land' (χωρίον τοῦτο); the Nile flows 'into this lake' (ἐς τὴν λίμνην ταύτην); the people in 'this land' (ἐν ταύτῃ) honour Zeus and Dionysus alone. There is also deixis encoding time: 'and next' (καὶ ἔπειτα) you will arrive into a smooth plane; 'and next' (καὶ ἔπειτα) you will disembark; 'again' (αὖτις) you will embark; 'and next' (καὶ ἔπειτα) you will arrive at Meroe (2.29).

Ps.-Longinus' account of the passage stops here, but the *Histories* continues to foreground the experience of the narratee on the path up the Nile.

> Sailing from this city you will come to the 'Deserters' in another period of time equal to that in which you came from Elephantine to the mother-city of the Ethiopians. (2.30.1: ἀπὸ δὲ ταύτης τῆς πόλιος πλέων ἐν ἴσῳ χρόνῳ ἄλλῳ ἥξεις ἐς τοὺς αὐτομόλους ἐν ὅσῳ περ ἐξ Ἐλεφαντίνης ἦλθες ἐς τὴν μητρόπολιν τὴν Αἰθιόπων)

---

[40] Török (2014), 84: 'But the historian does not pretend that he could present collective *akoē* statements from *locals* ... since he did not go to Nubia and did not meet Nubian informants either.'

[41] Aristid. *Or.* 36.41–63 critiques Herodotus' account and does so humorously by using the future or optative second person in the course of his discourse. Significantly, he characterizes Herodotus' style as using ψυχαγωγία. Cf. Ps.-Scylax's use of the second person, which is restricted to two instances and not part of a grouping of immersive verb forms, 67: μέχρι ἂν ἔλθῃς ἐφ' Ἱερόν. Ἀφ' Ἱεροῦ δὲ τοῦ στόματός ἐστι τοῦ Πόντου εὖρος στάδια ζ' ('until you come to Hieron. From Hieron the width of the mouth of the Pontos is seven stades'); and 100: καὶ ἐὰν προέλθῃς ἀπὸ θαλάττης ἀνώτερον, ἔστι Φασηλὶς πόλις καὶ λιμήν ('and if you advance to higher ground from the sea, there is the polis, Phaselis, and a harbour'). As Akujärvi (2012), 333, states: 'But in Herodotus' *Histories* there are some descriptions of larger territories where these participles are found in larger numbers, occasionally together with finite verb forms with subjects as indefinite as those of the participles.'

Authority, Experience, and the Vicarious Traveller 217

Simulated travel is further reinforced by the back-reference to the 'equal amount of time' it took 'you' to reach Meroe and to the region 'you came' from. Unique to this passage is the use of the past tense (ἦλθες) in a second-person address in the *Histories*; elsewhere, these are in the future tense. The aorist verb, however, creates a strong sense of internal temporal coherence for the journey of the narratee. The journey concludes with a path that peters out in a desert barren of people and knowledge. The narratee returns to the more distanced 'one': 'for one calculating' (συμβαλλομένῳ) the number of months for 'one traveling' (πορευομένῳ) from Elephantine to the Deserters is four (2.31).[42]

What is the effect of this passage in which, according to Ps.-Longinus, Herodotus turns hearing into sight? Herodotus has been walking the reader through his own journey in Egypt, but here the view through the camera lens is reversed, with the narratee as the agent of movement and experience, who walks and boats through geographical spaces the narrator has not. This reversal is a productive one. As de Jong has concluded, metalepsis in ancient texts is largely 'aimed at increasing the authority of the narrator and the realism of his narrative (rather than breaking the illusion)'.[43] This tallies well with the reception found in Ps.-Longinus, where the mimetic nature of the passage led to his punning on its persuasiveness. The realism of the journey is central to the narrative's authority effect. Insofar as the actual reader adopts the position of the narratee, hearsay is translated into a phenomenological episode of virtual travel. The verbs in this passage play an important role in generating a vivid spatial orientation. An egocentric perspective promotes self-relevance and, as cognitive research has shown, has the potential to generate stronger perceptual data in the 'mental tours' that it simulates.[44] Identification with the narratee's movements leads to a more immersive depiction of geography in the far south. This empathetic reading places the audience in the position of performing the historian's inquiry.[45]

Relevant too is the introductory comment on the journey, which highlights a dependence on hearsay, ἀκοή. In crafting a second-person narrative based on the reports of his informants, Herodotus might also be interpreted as re-enacting the response to his inquiries. Out of the passages we have looked at, this is the first time that the narrator is potentially to be

---

[42] On measuring and surveying this Egyptian space, Vasunia (2001), 89.   [43] De Jong (2009), 115.

[44] Brunyé et al. (2011), 663: 'situation models built during language comprehension differentially represent elements related to the spatial organisation of described environments, with relatively accurate and easily retrieved memories with the pronoun you'.

[45] For such narrative 'transgressions', McHale (1985), 93–5.

located beyond the Herodotean narrator; the 'I' implied by 'you' may be interpreted as an oral source. Herman's double-deixis is a useful concept here, as it exploits the tension of appeal to the reader that is also an appeal to a fictionalized narratee. In the journey to Meroe, second-person verbs apply simultaneously to a covert Herodotean 'I' as internal audience to his informants *and* to the actual reader. Blurring 'you' spurs reflection on the extent of readerly participation at stake even as it tropes the limits of hearsay.

Double-deixis is also present in a parallel voyage that explores the furthest reaches of the unknown world in the far *north* (4.16–31.2).[46] As in the journey up the Nile, the more distant reaches of the unseen north flag up the problem of sources. Of this region, Herodotus reports: 'I could not learn from anyone who claimed to be an eyewitness' (4.16.1). The poet Aristeas of Proconnesus had documented a path through Scythia to the mysterious Issedonian people in his epic poem, *Arimaspeia*. Herodotus assures us that even Aristeas did not, however, claim to visit the distant lands beyond Scythia and instead relied upon hearsay.[47] With these difficulties in mind the historian determines that 'as much as we were able to arrive at by hearsay of the most distant regions, all will be said' (4.16.2: ἀλλ' ὅσον μὲν ἡμεῖς [ἀτρεκέως] ἐπὶ μακρότατον οἷοί τε ἐγενόμεθα ἀκοῇ ἐξικέσθαι, πᾶν εἰρήσεται). This introduction has clear echoes of the earlier presentation of the geography of the far south:[48] ἄλλου δὲ οὐδενὸς οὐδὲν ἐδυνάμην πυθέσθαι. ἀλλὰ τοσόνδε μὲν ἄλλο ἐπὶ μακρότατον ἐπυθόμην, μέχρι μὲν Ἐλεφαντίνης πόλιος αὐτόπτης ἐλθών, τὸ δὲ ἀπὸ τούτου ἀκοῇ ἤδη ἱστορέων (2.29.1).[49] Again, the narrator makes reference to the absence of eyewitness accounts for lands distant in space and to his reliance on reporting. As in the virtual journey up the Nile, the path beyond Scythia is structured by a vicarious experience transforming sound into sight and embodied movement, in this case through the dative of reference participles.

[46] See Asheri, Lloyd, and Corcella (2007), 548, on the parallel; Lateiner (1989), 155–7; R. Thomas (2000), 56.

[47] On Herodotus' Aristaeus, S. West (2004), 44, who observes that the poet is portrayed as drawing a distinction between eyewitness and hearsay much as the historian does. The historical status of his trip to the Black Sea in general is not at stake for my purposes, but the conclusions of Armayor (1978a) are pessimistic.

[48] As is often noted, e.g. Trüdinger (1918), 19; Redfield (1985), 106–9. Cf. 2.16.2: ἀλλ' ὅσον μὲν ἡμεῖς ἀτρεκέως ἐπὶ μακρότατον οἷοί τε ἐγενόμεθα ἀκοῇ ἐξικέσθαι, πᾶν εἰρήσεται – the parallel is also cited by Benardete (1969), 106. The term ἀκοή occurs only five other times in the *Histories*, 1.38, 1.171, 2.29, 2.123, 2.148.

[49] For translation, see above, p. 215.

Authority, Experience, and the Vicarious Traveller 219

The path begins in the far west of Scythia, with the Hellenic Scythians and those Scythians who till the soil. The first-person singular falls away until the geographical description concludes.[50] After the move eastward into Scythia, the generic 'one' is appealed to: 'but for one crossing (διαβάντι) the Borysthenes river, first from the coast is Hylaea and from here other Scythia farmers live' (4.18.1). As the expedition moves further east, we are informed that 'for one who crosses (διαβάντι) the Panticapes river the Nomad Scythians dwell' (4.19.1). The exit from Scythia to the east is similarly marked, 'to one crossing (διαβάντι) the Tanais river, no longer is the country Scythia' (4.21).[51] The dative offers itself as a surrogate for the missing eyewitness testimony of the historian travelling east of Scythia.[52] In a discussion of the region north of the Budini, one is bidden to 'turn aside' (4.22: ἀποκλίνοντι) from the desert east to the Thyssagetae and again to 'turn aside' (4.22: ἀποκλίνοντι) further east to the land inhabited by Scythians who have revolted from the Royal Scythians. From this point, the land becomes stony and harsh and increasingly fantastic: 'to one crossing (διεξελθόντι) this rough country are men inhabiting the foothills of high mountains, who are said to be bald from birth' (4.23.2). Here the reader enters a wholly exotic, untrustworthy land: 'for one ascending' (ὑπερβάντι) the mountains, these men are said to have the feet of goats and to have six months of night (4.25.1).[53]

A description of the extremes of the Scythian climate closes the geography of the far north. The cold is biting for the majority of the year, a view that is confirmed by a proof that shifts narration into the second person: 'during these months you will not be able to make mud by pouring out water, but you will only make it by kindling a fire' (4.28.1: ἐν τοῖσι ὕδωρ ἐκχέας πηλὸν οὐ ποιήσεις, πῦρ δὲ ἀνακαίων ποιήσεις πηλόν).[54] The more distant generalized reader again gives way to a vivid set of second-person verbs, intensifying the role of the narratee traveling through Scythia

---

[50] An exception is found at 4.25.1, an intrusive rejection of the informants' statements that goat-footed men live in the mountains and that there are those for whom the night is six months long. The first-person plural ὅσον ἡμεῖς ἴδμεν is repeated: 4.17.2; 4.18.3; 4.20.2.

[51] Rivers play an especially important role in demarcating Scythian geography, S. West (2002), 441: 'The river system provides a topographical grid for Herodotus' location of different groups; the principle is sound, but his concept is implausibly schematic, with rivers regularly running down at right angles to the coast.' Cf. too Redfield (1985), 106–7; Hartog (1988), 12–19, 344–8, 351–3; Erbse (1992), 161; now Clarke (2018), 95–6, 98–106, 160–1.

[52] Hartog (1988), 353–4.

[53] Hartog (1988), 14: 'the further one goes in that direction, the less evidence of the human race is to be found'.

[54] On this passage as evidence of the exceptional nature of Scythian winters, Hartog (1988), 28–9; R. Thomas (2000), 65.

and bearing out that the frigid weather breaks the normal rules for the elements. As the *Histories* will continue to explain, in this region water becomes a second earth, and is frozen so fully that wagons are able to cross over entire seas. The cold makes it so that rain fails to fall at the customary time in winter, in contrast with the rest of the inhabited world. The above experiment corroborates these findings, and the transfer of the deictic centre to 'you' opens up the opportunity for the actual reader to identify with the narratee. The future tense, which we have seen is characteristic of this device in the *Histories*, projects the reader into the hypothetical visit to the frozen tundra beyond Scythia. As in Ethiopia, this takes place in the absence of the eyewitness testimony of the historian and with the explicit reflection on its origins in hearsay.[55]

In the journey north too, the enfranchisement of the narratee can be interpreted as part of a strategy of mimesis, with the *Histories* performing its sources. Flagging the report's status as hearsay immediately before proceeding into the account, with its suppression of the first person, supports this reading. The implied 'I' blurs into a double identification as Herodotus' informants and the Herodotean narrator. In this way, the narrative avoids a deterministic affirmation of Herodotus' conclusions; instead, authority is dispersed through the circuit of oral source, historian, and narratee.

A final passage that we shall examine occurs in the context of the origins of the Ionian Revolt and the attempts of the Milesian provocateur, Aristagoras, to bring Sparta's military might to bear on the coming Ionian conflict with Persia. Herodotus explains that Aristagoras detailed the journey from Sardis to Susa in an interview with the Spartan king, Cleomenes. In that discussion, with the help of a bronze map, he surveyed the rich, accessible territories en route to the Great King's residence in Susa (5.49). Spartan support for the campaign evaporates, however, after Cleomenes learns from Aristagoras that the distance of the journey inland is an eye-watering three months.

Aristagoras' map revealed 'the whole earth', 'all the sea', and 'all rivers', and in an impressive command of this technological innovation, the tyrant of Miletus uses it to move along the Royal Road, indicating its vast wealth.

---

[55] The narratee's complicity in sketching the rigidly geometric outline of the far north renders the country in impressive detail. This detail will be set in stark contrast to the wandering of the Great King, Darius, in his failed attempt to conquer Scythia. Ignorance of the geography of the north confounds the Persian onslaught, and it is the reader's intimate journey through this geography that will make that reversal all the more dramatic. More often it is considered unmappable, e.g. Purves (2010), 131–2; Clarke (2018), 26 n. 90.

Authority, Experience, and the Vicarious Traveller

He has only to point his finger to the map and explain the position and his interlocutor witnesses the transition into a new territory.[56] As Tim Rood has rightly observed, the 'account disturbs the contrast between map and text'.[57] That is, cartographic and hodological knowledge are combined. The dynamism of Aristagoras' speech and visual display piece is cut off, however, in the abrupt order of Cleomenes that he depart before the sunset. The *Histories* maintains the lively visual element conjured by Aristagoras' map, not through the deictic gesture of a finger on a map, but through the continual reference to the experiences of 'one' and 'you'.[58] First-person verbs disappear and after a description of traveling over Lydia and Phrygia, the actual reader is invited to be 'one crossing' (διαβάντι) into Cappadocia, and later, 'one journeying' (πορευομένῳ) up to Cicilia (5.52.2). From Cappadocia the narratee becomes the explicit surrogate for the progress with the future-tense verbs 'you will ride' (διεξελᾷς) through two mountain passes and 'you will pass' (παραμείψεαι) two fortified posts into Cilicia. Then, 'to one driving past these (διεξελάσαντι) and to one making (ποιευμένῳ) his way through Cilicia' the distance is carefully charted as three stades or fifteen and a half parasangs (5.52.2–3). Later, 'as one enters (ἐσβάλλοντι) into the Matenian land from this Armenian land' are thirty-four stades and 137 parasangs. 'From this land to one passing (μεταβαίνοντι) into Kissia' the distances are similarly given.

The departure of Aristagoras as internal narrator from Sparta arrests the forward momentum of the text and its representation of the Royal Road. Herodotus makes clear that 'it was not granted to him any longer to indicate (σημῆναι) the journey inland to the king' (5.51.3). But the expedition nonetheless continues – 'about this road, the story is as follows' (5.52.1) – with a redirection to immersive verbal forms. As we have seen, these can produce powerful simulations in terms of a mental mapping of the organization of space. First, the intensification of participation at this point constitutes a virtuoso performance of the power of Herodotus' text to produce a virtual landscape in the absence of Aristagoras' visual aid. As

---

[56] Pelling (2007a), 196, thoughtfully opposes the deictics of Aristagoras to Herodotus' textual display, which may be thought to 'do a better, less misleading job'.

[57] See Rood (2012a), 133, where he also notes: 'the map serves as a supplement to, not a replacement for, a hodological perspective'. The emphasis of Purves (2010), 132–50, is different, pointing out the tension between hodological and cartographic knowledge. Clarke (2003), 75 n. 17, discusses Polybius' rhetoric of autopsy and draws a parallel to Herodotus' excursus on the Royal Road, rightly seeing, however, that the latter does not claim autopsy.

[58] Branscome (2013), 134. Briant (2002), 357–9, on the royal roads of the empire and the controversial nature of Herodotus' account.

we saw above, the change of person can obscure the identification of 'you' and the implied 'I'. The march into the interior is at once Herodotus, but also an impersonation of the absent informant, Aristagoras. Note that the trip maintains the time limit that the tyrant has prescribed – ninety days (5.54.1) – although this is wrong. Herodotus afterward resumes his first-person narrative (5.54.2: λέγω) to correct Aristagoras' account by three days.[59] Significantly, the episode revolves around Cleomenes' choice *not* to travel east, and the determinism of these verbal forms stands in stark contrast to his rejection.

At this point it is possible to draw some conclusions. In this chapter, I have analysed Herodotus' embedding of a vicarious traveller through the second person and dative of reference 'one'. In each instance, this motif encourages the narratee to move from ignorance to new understanding. Already in antiquity, this was viewed as a highly immersive and experiential narrative strategy. Combining insights from ancient criticism, narratology, and cognitive science offers new understanding of this effect. On the basis of this framework, I have suggested that these verbal forms fashion an experiential text in which the actual reader is invited to become complicit in the forward momentum of the narratee's movement in space. 'You' is embedded into polemical passages, those in which the historian aims to shore up the weight of his own inferences – on, for example, the names of the Persians ending in sigma, the silting of Egypt, and the effect of environmental factors on skull density. In addition to this, in select passages the narratee takes part in a progressive journey through an elaborately detailed geographical space with the complete effacement of the first-person Herodotean narrator, as in the voyages to the far south and north. These episodes too elicit readerly participation in the represented world, but their explicit reliance on hearsay rather than the historian's eyewitness accounting opens up another possibility: they can be interpreted as a mimesis of responses from Herodotus' oral sources, with the identification of 'you' shifting between the Herodotean narratee and the actual reader, in an example of double-deixis.

---

[59] Stein ad 5.52: 'Die allgemeine Skizze dieser "Königsstraße" ... scheint derselben Karte, die der Erztafel des Aristagoras zu Grunde lag' ('The general outline of this "Royal Road" ... seems to be the same map as that which was the basis for the bronze one of Aristagoras'). Branscome (2013), 105–49, stresses the triumph of Herodotean inquiry over the deceptive display of Aristagoras; Zali (2015), 193–200, also highlights the deceptive nature of his language. Pelling (2007a), 195–6, 'Some may still prefer to think that Herodotus is supplementing Aristagoras' account without particularly correcting it; others will find the supplement so great as to *constitute* correction.' See further Pelling (2007a), 196 nn. 58 and 59.

Authority, Experience, and the Vicarious Traveller 223

All of this takes us back to the issue of authority and presents a new angle on the *Histories'* construction of its circuit of consent. The second person and the dative of reference make the text highly immersive. In these verb forms' determinism, they reaffirm the authority of the narrator; as Ps.-Longinus recognized, it is Herodotus who 'leads our souls'. Yet the experiential quality of the *Histories* is heightened in a different way in those passages in which the actual reader blurs in and out of 'you'. This ambiguity makes the attribution of the narratee the contingent product of the reader, whose role in negotiating identification takes the lead, and whose participation in Herodotus' workshop generates its own authority.

CHAPTER 11

Veni, vidi, vici
When Did Roman Republican Politicians Use the First-Person Singular?

Harriet I. Flower

Veni, vidi, vici
—A placard in Julius Caesar's triumph over Pontus in 46 BC[1]

This essay grows out of an ongoing interest in the first autobiographies written in Latin, the remains of which date to the early first century BC.[2] We have only small surviving fragments of the memoirs composed by four leading Roman senators in the 90s, 80s, and 70s BC. They are Quintus Lutatius Catulus (cos. 102), Marcus Aemilius Scaurus (cos. 115), Lucius Cornelius Sulla Felix (cos. 88, 80), and Publius Rutilius Rufus (cos. 105).[3] These men seem to have been the first Romans to write about their own lives in the first-person singular.[4] Their writings were circulated either in their own lifetimes or immediately after their deaths. They knew each other and were linked by complex networks of competition, mutual influence, and enmities sharpened by a harsh environment of political disintegration and civil war. In other words, this little group represents an intellectual milieu of sorts, operating at a rather specific time of political and military crisis.

---

*I would like to thank the following for help and advice with this chapter: Jackie Elliott, Michael Flower, Tony Woodman, and the editors of this volume. I would also like to thank John Marincola for over forty years of warm friendship and intellectual inspiration.

[1] Suetonius *Jul.* 37.2 assigns this saying to a placard in Caesar's Pontic triumph. Plutarch *Caes.* 50.2, *Mor.* 206e, and Appian *BC* 2.91 have him use the phrase in letters sent to friends in Rome. For discussion of the impact of the first person on a triumphal placard, see Östenberg (2013). For triumphal placards in general, see Östenberg (2009a), 68–96, 114–16, 127, 140, and (2009b), 163, 213–14.

[2] All dates are BC, unless otherwise indicated.

[3] Badian (1966) remains the classic discussion. See now also Walter (2003); C. Smith and Powell (2009); Candau (2011); and Tatum (2011). Three recent editions of the fragments are Chassignet (2004); Scholz, Walter and Winkle (2013); and Cornell et al. (2013 = *FRHist*).

[4] *Contra* Chassignet (2004), lxxxvi, who argues for a body of lost autobiographies in Latin written during the last generation of the second century, based on Tacitus *Ag.* 1.2–3. See now also Woodman with Kraus (2014) *ad loc.*

224

Republican Politicians and the First-Person Singular   225

Scaurus is traditionally listed as the first author, but this choice is based on Peter's edition of the fragments, which was arranged simply by birth date.[5] I have elsewhere argued for a different order, with Catulus 'publishing' first, around 100, followed by Scaurus in the late 90s, Sulla (posthumously) in the early 70s, and Rutilius Rufus also in the 70s, at the same time as or perhaps slightly after Sulla, whom Rutilius outlived by several years.[6] Regardless of their precise chronological order, these writings give us an insight into one possible response to the disintegration of the traditional political culture of the *nobiles*, namely, to tell your story for the contemporary moment, in your own words, and explicitly from your own point of view, albeit in different formats and on very varying scales. At the same time, they did not produce what anyone today would call a formal new 'genre' of Latin memoirs.[7]

Sulla's very detailed and extensive autobiography in twenty-two books remained unfinished at the time of his death, but was read, perhaps by many, throughout antiquity.[8] His highly partisan tone and baroque manner of self-presentation may have been responsible for discouraging others from this type of self-presentation. In effect, these first-person narratives did not launch a trend of writing autobiographies in Latin. As Cicero makes clear in his famous letter to L. Lucceius (*Fam.* 5.12), written in the mid-50s, an account of his achievements by another elite man in the third person would carry much more weight than anything that he could produce himself in the first person.[9] At this same time, Julius Caesar was sending his regular

---

[5] The order in Peter 1914 (originally published in the first edition of his fragments of the Roman historians in 1870) is Scaurus, Rufus, Catulus, and Sulla. This order is preserved by Suerbaum (2002), 450; Chassignet (2004); and Scholz, Walter, and Winkle (2013).

[6] H. I. Flower (2014) lists the authors in the following order: Catulus, Scaurus, Rutilius, and Sulla. C. Smith in *FRHist* has them as nos. 18 (Scaurus), 19 (Catulus), 21 (Rutilius) and 22 (Sulla), with Scaurus possibly publishing in the second century, distinctly earlier than the three others. It has been traditional to put Rutilius before Sulla, mainly because he was so much older, but they were probably writing around the same time. For Sulla's memoirs, see also H. I. Flower (2015a) and (2015b). For Rutilius' memoirs, see H. I. Flower (forthcoming).

[7] For discussion of genre, see Marincola (1999a); Baier (2005), 123 and 142; and Pelling (2009c).

[8] Twenty-three fragments of Sulla's memoirs survive. See Suerbaum (2002), 453–6 no. 173; Chassignet (2004), xcix–civ, 172–84, 240–7; Scholz, Walter, and Winkle (2013), 80–135, *FRHist* no. 22 (Christopher Smith). For further discussion, see C. Smith (2009) and Thein (2009). Most of the fragments are cited by Plutarch, especially in his biography of Sulla, but also in those of Marius and Lucullus. Other citing authors are Cicero, Valerius Maximus, Pliny the Elder, Tacitus, Aulus Gellius, and Priscian. Distinct influence can be detected in Sallust *Jug.* and Appian *BC*.

[9] L. Lucceius never complied with Cicero's request. Cicero himself had (already?) written an epic poem in Latin entitled *De consulatu suo*, which does not survive. In addition, he wrote a Greek version (*Att.* 1.20.6), which he sent to Posidonius to use for his Greek history (*Att.* 2.1.1–2). Cicero also soon published the speeches he had delivered in 63 (*Agr.*, *Mur.*, *Rab. Perd.*, and *Catil.* 1–4). In

dispatches from Gaul written in the third person.[10] Importantly, Sallust (*Cat.* 8) echoed a similar sentiment soon after both Caesar and Cicero had been killed and Republican government had collapsed in Rome.[11]

This thoroughly Roman aversion to first-person memoir was shaped by traditional practices of publicity and societal recognition. The format of the third-person eulogy was enshrined in Roman political culture, especially in the funeral *laudatio* delivered from the *rostra* in the forum for a recently deceased politician.[12] This eulogy might use either the third- or the second-person singular to refer to or to address the deceased directly. For a politician, this recognition by the community at large remained the ultimate accolade in Republican Rome. Similarly, inscriptions labelling honorific statues, buildings, religious dedications, or other monuments were also composed, almost without exception, in standard formats in the third person.[13]

With a view to finding a context within a Roman cultural framework for the highly experimental first-person narratives of the early first century BC, this essay will try to sketch the range of occasions and settings in which an elite Roman, such as Catulus (born around 150 BC) or Scaurus (who was probably at least a decade older than Catulus), would regularly have used the first-person singular to present himself to an audience beyond that of his immediate family and personal friends. Unfortunately, the slim evidence for the second century BC does not provide much precise detail, yet an outline can be made by adducing some examples from later sources that indicate standard practices and accepted norms. My discussion will move briskly from record books to legal documents, from letters to epigrams, from satire to epigraphical self-representation. At the end I will attempt a brief consideration of speeches, which provided the most obvious venues for public self-presentation in the first person, whether during their initial delivery or in a written form that circulated to a literate audience.

46, Cicero asserted that many more Romans were reading Xenophon's works than Scaurus' memoirs, which had become neglected (*Brut.* 132).

[10] Wiseman (1998) has argued decisively for a publication of Caesar's account of the Gallic wars in annual instalments during the 50s. For Caesar's use of the third person, see Marincola (1997), 196–205; Batstone and Damon (2006), 117–22 and 144–6; and Kraus (2009). For Caesar's use of the third person, especially in comparison to Xenophon's, see Pelling (2013).

[11] In the context of his choice to retire from politics and take up writing historiography (around 43–2), Sallust says: *optumus quisque facere quam dicere, sua ab aliis bene facta laudari quam ipse aliorum narrare malebat* ('Every excellent man would prefer deeds to words, would prefer his achievements to be praised by others than himself to write about others').

[12] For the slim fragments of the *laudationes*, see Kierdorf (1980), with discussion in H. I. Flower (1996), 128–58, and Suerbaum (2002), 518–23.

[13] For Republican inscriptions, see *ILLRP* and *CIL* 1^2 2.4 (1986) and earlier texts in 6.8.3 (2000). Östenberg (2013), 825–6, discusses the use of the third person in relation to the placards carried in triumphs.

Republican Politicians and the First-Person Singular 227

In the political sphere, a Roman magistrate would have made extensive use of the first person as a natural part of exercising his duties during his time in office. An example is provided by Cicero's quotation from Verres' account books, which he kept as praetor in Sicily (*Ver.* 1, 36–7).[14]

> ***ACCEPI:*** *VICIENS DVCENTA TRIGINTA QVINQVE MILIA QVADRINGENTOS DECEM ET SEPTEM NVMMOS. DEDI STIPENDIO, FRVMENTO, LEGATIS, PRO QVAESTORE, COHORTI PRAETORIAE HS MILLE SESCENTA TRIGINTA QVINQVE MILIA QVADRINGENTOS DECEM ET SEPTEM NVMMOS **RELIQVI***: *ARIMINI HS SESCENTA MILIA.*

> **I received**: 2,235,417 sesterces. I gave (expenses for the pay of soldiers, grain, legates, the proquaestor, and the praetorian cohort): 1,635,417 sesterces. **I deposited upon my departure**: at Ariminum 600,000 sesterces.

Cicero is naturally very critical of these accounts, but presumably they tell us something about standard format. Their first-person style of presentation is integral to their character as official records. In other words, they are guaranteed by the Roman governor of a province because they are *his* accounts. We may imagine that many account books of various kinds, both those kept publicly and those maintained for private estates or businesses, used this style.

A similar pattern of expression can be found in the earliest datable example of the new Bloomberg tablets from the excavations in London's financial district, which were undertaken between 2010 and 2013.[15] These 405 wooden tablets provide an invaluable glimpse of the commercial life of Roman London. Unlike the case of the Vindolanda tablets written in ink, the traces of writing on the new Bloomberg tablets remain scratched in the wood after the original wax layer has disappeared over time. In this example, which comes from soon after the initial Roman settlement, a freedman records his debt to another freedman in formal, legal wording.

> Nerone Claudio Caesar Augusto
> Germanico ii, L(ucio) Calpurnio Pisone
> co(n)s(ulibus) ui Idus Ianuarias
> Tibullus Venusti l(ibertus) scripsi et dico me
> debere Grato <S>puri l(iberto) (denarios) cu ex{s} pretio

---

[14] For Roman account books, see Rosillo López (2010), 111, and now the wide-ranging treatment of Roman accounting practices in Riggsby (2019).

[15] Tomlin (2016) is the first edition of these new tablets.

228 HARRIET I. FLOWER

> mercis quae uendita et tradita <est>
> quam pecuniam ei reddere debeo
> eiue ad quem ea res pertinebit

In the consulship of Nero Claudius Caesar Augustus Germanicus for the second time and of Lucius Calpurnius Piso, on the 6th day before the Ides of January (8 January AD 57): I, Tibullus the freedman of Venustus, have written and say that I owe Gratus the freedman of Spurius 105 denarii from the price of the merchandise that has been sold and delivered. This money I am due to repay him or the person whom the matter will concern.

(Tomlin (2016) WT44)

As in the case of Verres' accounts in Sicily, this IOU suggests a habitual formula used in financial instruments and transactions. With regard to the senate's business, one may cite the example of the *subscriptio* found at the end of the *Senatus Consultum de Cn. Pisone Patre* (copy A) from Spain.[16] This remarkably well-preserved and complete inscription on bronze includes the section below the *senatus consultum* itself in which the emperor Tiberius certifies the copy of the decree presented to him by his quaestor Aulus Plautius and assigns it for deposition in the official archives.

> Ti. Caesar Aug(ustus) trib(unicia) potestate XXII manu mea
> scripsi: velle me h(oc) s(enatus) c(onsultum), quod
> e<s>t factum IIII idus Decem(bres) Cotta et Messalla
> con(n)s(ulibus) referente me scri-
> ptum manu Auli q(uaestoris) mei in tabellis XIIII, referri in
> tabulas pub<l>icas.

I, Tiberius Caesar Augustus, in the twenty-second year of my tribunician power, have written in my own hand that I wish this decree of the senate, which was made on 10th December in the consulship of Cotta and Messalla (AD 20), on my motion, written by the hand of Aulus, my quaestor, on fourteen tablets, to be entered into the public record.

(*SCPP* 174–6)

This is the only surviving example of what would presumably have been a standard formula (or type of formula) used by many magistrates at different time periods, particularly to conclude a *senatus consultum* but also in other legal contexts. Once again, the use of the first person, in this case following the name of the official in question (in this instance the

---

[16] See Eck, Caballos, and Fernández (1996), *ad loc.*, with Cooley (2014).

Republican Politicians and the First-Person Singular 229

emperor), appears to be essential to the way the document functions; the *senatus consultum* is 'signed' in order to continue on its journey to an archive, and in this case also to be copied and distributed throughout the Roman Empire to the main towns and the winter camps of the armies.[17]

Other official business, especially with the senate, was conducted through correspondence between those in Rome and the many magistrates in the field.[18] These letters will obviously have become ever more frequent as the empire expanded and each magistrate will have written many during the course of a successful career. Letters containing official business might be addressed either to the consuls and other magistrates in Rome or to foreign leaders on behalf of Roman interests. Both Polybius and Livy mention many such letters but consistently present them in indirect discourse and as a summary.[19] Verbatim quotations from official or even unofficial Republican letters are very rare. Indeed, the earliest verbatim fragments seem to come from the much-debated extracts from letters attributed to Cornelia, mother of the Gracchi, and addressed to her son Gaius in the 120s BC. The quotations are preserved in the corpus of Cornelius Nepos.[20] Naturally, these are written in the first person and express an explicitly personal point of view, although they may originally have been written for circulation within an elite context rather than simply as private letters from mother to son. Regardless of the authenticity of these texts, the format is presumably what would be expected in elite circles.[21]

One of the few instances of verbatim quotations from a Roman magistrate is from the letter(s) of L. Caecilius Metellus (cos. 68), which he wrote as propraetor of Sicily in 70. Metellus addressed the consuls Pompey and Crassus, the praetor M. Mummius, and the quaestors in the city in a single communication:

---

[17] See *SCPP* lines 165–72 for the instructions to publish the inscription throughout the empire.

[18] Cugusi (1970) collects the references to Latin letters in literary sources. Cugusi (1973) presents examples of early letters in Latin on papyrus, of which there are few and none (so far) written by Roman elites.

[19] For example, Cn. Manlius Vulso (Polybius 21.44.1–3 and Livy 38.39.1–2).

[20] Several manuscripts of Nepos preserve two substantial fragments; see Horsfall (1989). Suerbaum (2002), no. 174, dates the Nepos fragments to 124, before Gaius' first tribunate. Cicero *Brut.* 211 had access to an edition of Cornelia's letters. Plutarch *CG* 13.2 was familiar with letters other than the ones in Nepos. See also Quintilian 1.1.6. Cornelia's letters are the first published letter collection we know of for a private individual that were circulated for a political motive.

[21] The authenticity of the Nepos fragments has been much debated, with more scholars now being willing to accept them as genuine or at least as re-edited versions of actual letters. For a brief introduction, see Instinsky (1971); Coarelli (1978); Hemelrijk (1999), 349–52; Hallett (2002), (2006), and (2018); and Dixon (2007), 26–9.

230   HARRIET I. FLOWER

decumas frumenti lege Hieronica vendidi . . .

I have sold the grain-tithes according to the law of Hiero

In reliquum tamen tempus vectigalibus prospexi . . .

I have taken steps, however, to secure the taxes for the future . . . (Cic. *Ver.* 2.3.123 and 128)

These examples attest to the pattern we would expect, namely, that the magistrate writes the letter in the first person in the same style we see in Cicero's own correspondence from his province of Cilicia twenty years later.[22] We may imagine that the well-known (type of) letter announcing a military victory, and setting the stage for the speech that a returning general would give to the senate to request a triumph, also spoke with the personal voice of the victorious commander, even as it will have included praise of other officers and the army as a whole.[23] Letters in Greek written by Roman magistrates, which survive in epigraphic sources, tended to use the first-person plural in the earlier second century, but the first-person singular by the teens.[24] Generalizations are dangerous since the surviving record is slim and random.

Still, it should come as no surprise that Q. Lutatius Catulus used the format of a letter, a first-person text that could be either personal or official, to write a narrative of his victories, as we know from a letter of Fronto to Lucius Verus in AD 163.[25] This 'memoir' was, therefore, a natural extension of an existing first-person genre associated with a specific political context. His 'open letter' will probably have drawn on other letters (and related speeches) he had written or delivered orally to the senate and to others. Catulus seems actually to have written two accounts: a letter in an elaborate style mentioned by Fronto (probably in the

---

[22] Letters from Cilicia can be found in *Fam.* Books 2 and 3.

[23] See Pelikan Pittenger (2008), 35–6, 299–302, for the mechanisms by which Republican generals sought a triumph, an honour that was awarded by the senate.

[24] For Greek letters sent by Roman magistrates in the East that use the first-person singular, see Sherk (1969), no. 43 Q. Fabius Maximus to Dyme in 115?; no. 48 C. Cassius to Nysa in 88–7; no. 49 L. Cornelius Sulla to the people of Cos (84 and 81).

[25] . . . *verum omnes, uti res postulat, breves nec ullam rerum gestarum expeditionem continentes. in hunc autem modum, quo scripsisti tu, extant Catuli litterae, quibus res a se iac<turi>s a<tque d>amni<s> sane gestas, at lauro merendas, <historico exemplo exposuit>; ve<rum> turgent elate <p>rolata teneris prope <v>erbis* (Van den Hout (1988), 124–5). 'But [the letters] were all short, as the subject demands, and did not contain any exposition of deeds that had been done. In the style, however, of your letter there is extant a letter of Catulus, in which he has recounted in the manner of a historian his own accomplishments, which were accompanied by losses and failures but still deserving of the laurel (i.e. of a triumph). But there is some bombast in the way [the letter] goes on at length in almost effeminate words.' For commentary, see Van den Hout (1999).

Republican Politicians and the First-Person Singular 231

first person) and a one-volume work addressed to the poet A. Furius in the third person, in the plain style of Xenophon, alluded to by Cicero (*Brut.* 132).[26]

Catulus was a highly cultured man who introduced innovations in a number of literary and artistic fields, including his elaborate public building plan in Rome, his delivery of the first public funeral oration for a woman (his mother Popilia), and his contribution as one of the very first elite Romans to compose epigrams in Latin on personal and erotic topics. Cicero, who greatly admired the elder Catulus and was a friend of his son of the same name, tells us that Rome reached a peak of Hellenism in the father's consulate in 102 BC.[27] Without taking this too literally, we can see the point Cicero is trying to make.

Catulus' epigram in praise of the famous comic actor Quintus Roscius provides a striking example of how the first person was coming to be used in new ways in the later second century BC. The epigram is a loose adaptation of Theocritus (18.26–8):[28]

> constiteram exorientem Auroram forte salutans
> cum subito a laeua Roscius exoritur,
> pace mihi liceat, caelestes, dicere uestra,
> mortalis uisus pulchrior esse deo.

By chance I had taken a stand facing East as I was greeting the Dawn, when suddenly Roscius came up on the left. If I may be allowed to say so, with your permission o gods, a mortal man appeared more beautiful than a god.

(Cicero *ND* 1.79)

---

[26] *Iam Q. Catulus non antiquo illo more, sed hoc nostro, nisi quid fieri potest perfectius, eruditus. Multae litterae, summa non vitae solum atque naturae sed orationis etiam comitas, incorrupta quaedam latini sermonis integritas; quae perspici cum ex orationibus eius potest tum facillime ex eo libro quem de consulatu et de rebus gestis suis conscriptum molli et Xenophontio genere sermonis misit ad A. Furium poetam, familiarem suum; qui liber nihilo notior est quam illi tres, de quibus ante dixi, Scauri libri* (*Brut.* 132). 'At that same period Quintus Catulus was a learned speaker, not in that antique manner but in this style of ours, or even better, if such a thing is possible. He was well read; he displayed the greatest affability not only in his life and his nature but also in his speaking style, there was a certain matchless purity to his spoken Latin. These qualities can be seen clearly in his (published) speeches but even more easily in that book which he wrote about his consulship and his achievements, in a smooth style reminiscent of Xenophon, and sent to Aulus Furius the poet, his friend. This book is no better known than those three that I spoke about before, the books by Scaurus.'

[27] Cicero *Arch.* 5 with Hillard (2001); Grüner (2004), 24–8; McDonnell (2006), 264; and Stroup (2010), 289–90.

[28] For Catulus' epigrams, Apuleius *Apol.* 9.6, and Gellius 19.9 with Blänsdorf (1995), 94–6; Courtney (2003), 75–8; and Grüner (2004), 20–3.

232 HARRIET I. FLOWER

Catulus boldly takes on the role of the romantic lover in a Hellenizing style. He was probably a generation older than Roscius, but the date of this epigram is unknown. In other words, Catulus may have been writing personal poetry before he published his autobiographical writings.

An influential, older contemporary of Catulus was the satirist Gaius Lucilius, who died in 102, the year when Catulus was consul.[29] Lucilius also came from an elite background but chose not to engage in politics or in business. He is credited with inventing the genre of Roman satire and of crafting a new role for the personal voice in Latin literature more generally.[30] Although the surviving fragments of his works are mostly very short, it is clear that his whole style was based on extensive use of the first person, in a wide range of literary settings from self-reflection to sharp criticisms of contemporary society. An example is provided by this much quoted snippet:

> publicanus vero ut Asiae fiam, ut scripturarius
> pro Lucilio, id ego nolo, et hoc uno muto omnia.
>
> (fr. 656–7K = 671–2M)

> I do not want to be a publican in (the province of) Asia or an accountant (working for a publican?) instead of being Lucilius, and I would not give everything in the world in exchange for this one thing.

Here we see Lucilius consciously using his stance of private citizen, a persona that is closely linked to his first-person voice. His topics included biographical narratives, such as the description of his journey from Rome to Sicily that took up the whole of Book 3 of the satires. Horace (S. 2.1.30–34) describes some of his poetry as being like a diary; parts of it may have been a more extended memoir in verse.[31] In other words, Lucilius could use the first person to define a personal perspective that contrasted with but also complemented the well-known 'I' of the magistrate speaking and writing in an official capacity. Lucilius' poetry is usually assigned to the 120s, a time when Catulus may also have been composing epigrams.[32]

---

[29] About 1,400 lines of Lucilius survive. The newest edition of the fragments is Christes and Garbugino (2015), with a concise introduction to the satires at 7–14. For further discussion of Lucilius' use of a personal voice, see Hass (2007); Goldberg (2010), 155–77; and Breed, Keitel, and Wallace (2018).

[30] Lucilius' precursors include Ennius (died c. 169; see Muecke (2005) for his satires) and Terence (active c. 170s–160s), whose prologues also contain autobiographical material. For Roman satire and Lucilius in general, see Christes (1986); Gruen (1992); Lefèvre (1997) and (2001); von Albrecht (1997), 241–66; Freudenburg (2001); and G. Manuwald (2001).

[31] Our view of Lucilius has been decisively shaped by Horace's enthusiasm for and emulation of him. See Christes (1989) and Rosen (2012).

[32] Lucilius' poetry is generally assigned to the period between the early 120s and his death in 102. The year of his birth has been variously placed in c. 180, 168, 159/158, or 148/147. For discussion, see Raschke (1979) and Christes and Garbugino (2015), 10–11.

Republican Politicians and the First-Person Singular

A few other suggestive examples of the first person in the late second century BC are provided by epigraphical evidence. One notable example is the *elogium* of Gnaeus Cornelius Scipio Hispanus from the famous tomb of the Scipios on the Via Appia. Another is the much-debated Polla *elogium*, apparently a second-century statue base from the Via Annia that records the achievements of an unnamed Roman magistrate in exercising Roman power in Sicily and Southern Italy. Each of these opens up its own particular world of self-expression, although the inscription from the tomb was visible to family members only and probably viewed only on limited occasions even by them.

The Scipio Hispanus buried here seems to be the praetor of 139 BC and was perhaps the first person to be buried in a new wing that was added to the older tomb.[33] There is no record of him holding the consulship, a circumstance that is usually taken to suggest that he died soon after 139. If this is correct, his epitaph provides valuable insight into the development of Latin personal epigrams in the early to mid 130s. Below the *titulus* that records his name and career (in descending order), appear two couplets in smaller letters:

> Cn. Cornelius Cn. f. Scipio Hispanus
> pr(aetor), aid(ilis) cur(ulis), q(uaestor), tr(ibunus) mil(itum) (bis),
>   (decem)vir stl(itibus) iudik(andis),
> (decem)vir sacr(is) fac(iundis)
> virtutes generis mieis moribus accumulavi
> progeniem genui; facta patris petiei.
> maiorum optenui laudem, ut sibei me esse creatum
> laetentur; stirpem nobilitavit honor.
>   (*CIL* 1.15 = 6.1293 and 37039i = *ILS* 6 = *ILLRP* 316)

Gnaeus Cornelius, son of Gnaeus, Scipio Hispanus
praetor, curule aedile, quaestor, military tribune twice,
one of ten (magistrates) for judging lawsuits,
one of ten (priests) for arranging sacred matters
I increased the manly virtues of my family by my own way of life, I begot offspring, I aimed to equal/equalled the achievements of my father. I maintained in my own right the renown of my ancestors so that they rejoice that I was their descendant; (my/an) official rank ennobled (my/a/the) lineage/offspring.

Despite the emphatic third person ending, the whole poem is obviously very much in the voice of Hispanus. Interestingly, it does not include

---

[33] For the epitaph of Scipio Hispanus, see *CIL* 1^2 15 = 6.1293 = 6.37039i = *ILS* 6 = *ILLRP* 316 = *CLE* 958. For discussion, see Massaro (1992), 38–40 and Courtney (1995), no. 13.

234 HARRIET I. FLOWER

mention of any names, nor of the specific details of his career. It both expresses traditional elite political values, framed by *virtute(s)* at the beginning and *honor* at the end, while giving voice to a very personal pride that just *sounds* completely different from the earlier *elogia* from the tomb.[34] This inscription is not often compared with Catulus' erotic epigrams or Lucilius' biting satires, but they all share what must at the time have been a distinctly 'modern' tone. Interestingly, there is also another fragment of an inscription from the same tomb that has a first-person verb (*vexei*) at the end.[35] Evidently, Hispanus was not the only one to speak for himself here.

By contrast with Hispanus' personal pride and family context, the unnamed magistrate who speaks in the Polla text strikes a much less individualistic note, while being equally pleased to advertise his accomplishments in the first person.[36]

VIAM **FECEI** AB REGIO AD CAPVAM ET

IN EA VIA PONTEIS OMNEIS MILIARIOS TABELARIOSQVE **POSEIVEI**. HINCE SVNT NOVCERIAM MEILIA LI CAPVAM XXCIIII MVRANVM LXXIIII COSENTIAM CXXIII VALENTIAM CLXXX AD FRETVM AD STATVAM CCXXXI REGIVM CCXXXVII5 SVMA AF CAPVA REGIVM MEILIA CCCXXI ET EIDEM PRAETOR IN

SICILIA FVGITEIVOS ITALICORVM **CONQVAEISIVEI REDIDEIQVE**

HOMINES DCCCCXVII EIDEMQVE

PRIMVS FECEI VT DE AGRO POPLICO ARATORIBVS CEDERENT PAASTORES FORVM AEDISQVE POPLICAS HEIC **FECE[I]**

I made a road from Rhegium to Capua and on that road **I placed** bridges (all of them), milestones, and *tabelarii*. From here to Nuceria 51 miles, to Capua 84 miles, to Muranum 74 miles, to Cosentia 123 miles, to Valentia 180 miles, to the Strait at the statue 231 miles, to Rhegium 237 miles. Total from Capua to Rhegium, 321 miles. And **I also, as praetor in Sicily, sought out** the fugitive slaves of Italian owners and restored them, 917

---

[34] For the earliest epigrams from the tomb of the Scipios, which use the second and third person, see *CIL* 1^2 6–9 = 6.1284–7 = *ILS* 1–3 = *ILLRP* 309–10 with Courtney (1995), nos. 9–13, and Massaro (2002). Morelli (2018), 431, argues that Roman aristocrats stopped using verse epitaphs around the end of the second century, once this format became more common amongst the general population.

[35] *CIL* 6.1292 = 37039h = 1^2.14 = *ILLRP* 315 = *ILS* 9 = *CLE* 10. This fragment is probably also from a verse epigram.

[36] For the Polla *elogium*, see *CIL* 1^2 638 = 10.6950 = *ILLRP* 454 = *II* 3.1.272 with Susini (1984) and Bernard, Damon, and Gray (2014), esp. 972–3, for the use of the first person in this inscription.

Republican Politicians and the First-Person Singular

individuals. And **I was also the first** – in connection with publicly owned land – to cause herdsmen to give way to plowmen. **I built** here a forum and public buildings.

The fragmentary state of the inscription and its unique character make it hard to interpret. It seems to present an amalgamation of different items usually found in a variety of epigraphic contexts. Is it an *elogium*? Is it a milestone? Is it a statue base? Is it really an expression of Roman imperial power, rather than simply an account of an individual career? For present purposes, it is the first-person usage across a range of subjects that is striking.

A brief summary is in order. Roman magistrates had naturally used the first person in a range of public settings, including political, legal, financial, and epistolary. The last three decades of the second century BC apparently saw an increased fashion for first-person self-presentation going beyond these traditional usages, whether in contexts that had previously favoured the third person or in new genres of personal expression, both in verse and in prose. Suggestive evidence comes from inscriptions, in prose and verse, and from personal poetry, including especially Hellenistic-style epigrams and the emerging genre of Roman satire. Interestingly, first-person narratives could be deployed to affirm traditional political and gentilicial values and roles *or* to critique Roman society from a more detached position – the position of an individual observer who had found his own voice to characterize particular, private aspirations and points of view. While Scipio Hispanus' *elogium* is usually dated to the early 130s, other surviving evidence seems to cluster in the 120s, a time of intense debate and societal tensions over the violent fate of Tiberius Gracchus and the outcome of his program of controversial land distributions. These usages clearly predate the first autobiographies in prose, which seem to be the two works of Catulus in circulation around 100.

The rather particular political and cultural climate of the decade of the 120s BC brings to mind the fiery oratory of Gaius Gracchus, the most prominent and innovative Roman orator, as far as we can tell, between Cato the Elder and Cicero.[37] Gaius was famous for his dramatic speaking style and lively engagement with his audience. Over a number of years, he boldly challenged those he held responsible for or complicit in the murder of his brother. His direct manner of speech made ample use of the first

---

[37] For Gaius Gracchus as an orator, see Malcovati in *ORF*⁴ no. 48 and G. Manuwald (2019), no. 48. Discussion can be found in Sciarrino (2007) and van der Blom (2016), 69–112 and 290–5 (a list of Gaius' public speeches).

person in emotional and vivid settings, enhanced by a range of personal and familial references. His speeches and pamphlets will have circulated both during this decade and then in various ways after his violent death. The following example offers a longer extract from a speech he gave as tribune of the plebs in 123:

> Ego ipse, qui aput vos verba facio, ut vectigalia vestra augeatis, quo facilius vestra commode et rem publicam administrare possitis, non gratis prodeo; verum peto a vobis non pecuniam, sed bonam existimationem atque honorem. Qui prodeunt dissuasuri ne hanc legem accipiatis, petunt non honorem a vobis, verum a Nicomede pecuniam; qui suadent ut accipiatis, hi quoque petunt non a vobis bonam existimationem, verum a Mithridate rei familiari suae pretium et praemium; qui autem ex eodem loco atque ordine tacent, hi vel acerrimi sunt; nam ab omnibus pretium accipiunt et omnis fallunt. (Gellius 11.10.1 = ORF4 48.44 dissuasio legis Aufeiae)

> I myself, who am making a speech to you arguing that you should increase your taxes, so that you may more easily serve your own best interests and administer the state, am not appearing free of charge. But I am seeking from you not money but a favourable reception and honour. Those who come forward to persuade you not to pass this law, do not seek honour but money from king Nicomedes. Those who argue in favour of your accepting it, these men also are not seeking a favourable reception from you, but a prize and payoff for their personal estates from king Mithridates. Those of the same rank and station who stay silent, they are the most acute, for they accept money from all and deceive everyone.

Shorter citations show a similar pattern of usage and help to create a fuller picture:

> Credo ego inimicos meos hoc dicturum. (Gellius 1.7.6 = ORF4 48.34 de P. Popillio Laenate circum conciliabula; also in 123)
> I believe my rivals would say this.

> Tu matri meae maledicas, quae me peperit?
> (Seneca *Dial.* 12.16.6 = *ORF*⁴ 48.65, in an unspecified *contio* at an unknown date)
> Are you saying bad things about my mother, who gave birth to me?

Nevertheless, Gaius' powerful and combative rhetoric should not distract us from realizing that in his day first-person oratory was actually not novel, at least in some traditional contexts. This is revealed most clearly in the fragments of Cato the Elder, a man born over seventy years before Gaius Gracchus.[38] Cato remains the best attested orator of the second century

---

[38] For Cato the Elder's speeches, see Malcovati in *ORF*⁴ no. 8. Astin (1978), 137–44, remains the classic treatment. Sciarrino (2011) treats Cato's prose works overall. See also T. J. Cornell in *FRHist*

Republican Politicians and the First-Person Singular 237

BC. Cicero knew of 150 published speeches; we have many fragments and titles of about eighty of these. Evidence for the range of topics Cato spoke about reveals types of situations in which first-person speeches were natural and often inevitable, and others where such interventions would have been more gratuitous and attention-getting.

A successful Roman politician's career was marked by standard rhetorical opportunities, such as the public speeches made by a candidate running for high office, the consul's speech of thanks to the people upon taking up office, and his speech at the end of his term in which he rehearsed his achievements. Without political parties or platforms, much of this rhetoric focused on the individual and his own story, his background, his character, his deeds, his overall suitability for office, all expressed in his own voice. Similarly, as we saw in the case of Catulus, a successful general would send home a letter detailing his victories, an account then reiterated and elaborated in a speech to the senate requesting a triumph and a subsequent public speech on the day of the actual celebration. In all these settings, the rhetorical first person was usual and often necessary; it ran in parallel with the 'I' of account books and other official communications that expressed the status and agency of the elite Roman.

A parallel set of circumstances arose in the law courts. Personal attacks were very common in the highly litigious atmosphere of Roman political life. Well before the days of permanent jury courts, Cato was constantly bringing suits or defending himself in court.[39] In many of these situations, he was called upon to give an account of himself or he deliberately chose to contrast his own behaviour, principles, and accomplishments with those of his political rivals. Law court speeches drew a crowd and we may imagine that many will have made a point of going to hear Cato perform as 'Cato', whether for the prosecution or for the defence. A successful Roman politician needed to present 'himself' in front of an audience, whether in the forum or in the senate house.

In addition, this habit of speaking for oneself also spilled over into other rhetorical contexts when the speaker was not talking about his own life. A good example is provided by the fragments of Cato's famous speech in

---

1:191–218, since some of the speeches were included in the *Origines*, as well as being circulated separately.

[39] Cato spoke frequently in the law courts, both as a prosecutor and as a defendant, but he was never himself convicted (Plin. *Nat.* 7.100; Plut. *Cat. ma.* 29.5, *vir ill.* 47.7).

238   HARRIET I. FLOWER

defence of the Rhodians, which was delivered in the senate in 167 BC.[40]
This is the best attested of his speeches. After the Rhodian ambassadors
had tried to persuade the senate not to declare war on them because they
had stayed neutral during Rome's bitter fight with King Perseus of
Macedon, Cato chose to argue in their favour. Here we have a prime
example of a speech about Roman foreign policy and a developing set of
power dynamics in the Eastern Mediterranean after the Roman victory at
Pydna. Cato, by now in his mid-sixties, had not fought in the recent war;
the issue being debated was not about him. Yet his use of the first person in
this speech opens up a world of characteristically Roman self-
representation. For example:

> Atque ego quidem arbitror Rodienses noluisse nos ita depugnare uti
> depugnatum est, neque regem Persen uinci. Sed non Rodienses modo id
> noluere, sed multos populos atque multas nations idem noluisse arbitror;
> atque haut scio an partim eorum fuerint, qui non nostrae contumeliae causa
> id noluerint euenire; sed enim id metuere, si nemo esset homo, quem
> uereremur, quidquid luberet, faceremus, ne sub solo imperio nostro in
> seruitute nostra essent. Libertatis suae causa in ea sententia fuisse arbitror.
> (*FRHist* 5 F88 = Peter F95b = Chassignet F3b = Cugusi F101 = *ORF*[4] 8
> F164)

> And indeed I think that the Rhodians did not want us to conclude the
> armed conflict in the way that this war turned out, nor did they want King
> Perseus to be defeated. But I think that it was not only the Rhodians who
> did not want this, but many people and many nations did not want it. And
> I am inclined to think that there were some of them who did not want it to
> happen, not as an insult to us, but because they were afraid that, if there
> were no man of whom we were fearful, we might do whatever we pleased,
> and in order not to be enslaved to us under our sole dominion. It was for
> the sake of their freedom that they had this opinion, I think.

In this case, the use of the first person makes a claim to insight while
creating empathy as it encourages the Roman audience to imagine themselves in the situation that the Rhodians and other Greeks find themselves
as they faced Rome's expanding role in the Eastern Mediterranean. It is a
rhetorical device that directly supports Cato's policy position, but from a
subjective point of view.

---

[40] For Cato's speech in defence of the Rhodians, see Gellius 6.3 with *ORF*[4] no. 8 F 163–9; Beck and
Walter (2001), 208–13; Cugusi and Sblendorio Cugusi (2001); Chassignet (2002), 93–5; Calboli
(2003), *FRHist* 5 F 87–93; and H. I. Flower (2020). The debate in the senate about a possible war
with Rhodes in 167 is recorded by Polybius 30.4; Livy 45.5.3 and 45.20.4-25.4; and Diodorus
30.24 and 31.5.

Republican Politicians and the First-Person Singular

Even more interestingly, Cato goes on to insert himself (and his children) into his famous saying about the well-known *superbia* (arrogance) of the Rhodians:[41]

> Rodiensis superbos esse aiunt id obiectantes, quod mihi et liberis meis minime dici uelim. Sint sane superbi. Quid id ad nos attinet? Idne irascimini, si quis superbior est quam nos? (*FRHist* 5 F93 = Peter F95g = Chassignet F3g = Cugusi F106 = *ORF*⁴ 8, 169)

> They say the Rhodians are arrogant, bringing a charge against them that I should absolutely not wish to have brought against me and against my children. So let them be arrogant! Why is that our business? Is that why you are angry, because someone is more arrogant than we are?

In this passage, he could have omitted the first-person intervention completely and have preserved the logic of his argument and the element of surprise in the punchline. I do think this is meant to be a saying with a humorous aspect, in the style of the *sententiae* he was so well known for. So why does Cato insert himself here? There is something of a delaying tactic at play. But this passage also exemplifies the vital role played by Cato's own persona in the delivery of the speech. In other words, it is not just the argument in favour of the Rhodians, but this argument as expressed specifically by the character 'Cato', a very well-known figure to this audience in the senate. The 'I' activates a sense of his personal *auctoritas*, as well as inserting Cato as a character in the story, a character with a specific point of view based on a set of well-articulated values. The way in which the 'I' is inserted gratuitously, as an interruption in a logical train of thought, only draws even more attention to this stylistic device.

Similar uses of the first person can be found in earlier speeches by Cato, notably the ones from his censorship in 184 BC. In a speech about women's use of luxury goods, specifically clothes and carriages, Cato apparently introduced himself as an example:[42]

---

[41] See now the comprehensive discussion of *superbia* in Baraz (2020), esp. 38–42.

[42] Here Cato speaks about a hypothetical situation in which he would not change his own habits as part of an argument that Roman women should not change theirs. In the same vein, when he expelled Manilius from the senate for public demonstrations of affection towards his wife, he added a joke about when he hugged his wife in public – only when thunder was heard (Plutarch *Cat. ma.* 17.7, not in *ORF*). Similarly, Cicero *Sen.* 42 records Cato describing how he personally felt about expelling L. Flaminius from the senate. Such personal asides seem to attract the attention of quoting authors.

> Nam periniurium siet, cum mihi ob eos mores, quos prius habui, honos detur, ubi datus est, tum uti eos mutem atque alii modi sim. (Prisc. GL ii p. 226 = *ORF⁴* 8.93)

> For it would be awful, if I had received recognition for my way of life, which I had been following earlier, but if when the recognition was awarded, at that moment I changed my habits and behaved in a different way.

As in so many other areas of Roman life, Cato had explored the potential of first-person speech acts well before these were exploited by later orators. In fact, the first-person voice is a key feature of Cato's rhetorical style across different occasions and audiences. It colours his delivery by setting up a complex network of expectations connected precisely with the character 'Cato', who is given special prominence as *the* authoritative speaker.

Many conclusions could be drawn from the disparate material assembled here. Three of these seem especially interesting to think about. All these pieces of evidence point to the fact that creating and performing a first-person narrative had traditionally been central to being a senator or an elected magistrate in Roman political culture for generations. Successful politicians sought and maintained political prominence in their own name; their repeated first-person interventions were built into a political career in the city and a leadership role in the army. Consequently, successful opinion makers, like Cato or Gaius Gracchus, also tended to make the most of these opportunities by extending first-person narratives into other contexts beyond the traditional or expected ones. Experimenting with the first person proved politically profitable throughout the second century BC. Meanwhile, the age of Gaius Gracchus and Gaius Lucilius was particularly fascinated with the first person as a means to address politics and society in new and critical ways. Violence and sacrilege had divided the Roman community into bitter factions, even as Rome's relationship with its Italian allies was beginning to fray. Both politicians (like Gracchus) and men who rejected public life (like Lucilius) found first-person self-expression a powerful and persuasive tool to work in the context of the anxieties of their times. The use of the first person is visible across a wide variety of literary genres and political persuasions in the late second-century milieu. Consequently, autobiographical first-person narratives, such as Catulus' letter about his achievements as consul and in defeating the Cimbri or Scaurus' more extensive account of his life in three books (*De vita sua*), can be seen to follow logically from Roman literary self-expression at the end of the second century.

CHAPTER 12

Self-Praise and Self-Presentation in Plutarch

Frances B. Titchener

It is true then, as Xenophon says, that the most pleasant sound that a man can hear is his own praise in another's mouth; but the most odious thing unto others is a man commending himself.
—Plutarch, *De se ipsum citra invidiam laudando* 539d[1]

In *Authority and Tradition in Ancient Historiography*, his influential work of 1997, John Marincola examined various ways in which historians used tradition to claim and bolster their own authority, identifying five specific techniques: (1) reference to 'gods and fortune', (2) a 'pretence of necessity', (3) 'commonness of action', (4) 'praise in the mouth of others', and finally (5) 'magnification of actions'. The dust jacket of the original volume features busts of Herodotus and Thucydides, fine historians both. As a biographer, Plutarch is not in the same league, but nevertheless he appears in the *index locorum* a satisfying thirty-seven times thanks to Marincola's own authoritative and expansive view of historiography. About one third of Marincola's Plutarch citations are to the *Lives*, and the rest to the *Moralia*, with the majority from *De se ipsum citra invidiam laudando* (hereafter *De se laudando*), the work that most Plutarchan scholars consult for Plutarch's view on self-presentation in the form of praise. In that essay, Plutarch gives us multiple situations when it is appropriate to praise oneself, and various techniques to avoid incurring ill will while doing so since self-praise is a tricky thing. Marincola sums up Plutarch's advice in *De se laudando* as 'praise the audience too (542a–b), ascribe some success to chance or god (542e–f), use slight corrections or amendments (ἐπανορθώσεσι) to others' praise of you (543a–b), throw in some short-comings (543f)'.[2] Plutarch (but not Marincola) includes a timely warning here about old men who 'once they have been drawn into admonishing others and rating unworthy habits and unwise acts . . .

[1] Trans. de Lacy and Einarson (1959).   [2] Marincola (1997), 177 n. 8.

241

242   FRANCES B. TITCHENER

magnify themselves as men who in the like circumstances have been prodigies of wisdom' (546f).[3]

The focus of this chapter, then, is the intersection of Plutarch and his use of self-praise as a technique of self-presentation to help create or assert authority in the context of Marincola's devices. This chapter thus supports his contention that ancient historians garnered authority with deliberate and careful self-presentation.

Marincola's Devices in Plutarch

In his 'The Historian's Deeds', Marincola identified and discussed 'some literary devices by which an author can shape his narrative in such a way as to mitigate his presence and achievement, since this seems to have been an important concern in antiquity: at the very least it must be conceded that ancient audiences listened differently when a man recorded his own achievements and when another did it for him'.[4] Let's look at those devices through Plutarch's writings.

1. Marincola begins with a reference to 'gods and fortune' in the sense of destiny. Attributing success to the gods diverted envy and also provided a convenient excuse, since if the gods wanted an outcome, they presumably were capable of making it happen. Plutarch is explicit that this is why

> great men ascribe to God and to Fortune a share in their successes, as Timoleon, who put down the tyrannies in Sicily, founded a sanctuary of Automatia (Chance); and Python, when he was admired and honoured by the Athenians for slaying Cotys, said 'God did this, borrowing from me the hand that did the deed.' And Theopompus, King of the Lacedaemonians, replied to the man who said that Sparta was preserved because the kings were fitted to rule, 'no, it is rather because the people are fitted to obey.' (*Praecepta gerendae reipublicae* 816e)[5]

But it is also true that Plutarch was a priest of Delphi who felt strongly that religion and religious ceremonies were an important part of any politically active individual's life.[6] He made a sharp distinction between religion and

---

[3] Trans. de Lacy and Einarson (1959).   [4] Marincola (1997), 206.
[5] Trans. H. N. Fowler (1936).
[6] Plutarch wrote three 'Delphic' essays. *De E apud Delphos* is a discussion of the various explanations for the three possible meanings of the Greek letter E on Apollo's temple at Delphi, namely 'five' (a significant number in mathematics, physiology, philosophy, and music), 'if' (people ask the oracle questions), and 'you are' (addressed to Apollo). *De Pythiae oraculis* (394d–409d) discusses the fact that oracles used to be delivered in hexameter verse, but are no longer, and concludes that the present time called for directness and simplicity rather than vagueness and riddling speech. It contains a guided tour of the Delphic statues and monuments, accompanied by anecdotes and former oracles as

superstition, defining superstition and atheism as the two extreme results of ignorance of the gods, as manifested in the personalities of those with soft and hard characters, respectively.[7] Superstition was worse than atheism because the atheist remains unmoved in respect to 'the divine', but the superstitious man is moved by the divine in the wrong way, by fear (*De superstitione* 165c). This fear lies at the heart of Plutarch's intense dislike of such credulity, believing as he did that it created a terror so intense that it completely debilitated and flattened the affected individual (*De superstitione* 165b).

We can see this attitude in the different ways Plutarch uses superstition to condemn the superstitious or praise those who are themselves free from superstition and who help free others, how he uses it to colour his presentation of others and himself. He casts his lot firmly with those who are free from superstition, offended by the implication of the gods as a source of pain and injury. He thought that such fear affected those ignorant of the causes of natural phenomena, but not those who understood such things (*Per.* 6.2), and that it was the mark of wise men and leaders to be able to counter the effects of superstition among his followers. Pericles, when an eclipse took place as he was sailing to Epidaurus on campaign, allayed the fears of his steersman by a rational explanation of the eclipse (*Per.* 35.2). Dion, in a similar situation, prevailed upon his seer Miltas to allay the fears of the soldiers, not by rational explanation this time but by favourable interpretation (*Dion* 24.1; *Nic.* 23.6). Nicias, by contrast, could not control his own fear, much less that of his soldiers (*Nic.* 23.1–4), and is condemned by Plutarch for this.

But fearing random fate (superstition) is not the same as acknowledging it as a variable, and Plutarch certainly does that, observing that people prefer to be defeated by luck rather than valour (*De se laudando* 542f) and adding to his condemnation of Crassus the fact that 'Crassus made so many blunders that he gave fortune no chance to favour him. We may not therefore wonder that his imbecility succumbed to the power of the Parthians, but rather that it prevailed over the usual good fortune of the Romans' (*Comp. Nic. et Crass.* 5.1).[8]

---

seen by young visitors, and essentially tries to defend the progressively declining reputation of the oracle. *De defectu oraculorum* (409e–438f) discusses but does not resolve the question of why the oracle was becoming obsolete (the gods were withholding information because humans had become evil, 413a; the oracles had become fewer because of the decline in population, 414a; the intermediary daemon had fled 418d).

[7] *De superstitione* 164e; see Titchener (2008).
[8] Trans. Perrin (1916). See Titchener (2014) on Plutarch and fate.

2. Marincola acknowledges that it can be useful to invoke a 'pretence of necessity'. Those who find themselves suddenly in the spotlight for heroic action often say something like, 'I just did what I had to do' or 'Anyone would have done the same' even when it is clear that is not true. This is clearly preferable to bragging that no one else could have done it or demanding recognition and money. Plutarch can be subtle about this, describing changes in lifestyle for the likes of Themistocles and Pericles as they entered public life and changed their public personas to that of expected sober and undemonstrative statesmen (*Them.* 2.5–3.1; *Per.* 7.4). But that is not really a pretence of necessity but a practical reality. In the case of Nicias, his over-the-top insistence on being too busy for anything as well as his employing a PR agent to spread news about town of exactly how busy he was was meant by Nicias to be an invocation of the pretence of necessity – it's not his choice; he can't help it (*Nic.* 5.3–4). Plutarch twists the knife a little by suggesting that Nicias was so extremely busy all the time that he could claim, just like Agamemnon, that he was a slave to the people. Agamemnon (Eur. *IA* 449–50) speaks these words right after the messenger brings in Agamemnon's daughter Iphigenia, who, brought to Aulis under pretext of marriage to Achilles, is in fact to be slaughtered by her father to pacify the goddess Artemis and secure fair sailing for his expedition against Troy. He must put on the yoke of necessity.[9] Comparing Agamemnon's sacrifice of his own daughter with being interrupted at dinner and bath is a subtle way of acknowledging and dismissing Nicias' attempt to invoke the pretence of necessity.

Sometimes it is harder to see whether or not there is pretence or true necessity. Plutarch allows that self-praise can be appropriate when under duress in certain situations, such as when reputation is under attack or one is in danger since danger protects the speaker from envy, although it is still risky. He contrasts the experience of Cicero and Scipio:

> The Romans again were annoyed with Cicero for frequently vaunting his success with Catiline; but when Scipio said that it ill befitted them to sit in judgement over Scipio, to whom they owed the power to sit in judgement for all mankind, they put garlands on their heads, escorted him to the Capitol, and joined him in the sacrifice. *For Cicero boasted not from necessity but for glory; whereas the peril of the other did away with envy.* (*De se laudando* 541a)[10]

---

[9] Aesch. *Ag.* 219: ἀνάγκας ἔδυ λέπαδνον.
[10] Trans. de Lacy and Einarson (1959), with my emphasis.

Self-Praise and Self-Presentation in Plutarch   245

3. 'Commonness of action allows for self-promotion without generating bad feeling.' In *Praecepta gerendae reipublicae*, Plutarch delivers political advice by relating that given to him by his father:

> I recollect that when I was still a young man I was sent with another as envoy to the proconsul; the other man was somehow left behind; I alone met the proconsul and accomplished the business. Now when I came back and was to make the report of our mission, my father left his seat and told me in private not to say 'I went,' but 'we went,' not 'I said,' but 'we said,' and in all other ways to associate my colleague in a joint report. *For that sort of thing is not only honourable and kind, but it also takes the sting out of any envy of our reputation.* (*Praecepta gerendae reipublicae* 816d, with my emphasis)[11]

Here Plutarch presents himself as the diligent young man he is advising his addressee, Menemachus, to become (see below). We know nothing of why Plutarch's companion was not there, but we do know that Plutarch himself completed his assigned task and returned home a successful young man, one on whom people could depend. Bragging about that fact would almost certainly provoke envy, but the Marincolan device of 'commonness of action', that is, linking his actions to that of another in order to diffuse any grudging suspicion, applies here.

This works only one way, with the actual performer elevating the non-performer. Plutarch shows us that when the non-performer tries to take over the action, it does not go so well, as we see from Crassus' fears about sharing his victory over Spartacus with Pompey and his relieving army, knowing that the palm will go to the one bringing help (*Crass.* 11). And he may have been right to be concerned! We don't have to look far in Plutarch's biographies for examples of the 'real' victor being denied his rightful credit by the excellent timing of his enemies (e.g. Cleon and Demosthenes at Pylos, *Nic.* 7.4–5).

4. 'Praise in the mouth of others' is an acceptable if transparent literary device. Marincola admits that this can be called 'Deception, perhaps, but a type sanctioned by long use, and one to which an ancient audience may have been far less hostile'.[12] Third-person narratives permit 'the author to place praise or admiration for his own actions into the mouth of another in a way that would be intolerable in a first-person account'.[13] Consider the

---

[11] Trans. H. N. Fowler (1936).

[12] Marincola (1997), 215, gives examples from Xenophon, Caesar, and Josephus in which these authors deflect potential envy of their achievements in this way.

[13] Marincola (1997), 214.

246   FRANCES B. TITCHENER

following passage in which Plutarch invokes the authority of his own life,
as a priest of Delphi, in order to make his point about the value of older
statesmen:[14]

> Now surely you know that I have been serving the Pythian Apollo for many
> Pythiads, but you would not say 'Plutarch, you have done enough sacrific-
> ing, marching in processions, and dancing in choruses, and now that you
> are older it is time to put off the garland and to desert the oracle on account
> of your age.' And so do not imagine that you yourself, being a leader and
> interpreter of the sacred rites of civic life, ought to give up the worship of
> Zeus of the State and of the Forum, rites to which you have for a long time
> been consecrated. (*An seni respublica gerenda sit* (792f)[15]

We are moved past being impressed at Plutarch's vigour and dedication,
something we might envy or feel negative about, and directed toward
admiration of his piety and concern for gods and religion, and we are
further filled with the desire to emulate, something Plutarch is very specific
about doing in writing the *Parallel Lives*. Another example comes from
where Plutarch presents himself as an active citizen, acting as a supervisor
of brick and sewer work:

> And no doubt I myself seem ridiculous to visitors in our town when I am
> seen in public, as I often am, engaged in such matters. But I am helped by
> the remark of Antisthenes which has been handed down to memory; for
> when someone expressed surprise that he himself carried a dried fish
> through the market-place, he said, 'Yes, but it's for myself'; but I, on the
> other hand, say to those who criticize me for standing and watching tiles
> being measured or concrete or stones being delivered, that I attend to these
> things, not for myself, but for my native place. (*Praecepta gerendae
> reipublicae* 811b)[16]

Here we see a modesty or self-deprecation quite common in Plutarch and
one of his favourite techniques to mitigate self-praise. Sometimes it is
conventional *recusatio*-style downplaying of talent, as in the opening of
Nicias where Plutarch entreats his audience not to think that he intended
to compete with the incomparable Thucydides, but that it would be
necessary to refer to the great historian in order to avoid accusations of
sloth or carelessness (*Nic.* 1.1). Plutarch begins by self-deprecating, but is
really claiming credit for being an active and involved citizen, giving of his

---

[14] Russell (1993), 428, distinguishes between the *Parallel Lives*: 'Self-reference in the *Lives* is generally
  intended simply to authorise a statement or claim to special knowledge', and the *Moralia*, 428: 'Self-
  disclosures in the *Moralia* are also generally intended to lend authority to a didactic point.'
[15] Trans. H. N. Fowler (1936).   [16] Trans. H. N. Fowler (1936).

own personal time, and risking ridicule in order to do what he believes is right. He uses words in the mouth of another, in this case Antisthenes, to claim some credit without seeming boastful.

The case of Fabius Maximus is also instructive. For instance, in *Fabius Maximus* (5.3), we learn that the great future dictator was not universally appreciated while avoiding Hannibal in the field:

> But for merely consuming time in this way he was generally despised by his countrymen, and roundly abused even in his own camp. Much more did his enemies think him a man of no courage and a mere nobody – all except Hannibal. He and he alone, comprehended the cleverness of his antagonist and the style of warfare which he had adopted.[17]

In this passage Plutarch seems to be diminishing Fabius by showing the Romans' hostility and contempt for Fabian tactics, but he redeems Fabius by praise from the great general Hannibal.

5. Finally, 'magnification of actions' is identified as a typical mechanism for ancient authors to avoid negative feeling towards their achievements. Marincola points out that 'Except for the openly partisan strain of Roman historiography ("our men fought brilliantly") the usual means of magnifying the greatness of one's achievements in a narrative is not direct praise but oblique references to one's opponents.'[18] For instance, in Plutarch's *Aristides* (10.1) we are told that Mardonius is 'formidable' (*phoberos*), largely through his well-placed confidence in his infantry, and yet the united Greeks will ultimately prevail at Plataea. At the end of his account of the battle, Plutarch observes that the Persian victims of the charging Spartans died courageously, seizing the spears with their bare hands (*Arist.* 18.3). Thus was the Greek victory at Plataea elevated by the stature of the enemy, both powerful and noble.

And not only military opponents are used in this way by Plutarch. Themistocles, born too late to fight at Marathon, was determined to match the honour and reputation of the great Miltiades, author of the Athenian victory, claiming that Miltiades' trophy would not let him sleep (*Them.* 3.4). And Julius Caesar famously wept as he contemplated Alexander's accomplishments at a similar age (*Caes.* 11.6). This behaviour – berating oneself for not having achieved greatness on the highest possible level – is what is currently known as the 'humblebrag' and is well-recognized as a rhetorical tactic.

---

[17] Trans. Perrin (1916).   [18] Marincola (1997), 215–16.

Plutarch's Presentation of Himself

If we want to learn about self-presentation in Plutarch, we must look to his works since most of what we know (or think we know) about Plutarch's life comes from those very works. Eunapius describes the challenge of this exercise without acknowledging the problems of distinguishing veracity:

> Clear and accurate accounts of the lives of these [philosophers] it was impossible to discover since, so far as I know, no one has written them. But their own writings were and still are sufficient records of their lives, filled as they are with such erudition and thorough research in the field of ethics and also that research which aspires to investigate the nature of things and disperses like a mist the ignorance of such as we are able to follow. Thus, for example, that marvellous man Plutarch records his own life in scattered notices throughout his books, and also that of his teacher ... he had the habit of inserting here and there in all his books what concerned himself and his master, so that if one has a keen eye for these things, following up obvious clues that present themselves, and carefully collects the details, one can learn most of the incidents of their lives.[19] (fr. 184 = Eunapius, *Vitae Sophistarum*, ii.7)

The following is some of what we know or believe we know about Plutarch from his own writings. He seems to have been a kind man, devoted to his family and friends, many of whom make appearances in the *Moralia*, and to have been active in public as well as political and religious life. He lived his long and productive life in Chaeronea, northwest of Athens, where he served as a priest of Delphi and in various capacities in connection with the Roman Empire. He tells us that he was a young man studying mathematics at the Academy when Nero visited Greece sometime around AD 67, meaning he must have been born around AD 46. In the dialogue *De E apud Delphos*, Plutarch describes Eustrophus making an argument from the position of the letter epsilon as fifth in the alphabet and its significance in counting by fives (πεμπάζειν).[20] He tells us, 'These words Eustrophus addressed to us not in jest, but for the reason that at this time I was devoting myself to mathematics with the greatest enthusiasm, although I was destined soon to pay all honour to the maxim "Avoid extremes," when I had once become a member of the Academy' (387f, 391e).[21] This is a vivid picture from an older scholar looking back on youthful enthusiasm, and this self-deprecation has been shown earlier

---

[19] I am indebted to the editors for this reference. [20] See note 5 for the number 5.
[21] Babbitt (1936).

Self-Praise and Self-Presentation in Plutarch 249

as typical of Plutarch's self-presentation to avoid giving offense, similar to the young Pliny continuing with his homework as Vesuvius erupted outside: 'I don't know whether I should call this courage or folly on my part (I was only seventeen at the time) but I called for a volume of Livy and went on reading as if I had nothing else to do. I even went on with the extracts I had been making' (*Ep.* 6.20).[22]

Despite the smallness of the town, Plutarch's home, Chaeronea, was hardly isolated, situated as it was in such a way that it was easily accessible via the Corinthian gulf to Italy, Macedonia, and hence the Black Sea, as well as Egypt and the Eastern Mediterranean, so friends and travellers from all those places would find it easy to visit him. Ultimately, he settled in Chaeronea 'lest it become even smaller' (*Dem.* 2.2). This may well have been a pretence of necessity in that Plutarch may not have cared for big cities, Rome in particular. Living in a big city was not necessary for living a virtuous and happy life, and he did not wish to compete in the international arena any more than was unavoidable through his local political work and his friendship with Roman officials like Sosius Senecio, perhaps because of a kind of apprehensive caution that should not be called by as strong a term as 'fear'. Yet his natural diplomacy preferred to accentuate the positive aspect of life in Chaeronea rather than deplore the negative aspects of hyper-urban life,[23] and accepting that Plutarch may have been employing Marincola's 'pretence of necessity,' we do not need to invent reasons why he, a proud Greek man, wanted to stay where he had always lived.

He was educated in philosophy at the Academy in Athens by Ammonius,[24] showing a staunch Platonism in most of his writings.[25] Later he travelled in Egypt,[26] visited Rome,[27] and undertook at least one tour of Northern Italy, during which he journeyed to Bedriacum, Brixellum, and Ravenna, where he saw Marius' statue. It is possible that he visited other cities in Italy and travelled extensively in Greece.[28] We infer that Plutarch must have died shortly after AD 119, the year in which a very aged (according to Eusebius) Plutarch was appointed *epitropos*, or caretaker, of Greece.[29]

---

[22] Radice (1969).   [23] For greater discussion, see Titchener (2002).

[24] *Them.* 32.6, *De E* 384c; *De ad. et am.* 48e.   [25] See Dillon (2014) on Plutarch's Platonism.

[26] *Quaest. conv.* 687c; cf. *De Is. et Os.* 351c–384b.   [27] *De cur.* 516a; *Publ.* 8.2, *Flam.* 1.1, *Dem.* 2.2.

[28] Including Tanagra (*Cons. ad ux.* 608b) Helicon (*Amatorius* 749b) Hyampolis in Phocis, Adepsus and Chalcis in Euboea, Patrae, Eleusis (*Quaest. conv.* 660d, 629f, 635a, respectively), and Sparta (*Lyc.* 18.2, *Ages.* 19.10).

[29] Eusebius, *Chron. ab. Abr.* 2135 for AD 119/20.

The collection of essays known collectively as the *Quaestiones convivales* have a special place in studies on Plutarchan self-presentation. These charming essays have in the past been the subject of descriptive rather than analytical scholarship, partly because their wide range of topics covered everything from dinner-table etiquette to debates on philosophy and natural history to rhetorical contests. Like much of Plutarch's work, the *Quaestiones convivales* have enjoyed a kind of rehabilitation and are now treated as independently worth investigation and not merely as a step in the development of miscellanistic literature. As I have argued elsewhere: 'Like that on much of sympotic literature in general, work on the *QC* became, and continues to become, more expansive and inclusive, largely through the influence of critical theories such as reader response theory, new historicism, and post-structuralism.'[30] These essays, well described as 'one of the most learned, and at the same time most personal literary creations of the prolific Chaeronean',[31] are now a prime source for clues to everything from Plutarch's opinion on drama (he hated it) to the names of his family members and other personal details that together can form a complex self-portrait.[32] The symposiastic context is crucial for understanding Plutarch as both leader (*pepaideuomenos*, symposiarch) and omniscient narrator,[33] partly because the *Quaestiones convivales* may or may not be transcripts, verbatim conversations. Does it matter? Elsewhere, I have argued that it does not:

> Plutarch's own phrasing hints at this. Early in the *Table Talk*, the participants are disputing the veracity of an anecdote under debate, claiming that discussion cannot resume unless it is known whether or not the event in question actually took place. The controversy is resolved when Philopappus says 'no problem because the discussion will provide occasion for practice, even if it provides nothing else useful' (1.10.2). In the same way, the reality described by Plutarch at the dinner parties is just as real for his purposes as a video recording. To insist on 'authenticity' or truth as an important lens through which to view the *Table Talk* is to fail to distinguish the differences between and among history, biography, and autobiography.[34]

This question of authentic self-presentation is complicated by the fact that Plutarch often appears as a character in the dialogues, sometimes younger than his actual age, and sometimes the subject of comments by others.[35] It is further complicated by the fact that Plutarch is vague about non-

---

[30] Titchener (2011), 36.   [31] Klotz (2007), 1.

[32] König (2011), 179: 'One of the things which makes the *Table Talk* so remarkable and memorable is the fact that it offers us such a multi-faceted portrayal of Plutarch himself.'

[33] König (2011), 180.   [34] Titchener (2010), 393.   [35] Russell (1993), 428.

Self-Praise and Self-Presentation in Plutarch 251

essential details like why his colleague in Rome could not join him for the meetings for which they had both travelled. Russell catalogues such omissions: 'What he does not tell us includes his age. We have no clear idea of when he was born.... We do not know what Plutarch looked like.... We do not know how many children he had, nor, except in very general terms, when he was in Rome or Egypt or how many times he made those journeys.'[36] Modern humans contemplating this limited self-disclosure would find these gaps disturbing, and that is one reason for the scholarly interest in Plutarch's self-disclosure. How can we know so much and so little at the same time? One way to shed light on the question might be to attempt to distinguish between genuine self-disclosure and tactical self-disclosure in an effort to garner details about Plutarch's personal life and family. The problem with this subjective approach becomes clear in, for example, Plutarch's *Consolatio ad uxorem*,[37] written to his wife after the death of their young daughter Timoxena. There are very personal and tender moments, such as when Plutarch, praising his wife for her tender maternal love, remembers how she had undergone breast surgery for injury from nursing. But the *consolatio* format was meant to be published and the essay has some strong didactic and rhetorical strands. It is not fiction, but it is hardly fact.

Returning to the *Quaestiones convivales* and the question of the extent to which those essays are a reliable source for details on Plutarch's own life, the most profitable course is to accept the idea that Plutarch, like the Muses, knows how to tell false or less true things as well as true, and that the more important question is why – why does it matter how many children he had, or how old he was? We know from the *Consolatio ad uxorem* that he was a grandfather at the time of his daughter Timoxena's death (608b). That is in many ways a much more useful thing to know (if true!) than how old Plutarch was. We can assume that he was already well-acquainted with death and loss in his family, and from his long marriage we can hope that it was a sustaining partnership. His relative position in life matters more than the number of years. Klotz illustrates this disconnect in response to the question of the veracity of Plutarch's self-presentation:

> Rather, we are supplied with multiple examples of philosophers at dinner, and multiple stages of the philosopher's development. We see Plutarch as mature thinker; and Plutarch as politician, as well as Plutarch as father, son, and respectful student. In the *Quaestiones Convivales*, the narrator's self-representation is not singular and static, nor does it move along a linear

---

[36] Russell (1993), 431.   [37] De Lacy and Einarson (1984).

chronological development in the course of the work. Plutarch depicts himself functioning in different relationship matrices, interacting constantly with various members of his family and close friends.[38]

Fair enough! And there is yet another reason to be cautious about Plutarch's self-disclosures. He always has a purpose, and that purpose is one way or another about edification through examples. I return to *Consolatio ad uxorem* as an example of how Plutarch takes the opportunity to weave his personal experience into generalized instruction on behaviour in public, counselling the avoidance of hysterics and dramatic display. As Roskam astutely observes,

> [W]e should bear in mind that Plutarch's self-disclosure is always closely connected with its argumentative context.... Some methodological caution is justified, then, although this does not imply that all of Plutarch's statements about himself and his experiences should a priori be regarded with great suspicion. They often provide a glimpse into his personality or an interesting snapshot from his life and can as such be used, with due caution, as an interesting source for Plutarch's daily activities and interests.[39]

This approach straddles the issue nicely, and it is impossible to dispute that the evidence from Plutarch about his personal details must be used cautiously but used nevertheless as we study the way he presents himself in his writing.

Plutarch's Presentation of His Civic Outlook

Since most of what scholars know (or think they know) about Plutarch, his life, and his relatives, comes from his own writings, we now turn to *An seni respublica gerenda sit* and the similar *Praecepta gerendae reipublicae,* to learn more about his civic outlook. These are essays about leadership with a particularly personal flavour, 'rightly prized as giving a rare insider's view of day-to-day politics in the Greek cities of the Roman Empire'.[40] *Praecepta gerendae reipublicae* is addressed to one Menemachus, a young man otherwise unknown to us. He is eager to enter public life, so eager that he does not have time to learn about statesmanship on his own through observation and daily life and therefore asks for advice from Plutarch, who is pleased to provide examples of statesmanship in action. *An seni respublica gerenda sit* is addressed to one Euphanes, an old man otherwise unknown to us. He seems to be consulting Plutarch about retirement from public

---

[38] Klotz (2007), 666.   [39] Roskam (2021).   [40] Trapp (2004), 189.

Self-Praise and Self-Presentation in Plutarch

life, a theme that also occurs in *Praecepta gerendae reipublicae*. The essays have much in common, and one can almost see the old man Euphanes of *An seni respublica gerenda sit* in *Praecepta gerendae reipublicae*: 'We might argue that the particular sort of guidance that the *Praecepta gerendae reipublicae* embodies is a textual counterpart of what the elderly politician in the *An seni respublica gerenda sit* ought to be giving. In other words, the *Praecepta gerendae reipublicae* could have been the textbook that the *An seni respublica gerenda sit* politician consulted when advising others.'[41] Despite their similarities, *An seni respublica gerenda sit* has a more positive feel than *Praecepta gerendae reipublicae* with the result that 'where the *Precepts* talked about seriousness of purpose in admonitory terms, the *Old Men* is exhortatory'.[42] It is here that we look for Plutarch's opinion on governance and leadership, much of which has to do with self-presentation and avoidance of envy.

Plutarch understands well the placating value of this kind of character-izing, as we see from his words in *Praecepta gerendae reipublicae,* an essay designed to give advice on ruling, in which he advises readers to avoid military battles as a way of bestowing praise; rather, they should praise acts of piety and strong ethical conviction. By comparing boasts about past victories in battle to small children dressing up, Plutarch may be striving to eliminate boasting behaviour from the Greek statesman's repertoire in order to promote harmony through controlling self-presentation:

> Furthermore, when we see little children trying playfully to bind their father's shoes on their feet or fit their crowns upon their heads, we only laugh, but the officials in the cities, when they foolishly urge the people to imitate the deeds, ideals, and actions of their ancestors, however unsuitable they may be to the present times and conditions, stir up the common folk, and, though what they do is laughable, what is done to them is no laughing matter, unless they are merely treated with utter contempt. Indeed there are many acts of the Greeks of former times by recounting which the statesman can mould and correct the characters of our contemporaries, for example, at Athens by calling to mind, not deeds in war, but such things as the decree of amnesty after the downfall of the Thirty Tyrants, the fining of Phrynichus for presenting in a tragedy the capture of Miletus, their decking their heads with garlands when Cassander refounded Thebes; how, when they heard of the clubbing at Argos, in which the Argives killed fifteen hundred of their own citizens, they decreed that an expiatory sacrifice be carried about in the assembly; and how, when they were searching the houses at the time of Harpalus' frauds, they passed by only one, that of a

[41] Xenophontos (2012), 86.   [42] Kemezis (2016–17), 113.

254 FRANCES B. TITCHENER

newly married man. By emulating acts like these it is even now possible to resemble our ancestors, but Marathon, the Eurymedon, Plataea, and all the other examples which make the common folk vainly to swell with pride and kick up their heels, should be left to the schools of the sophists. (*Praecepta gerenda reipublicae* 814b)[43]

In discussing Plutarch's suggested substitutions for Athenian civic pride, Cook points out that:

> these five exemplary events appear so suddenly and briefly in *Advice on public life* 814b that we may read past them without realizing how rare and unusual they are in Plutarch ... The rarity and seeming oddity of these scenes suggest that Plutarch did not casually pull these from his standard stock of historical exempla.... He chose them with unusual care ... *because the five exempla illustrate on a communal level Plutarch's constant advice to the individual statesman that he root out civic strife and maintain harmony through individual and public mildness and self-control* (πραότης).[44]

Control of self-presentation leads to control of the body politic.

Plutarch here rejects a sentimental, now out-of-date vision of Greece's past great military leaders in favour of private noble behaviour encouraging them to rise above using such standards as victory at Marathon as point of pride and look instead to internal measures. Modern times for a Greek living during the Roman Empire evidently required different kinds of men from those who led Greece to victory against Persia, or liberated Boeotia from Spartan occupation. Many of the 'great' heroes of the past, men who would appear to be suitable role models and national heroes, were consigned to the uses of history, not appropriate for modern icons. Greeks cannot compete with the Romans on a military basis and it is dangerous to try:

> You should arrange your cloak more carefully and from the office of the generals keep your eyes upon the orators' platform, and not have great pride of confidence in your crown, since you see the boots of the Roman soldiers just above your head. No, you should imitate the actors ... for to fail in one's part in public brings not mere hissing or catcalls or stamping of feet, but many have experienced 'The dread chastiser, axe that cleaves the neck'. (*Praecepta gerendae reipublicae* 813e–f)[45]

But there is still more of interest in the passage about Athenian pride in past victories like Marathon for insight into how Plutarch presents controversial material, which may be of interest to how he handles

---

[43] Trans. H. N. Fowler (1936).   [44] Cook (2004), 201, with my emphasis.
[45] Trans. H. N. Fowler (1936).

Self-Praise and Self-Presentation in Plutarch 255

self-presentation. The simile comes first – children dressing up – and the explanation later. The dynamic is that of a superior and inferior: child and parent, the masses and city officials. As 'we' laugh at the child dressing up, part of the comedy lies in the fact that the child has failed, and the child is not necessarily aware that these actions are comic. Thus, the Athenians puffing themselves up over ancient battles are the same as small children pulling on their fathers' shoes, and then thinking themselves dressed and ready for action. This is not very flattering to the Athenians, and the fact that the adult clothes in which these folks are dressing up are great battles of the Persian Wars is most startling.

It is almost impossible to believe that by Plutarch's day the *Marathonomachoi* were not officially revered, in a manner akin to what the United States in reference to World War II calls the 'greatest generation'. Why would Plutarch treat the memory of Greek victories in this way? Why would he adopt this harsh persona? Perhaps it was too dangerous to use those particular battles, even as long ago as they took place, for a partly Roman audience as examples of Athenian greatness against a numerically superior enemy. In *Bellone an pace clariores fuerint Athenienses*, Plutarch concludes that the Athenians were in fact greater in war than in peace, but there they are compared only against themselves (345c–351b). Or perhaps these battles, and the victories they secured, were too personal and painful of reminders to be experienced in front of others. Maybe Plutarch rejected military victories as a meaningful barometer of character during Roman occupation, where any Greek military victories would be seriously diminished, in the same way he rejects extreme displays of lamentation and grief.[46] Finally, this reaction against the glorious past may also be the reaction of a Greek living under Roman rule, who realizes that the military heyday of Greece is long over, that Marathon only delayed occupation, and that if Greece wishes to judge herself or be judged on military terms, she will surely be found wanting.

Here it is important to include Plutarch's Roman context as an element in understanding his self-presentation through words and outlook. He was a Roman citizen, living in a Roman province, travelling in Roman provinces, spending periods of time in the Rome of the emperors, and counting among his numerous friends many Romans, some of distinction. He may have loved his native Boeotia with an ardent patriotism; he may have been heir to Greek learning and thought; but the world in which he lived was now Greco-Roman, and he could not fail to be influenced by ideas that

---

[46] E.g. *Consolatio ad uxorem, passim,* de Lacy and Einarson (1959).

256 FRANCES B. TITCHENER

were Roman.[47] In reality, Plutarch was a 'Greek citizen in a Roman world', and he never forgot those Roman boots above his head. As Simon Swain put it:

> The Greeks were well aware that particular political acts of the past were not going to be repeated today in the Roman peace. It was the feeling, the spirit of their history and heritage that they were investing in. This was never political like a demonstration, a riot, or a sit-in. Nevertheless, in a society where it was possible to indicate priority in time and priority of authority by a single word (*arche*), the stability of intention to seem Greek and to be Greek with the past constantly in mind has a clear underlying political significance.[48]

Praecepta gerendae reipublicae and *An seni respublica gerenda sit* feel so personal largely because of Plutarch's own involvement in local government and as a priest, in Delphic matters, and his Platonism. It is also the case that Plutarch was a civic leader himself, so his thoughts on the subject are worth investigating more closely. Scholars in the past have argued that underlying peripatetic sources had become firmly embedded in Plutarch's thoughts, and were inextricable from his own,[49] while suggesting that Plutarch's viewpoint in these essays is so influenced by philosophy that he runs the risk of undermining the important need for citizens to compete for civic honours.[50] If that is true, and Plutarch's personal thoughts, however informed, are woven into these essays, then surely this is prime territory for clues to his self-presentation.

Early on in *Praecepta gerendae reipublicae*, Plutarch acknowledges that the state periodically makes do with bad leaders, likening such a choice to well-known cravings, like those of pregnant women for stones, or the seasick for salty pickles. He then goes on to describe a situation in Sparta where a good motion was made by a bad man, and the ephors, having turned it down, appointed by lot a good man to make the same motion so that it would be acceptable to the people, 'thus pouring, as it were, from a dirty vessel into a clean one. So great is the importance, in a free State, of confidence or lack of confidence in a man's character' (*Praecepta gerendae reipubliae* 801c).[51] In the *Parallel Lives*, Plutarch is at pains to demonstrate his subjects' characters through their actions, not to correct the historical record. If he had intended to write history in the

---

[47] Whether or not Plutarch can be considered an author of resistance literature is an enormous question, gaining increased attention and interest.
[48] Swain (1996), 88–9.   [49] Hershbell (2004), 156.   [50] Trapp (2004), 189.
[51] Trans. H. N. Fowler (1936).

Self-Praise and Self-Presentation in Plutarch 257

modern sense of the word, he would never have undertaken subjects such as Theseus, Romulus, Lycurgus, and Solon, and indeed the *Theseus-Romulus* pair begins with a disclaimer of sorts in which Plutarch acknowledges the fantastic nature of his subjects and their stories, but hopes that reason applied to mythology will yield history, or something that looks like history.

He tells us that he wrote the *Parallel Lives* to provide good examples for men to emulate, as is clear from the proems of *Timoleon* and *Aemilius,* and *Pericles*:

> It was for the sake of others that I first began to write biographies; but I find myself continuing and devoting myself to it for my own; the virtues of these great men providing me a sort of mirror in which I may see how to adjust and adorn my own life. (*Tim.* 1.1)[52]

> My method ... is by the rigor of inquiry and the habituation of writing to prepare my soul to accept the memories of the noblest and most outstanding individuals. (*Aem.* 1.1)[53]

> It is fitting for a man to pursue what is the best, not only to contemplate it, but to benefit from the contemplation.... This is inherent in virtuous deeds, which inject eagerness and zeal for imitation in those who search for them. (*Per.* 1.3)[54]

Notice that it was 'for the sake of others' that he began writing biographies; here we see the pretence of necessity used to establish authority and improve the audience. Plutarch presents to us fitting subjects for contemplation, and he presents himself as a willing and trustworthy guide.

This essay also includes some specific prescriptions for politicians successful according to the Plutarchan measure. Because public figures should be accessible, they needed to be aware that they were under constant scrutiny and act accordingly: 'But since you are henceforth to live as on an open stage, educate your character and put it in order; and if it is not easy wholly to banish evil from the soul, at any rate remove and repress those faults which are most flourishing and conspicuous' (800b).[55] Public figures should steer a middle course with friends, somewhere between the outlooks of Themistocles and Cleon. Cleon, 'when he first decided to take up political life, brought his friends together and renounced his friendship with them as something which often weakens and perverts the right and just choice of policy in political life. But he would have done better if he

---

[52] Trans. Perrin (1918).   [53] Trans. Perrin (1918).   [54] Trans. Perrin (1916).
[55] Trans. H. N. Fowler (1936).

FRANCES B. TITCHENER

had cast out from his soul avarice and life of strife and had cleansed himself of envy and malice; for the State needs, not men who have no friends or comrades, but good and self-controlled men' (806f).[56] Yet Themistocles,

> when someone said that he would govern well if he showed himself equally impartial to all, replied: 'May I never take my seat on such a throne that my friends shall not have more from me than those who are not my friends!' He also was wrong; for he put the government under pledge to his friendship, subordinating the affairs of the community and the public to private favours and interests. (*Praecepta gerendae reipublicae* 806f–807b)[57]

Plutarch sums up these different aspects of a statesman's public personality (accessibility, self-control, reserve with friends) as requiring 'attendance on superiors and enhancement of inferiors and honouring equals, but also greeting and acting friendly towards all alike' (816b).[58] We are reminded again of his Roman context and of his disdain for the reclusive Nicias.

Conclusion

Since authority in prose authors lacks the rhetorical or persuasive element enjoyed by poets from the invocation of the muse, it has been argued: 'That new model of authority expressed through prose did indeed place enormous weight on the future of the researcher, more so in many ways than that of the poet figure, who tends to hide behind the idea of divine inspiration.'[59] If the figure of the author or researcher is centre stage, the self-conscious presentation of that figure is an important part of the author's ability to make his point. Plutarch presents himself in his own works, particularly *An seni respublica gerenda sit*, *Praecepta gerendae reipublicae*, and the *Quaestiones convivales*, as a trusted figure by his careful use of all five of Marincola's devices – reference to 'gods and fortune', a 'pretence of necessity', 'commonness of action' and 'praise in the mouth of others', and finally, 'magnification of actions'. In this way Plutarch bolsters his own authority, validating Marincola's contention that ancient historians garnered authority with deliberate and careful self-presentation with a careful dose of self-praise.

---

[56] Trans. H. N. Fowler (1936)   [57] Trans. H. N. Fowler (1936).
[58] Trans. H. N. Fowler (1936).   [59] König (2011), 181.

PART IV

Generic Transformations

CHAPTER 13

Thucydides' Mytilenaean Debate
Political Philosophy or Authoritative History?

Paul Cartledge

Six decades ago (my chronology is as exact as that of Thucydides' 'pentekontaëtia'), A. ('Tony') Andrewes, Oxford's Wykeham Professor, laid down a number of markers for the ways in which a historian of late fifth-century BC Greece (such as he – and I) could or properly should make use of a famous pair of Thucydidean speeches, for purposes of historical reconstruction and analysis.[1] Since 1962, there has been a plethora of scholarship published on Thucydidean historiography in general, and on the speeches/rhetoric in particular, some of it very good, including great work by Andrewes himself in *Commentary* mode.[2] But the issues raised in and by the 'Mytilenaean Debate' and indeed by Thucydides' inchoate *History* as a whole have not gone away, and they will not do so any time soon.[3]

Italian philosopher Benedetto Croce once famously opined that every true history (as opposed to a dead chronicle) was contemporary history: 'Thus if contemporary history springs straight from life, so too does that history which is called non-contemporary, for it is evident that only an

---

*I am deeply grateful to the editors for their most gracious invitations to participate both in the conference (which I was unable to attend) and in this volume, and for their most helpful editorial interventions in an earlier draft of this essay. I first encountered our honorand in Cambridge some three decades ago, and we have kept our friendship alive since then, both at a distance and through meetings at regular intervals in New York; Washington, DC; Oxford; and back in Cambridge. It is a particular privilege and pleasure to offer this specially written essay to our profession's foremost historiographer and – probably – wit.

[1] Andrewes (1962).
[2] Samplings in Rengakos and Tsakmakis (2006); Rusten (2009); Morley and Harloe (2012); Balot, Forsdyke, and Foster (2017). A minimal selection would for me includes at least Stahl (2003 [1966]); Ste. Croix (1972); Andrewes in Gomme, Andrewes, and Dover (1945–81); Macleod (1983b); Connor (1984); and Hornblower (1991–2008), which is among much else a learned commentary upon Gomme, Andrewes, and Dover (1945–81).
[3] Symptomatic is the current preoccupation with the hare started by Graham Allison's 'Thucydides trap', correctly rubbished by Morley (2017).

261

interest in the life of the present can move one to investigate past fact.... "Every true history is contemporary history."[4]

That last sentence is printed in inverted commas, but I suspect this was a device for flagging it rather than acknowledging it as a quotation from somewhere else.[5] Thucydides, the contemporary historian par excellence from one historiographical point of view, could only have agreed and indeed applauded that sentiment. Except that, paradoxically – and Thucydides and paradox go together like the proverbial love and marriage – Thucydides was also the historian 'for all time' par excellence, as he himself proudly claimed (1.22.4) and as I shall hope to corroborate in a small way in this essay.

Eleven years after Andrewes' article was published, his future fellow-commentator on Thucydides, Kenneth Dover – one of the most acute and learned of the more recent Thucydidean critics – published a brilliant, short 'new survey' of Thucydidean scholarship, raising among many other issues that of the 'authority' of Thucydides. That is also the issue that I wish to re-open here.[6] By Thucydides' day (c. 455–400 BC) to include speeches in a work of 'history' (Herodotus' term, but a word Thucydides himself scrupulously avoided, preferring the legalistic-sounding *zetesis*) was more or less 'traditional' and de rigueur.[7] The questions for us, however, are these: what did Thucydides think he was doing or aiming to achieve by including speeches in *oratio recta*, as written up by himself; and, more particularly, how did writing them (up) effect, or affect, his authority as a, well, historian?[8]

Thucydides was certainly to this extent unusual, in that he explicitly set out in a prefatory way (1.22) a methodology he apparently claimed that he *had* followed – even though the work as he left it is incomplete in more than one sense; most noticeably, and relevantly, the final 'book'

---

[4] Croce (1921 [1919]), 12.   [5] With Peter Rhodes, pers. comm.

[6] Dover (1973), section II (I is Bibliography), is entitled 'Authority'. I pay homage to Marincola (1997), of course, but also to one of this volume's co-editors, Rood (2006b) (which is, however, devoted to exploring 'the way that Thucydides constructed his narratorial authority', 249, rather than my concern, the authoritativeness of a particular pair of the speeches).

[7] Walbank (1965 [1985]); cf. Debnar (2001); and on the Mytilenaean Debate specifically, Schmitz (2010). Not that there were all that many Greek 'historians' around by 400 BC: Scanlon (2015), esp. 121–5. For a defence of the absence of speeches from Book 8, as due to conscious and deliberate 'narrative artistry', see Liotsakis (2017). I am not persuaded.

[8] The obvious prompt for this tribute was Marincola (1997). For a parallel discussion of a Thucydidean speech, that of Alcibiades to the Spartan Assembly in 414 in Book 6, see Chlup (2006). There are critics who see Thucydides more or exclusively as a political theorist, even 'scientist', but I am not of their number. See further below and note 22.

Thucydides' Mytilenaean Debate

(Book 8, according to the ancient book division we follow) contains no speeches.[9] The key point, it seems to me, though, is this: that Thucydides apparently believed his credibility as regards accuracy (*akribeia*) and objectivity and, therefore, his authority or authoritativeness would be palpably diminished and at any rate certainly challenged if he had *not* followed the methodology that he prefatorily announced. What, then, did he mean or could he have meant by what he wrote at 1.22?

Here is the chapter in full, in what I consider to be the best available modern English translation, that by Jeremy Mynott (2013):

> As to what was said in speeches by the various parties either before they went to war or during the conflict itself, it was difficult for me to recall the precise details in the case of those I heard myself, just as it was for those who reported back to me on cases elsewhere. What I have set down is how I think each of them would have expressed what was most appropriate in the particular circumstances while staying as close as possible to the overall intention of what was actually said. As to the events of the war themselves, however, I resolved not to rely in my writing on what I learned from chance sources or even on my own impressions, but both in the cases where I was present myself and in those where I depended on others I investigated every detail with the utmost concern for accuracy. This was a laborious process of research, because eyewitnesses at the various events reported the same things differently, depending on which side they favoured and on their powers of memory. Perhaps the absence of the element of fable in my work may make it seem less easy on the ear; but it will have served its purpose well enough if it is judged useful by those who want to have a clear view of what happened in the past and what – the human condition being what it is – can be expected to happen again in the future in similar or much the same ways. It is composed to be a possession for all time and not just a performance-piece for the moment.

Note, to start off, that Thucydides begins the chapter with the methodological issue of the speeches *before* he turns to that of the narrative. Note too the careful distinctions drawn within the chapter: first, the contrast of the speeches with the facts of the narrative ('the events of the war themselves') with respect to the degree of potential accuracy; and then, second, that same contrast as perceived with regard to subjectivity/objectivity ('What I have set down is how *I think* each of them would have expressed' (my emphasis)). What in that last clause are the implicit or explicit meanings of τὰ δέοντα ('what was most appropriate in the

---

[9] Andrewes, appendix 1, 'Indications of incompleteness', in Gomme, Andrewes, and Dover (1945–81), v.361–83.

264   PAUL CARTLEDGE

particular circumstances'): appropriate or obligatory? And for whom, and in whose opinion?

Then there is the problem of how best to unpack ξύμπασα γνώμη: translated here as 'overall intention' but rendered/interpreted by others as overall burden or purport or general sense. Is the ξυμ- prefix inclusive or exclusive; that is, is the *gnome* meant to include all or most of the supporting argument(s), or is it to be thought of as general/overall in the sense of contrasted with the particular arguments? There are plenty of ambiguities, unfortunately, to chew on there.[10]

Over and above the linguistic-methodological quiddities of 1.22, why should one want to re-examine the Mytilenaean Debate in particular, among all the speeches or pairs of speeches that Thucydides wrote up, from the standpoint of interrogating the historian's authority? The answer, in one word, is – Diodotus. Like the Athenian Euphemus (an envoy speaking at a debate at Camarina on Sicily in winter 415/414 that Thucydides chose to write up in Book 6), whose very name ('fine speaker'?) has provoked the hypothesis that it is too good to be factually true, Diodotus ('Zeus's gift') appears nowhere else in Thucydides – nor in any other context in any other literary source. Is he (therefore) a *porte-parole* for the historian, or, more damagingly, a (mere) fiction?

Martin Ostwald has, I believe, made the best case, on the evidence then available, that he was not merely that; his suggestion that Diodotus was holding a major public elective office such as that of general or Hellenotamias is surely intrinsically plausible.[11] Moreover, one might also want to argue that any contemporary reader or hearer of Thucydides who had been present at the two Assembly meetings would have been at least surprised and therefore dismayed, if not incredulous, if Diodotus had been 'Diodotus', a mere Thucydidean fiction. For that artistic decision, surely, would have undermined or at any rate weakened his authority – his authoritativeness, which was indeed already vulnerable and impugned on other, purely descriptive, factual grounds.

However, just a couple of years ago a remarkable archaeological discovery was made in Kephisia, a northern suburb of Athens: a *skyphos* (drinking cup) of the second quarter of the fifth century BC inscribed with several names, each in a separate hand, including those of Pericles – and (one)

---

[10] Ste. Croix (my undergraduate Oxford tutor) (1972), 8–11, offers a useful conspectus of the range of possible shades of meanings. For his discussions of other key Thucydidean terminology, see his index, p. 434, s.v. 'Thucydides ... terminology'. See further Plant (1988); Porciani (1999); and Winton (1999).

[11] Ostwald (1979 [2009]).

Diodotus. To be sure, it is not 100 per cent certain that this 'Pericles' is *the* Pericles, but the presence here also of an Arriphron (the rare name of Pericles' grandfather and brother) makes it very likely, which means that this Diodotus could well be the homonymous grandfather of the Thucydidean Diodotus, if not a – by then pretty elderly – Diodotus.[12] All the same, *sub specie aeternitatis*, when judged in relation to the validity and impact of a loudly proclaimed *ktema es aiei*, the admittedly controversial authenticity or inauthenticity of Diodotus was and is a relatively minor matter, almost neither here nor there. And of course there is more to it than that, much more.

For the occasion of Thucydides' Mytilenaean Debate is the sole occasion in all the fifth century BC on which we know (so long as Thucydides can be relied upon, of course) that the Athenian Assembly reversed on meeting day 2 a decision it had taken on meeting day 1. Normally, indeed normatively, Assembly meetings lasted only the one day, or indeed just a portion thereof.[13] Thucydides, however, as simultaneously both historian and literary artist, wanted or even needed an occasion upon which to give to Cleon, or rather write-up for him, a full-blown, ideological-attitudinal speech. More specifically, he does so for a Cleon whom he (re)presents as if he were the false Pericles.[14] The Mytilenaean Debate therefore proved the perfect vehicle for Thucydides to reveal what he understood to be Cleon's ruling passion in all its – as he saw it – ingloriousness: namely, 'violence'.

Thucydides also wanted or needed a major 'paradeigmatic' empirical instance and occasion, within the framework of which he could meditate further on words he had placed in the mouths of anonymous (and therefore also controversially authentic) 'Athenians' speaking by invitation at a decisive pre-war assembly of the Spartans (1.73–8). Reflecting on the nature of interstate relations in general, they postulate that three dominant factors – fear, honour, and material interest (1.75.2, 76.3) – govern

---

[12] Chaniotis (2019), 26–7 (discussing *SEG* LXIII: 66); I am most grateful to Matt Simonton for drawing this to my attention. On graffiti as a genre, see Taylor (2011).

[13] For all matters to do with procedure in the Athenian *ekklesia*, see M. H. Hansen (1983–9).

[14] For Thucydides both 'as history' and, simultaneously, 'as literature', see Dover (1983 [2009]); Loraux (2011 [1980]); as 'between history and literature', Tsakmakis and Tamiolaki (2013). For his 'artfulness' as a 'reporter': Hunter (1973). For a penetrating, narratological vision, see Rood (1998): reviewed by J. Marincola, *BMCR* 2002.01.16; a highly original, Bakhtinian-dialogistical approach is offered by Dewald (2005) (but based on and incorporating a 1975 Berkeley doctoral thesis): reviewed by T. Rood, *BMCR* 2006.04.25. On Thucydides' Cleon, see especially Woodhead (1960).

266   PAUL CARTLEDGE

interstate relations within an alliance of a lopsided, imperial kind.[15] It is no coincidence, rather the opposite, that just those three concepts are invoked by Thucydides' two named speakers in his Mytilenaean Debate. In short, the Mytilene crisis of 427 fitted Thucydides' historiographical/political thought agenda to a 't'.

Nor is it any coincidence that adepts of international relations theory and analysis have so treasured this particular dimension of that Thucydidean agenda. But most of them have little or no conception of its political, intellectual, and artistic underpinnings. Thucydides chose to write up speeches only at what he considered key 'moments of decision'.[16] In this instance, what the Athenian *demos* in Assembly had to decide was what measures of reprisal to implement against a major (ship-contributing) revolted ally, and how to do so in such a way as both to prevent a recurrence of such a revolt and thereby to improve its own authority among the alliance as a whole. Just how important Thucydides considered this particular moment of decision in 427 to be can be inferred not only from his writing up of the Mytilenaean Debate but also from the fact that of all the Athenians' 150–200 allied states it is on the Mytilenaeans alone – that is, the ruling oligarchy of the *polis* of Mytilene – that Thucydides bestows the accolade of a speech.[17] This comes just a few chapters – though almost one whole year in elapsed real time – before the Mytilenaean Debate. In fact, although the whole work was arguably in some sense a prolonged meditation on empire, Book 3 is especially acutely so.[18]

How, then, should we judge the Mytilenaean Debate from the point of view of its author's 'authority'? The status, indeed, the very existence of Diodotus has, as noted, been put into question – probably, we now believe, unwarrantedly. But what are we to make of his allotted role within the dynamic of the Mytilenaean Debate as a whole? Thucydides reports that on day 1 the Assembly decided by a small margin to vote in favour of

---

[15] It may – or may not – be very significant that Thucydides' 'Athenians' alternate between using *deos* and *phobos*, both of which may be translated as 'fear', if with a variety of nuances according to context. I am grateful for discussion of this and many other points over the years with hyper-acute Thucydides expert Daniel Tompkins.

[16] Ste. Croix (1972), appendix IV.

[17] A standard work on 'the empire' is still Meiggs (1972). Two valuable collections: Low (2008); Ma et al. (2009). On oligarchy in classical Greece, see now definitively Simonton (2017). On justice and necessity, Rahe (2002) (full bibliography to that date at p. 27 n. 9). 'The Plataeans' are also given a speaking role in Book 3, but they were allies of a different, pre-imperial (519 BC) kind and besides were about to be upgraded to a form of Athenian citizens, following the temporary annihilation of their own city.

[18] Cogan (1981).

the severest punishment proposed for the Mytilenaean rebels and traitors. But he does not say either who proposed that motion or who else spoke in its support. In this, as in many other ways, he is no doubt an 'artful' reporter.[19] He states elliptically that the reason for holding the day 2 Assembly – that is, to spell it out as he did not feel the need to, the reason why the presiding prytany of the Council of 500 decided to reconvene it – was overridingly emotional, the dominant emotion being that of pity: for the original decision was felt, retrospectively, by sufficiently many of the participants to have been too cruel – and unjustly cruel. Yet Thucydides in his account of the day 2 Assembly meeting (which is what he reduces the actually much broader real debate over Mytilene to) reproduces or writes up no speech in which pity is the principal concern, or even the dominant note. Indeed, the note of pity, let alone empathy, is entirely absent from the first of the two written-up speeches (Cleon's) and is present only in a very minor key in the other (Diodotus').[20]

Instead, both of Thucydides' chosen speakers are represented as arguing – or (if we allow for subjective intention and intervention by the historian) are made to argue – in terms of what they claim to be and offer up as hardnosed pragmatism. That (im)balance suggests *ab initio* that Thucydides may be playing fast and loose with the facts of this prolonged Athenian Assembly meeting of 427; and that is so even if we grant, as is quite plausible, that on day 2 the most powerful and influential opposing speeches were indeed those of Cleon and Diodotus. However, it is of course also quite likely that it was a version of Cleon's original speech on day 1 that – just – tipped the balance of the Assembly's (initial) decision. On day 2 Cleon therefore would more likely have been *responding to* a speech arguing for rescindment of the first day's decision, such as Diodotus', rather than speaking before him, as represented in the Mytilenaean Debate of Thucydides' Book 3, and would have been attempting thereby to remind the Assembly of the reasons why, and the mindset in which, they had voted the way they did on day 1.

Finally, let us turn to consider in some detail the content of the two speeches, reminding ourselves of what was claimed by Thucydides at 1.22:

---

[19] Hunter (1973).

[20] On pity with special reference to the Mytilenaean Debate, Fulkerson (2008); on pity as a quality in ancient Greek culture, and specifically in politics, see Konstan (2005); typically, it was outweighed in the latter sphere by perceived self-interest, though the real Athenians prided themselves, for instance, on the pity they traditionally showed to suppliant strangers: Missiou (2004). It may or may not be relevant that there were several Greek words that could be translated 'pity', the two commonest being *oiktos* and *eleos*.

do we think that Cleon and Diodotus 'actually said' anything much like what Thucydides gives them to say, in the way he makes them say it, and/or do we think that, no matter how different reality and representation may have been in purely verbal terms, he does really convey the 'general/overall burden/intention' (*xympasa gnome*) of their respective argument(s)? If we are not convinced of Thucydides' substantive fidelity, and I do not mean to confine the argument to Thucydides' idiolect, what does that say for Thucydides' 'authority', always supposing that Thucydides really was aiming to make his speakers say what *in his opinion* the situation – including at least their situation as speakers, and the Assembly's occurrence and location within the domestic and international political moment – imperatively demanded (τὰ δέοντα, 'the necessary things')?[21]

One general interpretative rule laid down by Andrewes seems to be the right one to invoke first:[22] namely, the extent to which a speaker does stick to the *xympasa gnome* of 'what was actually said' or, conversely, deviates into irrelevancies and/or generalizations that may or may not have a telling application to the particular case in hand, may afford a useful clue to or yardstick for judging the argumentative fidelity of the Thucydidean speech to its supposed original. In this case, if we do invoke that rule, it is Diodotus' speech – not Cleon's – that raises the red flag of generalizing irrelevance. Its overall purport or argument, surely, is designed to moderate the Assembly's original, maximally harsh if not brutal decision, and above all to discriminate between the anti-Athenian ruling-elite Mytilenaeans and the pro-Athenian masses of the *demos* of the Mytilenaeans. Equally, it is sure that, although a disquisition on the effectiveness or otherwise of deterrence as a or the main motivation for and justification of punishment (of any kind, in any eventuality) would not in itself have been entirely out of place, the disproportionate length and inappropriately theoretical-philosophical character of Diodotus' impassioned attack upon the deterrence theory of punishment do jeopardize our view of Thucydides' authority as a truthful rather than 'artful' reporter.[23]

---

[21] Winnington-Ingram (1965). [22] Andrewes (1962).

[23] For Diodotus' 'deceit', see B. Manuwald (1979 [2009]); for his 'paradox', Debnar (2000); for his 'responsibility and accountability', Landauer (2019), 105–28; for Thucydides' (re)presentation of him (and Cleon) as 'ironic', L. Mitchell (2010); and for a moral-philosophical reading of the entire debate, Orwin (1984). On ideology and policy – including Thucydides' – see Cogan (1981). On the issue of punishment: Cohen (2005), esp. 175–82. My own introduction to the theoretical-philosophical issues involved in the concept and application of punishment was due to my New College Oxford philosophy tutor and mentor, Tony (later Lord) Quinton: see Quinton (1954 [2015]).

Thucydides' Mytilenaean Debate

Cleon's speech is seemingly the more realistic, or authentic, in two main ways. First, in spirit and tone it somewhat recalls the laconic intervention attributed to Spartan ephor Sthenelaidas (1.86) in the context of the decisive Spartan assembly debate held in 432 almost immediately prior to the outbreak of the Atheno-Peloponnesian War in 431, at least in its brutal and brutalizing violence of address.[24] It therefore bears out Thucydides' characterization of Cleon as an essentially and predominantly violent politician.[25] But, second and more important, it also designedly recalls the way that Thucydides' Pericles – for whom the historian writes no fewer than three speeches – does not shy away from telling the People in Assembly what he considered they needed to be told, rather than what they wanted to hear. At 2.65.7, in his obituary notice of Pericles, Thucydides confirms his own representation by making a point of praising the fact that – in direct contrast to his 'successors' as *demagogoi* – Pericles led the *demos* and was not led by them. In Cleon's Mytilenaean Debate speech that disinhibition cashes out as telling, almost ordering, the People to stick rigidly to their original decision, and so to let clemency – or indeed any discrimination of treatment among the citizen people of Mytilene – go hang.

In short, the Mytilene Debate for all its undoubted quotient of factuality does seem to me to lend significant weight overall to the view of those who argue that Thucydides is best classified not so much as a historian but rather as a political philosopher. Significant weight – but not, I think, decisive: few if any ancient historians would probably merit inclusion in the canon of historiography on the grounds of the factuality or otherwise of their speeches; but the enduring quality of Thucydides' speeches does not seem to me to depend chiefly on their factual accuracy, however much he himself vaunted that (consider only, but *imprimis*, the Funeral Speech (*epitaphios*) that is so often taken to be Pericles' very own *ipsissma verba*). Yet even so Thucydides is still, for me, an ancestor, although we historian descendants should surely all agree that he 'is not a colleague'.[26] At any rate, it seems to me entirely appropriate, for example, that Jeremy

---

[24] Debnar (2001).

[25] But see Woodhead (1960) for a persuasive corrective. On Cleon's 'hidden appeals', see Andrews (2000). On the rhetoric of Thucydides' Pericles, Zuccarini (2018). See further below.

[26] Loraux (2011 [1980]); like Hunter (1973) and Dover (1983 [2009]), Loraux too inveighs against the 'history *versus* literature' dichotomy. See above, note 14.

Mynott's Thucydides translation should have been published as a 'Cambridge Text in the History of Political Thought'.[27]

That view of Thucydides has, however, been vehemently attacked by Ste. Croix (1972) – with reason, and argument, as well as passion. But, even if one were to grant Ste. Croix's overall case, one would have to concede that there are exceptions to it, most glaringly the Melian Dialogue of Book 5. Here the very dialogue format is itself a clue – to the fact that this is at most para- or meta-historiography, history by other means than those proclaimed in 1.22.[28]

If that interpretation is right, however, there is an important doxographical corollary. Aristotle's preference for poetry over history, on the grounds that the former is the more 'serious' because more philosophically general, would seem to be both misplaced and misguided – at any rate in the case of Thucydides. Yet ironically enough it would seem to be precisely Thucydides' account of 'what Alcibiades did and had done to him' that occasioned Aristotle's negative judgement on all historiography as an intellectual genre, which perhaps serves to question the authority not of Thucydides but of Aristotle.[29] But that is a topic for another essay.

---

[27] For very different readings of Thucydides as a political philosopher, see, e.g., Grene (1946 [1965]) and Hawthorn (2014).

[28] The literature on the Melian Dialogue is immense; I retain a special fondness for Macleod (1983a [1974]), cited with other literature in Hussey (1985), 118 n. 1. Ste. Croix was especially critical of the approach to Thucydides' historiography taken by philosopher R. G. Collingwood (1946).

[29] Rhodes (1985); cf. Ste. Croix (1975 [1992]).

CHAPTER 14

Tradition, Innovation, and Authority
Caesar's Historical Ambitions

Kurt A. Raaflaub

Introduction and Purpose

Caesar is known as one of the most brilliant and successful generals in world history. In his *commentarii* he described two series of his wars. In the first, in Gaul from 58 to 50 BC, he extended the Roman frontier to the Atlantic, British Channel, and Rhine river. The seven books of his *Gallic War*, on which I focus in this essay, end with his victory over a pan-Gallic alliance under Vercingetorix in 52. The second series of campaigns was conducted in 49–48 in a civil war with Pompey in Italy, Spain, and the Balkan peninsula, culminating in Caesar's victory in Thessaly and the death of Pompey in Egypt. These campaigns are described in three books of the *Civil War*, ending with the outbreak of a new war with the Egyptian king's forces.[1] Pieces written by some of Caesar's officers provide additional information. The eighth book of the *Gallic War*, authored by Caesar's adjutant Hirtius (consul in 43), covers Caesar's last two years in Gaul, while the anonymous *Alexandrian, African,* and *Spanish Wars* describe a series of later wars and civil wars that took place

---

*To be able to count John among my former students and long since among my friends fills me with pride and joy. I am very happy to contribute this chapter to the volume celebrating the twenty-fifth anniversary of his seminal 1997 book, in gratitude for his friendship, for his pathbreaking scholarship, and for his service to our profession. Earlier versions of this chapter were presented in 2015 at the Summer Institute of the Classical Association of New England and in 2018–19 at the New England Ancient History Colloquium, to the European Network for the Study of Ancient Greek History, at Waseda University in Japan, the Universities of Cologne and Kiel, the University of Technology, Dresden, and the 'Marincola colloquium' in Martina Franca. I thank colleagues and audiences for their comments and suggestions, Deborah Boedeker for helpful advice, Giustina Monti and Scarlett Kingsley for the brilliant organization of the colloquium, and the editors for useful comments and suggestions. This is still work in progress. Space limitations force me to be brief and selective. With the editors' permission, a slightly different and expanded German version will be published in the Kieler Felix Jacoby-Vorlesungen. – Trans: *Gal.* and *Civ.*: Raaflaub (2017b).

[1] Described in the first part of the *Alexandrian War*. Parts of this work were possibly based on Caesar's drafts and notes: Gaertner and Hausburg (2013).

271

272 KURT A. RAAFLAUB

from 47 to 45 in Egypt, eastern Anatolia, the Adriatic, the province of Africa (modern Tunisia), and south-western Spain.[2]

One does not need to admire war, let alone civil war, to be fascinated by Caesar. The works he and his officers wrote about his campaigns offer rich insight into his art of generalship and the outstanding leadership qualities that enabled him to demand and receive from his army performance on the highest level year after year.[3] Still, if his works were only about military matters, they would be important but of limited interest. In fact, they are much more. They are also cultural histories teaching us, for example, what an eminent Roman considered the essence of being a Roman and of Rome's mission in the world.[4] And they were written by a man who was not satisfied with composing generals' reports. His works reflect a high level of narrative art.[5] This insight is not new. The purpose of this chapter is to support, expand, and enliven it by showing that this dimension of Caesar's work, aimed specifically at emulating the writing of history, is much broader and richer than has perhaps been seen before.[6]

Background

To understand Caesar the historian we need to be aware of some aspects of his life, career, and personality.[7] To begin with, his contemporaries also knew him as an exceptional intellectual and literary talent.[8] In Cicero's judgement, he equalled the best Roman orators.[9] He had a rare sense for style and the purity of the Latin language. His *De analogia* prompted Cicero to praise him as an unrivalled expert on correct Latinity.[10] His *commentarii* on the Gallic wars elicited much admiration for their unadorned elegance and precision of expression.[11]

Like other Roman leaders, Caesar admired Alexander the Great.[12] His ambition was further inflamed by the accomplishments of Pompey the Great in the East. After defeating Rome's long-standing nemesis, Mithridates VI, king of Pontus, Pompey had in the late 60s reorganized

---

[2] Cluett (2003), (2009); Gaertner and Hausburg (2013); Gaertner (2018).
[3] Goldsworthy (1998); Le Bohec (2001); Rosenstein (2009); De Blois (2017); see also Potter (2010).
[4] Raaflaub (2018).   [5] Recently, Batstone and Damon (2006); Riggsby (2006); Grillo (2012).
[6] On Caesar as historian, see Gelzer (1963) and Krebs (2017).
[7] Caesar biographies: Gelzer (1968); Meier (1995); Goldsworthy (2006); Billows (2009); see also Gruen (2009).
[8] See relevant chapters in Grillo and Krebs (2018).
[9] Cic. *Brut.* 261; also Quint. *Inst.* 10.1.114; Suet. *Jul.* 55.1.
[10] Cic. *Brut.* 252–61. *De analogia*: Garcea (2012).   [11] Hirt. *Gal.* 8 *praef.* 6; also Cic. *Brut.* 262.
[12] Plut. *Caes.* 12; Suet. *Jul.* 7.

Tradition, Innovation, and Authority

the eastern frontier of Rome's empire: establishing new provinces and rearranging dependent principalities ('client kingdoms'), he had created a deep security cordon against eastern threats.[13] In doing so, he had also raised the bar for public achievement: to be counted among the first in Rome, one now needed not only great victories but great conquests. More than ever, the path to the top led through success on the battlefield. When he became consul, Caesar thus secured for himself the governorships of three provinces (Transalpine Gaul, Cisalpine Gaul, and Illyricum) that covered the entire, and still vulnerable, northern frontier of Italy. Surely somewhere along that frontier troubles would break out that would offer him the chance of gaining military glory.

By family relation – his aunt had married Marius – and personal inclination Caesar was a *popularis*. His provocative style, demonstrative support for populist causes, and challenges to leading *optimates* and their policies earned him their hostility and unrelenting efforts to hinder his political advancement. His consulship in 59, gained with the help of Pompey and Crassus, was marked by disastrous fights with these 'conservative' enemies in the Senate. Unyielding resistance to his legislative agenda as well as his lack of patience, quick temper, and the pressures under which he acted induced him to use violent means to prevail in the assembly and to ignore religious objections to conducting public business when he wanted and needed to. All this made him vulnerable to prosecution. His enemies were determined to bring him to court at the earliest opportunity and to prevent any extension of his provincial commands, let alone his election for a second consulship ten years after the first. As governor, he seized the first opportunity to start a war and crossed the border into independent Gaul without Senate authorization – a step prohibited by a *lex Cornelia maiestatis* and a *lex Iulia repetundarum* (both perhaps no longer strictly observed) but justified by a Senate decree that explicitly obliged the governor of Transalpine Gaul to assist the Aedui and other Roman 'friends' if necessary and appropriate. If Caesar felt the need to justify his decisions very carefully, it was because of the uncompromising hostility of his enemies in the Senate, not because his war in Gaul violated Roman norms and views.[14]

---

[13] Pompey: Gelzer (1959); Greenhalgh (1980); Seager (2002).

[14] The Senate decree of 61: *Gal.* 1.35.4. The two laws: Cic. *Pis.* 49–50. The much-discussed 'Rechtsfrage' was, as so often, rather a question of power and legitimacy. Suet. *Jul.* 30.4 and Plut. *Caes.* 46.1 show that Caesar took the threat of a treason trial seriously, at least in retrospect and for the purpose of placing the blame entirely on his enemies' side, however unrealistic the prospects of a conviction were; for detailed studies, see Morstein-Marx (2007) and (2009). Rambaud (1966), 112,

Caesar's *Commentarii* and *Litterae* to the Senate

In 56 the Senate recognized Caesar's accomplishments by legally validating all of his actions in Gaul. In 55 his allies secured a five-year extension of his governorships. But when Caesar arrived in Gaul in 58 he knew that it was imperative to restore his damaged reputation and have his defences ready. His elaborate propaganda campaign comprised letters to senators and other leading personalities;[15] letters by his associates; financial favours for leading senators and officials in Rome, obliging them to defend his interests; building projects and acts of generosity toward the Roman populace; public meetings in which supportive officials stirred up public opinion in his favour; dispatches to the Senate; and the *commentarii*.

The title of Caesar's works probably was *C. Iulii Caesaris commentarii rerum gestarum* (*Caesar's Records of Achievements*).[16] A *commentarius* could be many things. The term probably did not apply to a clearly defined genre but was an umbrella term accommodating many types of records.[17] One of its purposes was to furnish materials or a draft that 'real historians' could elaborate upon. Cicero and Hirtius assume this for Caesar's *commentarii* but acknowledge that their literary quality would discourage historians from doing so.[18] At any rate, a *commentarius* 'could also be a full-scale independent account . . . written with care and *ornatio*, and meant for the same audience, and with some of the same purposes, as a large-scale narrative history'.[19] As a literary document, it was intended to describe and justify the author's achievements from his own perspective.

Caesar also wrote dispatches (*litterae*) to the Senate, at least at the end of every campaign season.[20] We do not know how elaborate they were. The only preserved examples of this genre, two of Cicero's gubernatorial letters in 51, do not provide much detail, but they were not year-end reports.[21] Since there was a steady flow of correspondence from Caesar's camps to

---

is sharply critical of Caesar; *contra*, among others, Gelzer (1968), 104–5; Gesche (1976), 89; see further Botermann (2007); Gruen (2009); Schauer (2016), 162–72.

[15] Osgood (2009), 338–48.   [16] E.g. Krebs (2017). No certainty is possible.

[17] Marincola (1997), 181: the term 'refers to anything that aids the memory'. See Rüpke (1992); Batstone and Damon (2006), 8–11; Riggsby (2006), 133–55; Schauer (2016), 92–5; Nousek (2018).

[18] Cic. *Brut.* 262; Hirt. *Gal.* 8 *praef.* 5; Raaflaub (2018), 17–18. The same is true for Cicero's *hypomnema* on his consulship, while Atticus' on the same topic was more traditional: *Att.* 2.1.1–2.

[19] Marincola (1997), 182.   [20] *Gal.* 2.35.4; 4.38.5; 7.90.8.

[21] *Fam.* 15.1–2. *Fam.* 15.4.2–10 (a private letter) resembles a year-end report (Mensching (1988), 39–40).

Tradition, Innovation, and Authority

Rome and back, to all kinds of people, including Caesar's enemies,[22] he wrote his Senate *litterae* for readers who had already heard a lot, both positive and negative. This must have prompted him to write in some detail to highlight his accomplishments, offer explanations, and correct misinformation. Apparently, he wrote these letters in the format of a *libellum memoriale*, a 'book containing records'; 'previously, consuls and generals had written right across the page, not in neat columns'.[23] This suggests care in presentation but says nothing about form or length. If, as is well attested, these *litterae* were read out to the Senate,[24] they must have been limited in length. Together with much other archival material (like reports of his sub-commanders), they underlie the elaborated *commentarii* that Caesar published.

Passages in the *Gallic War*, letters preserved in Cicero's corpus and elsewhere, senatorial inscriptions and *elogia*, and Augustus' *Res gestae* suggest that the style of such generals' reports was terse, mostly stringing brief sentences together asyndetically.[25] I doubt whether this applied to Caesar's letters as well. Naturally, we look for more substantial comparanda that may illuminate not necessarily form and style but content. A *commentarius* (the *African War*) composed by one of Caesar's high-ranking officers seems to retain, despite its length and detail, some of the characteristics of an officer's report to a superior (the *Spanish War*, by contrast, reveals the perspectives and partial knowledge of a lower-ranking officer).[26] Xenophon's *Anabasis* too is largely an elaborated general's report that, although it is long and uses some refined literary devices, reflects the narrative to be expected in such reports.[27] I take the combined characteristics of the *Bellum Africum* and *Anabasis* as a baseline of sorts that helps us recognize in how many ways Caesar's *commentarii* transcend a general's report.

How and when the *commentarii* were written and published is much debated. Good arguments are available both for unitary publication (probably in 51–50, shortly before Caesar's intended return to Rome) of the set

---

[22] E.g. *Gal.* 1.44.12; D.C. 38.35; Cicero's correspondence with his brother Quintus and others who served in Caesar's army; Osgood (2009), 338–40; Morello (2018).

[23] Suet. *Jul.* 56.6 (trans. R. Graves).

[24] E.g., *Civ.* 1.1.1; Cic. *Prov.* 11.27; more references in Lintott (1999), 77 n. 55. See Wiseman (2015), 100–1; Gerrish (2018), 354, for the likelihood that Caesar's letters were also read to the public.

[25] Fraenkel (1964). Cicero's letters: note 21; also *Att.* 5.20. See *Att.* 2.1.1 on the style of Atticus' *hypomnema* on Cicero's consulship: 'a trifle rough and unkempt' (trans. D. R. Shackleton Bailey). Richter (1977), 93–5, finds traces of Caesar's letter on the capitulation of Britain in *Gal.* 5.22.4–23.2 and Cic. *Att.* 4.18.5.

[26] On both *bella*, Gaertner (2018), 265–71.   [27] *Anabasis*: M. A. Flower (2012).

276   KURT A. RAAFLAUB

of seven books *and* for seriatim production and publication, year by year, in the winters following each campaign season.[28] Given Caesar's public relations needs, I feel strongly that the *commentarii* were written and published annually: they made him at least virtually present in Rome during his very long absence, when his personal presence would often have been crucially important; and they satisfied the curiosity and interest in *res gestae* and *historia* that is well attested even for the lower classes in Rome.[29]

For the same reason, the *commentarii* must have been disseminated very widely, in particular among those who were not a priori hostile to Caesar: senators, equestrians, elites in Italian and provincial towns, the middle and upper officer corps in the armies, urban populations in Rome and Italy, soldiers and veterans. Of course, most of these addressees read these texts not individually but in groups; Caesar's supporters may even have organized public readings.[30] Nor should we overlook that Caesar also wrote for an even larger audience (posterity), and that he may have had other purposes in mind as well.[31]

Given this diverse audience and the fact that many had already received bits of news from Gaul that were not always favourable,[32] it was critically important that Caesar could write with simple but 'refined elegance', displaying 'an absolutely unerring skill in explaining his plans and decisions'.[33] Moreover, he achieved greater effect by depersonalizing his narrative, making it look more objective, and creating a story that was attractive, dramatic, and easy to read. My thesis is that for these purposes Caesar not only massively elaborated his general's reports through the addition of material and detail, and wrote in an elegant and accessible style, but also applied a large number of literary or narrative devices that

---

[28] Unitary: e.g. Richter (1977), 49–75; Mensching (1988), 27–9; Schauer (2016), 91–104. Seriatim: e.g. Barwick (1967), 255–78, and especially Wiseman (1998) (who suggests, furthermore, that the crisis in the late fall of 54 forced Caesar to interrupt the annual series and publish Books 5 and 6 together in the winter of 53–52).

[29] Even so, perhaps the *commentarii* were brought out again as a unitary narrative in 51–50. This solution would help us reconcile the strong evidence for both ways of composition and publication. Kraus (2009), 160, seems to suggest something like this, and Hirtius' comment in *Gal.* 8 *praef.* 7 on how easily and fast Caesar completed the *commentarii* may refer to this effort to unite separately written pieces in one work. Interest in history: Wiseman (1998), 4–5; Gerrish (2018), 355 with ref. to Cic. *Fin.* 5.52; Plin. *Nat.* pref. 6; Plin. *Ep.* 4.7.2.

[30] Wiseman (1998), (2015), 102; see also Mensching (1988), 31–2; Rüpke (1992); Schauer (2016), 99–100; Gerrish (2018), 353–5.

[31] Posterity: Cic. *Marc.* 29. Owing to Caesar's didactic intent (at note 88), his *commentarii* also offered instruction to officers, thus serving as a military manual of sorts: by reading (as if watching) him, one learned. See Veith (1967); Campbell (1981); Rüpke (1992), 208–10.

[32] See at note 22.   [33] Hirtius, *Gal.* 8 *praef.* 4, 7.

Tradition, Innovation, and Authority

were typical of formal histories. He thereby elevated his *commentarii* to a level that emulated the writing of history.

Caesar's Models

Cicero claims that Roman historical works existing at the time were of rather poor literary quality.[34] This was changing shortly before and during his time, but even if Cicero exaggerated, it suggests that Caesar may not have been greatly inspired by those works. Yet he surely knew them, at least partially, and would have found some traits that he adopted, such as the use of speeches, an interest in ethnography and geography, or an obsession with precise numbers (for the size of armies, casualties, war captives, or people enslaved).[35]

But these very features are also typical of Greek historiography. As a highly educated person, Caesar, like Sallust, was familiar with the leading Greek historians, especially Thucydides.[36] Intertextual references to Thucydides are unmistakable – not in style but in narrative devices and historical insight. A good example is the adaptation of a scene during the naval battle in the harbour of Syracuse, which those not fighting themselves follow with rapt attention and passionate emotional engagement, while the fighters are driven to supreme efforts by knowing that all their officers and comrades are watching. Caesar describes something very similar during a naval battle on the south coast of modern Brittany and during a cavalry battle at Alesia.[37] Various details show that in his siege of Avaricum Caesar adapts elements of Thucydides' siege of Plataea.[38] Similarly, aspects of Caesar's handling of the Aeduan revolt in 52 are intertextually connected with Thucydides' account of the Athenian responses to the revolt of Mytilene in 427.[39]

In Thucydides, the Spartans remind the Athenians that a war should be ended when things are in balance; as soon as one side gains a decisive advantage, it will aim at complete victory. Caesar urges Scipio with the same argument to support his peace efforts.[40] Thucydides points to the

---

[34] Cic. *Leg.* 1.2.5–3.8.   [35] Chassignet (2018), 254–9, 261.

[36] Dionysius of Halicarnassus' essays against Thucydides attest to the latter's prominence in the period's historical thinking; see Pritchett (1975); Meister (2013), 53–66 (who does not consider Caesar). Sallust: Büchner (1960), 332–45; Syme (1964), 50–6, 245–8; Scanlon (1980); Meister (2013), 55–64.

[37] Thuc. 7.71; *Gal.* 3.14, 7.80. See also *Civ.* 2.3.4.   [38] Krebs (2016); *Gal.* 7.14–28; Thuc. 2.75–7.

[39] Gerrish (2013) with useful comments on intertextuality in historians, on which see also O'Gorman (2009).

[40] Thuc. 4.18, 20; *Gal.* 3.10.3–7; Pitcher (2018), 246.

reversal of values as a prime characteristic of civil strife; Caesar does the same when criticizing Scipio's abuses during the civil war.[41] Thucydides hints at the pitfalls of belittling and denigrating the enemy; so does Caesar.[42] Other possible Thucydidean echoes include a triple division among peoples;[43] tensions between aristocracy and the populace; a general's fight at the front, with mention of his shield; and the impression made on the besieged by the besiegers' speed in setting up siege engines.[44]

Of course, not all these cases are equally compelling. Some items must have been topoi from Herodotus through classical and Hellenistic historiography: already Herodotus' Mardonius belittles the Greeks, to the Persians' peril;[45] the fallacious claim that an action will be easy pervades the works of Herodotus, Thucydides, and Caesar.[46] Moreover, there are intertextual connections with Polybius and Herodotus as well. For example, the luxury found in Pompey's camp at Pharsalus reminds us of that in Mardonius' camp at Plataea: 'luxury is for the losers'.[47] But in some cases an intertextual connection between Caesar and Thucydides is clear and undeniable. I shall mention at the end another case that is crucial for my argument.[48]

Despite such conscious connections with leading Greek historians, however, Caesar equally consciously chose his own style. In contrast to Thucydides' dense, often austere, and abstract style, that seems to have been intended to be read rather than heard, and to Cicero's highly ornamented style,[49] Caesar wrote in a clear, simple, but elegant style that would be understandable to Romans of all classes. Moreover, his perspective developed. Limited campaigns against single nations or small-scale alliances ended in the defeat of a pan-Gallic coalition; 'Caesar's campaigns in defence of allies' became 'Caesar's war to conquer Gaul for Rome'. In the process, he created an increasingly powerful vision that forged out of multiple stories a coherent narrative of transforming a vast barbarian territory into a civilized province of the Roman Empire. This became the core of the message he strove to convey to his readers and the ultimate

---

[41] Thuc. 3.82.4; *Civ.* 3.32.3; Pitcher (2018), 244.
[42] Alcibiades in Thuc. 6.17; Labienus in *Civ.* 3.87.
[43] Thuc. 3.92.2; *Gal.* 1.1.1; Kraus (2009), 164, suggested by L. Edmunds.
[44] General: Brasidas in Thuc. 4.12.1; Caesar in *Gal.* 2.25.2. Besiegers' speed: *Gal.* 2.31.1; Thuc. 6.98.2; Pitcher (2018), 243–4. See Gaertner and Hausburg (2013), 122–39, for Thucydidean influences on the description of sea battles.
[45] Hdt. 7.9a–c.   [46] Pitcher (2018), 241–2.
[47] Polybius: Pitcher (2018), 239; see also note 89. Luxury: Hdt. 9.80.1; *Civ.* 3.96.1–2; quote: Pitcher, 242.
[48] At notes 110–17.   [49] *Att.* 2.1.1.

Tradition, Innovation, and Authority

justification of his actions in Gaul. Some of the methods he used to make this message even more compelling to his broad readership were borrowed from the historians.

Narrative Techniques Typical of History

I will now briefly describe the methods by which Caesar approximates his *commentarii* to works of history. Some of them concern narrative techniques; others emphasize specific content; some are well known, others apparently not; and there may be more.[50] I begin with narrative techniques.

The first method is the use of third-person narrative. Caesar generally writes: 'Caesar did,' not 'I did.' This strikes modern readers as odd, even as 'unnecessarily mannered'.[51] Governors' letters to the Senate were written in the first person;[52] Caesar's choice of the third person is thus deliberate. It separates Caesar the author/narrator from Caesar the actor and encourages the reader to see the actor's achievement from the outside.[53] In 'what has been called a "justifying narrative", in which the story itself, rather than any overt authorial comment, advances the writer's point of view', the 'third person may be viewed as a means of keeping the author's voice out of the text'.[54] It is thus a way to depersonalize and objectify the narrative, to allow evaluation of the actions it describes, and to lift it above the level of personal memoir (one of the functions of a *commentarius*) toward that of history, reflecting 'an attempt to provide a definitive account in the manner of an historian'.[55] Moreover, it was typical of Roman writers to refer to their army as 'our men' and to include themselves by emphasizing 'we' and 'us'. 'By using "us" and "our" for the Romans but "he" for Caesar, the narrator locates himself within his audience, conveying a sense that he is "one of us" reporting someone else's deeds.'[56] T. P. Wiseman adds a practical reason: 'If the commentaries were written to be delivered by a

---

[50] Some are mentioned e.g. by Kraus (2009), 164–5.   [51] Wiseman and Wiseman (1980), 14.

[52] Cicero's gubernatorial letters: note 21. Greek letters by Roman magistrates in the East: Sherk (1969), nos. 43, 48, 49. Thanks to Harriet Flower, whose chapter in this volume offers further valuable insights; see also Rambaud (1966), 19–23, on reports of officials. A letter written in the third person: Pl. *Ps.* 41–4 (thanks to Judith Hallet).

[53] Batstone and Damon (2006), 144–6; Riggsby (2006), 149–52; Schauer (2016), 114–23.

[54] Schadee (2018), 321 with n. 13.

[55] Marincola (1997), 198. Cic. *Fam.* 5.12.8; Sal. *Cat.* 8.5: third-person accounts authored by others are preferable to memoirs.

[56] Grillo (2018a), 166.

speaker at a public meeting, narrating Caesar's exploits to the People, the third-person form was unavoidable.'[57]

Third-person narrative was well known long before Caesar.[58] Thucydides applies it when mentioning his own writing and actions, aligning himself with all the other actors in his *History* – and he, like Caesar, only rarely uses the authorial 'I' for a personal comment. Xenophon too chooses it when describing his own leadership role, placing himself on the same level as all the other generals.[59] He goes even further in separating author and actor by attributing the *Anabasis* to another (most probably fictitious) author. Polybius, as Marincola points out, in all but his last books observes the difference between himself as the narrator, speaking in the first person, and the historical actor who appears in the third person. The particularly complex evidence in his work suggests that for Polybius 'history (as opposed perhaps to memoirs or other genres) demanded the third person for all participants'.[60]

The second narrative method is streamlining and focus, selection and omission, and arrangement. History consists of a kaleidoscope of events, decisions, actions, and actors. A general's report, I suppose, moved through these events in chronological and linear sequence (as the *Anabasis* and *African War* do). Caesar often does the same but with strict focus. In Book 1 he reports two campaigns, against the migrating Helvetii and the German warlord Ariovistus, both in self-contained narratives. He tells only what is relevant to these stories and omits everything else – not least many details of daily life and campaigning that show up in the *Anabasis* and *African War*. Caesar, like Thucydides, focuses strictly on the most important aspects of the most important events. His text thus hops from one highlighted dramatic episode to another: in Book 2 from the submission of the Remi to the defeat of the Belgae at the Axona, the subjection of the Suessiones, the victory over the heroic Nervii, and the conquest of the fortress of the Atuatuci. Such focus helps Caesar create a clearly structured, monumental narrative.

Of course, this method was also useful to filter out events that might reflect unfavourably on Caesar. His tendentiousness is visible precisely in what he chooses to tell, in what detail and with what emphasis, and what not to tell. 'Selective reporting is just as powerful a device of persuasion as

---

[57] Wiseman (1998), 8 n. 27.   [58] Marincola (1997), 175–205.
[59] M. A. Flower (2012), 52–3; see also Pelling (2013).
[60] Xenophon: M. A. Flower (2012), 53–5. Polybius: Marincola (1997), 188–92 (quote: 192).

Tradition, Innovation, and Authority

colorful packaging.'[61] In Book 8, Hirtius mentions two events that throw a negative light on Caesar and that he himself omits.[62] Yet efforts to prove that he systematically lied and distorted history have long become obsolete.[63]

Closely connected is the arrangement of Caesar's narrative: it is partly linear, following one event after another, but rarely day by day (unlike the *Anabasis* and the *African War*).[64] More importantly, Caesar's story is also arranged in blocs, tracing one development to a logical stopping point, then resuming another. By thus separating events that happened simultaneously and narrating them consecutively (as Thucydides does and Sallust will do), Caesar sacrifices chronology to narrative logic, which facilitates understanding. Thus Caesar must have learned as soon as he entered independent Gaul (if not much earlier) of Ariovistus' oppressive regime in eastern Gaul that deeply affected some of the nations involved in the Helvetian story. Still, he mentions these problems only after the conclusion of the Helvetian campaign, as an introduction to that against Ariovistus.[65] In the *Civil War*, Caesar describes his invasion of Italy to the point when he receives a personal message from Pompey, then pursues the ensuing peace negotiations to their failure about a month later, and only then returns to his military actions that had been going on in the meantime.[66]

Yet arrangement too could serve a political or propagandistic purpose. Caesar ends Book 2 with the triumphant conclusion that all of Gaul was pacified, which prompted the Senate to honour him with an unprecedented number of thanksgiving days. A late-year action – a legate's attempt to secure the upper Rhone valley and the Great St Bernard Pass – ended in failure and would have spoiled this positive ending. Caesar reports it at the beginning of Book 3, thus breaking the book-year coordination.[67]

The third narrative method is the use of speeches. This aspect of Caesar's works has been thoroughly discussed.[68] To lend speeches to historical actors was typical of Greek historiography and had its ultimate

---

[61] Damon (1994), 187. [62] *Gal.* 8.23.3–6, 24.3.

[63] Distortion: Barwick (1951); Rambaud (1966); contra: Collins (1972); see also Jervis (2017); Raaflaub (2017a); Krebs (2018).

[64] See further at notes 113–15.

[65] *Gal.* 1.30–32. The Aeduan leader Diviciacus had in 60 petitioned the Senate for help against Ariovistus: *Gal.* 1.31.9; Cic. *Div.* 1.90.

[66] *Civ.* 1.7–8; 1.9.1–11.3. [67] *Gal.*. 2.35.1, 4; 3.1–6.

[68] E.g. Rasmussen (1963) on the direct speeches; Grillo (2018b). For a detailed analysis of narrative content and purpose in the various forms of Caesarian speeches, see Adema (2017), 76–241.

model in Homer's epics.[69] Roman historians adopted this custom.[70] Such speeches were mostly entirely fictional or at least greatly condensed and rewritten in the author's style and with his emphasis. They played an important role in his historical interpretation, offering background and context, characterizing the enemy, introducing motives, explaining causes and concepts, juxtaposing conflicting viewpoints, moving the plot forward, and giving the narrative more immediacy. In a way that is comparable to the use of probability and fiction in the narrative,[71] speeches were (and were understood and accepted as) literary constructs that enriched and filled out the narrative.

Caesar uses short direct speeches or shouts as dramatic highlights. He inserts one very long direct speech (by the Arvernian leader Critognatus) just before the final showdown at Alesia, to throw light on the enemy's perspective and thus not merely to emphasize the cruelty and barbarism highlighted by the proposal of cannibalism for which the speech is mostly known.[72] Caesar himself addresses his audience in direct speech only once (and very briefly): when he announces his decision to accept Pompey's challenge at Pharsalus.[73]

But indirect speeches pervade his works. They serve some of the same purposes as direct speeches do in the Greek historians. In addition, they highlight, as does the narrative, the author's qualities and achievements as an 'omniscient, efficient, decisive and straightforward' general to whom 'war is something a human being can control, anticipate, plan and execute efficiently'.[74] The preference for indirect speech is probably to be explained by the identity of author and actor: it would have been awkward if Caesar had written his frequent speeches in direct oration. Indirect speeches are less formal; like the third-person narrative, they help 'depersonalize' the narrative and maintain critical distance, while preserving the advantage of using speeches. They 'present the narrator as factual and straightforward'.[75] In this respect, Caesar deviates from Roman predecessors (like Cato the Elder and Sulla) and Xenophon, who all tend to render their own speeches in direct oration.

---

[69] Marincola (2007c).   [70] Chassignet (2018), 257–8.

[71] See at note 87, and note M. A. Flower, Chapter 1 in this volume.

[72] *Gal.* 7.77; Schieffer (1972); Riggsby (2006), 107–26. See also two long direct speeches given to Curio, Caesar's favourite legate, at *Civ.* 2.31–2.

[73] *Civ.* 3.85.4.   [74] Adema (2017), 109–241, at 109, 231, 236–9.

[75] Grillo (2018b), 137; see Schauer (2016), 141–50. On Thucydides' use of indirect discourse, see Debnar (2013).

Tradition, Innovation, and Authority

The fourth narrative method is emphasis and the pursuit of overarching themes. Persistent emphasis placed on a few major themes serves interpretive purposes and enhances the work's cohesion, helping to connect pieces that were published separately. I offer two examples. The first is that Caesar, his officers, and, through them, his army constantly present themselves and act as representatives and servants of the Roman state and people. Quintus Cicero's response to rebels demanding a parley after attacking his camp is exemplary: 'It was not the custom of the Roman people to accept terms from an enemy who bore arms.'[76] Especially in Book 1, Caesar justifies his decisions by referring to his obligation to protect Roman allies, the Roman province, and Roman honour. Later, he even asks his second-in-command to come to his assistance if this can be done without harm to the *res publica.*[77] The 'interest of the Roman state or people' serves in such cases as a formula for the goals of the present campaign.

The second example concerns the suppression of the Gauls' liberty. The Romans too valued liberty. It thus seems surprising that Caesar allows the Gauls to emphasize often and strongly their desire to preserve their ancestral liberty.[78] The reason is, I suggest, that this helps him establish a higher level of purpose and highlight the historical aim he is pursuing in Gaul. By subjecting the peoples on their borders, the Romans pacify and civilize them (we think of Anchises' famous words in the *Aeneid*).[79] The sacrifice of the liberty of the defeated is necessary to create the peaceful, secure, and well-ordered world that Cicero envisions in *On the Consular Provinces* in 56:[80] this is Caesar's ultimate mission in Gaul.

The fifth narrative method is dramatization, well known from Greek historiography. Caesar uses every opportunity to create a dramatic and often intense, even gripping narrative. Examples abound.[81] He excels in this skill and increases the effect by applying literary techniques, such as retardation and peripety, to increase tension before the resolution of a crisis. When in the civil war of 49 Caesar's army in Spain suffers from extreme food shortage and he is about to find a way to resolve the crisis, he

---

[76] *Gal.* 5.41.7–8. [77] *Gal.* 5.46.4.

[78] Seager (2003), 22–6; Raaflaub (2018), 22–3; see Barlow (1998) on how Caesar undercuts Gallic insistence on liberty.

[79] Verg. *A.* 6.851–3. [80] *Prov.* 8.19, 12.30–14.34. This is also a main theme in Hirtius' Book 8.

[81] E.g. the battles against the Nervii (2.19–27) and at Alesia (7.84–8), the first landing in Britain (4.23–6), the disaster of Sabinus' camp (at notes 87–9), and the heroic defence and last-minute rescue of Cicero's camp (5.39–52). Mutschler (1975) offers useful analyses of dramatization. Gerrish (2018) discusses heroic resonances in dramatic scenes in *Gal.* Book 5. For dramatization in the *Bellum civile*, see Rowe (1967).

switches to describing contemporaneous events at Massilia, slowing the narrative down and letting us wait in growing tension until, suddenly, the course of events turns in Spain.[82] In the battle against the Nervii Caesar is surprised by the sudden enemy attack: 'Caesar had to do everything at once: raise the flag, which was the signal that the soldiers must rush to arms; have the trumpet blow the battle signal; summon the troops from their work; fetch back those who had gone out some distance . . .; deploy the battle line; urge on the troops; and give the signal to attack.'[83] Here it is acceleration, reporting in short, staccato-like sentences, that enhances the drama. In the same battle, the narrator's perspective turns from a broad, 'panoramic' overview of the battlefield to close-up views of specific episodes and in the end back to the panoramic view – a narrative technique applied already in the *Iliad*.[84]

In addition, a general's report probably suggested early on whether it aimed at praise for success or presented apologies for failure: the outcome was never in doubt. By contrast, a good historical narrative did not allow the readers to look into the future but kept them in the present, absorbed by drama and unexpected turns – although the author, of course, knew the outcome and might even mention it for specific purposes. Good history was not predetermined but open-ended.[85] This is true for Caesar's narrative as well. Although the readers might know the outcome from other sources, they did not find it in the narrative of the *commentarii* before it happened. This was a crucial condition for the dramatic quality of his text. Moreover, such open-endedness permitted the full appreciation of contingency and the power of chance.[86]

The sixth narrative method is free elaboration, use of probability, and fiction. Using rhetorical and factual elaboration, probability in reconstructing the course of events, and even fiction, Greek historians intended not to deceive the reader but to create a fuller narrative, enhance meaning, and convey essential lessons.[87] That Caesar did the same is somewhat unexpected, especially in a military context, but entirely plausible, at least when he had only minimal information about an event. In 54, Ambiorix and the Eburones attacked the camp of Sabinus and Cotta, which led to the withdrawal and subsequent ambush and annihilation of fifteen cohorts

---

[82] *Civ.* 1.48–59; also *Gal.* 5.44 with Schauer (2016), 157–61.   [83] *Gal.* 2.20.1.

[84] Latacz (1977), esp. 68–95; de Jong and Nünlist (2004).

[85] Grethlein (2010), 196–204, 240–54; (2013).

[86] Grethlein (2010), 252–4. Mensching (1988), 67–8, on Caesar's 'Unkenntnis der Zukunft'.

[87] So too Cic. *Brut.* 42. See Fornara (1971), 35–6; also Raaflaub (2010); Schauer (2016), 95–7; M. A. Flower, Chapter 1 in this volume.

Tradition, Innovation, and Authority

(about 5,000 men). Only a few soldiers (apparently no officers) survived as witnesses, and enemy captives were questioned later on.[88] Still, Caesar's report contains multiple speeches and intense debates in the commanders' war council, sharp contrasts in attitudes and behaviour of the two commanders (in council and battle), and other details that were at most partly knowable to those informants. Based on a rough outline of events, Caesar thus developed this episode into a dramatic and exemplary story about positive and negative attitudes, right and wrong (Roman and un-Roman) behaviour, good and bad leadership, and the impact of failing leadership on the troops' morale, discipline, and chance of survival.[89]

The seventh, and closely connected, narrative method is to focus on the exemplary nature and didactic purpose of history. Knowing that history remained interesting as long as it was meaningful to the present, Greek historians had long written with a didactic purpose, offering lessons for present and future readers. Roman historiography was emphatically exemplary. Thucydides' and Livy's programmatic statements on this issue are well known.[90] This very concern is pervasive in Caesar's work. The episode just discussed (Sabinus' failure to save his unit) offers an example. The contrasts established there within one camp remind us of the same Sabinus' excellent leadership in an independent command two years earlier and Quintus Cicero's exemplary defence of his camp – which in turn finds a sharp contrast in the same Cicero's failure and the near-destruction of his camp by a freak German attack a year later.[91] In both cases the previously successful legates fail when they do not strictly follow their commander's principles and orders.

For another example, in his self-portrait Caesar transcends justification and glorification by emphasizing generally valid traits that inspire identification and emulation.[92] Constantly thinking and acting as a representative of the Roman state and people and expecting the same from his army, he draws, in aggregate, a composite picture of ideal Romans and of the opposite, bad or 'un-Romans' and non-Romans. These contrasting portraits, based on patterns of behaviour and values, experience, and prejudice, have both an explanatory and ulterior purpose – which is to show Caesar replacing a world of barbarian instability with one of Roman order,

---

[88] *Gal.* 5.26–37; 5.36.6–7, 47.5, 52.4.
[89] Grillo (2018a), 163–5, sees here an intertextual connection with Polybius' description of the battle of Cannae.
[90] Thuc. 1.22.4 with Grethlein (2010), 268–79; Liv. *praef.* 9–10 with Chaplin (2000); Roller (2009).
[91] *Gal.* 3.17–19; 5.38–52; 6.32–42. On exemplarity in Caesar, see e.g. Nolan (2016).
[92] Caesar's self-portrait: Fairbank (2017); Batstone (2018); Raaflaub (2018), 22–7.

286   KURT A. RAAFLAUB

discipline, and stability.[93] Overall, Caesar's works impressively define true Romanness.

The following narrative methods focus more on content than technique but serve the same purpose of approximating Caesar's narrative to that of history proper.

The eighth narrative method is balanced reporting and showing respect for the enemy. Of the Helvetii Caesar writes: 'In that whole battle ... nobody saw a single enemy turn his back.' He describes the Nervii, who brought his army to the brink of defeat, and Vercingetorix, who defeated him at Gergovia and almost broke him at Alesia, with respect as worthy opponents. *Virtus*, a central Roman value, is generously attributed to both Gauls and Romans.[94] I doubt whether Caesar would have done the same in his Senate dispatches. Certainly, to emphasize enemy bravery enhanced the victor's achievement. But what mattered more in these letters were numbers – of enemies confronted, soldiers killed, towns and villages destroyed, and peoples subjected or enslaved – numbers that supported claims for a triumph, as is well attested in Caesar's triumph of 46.[95] In the *Anabasis* Xenophon scorns the enemy forces, as do Caesar's continuators, while both Herodotus and Thucydides write about the enemies' efforts with much respect and understanding.

Otherwise too, Caesar is even-handed in talking about Gallic values, customs, and beliefs, many of which the Gauls share with the Romans. His portrait of the Gauls is far from being simply prejudiced and clichéd. Even so, he does not tire of stressing their well-known weaknesses, their fickleness and treacherous nature.[96] They break agreements and oaths as easily as they make them – for which they deserve to be punished with utmost severity. This supports one of Caesar's main arguments.[97] The Germans (Ariovistus and the Usipetes and Tencteri) are yet a different matter.[98] Caesar describes them as deceptive, untrustworthy, and arrogant:[99] they must be removed from Gaul or, if they refuse to leave, eliminated altogether.

The ninth narrative method is the inclusion of decisions and events on the enemy side. This feature endows Herodotus' and Thucydides'

---

[93] See also at notes 78–80.
[94] *Gal.* 1.26.2; 2.27.3–5; Vercingetorix: often in Book 7. *Virtus:* Gruen (2011), 150–3.
[95] Plin. *Nat.* 7.92.
[96] For differentiated assessments, see Kremer (1994); relevant chapters in Welch and Powell (1998); Gruen (2011).
[97] Discussed at notes 78–80.   [98] *Gal.* 1.34–53; 4.7–15.
[99] E.g. *Gal.* 1.33.5, 36.6, 46.4, 47.6; 4.7.2–5, 9.3, 11.4, 13.4–6.

Tradition, Innovation, and Authority

narratives with depth and interpretive meaning. It is almost completely absent in the *Anabasis*, rare in the *African War*, and must have been absent in generals' reports that naturally focused on the leader's decisions and actions. At most, they mentioned enemy actions that added depth and contrast to those of the general, while enemy decisions appeared only in reports of messengers or deserters. Caesar, by contrast, pays considerable attention to the thinking, deliberations, decisions, and subsequent actions of his enemies. In Book 1, for example, he encapsulates this feature in speeches and messages attributed to enemy leaders (such as the Helvetian Divico or the German Ariovistus).[100] But in Book 7, with its extended and complex war between Caesar's Roman forces and Vercingetorix' pan-Gallic army, this dimension is prominently developed, describing diplomacy, speeches, debates, and preparations on the enemy side. This applies no less to the *Civil War*'s campaigns against Pompey and his generals.[101]

The tenth narrative method is the use of digressions. In his *litterae* Caesar would hardly have entertained the busy senators with tales of strange customs and phenomena. The *African War* contains no digressions. In the *Anabasis* Xenophon inserts descriptions of locations and customs, but not in the form of digressions.[102] But digressions were typical of Greek historiography and are found in earlier Roman historians.[103] Caesar offers digressions on geography and the customs of Gauls, Germans, and Britons.[104] Placed strategically in the text, they serve to enhance Caesar's achievement and prestige and satisfy the readers' curiosity but also to distract and manipulate them. Thus the long excursus on Gallic and German customs in Book 6 induces them to overlook that in his second crossing of the Rhine into German territory Caesar achieved virtually nothing.[105]

The eleventh narrative method is the use of causality and contingency. Causality in a general's report must be simple: it explains the general's moves, presumably claims responsibility for all successes for himself, while blaming the enemy for failures, and largely eliminates contingency.

---

[100] *Gal.* 1.13–14; 1.34–6, 42–5.
[101] *Gal.* 7.1–5, 7.8.4, 9.6, 14–15, 20–1, 29–31, 37–9, 63–4, 66, 75–8, 83, 89.1–2. *Civ.* 1.1–7, 17, 19–20, 38, 61, 67; 3.3–5, 18, 82–3, 86–7.
[102] *An.* 5.4.11–15, 27–34; 6.4.1–6 (thanks to Michael Flower).
[103] Dench (2007); Chassignet (2018), 254–6.
[104] Geography: Krebs (2006); Riggsby (2006), 21–45; (2018); Schadee (2008). Ethnography: Riggsby (2006), 47–71; Schauer (2016), 150–6; Schadee (2017).
[105] *Gal.* 6.11–28.

In contrast, Thucydides uses a sophisticated three-level causality that distinguishes between the factors that triggered the outbreak of the war, the causes that prompted war as a response to these factors, and the 'truest cause' that made war ultimately inevitable, no matter what actually caused it.[106] Caesar too allows for a complex causality, although he does not explicitly say so, often distinguishing between general dispositions or attitudes among the Gauls that were enhanced by the ambitions of individual leaders, were exploited in factional competitions for power, and broke through in a particular situation, causing tensions and strife within nations or even the outbreak of a war.[107]

Caesar further complicates causality by paying much attention to contingency in war. He acknowledges the role of the gods (as Xenophon does pervasively in *Anabasis*) and, much more prominently, of chance, Fortuna, whether it helps or opposes him: 'Fortune plays a great role in everything but has an even greater influence in warfare,' he writes.[108] According to Plutarch, for 'those who are forced to speak in their own praise' it is better to share their honour with chance and with god. 'For men would rather be bested by luck than by merit.'[109] The frequent mention of Fortuna thus moderates self-praise and acknowledges that even great generals cannot always succeed without luck.

The twelfth narrative method is the lack of precise dates, destinations, distances, and times. Caesar gives two precise dates in his seven books of the *Gallic War*, both at the very beginning, anchoring the start of his first campaign (against the Helvetii) in time and place: at Geneva on 28 March and 13 April 58 (of the traditional Roman calendar).[110] After that, he distinguishes only between warm and cold seasons and their suitability for campaigning. In the *Civil War* too, precise dates fix only the beginning of Caesar's Italian campaign on 7 January 49, and that against Pompey in the east on 4 January 48.[111] Very rarely does Caesar mention a time span, such as the fifteen days of his close pursuit of the Helvetii on their westward march.[112] Distance indications hardly exist. Often Caesar does not even mention his precise point of departure or destination.

Day-by-day accounts occur rarely, mainly in the final phase of campaigns, such as against Ariovistus, at Alesia, or in Spain in the civil war.[113] This feature dramatically increases the tension before the decision falls. In

---

[106] Thuc. 1.23.4–6.   [107] See e.g. *Gal.* 1.16–19; 5.3–4, 55–6; 7.4.
[108] *Gal.* 6.30.2; see also e.g. 6.42 or *Civ.* 3.26.4–27.2.
[109] Plut. *Mor.* 542e–f; see Marincola (1997), 206–11; also R. Gibson (2003); P.-B. Smith (2014).
[110] *Gal.* 1.6.4, 7.8.   [111] *Civ.* 1.5.2; 3.6.1.   [112] *Gal.* 1.15.5; also 2.2.5; 5.7.3.
[113] *Gal.* 1.47–51; 7.79–83; *Civ.* 1.63–84.

Tradition, Innovation, and Authority

the Italian campaign of 49 it brings out the speed of the advance.[114] Hence to Caesar a day-by-day account is a literary device, comparable to the rapid acceleration in short sentences used to describe a particularly dramatic scene.[115] By contrast, the *African War* generally sticks to a day-by-day account throughout. In the first part of the *Anabasis*, Xenophon offers precise locations and distances in a day-by-day sequence. Even in the second part, when his army marches through unknown territory, he mostly continues the day-by-day pattern.

Precise and militarily important logistical information must have been plentiful in Caesar's personal records. Its omission requires explanation. To be sure, Caesar was often moving in uncharted territory; events took place in areas that had no clear name; in independent Gaul there was no good road network; Caesar was feeling his way through the country with the help of scouts and various informers; and readers did not know the geography of Gaul anyway.[116] But I suspect an additional reason. Caesar's decision to date precisely only the beginnings of his wars suggests where his inspiration lies. Thucydides does exactly the same: he anchors the outbreak of the war he describes (and the end of its first ten-year phase) carefully in time, but otherwise distinguishes only between summers and winters – a dating method he considers more precise than that based on eponymous years that differed from polis to polis anyway – without giving any precise dates, distances, or times.[117] Greek historians had no other common dating choice; Romans did. Still, Caesar must have concluded, it was only generals who offered such details; real historians did not. Caesar knew what model he wanted to follow!

Conclusion

To sum up, Caesar employs a wide range of literary techniques that could hardly be found in generals' reports but are typical of formal histories. He thereby elevates his elaborated narrative onto a higher level and gives it an attractive and compelling shape that appeals to broad readerships. This enables him to convey most effectively his perspective on the events

---

[114] *Civ.* 1.11.4–27.   [115] See above at notes 83 and 84.

[116] Pelling (1981). Mensching (1988), 72–3, and Schauer (2016), 128–30, emphasize literary and aesthetic considerations.

[117] Precise dates (only by year and season, since local calendars differed widely): Thuc. 2.2.1; 5.19.1. Summers and winters: 5.20 (justifying this choice), 26.1. At 1.97.2 he criticizes Hellanicus for lack of precision in dates (thanks to Florian Sittig). Richter (1977), 45–6, refers to the tradition of Roman annalistic historiography that arranged wars in a series of summer campaigns.

290   KURT A. RAAFLAUB

described, the mission he is pursuing in Gaul for Rome, and the qualities and behaviour of exemplary Romans in contrast to those of bad Romans or non-Romans. He found his inspiration to some extent in earlier Roman historians but mostly among the eminent Greek ones and especially, it seems, in Thucydides.

Still, Caesar's works lack traits that are necessary for history proper:[118] a proem, a title that transcends the intimate connection with the author, statements on methodology, emphasis on the intention to pursue an objective truth, and an effort to reach beyond the narrow focus on Caesar's campaigns by including not only developments on the enemies' side but also the background of relevant events at least in Rome. The abundance of indirect discourse is also untypical. In Roman terms, 'a history had to be an essentially rhetorical work; to research the causes of deeds; to aim at the truth; and, in attributing an exemplary status to the past, it had to pursue a moral objective'.[119]

As we have seen, however, some of these categorical criticisms go too far: Caesar does explore the causes of deeds, he emphasizes exemplarity, and he orients himself after not only Roman but eminent Greek models. On the other hand, writing about, and drawing on the experience of, his own wars, battles, and communications with his army, he avoided the schematic, artificial battle descriptions and over-rhetoricized 'canned' speeches surrounding battles that became typical of historiography after Thucydides;[120] in this respect he ignored the objectivizing distance from the subject matter that was required of a historian and which he tried to create through some of the devices we discussed. At any rate, contemporaries compared but did not identify Caesar's works with history. Quintilian counts Caesar among orators, not historians.[121] Scholars today tend to dismiss as a 'pose' Hirtius' and Cicero's opinion that the *commentarii* were 'published to make sure that future writers would not lack knowledge of [the author's] enormous achievements'. Yet, Hirtius continues, Caesar's works 'have been received with such unanimous approval that future writers would seem to have been deprived of an opportunity rather than been offered one'.[122] I think this acknowledges that in terms of narrative quality and literary merit these texts had reached the level expected of histories – even if they were lacking in other and no less

---

[118] E.g. Krebs (2017); also Fornara (1983), 182–3; Schauer (2016), 97–9.
[119] Chassignet (2018), 250–1. Cic. *Or.* 2.62–4 highlights parts of a theory of history.
[120] See Thuc. 7.69.2 and Lendon (2017).   [121] Quint. *Inst.* 10.1.101–4, 114.
[122] Hirt. *Gal.* 8 *praef.* 5; Cic. *Brut.* 262; pose: Kraus (2009), 160–1; cf. Marincola (1997), 197–8.

Tradition, Innovation, and Authority

crucial respects. Cicero had a similar experience with his highly ornamented *hypomnema* on his consulship.[123] To perceive the gap that still separated Caesar's *commentarii* from fully developed histories it suffices to look at Sallust's *Jugurthine War*.

Yet Sallust and the other great late Republican historian, Livy, wrote after Caesar. If Cicero's claim that the Roman historical works existing at the time did not meet high literary expectations is only half correct, this background and the high praise Cicero bestows on Caesar's *commentarii* suggest that Caesar's literary achievement was very remarkable indeed.[124] Perhaps it even suggests that, at least to some extent, he was a pioneer in the development of Roman historical writing.

In conclusion, Caesar's *Gallic War* still shows traits that are typical of the broad category of *commentarius*. But it also integrates significant elements of historiography and thus is perhaps best characterized as a hybrid.[125] Scholars agree that Caesar expanded the frame of the category of *commentarius* but disagree about whether he broke it. Fornara, who thinks he did, concludes: 'In the hands of a man of brilliance and taste, this preliminary sketch became an art form in its own right.' Schauer even speaks of 'the invention of a new genre'.[126] It is tempting to think that Caesar, had he had the time and leisure, might have returned to the *Gallic War* and transformed it fully into a history of the conquest of Gaul for Rome – which he undoubtedly would have been capable of doing. But this seems highly unlikely and, in any case, was pre-empted by his assassination.[127] At the time, his needs were best served by a truly high-class *commentarius*. A real history would have pursued different goals and distracted from his immediate purposes.

---

[123] Cic. *Fam.* 5.12; *Att.* 1.19.10; 2.1.1–2.

[124] On the impact of this literary achievement on military memorials from the Renaissance to Napoleon, see Schadee (2018).

[125] Cf. Fornara (1983), 179, on Xenophon's *Anabasis*: 'a hybrid, proximate to history ... like Caesar's *Commentaries*'; Schauer (2016), 95: 'Zwitter'.

[126] Fornara (1983), 181; Flach (1985), 98, differs. Schauer (2016), 85; see also Richter (1977), 48: 'a new literary genre'.

[127] Asinius Pollio mentions the possibility that Caesar might have corrected errors, but not that he might have comprehensively revised his work (Suet. *Jul.* 56.4).

CHAPTER 15

Tradition and Authority in Philostratus' Lives of the Sophists

Ewen Bowie

Introduction

As the terms 'authority' and 'tradition' in my title suggest, in this chapter I try to ask of Philostratus' *Lives of the Sophists* some of the questions asked of Greek and Latin historians by John Marincola in his influential book *Authority and Tradition in Ancient Historiography.* These questions are related to ones that were asked by Thomas Schmitz in his chapter 'Narrator and Audience in Philostratus' *Lives of the Sophists*', published in 2009 but drafted several years earlier. Schmitz made a pre-publication draft available to Tim Whitmarsh when he was writing his shorter but comparably illuminating scrutiny of the narrator of the *Lives*, published in 2004 as part of chapter 32 of *Narrators, Narratees, and Narratives in Ancient Greek Literature.*[1] It is perhaps surprising that neither Schmitz nor Whitmarsh referred to Marincola, although both make many acute and persuasive points about how Philostratus establishes the narrator's authority, with Whitmarsh stressing – perhaps overstressing – the extent to which that authority is 'pedagogical',[2] and Schmitz arguing that 'His account of sophistic rhetoric aims to impress his readers with the knowledge and perspective of an insider'[3] and that 'It would be accurate . . . to describe the implied author's strategy of winning his reader's concurrence as one of intimidation.'[4] My excuse for going over some of this ground again is that my purpose is to examine not the narrator's persona in general – 'what sort of persona Philostratus envisages for his implied author'[5] – but the narrator's various strategies for convincing his readers that he is an authoritative historian of his chosen subject. From this

---

[1] Whitmarsh (2004); Schmitz (2009). See Whitmarsh (2004), 235 n. 33 for his access to Schmitz's draft. For an examination of a range of ancient authors' strategies for establishing their authority, see Marmodoro and Hill (2013).
[2] E.g. Whitmarsh (2004), 431, 439.   [3] Schmitz (2009), 49, cf. 56–7.   [4] Schmitz (2009), 65.
[5] Schmitz (2009), 51.

Tradition and Authority in Philostratus

perspective it does not matter whether he conceives his work as a history – and to me several features suggest that he sees himself as a quasi-Herodotean historian – or as a set of biographies, or as a fusion between these two genres, perhaps with a dash of doxography thrown in.[6] Nor does it matter for this investigation whether his accounts are in fact reliable,[7] though it is relevant to his procedures whether he himself believed that he was or was not offering reliable accounts.

Terminology

Philostratus[8] twice terms his historiographic (or biographic) activity ἑρμηνεύειν, touting himself as an interpretative intermediary between the tradition and the reader. Thus in the opening of his *Life* of Hermocrates of Phocaea he writes: 'Hermocrates of Phocaea is much celebrated in the world of the sophists, since he displayed greater natural power than all those I describe (ἑρμηνεύω).'[9] Philostratus uses the same verb when promising to help readers understand the style of Herodes: 'I shall also explicate (ἑρμηνεύσω) the man's language.'[10] Both these senses of ἑρμηνεύειν are found in post-classical Greek texts: so the literary critic who used precisely the noun ἑρμηνεία in his title περὶ ἑρμηνείας, often translated 'On Style', uses the verb of an author (not named) 'describing' a river,[11] while Galen uses it when criticizing Hippocrates because as a result of his ancient conciseness he 'explained' (ἑρμήνευσε) phenomena unclearly.[12] But it is significant that the verb ἑρμηνεύειν is also used of the rhetorical performances of sophists themselves. So Scopelianus is praised as a sophist 'who delivered his speeches (ἑρμηνεύσαντα) most

---

[6] For attempts to pin down the work's genre, cf. Jones (1974), 11 (denying that it is biographical and comparing Suetonius *De grammaticis et rhetoribus*); Swain (1991), 151 ('a sort of cross between biography and the blend of biography and doxography offered by Seneca (*Controversiae*) and Suetonius (*De grammaticis et rhetoribus*), Favorinus (*Apomnemoneumata*) and Diogenes Laertius'); Civiletti (2002), 31–7.

[7] On this important issue, see the different views of Jones (1974) and Swain (1991).

[8] For discussion of the four members of the same family named Philostratus and the problem of attributing to them the surviving works, cf. Rothe (1989), 1–5; Flinterman (1995), 5–14; De Lannoy (1997); Bowie (2009).

[9] *VS* 2.25.608. Like most scholars I refer to the *Lives* by the book and chapter (= *Life*) number of Kayser (1871) followed by the page number of Olearius' edition (1709). These allow a reader to navigate the Loeb edition of Wright (1921), which seems likely to remain the most widely accessible. I have not therefore added page numbers of the Oxford Classical Text edited by Stefec (2016). My translations of Philostratus are based on those of Wright (1921) but are in almost all cases modified, sometimes substantially.

[10] *VS* 2.1.565.   [11] Demetr. *Eloc.* 121.   [12] Gal. *Meth. Med.* 9.9 vol. 2 p. 498 = X 633 Kühn.

294 EWEN BOWIE

readily, most boldly and most grandly of any Greek of his time';[13] and lesser sophists are chastised for their inability to 'express (ἑρμηνεύειν) what they have conceived'.[14] The semantic range of the verb ἑρμηνεύειν suits Philostratus' mode of writing, which combines that of a stylistic critic with that of a biographic or historiographic narrator, and its use is also one of many strategies that embed him as a member of the sophistic movement he records.[15]

Another such strategy is his performative use of διαλέξομαι in the sentence 'I shall now discourse about the sophist Scopelianus,'[16] as if addressing not a reader holding a book-roll or codex but an audience attending a lecture or the informal sophistic performance called διάλεξις.

A quite different term that Philostratus often uses for his activity is ἀναγράφειν, 'to record', as if there are facts that he simply registers with no embellishment, far less distortion. Thus in his long life of Polemo he writes: 'I shall also record (ἀναγράψω) Polemo's witticisms, so that not even these may be seen to have been passed by.'[17] The term is used again in one of the most politically sensitive passages of the *Life* of Herodes, when (again implying that he is adhering to some historiographic principle) Philostratus introduces an episode with the following sentence: 'It is necessary (ἀνάγκη) that I also record (ἀναγράψαι) the reasons why Herodes offended the Athenians.'[18] He also uses the verb to introduce the *Life* of his teacher Proclus of Naucratis, linking it with the important claim to special knowledge: 'I shall record (ἀναγράψω) also Proclus of Naucratis, since I knew the man well.'[19] Finally, the self-description 'I have recorded' (ἀναγέγραφα) is used retrospectively of the *Lives* of Hadrianus and Aristides.[20]

---

[13] *VS* 1.21.515; again of Scopelianus at 520. [14] *VS* 1.19.511.

[15] For Philostratus' presentation of himself as a well-informed member of the profession whose stars' biographies he offers, see Schmitz (2009), 49.

[16] *VS* 1.21.514. Cf. Schmitz (2009), 52, elaborating the suggestion of Stephen Harrison that Philostratus' frequent first-person references to his compositional activity 'could be interpreted as mimicking the voice of the live performer'.

[17] *VS* 1.25.540. For the implication that Philostratus can be relied upon not to omit items of importance, see Schmitz (2009), 52.

[18] *VS* 2.1.549. Philostratus' appeal to 'necessity' (ἀνάγκη) here may evoke Herodotus' uses of the trope, (a) when excusing himself at 2.3.2 for mentioning divine matters he would prefer to omit – 'those of them I mention, I shall mention because compelled by my account' (ἐξαναγκαζόμενος ὑπὸ τοῦ λόγου) – and (b) when justifying his praise of Athens at 7.139.1: 'At this point I am driven by necessity to declare my judgement that the majority may disapprove of . . .' (ἐνταῦθα ἀναγκαίη ἐξέργομαι γνώμην ἀποδέξασθαι ἐπίφθονον πρὸς τῶν πλεόνων ἀνθρώπων . . .). As the editors point out to me, this passage is especially relevant given its context of Athens and φθόνος.

[19] *VS* 2.21.602.

[20] *VS* 2.23.605. Note also its use of 'recording' by Herodes at 1.25.538, below with note 25. None of Herodotus' three uses of ἀναγράφειν refers to his own authorial activity.

Knowledge

As the remark about Proclus emphasizes, the activity that Philostratus calls ἑρμηνεύειν or διαλέγεσθαι or ἀναγράφειν is one that he repeatedly claims to conduct on the basis of knowledge, thus aligning himself with the sophists of the fifth century BC to whom he ascribes such claims to 'know' in his preface. The first claim that *he*, Philostratus, knows, οἶδα, is indeed in that preface: 'Their fathers' names I have not added in all cases, indeed not, but only in the case of those who were the sons of illustrious men. For after all I know (οἶδα) that the sophist Critias also did not begin with the father's name as a rule.'[21] There follows shortly Philostratus' ascription of the claim 'I know' to fifth-century sophists: 'the ancient sophist speaks as one who knows (ὡς εἰδώς): at any rate, he introduces his speeches with such phrases as "I know" (οἶδα), or "I am aware" (γιγνώσκω), or "I have long observed" (πάλαι διέσκεμμαι)'.[22] But it is worth noting that the claim 'I know' (οἶδα) is one of several features that link Philostratus to Herodotus, in whose writing it is very frequent.[23]

Texts and Witnesses

On what basis does Philostratus suggest to readers of the *Lives* that *he* has a valid claim to 'knowledge'? For a start, he repeatedly quotes from sophists' speeches in a way that shows he has consulted texts, and occasionally he cites a written source for an event. Such citations are:

(a) A letter of Herodes Atticus to Varus (perhaps, but not certainly, the Varus of Perge whose *Life* is VS 2.6) cited for Polemo's theatrical self-presentation when declaiming: 'The theatricality the man deployed for his declamations is something one can also learn from Herodes by whom it is stated in one of his letters to Varus, and I shall set it out from that source.'[24]

(b) Something written by Herodes Atticus – perhaps, but not explicitly, the same letter – cited for the declamations with which Polemo impressed him over three days: '(Herodes says that) he was with him for three days. And Herodes also records (ἀναγράφει) the

---

[21] *VS* pref. 479.   [22] *VS* pref. 480.

[23] E.g. 1.5.3, 131.1, 140.2, etc. Thuc. uses οἶδα of his authorial knowledge only in the unusual passage 3.113.6. In Hdt. (ὡς) εἰδώς is rarer, but cf. 1.40.1, 193.4, 2.123.3, 171.1. Thuc. only has εἰδώς at 6.55.1 (of Hippias' seniority to Hipparchus).

[24] *VS* 1.25.537.

subjects of the declamations at which he was present.'[25] The term here used of Herodes' activity aligns the sophist whom Philostratus honoured with his longest *Life* with Philostratus himself, two of whose applications of it to his own writing come not long before and after this passage.[26]

(c) A letter of the emperor Marcus cited to refute the claim of 'some' (ἔνιοι) that Herodes was exiled to Oricum. Philostratus calls on the 'divine' (θεσπέσιον) Marcus as a witness (μάρτυρα), paraphrasing and quoting what he claims to be the relevant parts of a long and friendly letter from Marcus to Herodes.[27] He follows this, however, with an unattributed item – 'there is a story' (ἔστι δέ τις λόγος), an introduction with a Herodotean colour,[28] which he implicitly accepts concerning a letter of Herodes to the rebel Avidius Cassius.

(d) Written sources implied by Philostratus' wording when he registers Aristides' death: 'and some write that Aristides died at home' (ἀποθανεῖν δὲ τὸν Ἀριστείδην οἱ μὲν οἴκοι γράφουσιν).[29]

A little later in the *Life* of Herodes we encounter another mention of a specific source, an otherwise unknown Athenian, Ctesidemus, to whom I come shortly. But it is only once we have reached the later *Lives* in Book 2 that we can decide how Philostratus *might*, had he chosen, have distinguished between the quality and nature of his information for different periods within the time span he covers – although unlike Herodotus and Thucydides, Philostratus does not so choose. Had he done so, his division might have been as follows:

(a) For sophists whose careers overlapped with his own adolescent or adult lifetime he can claim or imply personal observation.

(b) For Hadrianus of Tyre, Aristides, and their generation – sophists who were nearing the end of their careers in the early 180s – he can claim the evidence of the Ephesian magnate Vedius Damianus, of his own teachers and of 'older men' (πρεσβύτεροι).

(c) For Herodes, as we have seen, he claims the written record of Herodes, some of that in the form of letters, and the eyewitness account of Ctesidemus.

I shall look at each category briefly, starting with Philostratus' own lifetime.

---

[25] *VS* 1.25.538.   [26] *VS* 1.25.514 and 2.1.549.

[27] *VS* 2.1.562–3: this is the only place where Philostratus terms supporting testimony a 'witness' (μάρτυς).

[28] Cf. Hdt 2.47.2, 'there is a story told about him by Egyptians' (ἔστι μὲν λόγος περὶ αὐτοῦ ὑπ' Αἰγυπτίων λεγόμενος); 3.3, 'this story is also told' (λέγεται δὲ καὶ ὅδε λόγος), etc.

[29] *VS* 2.9.585.

Tradition and Authority in Philostratus

Personal Observation

Regarding point (a): Although many of the vivid anecdotes in the *Lives* of sophists active in the Severan period and later could in principle be the result of Philostratus' personal observation, for example, the entertaining stand-off between Caracalla and Philiscus,[30] the earliest certain instance is in the *Life* of Proclus of Naucratis, whom he says was one of his teachers and someone he knew well.[31] His very full account of Proclus' intertwined academic and commercial career includes a lively picture of the arrangements in his school, which Philostratus must have attended in the later 180s.[32]

Personal observation resurfaces during the career of Antipater of Hierapolis, whom Philostratus had heard deliver epideictic orations, presumably towards the end of the second century: 'Although he could speak extempore, he did not neglect carefully prepared speeches either, but used to deliver for us (ἡμῖν) Olympian and Panathenaic orations.' Prima facie this suggests that Philostratus was present at first performances at Olympia and Athens, though it might simply refer to re-performance in an epideictic context elsewhere. But Philostratus undoubtedly spent much time in Athens, and he certainly implies his own presence there when Hippodromus replied eirenically to an attack by Proclus: 'And when Proclus of Naucratis composed an invective, unworthy of an old man, against all who were teaching at Athens, and included Hippodromus in this abuse, we expected (ἡμεῖς μὲν ᾠόμεθα) to hear a speech composed to echo what had been said. But he uttered nothing cheap, and delivered an encomium of fair-speaking.'[33]

A similar use of 'us' (ἡμῖν) also *implies* that he was present at a tense exchange between Heliodorus and Caracalla at some date between AD 211 and Caracalla's death in April 217: 'At this the Emperor sprang from his seat and called Heliodorus "a man such as I have never yet known, a new phenomenon such as has appeared only in my own time", and other epithets of this sort, and raising his hand he shook back the fold of his cloak. Now at first there came upon us (ἡμῖν) an urge to laugh, because we thought that the Emperor was really making fun of him.'[34]

Finally, towards the end of his two books, Philostratus implies he could have written with authority about contemporaries, but chose not to do so because friendship (φιλία) would be suspected of impeding objectivity:

[30] *VS* 2.30.623. [31] Above with note 19. [32] *VS* 2.21.604. [33] *VS* 2.27.617.
[34] *VS* 2.32.626.

298 EWEN BOWIE

'I should not write, for I would be disbelieved as favouring them, since they were my friends.'[35] As well as excusing Philostratus from the challenge of writing about close contemporaries this grand gesture leaves readers with the firm impression that he has set himself the reputable historian's target of writing *sine ira et studio* ('without anger or favour').

'I (have) heard'

Regarding point (b): For sophists active slightly earlier, between the AD 150s and 180s, information communicated orally by the Ephesian magnate and sophist Vedius Damianus is cited.[36] The first case concerns an anecdote about Aristides declaiming in Smyrna in AD 176 for the passing emperor Marcus: 'For as I heard (ἤκουον) from Damianus of Ephesus, the Emperor had already been visiting Smyrna for three days and since he had not yet seen Aristides he asked the Quintilii whether he had overlooked the man in the throng of those who came to greet him.'[37]

A little later Damianus is cited again for Aristides' sneaky preparations for extempore speeches: 'This too I heard (ἤκουον) from Damianus, that though in his discourses this sophist disparaged extempore speakers, nevertheless he so greatly admired extempore eloquence that he used to shut himself up in a room and work at it in private. And he used to work at a speech, repeating it again and again clause by clause and idea by idea.'[38] Only much later, in the *Life* of Damianus himself, do we read that all that Philostratus wrote about Aristides (*VS* 2.9) and Hadrianus of Tyre (*VS* 2.10) derived from Damianus: 'And in fact all that I have recorded (ἀναγέγραφα) about these men I have said having learned it from Damianus, who knew well both men's careers.'[39] That Damianus was a reliable source is emphasized by the phrase here 'who knew well' (εὖ εἰδότος), and that he supplied him with much information is implied by the statement that follows shortly that he privileged Philostratus with not simply one but a second and a third interview (συνουσία).[40] Despite the phraseology here, however, it seems that Damianus was not in fact Philostratus' only source. In the *Life* of Hadrianus he mentions that he knows (οἶδα) some former pupils who wept 'whenever they happened to remember this man (ὁπότε ἐς μνήμην τοῦ ἀνδρὸς τούτου καθίσταιντο)'

---

[35] *VS* 2.33.628.
[36] Whitmarsh (2004), 439, seems to exaggerate the extent to which '*VS* downplays the attribution of narratives to sources'.
[37] *VS* 2.9.582. [38] *VS* 2.9.583. [39] *VS* 2.23.605. Cf. above on Proclus with notes 19 and 31.
[40] *VS* 2.23.606.

Tradition and Authority in Philostratus

and who would imitate his voice, walk or elegant attire.[41] He also writes that Hadrianus came to Athens in Herodes' time 'as I have heard from my teachers' (ὡς γὰρ τῶν ἐμαυτοῦ διδασκάλων ἤκουον).[42]

For reports on earlier generations of sophists Philostratus most often cites simply 'some people' (τινες); but for sophists slightly older than Aristides and Hadrianus he twice cites 'my elders' (πρεσβύτεροι). Thus he writes that about Aristocles of Pergamum 'I shall set forth (δηλώσω) all that I have heard about him from men older than myself (τῶν πρεσβυτέρων ἤκουον).'[43] Finally, he cites πρεσβύτεροι for Philagrus' hostile reception in Athens, prefacing the anecdote with the phrase 'For as I have heard from my elders' (ὡς γὰρ τῶν πρεσβυτέρων ἤκουον).[44]

Regarding point (c), my third category, the earliest period of the second sophistic, from Nicetes of Smyrna to Herodes Atticus: For this he names, over and above the written sources we have encountered earlier, only two oral sources. In the *Life* of Dionysius of Miletus he writes that he should not omit what follows (μηδ' ἐκεῖνα παρείσθω) about an encounter between the ageing Dionysius and up-and-coming Polemo since he had heard it (ἠκροαμένῳ) from Aristaeus, the oldest of the Hellenes in his time and one who knew most about the sophists (πρεσβυτάτου τῶν κατ' ἐμὲ Ἑλλήνων καὶ πλεῖστα ὑπὲρ σοφιστῶν εἰδότος).[45] A reader may wonder whether this walking treasure-trove of information was drawn upon elsewhere by Philostratus, and if so, why it is only here that he is specifically named. Readers might also react similarly to the citation in the *Life* of Herodes of an Athenian Ctesidemus as somebody who, Philostratus writes, had *heard* Herodes explaining his ambition to cut a canal through the Isthmus of Corinth.[46] The circumstances of Ctesidemus' acquisition of this information – surely unlikely to be a secret – are set out in vivid detail that may distract the reader from asking who this otherwise unknown Ctesidemus was and whether what he told Philostratus decades later was to be believed:

> For as I have heard (ἤκουον) from Ctesidemus the Athenian, Herodes was driving to Corinth with Ctesidemus sitting by his side, and when he arrived at the Isthmus Herodes cried: 'Poseidon, I aspire to do it, but no one will let me!' Ctesidemus was surprised at what he had said and asked him why he had made the remark. Whereupon Herodes replied: 'I have long been striving to leave to men that come after me some proof ...'

---

[41] *VS* 2.10.587.

[42] *VS* 2.10.585. His teachers probably did not include Damianus; cf. Schmitz (2009), 55 with n. 22, against G. Anderson (1986), 4, and Rothe (1989), 92.

[43] *VS* 2.3.567.   [44] *VS* 2.8.579.   [45] *VS* 1.22.524.   [46] *VS* 2.1.552.

300   EWEN BOWIE

In each case Philostratus teases readers by playing what some historians treat as a trump card, a named source: but *these* named sources, Aristaeus and Ctesidemus, are unknown to us and were quite probably obscure to his first readers.

The claim to have 'heard' something without any source being named is twice made, first in the *Life* of Herodes, where Philostratus writes, 'I have heard (ἤκουον) the following concerning this Panathenaic festival.' He concludes his description of the Panathenaic ship and its mechanical progress by saying it finally reached the Pythion, 'where it is now moored' (οἷ νῦν ὥρμισται), hinting that its presence there at the time of writing in some way supports the account he has offered of its movements (which of course it does not).[47]

The second claim to have 'heard' something without any source being named comes in the *Life* of Ptolemy of Naucratis, where it is attached to one of two traditions between which Philostratus does not choose:[48]

> They used to call him 'Marathon'. As some have it, this was because he was enrolled in the deme Marathon at Athens, but I have heard (ἤκουον) from others that it was because in his Attic themes he often recalled those who risked their lives at Marathon.

Citation of Damianus, of πρεσβύτεροι, of Aristaeus and of Ctesidemus, and of unspecific τινες, does indeed add credibility to Philostratus' account of sophists of the Antonine period who had died before he himself was of an age to hear declamations; but it also alerts readers to the problem of Philostratus' sources for the previous century, to say nothing of the fifth and fourth centuries BC. Philostratus, however, reinforces the impression that he offers a *credible* account by offering alternative traditions, as he does with Ptolemy's nickname 'Marathon', more often introducing them with 'as some say' (ὡς ἔνιοί φασι).

Conflicting Traditions

Sometimes these alternatives are presented without endorsement of either. So it is with variant traditions on whether Dionysius of Miletus had very distinguished ancestors 'as some say' or was simply 'as some (say)' (ὡς τινες) of free birth.[49] In the case of Alexander of Seleucia's death Philostratus offers alternatives on place, age, and stage in his career,

---

[47] *VS* 2.1.550.   [48] *VS* 2.15.595.
[49] *VS* 1.22.521–2. For ὡς ἔνιοι, cf. 1.2.562 on Herodes' alleged exile.

Tradition and Authority in Philostratus 301

concluding with the remark that on these matters 'I have found nothing worth mentioning' (οὐδὲν εὗρον λόγου ἄξιον), a remark that evokes Herodotus and fosters the impression he had exacting standards for testing traditions.[50] On Aristides' death he writes: 'Some write (γράφουσιν) that Aristides died at home, and some in Ionia, some saying (φασιν) he had lived sixty years, others nearly seventy.'[51] The shift from 'write' to 'say' suggests that here, and quite probably in other places too, his use of 'they say' (φασιν) or 'as some say' (ὡς ἔνιοί φασι) may refer to consultation of written sources. Finally in discussing the number of Hermocrates' declamations (μελέται) and the age at which he died, Philostratus' uncertainty on these details is offset by total confidence in his assessment of his rhetorical promise:[52]

> There are extant perhaps eight or ten declamations by Hermocrates and a sort of short address which he delivered at Phocaea over the Pan-Ionian loving-cup. But let it be declared by me (ἐμοὶ δὲ ἀποπεφάνθω) that the eloquence of this stripling would have been such that no one could surpass it, had he not been cut off by an envious deity and prevented from reaching manhood. He died, as some have it, at the age of twenty-eight, though according to others he was only twenty-five, and the land of his fathers and the tombs of his fathers received him.

More often Philostratus introduces a tradition or traditions by, for example, 'they say' (φασι) only to reject them. This trademark of circumspect historiography is deployed as early as the preface to Book 1, perhaps programmatically. Here he reports traditions that trace the origins of sophistic rhetoric variously to Pericles, as 'some say' (οἱ μὲν ... φασίν), or to Pytho of Byzantium, 'but some ...' (οἱ δὲ ...), or to Aeschines 'but some ...' (οἱ δὲ ...); then Philostratus says, 'I think myself' (ἐμοὶ ... δοκεῖ) that Gorgias should be seen as the initiator of extempore speaking, offering as his reason for this view that 'when he appeared in the theatre at Athens he was bold enough to say, "Propose a theme"; and he was the first to utter this challenge'.[53]

Philostratus again insists on his superior knowledge of the history of sophistic in discussing Polus of Agrigentum, using 'they say' twice in four lines, the second time to reject what is said with an appeal to the inadequate evidence of Plato:[54]

---

[50] *VS* 2.5.576. λόγου ἄξιον is a term with a Herodotean pedigree; cf. 1.133.2, 2.138.2, 4.28.2, 8.35.2, 91, and λόγου ἄξιως at 6.112.3, 7.211.3.

[51] *VS* 2.9.585.   [52] *VS* 2.25.612.   [53] *VS* 1. pref. 482.   [54] *VS* 1.13.497, cf. Pl. *Grg.* 467b.

> Polus of Agrigentum, the sophist, was trained in the art by Gorgias, and for this he paid, as they say, very high fees; for in fact Polus was a wealthy man. And there are those who say (εἰσὶ δὲ οἵ φασι) that Polus was the first to use clauses that exactly balance, antitheses, and similar endings – a false claim, for such rhetorical ornament was already invented, and Polus merely employed it to excess. Hence Plato, to express his contempt for Polus because of this affectation, says: 'O polite Polus! to address you in your own style.'

This latter case, from a period long before Philostratus' oral traditions, is handled in something of the way Hellenistic and Greco-Roman scholars interpreted Homer and other canonical texts: the interpreter adduces another text that will support their own interpretation. Here, however, it is far from clear that the ludic address Plato puts in Socrates' mouth in the *Gorgias* supports Philostratus' position.

Rejecting Traditions and 'the Truer Explanation'

Rather different is Philostratus' rejection of things that had been said about his second-century sophists. The polemical tone in which such rejections are formulated was related by Schmitz to the practices of Alexandrian scholarship,[55] but comparably polemical rejections of others' views go back as far as Hecataeus and Herodotus.[56] There are several cases in the *Life* of Herodes Atticus.

Thus, after reporting that 'some say' (οἱ μὲν ... φασιν) that Heracles-Agathion was an earthborn Boeotian, Philostratus claims that Herodes himself 'says that he had heard him say' (ἀκοῦσαι λέγοντός φησιν) that his mother was a cowherd and his father Marathon, whose cult-statue is at Marathon.[57] It is unclear whether the reference to the statue at Marathon is a Philostratean footnote or part of Heracles-Agathion's communication to Herodes, but in either case it acts as a sort of anchor in the same way as the Panathenaic ship discussed above,[58] creating a fiduciary bridge between the tradition and the material world of the reader, and distracting from Philostratus' silence on just which work of Herodes offered him this nugget.

---

[55] Schmitz (2009), 53–4, citing (note 19) the *Life of Sophocles* 1 and observing that the connection between Philostratus and Alexandrian scholarship had already been made by Leo in 1901.
[56] E.g. Hecataeus *FGrHist* 1 F 1, Hdt. 2.2.5, 20.1, 4.36.2.   [57] *VS* 2.1.553.
[58] *VS* 2.1.550 with note 36.

Tradition and Authority in Philostratus

Later in the same *Life*, discussing the origins of Herodes' quarrel with the brothers Quintilii, Philostratus rejects two traditions and instead insists that his own explanation is 'more true':[59]

> His quarrel with the Quintilii began, as most people say (ὡς μὲν οἱ πολλοί φασι), over the Pythian festival, when they held different views about the musical competition; but as some (ὡς δὲ ἔνιοι) that it began with the jests that Herodes made to Marcus at their expense. For when he saw that, though they were Trojans, the Emperor thought them worthy of the highest honours, he said 'I blame Homer's Zeus also, for loving the Trojans.' But the truer reason is this (ἡ δὲ ἀληθεστέρα αἰτία ἥδε): when these two men were both governing Greece, the Athenians invited them to a meeting of the assembly, and made speeches to the effect that they were oppressed by a tyrant, meaning Herodes; and finally begged that what they had said might be passed on to the Emperor's ears.

Book 1 had already offered readers two similar instances where Philostratus insists that his own account is 'truer' but offers no evidence and little argument in its favour. Concerning Polemo's death, Philostratus rejects all the sites in Smyrna that 'are said' (λέγονται) to have been his burial place and offers an argument for it having been his ancestral tomb in Laodicea ad Lycum: 'But none of this is true, for if he had died in Smyrna there is not one of the marvellous temples there in which he would have been deemed unworthy to lie. But the following is truer (ἀλλ' ἐκεῖνα ἀληθέστερα), that he lies in Laodicea near the Syrian gate, where indeed too are the tombs of his ancestors.'[60] Here the words ἐκεῖνα ἀληθέστερα recall Thucydides 1.22.6, τὴν μὲν γὰρ ἀληθεστάτην πρόφασιν, also manifestly evoked earlier when Philostratus discusses the reasons for Scopelianus' estrangement from his father: 'The reasons (αἰτίαι) why his father, after being kind and indulgent to him, treated him harshly, are told (λέγονται) in many different versions, now this reason, now that, then more than one; but I shall set forth (δηλώσω) the truest reason (τὴν ἀληθεστάτην).'[61] The melodramatic tale of plotting against Scopelianus by his father's new wife and his cook is a good read; but neither here nor concerning the quarrel between Herodes and the brothers Quintilii are we ever given any reason for accepting it as 'truest'.

---

[59] *VS* 2.1.559.   [60] *VS* 1.25.543.

[61] *VS* 1.21.516. For other uses of the future 'I shall show' (δηλώσω), cf. also 1.21.515, 520, 1.22.523, 1.25.536, 537, 2.3.567, 2.26.613; for the past tense 'they have been shown' (δεδήλωται), 2.5.574–5; for the jussives 'let him be shown' (δηλούσθω), 2.5.574, 575, and 'let (a speech) show (his brilliance)' (δηλούτω), 2.9.584. I am not persuaded that the sense of the verb δηλοῦν is as strong as 'reveal' as suggested by Whitmarsh (2004), 436 with n. 37.

304 EWEN BOWIE

That is not strictly the case with Philostratus' rebuttal of those who 'say' (φασι) that Apollonius of Tyana fell in love with the beautiful mother of Alexander of Seleucia. But this rebuttal is no more than a general cross-reference to his *In Honour of Apollonius*, referring not to a particular passage but to the presentation of Apollonius in the work as a whole: 'In my work *In Honour of Apollonius* I have stated clearly in how many ways this story is incredible (ἀπίθανον).'[62]

Earlier in Book 1, however, Philostratus does offer argument of a sort for rejecting the allegation that Isocrates was an *aulos*-maker, using it to show that those who held this view were wrong: 'Those who think that Comedy attacked Isocrates because he was a maker of *auloi* are wrong (ἁμαρτάνουσιν); for though his father was Theodorus, who was known in Athens as an *aulos*-maker, Isocrates himself knew nothing about *aulos*-making or any other manual activity; and he would not have got the statue at Olympia if he had been employed in any low occupation.'[63]

Philostratus, the Authoritative Connoisseur of Style

Claims that others 'are wrong' can be reinforced by appeal to Philostratus' professional, sophistic sense of style. So concerning a work denied to Marcus of Byzantium he writes: 'Those who ascribe this discourse to Alcinous the Stoic fail to catch the style of his speech, and fail to catch the truth (διαμαρτάνουσι μὲν ἰδέας λόγου, διαμαρτάνουσι δὲ ἀληθείας), and are the most unjust of men, since they try to rob the sophist even of what is his own.'[64] On the same basis he pontificates on who did or did not teach Heraclides, offering concise judgements but no actual evidence: 'As for the teachers of Heraclides, Herodes is believed wrongly (οὐκ ἀληθῶς) to have been one, and among those who were genuinely his teachers are Hadrian and Chrestus; but let us not doubt that he heard Aristocles too.'[65]

One of the best cases of Philostratus' putting his personal reputation as a sophist on the line is his assessment of Herodes' style, which he relates to

---

[62] *VS* 2 5.570. For the correct title of the work on Apollonius, see Boter (2015). [63] *VS* 1.17.506.

[64] *VS* 1.24.528. Cf. his vehement ascription of *Araspas, lover of Pantheia* to the imperial secretary Celer and not, as supposed by the ignorant, to Dionysius of Miletus, *VS* 1.22.524. Failure to get the truth is, of course, a widespread charge levelled against predecessors in historical, philosophical, and medical writing as well as in historiography, where it appears (e.g.) in Plb. 2.12.2, 3.59.1, 5.31.1; cf. also Plut. *De def. or.* 15 = *Mor.* 417f πλεῖστον δὲ τῆς ἀληθείας διαμαρτάνουσιν οἱ Δελφῶν θεολόγοι, 'the religious expounders at Delphi are very far indeed from the truth'.

[65] *VS* 2.26.615. For first-person plural jussives, see both Whitmarsh (2004) and Schmitz (2009).

Tradition and Authority in Philostratus

his education. He introduces this critique with the first-person verb ἑρμηνεύσω, 'I shall ... explicate' (ἑρμηνεύσω), and supports neither his list of Herodes' teachers nor his stylistic critique with evidence:

> I shall also explicate the language of Herodes, addressing the character of his diction. I have already said that he counted Polemo, Favorinus, and Scopelianus among his teachers, and that he attended the lectures of Secundus the Athenian, but as to critics of writing he studied with Theagenes of Cnidus and Munatius of Tralles; and for the doctrines of Plato, with Taurus of Tyre. The structure of his work was suitably restrained, and its strength crept up on listeners rather than attacking them. He had a sonority combined with simplicity, and a tone recalling Critias; his ideas were such as would not be conceived by another; he had a comic fluency which was not dragged in, but drawn from his subjects themselves; his diction was pleasing, rich in figures and graceful, skilfully varying constructions; his tone was not vehement but smooth and firm, and his overall type of eloquence is like gold dust gleaming beneath a river's silver eddies.[66]

Earlier in Book 1 Philostratus had launched an attack, brimming with self-confident bluster, on the critics of Scopelianus, including the *Lives'* only use of λέγουσιν:[67]

> I will now discourse (διαλέξομαι) on the sophist Scopelian, but first I will castigate those who try to belittle the man, holding that he is unworthy of the sophistic circle and calling him dithyrambic and uncontrolled and thick-witted. Those who say (λέγουσιν) this about him are quibblers and sluggish and can muster no vigour in extempore eloquence.... Hence we must not be surprised if certain persons who are themselves tongue-tied, and have set on their tongues the 'ox of silence', who could not themselves conceive any great thought or sympathize with another who conceived one, should sneer at and revile one who delivered his speeches (ἑρμηνεύσαντα) most readily, most boldly, and most grandly of any Greek of his time.

These judgements of Herodes and Scopelianus are offered without specific examples. But sometimes Philostratus refers to specific speeches of a sophist to support his assessment. Thus after insisting that critics of Polemo's style are mistaken (διαμαρτάνουσι), he presents counter-examples that he thinks disproves (ἐλέγχει) them:[68]

> But they fail to understand the man who say that he handles attacks more skilfully than any other sophist, but is less skilful in making a defence. Such

---

[66] *VS* 2.1.564. For ἑρμηνεύειν, see above with notes 9–15.
[67] *VS* 1.21.514–5. For διαλέξομαι, cf. above p. 294 with note 16.
[68] *VS* 1.25.542–3. For imputation of error to others, cf. Schmitz (2009), 59.

306   EWEN BOWIE

a criticism is proved to be untrue by this and that declamation in which he speaks for the defence, but especially by the speech in which Demosthenes swears that he did not accept the fifty talents. For in establishing a defence so difficult to make, his ornate rhetoric and technical skill were fully equal to the argument. I observe the same error in the case of those who hold that he was not qualified to sustain simulated arguments, but was forced off the course like a horse for whom the ground is too rough, and that he deprecated the use of these themes when he quoted the maxim of Homer:

For hateful to me even as the gates of hell is he that hides one thing in his heart and utters another.

Perhaps he used to say this with a double meaning, and to illustrate by this allusion how intractable are such themes; nevertheless, these too he sustained with great skill, as is evident from his *Adulterer Unmasked* or his *Xenophon Refuses to Survive Socrates*; or his *Solon Demands That His Laws Be Rescinded after Peisistratus Has Obtained a Bodyguard*. Then there are the three on Demosthenes, the first where he denounced himself after Chaeronea, the second in which he pretends that he ought to be punished with death for the affair of Harpalus, lastly that in which he advises the Athenians to flee on their triremes at the approach of Philip, though Aeschines had carried a law that anyone who mentioned the war should be put to death.

Similarly, Philostratus pronounces judgement on Antipater's style based on having heard him deliver epideictic orations (ἡμῖν διῄει) and (implicitly) on having read letters he wrote as *ab epistulis graecis*, though neither here nor in his assessment of Herodes just quoted does he offer his readers samples of his subject's rhetoric:[69]

Though he had a talent for speaking extempore, he nevertheless did not neglect written work, but used to recite to us (ἡμῖν διῄει) Olympic and Panathenaic orations, and wrote an historical account of the deeds of the Emperor Severus, and when the latter appointed him Imperial Secretary, he wrote brilliantly in that post. For let me declare my opinion (ἐμοὶ μὲν γὰρ δὴ ἀποπεφάνθω) that, though there were many who declaimed or wrote history better than Antipater, no one wrote letters better than he, but, like a brilliant tragic actor who has a thorough knowledge of his profession, he always uttered what was worthy of the imperial persona.

Quotations from Sophistic Speeches

In the cases just discussed only titles or genres of composition are offered. But Philostratus also frequently quotes from sophists' speeches, implying,

[69] *VS* 2.24.607.

Tradition and Authority in Philostratus

as already said, that he had texts of these available to him, even if (as Civiletti points out) these quotations are rarely long enough to give readers a good understanding of the sophist's style.[70] Thus in the case of Varus of Perge a quotation supports Philostratus' commendation of his magnificent voice, which itself is based simply on hearsay (ἐλέγετο):[71]

> The character of his eloquence is as follows: 'When you arrive at the Hellespont do you call for a horse? When you arrive at Athos do you wish to sail? Man, do you not know the regular routes? You throw this handful of earth on the Hellespont, and think you that it will remain, when mountains do not remain?' It used to be said (ἐλέγετο) that he declaimed this in a magnificent and well-trained voice.

Likewise concerning Philagrus:[72]

> What rhythms he used in his declamations may be seen in his speech *To the Uninvited*; indeed he is said to have delighted in such rhythms: 'Friend, today I have seen you as you are, today you speak to me in arms and with a sword', and: 'The only friendship that I recognize comes from the assembly. So depart, friends, since this is the term we keep for you, and if ever we need allies, we will send for you – if ever we do.'

By the same token either speeches themselves or outcomes of speeches can implicitly be called as witnesses. Thus Philostratus cites an embassy speech of Scopelianus to Domitian in defence of his province's viticulture to 'show' his brilliance:[73]

> How he acquired fame in the contest on behalf of the vines, what he said shows (δηλοῖ): for the speech is among his most admired, and the outcome of the speech shows it too: for on its basis he won gifts which are customary from the emperor, and many compliments and commendations, and a brilliant generation of youths followed him to Ionia in love with wisdom.

The claim that a sophist's work 'shows' the correctness of Philostratus' account is made in two other places. Of Dio Philostratus writes: 'That he had also a talent for writing history, his *On the Getae* shows (δηλοῖ); he did indeed travel to the Getae during his wanderings.'[74] Similarly of the oeuvre of Antiochus of Aegeae:[75] 'He delivered extempore declamations, but he also tackled written compositions, as other works of his show (δηλοῖ), and especially his *History*: for in this he has made a display of his style and rhetoric.' In a comparable claim Philostratus uses the jussive subjunctive to urge that Aristides should not be judged by certain declamations 'but may

---

[70] Civiletti (2002), 17.   [71] *VS* 2.6.576–7.   [72] *VS* 2.8.580.
[73] *VS* 1.21.520. On δηλοῦν, see above with note 61.   [74] *VS* 1.7.487.   [75] *VS* 2.4.570.

308   EWEN BOWIE

his quality be shown (δηλούτω δὲ αὐτόν) by *Isocrates trying to dissuade the Athenians from reliance on the sea . . .'.*[76] Almost immediately he makes the same move using a different verb, writing: 'I know (οἶδα) several declamations that display (ἐνδεικνυμένας) this man's erudition.'[77]

Only superficially similar is the reverse, self-authenticating claim that Philostratus' own account 'shows' the brilliance of Alexander of Seleucia: 'For indeed Alexander was making his case with brilliant success, as what has been said shows (δηλοῖ).'[78]

The related impression that the biographer is simply guided by the facts at his disposal is given by the Herodotean remark at the opening of Theodotus' *Life*: 'My account calls me (καλεῖ με ὁ λόγος) to the sophist Theodotus.'[79]

The trope reappears at the opening of the *Life* of Damianus, linked here with a scathing dismissal of men he regards as lesser sophists: 'My account leads me (ἄγει με ὁ λόγος) to a man who became most renowned, Damianus of Ephesus – and let there be excluded from it such persons as Soter, Sosus, Nicander, Phaedrus, Cyrus, and Phylax, since these might rather be called the Greeks' toys than sophists worthy of mention.'[80]

Paratexts

We might reach the end of the *Lives* wondering how much of the account is reliable, whether at times Philostratus protests too much, whether he makes too ostentatious displays of his scepticism and his careful use of sources.[81] But a *subscriptio* such as Φιλοστράτου σοφιστῶν βίοι, 'Philostratus' *Lives of the Sophists*' – if there *was* such a *subscriptio* – might prompt us to return to the work's opening, the only place the author's

---

[76] *VS* 2.9.584. For Philostratus' use of first-person jussive subjunctives, see Schmitz (2009), 61 (with a list in n. 29), and for their function of 'steering' readers, Whitmarsh (2004), 436 with n. 36.

[77] *VS* 2.9.585.

[78] *VS* 2.5.572 – if this is how the passage should be understood. Elsewhere τὰ εἰρημένα is used of the quoted words of sophists, but since nothing of Alexander is quoted here it can only refer to Philostratus' own words.

[79] *VS* 2.1.566. Cf. Schmitz (2009), 51–2, noting the contrast with Philostratus' habitual transitions that are marked by first-person singular statements.

[80] *VS* 2.22.605. For the application of the criterion 'worth mentioning' (λόγου ἄξιον) cf. 2.5.576 (above p. 301). For the Herodotean ancestry, cf. Hdt. 1.95.1: 'My account (ὁ λόγος) next proceeds to enquire who this Cyrus was who brought down Croesus' Empire' (ἐπιδίζηται δὲ δὴ τὸ ἐνθεῦτεν ἡμῖν ὁ λόγος τόν τε Κῦρον ὅστις ἐὼν τὴν Κροίσου ἀρχὴν κατεῖλε); 4.30.1: 'For after all my account has sought out digressions from the start' (προσθήκας γὰρ δή μοι ὁ λόγος ἐξ ἀρχῆς ἐδίζητο).

[81] Cf. Schmitz (2009), 68: 'the text makes us constantly wonder whether we should trust this man or decry him'.

Tradition and Authority in Philostratus   309

name appears in the text. Even here it does not appear in the opening lines, as in the histories of Herodotus or Thucydides, nor, despite Philostratus' recurrent stance of an intrusive narrator, does he make biographic claims for himself and his career in his preface, as did Appian,[82] or in a second preface, as did Arrian.[83] Instead, the weight of arrogating authority is carried by a paratext in the form of a relatively short 'dedicatory' letter, addressed by Philostratus to Antonius Gordianus:[84]

> Flavius Philostratus to the most illustrious consul Antonius Gordianus
>
> I have recorded for you in two Books an account of certain men who pursued philosophy but ranked as sophists, and also of the sophists properly so called; partly because I know that your own family is connected with that profession, since Herodes the sophist was your ancestor; but also recalling the discussions we once had about sophists at Antioch, in the temple of Daphnaean Apollo. Their fathers' names I have not added in all cases, indeed not, but only for those who were the sons of illustrious men. For indeed I know that the sophist Critias too did not begin with the father's name, but only in the case of Homer mentioned his father, because what he was going to set forth was a marvel, namely, that Homer's father was a river. And further it would be no great piece of luck for one who desired to be really well informed, to know precisely who was a certain man's father and mother, yet fail to learn what were the man's own virtues and vices, and in what he succeeded or failed, whether by luck or judgement. This composition, best of proconsuls, will help to lighten the burdens on your mind, as Helen's mixing bowl did by its Egyptian drugs.
>
> Farewell, leader of the Muses.

This is one of only two places in the *Lives* where Roman *gentilicia* appear: the other, in the *Life* of Polemo, also involves the *nomen* Antonius, thus

---

[82] App. *praef.* 15: 'Who I am, who have written these things, many indeed know, and I have already indicated. To speak more plainly I am Appian of Alexandria, a man who has reached the highest place in my native country, and has been, in Rome, a pleader of causes before the emperors, until they deemed me worthy of being made their procurator. And if anyone has a great desire to learn more about my affairs there is a special treatise of mine on that subject' (trans. White, Loeb, adapted).

[83] Arr. *An.* 1.12.5: 'That, I declare, is why I myself have embarked on this history, not judging myself unworthy to make Alexander's deeds known to men. Whoever I may be, this I know in my favour; I need not write my name, for it is not at all unknown among men, nor my country nor my family nor any office I may have held in my own land; this I do set on paper, that country, family, and offices I find and have found from my youth in these tales. That is why I think myself not unworthy of the masters of Greek speech, since my subject Alexander was among the masters of warfare' (trans. Brunt, Loeb).

[84] *Pref.* 479–80. I am persuaded by Jones (2002) that this addressee is most probably the emperor Gordian III and the date of the *Lives*' completion ca. AD 242. For arguments that he was rather Gordian I, see among others Avotins (1978) and Flinterman (1995), 26–7.

EWEN BOWIE

linking Philostratus' dedicatee implicitly with the sophist to whom he gives his second longest *Life*, just as he is explicitly linked in the letter's long opening sentence with the subject of by far the longest *Life*, Herodes Atticus.[85]

Dedication of a more or less technical Greek literary work to a distinguished Roman had numerous precedents by the AD 240s.[86] For the writer's conscription of the dedicatee almost as a co-author we might compare how Aelianus Tacticus' letter to Trajan that precedes his *Tactica* implicates a consular Frontinus in its composition:[87]

> The Greeks' science of tactics, which began in Homer's time, Caesar Augustus Trajan, son of a god, is one of which many before me have written without having the trained mind I am credited with having in the sciences. So I conceived a wish to write of this science after persuading myself that future generations will give attention to my works in preference to the earlier ones. And since I had no understanding of the Romans' capacities and skills in this branch of study – for I must admit the truth – I was hesitant in relation to writing about and transmitting this knowledge in case it was obsolete and perhaps no longer of any practical use after the lessons that had been learned by you Romans. But since in the reign of your father, the god Nerva, I spent some days in Formiae in the house of the distinguished consular Frontinus, who has acquired renown for his military experience, and when I met him I found that he was no less enthusiastic about the knowledge that had been developed by Greeks, I began no longer to dismiss writing about tactics, thinking it would not have been taken seriously by Frontinus if it seemed to contain anything inferior to Roman organization.

The opening of Phrynichus' *Ecloge*, addressed to the *ab epistulis* Cornelianus, plays a similar game:[88]

> Phrynichus sends Cornelianus greetings
>
> While I admire your overall *paideia*, which you have cultivated outstandingly, beyond all men I have encountered, I have particularly admired the matter of your judgement concerning fine and acceptable words. So herein you asked for unacceptable words to be collected, and I have been able for now to include not all these, but only those that are in most common use

[85] *VS* 1.25.533. For the centrality of Herodes to Philostratus' choice of sophists as well as to the structure of the *Lives*, see Soria (1982); Civiletti (2002); Eshleman (2008).

[86] For an illuminating exploration of such prefaces, see König (2009); for an excellent discussion of the preface to the *Lives*, König (2014). For a wide-ranging discussion (with extensive bibliography) of the relations between Greek *pepaideumenoi* and 'Roman' patrons (especially in the city of Rome itself), see Bady (2021).

[87] Ael. *Tact. praef.*   [88] Phrynichus, *Ecloge*, pref.

Tradition and Authority in Philostratus

and confound ancient speech and attach much disgrace. You are not unaware, as in any other issue concerning *paideia*, that some people who have deserted our ancient vocabulary and taken refuge in ignorance furnish some witnesses to these words having previously been uttered by the ancients: but we focus not on mistakes but on the most acceptable of what is ancient. For if one were to put before them the choice whether they would wish their discourse to be ancient and precise way or newfangled and careless, they would agree at all costs to vote with us and be among the better party: for nobody is so wretched as to prefer the shameful to the fine. Farewell.

For the presumptuous way in which author and dedicatee are treated as comparable in *dignitas* by the formula of the standard epistolary greeting we may compare Pollux's prefatory letters addressed to Commodus, of which I offer the first (which precedes Book 1 of the *Onomasticon*) as an example:[89]

> Iulius Polydeuces sends greeting to Commodus Caesar
>
> Son of a good father, you have as inherited possessions both kingship and wisdom. And of wisdom some resides in the virtue of your mind, and some in your use of speech. Now of virtue you have a lesson in your father, and of speech, if he himself had leisure, he could have allowed you to have very little need of us. But since the safety of the inhabited world deprives him of leisure, I shall offer you at least one contribution to fine style. This book's title is *Onomasticon*, and it sets out synonyms that can be exchangeable and terms by which everything may be denoted. For the ambition has been to make a selection less with an eye to volume than to beauty. However this book has not comprised all words: for indeed it was not easy to include everything in a single book. And I shall begin where it most befits the pious to begin, with the gods: the remaining topics we shall arrange as each occurs to us. Farewell.

Conclusion

We have seen that Philostratus can exploit many techniques of securing authority for his work that are familiar from historiography ever since Herodotus and Thucydides. He can refer to eyewitnesses, to oral testimony, and to written accounts; he can quote from sophists' letters and speeches, though only rarely at any length (just as Thucydides' citation of the *Homeric Hymn to Apollo* at the end of his Book 3 is for him an unusual verbatim exploitation of a poetic text). In a way that is not open to

---

[89] Pollux, *Onomasticon*, pref.

political historians Philostratus can also display his sophistic virtuosity in voicing criticism of the subjects of his *Lives*, while he can risk silence on his own sophistic career and writings that might have authorized him to offer such critiques. In adopting this occasionally light touch, which is guided by the assumption that in the end of the day his readers *will* accept his versions of events and characters, I suggest that Philostratus expects sufficient authority to flow from his dedicatory letter's co-optation of the high-flying Antonius Gordianus in his new sophistic project.

PART V

Innovation within Tradition

CHAPTER 16

'When one assumes the ethos of writing history'
Polybius' Historiographical Neologisms

Giustina Monti

John Marincola has defined Polybius as 'a highly intrusive explicator' of his own narrative.[1] Polybius regularly interrupts the main narrative of events to explain and clarify what procedure he is following. Such intrusions always retain a historiographical flavour, and Polybius comes up with words or expressions used in a new way and with a new nuance, which I define as 'historiographical neologisms'. This chapter will show how Polybius inserts himself into a tradition (which he criticizes as well) in order to establish his own authority, and will highlight two ways: borrowing and revisiting terms from other genres – the much-discussed *apodeiktike historie* is a famous example[2] – to give them a historiographical nuance, or creating new ones.

I

Polybius opens his *Histories* with an apophasis: he will not praise the utility and importance of history, since virtually every single historian has already well stressed this concept and he does not want to revisit familiar ground.[3] Moreover, in an unusual way, he does not immediately proclaim his work's topic,[4] but he first states that his account will in any case attract

---

*Manuela Mari and Federico Santangelo deserve special thanks for bibliographical suggestions and valuable comments on earlier drafts of this chapter, which definitely contributed to its improvement. I would also like to thank Rhiannon Ash, Andrew Erskine, Michael Flower, Nino Luraghi, Chris Pelling, Kurt Raaflaub, Scott Scullion, and Tony Woodman, as well as my co-editors Scarlett Kingsley and Tim Rood for their helpful feedback. Last but not least, words are always not enough to thank John Marincola for his great support, mentorship, and advice over the years.

[1] Marincola (1997), 10.

[2] On this particular style and method, see Pédech (1964), 43–53; Petzold (1969), 3–20; and Musti (2010), 203–10.

[3] On these remarks, especially on 1.1.2, see Parmeggiani (2014), 180–8.

[4] Cf. Miltsios (2013), 7, who underlines that Polybius, by not indicating his identity and the subject of his work at the very beginning, 'deviates from the regular practice' of ancient historians.

315

316   GIUSTINA MONTI

readers due to the events' greatness and exceptionality.[5] This declaration of
intent is in one sense perfectly placed into a historiographical milieu,[6] but
at the same time Polybius is trying to differentiate his own work from
those of all his predecessors in the genre.[7]

Unlike them, Polybius states that he will be successful in pioneering a
universal history. Others' subjects had been limited because they were not
members of a country allowing them to write a proper universal history.
By contrast, Rome's conquests from 220 BC onward create what Polybius
defines as συμπλοκή (1.4.11),[8] thus the conditions for him to synopsise
and write *the* universal history in ways hitherto impossible. Polybius
assures his audience that a truthful historical work cannot but be a
universal one (1.4.7–11). Indeed, as noted by Meister, the aims of
Polybius' historiography, the identification of the truth, and the search
for causes 'can only be reached through a universal historical analysis'.[9] For
this reason Polybius begins his work with the events of the 140th
Olympiad (220/219 BC). Previously, he explains, events were 'scattered'
(σποράδας), whereas from this time history became organic (σωματοειδῆ)
and the events of Italy and Africa intertwined (συμπλέκεσθαι) with those
of Asia and Greece (1.3.3–4). Polybius expresses this concept by picking
up on the Hellenistic concept of history as a body,[10] a concept he reworks
by using, for the first time in a historiographical context, the adjective
σωματοειδής.[11]

With this assessment, Polybius is interested in drawing a clear-cut
demarcation line between different methods and approaches to history-
writing, with regard to the topic's choice: histories κατὰ μέρος ('by single
topic') versus 'universal' histories. Although historians have now the
opportunity to decide what kind of history they prefer to write, nevertheless Polybius suggests that if they write κατὰ μέρος, they (and their
audience) will have only a partial knowledge of the events (1.4.7–10):

---

[5] On this claim, a characteristic one of ancient historians, see Marincola (1997), 34–43.
[6] On the ancient historians' claim about their subject's greatness, see Marincola (1997), 34–43.
[7] On historians polemicizing with their predecessors, see, e.g., Mazzarino (1966), i.130–41; Canfora
   (1972), 73–8; Marincola (1997), 218–36; and Pani (2001), 95–102.
[8] The word alone means 'intertwining', which Polybius intends as 'intertwining of historical
   scenarios', a felicitous definition that I owe to Manuela Mari. On the concept of *symploke*, see
   Walbank (1975), 197–212.
[9] Meister (1992), 190.   [10] Walbank (1957), 43–4.
[11] Before Polybius, the adjective occurs in Plato (*Phd.* 81b–c, 81e, 83d, 86a, *Plt.* 273b, *Ti.* 31b, 36d,
   R. 532d); Aristotle ([*Pr.*] 936b); Ephorus (*FGrHist* 70 F 31b, referring to a god); and the historian
   and rhetorician Anaximenes (*Rhet.* 31.3, 36.16). On Polybius' philosophical education and his
   relationship with philosophy, see von Scala (1890), 86–255 and Scholz (2013), 285–300.

Polybius' Historiographical Neologisms 317

> In general, it seems to me that those who believe that they sufficiently comprehend the whole by means of histories κατὰ μέρος are in the same situation as people who, looking at the dismembered parts of a body that had been full of life and beautiful (ἐμψύχου καὶ καλοῦ σώματος γεγονότος διερριμμένα τὰ μέρη), deem themselves to have adequately been eyewitnesses of the creature's energy and beauty (ἱκανῶς αὐτόπται γίνεσθαι τῆς ἐνεργείας αὐτοῦ τοῦ ζώου καὶ καλλονῆς). Indeed, if someone (εἰ γάρ τις) could straightaway put the creature back together, give it its perfected form in both its shape and the beauty of life, and then show (ἐπιδεικνύοι) it again to those people, I think that all of them would quickly agree that they had been very far from the truth and similar to people who dream (τοῖς ὀνειρώττουσιν). For it is possible to get a sense of the whole from a part, but impossible to acquire knowledge and accurate understanding. Therefore, one must generally consider that history κατὰ μέρος contributes only a little to the understanding (ἐμπειρίαν) and trustworthiness of the whole.[12]

If the historiographical neologism σωματοειδής, used to describe the new Polybian way of writing history, appears to be a positive one, another historiographical neologism appearing in this passage might be defined as negative: the verb ὀνειρώσσω. Writers and consumers of traditional history are described as those who 'dream'. With this verb, Polybius establishes a simile to describe a particular historiographical approach and behaviour: historians writing histories κατὰ μέρος cannot reproduce the reality, that is to say the body-like structure of history (σωματοειδής), and are able to give only a foggy image of the events, while focussing on particulars rather than on the whole.

One might reflect upon the fact that the assessment must have a certain significance if Polybius nestles it into a crucial theoretical exposition on the importance of history at the beginning of his work, in a passage studded with philosophical terminology, which pointedly evokes two ancient philosophers as I shall show below. Indeed, the opposition of dream and sleep to truth readily recalls a memorable fragment of Heraclitus,[13] whose work Polybius knew in some form at least:[14] those who are awake live in a common universe (world order),[15] whereas those who sleep turn

---

[12] All translations are mine.

[13] Herodotus had already been inspired by Heraclitus, as has been recently shown by Darbo-Peschanski (2013), 87–91.

[14] This is demonstrated by his reference to the philosopher in two points of the *Histories* we now have (4.40.3; 12.27.1), where the historian is reflecting upon historical methodologies and on what might be the most useful to historical truth.

[15] The term κόσμος embraces a series of meanings that are not simple to translate with a unique term, but that seem to carry the idea of order.

themselves away from it (ἀποστρέφεσθαι) to their private sphere.[16] Furthermore, from Heraclitus' standpoint, people who live in their own worlds (i.e. those who are asleep) are far from truth, since their *logos* is ἄπιστος (untrustworthy), coming solely from their αἴσθησις (perception), at least according to Sextus Empiricus' tradition.[17] Besides, 'learning many things does not teach one how to possess intellect' (πολυμαθίη νόον ἔχειν οὐ διδάσκει):[18] in fact, 'Pythagoras extensively practised scientific research (ἱστορίην ἤσκησεν), more than all the other men, and, having made a selection of such writings, built his own wisdom, which was much learning (πολυμαθίην) and fraudulent artifice (κακοτεχνίην).'[19]

Polybius seems to echo even these last two statements when he observes that it is altogether unlikely that someone could apprehend (κατανενοηκέναι) the shape of the entire inhabited world, its whole setting and arrangement having visited each of the most notable cities one by one or having gazed at them drawn separately (1.4.6): historians who write works κατὰ μέρος are like such people who have knowledge of many things disjointedly, but they do not 'reach the intellect', to speak in philosophical terms.[20] All the more so as he explains his assessment with another simile, since his point is not only that separate knowledge of each single part does not allow historians to know the events in their complex entirety but also that this kind of learning is deceitful because it provides only perception: indeed, they are in a predicament equal to those people who, looking at the scattered parts of a body that was once beautiful and full of life, deem themselves to be adequate eyewitnesses (αὐτόπται) of its vitality and beauty (1.4.7).

However, the Polybian passage differs from Heraclitus in an important respect. The historian adds a further detail: Polybius' 'people who dream' can become aware of their status, whereas Heraclitus' 'asleep and dreamers' do not see any change or awareness in their miserable condition. Thus, the

---

[16] DK 12 B 89.

[17] DK 12 A 16, where Sextus Empiricus summarizes and explains Heraclitus. On the role of dream and sleep in Heraclitus, see Brillante (1986), 10–25.

[18] DK 12 B 40. Marincola (1997), 65, understands νόον ἔχειν as 'wisdom'; Graham (2008), 176–7, translates the phrase as 'understanding' and comments that 'people are like sleepwalkers who hear and see but do not comprehend. They seem to have experiences without becoming experienced.'

[19] DK 12 B 129. My own translation is adapted from Marcovich (1967) and Reale (2006). The fragment's authenticity was brought into question by Diels (1922), i.104, and the fragment was inserted among the spurious ones. More recently, the tendency is to consider it authentic: see, e.g., Marcovich (1967), 68–70, and Diano-Serra (1980), 176–7, with a discussion on previous literature.

[20] He will come back to this point later in his work: in 3.32, he draws attention to the point of view of readers, who cannot have complete and exact knowledge of the events if they try to understand them by reading many books on different topics, instead of just one book of universal history.

Polybius' Historiographical Neologisms

added value in Polybius' reflections is this realization, which occurs with the help of someone else who shows (εἰ γάρ τις . . . ἐπιδεικνύοι) them that looking separately at body parts is not the same as looking at an entire body full of living energy. Such a gain in consciousness is not a completely new concept, but above all it is found in a classic text: Plato's allegory of the cave (*R.* 514a–517a), to which Polybius' passage is clearly indebted. The men in the cave have the sole opportunity to see the shadows of real things projected onto the wall they face – as they are chained and unable to move –, and they think that such shadows represent reality; but, then, one of them succeeds in freeing himself, he leaves the dark cave and goes outside in the sunlight. Once there, he realizes that what he was watching before were not true objects, but mere images of them, which did not reflect the essence of the real ones. In the cave, where there is no light, truth is concealed, it is in darkness, whereas once the man liberates himself from misleading opinions by going outside in the light, truth reveals itself. As in Plato,[21] sight in Polybius is not unproblematically trustworthy. Indeed, people who look at dead limbs separately are still eyewitnesses, αὐτόπται, but not at all adequate, ἱκανῶς (1.4.7).

The association with Plato is even strengthened by the verb ὀνειρώσσω. This verb is completely absent until the middle of the fifth century, appearing for the first time in Hippocrates, and it was used not very often before Polybius.[22] Despite the general scarcity of the term in earlier writers, the author who employed it most frequently is Plato (eight times),[23] followed by Aristotle (four times)[24] and Polybius (four times).[25] Therefore, this verb, together with the concept it carries and the Polybian discussion, might be regarded as a joining link, since the passage is also characterized by a strong Aristotelian presence. The terms ἐνέργεια, ζῷον, and ἐμπειρία immediately bring to mind Aristotle,[26] and the fact that, in a passage where Polybius is reflecting on the genre of history, philosophical terms and allusions to Aristotle are embedded is thought-provoking, especially in relation to the importance of history-writing. All the more so, as Aristotle had reflected upon history and poetry, relegating the former to a minor role (*Poet.* 1451b): according to him, poetry is more

---

[21] See Tanner (1970), 88–90, and Sze (1977), 130.

[22] Indeed, there are only nineteen occurrences (out of the total of 259) before Polybius.

[23] *Cra.* 439c; *Tht.* 158b, *bis*; *R.* 476c, *bis*, 533b; *Leg.* 656b, 800a.

[24] *Div.Somn.* 463b; *GC* 335b; [*Pr.*] 957a; *Somn.Vig.* 453b.

[25] 1.4.8; 5.108.5; 12.12b.1; 18.15.13.

[26] See Walbank (1957), 45, for ζῷον; for ἐνέργεια, see Roveri (1964), 75–6. On Aristotle and ἐμπειρία, see Butler (2003), 329–50 and LaBarge (2006), 23–44.

320 GIUSTINA MONTI

philosophical and more serious than history, since it deals with general or universal truths, τὰ καθόλου, whereas history considers particulars or truths valid in their own right, τὰ καθ'ἕκαστον. In discussing this dichotomy, terms that are always antonyms in Aristotle's philosophical debate are applied, respectively, to history and poetry: in fact, τὸ καθόλου is generally opposed to τὸ καθ'ἕκαστον or, more interestingly for this analysis, to τὸ κατὰ μέρος.[27] Polybius flips the terminology over, assigning the positive one to history, although to a particular kind of history (the universal one), whereas the negative one, τὸ κατὰ μέρος, describes histories 'by single topic', which, in Polybius' mind, are not useful and give a distorted and incomplete view of the whole. Polybius seems to be trying to reverse Aristotle's negative assessment:[28] only a certain kind of history is inferior to tragedy, the one κατὰ μέρος, not universal history, which is the one and only possible way of writing a true historical account.

Consequently, it appears clear that Polybius is trying to establish his authority through the advertisement of his own universal history. To strengthen this self-positioning, he comes up with two opposite historiographical neologisms, the positive one to describe his own history, and the negative one to describe his competitors' kind of history. In effect, by stating that universal history is the ideal method of writing history, Polybius is also underlining that his history supersedes those of his predecessors, since he is the first to write it. Indeed, not only does he list previous topics and try to demonstrate that his subject of investigation (θεώρημα) is 'exceptionally great', παράδοξον καὶ μέγα (1.2.1),[29] but he also seems to allude to both Herodotus and Thucydides when, shortly before the similes of the world and of the body, he uses the terms τὸ θαυμάσιον and ὠφελιμώτατον, and the expressions εἰργάσατ'ἔργον and ἠγωνίσατ'ἀγώνισμα (1.4.1–5).[30]

---

[27] See LSJ, s.v. καθόλου.

[28] Cf. Zucchelli (1985), 303, who argues that Polybius underlines the universal character of his history to give an answer to Aristotle's bad judgement on history. See also Díaz-Tejera (1978), 44–6, who shows the textual closeness between Aristotle and Polybius: when the historian affirms that τὸ κατὰ μέρος does not give ἐπιστήμη, he is, in Díaz-Tejera's opinion, referring to Aristotle, *Metaph.* 1086b, ἄνευ μὲν γὰρ τοῦ καθόλου οὐκ ἔστιν ἐπιστήμην λαβεῖν.

[29] For a discussion on the meaning of παράδοξον θεώρημα, see Maier (2018), 55–74, who sees the expression 'as a perfect characterization of how Polybius perceived history' (72), given that it is an attempt to explain the events which at the same time cannot be systemized.

[30] Such terms are important since they recall both Herodotus' preface and Thucydides' methodological passage (1.22–3): more specifically, the declared subject of Herodotus' work are the great and marvellous deeds, ἔργα μεγάλα τε καὶ θωμαστά, of both the Greeks and the barbarians (1.p.); Thucydides uses the term ἔργα again, and highlights history's utility (ὠφέλιμα), since it is a possession for evermore and not a contest (ἀγώνισμα) composed for a momentary

Polybius' Historiographical Neologisms

Thus, Polybius is playing on two parallel levels, philosophy and history. As his history is universal, since it gathers and unifies different parts, in the same way his philosophy of history is universal and incorporates different philosophical voices to develop his own philosophy and to give a synoptic view of his achievement.[31]

II

The preceding section examined how the proemial passage allowed readers to understand that Polybius plays with two kinds of historiographical neologisms, positive and negative, depending on what he is writing about, whether on his own view of historiography or on others' ways of writing history. In the second part of this chapter, I shall analyse additional positive neologisms, namely those which Polybius uses to describe the best way of writing history.

The first, which will also appear as a sort of supporting pillar of Polybius' philosophy of history, is employed soon at the beginning of Book 1, in a passage (the first of many) where he criticizes two of his predecessors, Philinus of Akragas and Fabius Pictor. Polybius finds fault with them because they did not relate the truth as they should have, affected as they were by unintentional patriotic bias deriving from them acting as 'lovers' of their fatherlands (1.14.2). He reflects (1.14.5-6):

> But when someone assumes the disposition which is peculiar to history, he needs to forget everything of the sort, and often, if their actions demand this, speak well of his enemies and honour them with the highest praises, while confuting and even harshly reproaching his closest friends, whenever the errors of their conduct show this. Just as a living being is rendered useless in its entirety if one takes away the eyes from it, in the same way, if truth is removed from history, what is left of it becomes a useless tale.

The first phrase immediately catches the reader's attention. The expression ὅταν δὲ τὸ τῆς ἱστορίας ἦθος ἀναλαμβάνῃ τις appears to be a Polybian invention, since – to my knowledge – it does not occur in the Greek texts

---

performance (1.22.4). On the Polybian allusions to the Thucydidean κτῆμα ἐς αἰεί, see Nicolai (1995), 17–26. More recently, Rawlings (2016), 113–15, has supported his interpretation of Thuc. 1.22.4 looking at three Polybian passages (3.31.11–12; 9.1–2; and 38.4.5–8) and has hypothesized that Polybius was indeed interpreting Thucydides' assessments. On the relationship between Thucydides and Polybius, see also Luschnat (1970), 1294–6; Lehmann (1974), 165–70; and Rood (2012b), 50–67. See especially Thornton (2018), 99–109.

[31] This approach might also have been the result of his philosophical education, which looked at varied and diverse philosophers, as showed by von Scala (1890), 86–255.

we have at our disposal.[32] I have translated it as 'when someone assumes the disposition which is peculiar to history', and it can be literally translated as 'when one assumes the *ethos* of history'.[33] This particular procedure might be regarded and explained as being similar to the 'Stanislavski method' used by professional actors: just as they have to enter the character's soul and world by putting themselves in the place of the character, so does the historian need to enter the character proper to history.

Moreover, Polybius' remarks on the importance of truth in 1.14.6 are carefully set in a chiastic construction, so that the living being (ζώου) corresponds to history (ἱστορίας), and truth (τῆς ἀληθείας) is connected to the eyes (τῶν ὄψεων) of the living being, which leads the reader to recall the proemial passage where true history is actually compared to a lively being (1.4.7).

Thus, this particular 'phrasal neologism' is employed to define the way in which the Polybian historian works. While Philinus and Fabius were acting as 'lovers' by favouring their fatherlands in their accounts, Polybius does not act as a 'lover' blinded by love. Before Polybius, Plato and Theocritus had expressed a similar concept, the former explicitly speaking of the blindness peculiar to the lover,[34] and the latter linking Love/Eros to blindness, when in *Idyll* 10.19–20 he states that Plutus is not the only one to be blind, but the thoughtless Eros is also blind (τυφλὸς δ'οὐκ αὐτὸς ὁ Πλοῦτος, / ἀλλὰ καὶ ὡφρόντιστος Ἔρως).[35] Moreover, Polybius himself builds a connection between Philinus and Fabius' love and their blindness, when he concludes that history without truth is similar to a living being without eyes.

From this passage it is also apparent that the work of the historian has a moral weight, a concept which Polybius will better explain later (38.4). The methodological excursus is inserted almost at the end of Polybius' work, in the proemial passage of Book 38, a fragmentary book containing the events of 147/146 BC, the Achaean War (on which Polybius states that no disaster can stand comparison with what the Greeks suffered during

---

[32] The expression 'to assume the *ethos* of history' appears only in Plb. 1.14.5, and the phrase formed by the noun ἦθος and the adjective ἱστορικός appears only in Plb. 38.4.1.

[33] Schweighäuser (1822), *s.v.* ἦθος, translates it as '*historici personam suscipere*', whereas Mauersberger (2006), *s.v.* ἦθος, explains the phrase 'd.h. sich speziell als Historiker betätigen' (i.e. specialize as a historian), which – I believe – does not quite explain the sense Polybius is giving to this particular expression.

[34] *Leg.* 731e.

[35] As underlined by Gow (1952), ii.198, the representation of the god Eros as blind is 'highly unusual in antiquity'. See also Gilbert (1970), 304–5.

Polybius' Historiographical Neologisms 323

this war) and the Third Punic War with the fall of Carthage (38.4.1–2 and 38.4.8):

> Regarding this, it will be needless to marvel in case I might appear to offer a narrative on such events too declamatory and too zealous, and to transgress the character proper to historical narrative (ἐὰν παρεκβαίνοντες τὸ τῆς ἱστορικῆς διηγήσεως ἦθος ἐπιδεικτικωτέραν καὶ φιλοτιμοτέραν φαινώμεθα ποιούμενοι περὶ αὐτῶν τὴν ἀπαγγελίαν). And yet, some will perhaps rebuke me for writing in a quarrelsome tone, since it was my duty, more than anyone else, to conceal the faults of the Greeks.... on the contrary, the exposition through historical records (τὴν ... διὰ τῶν ὑπομνημάτων παράδοσιν) about the events meant for posterity should be left free from every kind of falsehood (ἀμιγῆ παντὸς ψεύδους ἀπολείπεσθαι), so that the readers should not receive a momentary pleasure in their ears, but rather be corrected in their minds so as not to fail in the same situations several times.

Polybius embellishes his statements with a connection of two other historiographical neologisms, παράδοσιν and ἀμιγῆ (38.4.8), with which he expresses the concept that a historical account must not be 'contaminated' by lies. I define them as 'historiographical neologisms' because both appear to have a particular meaning in a historiographical context that Polybius seems to invent. Indeed, the term παράδοσις rarely occurs before him and it does not have a historiographical nuance,[36] apart from Plato (*Leg.* 803a) and Aristotle (*SE* 184b) where it means 'transmission', thus a meaning that might be associated with a historical report. The adjective ἀμιγής occurs in Polybius only in this passage; before him, all occurrences appear in philosophers with the meaning of 'unmixed, pure'.[37] Thus, it might be the case that Polybius, drawing once again from the philosophical language, deliberately gives a new connotation to already existing, but very distinctive words in order to formulate new historiographical concepts and explain his own philosophy of history.

The importance of this passage is amplified by its position both in what appears to be the introductory part of a book and almost at the end of the

---

[36] Thuc. 1.9.4 and 3.53.1; Isocr. 17.16; Pl. *Leg.* 915d; Philistus *FGrHist* 556 F 53; Dem. *In Timocratem* 80; Dicaearchus F 89 Wehrli; Arist. *Pol.* 1309a, FF 119 and 437 Rose; Heraclides Ponticus F 91 Wehrli; Thphr. F 97.4 Wimmer; Epicurus F 20.2 Arrighetti; Andriscus *FGrHist* 500 F 3; Erasistratus FF 152 and 279 Garofalo; Chrysippus FF 42 and 173 von Arnim; Critodemus 5.2.113 and 8.3.102; Phylarchus *FGrHist* 81 F 56; Eratosth. [*Cat.*] 1.22.

[37] Pl. *Pol.* 265e and *Mx.* 245d; Arist. *de An.* 405a, 429a, 430a, *EN* 1173a, *HA* 638a, [*Mag. mor.*] 2.7.3, *Metaph.* 989b, *Ph.* 256b, [*Pr.*] 907a and 929a, *Spir.* 483b, *Top.* 119a; Xenocrates F 225 (Parente); Speusippus F 81a Tarán; Thphr. *Sens.* 67, 73, 76, *Igne* F 50, *CP* 6.8.5, 6.17.1; Chrysippus F 1103 von Arnim.

324   GIUSTINA MONTI

work as a whole, where concluding historiographical remarks might be added. In order to perform this task at the highest possible level, Polybius points to what seems to emerge as one of the most important historiographical features: the historian should be capable and have a wide range of competences, with most of them being 'practical' (such as knowledge of military techniques or geography).[38] Besides, his competence seems to spring from something that is less tangible, the historian's *ethos*, a concept Polybius alludes to when, at the very beginning of the passage, he mentions τὸ τῆς ἱστορικῆς διηγήσεως ἦθος, which he might apparently violate with his tone. Consequently, the message the reader takes away is that a historian is competent when he assumes the mental and moral disposition that is consonant with history. Unlike the previous passage, where he was criticizing Philinus and Fabius, here – at the end of his work – Polybius is speaking about himself, explaining that he had indeed followed his own recommendation because he is reprimanding his fellow citizens and denouncing their mistakes: thus, he presents himself as completely adopting the *ethos* of history. Therefore, he differs from Philinus and Fabius, who *wronged* the historical narrative because they were 'in love' with their fatherlands (1.14.2).

Hence, the work of the historian also has an ethical value. To be faithful to this moral value of history writing, Polybius' main concern consists in ascertaining the truth, and the search for truth and the criticism of lies, therefore, are not just part of the historical technique, but are mainly seen in relation to ethics.[39] Margherita Isnardi rightly affirms that *techne* and *ethos* are at the base of the Polybian historiographical procedure, where 'it is the *ethos* that creates the *techne*; the rule springs from the action'.[40] In the light of this, one could deduce that a proper history necessarily and naturally flows from the synthesis between *ethos* and *techne*, of which *ethos* constitutes the essential value.

The topic of 'moral history' in Polybius has been much discussed,[41] especially in relation to the fact that Polybius seems to have written his historical work to teach moral lessons to posterity.[42] However, from my

---

[38] See, e.g., the remarks at 12.3.2–6; 16.14.1–8; 16.17.9–18.3.   [39] Cf. Isnardi (1953), 104.
[40] Isnardi (1953), 106–7: 'E' cioè l'*éthos*, in definitiva, a creare la *téchne*; la regola scaturisce dall'azione.'
[41] See, e.g., Eckstein (1995).
[42] Eckstein (1995), 28 and 56, shows Polybius' celebration of what the scholar calls 'Aristocratic Ethos', in relation to both risky events and circumstances where honour and/or wealth were involved; Hau (2016), 23, defines Polybius as being 'obviously, explicitly and unashamedly a moral-didactic historian', in a chapter mainly concerned with Polybius' 'moral-didactic techniques' (40–2) and 'moral lessons' (42–71); B. J. Gibson (2018), 89–99, underlines that the

Polybius' Historiographical Neologisms

critical standpoint, the ethical worth of the historian's work – which Polybius appears to assign to the act of writing history – has not been fully grasped. Indeed, in light of the remarks in 1.14.5 and 38.4, it seems clear that also the process of writing is itself a matter of ethics, and this appears to be a completely new concept in ancient historiography. From Polybius' point of view, it is the historian's work in itself which has moral worth, apart from providing readers with examples of moral history. A corollary to this reflection is that, in this case, the historian and the politician seem to be placed at the same level: if historiography is an ethical practice, consequently the historical account will become ethical as well, and it will teach morally useful lessons. Moreover, since Polybius was indeed both a politician and a historian,[43] he was the best apt to write history, in his opinion, of course.

The upshot of these reflections is that one is unable to give a truthful account if they are trying to help or favour their friends. According to the Polybian axiom, history should be devoid of every kind of lie (38.4.8). The construction of the sentence τὴν (δ') ὑπὲρ τῶν γεγονότων τοῖς ἐπιγινομένοις διὰ τῶν ὑπομνημάτων παράδοσιν ἀμιγῆ παντὸς ψεύδους ἀπολείπεσθαι, which expresses this important concept and where the neologisms appear, is studied and polished. It starts with τὴν παράδοσιν, the object – or the subject depending on whether ἀπολείπεσθαι is interpreted as middle with the meaning of 'to leave to posterity' or passive – which encapsulates three expressions in attributive position defining the topic of the exposition (ὑπὲρ τῶν γεγονότων), the audience (τοῖς ἐπιγινομένοις), and the medium by which the tradition is handed down (διὰ τῶν ὑπομνημάτων); the verb is at the end (ἀπολείπεσθαι); and in the middle of the sentence there are the key words (ἀμιγῆ and the expression παντὸς ψεύδους). In addition, the statement, as if it were not historiographical enough, becomes even more interesting as it is followed by the re-elaboration of the Thucydidean concept of history being an everlasting teaching rather than a temporary pleasure. Furthermore, Polybius had used the verb ἀπολείπεσθαι in a negative sense accompanied by the word ἀλήθεια in the critique against histories κατὰ μέρος that were far from truth, as we have seen,[44] whereas he is here using it in a positive sense to describe how proper history should be far from

---

epideictic character of Polybius' work contains an ethical connotation as well, given that Polybius appears to be 'a bestower of praise or blame' (75).

[43] On the political dimension of the *Histories*, see Thornton (2013), 213–29.   [44] 1.4.8.

326 GIUSTINA MONTI

every lie. Hence, the reuse of the verb together with ψεῦδος renders the sentence suitable to describe how a good historical work should be.

III

The last set of neologisms describes negative historiographical praxis, in other words 'how *not* to write history'. Polybius often explains his methodology through the criticism of his predecessors. Polemic among historians is in fact one of the distinctive features of Greek historiography,[45] and the author who uses a systematic criticism of his predecessors more than anyone else is Polybius.[46] This procedure, which is a way of validating his own work and method, is not new in Greek historiography.[47]

This final section of the chapter will look at those neologisms with which Polybius comes up to criticize his predecessors and to impose even more his own authority as historian. It will underline that some historians' *wrong* behaviour and approach to the writing of history is a direct or indirect consequence of whether they assumed the *ethos* proper to history.

According to Polybius, there are historians who are not active men, which constitutes a sin against history and leads such historians to commit mistakes.[48] After having underlined and discussed (12.26d.2) that in Timaeus' work the political aspect of history is set aside with respect to the accounts of colonizations, foundations, and kinship ties, Polybius states (12.27a.1–4):

> After all, the political aspect of his history is made up of every sort of mistake, most of which we have gone through; we shall now expound the cause of the failing, a cause which seems unlikely to most people, but which will be found to be the truest of the accusations against Timaeus. He gives the impression of having been provided with the empirical capacity for the details and the ability in inquiry, and in short to have approached the writing of history with diligence, but in some matters no historian of

---

[45] See, e.g., Fairweather (1974), 247–9; Owen (1983), 15; Marincola (1997), 225–36; and Pani (2001), 95–102. More generally, on polemic in Hellenistic literature, see Isnardi (1953), 103–6; Brown (1958), 91; and Pearson (1987), 38.

[46] Cf. Pani (2001), 97, who defines Polybius' criticism as 'the most prolonged and systematic critique which has been preserved by the tradition'.

[47] Marincola (1997), 219, underlines the importance for ancient historians of defining themselves 'by contrast with a perceived or actual predecessor'. On this topic, see also Canfora (1971), 653–70. Pani (2001), 95–6, adds that apart from the obvious desire to make room for one's own historiographical work, there are genuine reasons, even though criticism is often dictated by a different political position or by rivalry and personal ill-will.

[48] In 3.59.4 Polybius praises the 'active men'.

Polybius' Historiographical Neologisms

renown appears to have been more inexperienced and more unfriendly-to-effort (ἀφιλοπονώτερος) [than Timaeus].

If Dante Alighieri had followed Polybius' line of reasoning, one would find poor Timaeus among the *ignavi* (uncommitted) in the vestibule of Hell.[49] In this case, the sin of Timaeus regards his research techniques, as he performed not all the procedures but only the easiest and least painful ones: indeed, he took his information only from reading books without any other kind of inquiry, such as autopsy or interviews of witnesses.[50]

These remarks come almost at the end of what remains of Book 12, a book mainly devoted, to judge from what is extant, to the critiques of the historian of Tauromenium. Here, Polybius' aim (so does he declare) is to find and explain the αἰτία of Timaeus' mistakes, which he has already commented on in the preceding passages. In this chapter and in the following ones, Polybius seems to draw a conclusion regarding the discussion of Timaeus' faults.

He charges Timaeus with being lazy, the opposite of the 'active men' he praised elsewhere (3.59.4), and he strengthens his statement by coming up with another of his neologisms, the adjective ἀφιλόπονος constructed by prefixing the privative alpha to φιλόπονος, an adjective which in poetry appears for the first time in Sophocles' *Ajax* 879,[51] where the chorus uses the adjective to modify the seamen busy in their sleepless hunts.[52] In prose, it is interesting that it is the adjective used to connote the hard-working animal par excellence, the ant (as opposed to the cicada) in the famous fable by Aesop.[53]

The neologism is the cherry on top of this discussion, where *Leitmotive* dear to Polybius recur, namely the theme of the historian's expertise, evoked by the terms ἐμπειρικήν and ἀπειρότερος, and the importance of inquiry.[54] Moreover, he highlights the issue of the historian's effort and the labour of writing history, a theme especially trendy among Hellenistic historians,[55] and in relation to which Polybius probably occupies a special

---

[49] Dante Alighieri, *Comedia, Inferno* III.22–69.   [50] 12.27.2–6.
[51] τίς ἂν φιλοπόνων / ἁλιαδᾶν ἔχων ἄϋπνους ἄγρας.
[52] Also, the connection in this Sophoclean passage between the adjective for being 'friendly-to-effort' and the idea of being sleepless (or, better, awake) is interesting with regard to the Polybian neologism, since the 'unfriendly-to-effort' Timaeus might reasonably be associated with someone who is not awake, thus with the asleep and dreaming people criticized in Polybius' preamble (1.4.8).
[53] Aesop. *Prov.* 2 (*The Ant and the Cicada*).   [54] 12.27a.3–4. See also 3.58; 4.39.11; 4.40.
[55] Indeed, according to Marincola (1997), 148, Herodotus 3.115.2 contains only an allusion and Thucydides 1.22.3 mentions it only in relation to the difficulty of providing the readers with an account deriving from different versions of the same story.

328   GIUSTINA MONTI

and preeminent place,[56] since it seems that before him only Theopompus (*FGrHist* 115 T 20a) and Timaeus (*FGrHist* 566 F 7) had mentioned it.[57] Thus, with this neologism Polybius perfectly inserts himself into a tradition, but at the same time he tries to overcome it to establish, once again, his own authority as historian and historical theorist.

Indeed, Polybius seems to go beyond a simple historiographical point, as the discussion here appears to be at a higher level, at a level I would define as 'historiography of historiography'. In fact, here he is not discussing how to relate a certain fact, but he opens up a discussion on the methodology of his colleague. Such reflections are more elevated thoughts than mere historiographical remarks. The first level of historiographical discussion might involve a reflection on how to find causes and historical facts, and on the historical methodology to find such causes and facts.[58] The second level might be to criticize previous historians for their mistakes and to correct them. Thus, by discussing the causes out of which a certain historian committed methodological errors, he moves the work to a completely different and higher level. In the light of this, one might gather that, according to Polybius, not only does the proper historian and historiographer discuss the causes of the facts, but he also enquires into the causes of methodology.

Another interesting element here is the fact that Polybius does search for the reason why Timaeus has committed such mistakes. Other historians do not look into the cause of their predecessors' errors when they criticize them: when Hecataeus, for example, declares that the accounts of the Greeks are numerous and ridiculous,[59] in the end he does not investigate the reason why the Greeks had written in such a way (so far as we know from the very fragmentary remains), whereas Polybius *troubles himself* to look into this and to find an explanation for the mistakes and the behaviour of his predecessor.

This procedure appears as a sort of reinforcement of the historiographical method, of the historian's role, and of what I have previously defined as the historian's ethic. Inasmuch as Polybius has assumed the *ethos* of writing history, inevitably he has a sort of professional distortion: he *must* search for causes in every aspect, regarding not only historical facts, but also – and especially – the causes of a flawed methodology. Hence, the criticism of an erroneous method does not suffice, since the Polybian

---

[56] Marincola (1997), 151, underlines that this idea was 'first clearly expressed by Polybius'.
[57] On the historian's efforts, see Marincola (1997), 148–58 and Pani (2001), 43–4.
[58] See, e.g., 3.6.4 and 22.18.11.   [59] *FGrHist* 1 F 1a.

Polybius' Historiographical Neologisms

329

historian has also the task of offering solutions and corrections, just as Polybius does, for example, in geographical discussions (3.57–8). Moreover, this quest for causes seems to be twofold: if fixing errors is only possible once the historian has established that there is actually a reason behind them, finding the cause is also helpful in demonstrating that the predecessor did indeed commit mistakes, and that this is not just a result of the harsh critiques of Polybius.

Thus, if one assumes the *ethos* of writing history, they should be ready to commit themselves to effort and sacrifices. Writing history is toilsome, and if one does not assume the proper *ethos*, they will not be ready to make sacrifices for history. But, apart from laziness, there are also other corollaries to not assuming the *ethos* proper to history. According to Polybius, such historians will run into several mistakes, because they will not write history as it should be done: they will pass over in silence important details, and they will chiefly be preoccupied with their style.

The concept of passing over in silence is highlighted by the neologism παρασιωπάω, a verb especially created to express a peculiar thought[60] and which can highlight both positive and negative concepts, depending on whether the historian has assumed the proper *ethos*. The first occurrence of this verb is found in Book 2 of the *Histories* (2.13.7), and Polybius uses it a total of eighteen times (apart from F 108, which is attributed to Polybius by modern scholars), of which nine have a historiographical nuance.[61]

---

[60] The verb constructed with παρά seems to give the idea of the relationship with the opinion or judgement of someone, if one thinks about παρά together with a proper personal name with the meaning of 'according to', for example παρ' Ἐφόρῳ (Plb. 9.2.4), or about the expression παρ' ἐμοί meaning 'in my judgement, in my view' (Hdt. 1.32.9). Moreover, παρά might also have the nuance of 'on the basis of, in consequence of'. See GE, *s.v.* Thus, the meaning of the Polybian neologism might be 'to pass over in silence on the basis of my judgement', also given the fact that, in 6.11.8, it is modified by the expression κατὰ κρίσιν.

[61] In 6.11.5 and 6.11.8, the cornerstone of the argument is not the act of omitting in itself, but omissions linked to the choice of the historian (6.11.8: παρασιωπᾶται κατὰ κρίσιν) – versus omissions due to ignorance (6.11.5: κατ'ἄγνοιαν παρασιωπᾶν) – namely the choice of when omitting is appropriate and when it is not; in 10.21.3, the verb seems to have a historiographical meaning, since Polybius underlines the importance of not 'passing over in silence' the education and ambitions of the protagonists of the events they are recounting; in 10.27.7, it carries a historiographical nuance, since Polybius reflects on the fact that both the description and the silence over the royal palace in Media might be embarrassing for the historian, given the exceptionality of the construction that might drive some to an exaggerated account; in 12.10.9, Polybius is arguing that Timaeus would have not passed over in silence a written document or a commemorative stele, should he find it; in 12.25b.4, the meaning of the verb is again related to history writing, as Polybius reflects on the fact that speeches and their causes should not be passed over in silence; in 16.14.4, Polybius underlines that it is necessary not to pass over in silence some events, because he needs to correct Zeno and Antisthenes; in 20.11.1, his remark is again historiographical, because he affirms that it is worthy not to pass over in silence what happened to Nicander, ambassador of the Aetolians; in 29.5.2, the historiographical meaning is given by the

330 GIUSTINA MONTI

Thus, what is at stake with this neologism is the assumption that the Polybian historian is the able historian who has the expertise to choose and to know when and what should be omitted, and this choice (the term used in 6.11.8 is κρίσις) might indicate not only the author's choice, but also their capacity for interpretation and/or judgement, their ability to distinguish useful omissions from damaging omissions, to estimate their value. Polybius will come back to the idea that ignorance might sometimes spring from the wrong approach to history in his criticism against Zeno, where he comments on his geographical and military ignorance (16.17.9 and 16.18.2–3):

> Then, for what might one reasonably blame Zeno? Because he cared more neither about inquiry of the events nor about the treatment of the subject, but rather about stylistic elaboration (περὶ τὴν τῆς λέξεως κατασκευὴν), and he shows that he often takes pride in this, exactly as many other renowned historians do?... Indeed, the aforementioned writer, in narrating the siege of Gaza and the battle between Antiochus and Scopas which took place at Panion in Coele-Syria, has clearly cared about stylistic elaboration (περὶ μὲν τὴν τῆς λέξεως κατασκευὴν) to such an extent that he has left no possibility of surpassing his sensationalism (τερατείας) even to those who create display compositions aimed at the astonishment (ἔκπληξιν) of the multitude, whereas he was so little concerned about the real events that the negligence and the inexperience (τὴν ἀπειρίαν) of this historian are likewise unsurpassable.

The phrasal neologism Polybius invents this time is the expression περὶ τὴν τῆς λέξεως κατασκευήν, which has been translated as 'stylistic elaboration'. Indeed, while the word κατασκευή alone is widely used in Polybius and in other previous and subsequent writers, it is Polybius who uses it for the first time in connection with λέξις, and in this passage only (16.17.9 and 16.18.2).[62]

Zeno's *apeiria* appears to be the direct consequence of the kind of *ethos* he has chosen for his history: paying attention to stylistic refinement is inversely proportional to historical research; the more one cares about style the more one will be negligent in giving a truthful account of events. Indeed, one of the key concepts here seems to be that conscientious

---

Polybian reflection on whether he should have passed over in silence the plot designed by Perseus and Eumenes II or written about it to explain the events. The remaining nine are: 2.13.7; 3.15.11; 3.21.1; 9.35.7; 22.4.17; 22.10.11; 24.10.7; 30.3.4; 30.23.4.

[62] After Polybius, Dionysius of Halicarnassus uses a similar expression in the meaning of 'artistry of the style' (*Isoc.* 13; *Th.* 27), 'adornments of the style' (*Dem.* 14; 24; 44). Moreover, the verb κατασκευάζω is used, for example, by Dion. Hal. *Is.* 7.2 (κατεσκεύασται τὸ δοκοῦν εἶναι ἀφελές) and Str. 1.2.6 (λόγος κατεσκευασμένος) with the meaning of 'to elaborate'. See LSJ and GE, *s.v.*

Polybius' Historiographical Neologisms

historians are characterized by moderation (16.17.10), whereas bad historians do not know how to use writing devices and fall into excess and exaggeration.

Thus, there seems to be a *fil rouge* connecting the following concepts in sequence: some historians have made mistakes and shown their inexperience because they made use of τερατεία and ἔκπληξις, and they employed such devices because they had attached importance only to style, a preoccupation derived from the *ethos* they had assumed, the *ethos* of a historian writing κατὰ μέρος. This chain of consequences is also valid the other way around: the assumption of the *ethos* of a historian writing κατὰ μέρος, after the same metaphorical route, will cause one to end up being ignorant and writing falsehoods.

Last, a flawed approach involves serious consequences: indeed, such historians are blind, they do not have the overall view of the events given by universal history, and they will be compelled to act in ways that will be the opposite of the correct historiographical approach.

The first concept is underlined by the neologism ἀσκεψία used by Polybius in his criticism against Phylarchus (2.63.5). This is a *hapax legomenon* especially created to criticize a previous historian and a previous tradition on grounds that bring together the concepts of sight and competence:[63] Phylarchus is blind (2.61.12). Moreover, he is ignorant and incompetent; indeed, Polybius also accuses him of ἀπειρία and ἄγνοια.[64]

The second and final concept is expressed by a series of neologisms in Book 7, and by two neologisms in Book 12, which belong to the same line of reasoning in relation to the considered choice of the historian, whether of topics or speeches. In 7.7.6–7, Polybius is criticizing historians who do not write universal history, and one of his points regards the wrong choice of the protagonists of their accounts:

> But it seems to me that those who write accounts in a κατὰ μέρος fashion, whenever they undertake the account of a circumscribed and narrow subject (ὑποθέσεις εὐπεριλήπτους ὑποστήσωνται καὶ στενάς), being badly off for facts (πτωχεύοντες πραγμάτων), are compelled to render small things great and to sprinkle them with many accounts not worthy of

---

[63] In 2.56.2, Polybius uses the adjective ἄσκεπτος, which occurs only twice in his work (2.56.2 and 30.21.9). Moreover, it does not occur very often in Greek texts. Before Polybius, there are only ten occurrences, but the term is never employed in a historiographical context: Ar. *Ec.* 258; Xen. *Mem.* 4.2.19; Pl. *Euthd.* 282c, *R.* 4.438a, *Tht.* 184a; Arist. *APo.* 89 b, *Pol.* 1274a; Ephippus Com., *Nau* F 1 Meineke; Arat. 1.1134 Martin; Clearchus F 63 Wehrli.

[64] 2.58.13; 2.62.2. Magnetto (2004) 15–17, underlines that it is Polybius who explicitly utilizes the term ἄγνοια in a historiographical and methodological context for the first time.

332   GIUSTINA MONTI

memory. Some of them fall into a similar mistake also due to lack of judgement (δι'ἀκρισίαν). Indeed, how much more reasonable it would be if someone, even concerning such topics, would allocate to Hiero and Gelo the account that fills up books and the superfluous additions to the narrative (τὸν ἀναπληροῦντα τὰς βύβλους καὶ τὸν ἐπιμετροῦντα λόγον τῆς διηγήσεως), while omitting Hieronymus!

The importance of this passage seems to be highlighted not only by the usage of εὐπεριλήπτους, *hapax legomenon* in Polybius (though most of his work is lost) and which, before him, was employed only by Aristoxenus in the fourth century,[65] but also by the three expressions ὑποθέσεις ... στενάς, πτωχεύοντες πραγμάτων, and ἀναπληροῦντα τὰς βύβλους, which are *hapax legomena* in extant Greek literature;[66] moreover, the phrase τὸν ἐπιμετροῦντα λόγον is employed only by Polybius.[67] The phrases in themselves are already interesting, but even more so is their frequency. Indeed, the presence of five expressions that can be better defined once again as Polybian neologisms, in just two paragraphs of a small chapter, sheds light on how carefully Polybius thought about this passage: he has thoroughly chosen the expressions to use in order to explain his point of view and to leave his readers with an unforgettable description.

The neologisms in Book 12 (12.25i.5 and 12.25i.7) relate to speeches and to the lack of considered choice of which speeches to report. Polybius criticizes Timaeus because he goes through all possible arguments and tries to come up with arguments on every subject (πρὸς πᾶσαν ὑπόθεσιν εὑρεσιλογῶν). Conversely, the good historian should always choose the appropriate arguments, though – Polybius admits – it is always difficult to determine what the occasion requires in any given case (ἔστι μὲν οὖν ὁ καιρὸς ἐν πᾶσι δυσπαράγγελτος). The two neologisms used here are the verb εὑρησιλογέω ('to try to come up with arguments')[68] and the adjective δυσπαράγγελτος ('difficult to determine', but also 'difficult to relate').

---

[65] Aristox. *Rhythmica* (lib.2) 22 Pighi.

[66] This fragment of Book 7 is quoted by two different sources: Constantinus Porphyrogenitus, *De virtutibus et vitiis*, ii.103, and *Suda*, *s.v.* Ἱερώνυμος (1200), where there is no mention of Polybius, but the lexicographer reports just the passage to explain the entry on Hieronymus.

[67] The expression occurs five times: in 7.7.7; in 12.28.10, where it does not carry a negative meaning as it is used to praise Ephorus, who had been criticized by Timaeus; in 15.34.1 and 15.35.1; finally, in 33.21.1, where Polybius is speaking about his own mistake in confuting and writing too much about what is clearly false. On how the ἐπιμετρῶν λόγος might be intended, see Bollansée (2005), 246.

[68] Schweighäuser (1822), *s.v.* translates '*confabulari*' or '*multa verba facere*'; Mauersberger (2003), *s.v.*, translates 'Argumente frei erfinden'. There are no occurrences of the verb before Polybius. There is only one occurrence of the noun εὑρησιλογία before Polybius, in Thphr. *Phys. op.* 12.

Polybius' Historiographical Neologisms

The first term seems to show that Polybius' critique is perhaps orchestrated in a rather shrewd way, if one thinks that εὑρησιλογέω, apart from the meaning of 'to look for arguments', might involve a rhetorical acceptation, given that it is linked to the verb εὑρίσκω (which might also mean 'to invent'), whose Latin equivalent is *invenio*, from which *inventio* is formed.[69] While the verb εὑρίσκω alone might indicate a positive concept, when – for example – one searches for truth or for facts, consequently underlining the efforts of the research, as Polybius highlights,[70] the newly created verb does not seem to carry a positive meaning at all. The second term is a *hapax legomenon* and it does seem to express exactly the opposite concept of the one expressed by εὑρησιλογέω: indeed, while trying to find all possible arguments is wrong, useless, and easy (something that everyone can do, 12.25i.9: ἐν μέσῳ ... καὶ κοινόν), to make a selection of the most useful arguments required by that particular occasion is difficult, might be attained only if the historian has gained enough experience (12.25i.7: ἐκ τῆς αὐτοπαθείας καὶ τριβῆς), and – if one follows Polybius' line of reasoning – requires a great deal of effort.

Thus, a wrong choice will lead the historian to a wrong approach: they will lose the overall view of their subject matter and will lose sight of the most important elements to the extent that they will lack good judgement, be unable to choose the right topics or speeches to relate, and be led to exaggerate their accounts.

IV

This chapter has looked at the ways in which Polybius tried to insert himself into a tradition and, at the same time, to create his own philosophy of history, notably through the invention of new words and concepts to express his own ideas. Another interesting aspect of his neologisms is the fact that they are different, in the sense that we do not find positive neologisms characterizing positive ideas and their antonyms characterizing negative ideas. On the contrary, neologisms expressing positive and negative concepts belong to completely different semantic categories. Positive neologisms seem to belong mostly to an 'ethical' category, with the ideas of assuming the *ethos* proper to history and of an account 'purified' by every single falsehood. As for the negative neologisms, the first element one might notice is that they belong to the semantic sphere of the 'no': Polybius' *bad colleagues* are characterized by a refusal to make an effort

---

[69] Cf. εὕρεσις, 'invention'.   [70] See, e.g., 3.58–9 and 12.27a.1–4.

(ἀφιλόπονος) and by the fact that they are not able to see (ἀσκεψία). Other neologisms seem to belong to the sphere of the way in which historians write accounts: they do not care about omissions and are preoccupied with stylistic elaboration rather than facts, which will cause them to emphasize and render events or characters greater than they really are; thus, such historians will also be like dreamers. If sight is one of the most important parts of history, the bad historian is not able to see and examine. If history is effort, the bad historian is lazy and is not committed to effort. If historians do not 'see' or work hard, the result is that they omit and sometimes omit in a deliberate way because they do not want to do the toilsome research that history requires.

Last, it is worth noting that negative neologisms are more numerous than the positive ones. It might then appear clear that Polybius' intention is to affirm his own authority to the detriment of his colleagues. Thus, the authoritative historian is exemplified and defined mostly by contrast: being what others are not, the authoritative historian overcomes tradition by innovating it.

CHAPTER 17

How Tradition Is Formed
From the Fall of Caesar to the Rise of Octavian

Mark Toher

Looking back on the year 44 from the comparative calm of March 43 BC, Cicero described it as a *caecum tempus* (*Fam.* 12.25.3). But in addition to being a time of confusion for those who lived through it, the assassination of Caesar and the ensuing eight months brought transformations in fortune that produced the men who would dictate events in Roman history over the next dozen years.

In January of the year 44 the former Pompeians M. Iunius Brutus and G. Cassius Longinus became praetor *urbanus* and praetor *peregrinus*, respectively, and both could reasonably expect consulships in the coming years. Instead, by the end of the summer, they had been stripped of their praetorships and had to abandon Italy as a place too dangerous for their personal safety. In March 44 Cicero had been in political retirement for over a year, devoting his considerable energy to the composition of rhetorical and philosophical treatises. But by November he had found in Caesar's heir a pawn with which to confront Antonius on the battlefield, and he was once again the conscience and voice of the Senate, by then well into the fatal eloquence of his *Philippics*.

The times presented opportunities to more than one young man of ambition. P. Cornelius Dolabella donned the garb of consul on the day of the Dictator's murder as the victim's successor. Although his appointment as consul *suffectus* to Caesar had been blocked by Antonius at the time, by June both the assassins and Antonius had consented to Dolabella's consulship and he was allotted the important province of Syria, along with the command of a substantial army. At the same time, Dolabella had become the favourite of timid Republicans for his energetic suppression of popular demonstrations in Caesar's memory. In July of 44, this twenty-something consul looked to profit most from the upheaval of the Ides. But by November Dolabella was long gone to the East, no longer a factor in the momentous events in Rome and Italy. Within a year he would die by his own hand.

In March of 44, Sextus Pompeius, the renegade son of Caesar's old enemy, was isolated but defiant and dangerous in Spain. By the summer he had come to an accommodation with the newly arrived governor of Spain, M. Aemilius Lepidus, an accommodation that included his appointment as *praefectus classis et orae maritimae* within a year. On the Ides of March, Marcus Antonius was consul. Following ominous precedent, he extorted from the Senate and people of Rome a large army and a five-year proconsulship in the Gallic provinces. And then there was the greatest transformation of all. In March, Gaius Octavius was an eighteen-year-old in Apollonia in north-western Greece, a few months into his first experience of life in a military camp. By November he had transformed into Gaius Julius Caesar and, in command of a private army, had already marched on Rome.

The period is both epilogue and prologue, inevitably overshadowed by what came before and what followed. But these months present an opportunity to examine how the historiographical tradition on crucial events evolved over two centuries. Two layers of ancient historiographical tradition are extant for the period October 45 to October 44. One is in the contemporary or near contemporary evidence in Cicero and in the biography of Augustus by Nicolaus of Damascus, and the other in the later narratives of these events by the biographers Suetonius and Plutarch and the historians Appian and Cassius Dio.

Ronald Syme in *The Roman Revolution* presented what is still the most compelling modern account of the years 60 to 27 BC. His inspiration was the history of C. Asinius Pollio, of which Peter could find but ten passages for his collection of the fragments of Roman historians.[1] Nevertheless, Pollio provided the example, which when combined with the abundance of historical material 'encourages the attempt to record the story of the Roman Revolution and its sequel ... from the Republican and Antonian side',[2] which seems to suggest that Syme's narrative of events would, in a sense, resurrect the lost history of Pollio by use of later writers.

This approach of traditional *Quellenkritik* can obscure significant facts. For example, Plutarch reports that immediately after the murder of Caesar, M. Antonius fled the scene disguised as a slave or plebeian (Plut. *Ant.* 14.1; also App. *BC* 2.118/496). But the Augustan author Nicolaus, who mentions that some men changed their clothing to escape after the

---

[1] Peter (1906), 67–70. The new edition of the Roman historical fragments assigns thirteen fragments to Pollio; cf. Cornell (2013), 2 no. 56.

[2] Syme (1939), 6–7.

How Tradition Is Formed   337

assassination, has nothing about Antonius doing so (*FGrHist* 90 F 130.95). Traditional 'vertical' source criticism might explain the discrepancy between the different accounts by the fact that Plutarch and Appian followed a source not known or used by Nicolaus. But the situation becomes more complicated when we consider that Cicero claims that Antonius fled from the Senate house, but he too does not mention Antonius disguising himself in demeaning costume (*Phil.* 2.88). The obvious explanation would seem to be that when Cicero and Nicolaus composed their accounts, the story of Antonius fleeing in such a disguise was not in circulation. For had it been, two authors so hostile to Antonius as were Cicero and Nicolaus would surely have included the demeaning episode. It seems reasonable then to conclude that even after the Augustan era, the historiographical tradition on the assassination of Caesar and its aftermath was still evolving; episodes and details were still being invented. One might explain the story of Antonius' escape in servile costume as the ironic inversion of the genre of proscription stories – many of them surely later inventions – found in Appian, in which Antonius' victims escaped his murderous agents by disguising themselves as slaves.[3] In fact, Antonius in servile disguise seems to have become something of a motif in the late tradition, since Plutarch (*Ant.* 5.9) tells us that as tribune Antonius used servile disguise to escape from Rome just before the outbreak of the civil war in 49 BC. Or possibly we should connect the image of Antonius as a disguised slave with his reputation as enslaved to Cleopatra.

Whatever its inspiration, this minor detail in Plutarch about Antonius' behaviour after the assassination of Caesar suggests that it might be profitable to think about the historiographical tradition between March and November of 44 in terms of an earlier tradition as represented by evidence in Cicero and Nicolaus, who are in agreement on almost all episodes that both their accounts have in common, and a later, more elaborate tradition that emerges for us only 150 years or more after the events and that is best represented in Appian's history of the period. With this premise, this essay has two purposes. First, to show that the characterization of Caesar and the conspirators in the Augustan writer Nicolaus contrasts significantly with the depiction of Caesar and the assassins in the later tradition, and that this contrast in turn suggests reconsideration of the historicity of Caesar's depiction in the later tradition. And second, to consider the later tradition on events after Caesar's assassination presented in Appian and to explain errors in his account that are ignored or accepted

---

[3] App. 4.13/52, 44/185, 48/204–5, and 49/210–14.

338 MARK TOHER

without explanation by modern historians formulating their own narratives of the events of the summer and autumn of 44 BC.

Our earliest narrative of Caesar's assassination and its consequences is found in the *Bios Kaisaros* of Nicolaus of Damascus. Nicolaus had a personal relationship with Augustus, who named a type of date or fig a 'Nikolaos' because its colour and sweet taste reminded the Princeps of the complexion and disposition of his friend.[4] For over a decade Nicolaus was also the trusted advisor and envoy of Herod the Great in Jerusalem, and it must have been in this capacity that Augustus came to know Nicolaus. On more than one occasion Nicolaus had defended the illegal (and occasionally murderous) domestic and foreign policy of Herod to Augustus and other Roman magistrates. It is speculative but tempting to think that it was to Nicolaus that Augustus confided his candid assessment of Herod: he would rather be Herod's pig than his son.[5]

Probably the most evocative depiction of Caesar is found in the work of Shakespeare, but Shakespeare was not the first author to characterize Caesar through the conspiracy against him and his assassination. In his adulatory biography of Augustus, Nicolaus of Damascus uses the same strategy in an excursus that provides a detailed description of how the conspiracy formed against Caesar and of his murder. Like Shakespeare's frail Caesar, who is deaf in one ear, has to be saved in a swimming race, and faints in public, Nicolaus' Caesar is vulnerable in ways that are not apparent in the rest of the ancient tradition.[6]

Nicolaus' Caesar is excitable in a distinctly un-Roman way. When Caesar learns that Octavian is critically ill, he rushes from dinner without his shoes (F 130.20), something characteristic of distraught women in ancient Greek literature.[7] Nicolaus' Caesar is indecisive and passive. On the morning of the Ides, he cannot decide whether to enter the Senate: his friends advise against it, but Decimus Brutus cajoles Caesar and leads him by the hand into the fatal meeting. Nicolaus says that the Dictator followed in silence (F 130.83–7). Caesar was also politically inept due to his years away from Rome on campaign, and Nicolaus ascribes the success of the conspiracy to the fact that Caesar was by nature straightforward in character (F 130.67: ἁπλοῦς ὢν τὸ ἦθος and ἄπειρος πολιτικῆς τέχνης διὰ

---

[4] *FGrHist* 90 T 13; for the evidence on Nicolaus' relationship with Augustus, cf. Toher (2017), 19–20.

[5] Macr. *Sat.* 2.4.11: *melius est Herodis porcum esse quam filium.*

[6] Cf. Toher (2017), 34–35, 37, 39, 202, 274–75, and 283–85.

[7] Cf. Hesiod, *Op.* 345; Aesch. *PV* 135; Pind. fr. 169.36 (Snell-Maehler); Theoc. 24.36; Ap. Rhod. 4.43; and Bion 1.21; also Toher (2017), 202.

τὰς ἐκδήμους στρατείας) and unsuspecting (F 130.59: ἀνύποπτος): he failed to see that those honouring and praising him were in fact conspiring against him. Rather than fate, which plays a dominant role in the story of Caesar's downfall in the later sources, in Nicolaus it was more the indecision of Caesar that led to his assassination.

Nicolaus' depiction of Caesar is in significant contrast to the fairly consistent characterization of Caesar that emerges from the biographical genre at the beginning of the second century AD and that seems to have been adopted by the historians Appian and Dio. That Caesar is a dynamic hero of almost tyrannical ambition, who is perceptive and cynical enough to realize that the honours voted him in his last year were not due to the goodwill of those who proposed them.[8] As Plutarch says (*Caes.* 58.2), each success only increased Caesar's desire for more ambitious undertakings; it was in his character to do great things and seek constantly for fame. In the later sources on Caesar the only reasonable explanation of how a conspiracy could succeed against such a great man was fate itself. Yet his confidence and courage (*tharsos*) were such that even the portents and omens of the gods held no terror for him.[9]

Nicolaus' depiction of an imperceptive victim susceptible to manipulation is highlighted by contrast with his elaborate analysis of the conspirators and their motivations. Nicolaus' discussion of this issue is singular in the ancient sources, and once again it differs significantly from the assessment found in the later authors. The later tradition is quite consistent in presenting three factors as crucial in the formation and execution of the conspiracy: first, resentment of Caesar's honours and his status; second, the fear that Caesar planned to make himself king; and third, the central role of Marcus Brutus as an initially reluctant conspirator urged on by Cassius and others to undertake his ancestral obligation of tyrannicide.[10]

The grievances of the conspirators in Nicolaus are more varied and complicated, and there is no evidence of men driven to tyrannicide by Brutus' Republican ideology and the threat of Caesar's kingship. Some are resentful of the power of Caesar, especially those who aspire to it

---

[8] On Caesar's ambition: Plut. *Caes.* 69.1, also 4.3–4 and 6.3; *Ant.* 6.1–3; Suet. *Jul.* 30.5; his perception: D.C. 43.15.1.

[9] On fate as the explanation for the success of the conspirators and Caesar's assassination, cf. Plut. *Caes.* 63.1 and 66.1–3; Appian *BC* 2.116/489; Florus 2.13.94; and D.C. 44.18.4. Caesar's lack of superstition: Suet. *Jul.* 81.4 and Appian *BC* 2.116/488.

[10] Resentment of Caesar's honours and status: Suet. *Jul.* 76.1; Plut. *Caes.* 57.2–3; D.C. 44.1–3. Caesar's kingship: Suet. *Jul.* 80.3; Plut. *Caes* 60.1; Appian 2.111/462–63; D.C. 44.14; role of Brutus: Plut. *Brut.* 8–10, 13 and *Caes.* 62; D.C. 43.45.4 and 44.12–14.1.

340   MARK TOHER

themselves (F 130.60 and 64), but just as many proclaim loyalty to Republican government only as a pretext for personal complaints. Many had lost relatives, property, and office through Caesar's victory in the civil war. They were out for vengeance. Nicolaus does not present the moral drama of Brutus' evolution into a conspirator that is found in the later sources. In Nicolaus, it is the reputation of Brutus' *gens* more than the man himself that moves some to join the conspiracy (F 130.61), and it is more often alleged as a pretext than as a real motivation. Furthermore, despite the fact that Nicolaus describes in detail which of the assassins attacked Caesar and how, Brutus plays no significant role in the actual attack on Caesar. By contrast, Brutus is the central figure in the drama of the attack in the later tradition, where either Caesar despairs of his life and veils his head when he sees Brutus with his dagger (Plut. *Caes.* 66.12, *Brut.* 17.6, and App. *BC* 2.117/493) or he addresses his dying words to Brutus: 'you too, my son'.

In Nicolaus, the significant grievance of the conspirators is resentment of Caesar's *clementia*. The former Pompeians, from men of the highest station like Brutus and Cassius to common soldiers, all resent having been granted by Caesar what would have remained theirs had they been victorious in their war against him. Conversely, those who had been loyal to Caesar from the beginning resented former enemies receiving salaries and positions that were equal to or better than their own (F 130.60 and 62–3). Some of the earlier sources do mention Caesar's practice of clemency as an ingredient in his downfall,[11] but only because Caesar had failed to eliminate his future murderers when he had the opportunity.

Nicolaus is unique in explaining the conspiracy against Caesar through his *clementia* and the resentment it aroused among both its recipients and his allies. Although Plutarch does present an anecdote that illustrates such resentment on the part of the assassin Ligarius (Plut. *Brut.* 11.1–3), the later sources explain the conspiracy as due to the leadership of Brutus and ideological opposition to tyranny.

Nicolaus, however, focuses on an interlocking set of motives that ultimately find their origin in ambition and revenge to explain the variety of men who came together to murder Caesar. The difference between Nicolaus' analysis of the conspiracy and that in later sources is encapsulated in the later tradition's explanation of why the conspirators decided not to kill Antonius along with Caesar: the idea was dropped because to kill Antonius would have suggested that the liberators acted out of selfish

---

[11] *Bell. Afric.* 86.2, 88.6, and 92.4; Sal. *Cat.* 54.3; Vell. 2.52.4–6; and Sen. *De Ira* 2.23.4.

How Tradition Is Formed

motives of ambition and desire for power, which is to say, just the motives that Nicolaus ascribes to the conspirators.[12] In the later tradition such a base motive is assigned only to Cassius by Plutarch,[13] and is mentioned only to contrast with the lofty ideals of Brutus.

When we take Nicolaus' account on its own, it presents a coherent and reasonable narrative that reflects an early stage in the formation of the tradition on Caesar, before the conspiracy and his assassination had been reduced to a simple confrontation between implacable ambition and resolute tyrannicide. Nicolaus' presentation of Caesar as the imperceptive victim of ruthless and cunning enemies seems to have been his own invention, not something he derived from a lost source on Caesar and his assassination. Conspiracy against a weak and imperceptive ruler by more ruthless and ambitious rivals was a motif in Nicolaus' universal history. In his account of Syrian history, a weak king inspires a virile commander of his army to conspiracy (F 2). In his account of the history of Sicyon, Nicolaus describes Isodemus, a ruler who is driven from his position and his city by his more intelligent and ambitious brother, in terms that are very similar to those he uses of Caesar in his life of Augustus: Isodemus was simple and guileless (F 61). And in his account of Cyrus' rise to power, Nicolaus tells the story of a clever, courageous Persian who murders an unsuspecting but faithful companion of Cyrus so that the victim might not inadvertently reveal the dream that portended Cyrus' rise to the kingship (F 66.16–19). Furthermore, the motif of a vulnerable king who becomes the object of conspiracy by those closest to him is prominent in the Herodian books of Josephus' *Antiquitates Judaicae*, and it is generally agreed that Nicolaus' account of the reign of Herod would have been a main source for Josephus' account of the era. In light of this evidence, it is hardly likely that Nicolaus simply adopted a characterization of Caesar from another source. Explanation of his depiction of Caesar is to be sought elsewhere.

Nicolaus spent at least ten years as a close associate of Herod in Jerusalem, where conspiracy and murder were endemic in domestic and political affairs. As advisor to the king, Nicolaus was involved in the worst of it. Herod prosecuted and executed three of his sons for conspiracy on two different occasions in 7 and 4 BC, and twenty-five years before that he had executed his beloved wife Mariamme, the mother of two of the

---

[12] Appian 3.33/129; also Vell. 2.58.2, Plut. *Ant.* 13.3 and *Brut.* 18.2–4, and D.C. 44.19.2.
[13] Cassius resented Caesar because the Dictator had stolen some lions of his at Megara; cf. Plut. *Brut.* 8.5–6.

executed sons. Nicolaus advised the king in 7 BC against executing his victims, but in 4 BC he joined the king in prosecuting his son Antipater for conspiracy before a Roman council. The murderous domestic situation of the increasingly paranoid Herod would have given his advisor much experience in the motives and formation of conspiracies against autocratic authority. Based on this experience Nicolaus apparently concluded that a significant factor in the generation of conspiracy was the perceived weakness of the individual who was the target. In a similar way, Nicolaus' analysis of the various interests and motives of the different groups that came together to form the conspiracy against Caesar also indicates personal experience with such plotting. His analysis, which focuses on ambition and resentment, is certainly more in accord with Roman political culture than the fantasy of the later tradition, where anonymous letters left at Brutus' tribunal and pasted on statues of his ancestors become a critical factor in the formation of the conspiracy.[14]

In depicting Caesar and his assassins, Nicolaus had an advantage as an 'outsider'. Nicolaus was unaffected by such parochial Roman concerns as *libertas*, the *res publica*, or even *dignitas* – all concepts inescapable for an author writing in the Roman historiographical tradition. When the prism of kingship, the nostalgic glory of the *res publica*, and the noble act of tyrannicide are removed, the assassination of Caesar could be seen for what it was, a crude, violent play for power within the Roman governing class, but one that went badly awry. It is interesting to note in this regard that Nicolaus was deeply learned in Greek philosophy (cf. FF 132(2) and 138), and yet *eleutheria* and other such Greek concepts as supposedly infected philhellene opponents of Caesar are utterly lacking in Nicolaus' account of the conspiracy.

The illegal and violent triumviral career of Octavian gave Roman historians pause for years after. A favourite poet of the Princeps knew that it was a smouldering subject, full of danger for any who might attempt its narrative (Hor. *Carm.* 2.1.1–9). Livy (*per.* 121) did not publish his account of the year 43 BC until Augustus was dead. And even after this the future Princeps Claudius omitted the triumviral years in his Roman history, on the advice of his grandmother Livia (Suet. *Cl.* 41.2). But it was not so for Nicolaus, a man who had defended the violent career and illegal acts of a Roman client-king to the Romans themselves. His characterization of Julius Caesar provided the means whereby Nicolaus could justify

---

[14] Plut. *Caes.* 62.7 and *Brut.* 9.6–7 and 10.6; Appian *BC* 2.112/469 and 113/472; D.C. 44.12.3. These 'motives' would seem to be more in accord with the political culture of the authors' eras.

Octavian's opening moves in the months after the assassination of Caesar. A significant theme in Nicolaus' biography is the evolving perception of Octavian as he confronts the ruthless intrigues of Antonius and others who would deny him his rightful succession to the power and position of his murdered *pater*. Unlike Caesar, the young heir was able to perceive insidious danger, and so took drastic action to avoid his fate: he raised his own army (F 130.131).

In the later tradition, Appian provides the most detailed account of the events from March to November of 44 BC. The Teubner edition of Appian devotes seventy-eight pages to cover what Dio covers in about ten chapters and what Plutarch and Suetonius each cover in a chapter or less.[15] But there are significant problems with Appian's account. Most obvious are the chronological errors that are easily detected by comparison with Cicero's letters and orations. Appian (*BC* 3.25/94) puts the abolition of the Dictatorship by Antonius to mid-July and explains it as an act of appeasement to the Senate for granting him command of the armies in Macedonia. But Cicero (*Phil.* 1.3 and 2.91) makes it clear that abolition of the Dictatorship was one of Antonius' first acts in April or May and it had no connection with his gaining command of the armies in Macedonia. Cicero (*Att.* 14.14.4) knew by late April that Antonius was plotting to get Gaul as his provincial command at the meeting of the Senate on 1 June, yet Appian (*BC* 3.30/117–19) places the plebiscite on the Gallic provinces in mid-July. Appian puts the confrontation between Octavian and Antonius over the display of Caesar's chair and crown at the Ludi Cereales in mid or late July (3.28/105–8), but we know from the Roman calendar that the Ludi Cereales was celebrated in mid-April.

Appian's imprecise chronology is not simply a matter of pedantic correction. In a period of rapid and unexpected development of events, it matters in what context and chronological relation events are placed. In Appian, the consul Antonius is relatively inactive until the middle of the summer, but then he is confronted with Octavian's impertinent public claim to Caesar's estate. It is only after these affronts that Antonius undertakes the highly significant acts of abolishing the dictatorship, moving to get the Gallic provinces and suppressing Octavian's display at the Ludi Cereales, acts that he had in fact performed within a few weeks of the assassination of Caesar. Appian's chronological errors here are not just a function of imprecision nor are they to be explained by Appian's self-acknowledged aversion to providing dates for everything (*Praef.* 1.13/50).

---

[15] Appian *BC* 2.118/494–3.42/174; D.C. 45.3–9 and 11–13.1, Suet. *Aug.* 10 and Plut. *Ant.* 16.

344   MARK TOHER

Appian's chronology tends to excuse Antonius' controversial actions by putting all of them after Antonius found himself in a serious confrontation with an ambitious and aggressive Octavian over the leadership of the Caesarians.

That there may be some pro-Antonian bias in Appian's account of the triumviral era has been generally recognized, but in addition to his chronology, there are other, more significant problems in Appian's account that become obvious and explicable only when they are analysed in relation to the earlier historiographical tradition as it is presented in Cicero and Nicolaus.

According to Appian, Antonius and Octavian had an acrimonious first meeting in Rome (*BC* 3.14/50–21/77), in which Antonius summarily dismissed Octavian's claim as heir to money from the estate of Caesar that was in Antonius' control. Octavian then publicized Antonius' withholding of Caesar's estate by engaging in an ostentatious auction of his own property and that of his immediate family to finance the payment of Caesar's legacy of 300 sesterces per citizen. By such direct appeal to the people, the young heir both created a political base for himself and undermined the consul's status as the leader of the Caesarians (*BC* 3.23/ 87–9). In the next two months, Antonius twice blocked Octavian's attempts to display the paraphernalia of Caesar at public games (*BC* 3.28/105–8), and by the end of July the acrimony between the two leaders of the Caesarians induced Antonius' military tribunes to demand that he and Octavian reconcile (*BC* 3.29/111–14). Appian says that Antonius and Octavian agreed to meet, and after some mutual recrimination they formed an alliance.

The immediate profit for Antonius came in the form of Octavian's support for the bill that gave Antonius the Gallic provinces as his provincial command. Appian says that although the plebeians were incensed against Antonius (presumably because of his months of compromise with the assassins and his treatment of Octavian), the bill passed because of Octavian's efforts on Antonius' behalf with the demos. But when it seemed that Octavian would stand for election to a vacant tribune's position, Antonius ingratiated himself with the Senate by vowing to block any illegal act of Octavian (*BC* 3.30/115–21).

Now, openly under attack by Antonius, Octavian sent agents among Caesar's colonists and the troops to cause disaffection from Antonius and support for himself (*BC* 3.31.120–3). Once again, according to Appian, the military tribunes intervened and demanded from Antonius that he reconcile yet again with Octavian. After a long speech in which Antonius

How Tradition Is Formed 345

defended his actions to the tribunes, Antonius agreed once more to meet with Octavian, this time on the Capitol, and a second reconciliation and a second alliance were the result (*BC* 3.32/124–56). This second reconciliation, like the first, is difficult to date. But they both had to occur after late July and before or during the very early days of October, since it was in the first week of October that reports circulated of an assassination plot against Antonius, and many suspected Octavian to be the perpetrator (*BC* 3.39/157–9). This led to the final breach between consul and heir: Antonius went to Brundisium to take command of legions arriving there from Greece (*BC* 3.40/164) and by mid-October Octavian was recruiting a private army among Caesar's veterans in Campania (*BC* 3.40/164–6). By November, Octavian was back in Rome with a private army that Appian estimated at 10,000 men. There he was presented to a *contio* of citizens and soldiers by the tribune Cannutius and he delivered a speech in which he justified raising an army to protect himself against Antonius and swore that, as an obedient servant of his country, he was ready to confront Antonius (*BC* 3.41/167–9).

But the *contio* and speech turned out to be a spectacular miscalculation according to Appian. When the troops were confronted with the prospect of a war against Antonius rather than avenging Caesar, they simply turned around and deserted Octavian. Fortunately for Octavian the recruits soon remembered the toils of agriculture and the rewards of military service, and the cash already given and promised by Octavian. And so, as the fickle multitude will do, of their own accord the troops returned to Octavian (*BC* 3.42/170–4).[16]

We can only control Appian's account by comparison with the earlier accounts of the same events down to November of 44. But there is ample material for bemusement. There are four significant episodes in Appian that have no parallel in the early tradition as presented in Nicolaus and Cicero: the double reconciliations of Antonius and Octavian arranged by the military tribunes; that Octavian was the ally and agent by whom Antonius got the Gallic provinces as his provincial command; that Octavian attempted to stand for the tribunate and Antonius opposed him; and finally that Octavian's newly recruited army deserted him at Rome.[17] Nicolaus (F 130.115–19) does mention a reconciliation arranged

[16] Despite Appian's somewhat strange account of Octavian's miscalculation, this event was crucial for Octavian and his understanding of the troops and their motives; cf. Havener (2016), 19–21.

[17] Reconciliations: App. *BC* 3.29/112–30/115 and 3.32/124–39/156; assignment of Gallic provinces: App. *BC* 3.30/117–19; tribunate: App. *BC* 3.31/120; also Suet. *Aug.* 10.1, Plut. *Ant.* 16.5 and D.C. 45.6.1–3; troops desert Octavian: App. *BC* 3.41/167–42/174.

346   MARK TOHER

by the military tribunes, but he has only one such episode. Neither he nor
Cicero say anything about Octavian acting to get Antonius his provincial
command in Gaul, nor do they know of Octavian standing for the
tribunate; and Cicero has no mention of the disastrous effect of
Octavian's speech to the troops, although he does remark in his correspondence on its vehemence (*Att.* 16.15.3). When we turn to the other
ancient writers of the later tradition on these events, Appian's account still
remains singular. Plutarch, Dio, and Suetonius all mention that Octavian
attempted to stand for the tribunate, and Plutarch does mention the
reconciliation on the Capitol. But none of these writers mentions a first
reconciliation between the two, nor is there any mention that Octavian
was instrumental in Antonius' passing of his bill for the Gallic provincial
command. Dio (45.12.3–6) is the only other source that describes the
contio at Rome organized by Cannutius, but he knows nothing of a
desertion by Octavian's troops. In fact, in his account, the *contio* is a
complete success for Octavian.

But what may be even more surprising is how scholars fail to address
these problems in the sources. In *The Roman Revolution* Ronald Syme is
careful to avoid using Appian in his chapter entitled 'Caesar's Heir'. He
mentions in a footnote the 'vague, various and inconsistent' evidence on
Octavian and the tribunate, but otherwise he does not cite Appian on any
significant event. It is striking, however, that in his following chapter on
Octavian's first march on Rome, Syme accepts without comment or
qualification Appian's description of Octavian's inept performance at
Cannutius' *contio* and the desertion of his men. He describes Octavian
retreating from Rome 'with despair in his heart'.[18] T. Rice Holmes accepts
without discussion that Octavian did attempt to stand for the tribunate
and that he was deserted by his troops, but remains silent about Octavian's
co-operation with Antonius on the provincial bill and has no discussion of
the problem of the double reconciliation.[19] Turning to more recent
accounts, Dietmar Kienast in the third edition of his indispensable narrative cum *Forschungsbericht* of the Augustan era has no mention of
Octavian's support for the bill giving Antonius the province of Cisalpine
Gaul in Appian; and he agrees with Syme's assessment of Octavian's
candidacy for the tribunate as vague and doubtful but also, like Syme,
accepts the desertion of Octavian's troops at Rome.[20] In his full biography
of Augustus, Jochen Bleicken attempts to deal with Appian's claim that

---

[18] Syme (1939), 120 and 125.   [19] Holmes (1928), 26–7 and 31.
[20] Kienast (2009), 23–4 and 29.

How Tradition Is Formed 347

Octavian worked with Antonius to get his provincial command changed. Bleicken's explanation is that Octavian was happy to do so to get Antonius out of Rome. He accepts without comment Octavian standing for the tribunate and suffering the embarrassing desertion of his recruits when he leads them to Rome, as does Elizabeth Rawson in her chapter on the year 44 for the second edition of *The Cambridge Ancient History*.[21]

Significant points emerge from this survey of respected scholarship on these events. No one lends credence to Appian's account of two reconciliations between Octavian and Antonius, and opinion is divided but generally against Octavian as an ally in passing Antonius' bill for the Gallic command. On the other hand, there is some acceptance of the claim that Octavian seriously considered standing for election to the tribunate (probably because it is also mentioned by Plutarch, Suetonius, and Dio), and there is general acceptance of Appian's account of the troops deserting Octavian after the *contio* in Rome. There seems to be a gradation of credence accorded to Appian's account by modern scholars. And that leads to a second point: none of these scholars attempts to explain (with the single exception of Bleicken on Octavian's support for Antonius' bill) why they incorporate some aspects of Appian's account but pass over in silence episodes that they seemingly think are unhistorical. This is especially obvious in the case of the desertion at the *contio*: why accept Appian's version over that in Dio, where Octavian's address is a success? So, there is a loose consensus among scholars as to what we can accept from Appian in the period March to November of 44, but there is effectively no justification offered for the consensus.

The problem becomes more obvious when we consider that none of these significant episodes in Appian is mentioned in either Cicero or Nicolaus, and their combined silence on all of them cannot be ignored or easily dismissed. Are we to accept that Octavian was going to make a run for the tribunate in the summer of 44 and Cicero did not know about it, or had he known, that he had no occasion to remark on it in the voluminous correspondence that he seems to have carried on almost daily

---

[21] Bleicken, (1998), 77, 94–5 and 96–9, and Rawson (1994), 472 and 478. Respected scholars of the late nineteenth century are also inconsistent: Drumann and Groebe (1899) accept the Gallic command alliance since Octavian had no choice but to support Antonius against D. Brutus' claim to the province (1.120 and 4.268); they believe that Octavian stood for the tribunate (1.92–3) and accept Appian's account of the *contio* (1.158–9). Gardthausen (1891) has nothing on the double reconciliation of Octavian and Antonius or their alliance on the Gallic command, and nothing on Octavian standing for the tribunate; but they do give qualified endorsement to Appian's version of Octavian's disastrous *contio*, saying that although the troops deserted him, Octavian was easily able to make up the losses by recruitment in the north (1.70–1).

throughout the summer of 44? Furthermore, why would Nicolaus not have mentioned it, especially if it was a move that was vehemently opposed by Nicolaus' arch villain and so would provide one more item for the catalogue of injustices perpetrated by Antonius against Caesar's heir? And this especially, since in his account Appian says that Antonius' opposition to Octavian's standing for the tribunate was seen as an act of gross ingratitude due to Octavian's earlier support of Antonius' bill for his provincial command. Cicero was interested in Antonius' manoeuvres with regard to the Gallic provinces and is concerned as early as late April about Antonius' scheming in this regard (*Att.* 14.4.4). Is it likely that Cicero would have been ignorant of or passed over in silence in his letters and speeches an alliance between the consul and the newly arrived heir that enabled Antonius to get his desired provincial command? Why would Nicolaus pass over a golden opportunity to demonstrate Octavian's attempt to co-operate with and show respect for Antonius, a claim he makes repeatedly in his biased account of the relationship between Octavian and Antonius? And what of Appian's account of Octavian's disastrous *contio*? Cicero actually refers to the vehemence of Octavian's speech at the *contio* in a letter to Atticus (*Att.* 16.15.3), but he says nothing about a catastrophic political mistake by Octavian and the desertion of his troops. It is very unlikely that such a desertion of Octavian by his troops as described by Appian could have occurred and that Cicero would not have known about it or failed to remark on it. Furthermore, Dio's account of the *contio* confirms the silence of Cicero about any such desertion.

The *argumentum e silentio* in this case seems plausible. Appian's account of the summer and autumn of 44 presents four significant episodes that are not found in the early tradition reconstructed from the combined evidence of Cicero and Nicolaus, and even in the later tradition, only one of Appian's four episodes (Octavian standing for the tribunate) is confirmed by other authors. It is fair to say that Appian's account of this period is our fullest and most detailed – and also the most suspect.

To begin with, the first reconciliation of Octavian and Antonius in Appian is clearly a doublet from the later reconciliation that both Nicolaus and Plutarch mention, and it can explain another highly improbable episode in Appian, that is, how Octavian came to support the bill that changed Antonius' provincial command. That this episode is also unhistorical seems plausible due to the silence of all other sources on it and by the sheer improbability of it. If Antonius and Octavian did not meet until late May, then that would leave less than ten days for them to quarrel, make up, and then ally to propose Antonius' bill, which was passed on

How Tradition Is Formed 349

either the first or second of June. And this of course assumes that Octavian had developed by late May the large following among the urban plebs that becomes evident only in August and September and probably was due to his public displays at the games of July and his ongoing payment of Caesar's legacy after that. Therefore, the first reconciliation in Appian and his account of Octavian's support of Antonius' bill are likely unhistorical.

The veracity of Octavian's standing for the tribunate, mentioned by all four sources of the later tradition and generally accepted in the modern narratives of the era, is also suspect.[22] Octavian was eighteen years old and a patrician, thus doubly disqualified by age and status for election to the office. The election of teenagers to high magistracies (at least teenagers who were not at the head of a large army that had just taken Rome) was an innovation of the Augustan era, and for an eighteen-year-old to canvass for the tribunate in the 40s BC would have been unacceptable even by the notorious standards of late Republican political behaviour. Furthermore, there is significant discrepancy in what the authors report. Dio, Plutarch, and Suetonius say, without elaboration, that Octavian stood for the tribunate and that his election was opposed and prevented by Antonius. Appian, however, says that Octavian actually supported another candidate for the vacant position, but the demos sensed that Octavian himself actually wanted to be tribune and so proposed to cast their votes for him. At this point Antonius, to ingratiate himself with the Senate, announced that he would use the full power of his office to prevent Octavian from doing anything illegal.[23] In this case, it is Appian who provides the clue to what might have happened. Octavian never actually stood for the tribunate, but there was a rumour of his intending to do so or even a spontaneous, aborted effort on his behalf that subsequently transformed in the later historical tradition into an unsuccessful run for the office due to Antonius' opposition.

Finally, the story, almost universally accepted by modern narratives, that Octavian's recruits deserted him after his speech is probably the most significant of all the singular episodes that Appian retails from the year 44. For if it were true, as Bleicken notes, then Octavian's political existence, even his life, hung by a hair.[24] And therein lies the problem. What did Octavian do at this dangerous turn to recover? According to Appian – and according to the modern scholars who accept the story – he did nothing. The rebellious troops went home, became bored with their

---

[22] Cf. note 20.   [23] App. *BC* 3.31/120.   [24] Bleicken (1998), 98–9.

agricultural chores, and pined for the life and rewards of the legionary camp. And so they flocked back to Octavian's banner of their own accord (App. 3.42/170–4). One need not comment on such a scenario except to say that it is tactfully left out of all the modern discussions cited here that do accept the rest of Appian's description of the episode. The sheer improbability of the story as Appian presents it, the contradictory account of the same episode in Dio (45.12.3–6), and the contemporary silence of Cicero on such a momentous and threatening development argue strongly against its historicity.

The ides of March 44 and its results provide evidence that ancient tradition does form over time, even in the context of momentous and memorable events, and evidence of this formation can be detected through a comparison of the early and later traditions on events. That tradition forms over time may seem obvious, but it does not seem to be a factor that is incorporated into modern accounts of the year 44, where even the best scholars pick and choose which episodes from the ancient authors they accept or reject without discussion or justification. To explain *how* the ancient tradition is formed is a more difficult and speculative task.

Although Nicolaus' account is essentially the same with regard to the facts as the accounts in later authors, Nicolaus' depiction of Caesar and his assassins – his imperceptive victim surrounded by calculating and resentful enemies – suggests that the dynamic Caesar of the biographical tradition confronted by the *liberator* Brutus is, at least to some degree, a construct of Roman parochial interests that focused on the assertion of *dignitas* and the prerogatives of *libertas* and the *res publica*. This in turn leads to the possibly disturbing conclusion that our 'historical' Caesar as derived from the later sources is something of an image itself. The very consistency in the later tradition on the uncomplicated depiction of Caesar as a dynamic, tragic hero and the matching depiction of Brutus as a tortured idealist is prima facie evidence of this. Such vignettes in the biography of Caesar as Sulla seeing many Mariuses in the teenage Caesar or Caesar, the governor of Spain, weeping in self-reproach over the accomplishments of Alexander suggest more the invention of tradition than evidence of historical fact. Nicolaus' account of Caesar and his assassination lacks the epochal tone of the later tradition. His vulnerable Caesar and ruthless conspirators do not personify the crisis that Caesar's career introduced into the political culture of the late Roman Republic. Nicolaus' own experience at the court of Herod the Great taught him that even the worst autocratic rulers could be managed, and his cultural outlook easily accommodated a *rex*. Furthermore, there is his chronological perspective. If we are to accept

How Tradition Is Formed 351

one generally held view, Nicolaus wrote his biography of Augustus as early as the late 20s BC,[25] just a little over twenty years after Caesar's assassination, and much too early for contemporaries to perceive the full significance of that event for Roman history. Octavian had only just become Augustus, and while clearly the victor over all challengers, how long that would remain the case could not be foreseen then. An adulatory biography by a loyal and experienced friend might usefully contain an extended representation of the *Realien* of conspiracy and assassination for the benefit of the new Princeps. It is impossible to assess the specific roles of such figures as Pollio or Livy in the formation of the tradition concerning Caesar. But whatever those roles were, it would take time, much time, before the course of Roman history revealed the momentous significance of the events of the Ides of March. Only then would it be possible for the Roman historiographical tradition to formulate a coherent moral portrait of the culmination of the Republican epoch in which the ongoing and destructive confrontation between Roman aristocratic ambition for power and status and the countervailing resistance of *libertas* became personified in Caesar and his assassins. But for Nicolaus – this 'outsider' who was writing much closer to the events and who was himself very close to those who benefitted from them – Caesar was a victim of his own military ambition and the ambitions of those closest to him. Hardly a hero, and his murderers hardly noble. After all, in such circumstances even Herod himself had been able to survive.

Appian presents four significant episodes in his narrative of the eight months after the Ides of March. None is mentioned by Cicero or Nicolaus, only one finds confirmation in other ancient writers, and some have become part of the modern scholarly accounts of the era. It has been suggested above that the story of Antonius escaping on the Ides in servile disguise must have come into the tradition after the time of Augustus. In a similar way, the four, far more significant episodes in Appian also may have entered the tradition after the age of Augustus.

Appian's account of the triumviral era shows clear signs of later rhetorical embellishment. He provides an elaborate collection of proscription stories, sentimental and harrowing accounts of the victims of the triumvirs arranged in neat categories.[26] While some of the proscription stories may be true, taken as a whole they reflect more the invention of later tradition

---

[25] Jacoby (1926), 263–5.
[26] App. *BC* 4.12/45–51/223; Syme (1939), 190 n. 6, noted that this peculiar sub-genre of proscription stories went some way towards compensating for the lack of Roman prose fiction.

than historical truth. Furthermore, Appian devotes almost a third of his account of events from the Ides of March to the end of the year 44 to three speeches by Antonius and Piso in defence of Antonius' policy. This clear evidence of rhetorical embellishment in Appian suggests the origin of three of the four episodes discussed above and found only in Appian. Octavian's support for Antonius' bill on the Gallic provinces, his candidacy for the tribunate, and his performance in the *contio* in Rome were all occasions when a speech by Octavian would have been appropriate. Long after Pollio, Livy, and Augustus were gone from the scene, Horace's glowing embers of the triumviral era burned on, at least rhetorically. It is not hard to imagine that such invented episodes – as Octavian supporting Antonius' crucial bill for the Gallic provinces or Octavian standing for the tribunate against Antonius' opposition – would have provided suitable contexts for a speech assignment for an advanced student in the rhetorical schools of the Julio-Claudian era and later.[27] We know that Antonius remained a figure of interest in later eras, if for no other reason than the popularity of Cicero's *Philippics*. The irony is that by the time of Nero or Domitian, the triumviral era, which seems to have been out of bounds for historians until well into the first century AD, may have become the rhetorical battleground on which old issues and new 'what if' scenarios were played out, and some of those scenarios seem to have found their way into the later historical tradition on the year 44.

[27] Saller (1980), 71.

CHAPTER 18

Burn Baby Burn (Disco in Furneaux)
Tacitean Authority, Innovation, and the Neronian Fire
(Annals 15.38–9)

Rhiannon Ash

Introduction

John Marincola's remarkable monograph *Authority and Tradition in Ancient Historiography* (1997) was inspired by a simple question. What do ancient historians tell us about themselves?[1] This culminated in a study illuminating the complex and evolving processes whereby historical writers sought to imitate and manipulate traditions established by their predecessors as a strategy to underpin their own authority – and ultimately to persuade their readers.

By 'predecessors' Marincola had in mind primarily narrative historians, but he urges that 'it is salutary to remember also that this was hardly the sole source of knowledge about the past for the ancients: there were oral traditions, family traditions, pictorial representations of the past, the words of panegyricists, and monuments commemorating (or purporting to commemorate) great historical actions'.[2] That rich repository of different resources allowing ancients access to (a version of) their past naturally also includes the genre of epic and other kinds of poetry. Particularly in a Roman setting, where narrative history developed comparatively late and where the first Roman historical work was 'not a prose history but an epic poem by C. Naevius on the First Punic War',[3] there was strong potential for epic to provide material and *topoi* familiar to audiences, which creative historians could then exploit to enhance their own authority.[4] As Jackie

---

*Special thanks are due to Luke Pitcher for the whimsical pun in the title (which will remain puzzling for those not familiar with the 1976 song 'Disco Inferno' by The Trammps). I am enormously grateful to Giusy Monti and Scarlett Kingsley for organizing the splendid conference in Puglia in April 2019, which resulted in this volume – and to all three co-editors for their hard work in bringing this final volume to fruition. John Marincola, the honorand of the conference, has been the most genial friend and wonderful colleague for many years.

[1] Marincola (1997), xi.   [2] Marincola (1997), 20.   [3] Marincola (1997), 26.

[4] The fusion between historiography and poetry is a rich topic. See, for example, the essays in Levene and Nelis (2002), especially Wiseman's article, and in Miller and Woodman (2010). Simonides' Plataea elegy is a fascinating example from the fifth century BC (Boedeker (1996)).

353

Elliott aptly observes, historians' engagement with material from epic was a way of 'reflecting tradition as the repository of the true past and using it to assert the validity and relevance of that truth with regard to the lived and the textual present'.[5]

This chapter sets out to analyse one particularly brilliant and provocative piece of historical narrative that crystallizes and brings into focus many broader issues raised by Marincola, issues surrounding a historian's techniques of establishing their own authority, their rhetorical strategies of persuasion, their relationship to previous historical sources, their importing material from genres other than history, and their self-positioning along the spectrum between imitation and originality. The narrative in question is Tacitus' memorable account of the great fire that devastated Rome in AD 64 – an infamous disaster for which Nero (may or) may not have been responsible.[6] Tacitus' account builds on multiple layers of previous historical representations of that fire in the fifty or more years between his own version in the *Annals* (probably published at some point after the Trajan's death in AD 117) and the real lived experiences of eyewitness survivors from AD 64.[7] Yet it also draws creatively on fictionalized fires from epic and elsewhere – descriptions long predating the fire of AD 64 – which offered familiar models and rich literary inspiration.

The structure of this chapter is simple. I first offer some brief contextual analysis of the AD 64 fire in relation to other major fires in the first century AD; I then consider the potential impact of literary accounts of disaster on an audience's emotions and how this emotive material plays out in a historiographical setting; and finally, I deliver a detailed reading of Tacitus' version of the fire, drawing out distinctive touches against parallel versions in Suetonius and Cassius Dio. Tacitus clearly wanted his own

---

[5] Elliott (2015), 287. One of Marincola's many services to the field of historiography has been his tireless work together with the late John Moles on the electronic journal *Histos* (groundbreaking both in format and focus), which published Elliott's article.

[6] Three important studies examine the Neronian fire. Closs (2020) is a wide-ranging study in politics, poetics, and imagery, engaging with the intersection of fire, city, and ruler in the imperial era: chapter 5 analyses Tacitus' version of the fire. A. A. Barrett (2020) considers the reality of the fire based on a range of archaeological and numismatic evidence and questions Nero's responsibility for starting it. Walsh (2019) looks at the fire in detail, setting it against the backdrop of other urban disasters unleashed on Rome and its inhabitants.

[7] If we accept a broad-brush date (i.e. that the *Annals* was not completed before Trajan's death in AD 117), this means that around fifty-three years had elapsed since the AD 64 fire. Potter (1991), 287–90, surveys three possible dates of composition: (i) written between 108 and 116; (ii) written over more than a decade but postdating Trajan's death; (iii) written between 112 and sometime after 117. He concludes (290): 'Tacitus was plainly a slow and painstaking author, and it is therefore likely that the *Annales* as we have them were not completed before the death of Trajan in 117.'

Burn Baby Burn (Disco *in Furneaux*)

superimposed version of the disaster to outshine previous accounts. Exploiting and innovating on traditions laid down by his predecessors was an ideal way for him to achieve this pre-eminence and to stamp his own authority on the material, thereby inscribing his own account into the tradition of fire narratives as a reference point for future historians.

Fire in the First Century AD: Real and Imagined Blazes

Unfortunately, accidental urban fires were endemic in the ancient world.[8] Aulus Gellius, as a prelude to quoting verbatim from Claudius Quadrigarius' *Annals* about the fireproof qualities of wood smeared with alum, casually describes seeing a tall block of flats burning and the surrounding neighbourhood in flames as he and some friends walk through Rome (15.1.2).[9] Vitruvius even advises that in constructing a city, Vulcan's shrine should be located outside the walls so that buildings are freed from the fear of fires (1.7.1).[10] Despite Augustus having organized *uigiles* in Rome as a fire brigade (AD 6) and Claudius subsequently doing so at Ostia and Puteoli, nonetheless accidents were inevitable in a society relying on fire for warmth and cooking.[11] Just to highlight a few examples, there had been huge conflagrations at Colonia Agrippinensis in AD 58 (Tac. *Ann.* 13.57.3), at Lugdunum probably in AD 64 (Sen. *Ep.* 91; Tac. *Ann.* 16.13.3), in Rome again in AD 80 (Suet. *Tit.* 8, *Dom.* 5; D.C. 66.24; cf. Mart. 5.7), and at Nicomedia in c. AD 110 'an utterly massive fire' (*uastissimum incendium*, Plin. *Ep.* 10.33).[12] Accounts of all these different disasters could have informed Tacitus' narrative of the AD 64 fire (albeit anachronistically).

---

[8] Ramage (1983) considers various urban problems including crime, traffic problems, noise pollution, unhealthiness, air pollution, flooding, and fire ('the most serious problem', 74). He distinguishes between 'the great conflagrations such as those of Nero in AD 64 or Titus in AD 80' and the 'thousands of lesser fires each year' (74).

[9] Claudius Quadrigarius *FRHist* 24 F 84 about Sulla's siege of the Piraeus (87–86 BC).

[10] Vitruvius also discusses how susceptible various wood and stones are to fire (2.7.2, 2.9.6, 2.9.14, 2.9.16).

[11] On Augustus and the *uigiles*, see Suet. *Aug.* 30.1, with Wardle (2014), 241; O. Robinson (1977); Daugherty (1992); Sablayrolles (1996), 24–37; *OCD*[3] *uigiles*). On Claudius and Ostia/Puteoli, see Suet., *Cl.* 25.2, with Sablayrolles (1996), 45–6. See further Ash (2007), 260–1. Rainbird (1986) discusses the fire stations of imperial Rome.

[12] The fire at Lugdunum is probably the one mentioned by Tacitus (*Ann.* 16.13.3). It perhaps happened sometime between July and September AD 64. Lugdunum's citizens had given four million HS to Rome after the fire, and Nero then gave Lugdunum the same sum after the devastating fire there. Closs (2020) in chapter 3 perceptively reads the Lugdunum fire as a form of displaced commentary by Seneca on Rome's recent devastation by fire.

Descriptions of urban fires appear in many works across a range of genres, creating the impression that such blazes were a regular blight on city life.[13] Yet authors operating in historiography and epic also describe fires that were not accidental – those fires set deliberately during 'the sackings of cities' (*expugnationes urbium*, Tac. *Ann.* 4.32.1) as the culmination of military operations, with the 'patient zero' of Troy being the archetype.[14] From Troy's ashes, depictions of the *urbs capta* and its destruction cascade and evolve as a distinct historiographical motif, with accounts of the sacking of Carthage (146 BC) and Corinth (146 BC) emerging as particularly significant manifestations of this theme.[15] As Purcell observes, 'Other cities reduced in war, though terribly damaged, might rise again; but in 146 it was considered essential that there should never again be a Corinth or a Carthage.'[16]

One city that did rise again after a sack was Rome itself. Rome too had become part of this narrative fabric of sackings, most notably when the Gauls invaded (390 BC): the experience and descriptions of those (later) destructive fires in Carthage and Corinth were probably projected backwards, anachronistically serving as narrative filters for the fire in Rome in 390 BC, even if in some accounts a sense of national shame limited the fire's extent, with the flames sparing the Capitol and destroying only parts of the city below (Liv. 5.39–55).[17] The Gauls unleashed a fire that drew later historians (like moths) to narrate this moment of intense national crisis. So, Claudius Quadrigarius (*FRHist* 24) almost certainly started his work with the Gallic sack, thereby establishing this trauma as a low point from which collective Roman energy and ambition saw its people rise to impressive new heights.[18]

---

[13] For some other accounts and notices of fires, see Liv. 24.47.15, 26.27.1–3, 30.26.5; Fron. *Aq.* 1, 18.2; Tac. *Ann.* 4.64.1, 6.45.1, 12.58, 13.57.3, 16.13.3; Suet. *Vit.* 8.2, *Vesp.* 8.5, *Tit.* 8.3; Juv. 3.197–222 (with Mayor (1872), 172; van den Berg (2003), 443–77; Woodman (2017), 266). Sablayrolles (1996), 771–802, assembles evidence for eighty-eight fires in Rome from the sixth century BC to AD 410. Canter (1932) is useful.

[14] See Kraus (1994); Woodman (2012), 387–92. On *expugnationes urbium* as a staple of historiography, see Martin and Woodman (1989), 171. Hom. *Il.* 9.593 casts fire as standard in such narratives of sacking cities.

[15] See Paul (1982); A. Ziolkowski (1993); and Purcell (1995). Rossi (2002) considers how Virgil uses the *Vrbs Capta* trope in *A.* 2.

[16] Purcell (1995), 141.

[17] Cf. *Capitolio atque arce incolumi* (Liv. 5.53.9). See Skutsch (1953) and (1978); Malloch (2013), 355–7.

[18] *FRHist* 24 F1–2 ('Claudius deviated from his predecessors . . . in not beginning his history with the origins of Rome; he started instead with the Gallic invasion and occupation of Rome in 390', Briscoe, *FRHist* 1.289).

The horror and human cost of fires could exercise a peculiar fascination in audiences, so that Tacitus flags the 'city devastated by fires', *urbs incendiis uastata* (*Hist.* 1.2.2), as a dark attraction.[19] Yet since various historians (including Tacitus himself at *Hist.* 3.71 on the burning of the Capitoline temple in AD 69) and writers of epic (Virgil *A.* 2 on Troy) memorably narrate destructive urban fires in a military setting, there was a risk that sophisticated readers had seen it all before. Tacitus needed all his creative powers to deliver a successful version of this fire – it had to be compelling, but not too sensational or hackneyed. Hence, as Keitel notices, 'he does not lace his account with reminiscences from Livy' (i.e. the Gallic sack), nor generally does he 'evoke the fall of Troy, aside from Nero's musical performance'.[20] Other powerful models of disasters involving fires were also available to Tacitus, including Vesuvius' eruption in AD 79 (Plin. *Ep.* 6.16, 6.20), covered in the *Histories*' missing books and billed as an attraction in the preface (*Hist.* 1.2.2).[21] This deadly volcanic eruption was an anachronistic reference point for the AD 64 fire, but it still spoke to Tacitus' contemporaries – and so he embeds in the fire narrative verbal details creating associations with Vesuvius.[22]

Another element present in Tacitus' creative melange is the hyperbolic world of the declaimers. So, Tacitus' version of the city's reconstruction after the Neronian fire includes expressive verbal and conceptual echoes of Papirius Fabianus' indignant speech (relayed by Seneca the Elder) denouncing wealth as even having corrupted the city's very buildings:

> tanta altitudo aedificiorum [cf. *Ann.* 15.43.1, aedificiorum altitudine] est tantaeque uiarum angustiae [cf. *Ann.* 15.38.3, artis itineribus][23] ut neque aduersus ignem praesidium nec ex ruinis ullam in partem effugium [cf. *Ann.* 15.38.6, effugio] sit. (Sen. *Con.* 2.1.11)

> Such is the great height of the buildings and such the narrowness of the streets that there is neither any protection against fire nor an escape from collapsing buildings to any section.

Tacitus' account of the AD 64 fire and its aftermath clearly includes lexical echoes of this passage from Fabianus' declamation. This rhetorical *color*

---

[19] Damon (2003), 88.

[20] Keitel (2010), 344. Nonetheless, further hints of the fall of Troy may be present (Ash (2018), 183–4, on *patente effugio, Ann.* 15.38.6).

[21] Damon (2003), 87–8. See the excellent discussion of Berry (2008).

[22] Ash (2018), 38.4n. *lamenta . . . feminarum*; 38.5n. *respectant*; 39.1n. *haurirentur*.

[23] This is a conceptual rather than a verbal echo. Edwards (2011), 653, points to its 'evoking the labyrinthine ways of Virgil's burning Troy (*Aen.* 2.736–7)'.

reminds us of the diverse literary material from different genres available to him for enriching his account.

Literary Accounts of Disaster and the Emotions

Reporting on any disaster (ancient or modern) raises questions about the boundaries of good taste and about an audience's potential range of emotional responses to such a narrative. It also introduces an issue central to historiography, namely, the risk that a historical narrative might be perceived as sensationalizing. Furthermore, even considering average mortality rates in the ancient world, some of the *Annals'* first readers could themselves have experienced the Neronian fire, or lost relatives and friends there.[24] So the AD 64 fire was still personally emotive for survivors and more generally resonant for Tacitus' contemporaries; and for Tacitus himself, this could be an advantage or disadvantage, depending on his handling of this episode. Many readers would be living and working in the revamped city that had emerged from the flames. Indeed, the very newness of the city's layout would vividly remind people of the destruction; and in the intervening period other visual triggers and memorials such as Domitian's altars to Vulcan (the so-called *arae incendii Neroniani*) would ensure that the fire's emotional legacy was still alive.[25] From Domitian's principate, we have boundary markers specifying preventative fire-clearance zones where building was forbidden so as to pre-empt further disasters.[26] People would have remembered the AD 64 fire.

Even for those who had not directly experienced the fire, a historian's *auctoritas* could crumble if events were narrated so as to stir discreditable associations with predecessors in the genre, particularly Hellenistic historiography (or 'tragic history' as it is sometimes called, i.e. historical writing sometimes deemed too ready to evoke the emotions of pity and fear associated with tragedy). Roman historians, particularly sensitive about such risks, often pre-emptively apologize for or express unease about

---

[24] Tacitus' first readers might have included people in their sixties who had witnessed the fire as children, and even older survivors (cf. Plin. *Nat.* 7.153–64, with Beagon (2005), 357–74, on human longevity). As Edwards (2011), 656, reminds us, the fire also occurred early in Tacitus' own lifetime (born between AD 56 and AD 58).

[25] See Closs (2016) on these monumental altars dedicated to Vulcan in fulfilment of a vow dating back to the Neronian fire, and probably intended to dampen bad publicity from another devastating fire from AD 80. Mart. 5.7 (with Howell (1995), 83–4), a prayer to Vulcan where Rome is compared with a phoenix rising from the ashes, looks like it refers to Domitian's restoration of the cityscape after that fire.

[26] *CIL* 6.30387a, 30387b = *ILS* 4914, 30387c, with Shaw (2015), 90.

Burn Baby Burn (Disco in Furneaux) 359

including material potentially evocative of this dubious narrative mode. The crucial passage for such issues and for the debate about 'tragic history' is Polybius' famous critique of Phylarchus' historical writing, in particular his account of the Achaeans' cruel treatment of the Mantineans when they surrendered their city (223 BC):[27]

> [7] In his [Phylarchus'] eagerness to arouse the pity and attention of his readers he treats us to a picture of clinging women with their hair dishevelled and their breasts bare, or again of crowds of both sexes together with their children and aged parents weeping and lamenting as they are led away to slavery. [8] This sort of thing he keeps up throughout his history, always trying to bring the horrors vividly before our eyes.... [10] A historical author should not try to thrill his readers by such exaggerated pictures, nor should he, like a tragic poet, try to imagine the probable utterances of his characters or reckon up all the consequences probably incidental to the occurrences with which he deals, but he should simply record what really happened and what really was said, however commonplace. (Plb. 2.56.7–8, 10)

This famous passage's nuances and place in the evolution of historiography have been much discussed, particularly by scholars seeking to downgrade 'tragic history' as a distinct school.[28] However that may be, in the context of my current analysis, Polybius' critique indicates that a historian embarking on a disaster narrative faces challenges in striking the right tone: too much focus on emotive details risked associations with entertainment and tragic poetry, but avoiding hyperbole and recording what really happened might generate a commonplace account, unpalatable to readers familiar with the tradition and primed to expect a purple passage. After all, historians before Tacitus had written about the fire.[29] Tacitus must have wanted his own superimposed version of the disaster narrative to outshine the accounts in his sources. Disaster narratives too have their own distinctively grim rivalry via the scale of devastation, number of casualties, and so

---

[27] On these events, see Champion (2004), 125–6; and on the passage, Walbank (1957), 259–63.

[28] See Marincola (2003), 285–315. Walbank (1960) outlines how Schwartz (1897) and Scheller (1911) developed the theory that tragic history derived from the Peripatetics who had overturned Aristotle's clear distinction between history and tragedy (*Po.* 9). Ullman (1942) challenged this view but was himself challenged by von Fritz (1957). Farrington (2008) explores such issues further. Rossi (2002), 232–3, is illuminating on tragic history, as are Zucchelli (1985) and Marincola (2010) and (2013).

[29] Three possibilities are (i) Pliny the Elder (*FRHist* 80) in his continuation of the history of Aufidius Bassus, (ii) Seneca's friend Fabius Rusticus (*FRHist* 87), and (iii) the senator Cluvius Rufus (*FRHist* 84), Nero's herald at the Neronia in Rome in 65 (Suet. *Nero* 21.1–2), who accompanied the emperor on his tour of Greece (D.C. 63.14.3).

360   RHIANNON ASH

on.[30] With a standout disaster such as the AD 64 fire, there was considerable scope for subsequent disaster narratives of the same event to compete with earlier versions in a disturbing dynamic of 'my version of the disaster is bigger/worse/more destructive/more shocking than yours'.[31] *Aemulatio* shaped historiography, and disaster narratives often show a strong competitive drive marked by hyperbole and striving for stylistic heights. For example, the great fire of London (1666) inspired the diarist John Evelyn to some elevated description. His entry for 3 September includes the following:

> God grant mine eyes may never behold the like, who now saw above ten thousand houses all in one flame, the noise & crakling & thunder of the impetuous flames, the shreeking of Women & children, the hurry of people, the fall of towers, houses & churches was like an hideous storme, & the aire all about so hot & inflam'd that at the last one was not able to approch it, so as they were force'd [to] stand still, and let the flames consume on which they did for neere two whole mile[s] in length and one in bredth. The Clowds also of Smoke were dismall, & reached upon computation neere 50 miles in length.[32]

Evelyn here elevates his usual diarist's style in a muscular way to capture the horrors of the disaster.

Tacitus on the Fire

So how does Tacitus go about narrating 'the most extensive disaster-narrative in the extant *Annals*'?[33] With the illuminated shadows of the banquet organized by Tigellinus (15.37.1–3) and the blazing torches of Nero's transgressive wedding to Pythagoras (15.37.4) still fresh in our minds' eyes, Tacitus now turns to the infamous fire in Rome, with the powerful and arresting opening: 'Disaster followed' (*sequitur clades*, 15.38.1). As is clear, the verb choice projects a causal connection with the decadent events narrated in the previous chapter – what Waddell calls a 'cinematic quick cut', artfully linking sections of the narrative – and *clades*

---

[30] E.g. Diod. Sic. 17.14.1 (capture of Thebes). This competitive drive of disaster narratives to measure things recalls narratives of wars and battles. Cf. Rubincam (2003) and (2008).

[31] This passion for enumeration also marks accounts of the great fire of London (1666): 'It has been estimated that the fire consumed 13,200 houses, St Paul's Cathedral, 87 parish churches, 6 consecrated chapels, the Guildhall, the Royal Exchange, the Custom House, 52 company halls, various markets and prisons, 3 gates and 4 stone bridges' (J. Richardson (2000), 144).

[32] De la Bédoyère (1995), 154.   [33] Keitel (2010), 342; cf. (2009), 136–8.

suggests a military disaster.[34] Shannon-Henderson sees Tacitus' powerful introduction of the fire using 'causal *sequor*' as suggestive of it being a prodigious event, with hints of divine wrath in play in light of Nero's aberrant conduct.[35] The central portion of Tacitus' account of the fire (15.38–9) falls into three distinct units, the first running as follows:

38 (1) sequitur clades, forte an dolo principis incertum (nam utrumque auctores prodidere), sed omnibus, quae huic urbi per uiolentiam ignium acciderunt, grauior atque atrocior. (2) initium in ea parte circi ortum, quae Palatino Caelioque montibus contigua est, ubi per tabernas, quibus id mercimonium inerat, quo flamma alitur, simul coeptus ignis et statim ualidus ac uento citus longitudinem circi conripuit. neque enim domus munimentis saeptae uel templa muris cincta aut quid aliud morae interiacebat. (3) impetu peruagatum incendium plana primum, deinde in edita adsurgens et rursus inferiora populando anteiit remedia uelocitate mali et obnoxia urbe artis itineribus hucque et illuc flexis atque enormibus uicis, qualis uetus Roma fuit.

(1) There followed a disaster – whether by chance or by the princeps' cunning being uncertain (authors have transmitted each alternative), but one more serious and frightening than any which have befallen this City through violent fires. (2) Its beginning arose in that part of the circus which adjoins the Palatine and Caelian hills, where, among shops in which there was that kind of merchandise by which flames are fed, the fire had no sooner started than gathered strength and, fanned by the wind, took hold along the length of the circus. There were no houses enclosed by fortifications or temples girded by walls, nor did any other form of hindrance lie in its path. (3) In its attack the conflagration – ranging across the level at first, then surging to the heights and contrariwise ravaging the depressions – outstripped all remedies in the speed of its malignancy and with the City being susceptible owing to its confined streets winding this way and that, and its irregular blocks, as was the nature of old Rome.[36]

Tacitus' cagey opening, conceding that the fire may or may not have been started by Nero, masterfully wrong-foots his audience's expectations, boldly stirring interest. His apparent *dubitatio* distinguishes him from other sources, who unambiguously assert Nero's responsibility.[37] So

---

[34] Waddell (2013), 486–8. See Edwards (2011), 653, on the causal connection and Ash (2018), 106 and 179, on the lexical register of *clades*.

[35] Shannon-Henderson (2019), 319. See further Shannon (2012) on how such issues play out subsequently in *Annals* 15.41–7.

[36] The translation is by Woodman (2004), as are later extracts.

[37] Walsh (2019), 78–85, considers responsibility for the fire through the device of a mock court case. *Dubitatio* ('hesitation') is a useful device: 'The posed indecision has a rhetorical force characteristic of and crucial to Tacitus' narrative' (Whitton (2011), 274). Tacitus similarly swims against the tide

362 RHIANNON ASH

Suetonius uses a third-person singular verb (*incendit urbem*, *Nero* 38.1) for the fire's start, while in Dio, Nero dispatches arsonists around the city ('he secretly sent out men who pretended to be drunk or made other kinds of trouble, and caused them at first to set fire to one or two or even several buildings in different parts of the city', 62.16.2).[38] Tacitus' prominent authorial focus on two possibilities (accident vs imperial arson) places questions of causation centre-stage and showcases his own impartiality, whatever his real views.[39] Such poses can be strategically useful in projecting a certain kind of impartial authorial identity, but as Kuukkanen stresses, 'historiography is not categorically either subjective or objective, but always lies somewhere in between these extremes'.[40]

Tacitus' formulation also recalls Livy's version of Camillus' speech after the Gallic sack (390 BC) seeking to deter his listeners from abandoning Rome. Camillus pitches a counterfactual argument about potential fires in Veii (the Romans' proposed destination): 'suppose that by crime or by chance fire should break out at Veii' (*si fraude si casu Veiis incendium ortum sit*, Liv. 5.54.1).[41] Since there will be urban blazes wherever they go, why not stay in Rome? Yet where Camillus talks hypothetically about future arson in another city, Tacitus analyses the cause of a real fire that has already broken out in Rome; and where Camillus is subsequently heralded as the 'second founder of the city' (*conditor alter urbis*, Liv. 5.49) for preventing people from abandoning Rome after the Gallic sack, Nero suffers *infamia* because he is thought to exploit fire to seek the 'glory of founding a new city' (*condendae nouae urbis . . . gloriam*, *Ann.* 15.40.2).[42] Nero becomes a warped recasting of a much more positive archetype, and the implicit contrast brings into focus a broad question. Will Tacitus by this opening really lay foundations to exonerate Nero? For now, his

---

in expressing doubts about those responsible for burning the Capitol in AD 69 (*hic ambigitur . . .*, *Hist.* 3.71.4). Other sources blamed the easy target, the Vitellians who lost the war (Joseph. *BJ* 4.649; Suet. *Vit.* 15.3; D.C. 64.17; Wellesley (1972), 16–18).

[38] See too Plin., *Nat.* 17.5, [Sen.] *Oct.* 831.

[39] B. J. Gibson (2010), 30–1, usefully discusses causation in historiography.

[40] Kuukkanen (2015), 169–70.

[41] Closs (2020), 367, compares Virgil's Aeneas introducing his account of the fall of Troy: *sive **dolo** seu iam Troiae sic **fata** ferebant* (*A.* 2.34). Cf. ***forte** an **dolo** principis . . . **ortum*** (Tac. *Ann.* 15.38.1).

[42] Gaertner (2008), 37–8, analysing how Augustus (amongst others) appropriates the paradigm of Camillus for his own political purposes, discusses various representations of Camillus as a second founder after Romulus. Tacitus presents people in AD 64 explicitly comparing the start dates of the Neronian fire and the Gallic sack (*Ann.* 15.41.2, with Ash (2018), 192–3), but seems sceptical about whether such synchronism of notable events is significant. See Edwards (2011), 654, on the possible resonances of Tacitus' evocation of Camillus.

Burn Baby Burn (Disco *in Furneaux*)   363

audience is left in suspended animation, but the intriguing possibility that Nero is blameless is a well-judged opening gambit.

Next, Tacitus activates a trope more familiar from a different area of historiography. When he announces that the disaster was more serious and destructive than all previous damage inflicted on the city through violent fires, he recalls a topos from historical prefaces, namely, the assertion that the war about to be described is the greatest conflict ever.[43] Insisting beforehand on a war's severity is common in historical prefaces, such as Sallust claiming, 'The war I am about to write is that which the Roman people waged with Jugurtha, king of the Numidians, first of all because it was great and fierce and of only sporadic success' (*bellum scripturus sum quod populus Romanus cum Iugurtha rege Numidarum gessit, primum quia magnum et atrox uariaque uictoria fuit, Iug.* 5.1);[44] and likewise in prefatory sections within historical narratives when Livy trumpets the conflict against Hannibal as 'the war which was the most memorable of all those ever fought' (*bellum maxime omnium memorabile quae umquam gesta sint,* Liv. 21.1.1).[45] Tacitus' opening therefore implicitly likens the conflagration to a war (an alignment already suggested by *clades*) and prepares the way to cast the fire as an invading army (an important metaphorical strand running through his whole account).[46] Seneca likewise characterized the fire at Lugdunum as unleashing even worse terrors than war: 'during peacetime something so momentous has happened which even during a war could not be feared' (*in tanta pace quantum ne bello quidem timeri potest accidit, Ep.* 91.2). In contrast, Tacitus leaves the comparison hovering indirectly, but increasingly peppers his narrative with vocabulary suggesting the military sphere (*clades, impetu, peruagatum, populando, circumueniebantur, uociferanbantur, cladibus*). In introducing the fire in comparative terms as *grauior atque atrocior*, Tacitus also activates rivalry with predecessors describing other blazes, such as Thucydides on the superlative fire at Plataea, 'the largest man-made (χειροποίητον) conflagration that anyone had ever seen up to that time' (2.77.4), or Seneca calling the fire at Lugdunum 'a disaster which was unexpected and almost

---

[43] Suetonius and Dio offer no similar opening gambit.

[44] Velleius Paterculus 2.11.1 avoids this aggrandising claim about the war, instead transferring it to Metellus, the best general.

[45] Levene (2010), 3–4, discusses the expectations raised by this assertion.

[46] See Jaeger (1999), 169, on the 'guiding metaphor' as a device to help readers identify patterns latent in a narrative. Woodman (2006) analyses metaphor in the other direction, considering the network of imagery (medicine and madness) marking the rebellious armies in Tacitus *Annals* 1. Goodyear (1972), 215–16, examines the recurrent fire imagery applied to these mutinous soldiers. Suetonius includes an actual siege-engine in his version of the fire (*Nero* 38.1).

(*paene*) unheard of (*Ep.* 91.1).[47] Tacitus' assessment of the AD 64 fire as the most terrible and destructive fire Rome had ever experienced is supremely confident, but leaves open the possibility that subsequent fires in Rome (e.g. the firing of the Capitol in AD 69) would be even more substantial.

After this arresting opening, Tacitus presents the fire's outbreak, showing a level of interest in Rome's topographical detail as the backdrop to the fire – an element absent from the parallel versions in Suetonius and Cassius Dio. According to Tacitus, the fire began in the Circus Maximus, surely a suggestive detail, as the fire's topography meshes with Nero's personality: 'even from earliest youth, Nero burned with enthusiasm (*flagrauit*) for the horses' (Suet. *Nero* 22.1).[48] Tacitus' description of the fire's outbreak is also linguistically striking because of mimetic syntax.[49] So, the elaborate and sprawling opening, marked by pleonasm (*initium* + *ortum*) and thick with layered relative clauses (*quae, quibus, quo*), mimics time passing slowly as the fire comes to life. Then the tempo changes drastically: 'the fire had no sooner started than gathered strength and, fanned by the wind, took hold along the length of the circus' (*simul coeptus ignis et statim ualidus ac uento citus longitudinem circi corripuit*, 15.38.1). Verbal ellipse and encircling alliteration of '*c*' mirrors the ruthless speed of the fire taking hold. One elegant detail is Tacitus' allusion to Virgil in the *Georgics* and the *Aeneid* describing chariot races, as he aligns the racing fire with those speedy chariots normally hurtling through the Circus Maximus.[50]

Tacitus further complicates the issue of Nero's responsibility in two ways. First, he acknowledges that chance also contributed to this devastating disaster via the wind, which fanned and spread the fire at a formative stage. Cassius Dio also accentuates the wind, but only at his narrative's finale: 'a wind caught up the flames and carried them indiscriminately against all the buildings that were left' (62.17.2).[51] Second, Tacitus introduces a further rational and analytical dimension by acknowledging that the old city's ramshackle layout, with its narrow winding streets,

---

[47] *paene* seems wryly self-aware, as Seneca subtly concedes that big fire descriptions were a trope.

[48] Tacitus also enjoys *flagrare*, 'one of the most extravagantly metaphorical words in Tacitus' vocabulary' (Closs (2020), 354).

[49] Lateiner (1990) discusses mimetic syntax.

[50] *longitudinem **circi corripuit*** (Tac. *Ann.* 15.38.1): cf. ***campum*** / ***corripuere*** ... *currus* (Verg. *G.* 3.103–4, *A.* 5.144–5). See Mynors (1990), 198, on *corripere* 'used of setting out vigorously over a space, as though one seized upon its nearer edge before devouring it'.

[51] Cf. Thomas Vyner's eyewitness account of the great fire of London (1666), emphasizing the strong westerly wind: 'But now the fire gets mastery and burns dreadfully; and God with his great bellows blows upon it!' (J. Richardson (2000), 142).

Burn Baby Burn (Disco *in Furneaux*)

facilitated the spreading of the fire (*artis itineribus hucque et illuc flexis atque enormibus uicis, qualis uetus Roma fuit*).[52] This elaborate language has mythical and poetical colour, evoking the winding maze from which Theseus escapes after killing the minotaur ('as he emerged from the windings of the labyrinth', *labyrintheis e flexibus egredientem*, Cat. 64.114), or Daedalus' ingenious labyrinth ('Daedalus ... constructed the work, confused the usual ways and deceived the eyes by a conflicting maze of diverse, winding paths', *Daedalus ... / ponit opus turbatque notas et lumina flexa / ducit in errorem uariarum ambage uiarum*, Ov. *Met.* 8.159–61).[53] Tacitus' Rome is cast as a bewildering space, with unclear escape routes from a city whose confusing layers reflect physical accretions over huge swathes of time:[54] Nero is not responsible for this cityscape (however much he is condemned for shaping its successor). Tacitus' topographical focus also recalls the legacy of previous historical trauma, as Rome's unsystematic layout in AD 64 springs from the city's chaotic reconstruction after the Gallic sack (390 BC):

> festinatio curam exemit vicos dirigendi, dum omisso sui alienique discrimine in vacuo aedificant. ea est causa ut veteres cloacae, primo per publicum ductae, nunc privata passim subeant tecta, formaque urbis sit occupatae magis quam divisae similis.
>
> haste eliminated any concern for making the streets straight, and people built in empty space without distinguishing between their own and others' properties. This is why the ancient sewers, initially laid out through public domain, now run beneath private houses everywhere, and why the city's form resembles one seized rather than demarcated by planning. (Liv. 5.55.4)

This is a curious ending to Livy's first pentad, catapulting his readers into the Augustan present: the twilight zone of the underground sewers preserves the original historical divisions between public and private space in the city before 390 BC, which was drastically altered above ground in the chaotically rebuilt city, while the figurative focus on *urbs occupata* reminds readers of the fate that Rome narrowly avoided at the Gauls' hands.[55] Tacitus' emphasis on the historic layout of 'old Rome' foregrounds a point for which Nero is not responsible – and indeed contrasts with Suetonius'

---

[52] Suetonius is briefer (*angustiis flexurisque uicorum*, *Nero* 38.1).

[53] See Reed Doob (1990), 17–38, on these and other labyrinths.

[54] See Gowers (1995), 23, on Rome as a 'perennial palimpsest'.

[55] Livy's focus on the *cloacae* recalls the wretched plebeians forced to dig underground, constructing Tarquinius Superbus' sewers (1.59.9). Cf. Plin. *Nat.* 36.107–8 (blaming Tarquinius Priscus). The Cloaca Maxima was big enough for Agrippa to sail through it to the Tiber in 33 BC (D.C. 49.43.1).

366   RHIANNON ASH

claim that Nero burned the city 'since he was displeased by the ugliness of
the old buildings and by the narrow winding streets' (*quasi offensus
deformitate ueterum aedificiorum et angustiis flexurisque uicorum*, *Nero*
38.1).[56]

After this apparently even-handed and analytical opening, Tacitus
changes gears in the central section:

> 38 (4) ad hoc lamenta pauentium feminarum, fessa aetate aut rudis puer-
> itiae, quique sibi quique aliis consulebat, dum trahunt inualidos aut opper-
> iuntur, pars mora, pars festinans, cuncta impediebant. (5) et saepe, dum in
> tergum respectant, lateribus aut fronte circumueniebantur, uel si in prox-
> ima euaserant, illis quoque igni correptis, etiam quae longinqua crediderant
> in eodem casu reperiebant. (6) postremo, quid uitarent quid peterent
> ambigui, complere uias, sterni per agros; quidam amissis omnibus fortunis,
> diurni quoque uictus, alii caritate suorum, quos eripere nequiuerant, qua-
> muis patente effugio interiere. (7) nec quisquam defendere audebat, crebris
> multorum minis restinguere prohibentium, et quia alii palam facies iacie-
> bant atque esse sibi auctorem uociferabantur, siue ut raptus licentius
> exercerent seu iussu.

> (4) In addition, the lamentations of the panic-stricken – of women, those
> worn out by age or in their raw youth – and individuals who paid heed to
> themselves or to others, as they dragged the infirm or waited for them,
> impeded everything, some by dilatoriness, others hurrying. (5) And often,
> while they looked back to the rear, they were surrounded on the flanks or in
> front, or, if they emerged in some nearby area, with the fire having taken
> hold there too they discovered that even places which they had believed
> distant from it were in the same predicament. (6) Finally, in two minds as
> to what they should avoid and what they should make for, they filled the
> roads or scattered over the fields. Some perished after the loss of all their
> fortune and even that of their daily livelihood, others from affection for the
> relatives whom they had been unable to rescue; yet in both cases escape had
> been open. (7) Nor did anyone dare to fight back the fire, given the
> frequency of threats from the numbers who prevented quenching it, and
> because others openly threw torches and shouted that they had authoriza-
> tion – whether to conduct their looting more licentiously or by order.

This is where the emotions hit. Tacitus' carefully compartmentalized
narrative is very effective. Whereas the first section had addressed practical
questions (how the city's layout and the random factor of the wind had
exacerbated the fire), only now does Tacitus document the impact on the
people. That pointed division not only asserts his *auctoritas* as a

---

[56] This is taking *quasi* as causal (*OLD quasi* 5a).

Burn Baby Burn (Disco in Furneaux) 367

dispassionate, rational historian, but also allows him to build to an emotional climax: for, after methodically considering causes and explanations, he then shifts direction and zooms in on the disaster's human cost.[57] This layout also contributes significantly to anticipation and foreboding. We must wonder, throughout the first section about the city's fabric, what impact this fire will have on its inhabitants.[58] Contrast this with Dio's opening gambit, relaying verbatim in *oratio recta* people's bursts of bemused exclamation (62.16.3) and thus disregarding Polybius' warning that historians should avoid recreating characters' probable utterances (2.56.10).[59] Tacitus instead restricts himself to conveying women's *lamenta* in impressionistic, general terms. Quintilian, explaining how best to narrate an *urbs capta* falling, recommends emphasizing wailing women and children (*infantium feminarumque ploratus*, 8.3.68), but in his enumeration of telling points to include, this detail is the finale after a general backdrop of *flammae*, *fragor*, and *sonus*. Tacitus, with his sharp eye and rhetorical training, seems to have taken note.

Tacitus also avoids or adds nuance to some more grimy, prosaic details found in Dio, such as some people's efforts to rescue their possessions and others stealing property (62.16.6). Rome's citizens in Tacitus' account are more honourable than their counterparts in Dio – a point that stands out because elsewhere Tacitus is often caustic about the lower classes in an urban setting.[60] Finally, Tacitus adds a poignant touch (absent from Dio and Suetonius) that some people died in distress about failing to rescue

---

[57] This mirrors wider patterns; e.g. in Tacitus' account of Vitellius' imperial challenge (AD 69), dispassionate analysis of causes (*nunc initia causasque motus Vitelliani expediam*, 'now I will lay out the beginnings and causes of the Vitellian movement', *Hist.* 1.51.1) precedes the emotive presentation of consequences. Likewise, Tacitus stresses the importance of investigating not just *casus euentusque rerum* ('occurrences and outcomes of events') but *ratio etiam causaeque* ('also the reason and causes', *Hist.* 1.4.1): 'the emphasis on explanation . . . links *Hist.* to a tradition of ancient historiography indebted to Polybius, which defined itself in the Roman world by opposition to the first generation of "annalistic" histories that simply recorded each year's events' (Damon (2003), 101).

[58] Diodorus Siculus, probably drawing on Hellenistic historians Cleitarchus and Duris of Samos (Rossi (2002), 233; Marincola (1997), 243 n. 129 on Diodorus' explicit citations), opens immediately with the slaughter of inhabitants during the sacks of Thebes (17.13.1), Persepolis (17.70.2), and Segesta (20.71.2). For the sack of Syracuse, Diodorus Siculus even offers a *praeteritio* about avoiding artificially tragic history (19.7.4) despite opening with the inhabitants' slaughter (19.7.1). See too *Rhet. Her.* 4.39.

[59] Quoted above, p. 359.

[60] See Newbold (1976); and Pelling (2009b), 159, on the 'suite of traditional aristocratic values' tangible in Tacitus' narrative. The editors of this volume raise the question of *raptus* at 15.38.7, but this detail is associated with a distinct dubious sub-group that is directly at odds with the honourable populace. See Walsh (2019), 47, on these gangs attempting to prevent people from fighting the fire.

368 RHIANNON ASH

loved ones, even though escape was possible.[61] This general observation allows comparisons with a crucial and emotive sequence from Virgil *Aeneid* 2, when Anchises stubbornly refuses to leave Troy and Aeneas almost gives up and dies with him in the city (*A.* 2.634–70). The link is not drawn explicitly, but Tacitus deftly hints at this scene from the epic tradition to align the victims of the AD 64 fire with Anchises and Aeneas.[62]

This central panel again deploys mimetic grammar and syntax to reinforce the impression of chaos and human misery: we are buffeted by ellipse of verbs (*lamenta* [sc. *fuerunt*]), abrupt changes of construction (*fessa aetate* [ablative of quality] *aut rudis pueritiae* [genitive of quality]), verbs with vivid present tenses (*trahunt, respectant*), historic infinitives (*complere, sterni*), anaphora (*quid . . . quid*) and deliberate imbalance (as in *pars mora pars festinans*, shifting from a descriptive ablative to a present participle).[63] Last but not least, Tacitus again equivocates about Nero's responsibility by acknowledging that although arsonists might have been under orders, equally this could have been their excuse to plunder unhampered.

The third section sees Tacitus manipulating his audience's preconceptions especially provocatively in light of alternative traditions about responsibility for this fire:

> **39** (1) eo in tempore Nero Anti agens non ante in urbem regressus est, quam domui eius, qua Palatium et Maecenatis hortos continuauerat, ignis propinquaret. neque tamen sisti potuit, quin et Palatium et domus et cuncta circum haurirentur. (2) sed solacium populo exturbato ac profugo campum Martis ac monumenta Agrippae, hortos quin etiam suos patefacit et subitaria aedificia exstruxit, quae multitudinem inopem acciperent; subuectaque utensilia ab Ostia et propinquis municipiis, pretiumque frumenti minutum usque ad ternos nummos. (3) quae quamquam popularia in inritum cadebant, quia peruaserat rumor ipso tempore flagrantis urbis inisse eum domesticam scaenam et cecinisse Troianum excidium, praesentia mala uetustis cladibus adsimulantem.

> At the time, Nero was at Antium, not returning to the City until the fire neared the house of his by which he had linked the Palatium with Maecenas' Gardens; yet it still could not be stopped from consuming the Palatium and house and everything around about. But, as a relief for the evicted and fugitive people, he opened up the Plain of Mars and the

---

[61] This is more extreme than Quintilian's suggested focus on 'some in doubt whether to flee' (8.3.68). See too Hutchinson (2020), 140–2, on Tacitus' depiction of movement in this passage.

[62] The association is triggered not by a verbal echo but by overlapping context, although earlier in the passage *fessa aetate* recalls Virgil's Anchises, *fessum aetate parentem* (*A.* 2.596). See further Damon (2010) on such issues.

[63] See Ash (2018), 182–4.

Burn Baby Burn (Disco *in Furneaux*)

monuments of Agrippa, in fact even his own gardens, and he set up improvised buildings to receive the destitute multitude; and comestibles were sailed up from Ostia and nearby municipalities, and the price of grain was reduced to three sesterces. All of which, though intended to be popular, proved unavailing, because a rumour had spread that at the very time of the City's blaze he had actually mounted his domestic stage and sung of the extirpation of Troy, assimilating present calamities to olden disasters.

That opening temporal marker *eo in tempore* significantly underscores that precisely when Rome was burning, Nero was at Antium.[64] Not that Nero's absence is straightforwardly commendable (nor does it guarantee innocence), but it does differ from the parallel tradition. In Suetonius and Dio, Antium is not mentioned, and the clear implication is that Nero is present in Rome throughout the fire, although without helping the populace. We can compare here an eyewitness to the great fire of London (1666) commenting on James, Duke of York, leading the fire-fighting: 'The Duke of York hath won the hearts of the people with his continual and indefatigable pains day and night in helping to quench the Fire.'[65] In Suetonius and Dio, third-person singular verbs with Nero as subject and agent cluster at the start of the fire narrative.[66] Yet Tacitus defers naming the emperor as a direct participant in the action until now. Although Nero's dubious involvement was considered possible (*dolo principis*, 15.38.1; *iussu*, 15.38.7), both potentially damning instances are balanced by alternative explanations denying his culpability (*forte*, 15.38.1; *ut raptus licentius exercerent*, 15.38.7).[67] Given sensational stories of Nero singing about Troy's destruction while watching Rome burn, Tacitus' delayed announcement that Nero was at Antium when the fire started is unexpected. Even when the emperor returns to Rome, the notorious performance is not immediately highlighted. Instead, Tacitus enumerates in detail Nero's relief measures for the people, without suggesting that there is anything hypocritical or insincere about them. Indeed, when Tacitus calls these interventions *popularia*, he means that they were 'intended to be popular', despite the fact that they were not – and the reason for that

---

[64] Antium (*OCD*³), mod. Anzio, about twenty miles south of Ostia, became a fashionable coastal resort under Augustus, who had an imperial villa there (as did Agrippina the Younger, Tac. *Ann.* 14.3.1). Nero lavishly rebuilt the harbour (Suet. *Nero* 9) and made it a colony for veterans (AD 61; Tac. *Ann.* 14.27.2; Suet. *Nero* 9).

[65] Tinniswood (2003), 80, quoting from an eyewitness' letter.

[66] *nec ... pepercit*; *inquit*; *fecit*; *incendit* (Suet. *Nero* 38.1) and ἐπεθύμησεν; ἐμακάριζεν; διαπέμπων; ὑπεπίμπρα (D.C. 62.16.1).

[67] Whitehead (1979), 492, discussing Tacitus and loaded alternatives, acknowledges the subtlety of both examples but categorizes them as 'probably or certainly' emphasizing the second alternative.

370 RHIANNON ASH

failure was that 'a rumour had spread' (*peruaserat rumor*) that Nero had sung about Troy's destruction. The verb's pluperfect tense anchors the rumour *before* the relief effort, suggesting its speedy dissemination.[68] Tacitus avoids saying that Nero's performance really happened, whereas Suetonius and Dio convey it as fact.[69] And various other details downgrade the transgressive nature of Nero's performance. In Tacitus Nero performs on a *domestica scaena* in the palace, but authors in the parallel tradition give more conspicuous locations: the top of the Tower of Maecenas (Suet. *Nero* 38.2) or the roof of the palace (D.C. 62.18.1). Their flashy Nero dons formal costume (*in illo scaenico habitu*, Suet., *Nero* 38.2; τὴν σκευὴν τὴν κιθαρῳδικήν, D.C. 62.18.1), a detail completely omitted by Tacitus. As a final elegant touch, Tacitus introduces ring composition, where Nero likens 'present troubles' (*praesentia mala*) with 'ancient disasters' (*uetustis cladibus*): the aggrandizing plurals applied to Nero trump Tacitus' authorial singular (*clades*) at the narrative's opening – or so the rumour goes. In some sense the plurals are apt, since the fire is not quite over: one further outbreak looms (15.40.1). That too exacerbates Nero's *infamia* as he 'seemed' (*uidebatur*, 15.40.2) to seek the glory of founding a new city named after himself. Yet Tacitus holds back from endorsing that interpretation, but presents it as a common belief.

Conclusions

So, where does this close reading leave us? Earlier I highlighted the inherently competitive nature of disaster narratives in ancient texts, particularly within historiography where the agonistic drive was especially pronounced. Impressively, Tacitus competes both with his predecessors' accounts (no longer extant) and (paradoxically) even with himself. Earlier purple passages such as *Histories* 3.71, the burning of the Capitol during the civil wars, and the (no longer extant) account of Vesuvius' eruption, would have set the bar high, as readers turned their attention to his version

---

[68] Hardie (2012), 307, comments: 'Comparing latter-day disasters with the sack of Troy is something that Romans other than Nero also do, not least historians such as Livy and Tacitus, who in *Histories* 3 hints that the sack of Cremona and of the Capitoline Temple of Jupiter are repetitions of the sack of Troy.' The significant difference is the chronological gap of forty years between Tacitus publishing the *Histories* (c. AD 109) and the calamities described. John Evelyn described the great fire of London creating 'ruines resembling the picture of Troy' (de la Bédoyère (1995), 154).

[69] 'Other sources squarely blame Nero (Plin., *Nat.* 17.5, [Sen.], *Oct.* 831, Suet., *Nero* 38, D.C. 62.16.1): after all, he benefited, since the fire made space for his Golden House (a *cui bono* rationalization; Cic. *S. Rosc.* 84, *Phil.* 2.35)' (Ash (2018), 177).

Burn Baby Burn (Disco *in Furneaux*)

of the famous AD 64 fire. If we accept that traditional versions of this fire were marked by hyperbole and emotion – and a willingness straightforwardly to blame Nero, then we can see that Tacitus' response is designed to strengthen his historiographical authority in two ways.

First, Tacitus foregrounds old Rome's physical layout and chance factors such as the wind in his own analysis of the disaster, thereby projecting himself as a cool-headed and rational historian. That restrained stance also brought fringe benefits by closing down potential associations with sensationalizing modes of historiography and by expressing sensitivity towards the boundaries of good and bad taste.

Second, Tacitus' repeated posture of reluctance to blame Nero squarely for the disaster is startling and marks him out from the parallel tradition. Throughout this disaster narrative, Tacitus is competing with other historians (past, present, and future). Rather than directly blaming Nero, Tacitus allows scope for other explanations and thus comes across as more balanced, thereby making a play for the longevity of his own account. Yet despite allowing the possibility that Nero himself did not start the fire and revel in performing the notorious song, Tacitus' veneer of impartiality and objectivity may be just that. Nero hardly emerges unscathed from these chapters. Tacitus quickly piles on moral pressure subsequently when presenting the construction of Nero's Golden House: 'However, Nero took advantage of the ruin of his fatherland and built a house' (*ceterum Nero usus est patriae ruinis extruxitque domum, Ann.* 15.42.1). The pejorative connotation of *usus est* here is clear. Although it is not the same as saying that Nero set the fire to clear space for his Golden House, it is still damning, and discreditably echoes the opening of Tigellinus' banquet: 'He treated the whole city as if it were his private house' (*totaque urbe quasi domo uti, Ann.* 15.37.1). This sort of suggestive and interconnected language is typical of Tacitus, using pinpricks rather than a sledge-hammer.

In that connection it is crucial that Tacitus casts Nero's performance during the disaster as rumour, not fact. This detail takes on an intriguing significance subsequently: rumours matter, and can significantly influence people's beliefs and behaviour. During the unsuccessful Pisonian conspiracy, the centurion Subrius Flavus explains why he abandoned his military oath to Nero: 'I began to hate you after you became the killer of your mother and wife, charioteer, actor, and fire-starter' (*odisse coepi, postquam parricida matris et uxoris, auriga et histrio et incendiarius extitisti, Ann.* 15.67.2). Tacitus purportedly relays the soldier's direct words. Damning nouns trace Nero's abuses in broadly chronological order, culminating in *incendiarius*. Whatever the reality, Subrius Flavus believed that Nero started the fire. This is the crucial factor, since that belief prompted him to join the conspiracy. As Gibson observes in an important article about Tacitean rumours, 'perceptions can be just as important as more concrete realities in determining subsequent events'.[70] Even Nero's suicide may, paradoxically, have been premature, as Tacitus clarifies in an extraordinary comment: 'Nero was driven out by messages and rumours more than by fighting' (*Nero nuntiis magis et rumoribus quam armis depulsus*, *H*. 1.89.2). Tacitus engages brilliantly with previous versions of the fire in the historical tradition and enriches his narrative by subtle allusions to the emotive archetypal destruction of Troy from the epic tradition. This affords us simultaneous glimpses of the potentially mundane reasons for the deadly fire's evolution and people's readiness to cast it as an epic disaster unleashed by their emperor. The collective drive to blame someone after a disaster and to 'learn lessons' is an overpowering response. Tacitus, seeking to enhance his authority, goes against the grain and uses the tradition to shape an account whose most original and innovative feature is the possibility that Nero is innocent. It took a bold historian with a remarkable level of confidence in his own *auctoritas* to offer that reading.

[70] B. J. Gibson (1998), 129.

CHAPTER 19

The Authority to Be Untraditional

Christopher Pelling

I

You do not hold an inquest into a book more than twenty years later unless it was a gamechanger. That is not just because John Marincola's *Authority and Tradition* is where you go first to find out what the historians said about what they were doing. It is also because it ranged so surefootedly over such a wide range that it opened many new perspectives and corrected many old mistakes – whether Caesar's use of the third-person in the *Commentarii* was just the sort of thing one did, for instance, or a bold unobvious choice (H. Flower, Chapter 11 in this volume); or what difference Rome's preoccupation with social status made to the way historians framed their projects.

This chapter is a meditation on that word 'gamechanger'. It has been observed that those who break with an age are then remembered as most symbolic of that age[1] – a thought-provoking idea if we think of, for example, Thucydides or Tacitus. That makes it more difficult to think of a gamechanger in the terms appropriate to the time. The word is modern, and so is the phrase 'paradigm shift'. The *Oxford English Dictionary* dates the first use of each to 1962, with 'paradigm shift' originating in discussion of Copernicus, Newton, and Einstein, and 'gamechanger' in Minnesota baseball. But the concept may not be alien to ancient historiography, at least if one recalls how often we talk of authors 'defining' or 'positioning themselves against' something else: to

---

* I am most grateful to Mike Brearley, Luke Pitcher, and Rhiannon Ash for valuable help and comments. My greatest thanks are due to John Marincola himself, for all those hours – educational, editorial, and above all convivial – that we have spent together over the years.
[1] Knausgaard (2019), 18, discussing the art of Edward Munch: 'only those works that break with the era come to be seen as typical of the era': quoted by Mike Brearley, in a talk given in London on 1 April 2019, just before the conference that was the origin of this volume. Brearley, captain of the England cricket team in the 1970s and 1980s and now an experienced psychoanalyst, was talking about both cricket and psychotherapy.

373

374   CHRISTOPHER PELLING

take one example, Herodotus has been seen as defining himself against earlier *logographoi*, against Homer, against commemorative oratory and the poets in general, or 'Aesopic' low literature, or 'other purveyors of mythical material', or proto-biography;[2] to take another, Suetonius as positioning his biography against historiography itself.[3] And it is not just modern scholars who speak in such terms. Tacitus does it too, contrasting himself with all those Republican writers who enjoyed such lush topics as tribunicial agitation or corn laws (*Ann* 4.32: below, p. 386); Plutarch firmly proclaims 'it is not histories we are writing but Lives' (*Alex.* 1.2: below, p. 389); and there are many others. Marincola could indeed entitle a whole chapter 'The Lonely Historian' (1997, ch. 5), as these bold pioneers set out on their path and mark their distance from the herd or the pack.

There were dangers here as well. When Plutarch is about to trample on Thucydidean ground in the *Nicias*, he hopes that nobody will mistake him for suffering from Timaeus-disease – Timaeus, who hoped to show himself smarter than Thucydides and more sophisticated than Philistus, and in fact just made himself ridiculous (more precisely, ὀψιμαθὴς καὶ μειρακιώδης, a nice blend of 'late learning' – too little, too late – and 'adolescent' naïveté: *Nicias* 1). Similarly in the *Artaxerxes*: 'one would be crazy' to attempt to rival Xenophon by giving a full narrative of the battle of Cunaxa, rather than just adding a few details he missed (*Artax.* 8.1–2) – not least that it was the battle of Cunaxa! Xenophon did not give it a name or a place.[4] When you tilt at the acknowledged greats, you need to be sure not just of your ground but that your audience too feels that you have some right to that ground. Who do you think you are to fiddle with a heavyweight and highly respected tradition? Why, you are just one of those 'academic nonentities who have dared to take the measure of their literary betters'.[5] This chapter will investigate some of the ways that authors build the 'authority' to set themselves against the tradition and the traditional greats without being ridiculous.

True, there is often some balancing act, as authors set themselves *within* the tradition as well. Marincola convincingly argued that Posidonius could both be Polybius' continuator and write a conspicuously different type of

---

[2] Homer: bibliography in Pelling (2006b). Commemorative oratory and the poets: Grethlein (2010); cf. Marincola (2006), esp. 14, 21–2. Aesopic 'low' literature: Kurke (2011); cf. Griffin (1990). 'Other purveyors of mythical material': Baragwanath and de Bakker (2012b), 31. Stesimbrotus and Ion: Pelling (2007c).
[3] Suetonius: Wallace-Hadrill (1983).   [4] Huitink (2019), 209–13.
[5] A phrase used in a *Times Literary Supplement* review (15 March 2019, p. 33): it was used ironically, and was less unfriendly to its target than it sounds.

The Authority to Be Untraditional

history, with lots more cultural interest, and Ammianus could do the same for Tacitus.[6] One further objection to framing the inquiry in these terms is that it risks misunderstanding how genre works. There is an issue anyway about how far we should talk about 'genre' for the earliest Greek historians, or for any early prose: poetry can tie its 'generic' qualities to particular performance contexts, but that does not really work for prose. Even once we can talk about 'history' as a genre – possibly as late as Aristotle's *Poetics* (1451a36–b11) – genre is never that constricting; we have become used to thinking about genre as a moving target, 'more a pigeon than a pigeonhole',[7] where authors place themselves in a generic tradition while subtly moving on to do something a little different as well. Perhaps indeed they have to do this if a work is not to be wholly bewildering. It can even be made expressively questionable whether a genre can shift enough to accommodate what an author is trying to do with it: Marincola has written about that in the case of Tacitus' *Agricola* – is it really possible to write a biography of a non-imperial figure when author and subject are working under an imperial system?[8] One can raise a mirroring question with the big men of the late Republic: can one keep any boundary between history and biography when so vast a figure as Julius Caesar turns Rome's story into his own?[9] There are also texts like Xenophon's *Cyropaedia* or Philostratus' *Life of Apollonius*, where readers are left to work out as they go along what sort of work this is, and in particular how true all this is supposed to be. There we cannot really talk of 'gamechanging', rather of setting up a game where one of the players, the reader, has to work out the rules while already playing it. So, someone might say, we cannot really separate out the gamechangers: they are all doing it, to a degree. Perhaps that is right – but some do it more, and more explicitly, than others. The emphasis in programmatic remarks often falls on 'others have done it, but I can do it better' or 'I can do it too, for a different period'; but here the focus will be on those cases where the emphasis – our emphasis, usually their emphasis too – will be more 'what those others did is all very well, but I am going to do something different'.

II

Where to start? Perhaps it should be with Herodotus on Hecataeus: there is plenty to say, or at least to speculate, about that. But we are on a little

---

[6] Marincola (1997), 239, 254–6. [7] A. Fowler (1982), 34 [8] Marincola (1999a), 318–20.
[9] Pelling (2006a).

firmer ground with Thucydides' relation to Herodotus. At that stage it is probably still wise to talk about the relation to the great predecessor rather than to any 'genre' as a whole.

It is generally assumed that Thucydides has Herodotus in particular in mind at 1.20–1, when he snipes at the mistakes made when people are too uncritical of oral transmission. It is also often thought that Herodotus is his principal target there when he corrects a couple of particular misapprehensions, first that Spartan kings have two votes and second that there is such a thing as a Pitanate λόχος (1.20.3); that is less certain, and whatever his target it is also unclear that Thucydides is fair or correct in those criticisms. In our respective Herodotus commentaries M. A. Flower and Marincola are as cautious about the Pitanate λόχος (9.53.2) as Hornblower and Pelling are about the Spartan kings (6.57.5).[10] Still, it is unlikely to be coincidence that Herodotus treated both those cases, and it is not particularly controversial to say that Thucydides too is 'defining himself against' alternatives at 1.20–1: he will not be like the poets and exaggerate, nor like 'the logographers' and sacrifice truth for attractiveness. So it is not a stretch to see him as positioning himself against Herodotus too, especially as he goes on to compare his own topic with the Persian Wars in 1.23 and especially as the Pentekontaetia will pick up the story (1.89) almost but not quite at the point where Herodotus stopped. This is surely right, but the exact character of this 'positioning' is quite hard to pin down.

Thucydides' other example here of a common mistake already suggests that it is complicated. That is the popular misapprehension about the Peisistratids, with people thinking that Hipparchus was tyrant when Harmodius and Aristogeiton killed him and not realizing the full story (1.20.2). Thucydides comes back to this again at 6.54–9, giving a much fuller version there along the same lines, probably with a verbal echo of the passage in Book 1.[11] Herodotus again might surely be expected to be in his sights, for Herodotus treated the tyrant-killing, or brother-of-the-tyrant-killing, in his Book 5. But, as again is often pointed out, in fact Herodotus and Thucydides are here on the same side, at least on the important points that Hippias, not Hipparchus, was tyrant (Hdt. 5.55.1, Thuc. 1.20.2, 6.54.2), and that the tyranny continued for four years after the assassination (Hdt. 5.55.1, Thuc. 6.59.4). Thucydides even echoes Herodotus in

---

[10] M. A. Flower and Marincola (2002), 202; Hornblower and Pelling (2017), 165.

[11] 6.54.1, where 'about their own tyrants' echoes 'in their own country' (1.20.2) and 'they say nothing accurate' echoes 'accept without investigation' (1.20.2).

his insistence that the earlier phases of the tyranny were praiseworthy, extending Herodotus' positive verdict on Peisistratus (Hdt. 1.59.6) to include his sons (6.54.6) – but only up to 514 BC, and then again there is a similar insistence that the final years were much worse (Hdt. 5.62.2, 6.123.2, Thuc. 6.59.2). The same could be said about the Pausanias and Themistocles excursus at the end of Book 1 and about the Cylon episode that comes just before it:[12] there are one or two mild corrections of fact – commentators have fastened on these – but they do not amount to much and it is not at all clear that Thucydides always gets these right. So Herodotus may well be 'in mind', as I put it earlier, but if so Thucydides is sniping as much with him as against him.

More interesting is the style in which all these episodes are couched. 'Here the lion laughed', said the Scholiast on the Cylon episode, and the lively narrative in all three episodes – indeed, four, as one can add the story of Themistocles and the walls that begins the Pentekontaetia[13] – is unlike the austere manner of many of Thucydides' excursuses and bears comparison with Herodotus at his best. There are also some Herodoteanisms of style and manner, as has long been recognized and as Rosaria Munson in particular has spelled out for Pausanias and Themistocles; Rosalind Thomas, Victor Parker, and Tim Rood have done the same for Cylon.[14] Simon Hornblower also pointed out some of these for the Peisistratid excursus,[15] and a few more will be found in my own 'green and yellow' commentary on Thucydides 6.[16] There is also the highest concentration of women of anywhere in Thucydides, another Herodotean characteristic;[17] there is a new stress too on the erotic angle with Harmodius and Aristogeiton[18] – nothing of that in Herodotus, though we would normally think of Herodotus as the one to inject a personal element into high politics. So, yes, Thucydides is doing a pretty good job of out-Herodotusing Herodotus here,[19] rather as, arguably, Herodotus was making a point of out-Hecataeusing-Hecataeus. Perhaps, again like Herodotus with

---

[12] Pausanias and Themistocles: 1.128–38; Munson (2012), 250–6. Cylon: 1.126–7; Rood (2013).

[13] 1.90–2: cf. Blösel (2012), 216–18; Tsakmakis (1995), 74–6.

[14] Munson (2012), and cf. also Nicolai (2001); R. Thomas (1989), 272–81 ('we thus have a tale we might rather expect from Herodotus, with a visit to Delphi, a deceptive oracle and failed coup because the oracle was misinterpreted' (274)); Parker (2004), 131–41; Rood (2013); see also Hornblower (1991–2008), i.206–7.

[15] Hornblower (1991–2008), iii.438–9.   [16] Pelling (2022), 219–34.

[17] Even though they still remain marginal to the manoeuvrings of the men: Shannon-Henderson (2018), 94–5.

[18] Hornblower (1991–2008), iii.436–8.

[19] As Parker (2004), 135–6, puts it; cf. Rood (2013), 130 n. 36.

378   CHRISTOPHER PELLING

Hecataeus, he is also projecting his ability to do the same as Herodotus but
with a sharper critical edge, for instance, in his extraction of history from
inscriptions at 6.59: Herodotus cited inscriptions often enough, but with
mixed results. But the critical edge is not *much* sharper, and in fact
Thucydides' inscriptional argument is really not very good.[20] Once again
the main impression is that the two authors are far more similar than they
are different.

   We also have to see what the various episodes are doing in their
Thucydidean context, and that is what commentators these days increasingly scratch their heads over. Answers can be given, for the cases at the
end of Book 1 probably focusing on the narrative entry of Pericles and for
Book 6 something to do with Alcibiades, or more particularly the behaviour of the *demos* vis-à-vis Alcibiades. We also have to ask the point of the
stylistic Herodoteanism. Is it parody? Perhaps – but if so, it is not a
dismissive sort of parody; that would risk undermining the serious analysis
of the distant past that Thucydides is giving in all these passages. It is more
a feeling that this is the appropriate style for that sort of material and that
sort of history, and it goes with an insight that history has changed and the
way of writing it will change with it. Perhaps, indeed, we could find
something of the same insight within Herodotus himself: telling of
Alcmaeon's gold-strike at Croesus' court (6.125) and Agariste's marriage
(6.126–31) requires a different narrative style from the tenser and more
compressed action of Marathon that came a few chapters before, and for
that matter from the combative remarks on the Alcmaeonids and the
shield that have come in between (6.121–4).[21] And this is a point that
will come back for other writers too. When we find a gamechanger
historian, that can be a reflection not just of historians thinking they can
do the same past in a different way. It can also be the insight that different
pasts require different historiographies.

   So far, then, we are seeing the usual balance between compliment and
criticism, between homage and challenge that we find in any sort of
imitatio, but with a tilting of the scales towards the homage and the
compliment. One could say the same about the Archaeology. Some have
talked in more general terms of Thucydides' 'ideological rejection of
Herodotus and of Herodotus' way of doing history'[22] – but is he so
dismissive, at least for the earlier period? We could equally say that he
takes over Herodotus' techniques and pushes them further: yes, in the

[20] See e.g. Cawkwell (1997), 11.   [21] Hornblower and Pelling (2017), 14, 272.
[22] Munson (2012), 244, citing Greenwood (2006), 7, who in turn cites Ober (1998), 62–3.

The Authority to Be Untraditional

Archaeology he puts different questions to the material and adds different emphases – the importance of wealth and of sea power, neither of them points with which Herodotus would disagree, or the reasons for the sitings of cities – but does so with versions of Herodotus' own suite of techniques, sight (ὄψις), intelligence (γνώμη), and enquiry (ἱστορία).[23] There are the elaborate arguments from 'reasonability' (εἰκός) that one might expect of a child of the sophistic age, but does not Herodotus use εἰκός arguments too?[24] Helen could not have been at Troy, for if she had been the Trojans would have given her back (2.120.1–2); Scyllias could not have swum underwater because it was too far, and *I* think he went in a boat (8.8.1).

What of Thucydides' famed critical rigour? It is Herodotus who makes Polycrates 'the first Greek we know of' who attained θαλασσοκρατίη ('mastery of the sea'), adding a mention of Minos only in a qualifying clause, someone who belonged before 'the human generation' (3.122.2). Thucydides echoes Herodotus' language in his own treatment of Minos (1.4), but is more inclined to treat this as a matter of raw historical fact.[25] It is Thucydides, too, who thinks that Homer can be quarried for historical insight, even if one needs to beware poetic exaggeration (1.10.3) and to provide a harder-edged reason for Agamemnon's ability to launch so many ships, one more in line with Thucydides' view of the continuities of human nature.[26] Contrast Herodotus, who emphasizes that epic poetry imposes its own plot demands (2.116.1) and is prepared to doubt even so basic an element of the story as the presence of Helen at Troy.[27]

It is hard, then, to accept that Thucydides really believes that 'contemporary history is the only possible history'.[28] It would be better to say that he is mapping out the ways you can write even earlier history than Herodotus had done,[29] using techniques and materials that have more in

---

[23] So also Munson (2017), 258, 'exceptionally close' to Herodotus' procedures.

[24] 'Herodotus' technique of drawing inferences about the past is strikingly similar to Thucydides'', Rood (2006b), 236.

[25] Irwin (2007), esp. 190–1; cf. also Nicolai (2001), 270; Rood (2019), 335, and Chapter 3 in this volume.

[26] Kallet (2001), 113–14; cf. de Romilly (1967), ch. 4, esp. 260–2, 276–8 = (2012), 156–7, 166–7; Parry (1972b [1989]), 53–4; Hunter (1980), esp. 193–4, 202–4; Tsakmakis (1995), 46–7; Raaflaub (2016), 605; Saxonhouse (2017), 340–4; van Wees (2017), esp. 50–2, on various Thucydidean distortions in his arguments from Homer.

[27] Gomme in Gomme, Andrewes, and Dover (1945–81), i.; Hunter (1980), 192–3; and esp. Marcozzi–Sinatra–Vannicelli (1994). Still, one should not overstate the differences between Herodotus and Thucydides here; I discuss this more fully in Pelling (forthcoming a).

[28] Nicolai (2001), 283; similarly Moles (2001), 198, 'only contemporary history can be done properly'.

[29] Cf. Marcozzi, Sinatra, and Vannicelli (1994) on Thucydides' greater willingness to extract historically useful material from Homeric epic (above, note 23): 'we might say that Thucydides

380   CHRISTOPHER PELLING

common with Herodotus than with those that Thucydides will be using
for his contemporary history. One could never, for instance, imagine him
citing Aristophanes when he came to write of Pericles or Cleon in the way
that he cites Homer for Agamemnon, largely because a much more
rigorous interrogation of ἀκοή becomes possible with multiple informants.
To put it in Aristotelian terms (*EN* 1 1094b.11–14), the degree of
attainable precision (ἀκρίβεια) depends on the available material (ὕλη),
but he is still content that he has found out the truth about that earlier
material 'sufficiently, given that they happened a long time ago' (ὡς
παλαιὰ εἶναι ἀποχρώντως, 1.21.1).[30] We could even see the Book
6 Peisistratid excursus as presenting a test case to show that you can find
out the truth even in an extreme case, one where confusion and partisanship had particularly distorted popular tradition. Perhaps that goes for
Cylon too, for where there is material that figures in only one of the two
authors it is always Thucydides who offers it.[31]

There is plenty, then, to show how Thucydides is building that 'authority' and barricading himself against that awkward question, who are you to
set yourself up against the great Herodotus? Why, I'm someone who can
play the Herodotus game too, but for the rest of the work I'm choosing not
to do it.

So how is he going to do it? What will be different? One way we have
already seen: the exploitation of the different and wider source material
that contemporary history can offer. Other ways are mapped out in the
methodological chapters 1.20–3, but this is not the place to go into those.
Others again will emerge only as the narrative progresses, such as the
absence of any divine management: not every first-time reader would have
anticipated this after the emphasis on earthquakes and eclipses and natural
disasters in 1.23.3. Still, we have already seen enough to make it doubtful
whether he is sniping at Herodotus in particular with his claim to have
produced 'a possession for ever more than a prize-piece for immediate
hearing' (κτῆμά τε ἐς αἰεὶ μᾶλλον ἢ ἀγώνισμα ἐς τὸ παραχρῆμα ἀκούειν
ξυγκεῖται, 1.22.4). If Herodotus is particularly in mind there, it may be as

---

would have accused Herodotus of throwing the baby out with the bathwater' ('di aver gettato via,
con l'acqua, anche il bambino', 173).

[30] Cf. now Rawlings (2021), esp. 195, arguing that Thucydides' careful distinction in 1.22 between
what he claims (a) for the λόγοι spoken 'either before the war or after its outbreak' and (b) for the
ἔργα 'done in the war' acknowledges that all events before 431, including the Pentekontaetia as well
as the Archaeology, could not be investigated with the same thoroughness and rigour as those of the
war itself.

[31] Parker (2004), 133.

much as an ally as a target, for one could reasonably see Herodotus' work too as a 'possession for ever', given his concern to ensure that human achievements should not become 'wiped out through time' (τῷ χρόνῳ ἐξίτηλα, Hdt. proem). For that matter, Thucydides need not be denying that either work is a 'prize-piece for immediate hearing' *as well*. This is not the only Thucydidean comparison to say that something is more A than B, or not so much B as A, without excluding that it can be both.[32]

Still, there is certainly plenty of Herodotus in the air, and especially in 1.23. That contrast of Thucydides' war with τὰ Μηδικά could hardly fail to stir Herodotean thoughts; several of the natural phenomena mentioned – earthquakes, eclipses, dislocations of populations (1.23.6) – are also pretty frequent in Herodotus. Maybe even the famous contrast of αἰτίαι ('causes', 'grievances') and ἀληθεστάτη πρόφασις ('truest explanation') has more of a Herodotean tinge than is often recognized. That is not just because the precise analysis – Spartans fearing the growth of Athenian power and striking pre-emptively – is in line with Herodotean thinking: that is why Croesus moves on Cyrus (Hdt. 1.46.1) and why Sparta thinks of strangling the infant democracy at Athens (5.91.1). It has also been observed that Thucydides has switched the words around, as αἰτία tends to be used elsewhere of a truer cause and πρόφασις of something closer to (but not exactly or not always) a 'pretext', though both can be used of both.[33] If there is a switch, it is natural enough to put it down simply to Thucydidean cussedness or, more politely, to a desire to arrest the audience's attention and alert them to something more fundamental here than a contrast of 'truth' and 'pretext', and there is something in those explanations. But it is also true that Herodotus' proem too homes in on 'the αἰτίη for their coming to fight another' (a phrase that may be echoed in Thucydides' 'so that nobody should ever need to ask about the origins of so great a war among the Greeks', 1.23.5), and then Herodotus' narrative picks up that αἰτίη with the Persians saying the Phoenicians were αἰτίους and so on (1.1–4); asking for an αἰτίη encourages this sort of 'who started it?', 'who's to blame?' narrative, but it will soon be overlaid by something that carries more explanatory power.[34] One could say something similar about Thucydides' narrative: ἐς τὸ φανερὸν λεγόμεναι αἰτίαι (1.23.6)

---

[32] Nor the only one of these Thucydidean comparisons where that nuance has often been missed: other famous cases are 1.9.1, 1.88.1, and 2.65.11 (οὐ τοσοῦτον ... ὅσον), 6.31.4 (μᾶλλον ... ἤ), and 7.57.1 (οὐ ... μᾶλλον ἤ). Cf. Hornblower (1991–2008), i.31 and 61.

[33] Sealey (1957), 4 ('a suggestion of oxymoron'); Heubeck (1980); Pelling (2019), 83 and 261–2 n. 22.

[34] Pelling (2019), ch. 2.

382 CHRISTOPHER PELLING

provides the rubric for the 'grievances that were openly talked about' to come first, Corcyra and Potidaea, before the narrative moves on to something deeper, something that will require the Pentekontaeteia to trace.

Hartmut Erbse once observed that this was an especially appropriate context for Herodotus to be strongly in the air, at the point where Thucydides changes gear and moves on to the linear narrative, interspersed with speeches, that is more in keeping or in rivalry with Herodotus (or at least with his final books).[35] I dare say that is right. But it is not so much a matter of pushing Herodotus off his pedestal, more of asking him to budge up a little to make room for Thucydides too.

III

The rest of this chapter will jump around among different writers of different periods: this too is appropriate in a tribute to John Marincola, who did the same so brilliantly in *Authority and Tradition*.

First, Polybius. Thucydides, I have suggested, is respectful of Herodotus; one cannot claim that Polybius is as respectful of Timaeus, Phylarchus, and Fabius. On the contrary, one way in which Polybius establishes his own authority is through those aggressive put-downs.[36] It is arguable, though, that he is as respectful of Thucydides himself, if one considers the trouble he takes to adapt and expand Thucydides' framework of causation to fit his own history: he is placing himself within a tradition, not just 'defining himself against' those deficient rivals. What he also gives is an unusually explicit statement of why a particular sort of historiography is needed to suit the events he will be describing. Treating the fifty-three years in which Rome grew to power means that history too has to be universal (hence some later gestures of politeness to Ephorus, his universal predecessor, even when there is some one-upmanship too[37]); the bitty, κατὰ μέρος historiography that others wrote is no good for that, because the whole of the Mediterranean world is coming together (1.4). We can trace a development within the History itself as that growth of Rome is tracked, especially in the later books that he added to his original plan

---

[35] Erbse (1953), 59. For Erbse this was a matter of marking out his distance from Herodotus; it will be clear that I would put it differently.

[36] The classic treatment of Polybian polemic is Walbank (1962 [1985]), but for Polybius' criticisms of Phylarchus, see especially Marincola (2013). See also Monti, Chapter 16 in this volume.

[37] 4.20.5, 5.33.2, 6.45.1, 34.1.3; he defends Ephorus against Timaeus, 12.4a.3–6, 23.1 and 8, 12.28.8–12, cf. 12.27.7; he is critical, however, of Ephorus' understanding of land warfare, 12.25f.

The Authority to Be Untraditional

(3.4.1–8), and different questions are provoked as the events play out: in the early books the focus rests on the factors that made Rome so successful (this is why Book 6 is necessary), in the later books on what sort of moral verdict will be appropriate for later generations to pass (and hence the elaborate framework set out at 36.9). The teleology has shifted: for the first thirty books, the narrative has driven towards the firm end-point of Roman domination; in the last ten, who knows what the future may now hold?[38] The style, pace, and focus of the narrative change accordingly. An extra dimension is also added to those later books because Polybius himself – the flesh-and-blood Polybius, not just a disembodied 'narrator' – becomes a witness and a player, and that too is a way of creating a new authority, or rather of enhancing the authority that his earlier text has already built.[39] (One implication of *Authority and Tradition* is the complication it suggests about any distinction of 'author' and 'narrator', at least for historiography: 'where moderns might speak of a narrator or implied narrator, the ancients spoke of the man himself' (Marincola (1997), 132), and there were good reasons for that.[40] This is a large topic, but not one for here.)

So Polybius gives us three important themes: the way that historical change conditions historiographic change, so that the literary gamechanging is not just a way of showing off one's personal cleverness but a response to real-world events; the way that a work can itself change its texture as it works its way through those events; and the question of how far the writer's real-life experience is a further way of building that authority. He was there, and so he really knows what it was like.

Those three strands can interact in a number of ways. Take, for instance, Cassius Dio's justification for describing a particularly vulgar day when Commodus killed 100 bears in the amphitheatre.

> Let no one think that I am sullying the majesty of history when I write such things. I would not have mentioned them otherwise, but since they came from the emperor himself, and I myself was present and took part and saw and heard and discussed them, I thought it proper to suppress none of them, but to hand down even these things to the memory of those who shall live hereafter, as if they were great and important events. And, indeed, all the other events that took place in my lifetime I shall recount in more

---

[38] See Grethlein (2013), ch. 7, and esp. Wiater (2016).

[39] On such uses of extra-textual experience to build 'authority', see esp. Marincola (1997), 133–48. I discuss the interaction of Polybius-as-narrator and Polybius-as-actor – 'I-Polybius' and 'he-Polybius' – more fully in Pelling (forthcoming b).

[40] Cf. Pelling (2009b), 149 and n. 5.

> detail than earlier events, since I was present at them, and know no one else,
> of those who can write a record worthy of events, who knows so accurately
> about them as I. (D.C. 72[73].18.3–4, trans. Marincola (1997), 92)

History itself has lost its dignity, thanks to the antics of Commodus, and Dio's history needs to mirror that; future generations need to know about this too if they are to understand the relations between ruler and senator.[41] The game has indeed changed. And if anyone is going to write about it, Dio is the man, because he was there and knows better than anyone. That is our third strand: personal experience.

The same will be true of the incident a few chapters later, when Commodus chops off an ostrich head, comes up to where Dio was sitting, and waves it around, waggles his sword, and grins. What was a senator to do? The answer: chew some laurel leaves from your garland to stop yourself laughing (D.C. 72[73].21). Not dignified behaviour for a senator, not dignified writing for a historian,[42] but once again what else could he do? It makes a difference too that this comes so late in the History, once Dio has shown himself so capable of responding to the dignity expected of the historiographic genre when it was called for. He has indeed already changed the game once, with the shift from Republic into Empire, partly because of the reduced accessibility to what's going on (53.19) and partly because the texture of the principate requires a shift to a new, more 'biostructuring' technique.[43] If anyone has the right to lower the tone, it is someone who has written like this as well as seeing how history has changed.

Such shifts in narrative style go a long way back. Xenophon's *Hellenica* changes its texture too, with the first books continuing Thucydides but the final books moving further away from any Thucydidean model.[44] The old habit was to explain that in terms of Xenophon's personal development, and perhaps of different phases of composition; we are now more inclined to explain that too in terms of a response to the shifting texture of events, with the simpler model of Thucydides' two power blocs no longer enough to provide a framework. History is seen to be moving closer to that

---

[41] Marincola (1997), 91–2.

[42] 'It is difficult to imagine Tacitus describing his own mastication under any circumstances', Gleason (2011), 49 n. 63.

[43] I plead guilty to introducing the ugly word: Pelling (1997a). Luke Pitcher points out to me too the interesting passage at App. *Ill.* 30.87, where Appian contrasts imperial rule (where achievements belong to the emperors) and the Republic (where they are shared by the people): that affects the way he has chosen to organize his material.

[44] See e.g. Dillery (1995), 146–7.

The Authority to Be Untraditional

unpredictable messiness that he ends by finding characteristic of life after Mantinea, so chaotic that it was not yet possible to disentangle the threads (7.5.26–7). Egidia Occhipinti has recently made a related case about the *Hellenica Oxyrhynchia*.[45] We can go back again to Thucydides himself, and explain the different character of Book 8 in that way;[46] or to Herodotus, and argue that different narrative shapes were needed for Persian history, given a strong linear direction by the will of the king, and for the messy and fractured interactions of the Greek *poleis*;[47] or forward again to Livy, and how the completion of the Hannibalic books makes clear to him the vastness of the scale on which he needs to operate (31.1.1–5); or to Tacitus, and Judith Ginsburg's thesis that the texture changes as the *Annals* go on, moving away from the annalistic form as the Republic fades into the distance;[48] or even further back to Homer, and muse on the different textures of *Iliad* and *Odyssey*, the world of war and the world of peace, with differing qualities needed to survive in both and different manners to describe both – though for Homer the manner of 'building authority' is very different, and we would have to bring in the Muse. *Autres temps, autres moeurs*, and that goes for the *moeurs* of historiography too.

IV

Let us dwell on Tacitus for a little longer. Building one's authority is less necessary if one has already produced a major work of a similar kind. Most of the authors we have are one-text wonders, at least as far as surviving texts are concerned, but not all of them: it will not be coincidence that it tends to be the earlier publications that work hardest to build up authority in terms of the writer's extra-textual career, especially if they also defend doing something unconventional. Thus it is the *Bellum Catilinae* (3.3–4.2) that has more than the *Bellum Iugurthinum* (4.3) on Sallust's aborted public career, and that is also where he defends his decision to write *carptim*, monographs rather than annals. The same is true of Tacitus: it is the *Agricola* (1.2–3) and then especially the *Histories* (1.1) where the proems do more to link Tacitus' personal circumstances with his subject matter, and the *Histories*' proem intricately projects his own knowledge of events as an insider while at the same time distancing himself from writers who either knew nothing of high politics or were too implicated to avoid

---

[45] Occhipinti (2016).   [46] Rood (1998), ch. 11; Dewald (2005), ch. 6, esp. 144.
[47] Pelling (2019), 200–1.   [48] Ginsburg (1981).

386   CHRISTOPHER PELLING

partisanship. By the time of the *Annals* there is no need for him to do that: *sine ira et studio, quorum causas procul habeo* (*Ann.* 1.1.3) is as much about the distance in time from the subject material as about Tacitus himself, and a more direct mention of his experience is delayed until a passing remark at 11.11.1.

In both major works, though, Tacitus uses his proems to position himself against earlier treatments. In the *Histories*, the nature of the principate brings the danger not just of 'ignorance of the state as something alien' (*inscitia rei publicae ut alienae*) – something Tacitus is free from because of those public offices he goes on to recount – but also of 'a taste for acquiescence or again hatred for the men of power', *libido adsentandi aut rursus odium aduersus dominantis* (*Hist.* 1.1.1–2); you have to be either hostile or servile, *infensus uel obnoxius*. In the *Annals* proem he looks back on the Julio-Claudian principate and regards it as marked by 'the insidious spread of toadying' (*gliscente adulatione*); writers then treated individual reigns with fear, *metus*, or, retrospectively, with hatred, *odia* (*Ann.* 1.1.2). All those points are telling about the atmosphere of the reigns as well as the writers, and so once again changing times produce changing historiography: but in these cases the linkage of the material with the appropriate historiography *diminishes* the authority of those rival authors rather than building it.

The more elaborate self-definition comes at *Annals* 4.32–3, that famous comparison of his narrative with those telling of the Republican glory days. Tony Woodman brings out how many of the traditional themes are turned on their heads.[49] These events are small, barely worth recording, rather than great (μεγάλα) and memorable (ἀξιομνημόνευτα); there is no glory here; there is not even variety, just the monotony that comes with repeated scenes of the same type; and even then you risk offence because people find in your writings replicas of their own vices. We then move, appropriately enough, to the hounding of the historian Cremutius Cordus (4.34–5).

Of course Tacitus is stretching things here. Were the treason trials of the Empire really so boring and repetitious compared with those of the late Republic? Not if we judge from Pliny, though admittedly he is talking of a later generation. But in any case Tacitus could not have said all this about the *Histories*, and the proem there blazoned its material in very different terms (*Hist.* 1.2), ones thoroughly in line with the expectations of Republican historiography.[50] That work was certainly not short of many

---

[49] Woodman (2018), 172–3.
[50] Woodman (1988), 165–7 = (1998), 109–11; cf. Moles (1998), 103.

The Authority to Be Untraditional

of the features that he describes here as missing in the *Annals*, *ingentia bella* ('vast wars'), *expugnationes urbium* ('stormings of cities'), *uarietates proeliorum* ('vicissitudes of battles'), *situs gentium* ('geographical settings'), and *clari ducum exitus*[51] ('famous' – or indeed sometimes infamous – 'deaths of the leaders'); there would have been plenty more too to relieve any monotony, Vesuvius included. We may well be supposed to think of that earlier work of his own as well as of the great Republican heavyweights.[52] Might too 'those things that might appear trivial, but from which great movements often begin' (4.32.2) presage the momentous events of 68–69 AD, so memorably described in the *Histories*? If so, *pace* Woodman,[53] the reference will have relevance to the 'great movements' reached in the closing books of the *Annals* as well as being primarily about the Tiberius books. If, then, we do think of the *Histories*, this is a further case where an author has shown that he can write in more traditional ways before moving the genre on to something that, at least as he presents it himself, is more unconventional.

This is also a further example of linking the history to the historiography. You cannot write Republican historiography any more, not when you have events like this to describe. Perhaps, too, it took a further change in the times to make such writing possible at all. At least, that is what the proem of the *Histories* suggested:

> If I live long enough, I have reserved for my old age the richer and less troublesome material of the principate of the deified Nerva and the rule of Trajan, in this rare delight of the times when you can think what you like and say what you think. (*Hist.* 1.1.4)

He never wrote those books, whether or not it was age that prevented him. But it could still, perhaps, be that delight of the times – the age, and maybe his own old age too – that enabled him to say what he really thought about the age of Tiberius, Gaius, Claudius, and Nero. In that case the linkage of historiographic manner to historical texture relates not just to the time described, several generations ago, but also to the time of writing, the here-and-now.

---

[51] Rhiannon Ash points out to me the expressively transferred epithet here, commenting that 'you would expect the generals to be famous rather than their deaths, but that may be precisely the point'.

[52] Woodman (1988), 185 = (1998), 135: 'The change will have seemed particularly striking to those readers of the *Annals* who were already acquainted with the *Histories*.'

[53] Woodman (2018), 173–4 on 4.32.1.

388 CHRISTOPHER PELLING

Still, is that link so straightforward? Again as Woodman stresses and as Moles and O'Gorman have brought out,[54] the progression of the argument in 4.33 is very odd. In the old days the way to seem canny and provide useful guidance was to understand the way the Republican system worked: one needed to grasp what senators and optimates were like. Now everything has changed, with the necessity of one-man rule, and so ... And so what? We would expect the answer to be 'the equivalent nowadays is understanding the top man: how do you handle a *princeps* if you want to be successful, or indeed to survive?' But he does not say that; instead, he goes on to talk of the offence you might cause to lots of people, the biological or moral descendants of those who were 'punished or disgraced' at the time. What do we make of that? Is it that the real equivalent is not understanding the *princeps* but understanding his whole coterie, all the satellites that really run things, and that is the real core of the system? Maybe. Or is he just building the transition to Cremutius Cordus, and the clash between one man who was 'punished' and the accusers who merited 'disgrace'? Again, maybe. Or, most interestingly of all, do we sense the swerve in the argument, and infer that it would still be too dangerous for Tacitus to spell out where his own analogy is taking him? Might the current emperor, Trajan or perhaps Hadrian, not take kindly to an implication that he was the new Tiberius and there needed to be lessons on how to handle him? If so, that too prepares for Cremutius Cordus, but in a different way. Historians still have to watch their tongues, and you can see what I did there, what I, Tacitus, had to do.

If that is right, that might now cast a different light on those bland comments in the *Histories'* proem on these serene days of Nerva and Trajan where you can think what you like and say what you think. Well, he would say that, wouldn't he, because that is the sort of thing you had to say[55] – but no wonder that he still won't write about them, not yet. There may be disingenuousness too in the notion that it is this new freedom of speech that allows him to write like this: might not denigration of their predecessors be exactly what Nerva and Trajan wanted?[56] In both passages the implications take a lot of teasing out, but then the best figured speech always carries a dose of deniability. But if anyone catches a hint of any such thing in either passage, we have an even subtler way of reinforcing that 'authority' to write as he does, in such an oblique and un-

---

[54] Moles (1998), 129–34; O'Gorman (2000), 99–100.
[55] So, briefly, Moles (1998), 132, following Ahl (1984), 207; cf. Pelling (2009b), 150.
[56] Marincola (1999b), 400.

The Authority to Be Untraditional   389

Republican way. He should know what it is like to live under such a regime, for he still does. *Autres moeurs*, then, from the Republic, both for ruling and for writing; but not so *autres* now, under Trajan or Hadrian, from the days of the first emperors.

V

Does Plutarch belong here at all, given that he stresses that he is not writing history but is writing biography (*Alex.* 1.2)? I think he does: it is indeed interesting that it is history (or rather histories) rather than earlier biographies that he there defines himself against, just as in *Theseus* he talks of 'making myth look like history', not like biography (*Thes.* 1), and just as it is Thucydides who is in his eyeline in the *Nicias* passage with which we began (*Nic.* 1, p. 374). Probably it was already possible to think of biography as a 'genre', given that Nepos too could snappily contrast 'narrating the man's life' with 'writing history' (*Pelopidas* 1.1) and refer to 'this kind of writing' (*hoc genus scripturae*, Nep. proem), but it was a very loose genre. In fact Plutarch probably was not much like any of his predecessors,[57] but positioning himself either within or against that generic tradition would not have been very easy or informative. Saying that he wasn't writing history conveyed a clearer idea of what the audience should and should not expect, and it is no coincidence that this clear statement comes before the *Lives* of Alexander and Caesar, world dominators whose doings were very much material for historians.

Plutarch certainly does some of the things that we have seen done by others. He chooses not to write history, but it is not because he cannot or does not know how to: he wrote the treatise *How We Are to Judge Historical Truth* (πῶς κρινοῦμεν τὴν ἀληθῆ ἱστορίαν, Lampr. Cat. 124) as well as the extant *On Herodotus' Malice*, with its elaborate initial cataloguing of eight historiographic principles (855b–856e). He is very happy to engage head-on with his historical sources on their own ground, and to ferret out new facts that they had missed.[58] That is what he promises to do in the *Nicias* proem, 'collecting material that is not well-known but scattered among authors other than Thucydides, and found on ancient dedications and decrees' (*Nic.* 1.5), and he does a fair amount of that later in that *Life*.[59] It is notable too that some of his most monstrous

---

[57] Pelling (2023).   [58] Pelling (1990 [2002]).

[59] Pelling (1990 [2002]), 25 with n. 16 = (2002b), 146 with 164 n. 19; (1992 [2002]), 10–17 = (2002b), 117–22.

390   CHRISTOPHER PELLING

demonstrations of historical erudition come towards the beginnings or the ends of *Lives* or in some cases both beginnings and ends (*Aristides* and *Solon*) – that is, close to the proems and epilogues where Plutarch's personal voice is most loudly heard. The learned historical virtuoso is certainly part of his self-presentation.

So he could write history, but he does not. He tells us a fair bit in those proemial passages about *how* he is setting about writing biography, favouring all those characterizing small things and anecdotes; what he does not do, at least in the proems that we have, is tell us *why* – why not write history, given that he knows how to do it?

An idea of what he might have said comes in a famous passage of the *Advice on Public Life*:[60]

> We laugh at small children when they try to pull on their fathers' boots and wear their crowns; but what of the leaders in the cities, when they stupidly stir up the ordinary people and encourage them to imitate their ancestors' achievements and spirit and exploits, even though those are all quite out of keeping with present circumstances? Their behaviour may be laughable, but the consequences they suffer are no laughing matter.... There are many other deeds of the Greeks of old which one may recount to mould the characters of the people of today and give them wisdom. At Athens, for instance, one might remind them not of their deeds of war, but of the nature of the amnesty decree under the Thirty; or of the way they fined Phrynichus for his tragedy about the fall of Miletus; or of how they wore crowns when Cassander refounded Thebes, but when they heard of the clubbing at Argos, with the Argives killing 1,500 of their fellow-citizens, they gave orders for a procession of purification around the whole assembly; or of the episode during the Harpalus affair, when they were searching the houses but passed by the one of the newly wedded bridegroom. Even now one can imitate these things, and make oneself like one's ancestors; as for Marathon and Eurymedon and Plataea, and all those examples which make the ordinary people swell up and fill them with shallow ostentation – we should leave them in the schools of the sophists. (*Advice on Public Life* 814a–c)

Perhaps indeed he did say something like that, as we do not have the proem to the opening pair *Epaminondas and Scipio*. In any case, that passage indicates the pattern of his thinking, and this too relates his different way of writing history to the nature of the history itself, in this case the history of his own time. Doing the traditional things with the great events was simply too dangerous. Plutarch might be too good at it,

---

[60] See Titchener, Chapter 12 in this volume.

too successful in his moral inspiration, and make his listeners too uppity. You always need to remember 'those most powerful people above', as he describes the Romans in a haunting phrase in the very next sentence of the *Praecepta* (814c). There are still things to get out of history, but it is likely to be the little things, the words and the jests (as he puts it in *Alex.* 1), that serve you best. Avoid the 'battles where tens of thousands die' – otherwise you might stir up another. And it was Plutarch's own grasp of history, projected through his work with such 'authority', that showed him the dangers as well as the brilliance of historiographic 'tradition', and suggested a better and wiser path to take.

VI

John Marincola sorted into various categories the ways in which historians would generally mark themselves out from their predecessors.[61] They might complain about the gaps or the brevity of their accounts; they might criticize the inaccuracies; they might be scornful of the style; most often of all, they might convict the earlier writers of partisan bias. Certainly, many examples of such polemic can be found in the authors we have been discussing, but here we have found arguments of a rather different stamp. That is understandable, as Marincola's categories dealt more with 'I can do the same sorts of thing better' claims while we have been more concerned with 'I can do something rather different'. Not that those categories are wholly absent: Thucydides' ventures into earlier history and Plutarch's into historical argumentation show that they could indeed match predecessors on their own ground, though both do so with more courtesy and respect than we see in many of Marincola's examples. Those claims to personal experience, Polybius' and Dio's in particular, also suggest that they can be fuller and more accurate than others, even if that same involvement cannot shield them from suspicion of bias. But the most striking feature of our cases is the frequency with which they focus on the texture of the history itself. The game that has changed is a historical one; in several cases the narrative has even shown it changing before our eyes. History may be what the historian makes of it, but it is also history that makes and moulds the historian.

---

[61] Marincola (1999b), 395–6; cf. his fuller listing of examples in Marincola (1997), ch. 5, including valuable distinctions between contemporary and non-contemporary historians and between Greek and Latin.

Bibliography

Aalto, P. (1949) *Untersuchungen über das lateinische Gerundium und Gerundivum* (Helsinki: Suomalainen Tiedeakatemia).

Aarne, A. (1910) *Verzeichnis der Märchentypen*, Folklore Fellows Communications 3 (Helsinki: Suomalainen Tiedeakatemia).

Aarne, A. and Thompson, S. (1961) *The Types of the Folktale: A Classification and Bibliography*, Folklore Fellows Communications 184 (Helsinki: Suomalainen Tiedeakatemia).

Adema, S. M. (2017) *Speech and Thought in Latin War Narratives: Words of Warriors* (Leiden: Brill).

Adler, W. (2009) 'The *Cesti* and Sophistic Culture in the Severan Age,' in M. Wallraff and L. Mecella (eds.), *Die Kestoi des Julius Africanus und ihre Überlieferung* (Berlin: De Gruyter), 1–15.

Adorjáni, Z. (2014) *Pindars sechste olympische Siegesode. Text, Einleitung und Kommentar*, *Mnemosyne* Supplement 370 (Leiden: Brill).

Ager, S. L. (1993) 'Why War?: Some Views on International Arbitration in Ancient Greece', *Echos du Monde Classique/Classical Views* 37, 1–13.

Ahl, F. (1984) 'The Art of Safe Criticism in Greece and Rome', *AJPh* 105, 174–208.

Akujärvi, J. (2005) *Researcher, Traveller, Narrator: Studies in Pausanias' Periegesis* (Stockholm: Almqvist & Wiksell International).

(2012) 'One and "I" in the Frame Narrative: Authorial Voice, Travelling Persona and Addressee in Pausanias' *Periegesis*', *CQ* 62, 327–58.

Allan, R. J., de Jong, I. J. F., and de Jonge, C. C. (2017) 'From *Enargeia* to Immersion: The Ancient Roots of a Modern Concept', *Style* 51, 34–51.

Allison, G. (2017) *Destined for War: Can America and China Escape Thucydides's Trap?* (New York: Houghton Mifflin).

Aly, W. (1969) *Volksmärchen, Sage und Novelle bei Herodot und seinen Zeitgenossen*, 2nd, revised ed., ed. L. Huber (Göttingen: Vandenhoeck & Ruprecht).

Ampolo, C. (1994) 'La città dell'eccesso: Per la storia di Sibari fino al 510 a.C.', in A. Stazio and S. Ceccoli (eds.), *Sibari e la Sibaritide. Atti del trentaduesimo convegno di studi sulla Magna Grecia, Taranto–Sibari 7–12 ottobre 1992* (Naples: Istituto per la storia e l'archeologia della Magna Grecia), 213–54.

Bibliography

Anderson, G. (1986) *Philostratus: Biography and Belles Lettres in the Third Century A.D.* (London: Routledge).

(2018) *The Realness of Things Past: Ancient Greece and Ontological History* (Oxford: Oxford University Press).

Anderson, J. G. C. (1938) *Tacitus: Germania* (Oxford: Clarendon Press).

Anderson, M., Cairns, D., and Sprevak, M. (eds.) (2019) *Distributed Cognition in Classical Antiquity*, The Edinburgh History of Distributed Cognition, vol. 1 (Edinburgh: Edinburgh University Press).

Andrewes, A. (1962) 'The Mytilene Debate: Thucydides 3.36–49', *Phoenix* 16, 64–85.

Andrews, J. A. (2000) 'Cleon's Hidden Appeals', *CQ* 50, 45–62.

Archibald, Z. H. (1998) *The Odrysian Kingdom of Thrace: Orpheus Unmasked* (Oxford: Oxford University Press).

Armayor, O. K. (1978a) 'Did Herodotus Ever Go to the Black Sea?', *HSCP* 82, 45–62.

(1978b) 'Did Herodotus Ever Go to Egypt?', *Journal of the American Research Center in Egypt* 15, 59–73.

(1980) 'Sesostris and Herodotus' Autopsy of Thrace, Colchis, Inland Asia Minor, and the Levant', *HSCP* 84, 51–74.

(1985) *Herodotus' Autopsy of the Fayoum: Lake Moeris and the Labyrinth of Egypt* (Amsterdam: J. C. Gieben).

Armstrong, P. (ed.) (2013) *Authority in Byzantium*, Publications of the Centre for Hellenic Studies, King's College London, 14 (Farnham: Ashgate).

Ash, R. (2007) *Tacitus Histories II* (Cambridge: Cambridge University Press).

(2018) *Tacitus Annals Book XV* (Cambridge: Cambridge University Press).

Asheri, D. (1988) 'Carthaginians and Greeks', in J. Boardman, N. G. L. Hammond, D. M. Lewis, and M. Ostwald (eds.), *The Cambridge Ancient History,* vol. 4: *Persia, Greece, and the Western Mediterranean c. 525 to 479 BC²* (Cambridge: Cambridge University Press), 766–75.

Asheri, D., Lloyd, A., and Corcella, A. (2007) *A Commentary on Herodotus Books I–IV*, ed. O. Murray and A. Moreno (Oxford: Oxford University Press).

Asmis, E. (1986) '*Psychagogia* in Plato's *Phaedrus*', *Illinois Classical Studies* 11, 153–72.

Astin, A. (1978) *Cato the Censor* (Oxford: Oxford University Press).

Athanassaki, L. (1990) 'Mantic Vision and Diction in Pindar's Victory Odes' (PhD thesis, Brown University).

(2003) 'A Divine Audience for the Celebration of Asopichus' Victory in Pindar's *Fourteenth Olympian Ode*', in G. W. Bakewell and J. P. Sickinger (eds.), *Gestures: Essays in Ancient History, Literature and Philosophy Presented to Alan L. Boegehold on the Occasion of His Retirement and His Seventy-Fifth Birthday* (Oxford: Oxbow Books), 3–15.

394 Bibliography

(2009) [=Αθανασάκη Λ.] ἀείδετο πᾶν τέμενος. Οι χορικές παραστάσεις και το κοινό τους στην αρχαϊκή και πρώιμη κλασική περίοδο (Herakleion: University of Crete Press).

(2014) 'The Creative Impact of the Occasion: Pindar's Songs for the Emmenids and Horace's *Odes* 1.2 and 4.2', in D. Cairns and R. Scodel (eds.), *Defining Greek Narrative* (Edinburgh: Edinburgh University Press), 197–225.

(2018) 'ἐν ζαθέῳ χρόνῳ: Ritual Interaction of Mortals and Immortals in Pindaric Choral Performance', in L. Athanassaki, C. Nappa, and A. Vergados (eds.), *Gods and Mortals in Greek and Latin Poetry: Studies in Honor of Jenny Strauss Clay*, Ariadne Supplement 2, 81–117.

(2022) 'The Lyric Chorus', in L. Swift (ed.), *A Companion to Greek Lyric Poetry* (Oxford: Wiley Blackwell), 3–18.

Avlamis, P. (2019) 'Contextualizing Quintus: The Fall of Troy and Cultural Uses of the Paradoxical Cityscape in *Posthomerica* 13', *TAPA* 149, 149–208.

Avotins, I. (1978) 'The Date and the Recipient of the *Vitae Sophistarum* of Philostratus', *Hermes* 106, 242–7.

Babbitt, F. C. (1936) *Plutarch's Moralia V* (Cambridge, MA: Harvard University Press).

Badian, E. (1966) 'The Early Historians', in T. A. Dorey (ed.), *Latin Historians* (London: Routledge), 1–38.

(1993) 'Thucydides and the Outbreak of the Peloponnesian War', in E. Badian (ed.), *From Plataea to Potidaea: Studies in the History and Historiography of the Pentekontaetia* (Baltimore, MD: Johns Hopkins University Press), 125–62.

Bady, C. (2021) 'La Rome des *pepaideumenoi*. Mobilité, patronage et sociabilité des élites intellectuelles hellénophones dans la Rome du Haut-Empire (31 av. J.-C.–235 ap. J.-C.)' (doctoral thesis, Paris X – Nanterre).

Baier, T. (2005) 'Autobiographie in der späten römischen Republik', in M. Reichel (ed.), *Antike Autobiographien: Werke – Epochen – Gattungen* (Cologne: Böhlau), 123–42.

Bakhtin, M. M. (1981) *The Dialogic Imagination: Four Essays* (Austin: University of Texas Press).

Bakker, E. J. (2002) 'The Marking of History: Herodotus' *Historiēs apodexis*', in E. J. Bakker, I. J. F. de Jong, and H. van Wees (eds.), *Brill's Companion to Herodotus* (Leiden: Brill), 1–32.

(ed.) (2017) *Authorship and Greek Song: Authority, Authenticity, and Performance* (Leiden: Brill).

Balot, R., Forsdyke, S., and Foster, E. (eds.) (2017) *The Oxford Handbook of Thucydides* (Oxford: Oxford University Press).

Baragwanath, E. (2008) *Motivation and Narrative in Herodotus* (Oxford: Oxford University Press).

(2013) 'Herodotos and the Avoidance of Hindsight', in A. Powell (ed.), *Hindsight in Greek and Roman History* (Swansea: Classical Press of Wales), 25–48.

Bibliography

Baragwanath, E. and de Bakker, M. (eds.) (2012a) *Myth, Truth, and Narrative in Herodotus* (Oxford: Oxford University Press).

(2012b) 'Introduction', in E. Baragwanath and M. de Bakker (eds.), *Myth, Truth, and Narrative in Herodotus* (Oxford: Oxford University Press), 1–57.

Baraz, Y. (2020) *Reading Roman Pride* (Oxford: Oxford University Press).

Barker, E., Bouzarovski, S., Pelling, C., and Isaksen L. (eds.) (2016) *New Worlds out of Old Texts: Developing Techniques for the Spatial Analysis of Ancient Narratives* (Oxford: Oxford University Press).

Barlow, J. (1998) 'Noble Gauls and Their Other in Caesar's Propaganda', in K. Welch and A. Powell (eds.), *Julius Caesar as Artful Reporter: The War Commentaries as Political Instruments* (London: Duckworth; Swansea: Classical Press of Wales), 139–70.

Barnes, Jonathan (ed.) (1984) *The Complete Works of Aristotle: The Revised Oxford Translation*, 2 vols. (Oxford: Oxford University Press).

Barnes, Julian (1984) *Flaubert's Parrot* (London: Cape).

Barrett, A. A. (2020) *Rome Is Burning: Nero and the Fire That Ended a Dynasty* (Princeton, NJ: Princeton University Press).

Barrett, J. (2002) *Staged Narrative: Poetics and the Messenger in Greek Tragedy* (Berkeley: University of California Press).

Barwick, K. (1951) *Caesars Bellum Civile. Tendenz, Abfassungszeit und Stil* (Berlin: Akademie Verlag).

(1967) 'Zur Entstehungsgeschichte des Bellum Gallicum', in D. Rasmussen (ed.), *Caesar* (Darmstadt: Wissenschaftliche Buchgesellschaft), 255–78.

Bascom, W. (1975) 'The Forms of Folklore: Prose Narratives', *The Journal of American Folklore* 307, 3–20.

Batstone, W. (2018) 'Caesar Constructing Caesar', in L. Grillo and C. B. Krebs (eds.), *The Cambridge Companion to the Writings of Julius Caesar* (Cambridge: Cambridge University Press), 43–57.

Batstone, W. and Damon, C. (2006) *Caesar's Civil War* (Oxford: Oxford University Press).

Beagon, M. (2005) *The Elder Pliny on the Human Animal: Natural History Book 7* (Oxford: Oxford University Press).

Beck, H. and Walter, U. (eds.) (2001) *Die frühen römischen Historiker. 1: Von Fabius Pictor bis Cn. Gellius* (Darmstadt: Wissenschaftliche Buchgesellschaft).

Bell, A. and Ensslin, A. (2011) '"I know what it was. You know what it was": Second-Person Narration in Hypertext Fiction', *Narrative* 19, 311–29.

Benardete, S. (1969) *Herodotean Inquiries* (Dordrecht: Springer Netherlands).

Bernard, S., Damon, C., and Grey, C. (2014) 'Rhetorics of Land and Power in the Polla Inscription (*CIL* 1^2 638)', *Mnemosyne* 67, 953–985.

Berry, D. (2008) 'Letters from an Advocate: Pliny's "Vesuvius" Narratives (*Epistles* 6.16, 6.20)', *Papers of the Langford Latin Seminar* 13, 297–313.

Billault, A. (2000) *L'univers de Philostrate* (Bruxelles: Latomus).

Billows, R. A. (2009) *Julius Caesar: The Colossus of Rome* (London: Routledge).

396 Bibliography

Biriotti, M. and Miller, N. (eds.) (1993) *What Is an Author?* (Manchester: Manchester University Press).

Birke, D. (2015) 'Author, Authority and "Authorial Narration": The Eighteenth-Century English Novel as a Test Case', in D. Birke and T. Köppe (eds.), *Author and Narrator: Transdisciplinary Contributions to a Narratological Debate* (Berlin: De Gruyter), 99–111.

Blänsdorf, J. (1995) *Fragmenta Poetarum Latinorum Epicorum et Lyricorum praeter Ennium et Lucilium, post Wilhelm Morel novis curis adhibitis edidit Carolus Buechner (ed. tertiam auctam cur. Jürgen Blänsdorf)* (Stuttgart: Teubner).

Bleckmann, B. (2006) *Fiktion als Geschichte: Neue Studien zum Autor der Hellenika Oxyrhynchia und zur Historiographie des vierten vorchristlichen Jahrhunderts* (Göttingen: Vandenhoeck & Ruprecht).

Bleicken, J. (1998) *Augustus: Eine Biographie* (Berlin: Alexander Fest Verlag).

Block, E. (1982) 'The Narrator Speaks: Apostrophe in Homer and Vergil', *TAPA* 92, 7–21.

Blösel, W. (2012) 'Thucydides on Themistocles: A Herodotean Narrator?', in E. Foster and D. Lateiner (eds.), *Thucydides and Herodotus* (Oxford: Oxford University Press), 215–40.

Boedeker, D. (1987) 'The Two Faces of Demaratus', *Arethusa* 20, 185–201.

(1996) 'Heroic Historiography: Simonides and Herodotus on Plataea', *Arethusa* 29, 223–42.

(2002) 'Epic Heritage and Mythical Patterns in Herodotus', in E. J. Bakker, I. J. F. de Jong, and H. van Wees (eds.), *Brill's Companion to Herodotus* (Leiden: Brill), 97–116.

(2003) 'Pedestrian Fatalities: The Prosaics of Death in Herodotus', in P. Derow and R. C. T. Parker (eds.), *Herodotus and His World: Essays from a Conference in Memory of George Forrest* (Oxford: Oxford University Press), 17–36.

(2006) 'Voiceless Victims, Memorable Deaths in Herodotus', *CQ* 56, 393–403.

(2011) 'Persian Gender Relations as Historical Motives in Herodotus', in R. Rollinger, B. Truschnegg, and R. Bichler (eds.), *Herodot und das Persische Weltreich = Herodotus and the Persian Empire, Akten des 3. Internationalen Kolloquiums zum Thema* Vorderasien im Spannungsfeld klassischer und altorientalischer Überlieferungen, *Innsbruck, 24.–28. November 2008*, Classica et Orientalia 3 (Wiesbaden: Harrassowitz), 211–35.

(2015) 'Two Tales of Spartan Envoys', in C. Clark, E. Foster, and J. Hallett (eds.), *Kinesis: The Ancient Depiction of Gesture, Motion, and Emotion: Essays for Donald Lateiner* (Ann Arbor: University of Michigan Press), 103–115.

Bollansée, J. (2005) 'Historians of Agathocles of Samus: Polybius on Writers of Historical Monographs', in G. Schepens and J. Bollansée (eds.), *The Shadow of Polybius: Intertextuality as a Research Tool in Greek Historiography: Proceedings of the International Colloquium, Leuven, 21–22 September 2001* (Leuven: Peeters), 237–53.

Bolte, J. and Polívka, J. (1915) *Anmerkungen zu den Kinder- und Hausmärchen der Brüder Grimm*, 2nd ed., vol. 2 (Leipzig: Theodor Weicher).

Bibliography

Bonheim, H. (1983) 'Narration in the Second Person', *Recherches Anglaises et Américaines Strasbourg* 16, 69–80.

Bosworth, A. (2003) 'Plus ça change . . . : Ancient Historians and Their Sources', *ClAnt* 22, 167–198.

Boter, G. (2015) 'The Title of Philostratus' *Life of Apollonius of Tyana*', *JHS* 135, 1–7.

Botermann, H. (2007) 'Gallia pacata – perpetua pax. Die Eroberung Galliens und der "gerechte Krieg"', in E. Baltrusch (ed.), *Caesar* (Darmstadt: Wissenschaftliche Buchgesellschaft), 137–58.

Bowie, A. M. (2007) *Herodotus Histories Book VIII.* Cambridge Greek and Latin Classics (Cambridge: Cambridge University Press).

Bowie, E. L. (2009) 'Philostratus: The Life of a Sophist', in E. L. Bowie and J. Elsner (eds.), *Philostratus* (Cambridge: Cambridge University Press), 19–32.

Bradley, P. J. (2010) 'Irony and the Narrator in Xenophon's *Anabasis*', in V. J. Gray (ed.), *Xenophon: Oxford Readings in Classical Studies* (Oxford: Oxford University Press), 520–52.

Branscome, D. (2010) 'Herodotus and the Map of Aristagoras', *ClAnt* 29, 1–44.
  (2013) *Textual Rivals: Self-Presentation in Herodotus' Histories* (Ann Arbor: University of Michigan Press).

Breed, B., Keitel, E., and Wallace R. (eds.) (2018) *Lucilius and Satire in Second-Century BC Rome* (Cambridge: Cambridge University Press).

Briant, P. (2002) *From Cyrus to Alexander: A History of the Persian Empire*, trans. Peter T. Daniels (Winona Lake, IN: Eisenbrauns).

Brillante, C. (1986) 'Il sogno nella riflessione dei presocratici', *MD* 16, 9–53.

Brock, R. (2003) 'Authorial Voice and Narrative Management in Herodotus', in P. Derow and R. C. T. Parker (eds.), *Herodotus and His World: Essays from a Conference in Memory of George Forrest* (Oxford: Oxford University Press), 3–17.

Brosius, M. (2000) *The Persian Empire from Cyrus II to Artaxerxes I* (London: London Association of Classical Teachers).

Brown, T. S. (1958) *Timaeus of Tauromenium* (Berkeley: University of California Press).

Brugnone, M. A. (1995) 'In margine alle tradizioni ecistiche di Massalia', *PdP* 50, 46–66.

Brunt, P. A. (1976) *Arrian. Anabasis Alexandri Books i–iv*, Loeb Classical Library 236 (Cambridge, MA: Harvard University Press).
  (1993) 'The Megarian Decree', in P. A. Brunt (ed.), *Studies in Greek History and Thought* (Oxford: Clarendon Press), 1–16.

Brunyé, T. T., Ditman, T., Mahoney, C. R., Augustyn, J. S., and Taylor, H. A. (2009) 'When You and I Share Perspectives: Pronouns Modulate Perspective Taking during Narrative Comprehension', *Psychological Science* 20, 27–32.

Brunyé, T. T., Ditman, T., Mahoney C. R., and Taylor, H. A. (2011) 'Better You Than I: Perspectives and Emotion Simulation during Narrative Comprehension', *Journal of Cognitive Psychology* 23, 659–66.

Bibliography

Brunyé, T. T., Ditman, T., Giles, G.E., Holmes, A., and Taylor, H.A. (2016) 'Mentally Simulating Narrative Perspective Is Not Universal or Necessary for Language Comprehension', *Journal of Experimental Psychology: Learning, Memory, and Cognition* 42, 1592–605.

Büchner, K. (1960) *Sallust* (Heidelberg: Winter).

Bühler, K. (1982) 'The Deictic Field of Language and Deictic Words', in R. J. Jarvella and W. Klein (eds.), *Speech, Place, and Action: Studies of Deixis and Related Topics* (Chichester: Wiley-Blackwell), 9–30.

Bundy, E. L. (1962) *Studia Pindarica, I–II: The Eleventh Olympian Ode: The First Isthmian Ode* (Berkeley: University of California Press).

Burkert, W. (1979) *Structure and History in Greek Mythology and Ritual* (Berkeley: University of California Press).

(1985 [2013]) 'Herodot über die Namen der Götter: Polytheismus als historisches Problem', *MH* 43, 121–32, translated in R. V. Munson (ed.), *Herodotus: Oxford Readings in Classical Studies,* vol. 2 (Oxford: Oxford University Press), 198–209.

(1990) 'Herodot als Historiker fremder Religionen', in G. Nenci and O. Reverdin (eds.), *Hérodote et les peuples non grecs*, Entretiens sur l'antiquité classique 35 (Vandoeuvres-Geneva: Fondation Hardt), 1–39.

(1991) *Wilder Ursprung. Opferritual und Mythos bei den Griechen* (Berlin: Wagenbach).

Burton, P. J. (2008) 'Livy's Preface and Its Historical Context', *Scholia* 17, 70–91.

Butler, T. (2003) ''Εμπειρία in Aristotle', *SJPh* 41, 329–50.

Byre, C. S. (1991) 'The Narrator's Addresses to the Narratee in Apollonius Rhodius' *Argonautica'*, *TAPA* 121, 215–27.

Calame, C. (2003) *Myth and History in Ancient Greece: The Symbolic Creation of a Colony*, trans. D. W. Berman (Princeton, NJ: Princeton University Press).

(2005) *Masks of Authority: Fiction and Pragmatics in Ancient Greek Poetics* (Ithaca, NY: Cornell University Press).

Calboli, G. (2003) *Marci Porci Catonis Oratio pro Rhodiensibus*[2] (Bologna: Pàtron).

Cameron, A. (2004) *Greek Mythography in the Roman World* (Oxford: Oxford University Press).

Campbell, J. (1981) 'Teach Yourself How to Be a General', *JRS* 77, 13–29.

Candau, J. M. (2011) 'Republican Rome: Autobiography and Political Struggle', in G. Marasco (ed.), *Political Autobiographies and Memoirs in Antiquity: A Brill Companion* (Leiden: Brill), 121–59.

Canfora, L. (1971) 'Il ciclo storico', *Belfagor* 26, 653–70.

(1972) *Totalità e selezione nella storiografia classica* (Rome: Laterza).

(1991) 'L'inizio della storia secondo i Greci', *QS* 33, 5–19.

Canter, H. V. (1932) 'Conflagrations in Ancient Rome', *CJ* 27, 270–88.

Cartledge, P. and Greenwood, E. (2002) 'Herodotus as a Critic: Truth, Fiction, Polarity', in I. J. F. de Jong and H. van Wees (eds.), *Brill's Companion to Herodotus* (Leiden: Brill), 351–71.

Bibliography

Caterine, C. L. (2015) '*Si credere velis*: Lucan's Cato and the Reader of the *Bellum Civile*', *Arethusa* 48, 339–67.

Cawkwell, G. (1997) *Thucydides and the Peloponnesian War* (London: Routledge).

Ceccarelli, P. (2016) 'Charon of Lampsakos (262)', in *Brill's New Jacoby* (Leiden: Brill), online publication.

Ceulemans, R. and De Leemans, P. (2015) *On Good Authority: Tradition, Compilation and the Construction of Authority in Literature from Antiquity to the Renaissance* (Turnhout: Brepols).

Chadwick, H. (2001) *The Church in Ancient Society: From Galilee to Gregory the Great* (Oxford: Oxford University Press).

Chamberlain, D. (1999) '"We the others": Interpretive Community and Plural Voice in Herodotus', *ClAnt* 20, 5–34.

Chambers, R. (1984) *Story and Situation: Narrative Seduction and the Power of Fiction* (Minneapolis: University of Minnesota Press).

Champion, C. B. (2004) *Cultural Politics in Polybius' Histories* (Berkeley: University of California Press).

Chandler, C. (2006) *Philodemus On Rhetoric. Books 1 and 2: Translation and Exegetical Essays* (London: Routledge).

Chaniotis, A. (2019) 'Epigraphy of the Night', in C. F. Norena and N. Papazarkadas (eds.), *From Document to History: Epigraphic Insights into the Greco-Roman World* (Leiden: Brill), 13–36.

Chantraine, P. (1968) *Dictionnaire étymologique de la langue grecque: Histoire des mots*, vol. 1 (Paris: Klincksieck).

Chaplin, J. D. (2000) *Livy's Exemplary History* (Oxford: Oxford University Press).

Chaplin, J. D. and Kraus, C. S. (eds.) (2009) *Livy: Oxford Readings in Classical Studies* (Oxford: Oxford University Press).

Chassignet, M. (2002) *Caton. Les Origines. Fragments* (Paris: Les Belles Lettres).

  (2003) 'La naissance de l'autobiographie à Rome: *Laus sui* ou *apologia de vita sua*?', *REL* 81, 65–78.

  (2004) *L'annalistique romaine*, vol. 3: *L'annalistique récente, l'autobiographie politique* (Paris: Les Belles Lettres).

  (2018) 'Caesar and Roman Historiography Prior to the *Commentarii*', in L. Grillo and C. B. Krebs (eds.), *The Cambridge Companion to the Writings of Julius Caesar* (Cambridge: Cambridge University Press), 249–62.

Chlup, J. T. (2006) 'The Rhetoric of Authority: Alcibiades' Speech to the Spartans in Thucydides', *CEA* 42, 299–325.

Christ, M. R. (1994) 'Herodotean Kings and Historical Inquiry', *ClAnt* 13, 167–202.

Christes, J. (1986) 'Lucilius', in J. Adamietz (ed.), *Die römische Satire* (Darmstadt: Wissenschaftliche Buchgesellschaft), 57–122.

  (1989) 'Der frühe Lucilius und Horaz. Eine Entgegnung', *Hermes* 117, 321–6.

Christes, J. and Garbugino, G. (2015) *Lucilius, Satiren, Lateinisch und Deutsch* (Darmstadt: Wissenschaftliche Buchgesellschaft).

Civiletti, M. (2002) *Filostrato. Vite dei sofisti* (Milan: Bompiani).

Bibliography

Clarke, K. (1999) *Between Geography and History: Hellenistic Constructions of the Roman World* (Oxford: Clarendon Press).

(2003) 'Polybius and the Nature of Late Hellenistic Geography', in J. S. Yanguas and E. T. Pagola (eds.), *Polibio y la Península Ibérica*, Revisiones de Historia Antigua 4 (Vitoria: Universidad del País Vasco, Servicio Editorial), 69–87.

(2018) *Shaping the Geography of Empire: Man and Nature in Herodotus' Histories* (Oxford: Oxford University Press).

Closs, V. M. (2016) '*Neronianis Temporibus*: The So-Called *Arae Incendii Neroniani* and the 64 Fire in Rome's Monumental Landscape', *JRS* 106, 102–23.

(2020) *While Rome Burned: Fire, Leadership, and Urban Disaster in the Roman Cultural Imagination* (Ann Arbor: University of Michigan Press).

Cluett, R. (2003) 'In Caesar's Wake: The Ideology of the Continuators', in F. Cairns and E. Fantham (eds.), *Caesar against Liberty: Perspectives on His Autocracy* (Cambridge: Cairns), 118–31.

(2009) 'The Continuators: Soldiering Oon', in M. Griffin (ed.), *A Companion to Julius Caesar* (Oxford: Wiley-Blackwell), 192–205.

Coarelli, F. (1978) 'La statue de Cornélie, mère des Gracques et la crise politique à Rome au temps de Saturninus', in H. Zehnacker (ed.) *Le dernier siècle de la république romaine et l'époque augustéenne* (Strasbourg: Association pour l'étude de la civilisation romaine), 13–28.

Cobet, J. (2002) 'The Organization of Time in the *Histories*', in E. J. Bakker, I. J. F. de Jong, and H. van Wees (eds.), *Brill's Companion to Herodotus* (Leiden: Brill), 387–412.

Cogan, M. (1981) 'Mytilene, Plataea and Corcyra: Ideology and Policy in Thucydides, Book Three', *Phoenix* 35, 1–21.

Cohen, D. (2005) 'Theories of Punishment', in M. Gagarin and D. Cohen (eds.), *The Cambridge Companion to Ancient Greek Law* (Cambridge: Cambridge University Press), 170–90.

Collingwood, R. G. (1946) *The Idea of History* (Oxford: Oxford University Press).

Collins, J. H. (1972) 'Caesar as Political Propagandist', in H. Temporini (ed.), *Aufstieg und Niedergang der römischen Welt*, vol. I.1 (Berlin: De Gruyter), 922–66.

(2012) 'Prompts for Participation in Early Philosophical Texts', in E. Minchin (ed.), *Orality, Literacy and Performance in the Ancient World*, Mnemosyne Supplement 335 (Leiden: Brill), 151–82.

Connor, W. R. (1962) 'Charinus' Megarean Decree', *AJPh* 53, 225–46.

(1984) *Thucydides* (Princeton, NJ: Princeton University Press).

Conti, N. (2006) *Natale Conti's Mythologiae*, trans. and ed. J. Mulryan and S. Brown, 2 vols. (Tempe, AZ: Arizona Center for Medieval and Renaissance Studies).

Cook, B. (2004) 'Plutarch's "Many Other" Imitable Events: *Mor.* 814B and the Statesman's Duty', in L. de Blois, J. Bons, T. Kessels, and D. M. Schenkeveld (eds.), *The Sstatesman in Plutarch's Works: Proceedings of the*

Sixth International Conference of the International Plutarch Society, Nijmegen/ Castle Hernen, May 1–5, 2002, vol. 1: Plutarch's Statesman and His Aftermath: Political, Philosophical, and Literary Aspects, Mnemosyne Supplement 250 (Leiden: Brill), 201–10.

Cooley, A. (2014) 'Paratextual Perspectives upon the *Senatus Consultum de Cn. Pisone Patre*', in L. Jansen (ed.), *The Roman Paratext: Frame, Texts, Reader* (Cambridge: Cambridge University Press), 143–55.

Cornell, T. J. (2009) 'Cato the Elder and the Origins of Roman Autobiography', in C. Smith and A. Powell (eds.), *The Lost Memoirs of Augustus and the Development of Roman Autobiography* (Swansea: Classical Press of Wales), 15–40.

Cornell, T. J., Bispham, E., Rich, J. W., and Smith, C. J. (eds.) (2013) *The Fragments of the Roman Historians*, 3 vols. (Oxford: Oxford University Press).

Courtney, E. (1995) *Musa Lapidaria. A Selection of Latin Verse Inscriptions*, American Classical Studies, no. 36 (Atlanta, GA: Scholars Press).

  (2003) *The Fragmentary Latin Poets*, revised ed. (Oxford: Oxford University Press).

Cowan, R. (2018) 'You Too: The Narratology of Apostrophe and Second-Person Narrative in Virgil's *Georgics*', *Arethusa* 51, 269–98.

Croce, B. (1921 [1919]) *Teoria e storia della storiografia*, 2nd ed., trans. D. Ainslie as *Theory and History of Historiography* (London: Wentworth Press).

Cugusi, P. (1970) *Epistolographi Latini Minores*, 2 vols. (Turin: Paravia).

  (1973) 'Le più antiche lettere papiracee latine', *Atti della Accademia delle Scienze di Torino* 107, 641–92.

Cugusi, P. and Sblendorio Cugusi, M. T. (2001) *Opere di Marco Porcio Catone Censore*, vol. 1 (Turin: UTET).

D'Alessio, G. B. (2020) 'Dancing with the Dogs: Mimetic Dance and the Hyporcheme (on Pind. fr. *107 M = Simonides 255 Poltera)', in P. Agócs and L. Prauscello (eds.), *Simonides Lyricus. Essays on the 'Other' Classical Choral Lyric Poet*, CCJ Supplement 42 (Cambridge: Cambridge Philological Society), 59–80.

Damon, C. (1994) 'Caesar's Practical Prose', *CJ* 89, 183–94.

  (2003) *Tacitus Histories Book I* (Cambridge: Cambridge University Press).

  (2010) 'Déjà vu or déjà lu? History as Intertext', *Papers of the Langford Latin Seminar* 14, 375–88.

D'Angour, A. (1997) 'How the Dithyramb Got Its Shape', *CQ* 47, 331–51.

Dannenberg, H. P. (2004) 'A Poetics of Coincidence in Narrative Fiction', *Poetics Today* 25, 399–436.

  (2008) *Coincidence and Counterfactuality: Plotting Time and Space in Narrative Fiction* (Lincoln: University of Nebraska Press).

Darbo-Peschanski, C. (2013) 'Herodotus and *Historia*', in R. V. Munson (ed.), *Herodotus: Oxford Readings in Classical Studies*, vol. 2 (Oxford: Oxford University Press), 78–105.

Bibliography

Daugherty, G. N. (1992) 'The *Cohortes Vigilum* and the Great Fire of AD64', *CJ* 87, 229–40.

Davidson, J. (1997) *Courtesans and Fishcakes: The Consuming Passions of Classical Athens* (London: HarperCollins).

Dawson, W. R. (1986) 'Herodotus as a Medical Writer', *BICS* 33, 87–96.

Day, J. W. (2010). *Archaic Greek Epigram and Dedication: Representation and Reperformance* (Cambridge: Cambridge University Press).

de Blois, L. (2017) 'Caesar the General and Leader', in K. Raaflaub (ed.), *The Landmark Julius Caesar* (New York: Pantheon), app. X: web essay at www .landmarkcaesar.com.

de Jong, I. J. F. (2002) 'Narrative Unity and Units', in E. J. Bakker, I. J. F. de Jong, and H. van Wees (eds.), *Brill's Companion to Herodotus* (Leiden: Brill), 245–66.

    (2004) 'Herodotus', in I. J. F. de Jong, R. Nünlist, and A. Bowie (eds.), *Narrators, Narratees, and Narratives in Ancient Greek Literature: Studies in Ancient Greek Narrative* (Leiden: Brill), 102–14.

    (2009) 'Metalepsis in Ancient Greek Literature', in J. Grethlein and A. Rengakos (eds.), *Narratology and Interpretation: The Content of Narrative Form in Ancient Literature* (Berlin: De Gruyter), 87–116.

    (2013 [1999]) 'Narratological Aspects of the *Histories* of Herodotus', in R. V. Munson (ed.), *Herodotus: Oxford Readings in Classical Studies,* vol. 1 (Oxford: Oxford University Press), 253–91.

    (2014a) *Narratology and Classics: A Practical Guide* (Oxford: Oxford University Press).

    (2014b) 'The Anonymous Traveler in European Literature: A Greek Meme', in D. Cairns and R. Scodel (eds.), *Defining Greek Narrative*, Edinburgh Leventis Studies 7 (Edinburgh: Edinburgh University Press), 314–33.

de Jong, I. J. F. and Nünlist, R. (2004) 'From Bird's Eye View to Close-Up: The Standpoint of the Narrator in the Homeric Epics', in A. Bierl, A. Schmitt, and A. Willi (eds.), *Antike Literatur in neuer Deutung* (Munich: Saur), 63–83.

de Jonge, C. C. (2015) 'Grammatical Theory and Rhetorical Teaching', in F. Montanari, S. Matthaios, and A. Rengakos (eds.), *Brill's Companion to Ancient Greek Scholarship*, 2 vols. (Leiden: Brill), 979–1011.

    (2020) 'Ps.-Longinus on Ecstasy: Author, Audience, and Text', in J. Grethlein, L. Huitink, and A. Tagliabue (eds.), *Experience, Narrative, and Criticism in Ancient Greece* (Oxford: Oxford University Press), 148–71.

de la Bédoyère, G. (1995) *The Diary of John Evelyn* (Woodbridge: Boydell).

de Lacy, P. and Einarson, B. (eds.) (1959) *Moralia, VII: 523C–612B* (London: Heinemann).

    (eds.) (1984) *Plutarch's Moralia VII* (Cambridge, MA: Harvard University Press).

de Lannoy, L. (1997) 'Le problème des Philostrate. État de la question', in *Aufstieg und Niedergang der römischen Welt II 34.3* (Berlin: De Gruyter), 2362–449.

Bibliography

de Romilly, J. (1967) *Histoire et raison chez Thucydide* (Paris: Les Belles Lettres), translated by E. T. Rawlings as *The Mind of Thucydides* (Ithaca, NY: Cornell University Press, 2012).

(1971) 'La vengeance comme explication historique dans l'oeuvre d'Hérodote', *REG* 84, 314–57.

(2012) *The Mind of Thucydides*, trans. E. T. Rawlings (Ithaca, NY: Cornell University Press).

de Sélincourt, A. (1960) *Livy: The Early History of Rome* (Harmondsworth: Penguin Books).

Debnar, P. A. (2000) 'Diodotus' Paradox and the Mytilene Debate (Thuc. 3.37–49)', *RhM* 143, 161–78.

(2001) *Speaking the Same Language: Speech and Audience in Thucydides' Spartan Debates* (Ann Arbor: University of Michigan Press).

(2013) 'Blurring the Boundaries of Speech: Thucydides and Indirect Discourse', in A. Tsakmakis and M. Tamiolaki (eds.), *Thucydides between History and Literature* (Berlin: De Gruyter), 271–85.

DelConte, M. (2003) 'Why You Can't Speak: Second-Person Narration, Voice, and a New Model for Understanding Narrative', *Style* 37, 204–19.

Delarue, F. (1998) 'Sur la préface de Tite-Live', *Vita Latina* 151, 44–58.

Dench, E. (2007) 'Ethnography and History', in J. Marincola (ed.), *A Companion to Greek and Roman Historiography* (Oxford: Blackwell), 493–503.

Detienne, M. (1986) *The Creation of Mythology*, trans. M. Cook (Chicago: University of Chicago Press; originally published in French in 1981).

Dewald, C. (1985) 'Practical Knowledge and the Historian's Role', in M. Jameson (ed.), *The Greek Historians: Papers Presented to A. E. Raubitschek* (Saratoga, NY: ANMA Libri), 47–63.

(1987) 'Narrative Surface and Authorial Voice in Herodotus' Histories', in D. Boedeker (ed.), *Herodotus and the Invention of History*, Arethusa 20 (Buffalo: State University of New York), 147–70.

(1993) 'Reading the World: The Interpretation of Objects in Herodotus' Histories', in R. Rosen and J. Farrell (eds.), *Nomodeiktes: Festschrift for Martin Ostwald* (Ann Arbor: University of Michigan Press), 55–70.

(1999) 'The Figured Stage: Focalizing the Initial Narratives of Herodotus and Thucydides', in T. M. Falkner and J. J. Peradotto (eds.), *Contextualizing Classics: Ideology, Perfomance, Dialogue: Essays in Honor of John J. Peradotto* (Lanham, MD: Rowman & Littlefield), 221–52.

(2002) '"I didn't give my own genealogy": Herodotus and the Authorial Persona', in E. J. Bakker, I. J. F. de Jong, and H. van Wees (eds.), *Brill's Companion to Herodotus* (Leiden: Brill), 267–89.

(2003) 'Form and Content: The Question of Tyranny in Herodotus', in K. Morgan (ed.), *Popular Tyranny: Sovereignty and Its Discontents in Ancient Greece* (Austin: University of Texas Press), 25–58.

(2005) *Thucydides' War Narrative: A Structural Study* (Berkeley: University of California Press).

Bibliography

(2006a) 'Humour and Danger in Herodotus', in C. Dewald and J. Marincola (eds.), *The Cambridge Companion to Herodotus* (Cambridge: Cambridge University Press), 145–64.

(2006b) 'Paying Attention: History as the Development of a Secular Narrative', in S. Goldhill and R. Osborne (eds.), *Rethinking Revolutions through Ancient Greece* (Cambridge: Cambridge University Press), 164–82.

(2007) 'The Construction of Meaning in the First Three Historians', in J. Marincola (ed.), *A Companion to Greek and Roman Historiography*, vol. 1 (Malden, MA: Blackwell), 89–101.

(2011) 'Happiness in Herodotus', *Symbolae Osloensis* 85, 18–39.

(2013 [1997]) 'Wanton Kings, Pickled Heroes, and Gnomic Founding Fathers: Strategies of Meaning at the End of Herodotus's *Histories*', in R. V. Munson (ed.), *Herodotus: Oxford Readings in Classical Studies,* vol. 1 (Oxford: Oxford University Press), 379–402.

(2013 [1981]) 'Women and Culture in Herodotus' *Histories*', in R. V. Munson (ed.), *Herodotus: Oxford Readings in Classical Studies,* vol. 2 (Oxford: Oxford University Press), 151–82.

(2015) '"The medium is the message": Herodotus and His Logoi', in R. Ash, J. Mossman, and F. B. Titchener (eds.), *Fame and Infamy: Essays for Christopher Pelling on Characterization in Greek and Roman Biography and Historiography* (Oxford: Oxford University Press), 67–82.

Dewald, C. and Kitzinger, R. (2015) 'Speaking Silences in Herodotus and Sophocles', in C. A. Clark, E. Foster, and J. P. Hallett (eds.), *Kinesis: The Ancient Depiction of Gesture, Motion, and Emotion. Essays for Donald Lateiner* (Ann Arbor: University of Michigan Press), 86–102.

Dewald, C. and Marincola, J. (eds.) (2006) *The Cambridge Companion to Herodotus* (Cambridge: Cambridge University Press).

Diano, C. and Serra, G. (1980) *Eraclito. I Frammenti e le Testimonianze* (Milan: Fondazione Lorenzo Valla, Mondadori).

Díaz-Tejera, A. (1978) 'Concordancias terminológicas con *La Poética* en la historia universal: Aristóteles y Polibio', *Habis* 9, 33–48.

Diels, H. (1922) *Die Fragmente der Vorsokratiker*, 4th ed. (Berlin: Weidmann).

Diggle, J. (2004) *Theophrastus: Characters* (Cambridge: Cambridge University Press).

Dillery, J. (1995) *Xenophon and the History of His Times* (London: Routledge).

Dillon, J. (2014) 'Plutarch and Platonism', in M. Beck (ed.), *A Companion to Plutarch* (Chichester: Wiley-Blackwell), 61–72.

Ditman, T., Brunyé, T. T., Mahoney, C. R., and Taylor, H. A. (2010) 'Simulating an Enactment Effect: Pronouns Guide Action Simulation during Narrative Comprehension', *Cognition* 115, 172–8.

Dixon, S. (2007) *Cornelia, Mother of the Gracchi* (London: Routledge).

Dougherty, C. (1993) *The Poetics of Colonization: From City to Text in Archaic Greece* (Oxford: Oxford University Press).

Bibliography

Dover, K. J. (1973) *Thucydides, Greece & Rome* New Surveys in the Classics 7 (Oxford: Clarendon Press).

(1983 [2009]) 'Thucydides "as History" and "as Literature"', *History & Theory* 22, 54–63, reprinted in J. S. Rusten (ed.), *Thucydides* (Oxford: Oxford University Press), 44–59.

Drumann, W. and Groebe, P. (1899) *Geschichte Roms*, vol. 1^2 (Berlin: Borntraeger).

Duchemin, J. (1955) *Pindare: Poète et prophète* (Paris: Les Belles Lettres).

Eberhardt, W. (1959) 'Der Melierdialog und die Inschriften ATL A 9 (*IG* I2 63 +) und *IG* I2 97 +', *Historia* 8, 284–314.

Eck, W., Caballos, A., and Fernández, F. (1996) *Das senatus consultum de Cn. Pisone patre* (Munich: Beck).

Eckstein, A. M. (1995) *Moral Vision in the Histories of Polybius* (Berkeley: University of California Press).

Edwards, C. (2011) 'Imagining Ruins in Ancient Rome', *European Review of History – Revue européenne d'histoire* 18, 645–61.

Eidinow, E. (2011) *Luck, Fate and Fortune: Antiquity and Its Legacy* (London: I. B. Tauris).

(2016) 'Popular Theologies: The Gift of Divine Envy', in E. Eidinow, J. Kindt, and R. Osborne (eds.), *Theologies of Ancient Greek Religion* (Cambridge: Cambridge University Press), 205–32.

Elliott, J. (2015) 'The Epic Vantage-Point: Roman Historiographical Allusion Reconsidered', *Histos* 9, 277–311.

Erbse, H. (1953) 'Über eine Eigenheit thukydideischer Geschichtsbetrachtung', *RhM* 96, 38–62.

(1992) *Studien zum Verständnis Herodots* (Berlin: De Gruyter).

Eshleman, K. J. (2008) 'Defining the Circle of Sophists: Philostratus and the Construction of the Second Sophistic', *CP* 103, 395–413.

Evans, J. A. S. (1987) 'The Faiyum and the Lake of Moeris', *AHB* 92, 66–74.

(2013 [1980]) 'Oral Tradition in Herodotus', in R. V. Munson (ed.), *Herodotus: Oxford Readings in Classical Studies*, vol. 1 (Oxford: Oxford University Press), 113–23.

Everson, J. (2011) 'Il Mambriano di Francesco Cieco da Ferrara – fra tradizione cavalleresca e mondo estense', in G. Venturi (ed.), *L'uno e l'altro Ariosto: In corte e nelle delizie* (Florence: Olschki), 153–73.

Fairbank, K. (2017) 'Caesar's Portrait of "Caesar"', in K. Raaflaub (ed.), *The Landmark Julius Caesar* (New York: Pantheon), app. EE: web essay at www .landmarkcaesar.com.

Fairweather, J. (1974) 'Fiction in the Biographies of Ancient Writers', *AncSoc* 5, 231–75.

Farrington, S. T. (2008) 'As the Tragic Poets Do: Polybius' Conception of Tragedy and Its Relationship to "Tragic History"' (PhD dissertation, University of Colorado).

Feeney, D. C. (1991) *The Gods in Epic: Poets and Critics of the Classical Tradition* (Oxford: Clarendon Press).

406 Bibliography

(2007) *Caesar's Calendar: Ancient Time and the Beginnings of History* (Berkeley: University of California Press).

Fehling, D. C. (1989) *Herodotus and His 'Sources': Citation, Invention and Narrative Art* (Leeds: Francis Cairns), English trans. by J. G. Howie of a revised version of *Die Quellenangaben bei Herodot* (Berlin: De Gruyter, 1971).

Fisher, N. R. E. (2002) 'Popular Morality in Herodotus', in E. J. Bakker, I. J. F. de Jong, and H. van Wees (eds.), *Brill's Companion to Herodotus* (Leiden: Brill), 199–224.

(2003) 'Let Envy Be Absent: Envy, Liturgies, and Reciprocity in Athens', in D. Konstan and N. K. Rutter (eds.), *Envy, Spite and Jealousy: The Rivalrous Emotions in Ancient Greece*, Edinburgh Leventis Studies 2 (Edinburgh: Edinburgh University Press), 181–215.

(2010) 'Kharis, Kharites, Festivals, and Social Peace in the Classical Greek City', in R. M. Rosen and I. Sluiter (eds.), *Valuing Others in Classical Antiquity*, Mnemosyne Supplement 323 (Leiden: Brill), 71–112.

Flach, D. (1985) *Einführung in die römische Geschichtsschreibung* (Darmstadt: Wissenschaftliche Buchgesellschaft).

Flinterman, J.-J. (1995) *Power, Paideia and Pythagoreanism: Greek Identity, Conceptions of the Relationship between Philosophers and Monarchs and Political Ideas in Philostratus' Life of Apollonius* (Amsterdam: Gieben).

Flower, H. I. (1992) 'Thucydides and the Pylos Debate (4.27–29)', *Historia* 41, 40–57.

(1996) *Ancestor Masks and Aristocratic Power in Roman Culture* (Oxford: Oxford University Press).

(2014) 'Memory and Memoirs in Republican Rome', in K. Galinsky (ed.), *Memoria Romana: Memory in Rome and Rome in Memory*, Memoirs of the American Academy in Rome, supplement 10 (Ann Arbor: University of Michigan Press), 27–40.

(2015a) 'Sulla's Memoirs as an Account of Personal Religious Experiences', *Religion in the Roman Empire* 1, 297–320.

(2015b) 'The Rapture and the Sorrow: Characterization in Sulla's Memoirs', in R. Ash, J. Mossman, and F. B. Titchener (eds.), *Fame and Infamy: Essays for Christopher Pelling on Characterization in Greek and Roman Biography and Historiography* (Oxford: Oxford University Press), 209–23.

(2020) 'The Freedom of the Rhodians: Cato the Elder and Demosthenes', in C. Balmaceda (ed.), *Libertas and Res Publica in the Roman Republic* (Leiden: Brill), 84–103.

(forthcoming) 'Self-Representation in a Time of Civil Strife: Publius Rutilius Rufus' *de vita sua*', in W. Havener and U. Gotter (eds.), *A Culture of Civil War? Bellum Civile in the Late Republic and Early Empire, HABES* (Steiner: Stuttgart).

Flower, M. A. (1994) *Theopompus of Chios: History and Rhetoric in the Fourth Century BC.* (Oxford: Oxford University Press).

(2000) 'From Simonides to Isocrates: The Fifth-Century Origins of Fourth-Century Panhellenism', *ClAnt* 19, 65–101.

(2006) 'Herodotus and Persia', in C. Dewald and J. Marincola (eds.), *The Cambridge Companion to Herodotus* (Cambridge: Cambridge University Press), 274–89.

(2007) 'The Size of Xerxes' Expeditionary Forces', in R. Strassler (ed.), *The Landmark Herodotus: The Histories*, app. R (New York: Pantheon), 802–6.

(2012) *Xenophon's Anabasis, or The Expedition of Cyrus* (Oxford: Oxford University Press).

(2017) 'Xenophon as a Historian', in M. A. Flower (ed.), *The Cambridge Companion to Xenophon* (Cambridge: Cambridge University Press), 301–22.

Flower, M. A. and Marincola, J. (eds.) (2002) *Herodotus Histories Book IX*, Cambridge Greek and Latin Classics (Cambridge: Cambridge University Press).

Fludernik, M. (1993) 'Second-Person Fiction: Narrative You as Addressee and/or Protagonist', *Arbeiten aus Anglistik und Amerikanistik* 18, 217–47.

(1994) ' Introduction: Second-Person Narrative and Related Issues', in H. F. Mosher (ed.), 'Second-Person Narrative', special issue of *Style* 28.3, 281–311.

(1996) *Towards a 'Natural' Narratology* (London: Routledge).

Fontenrose, J. (1978) *The Delphic Oracle* (Berkeley: University of California Press).

Fornara, C. W. (1971) *Herodotus: An Interpretative Essay* (Oxford: Oxford University Press).

(1983) *The Nature of History in Ancient Greece and Rome* (Berkeley: University of California Press).

(2013 [1971]) 'Herodotus' Perspective', in R. V. Munson (ed.), *Herodotus: Oxford Readings in Classical Studies*, vol. 1 (Oxford: Oxford University Press), 321–33.

Foster, B. O. (1919) *Livy* (Loeb edition), vol. 1 (London: William Heinemann; New York: G. P. Putnam's Sons).

Fowler, A. (1982) *Kinds of Literature: An Introduction to the Theory of Genres and Modes* (Cambridge, MA: Harvard University Press).

Fowler, H. N. (1936) *Plutarch's Moralia X* (Cambridge, MA: Harvard University Press).

Fowler, R. (2000) 'P. Oxy. 4458: Poseidonios', *ZPE* 132, 133–42.

(2000–13) *Early Greek Mythography*, 2 vols. (Oxford: Oxford University Press).

(2006a) 'Herodotus and His Prose Predecessors', in C. Dewald and J. Marincola (eds.), *The Cambridge Companion to Herodotus* (Cambridge: Cambridge University Press), 29–45.

(2006b) 'How to Tell a Myth: Genealogy, Mythology, Mythography', *Kernos* 19, 35–46.

(2010) 'Gods in Early Greek Historiography', in J. N. Bremmer and A. Erskine (eds.), *The Gods of Ancient Greece: Identities and Transformations* (Edinburgh: Edinburgh University Press), 318–34.

408 *Bibliography*

(2011) '*Mythos* and *Logos*', *JHS* 131, 45–66.

(2013) *Early Greek Mythography,* vol. 2: *Commentary* (Oxford: Oxford University Press).

(2013 [1996]) 'Herodotos and His Contemporaries', in R. V. Munson (ed.) *Herodotus: Oxford Readings in Classical Studies,* vol. 1 (Oxford: Oxford University Press), 46–83.

Fraenkel, E. (1964) 'Eine Form römischer Kriegsbulletins', in E. Fraenkel (ed.), *Kleine Beiträge zur klassischen Philologie,* vol. 2 (Rome: Edizioni di Storia e Letteratura), 69–73.

Fränkel, H. (1975) *Early Greek Poetry and Philosophy* (Oxford: Blackwell).

Freudenburg, K. (2001) *Satires of Rome: Threatening Poses from Lucilius to Juvenal* (Cambridge: Cambridge University Press).

Fulkerson, L. (2008) 'Emotional Appeals in the Mytilenean Debate', *SyllClass* 19, 115–54.

Gaertner, J. F. (2008) 'Livy's Camillus and the Political Discourse of the Late Republic', *JRS* 98, 27–52.

(2018) 'The Corpus Caesarianum', in L. Grillo and C. B. Krebs (eds.), *The Cambridge Companion to the Writings of Julius Caesar* (Cambridge: Cambridge University Press), 263–76.

Gaertner, J. F. and Hausburg, B. (2013) *Caesar and the Bellum Alexandrinum: An Analysis of Style, Narrative Technique, and the Reception of Greek Historiography* (Göttingen: Vandenhoeck & Ruprecht).

Garcea, A. (2012) *Caesar's* De Analogia: *Edition, Translation, and Commentary* (Oxford: Oxford University Press).

Gardthausen, V. (1891) *Augustus und seine Zeit* (Aalen: Scientia Verlag).

Gelzer, M. (1959) *Pompeius,* 2nd ed. (Munich: Bruckmann).

(1963) 'Caesar als Historiker', in M. Gelzer (ed.), *Kleine Schriften,* vol. 2 (Wiesbaden: Steiner), 307–35.

(1968) *Caesar: Politician and Statesman* (Cambridge, MA: Harvard University Press).

Gera, D. L. (2000) 'Two Thought Experiments in the *Dissoi Logoi*', *AJPh* 121, 21–45.

Gerrish, J. (2013) '*Civitatem recipit*: Responding to Revolt in Thucydides 3 and Caesar's *Bellum Gallicum* 7', *New England Classical Journal* 40, 69–85.

(2018) 'Heroic Resonances in Caesar's *Bellum Gallicum* 5', *CW* 111.3, 351–70.

Gesche, H. (1976) *Caesar* (Darmstadt: Wissenschaftliche Buchgesellschaft).

Gibson, B. J. (1998) 'Rumours as Causes of Events in Tacitus', *Materiali e iscussion per l'analisi dei testi classici* 40, 111–29.

(2010) 'Causation in Post-Augustan Epic', in J. F. Miller and A. J. Woodman (eds.), *Latin Historiography and Poetry in the Early Empire: Generic Interactions* (Leiden: Brill), 29–47.

(2018) 'Praise in Polybius', in N. Miltsios and M. Tamiolaki (eds.), *Polybius and His Legacy* (Berlin: De Gruyter), 75–101.

Gibson, R. (2003) 'Pliny and the Art of (In)offensive Self-Praise', *Arethusa* 36, 235–54.

(2020) *Man of High Empire: The Life of Pliny the Younger* (Oxford: Oxford University Press).

Gilbert, C. D. (1970) 'Blind Cupid', *Journal of the Warburg and Courtauld Institutes* 33, 304–5.

Gilmartin, K. (1975) 'A Rhetorical Figure in Latin Historical Style: The Imaginary Second Person Singular', *TAPA* 105, 99–121.

Ginsburg, J. (1981) *Tradition and Theme in the Annals of Tacitus* (New York: Arno Press).

Ginzburg, C. (2012) 'The Bitter Truth: Stendhal's Challenge to Historians', in C. Ginzburg, A. Tedeschi, and J. Tedeschi (eds.), *Threads and Traces: True False Fictive* (Berkeley: University of California Press), 137–50.

Gleason, M. (2011) 'Identity Theft: Doubles and Masquerades in Cassius Dio's Contemporary History', *ClAnt* 30, 33–86.

Glenberg, A. M. and Kaschak, M. P. (2002) 'Grounding Language in Action', *Psychonomic Bulletin & Review* 9, 558–65.

Goldberg, S. (2010) *Constructing Literature in the Roman Republic* (Cambridge: Cambridge University Press).

Goldknopf, D. (1972) *The Life of the Novel* (Chicago: University of Chicago Press).

Goldman, M. L. (2015) 'Associating the *aulêtris*: Flute Girls and Prostitutes in the Classical Greek Symposium', *Helios* 42, 29–60.

Goldsworthy, A. (1998) '"Instinctive Genius": The Depiction of Caesar the General', in K. Welch and A. Powell (eds.), *Julius Caesar as Artful Reporter: The War Commentaries as Political Instruments* (London: Duckworth; Swansea: Classical Press of Wales), 193–219.

(2006) *Caesar: Life of a Colossus* (New Haven, CT: Yale University Press).

Gomme, A. W., Andrewes, A., and Dover, K. J. (1945–81) *A Historical Commentary on Thucydides*, 5 vols. (Oxford: Clarendon Press).

Goodyear, F. R. D. (1972) *The Annals of Tacitus*, vol. 1 (Cambridge: Cambridge University Press).

Gorman, R. G. and Gorman, V. B. (2007) 'The *Tryphê* of the Sybarites: A Historiographical Problem in Athenaeus', *JHS* 127, 38–60.

Gorman, V. B. (2001) *Miletos, the Ornament of Ionia: A History of the City to 400 B.C.E.* (Ann Arbor: University of Michigan Press).

Gould, H. E. and Whiteley, J. L. (1952) *Livy Book 1* (London: Macmillan).

Gould, J. (1985) 'On Making Sense of Greek Religion', in P. E. Easterling and J. V. Muir (eds.), *Greek Religion and Society* (Cambridge: Cambridge University Press), 1–33, reprinted in J. Gould, *Myth, Ritual, Memory and*

410   *Bibliography*

Exchange: Essays in Greek Literature and Culture (Oxford: Oxford University Press, 2001), 203–34.

(1989) *Herodotus* (London: Weidenfeld and Nicolson).

(1994) 'Herodotus and Religion', in S. Hornblower (ed.), *Greek Historiography* (Oxford: Oxford University Press) 91–106, reprinted in J. Gould, *Myth, Ritual, Memory and Exchange: Essays in Greek Literature and Culture* (Oxford: Oxford University Press, 2001), 283–303.

(2001) *Myth, Ritual, Mmemory and Exchange: Essays in Greek Literature and Culture* (Oxford: Oxford University Press).

(2003) 'Herodotus and the "Resurrection"', in P. Derow and R. C. T. Parker (eds.), *Herodotus and His World: Essays from a Conference in Memory of George Forrest* (Oxford: Oxford University Press), 297–302.

Gow, A. S. F. (1950–1952) *Theocritus*, vol. 1: *Introduction, Text and Translation*; vol. 2: *Commentary, Appendix, Indexes and Plates* (Cambridge: Cambridge University Press).

Gowers, E. (1995) 'The Anatomy of Rome from Capitol to Cloaca', *JRS* 85, 23–32.

Grafton, A. T. (1983–93) *Joseph Scaliger: A Study in the History of Classical Scholarship* (Oxford: Oxford University Press).

Graham, D. W. (2008) 'Heraclitus: Flux, Order, and Knowledge', in P. Curd and D. W. Graham (eds.), *The Oxford Handbook of Presocratic Philosophy* (Oxford: Oxford University Press), 169–84.

Green, P. (2010) *Diodorus Siculus: The Persian Wars to the Fall of Athens: Books 11–14.34 (480–401 BCE)* (Austin: University of Texas Press).

Greenblatt, S. (1991) *Marvelous Possessions: The Wonder of the New World* (Chicago: University of Chicago Press).

Greenhalgh, P. (1980) *Pompey: The Roman Alexander* (Columbia: University of Missouri Press).

Greenwood, E. (2006) *Thucydides and the Shaping of History* (London: Duckworth).

Grene, D. (1946 [1965]) *Greek Political Theory: The Image of Man in Plato and Thucydides* (Chicago: University of Chicago Press).

Grethlein, J. (2009) 'How Not to Do History: Xerxes in Herodotus' *Histories*,' *AJPh* 130, 195–218.

(2010) *The Greeks and Their Past: Poetry, Oratory and History in the Fifth Century BCE* (Cambridge: Cambridge University Press).

(2012) 'Xenophon's *Anabasis* from Character to Narrator', *JHS* 132, 23–40.

(2013) *Experience and Teleology in Ancient Historiography: 'Futures Past' from Herodotus to Augustine* (Cambridge: Cambridge University Press).

(2017) *Aesthetic Experiences and Classical Antiquity: The Significance of Form in Narratives and Pictures* (Cambridge: Cambridge University Press).

(2018) 'The Dynamics of Time: Herodotus' *Histories* and Contemporary Athens before and after Fornara', in T. Harrison and E. Irwin (eds.), *Interpreting Herodotus* (Oxford: Oxford University Press), 223–42.

Bibliography

(2020) 'World and Words: The Limits to *mimesis* and Immersion in Heliodorus' *Ethiopica*', in J. Grethlein, L. Huitink, and A. Tagliabue (eds.), *Experience, Narrative, and Criticism in Ancient Greece: Under the Spell of Stories* (Oxford: Oxford University Press), 127–47.

Grethlein, J. and Huitink, L. (2017) 'Homer's Vividness: An Enactive Approach', *JHS* 137, 67–91.

Grethlein, J., Huitink, L., and Tagliabue, A. (eds.) (2020) *Experience, Narrative, and Criticism in Ancient Greece: Under the Spell of Stories* (Oxford: Oxford University Press).

Griffin, J. (1990) 'Die Ursprünge der Historien Herodots', in W. von Ax (ed.), *Memoria rerum veterum: Neue Beiträge zur antiken Historiographie und alten Geschichte. Festschrift für Carl Joachim Classen zum 60. Geburtstag* (Stuttgart: Steiner), 51–82, translated as 'The Emergence of Herodotus', *Histos* 8 (2014), 1–24.

(2006) 'Herodotus and Tragedy', in C. Dewald and J. Marincola (eds.), *The Cambridge Companion to Herodotus* (Cambridge: Cambridge University Press), 46–59.

Griffiths, A. (1989) 'Was Cleomenes mad?', in A. Powell (ed.), *Classical Sparta* (London: Routledge), 51–78.

Grillo, L. (2012) *The Art of Caesar's* Bellum Civile*: Literature, Ideology, and Community* (Cambridge: Cambridge University Press).

(2018a) 'Literary Approaches to Caesar: Three Case Studies', in L. Grillo and C. B. Krebs (eds.), *The Cambridge Companion to the Writings of Julius Caesar* (Cambridge: Cambridge University Press), 157–69.

(2018b) 'Speeches in the *Commentarii*', in L. Grillo and C. B. Krebs (eds.), *The Cambridge Companion to the Writings of Julius Caesar* (Cambridge: Cambridge University Press), 131–43.

Grillo, L. and Krebs, C. B. (eds.) (2018) *The Cambridge Companion to the Writings of Julius Caesar* (Cambridge: Cambridge University Press).

Grimm, J. and Grimm, W. (1812–15) *Kinder- und Hausmärchen*, 1st ed. in 2 vols. (Berlin: Realschulbuchhandlung).

Grote, G. (1904–7) *History of Greece* (London: John Murray); orig. pub. 1846–56.

Gruen, E. S. (1992) 'Lucilius and the Contemporary Scene', in E. S. Gruen (ed.), *Culture and National Identity in Republican Rome* (London: Duckworth; Ithaca, NY: Cornell University Press), 272–318.

(2009) 'Caesar as a Politician', in M. Griffin (ed.), *A Companion to Julius Caesar* (Oxford: Wiley-Blackwell), 23–36.

(2011) *Rethinking the Other in Antiquity* (Princeton, NJ: Princeton University Press).

Grüner, A. (2004) *Venus Ordinis: Der Wandel von Malerei und Literatur im Zeitalter der römischen Bürgerkriege* (Paderborn: Schöningh).

Gulick, C. B. (1927) *Athenaeus: The Deipnosophists, Volume I, Books 1–3.106e* (Cambridge, MA: Harvard University Press).

Bibliography

Guthrie, W. K. C. (1965–81) *A History of Greek Philosophy*, 6 vols. (Cambridge: Cambridge University Press).

Guzzo, P. G. (2010) 'Intorno a Lampsake: Ipotesi di un modello foceo', *Incidenza dell'antico* 8, 197–212.

Hägg, T. (2012) *The Art of Biography in Antiquity* (Cambridge: Cambridge University Press).

Hallett, J. P. (2002) 'Women Writing in Rome and Cornelia, Mother of the Gracchi', in L. J. Churchill, P. R. Brown, and J. E. Jeffrey (eds.), *Women Writing Latin from Roman Antiquity to Early Modern Europe,* vol. 1 *Women Writing Latin in Roman Antiquity, Late Antiquity, and the Early Christian Era* (London: Routledge), 13–24.

(2006) 'Introduction: Cornelia and Her Maternal Legacy', *Helios* 33.2, 119–47.

(2018) '*Oratorum Romanorum Fragmenta Liberae Rei Publicae*: The Letter of Cornelia, *Mater Gracchorum* and the Speeches of her Father and Son', in C. Gray, A. Balbo, R. M. A. Marshall, and C. E. W. Steel (eds.), *Reading Republican Oratory. Reconstructions, Contexts, Receptions* (Oxford: Oxford University Press), 309–18.

Halliwell, S. (1991) 'The Uses of Laughter in Greek Culture', *CQ* 41, 279–96.

(2012) *Between Ecstasy and Truth: Interpretations of Greek Poetics from Homer to Longinus* (Oxford: Oxford University Press).

Hammond, N. G. L. (1972) *A History of Macedonia*, vol. 1 (Oxford: Clarendon Press).

Hansen, M. H. (1983–9) *The Athenian Ecclesia*, 2 vols. (Copenhagen: Museum Tusculanum Press).

Hansen, W. (2002) *Ariadne's Thread: A Guide to International Tales Found in Classical Literature* (Ithaca, NY: Cornell University Press).

Hardie, P. (2012) *Rumour and Renown: Representations of* Fama *in Western Literature* (Cambridge: Cambridge University Press).

Harrison, T. (2000) *Divinity and Herodotus: The Religion of Herodotus* (Oxford: Oxford University Press).

(2002) 'The Persian Invasions', in E. J. Bakker, I. J. F. de Jong, and H. Van Wees (eds.), *Brill's Companion to Herodotus* (Leiden: Brill), 551–78.

(2003) 'The Cause of Things: Envy and the Emotions in Herodotus' *Histories*', in D. Konstan and K. Rutter (eds.), *Envy, Spite and Jealousy: The Rivalrous Emotions in Ancient Greece* (Edinburgh: Edinburgh University Press), 143–63.

Hartog, F. (1988) *The Mirror of Herodotus: The Representation of the Other in the Writing of History* (French original: Le miroir d'Herodote [Paris: 'Editions Gallimard, 1980]), trans. J. Lloyd (Berkeley: University of California Press).

Hass, K. (2007) *Lucilius und der Beginn der Persönlichkeitsdichtung in Rom* (Stuttgart: Steiner).

Hau, L. I. (2016) *Moral History from Herodotus to Diodorus Siculus* (Edinburgh: Edinburgh University Press).

Bibliography 413

Haubold, J. (2013) *Greece and Mesopotamia. Dialogues in Literature* (Cambridge: Cambridge University Press).

Havener, W. (2016) *Imperator Augustus: die diskursive Konstituierung der militärischen persona des ersten römischen princeps* (Stuttgart: Steiner).

Hawthorn, G. (2014) *Thucydides on Politics: Back to the Present* (Cambridge: Cambridge University Press).

Helmbold, W. C. (1939) *Plutarch's Moralia VI* (Cambridge, MA: Harvard University Press).

Hemelrijk, E. A. (1999) *Matrona Docta: Educated Women in the Roman Élite from Cornelia to Julia Domna* (London: Routledge).

Henderson, W. J. (1992) 'Pindar Fr. 140B Snell-Maehler: The Chariot and the Dolphin', *Hermes* 120.2, 148–58.

Henrichs, A. (1994/5) '"Why Should I Dance?": Choral Self-Referentiality in Greek Tragedy', in H. Golder (ed.), 'The Chorus in Greek Tragedy and Culture', special issue of *Arion: A Journal of Humanities and the Classics, Third Series* 3.1, 56–111.

Hepperle, A. (1956) 'Charon von Lampsakos', in *Festschrift für Otto Regenbogen zum 65. Geburtstage* (Heidelberg: n.p.), 67–76.

Herkommer, E. (1968) 'Die Topoi in den Proömien der römischen Geschichtswerke' (dissertation, University of Tübingen).

Herman, D. (1994) 'Textual *You* and Double Deixis in Edna O'Brien's *A Pagan Place*', *Style* 28, 378–410.

Hershbell, J. P. (2004) 'Plutarch's Political Philosophy: Peripatetic and Platonic', in L. de Blois, J. Bons, T. Kessels, and D. M. Schenkeveld (eds.), *The Statesman in Plutarch's Works: Proceedings of the Sixth International Conference of the International Plutarch Society, Nijmegen/Castle Hernen, May 1–5, 2002,* vol. 1: *Plutarch's Statesman and His Aftermath: Political, Philosophical, and Literary Aspects, Mnemosyne* Supplement 250 (Leiden: Brill), 151–62.

Heubeck, A. (1980) 'Πρόφασις und keine Ende (zu Thuk. 1.23)', *Glotta* 58, 222–36.

Heurgon, J. (1970) *Tite-Live: Ab Vrbe Condita Liber Primus,* 2nd ed. (Paris: Presses Universitaires de France).

Hillard, T. W. (2001) 'Popilia and the *Laudationes Funebres* for Women', *Antichthon* 35, 45–63.

Holmes, T. R. (1928) *The Architect of the Roman Empire* (Oxford: Humphrey Milford).

Horden, P. and Purcell, N. (2000) *The Corrupting Sea* (Oxford: Blackwell).

Hornblower, S. (1991–2008) *A Commentary on Thucydides,* 3 vols. (revised editions, vols. 1 and 2, 1997 and 2004) (Oxford: Clarendon Press).

  (1994) *Greek Historiography* (Oxford: Clarendon Press).

  (2003) 'Panionios of Chios and Hermotimos of Pedasa (Hdt. 8.104–6)', in P. Derow and R. C. T. Parker (eds.), *Herodotus and His World: Essays from a Conference in Memory of George Forrest* (Oxford: Oxford University Press), 37–57.

414 *Bibliography*

(2004) *Thucydides and Pindar: Historical Narrative and the World of Epinikian Poetry* (Oxford: Oxford University Press).

Hornblower, S. and Pelling, C. (2017) *Herodotus:* Histories, *Book VI* (Cambridge: Cambridge University Press).

Horsfall, N. (1974) 'Virgil's Roman Chronography: A Reconsideration', *CQ* 24, 111–15, reprinted in N. Horsfall, *Fifty Years at the Sibyl's Heels: Selected Papers on Virgil and Rome* (Oxford: Oxford University Press, 2020), 34–9.

(1981) 'Some Problems of Titulature in Roman Literary History', *BICS* 28, 103–14.

(1989) *Cornelius Nepos, a Selection Including the Lives of Cato and Atticus* (Oxford: Clarendon Press).

How, W. W. and Wells, J. (1912, rev. 1928) *A Commentary on Herodotus*, 2 vols. (Oxford: Oxford University Press).

Howe, A. (2013) *Byron and the Forms of Thought* (Liverpool: Liverpool University Press).

Howell, P. (1995) *Martial Epigrams V* (Warminster: Aris and Phillips).

Huitink, L. (2019) '"There was a river on their left-hand side": Xenophon's *Anabasis*, Arrival Scenes, Reflector Narrative and the Evolving Language of Greek Historiography', in A. Willi and P. Derron (eds.), *Formes et fonctions des langues littéraires en Grèce ancienne*, Entr. Hardt 65 (Vandoeuvres-Genève: Fondation Hardt), 185–226.

Hunter, V. J. (1973) *Thucydides: The Artful Reporter* (Toronto: Hakkert).

(1980) 'Thucydides and the Uses of the Past', *Klio* 62, 190–219.

(1982) *Past and Process in Herodotus and Thucydides*. Princeton, NJ: Princeton University Press.

Hurst, A. (1975) 'Prose historique et poésie. Le cas de Charon de Lampsaque', in I. Fischer (ed.), *Actes de la XIIe conférence international d'études classiques* Eirene, *Cluj-Napoca, 2–7 octobre 1972* (Amsterdam: Hakkert), 231–7.

Hussey, E. L. (1985) 'Thucydidean History and Democritean Theory', *History of Political Thought* 6, 118–38.

Hutchinson, G. O. (2020) *Motion in Classical Literature: Homer, Parmenides, Sophocles, Ovid, Seneca, Tacitus, Art* (Oxford: Oxford University Press).

Immerwahr, H. (2013 [1956]) 'Aspects of Historical Causation in Herodotus', in R. V. Munson (ed.), *Herodotus: Oxford Readings in Classical Studies*, vol. 1 (Oxford: Oxford University Press), 157–93.

Instinsky, H. U. (1971) 'Zur Echtheitsfrage der Brieffragmente der Cornelia, Mutter der Gracchen', *Chiron* 1, 177–89.

Irwin, E. (2007) 'The Politics of Precedence: First "Historians" on First "Thalassocrats"', in R. Osborne (ed.), *Debating the Athenian Cultural Revolution: art, Literature, Philosophy, and Politics 430–380 BC* (Cambridge: Cambridge University Press), 188–223.

Bibliography

Isaac, B. (1986) *The Greek Settlements in Thrace until the Macedonian Conquest* (Leiden: Brill).

Iser, W. (1978) *The Act of Reading: A Theory of Aesthetic Response* (Baltimore, MD: Johns Hopkins University Press).

Isnardi, M. (1953) 'Τέχνη e ἦθος nella metodologia storiografica di Polibio', *SCO* 3, 102–10.

Jacoby, F. (1902) *Apollodors Chronik: Eine Sammlung der Fragmente* (Berlin: Weidmann).

   (1909) 'Über die Entwicklung der griechischen Geschichtsschreibung und den Plan einer neuen Sammlung der griechischen Historikerfragmente', *Klio* 9, 80–123.

   (1913) 'Herodotos', *RE* Suppl. 2, 205–520.

   (1922) 'Ktesias', *RE* 11, 2032–37.

   (1926) *Die Fragmente der griechischen Historiker. Zweiter Teil C: Kommentar zu Nr. 56–105* (Leiden: Brill).

   (1943) *Die Fragmente der griechischen Historiker,* vol. IIIa, *Kommentar* (Leiden: Brill).

   (1949) *Atthis: The Local Chronicles of Ancient Athens* (Oxford: Clarendon Press).

   (1956) 'Charon of Lampsakos', originally *SIFC* 15 (1938), 207–42, quoted from H. Bloch (ed.), *Abhandlungen zur griechischen Geschichtsschreibung* (Leiden: Brill), 178–206.

   (2015) *On the Development of Greek Historiography and the Plan for a New Collection of the Fragments of the Greek Historians*, trans. M. Chambers and S. Schorn (*Histos* Supplement 3, Newcastle upon Tyne).

Jaeger, M. (1999) 'Guiding Metaphor and Narrative Point of View in Livy's *Ab Vrbe Condita*', in C. S. Kraus (ed.), *The Limits of Historiography: Genre and Narrative in Ancient Historical Texts* (Leiden: Brill), 169–95.

Jervis, A. (2017) 'The *Gallic War* as a Work of Propaganda', in K. Raaflaub (ed.), *The Landmark Julius Caesar* (New York: Pantheon), app. HH: web essay at www.landmarkcaesar.com.

Jones, C. P. (1974) 'The Reliability of Philostratus', in G. W. Bowersock (ed.), *Approaches to the Second Sophistic: Papers Presented at the 105th Annual Meeting of the American Philological Association* (University Park: Pennsylvania State University Press), 11–16.

   (2002) 'Philostratus and the Gordiani', *MedAnt* 5, 759–67.

Judson, L. (1991) 'Chance and "Always for the Most Part" in Aristotle', in L. Judson (ed.), *Aristotle's Physics: A Collection of Essays* (Oxford: Oxford University Press), 73–99.

   (1998) 'What Can Happen When You Eat Pungent Food', in N. Avgelis and F. Peonidis (eds.), *Aristotle on Logic, Language and Science* (Thessaloniki: Sakkoulas Publications), 185–204.

Kacandes, I. (1990) 'Orality, Reader Address and "Anonymous You": On Translating Second Person References from Modern Greek Prose', *Journal of Modern Greek Studies* 8, 223–43.

(1993) 'Are You in the Text?: The "Literary Performative" in Postmodernist Fiction', *Text and Performance Quarterly* 13, 139–53.

Kagan, D. (1969) *The Outbreak of the Peloponnesian War* (Ithaca, NY: Cornell University Press).

(2009) *Thucydides: The Reinvention of History* (New York: Viking).

Kahane, A. (2005) *Diachronic Dialogues: Authority and Continuity in Homer and the Homeric Tradition* (Lanham, MD: Lexington Books).

Kajanto, I. (1957) *God and Fate in Livy* (Turku: Turun Yliopiston Kustantama).

Kallet, L. (2001) *Money and the Corrosion of Power in Thucydides: The Sicilian Expedition and Its Aftermath* (Berkeley: University of California Press).

Karttunen, K. (2002) 'The Ethnography of the Fringes,' in E. J. Bakker, I. J. F. de Jong, and H. van Wees (eds.), *Brill's Companion to Herodotus* (Leiden: Brill), 457–74.

Kayser, C. L. (1870–1) *Flavii Philostrati opera auctiora*, 2 vols. (Leipzig: Teubner, reprinted in 1985).

Keitel, E. (2009) '"Is Dying So Very Terrible?": The Neronian *Annals*', in A. J. Woodman (ed.), *The Cambridge Companion to Tacitus* (Cambridge: Cambridge University Press), 127–43.

(2010) 'The Art of Losing: Tacitus and the Disaster Narrative', in C. S. Kraus, J. Marincola, and C. Pelling (eds.), *Ancient Historiography and Its Contexts: Studies in Honour of A. J. Woodman* (Oxford: Oxford University Press), 331–52.

Kemezis, A. M. (2011) 'Narrative of Cultural Geography in Philostratus' *Lives of the Sophists*', in P. Fleury and T. Schmidt (eds.), *Regards sur la Seconde Sophistique et son époque* (Toronto: University of Toronto Press), 3–22.

(2014) *Greek Narratives of the Roman Empire under the Severans: Cassius Dio, Philostratus and Herodian* (Cambridge: Cambridge University Press).

(2016–17) '"Inglorius Labor"?: The Rhetoric of Glory and Utility in Plutarch's *Precepts* and Tacitus' *Agricola*', *CW* 110, 87–117.

Keulen, W. (2006) *Gellius the Satirist: Roman Cultural Authority in Attic Nights* (Leiden: Brill).

Kienast, D. (2009) *Augustus: Prinzeps und Monarch*, 4th ed. (Darmstadt: Primus Verlag).

Kierdorf, W. (1962) 'Zum Melier-Dialog des Thukydides', *RhM* 105, 253–6.

(1980) *Laudatio funebris: Interpretationen und Untersuchungen zur Entwicklung der römischen Leichenrede* (Meisenheim: Hain).

Kirwan, C. (1993) *Aristotle, Metaphysics Books Γ, Δ and E*, 2nd ed. (Oxford: Clarendon Press).

Klotz, F. (2007) 'Portraits of the Philosopher: Plutarch's Self-Presentation in the *Quaestiones Convivales*', *CQ* 57, 550–7.

Klotz, F. and Oikonomopoulou K. (eds.) (2011) *The Philosophers' Banquet: Plutarch's Table Talk in the Intellectual Culture of the Roman Empire* (Oxford: Oxford University Press).

Knausgaard, K. O. (2019) *So Much Longing in So Little Space: The Art of Edvard Munch*, trans. I. Burkey, Norwegian original 2017 (New York: Penguin, London: Harvill Secker).

Bibliography

König, J. (2009) 'Conventions of Prefatory Self-Representation in Galen's *On the Order of My Own Books*', in C. Gill, T. J. G. Whitmarsh, and J. Wilkins (eds.), *Galen and the World of Knowledge* (Cambridge: Cambridge University Press), 35–58.

    (2011) 'Self-Promotion and Self-Effacement in Plutarch's *Table Talk*', in F. Klotz and K. Oikonomopoulou (eds.), *The Philosopher's Banquet: Plutarch's Table Talk in the Intellectual Culture of the Roman Empire* (Oxford: Oxford University Press), 179–203.

    (2014) 'Images of Elite Communities in Philostratus: Re-reading the Preface to the *Lives of the Sophists*', in J. M. Madsen and R. Rees (eds.), *Roman Rule in Greek and Latin Writing: Double Vision* (Leiden: Brill), 246–70.

Konstan, D. (1987) 'Persians, Greeks and Empire', in D. Boedeker (ed.), 'Herodotus and the Invention of History', special issue of *Arethusa* 20, 59–73.

    (2005) 'Pity and Politics', in R. Hall Sternberg (ed.), *Pity and Power in Ancient Athens* (Cambridge: Cambridge University Press), 48–66.

Kowalzig, B. (2007) *Singing for the Gods: Performances of Myth and Ritual in Archaic and Classical Greece* (Oxford: Oxford University Press).

Kraay, C. M. and Moorey, P. R. S. (1981) 'A Black Sea Hoard of the Late Fifth Century BC', *NC* 141, 1–19.

Kraus, C. S. (1994) '"No Second Troy": Topoi and Refoundation in Livy Book V', *TAPA* 164, 267–89.

    (2009) 'Bellum Gallicum', in M. Griffin (ed.), *A Companion to Julius Caesar* (Oxford: Wiley-Blackwell), 159–74.

Krebs, C. B. (2006) '"Imaginary Geography" in Caesar's *Bellum Gallicum*', *AJPh* 127, 111–36.

    (2016) 'Thucydides in Gaul and Signposting in the *Gallic War*. The Sieges of Plataea and Avaricum', *Histos* 10, 1–11.

    (2017) 'Caesar the Historian', in K. Raaflaub (ed.), *The Landmark Julius Caesar* (New York: Pantheon), app. DD: web essay at www.landmarkcaesar.com.

    (2018) 'More Than Words. The *Commentarii* in Their Propagandistic Context', in L. Grillo and C. B. Krebs (eds.), *The Cambridge Companion to the Writings of Julius Caesar* (Cambridge: Cambridge University Press), 29–42.

Kremer, B. (1994) *Das Bild der Kelten bis in Augusteische Zeit. Studien zur Instrumentalisierung eines antiken Feindbildes bei griechischen und römischen Autoren* (Wiesbaden: Steiner).

Krentz, P. (1982) *The Thirty at Athens* (Ithaca, NY: Cornell University Press).

    (ed.) (1995) *Xenophon: Hellenika II.3.11–IV.2.8* (Warminster: Aris and Phillips).

Kuhn-Treichel, T. (2020–1) 'Pindar's Poetic "I" and the Muses: Metaphorical Role Characterization in Different Genres', *CJ* 116.2, 152–71.

Kühner, R. and Stegmann, C. (1962) *Ausführliche Grammatik der lateinischen Sprache,* vol. 2 *Satzlehre. Parts 1 and 2,* 4th ed., repr. (Munich: Max Hueber Verlag).

Bibliography

Kurke, L. (1988) 'The Poet's Pentathlon: Genre in Pindar's First Isthmian', *GRBS* 29, 97–113.

(1989) 'Καπηλεία and Deceit: Theognis 59–60', *AJPh* 110, 535–44.

(1991) *The Traffic in Praise: Pindar and the Poetics of Social Economy* (Ithaca, NY: Cornell University Press).

(2011) *Aesopic Conversations: Popular Tradition, Cultural Dialogue, and the Invention of Greek Prose* (Princeton, NJ: Princeton University Press).

Kuukkanen, J.-M. (2015) *Postnarrativist Philosophy of Historiography* (Houndmills: Palgrave Macmillan).

Kyle, D. G. (2008) 'Herodotus on Ancient Athletics, Olympia, and Egypt', in P. Mauritsch, W. Petermandl, R. Rollinger, and C. Ulf (eds.), *Antike Lebenswelten. Konstanz – Wandel – Wirkungsmacht. Festschrift für Ingomar Weiler.* Phillippika: Marburger altertumskundliche Abhandlungen 25 (Wiesbaden: Harrassowitz), 149–59.

LaBarge, S. (2006) 'Aristotle on Empeiria', *AncPhil* 26, 23–44.

Lamarque, P. (1990) 'The Death of the Author: An Analytical Autopsy', *The British Journal of Aesthetics* 30, 319–31.

Landauer, M. (2019) *Dangerous Counsel: Accountability and Advice in Ancient Greece* (Chicago: University of Chicago Press).

Lanser, S. (1992) *Fictions of Authority: Women Writers and Narrative Voice* (Ithaca, NY: Cornell University Press).

Laqueur, R. (1907) 'Zur Griechischen Sagenchronographie', *Hermes* 42, 513–32.

Larcher, P.-H. (1786) (trans.) *Histoire d'Hérodote*, 7 vols. (Paris).

Lardinois, A. (1996) 'Who Sang Sappho's Songs?', in E. Green (ed.), *Reading Sappho: Contemporary Approaches* (Berkeley: University of California Press), 150–72.

Latacz, J. (1977) *Kampfparänese, Kampfdarstellung und Kampfwirklichkeit in der Ilias, bei Kallinos und Tyrtaios* (Munich: Beck).

Lateiner, D. (1977) 'No Laughing Matter: A Literary Tactic in Herodotus', *TAPA* 107, 173–82.

(1989) *The Historical Method of Herodotus* (Toronto: University of Toronto Press).

(1990) 'Mimetic Syntax: Metaphor from Word Order Especially in Ovid', *AJPh* 111, 204–37.

(2012) 'Herodotos the Pathographer: Persian and Hellenic Grief Displays', *Scripta Classica Israelica* 31, 133–50.

Le Bohec, Y. (2001) *César chef de guerre: César stratège et tacticien* (Monaco: Rocher; reprint Paris: Tallandier, 2019).

Lefèvre, E. (1997) 'Die Literatur der republikanischen Zeit', in F. Graf (ed.), *Einleitung in die lateinische Philologie* (Stuttgart: Teubner), 165–91.

(2001) 'Lucilius und die Politik', in G. Manuwald (ed.), *Der Satiriker Lucilius und seine Zeit* (Munich: Beck), 139–49.

Lefkowitz, M. R. (1991) *First-Person Fictions: Pindar's Poetic 'I'* (Oxford: Clarendon Press).

Bibliography

Legrand, Ph.-E. (1932–54) (ed. and trans.) *Hérodote:* Histoires (Paris: Les Belles Lettres).

Lehmann, G. A. (1974) 'Polybios und die ältere und zeitgenössische Geschichtsschreibung: Einige Bemerkungen', in E. Gabba (ed.), *Polybe,* Entretiens sur l'Antiquité Classique, XX (Vandoeuvres-Genève: Fondation Hardt), 145–205.

Lendon, J. E. (2009) 'Historians without History: Against Roman Historiography', in A. Feldherr (ed.), *The Cambridge Companion to the Roman Historians* (Cambridge: Cambridge University Press), 41–62.

(2017) 'Battle Description in the Ancient Historians', *G&R* 64, 39–64, 145–67.

Leumann, M., Hofmann, J. B., and Szantyr, A. (1972) *Lateinische Grammatik,* vol. 2 *Syntax und Stilistik,* revised ed. (Munich: Beck).

Levene, D. S. (2010) *Livy on the Hannibalic War* (Oxford: Oxford University Press).

Levene, D. S. and Nelis, D. P. (eds.) (2002) *Clio and the Poets: Augustan Poetry and the Traditions of Ancient Historiography* (Leiden: Brill).

Leyden, W. M. von (1949–50) '*Spatium historicum*: The Historical Past as Viewed by Hecataeus, Herodotus and Thucydides', *Durham University Journal* 11, 89–104.

Lilie, R.-J. (2014) 'Reality and Invention: Reflections on Byzantine Historiography', *Dumbarton Oaks Papers* 68, 157–210.

Lintott, A. (1999) *The Constitution of the Roman Republic* (Oxford: Oxford University Press).

Liotsakis, V. (2017) *Redeeming Thucydides' Book VIII: Narrative Artistry in the Account of the Ionian War,* Trends in Classics 48 (Berlin: De Gruyter).

Llewellyn-Jones, L. (2010) 'Introduction', in L. Llewellyn-Jones and J. Robson (eds.), *Ctesias' History of Persia: Tales of the Orient* (London: Routledge), 1–87.

Lloyd, A. B. (1975–88) *Herodotus Book Two,* 3 vols. (Leiden: Brill).

(1988) 'Herodotus' Account of Pharaonic History', *Historia* 37, 22–53.

(1995) 'Herodotus on Egyptian Buildings: A Test Case', in A. Powell (ed.), *The Greek World* (London: Routledge), 273–300.

Lloyd, M. (1984) 'Croesus' Priority: Herodotus 1.5.3', *Liverpool Classical Monthly* 9, 11.

Loomis, W. T. (1992) *The Spartan War Fund: IG V 1, 1 and a New Fragment* (Stuttgart: Steiner).

Loraux, N. (1980 [2011]) 'Thucydides Is Not a Colleague' (French original 1980), repr. in translation in J. Marincola (ed.), *Greek and Roman Historiography* (Oxford: Oxford University Press), ch. 1.

Loukopoulou, L. (2004) 'Thracian Chersonesos', in M. H. Hansen and T. H. Nielsen (eds.), *An Inventory of Archaic and Classical Poleis* (Oxford: Oxford University Press), 900–11.

Low, P. A. (ed.) (2008) *The Athenian Empire* (Edinburgh: Edinburgh University Press).

Bibliography

Lubtchansky, N. (1993) 'La valse tragique des cavaliers sybarites selon Aristote', *Annali di Archeologia e Storia Antica/Dipartimento di Studi del Mondo Classico e del Mediterraneo Antico* 15, 31–57.

(2005) *Le cavalier tyrrhénien. Représentations équestres dans l'Italie archaïque*, BEFAR 320 (Paris: De Boccard).

Luce, T. J. (1977) *Livy: The Composition of His History* (Princeton, NJ: Princeton University Press).

(1989) 'Ancient Views on the Causes of Bias in Historical Writing', *CP* 84, 16–31, reprinted in J. Marincola (ed.), *Greek and Roman historiography* (Oxford: Oxford University Press), 291–313.

(1998) *Livy. The Rise of Rome: Books One to Five* (Oxford: Oxford University Press).

Luckenbill, D. D. (1924) *The Annals of Sennacherib*, Oriental Institute Publications 2 (Chicago: University of Chicago Press).

Lund, A. A. (1989) 'Zu drei unechten Stellen in den *Ann.* des Tacitus', *Mnemosyne* 42, 124–8.

Luraghi, N. (2001a) 'Introduction', in N. Luraghi (ed.), *The Historian's Craft in the Age of Herodotus* (Oxford: Oxford University Press), 1–15.

(2001b) 'Local Knowledge in Herodotus' *Histories*', in N. Luraghi (ed.), *The Historian's Craft in the Age of Herodotus* (Oxford: Oxford University Press), 138–60.

(2006) 'Meta-historiê: Method and Genre in the *Histories*', in C. Dewald and J. Marincola (eds.), *The Cambridge Companion to Herodotus* (Cambridge: Cambridge University Press), 76–91.

(2013 [2005]) 'The Stories before the *Histories*: Folktale and Traditional Narrative in Herodotus', in R. V. Munson (ed.), *Herodotus: Oxford Reading in Classical Studies,* vol. 1 (Oxford: Oxford University Press), 87–123, revised and updated translation of 'Le storie prima delle *Storie*. Prospettive di ricerca', in M. Giangiulio (ed.), *Erodoto e il 'modello erodoteo'. Formazione e trasmissione delle tradizioni storiche in Grecia* (Trento: Università degli Studi di Trento, 2005), 61–90.

(2014) 'Ephorus in Context: The Return of the Heraclidae and Fourth-Century Peloponnesian Politics', in G. Parmeggiani (ed.), *Between Thucydides and Polybius: The Golden Age of Greek Historiography* (Washington, DC: Center for Hellenic Studies), 133–51.

Luschnat, O. (1970) 'Thukydides der Historiker', *Paulys Realencyclopädie der classischen Altertumswissenschaft* Supplementband 12, 1085–354.

Ma, J., Papazarkadas, N., and Parker, R. (eds.) (2009) *Interpreting the Athenian Empire* (London: Duckworth).

MacLachlan, B. (1993) *The Age of Grace: Charis in Early Greek Poetry* (Princeton, NJ: Princeton University Press).

Macleod, C. W. (1983a [1974]) 'Form and Meaning in the Melian Dialogue', *Historia* 23, 385–400, reprinted in O. Taplin (ed.), *The Collected Essays of Colin Macleod* (Oxford: Clarendon Press), 52–67.

Bibliography

(1983b [1978]) 'Reason and Necessity: Thucydides III 9–14, 37–48', *JHS* 98, 64–78, reprinted in O. Taplin (ed.), *The Collected Essays of Colin Macleod* (Oxford: Clarendon Press), 88–102.

Magnetto, A. (2004) 'Agnoia, ignoranza, errore', in L. Porciani (ed.), *Lexicon historiographicum Graecum et Latinum (LHG&L)*, vol. I (Pisa: Edizioni della Normale), 14–18.

Maier, F. K. (2018) 'Past and Present as *paradoxon theōrēma* in Polybius', in N. Miltsios and M. Tamiolaki (eds.), *Polybius and His Legacy* (Berlin: De Gruyter), 55–74.

Malitz, J. (2006) 'Klassische Philologie', in E. Wirbelauer (ed.), *Die Freiburger Philosophische Fakultät 1920–1960. Mitglieder – Strukturen – Vernetzungen* (Freiburg: Verlag Karl Alber), 303–64.

Malkin, I. (1990) 'Territorialisation mythologique: Les autels des Philènes en Cyrénaïque', *DHA* 16, 219–29.

(2011) *A Small Greek World: Networks in Ancient Mediterranean* (Oxford: Oxford University Press).

Malloch, S. J. V. (2013) *The Annals of Tacitus Book 11* (Cambridge: Cambridge University Press).

Mallon, Th. (2011) 'Fictions of Alternative History', *The New Yorker*, November 21.

Maltby, R. (1991) *A Lexicon of Ancient Latin Etymologies* (Leeds: Francis Cairns Publications).

Manuwald, B. (1979 [2009]) 'Diodotus' Deceit (on Thucydides 3.42–48)', trans. J. S. Rusten, in J. S. Rusten (ed.), *Thucydides* (Oxford: Oxford University Press), 241–60.

Manuwald, G. (ed.) (2001) *Der Satiriker Lucilius und seine Zeit* (Munich: Beck).

(2019) *Fragmentary Republican Latin,* vol. 4 *Oratory, Part 2* (Cambridge, MA: Harvard University Press).

Marasco, G. (1984) 'L'apologia di Q. Lutazio Catulo e la tradizione sulla guerra cimbrica', *Giornale Filologico Ferrarese* 7, 75–84.

(ed.) (2011) *Political Autobiographies and Memoirs in Antiquity: A Brill Companion* (Leiden: Brill).

Marcovich, M. (1967) *Heraclitus: Greek Text with a Short Commentary* (Merida: Los Andes University Press).

Marcozzi, D., Sinatra, M., and Vannicelli, P. (1994) 'Tra epica e storiografia: Il Catalogo delle navi', *Studi Micenei ed Egeo-Anatolici* 33, 163–74.

Margolin, U. (1993) 'Narrative "You" Revisited', *Language and Style* 23, 1–21.

Marincola, J. (1987) 'Herodotean Narrative and the Narrator's Presence', *Arethusa* 20, 121–37.

(1994) 'Plutarch's Refutation of Herodotus', *AW* 25, 191–203.

(1997) *Authority and Tradition in Ancient Historiography* (Cambridge: Cambridge University Press).

(1999a) 'Genre, Convention, and Innovation in Greco-Roman Historiography', in C. S. Kraus (ed.), *The Limits of Historiography: Genre and Narrative in Ancient Historical Texts* (Leiden: Brill), 281–324.

422 *Bibliography*

(1999b) 'Tacitus' Prefaces and the Decline of Imperial Historiography', *Latomus* 58, 391–404.

(2001) *Greek Historians, Greece & Rome* New Surveys in the Classics 31 (Oxford: Oxford University Press).

(2003) 'Beyond Pity and Fear: The Emotions of History', *AncSoc* 33, 285–315.

(2006) 'Herodotus and the Poetry of the Past', in C. Dewald and J. Marincola (eds.), *The Cambridge Companion to Herodotus* (Cambridge: Cambridge University Press), 13–28.

(2007a) 'Aletheia', in C. Ampolo, U. Fantasia, and L. Porciani (eds.), *Lexicon Historiographicum Graecum et Latinum*, vol. 2 (Pisa: Edizioni della Normale), 7–29.

(2007b) 'Odysseus and the Historians', *SyllClass* 18, 1–79.

(2007c) 'Speeches in Classical Historiography', in J. Marincola (ed.), *A Companion to Greek and Roman Historiography*, vol. 1 (Oxford: Blackwell), 118–32.

(2007d) 'The Persian Wars in Fourth-Century Oratory and Historiography', in E. Bridges, E. Hall, and P. J. Rhodes (eds.), *Cultural Responses to the Persian Wars* (Oxford: Oxford University Press), 105–26.

(ed.). (2007e) *A Companion to Greek and Roman Historiography* (Oxford: Blackwell).

(2010) 'Aristotle's *Poetics* and "Tragic History"', in S. Tsitsiridis (ed.), *Parachoregema: Studies on Ancient Theatre in Honour of Professor Gregory M. Sifakis* (Heraklion: Crete University Press), 445–60.

(2013) 'Polybius, Phylarchus, and "Tragic History": A Reconsideration', in B. J. Gibson and T. Harrison (eds.), *Polybius and His World: Essays in Memory of F. W. Walbank* (Oxford: Oxford University Press), 73–90.

(2013 [2007]) 'Herodotus and Odysseus', in R. V. Munson (ed.), *Herodotus: Oxford Readings in Classical Studies*, vol. 2 (Oxford: Oxford University Press), 109–32.

(2015a) 'Defending the Divine: Plutarch on the Gods of Herodotus', in A. Ellis (ed.), *God in History: Reading and Rewriting Herodotean Theology from Plutarch to the Renaissance*, Histos Supplement 4 (Newcastle: University of Newcastle), 41–83.

(2015b) 'Plutarch, Herodotus, and the Historian's Character', in R. Ash, J. Mossman, and F. B. Titchener (eds.), *Fame and Infamy: Essays for Christopher Pelling on Characterization in Greek and Roman Biography and Historiography* (Oxford: Oxford University Press), 83–96.

(2017) *On Writing History from Herodotus to Herodian* (London: Penguin Random House).

Marmodoro, A. and Hill, J. (eds.) (2013) *The Author's Voice in Classical and Late Antiquity* (Oxford: Oxford University Press).

Martin, R. H. and Woodman, A. J. (1989) *Tacitus Annals 4* (Cambridge: Cambridge University Press).

Martini, E. (2016) *Un romanzo di crisi: Il* Mambriano *del Cieco da Ferrara* (Florence: Società Editrice Fiorentina).

Bibliography

Maslov, B. (2015) *Pindar and the Emergence of Literature* (Cambridge: Cambridge University Press).

Massar, N. (2010) '"Choose Your Master Well": Medical Training, Testimonies and Claims to Authority', in M. Horstmanshoff (ed.), *Hippocrates and Medical Education: Selected Papers Read at the XIIth International Hippocrates Colloquium, Universiteit Leiden, 24–26 August 2005* (Leiden: Brill), 169–86.

Massaro, M. (1992) *Epigrafia metrica latina in età repubblicana,* Quaderni di *Invigilata Lucernis,* vol. 1 (Bari: Istituto di Latino, Università di Bari).

(2002) 'Il "ciclo degli Scipioni" e le origini della epigrafia metrica latina', in J. del Hoyo Calleja and J. Gómez Pallarès (eds.), *Asta ac pellege: 50 años de la publicación de 'Inscripciones Hispanas en verso' de S. Mariner* (Madrid: Signifer Libros), 17–37.

Mauersberger, A. (1956–) *Polybios-Lexikon* (Berlin: Akademie Verlag).

Mayor, J. E. B. (1872) *Thirteen Satires of Juvenal with a Commentary,* vol. 1 (London: Macmillan).

Mazzarino, S. (1966) *Il Pensiero Storico Classico,* 3 vols. (Bari: Laterza).

Mazzucchi, C. M. (1992) *Dionisio Longino: Del sublime* (Milan: Vita e pensiero).

McDonnell, M. A. (2006) *Roman Manliness:* Virtus *and the Roman Republic* (Cambridge: Cambridge University Press).

McHale, B. (1985) '"You used to know what these words mean": Misreading *Gravity's Rainbow*', *Language and Style* 18, 93–118.

(1992) *Constructing Postmodernism* (London: Routledge).

Meeus, A. (2017) 'Ctesias of Cnidus: Poet, Novelist or Historian?', in I. Ruffell and L. I. Hau (eds.), *Truth and History in the Ancient World: Pluralising the Past* (New York : Routledge), 172–201.

Meier, C. (1995) *Caesar* (New York: Basic Books).

Meiggs, R. (1972) *The Athenian Empire* (Oxford: Clarendon Press).

Meijering, R. (1987) *Literary and Rhetorical Theories in Greek Scholia* (Groningen: Egbert Forsten).

Meineck, P., Short, W. M., and Devereaux J. (eds.) (2019) *The Routledge Handbook of Classics and Cognitive Theory* (London: Routledge).

Meister, K. (1992) *La Storiografia Greca: Dalle Origini alla fine dell'Ellenismo* (Rome: Laterza).

(2013) *Thukydides als Vorbild der Historiker: Von der Antike bis zur Gegenwart* (Paderborn: Schöningh).

Mensching, E. (1988) *Caesars Bellum Gallicum: Eine Einführung* (Frankfurt am Main: Diesterweg).

Meyer, E. A. (1997) 'The *Outbreak of the Peloponnesian War* after Twenty-Five Years', in C. D. Hamilton and P. M. Krentz (eds.), *Polis and Polemos: Essays on Politics, War and History in Ancient Greece, in Honor of Donald Kagan* (Claremont, CA: Regina Books), 23–54.

Meyer, Ed. (1899) *Forschungen zur alten Geschichte,* vol. 2 (Halle: M. Niemeyer).

Mikalson, J. (2003) *Herodotus and Religion in the Persian Wars* (Chapel Hill: University of North Carolina Press).

424

Bibliography

Mildorf, J. (2006) 'Reconsidering Second-Person Narration and Involvement', *Language and Literature* 25, 145–58.

Miles, G. B. (1995) *Livy: Reconstructing Early Rome* (Ithaca, NY: Cornell University Press).

Miller, J. F. and Woodman, A. J. (2010) *Latin Historiography and Poetry in the Early Empire: Generic Interactions* (Leiden: Brill).

Miltsios, N. (2013) *The Shaping of Narrative in Polybius* (Berlin: De Gruyter).

Minar, E. L., Sandbach, F. H., and Helmbold, W. C. (1961) *Plutarch: Moralia, Volume 9: Table-Talk, Books 7–9. Dialogue on Love*, Loeb Classical Library 425 (Cambridge, MA: Harvard University Press).

Missiou, A. (2004) *The Subversive Oratory of Andokides: Politics, Ideology and Decision-Making in Democratic Athens* (Cambridge: Cambridge University Press).

Mitchell, L. (2010) 'Cleon and Diodotus: Masters of Thucydidean Irony', *Pegasus* 53, 10–14.

Mitchell, S. A. (1987) 'The Sagaman and Oral Literature: The Icelandic Traditions of Hjörleifr inn kvensami and Geirmundr heljarskinn', in J. M. Foley (ed.), *Comparative Research in Oral Traditions: A Memorial for Milman Parry* (Columbus, OH: Slavica), 395–423.

Mitsis, P. and Tsagalis, C. (eds.) (2010) *Allusion, Authority, and Truth: Critical Perspectives on Greek Poetic and Rhetorical Praxis* (Berlin: De Gruyter).

Moggi, M. (1972) 'Autori greci di *Persikà*, I: Dionisio di Mileto', *ASNP* 2, 433–68.

(1977) 'Autori greci di *Persikà*, II: Carone di Lampsaco', *ASNP* 7, 1–26.

Moles, J. (1993a) 'Livy's Preface', *PCPhS* 39, 141–68, reprinted in J. D. Chaplin and C. S. Kraus (eds.), *Livy: Oxford Readings in Classical Studies* (New York: Oxford University Press 2009), 49–87.

(1993b) 'Truth and Untruth in Herodotus and Thucydides', in C. Gill and T. P. Wiseman (eds.), *Lies and Fiction in the Ancient World* (Austin: University of Texas Press), 88–121.

(1996) 'Herodotus Warns the Athenians', in F. Cairns and M. Heath (eds.), *Papers of the Leeds International Latin Seminar*, vol. 9 *Roman Poetry and Prose, Greek Poetry, Etymology, Historiography* (Leeds: Cairns), 259–84.

(1998) 'Cry Freedom: Tacitus *Annals* 4.32–35', *Histos* 2, 95–184.

(2001) 'A False Dilemma: Thucydides' History and Historicism', in S. J. Harrison (ed.), *Texts, Ideas, and the Classics: Scholarship, Theory, and Classical Literature* (Oxford: Oxford University Press), 195–219.

(2011) 'Luke's Preface: The Greek Decree, Classical Historiography and Christian Redefinitions', *New Testament Studies* 57, 461–82.

Möller, A. (2005) 'Epoch-Making Eratosthenes', *GRBS* 45, 245–60.

Momigliano, A. (1978) *Alien Wisdom: The Limits of Hellenization* (Cambridge: Cambridge University Press).

(1981) 'The Rhetoric of History and the History of Rhetoric: On Hayden White's Tropes', *Comparative Criticism* 3, 260–1.

(2013 [1966]) 'The Place of Herodotus in the History of Historiography', in R. V. Munson (ed.), *Herodotus: Oxford Readings in Classical Studies*, vol. 1 (Oxford: Oxford University Press), 31–45.

Morelli, A. M. (2007) 'Hellenistic Epigram in the Roman World: From the Beginnings to the End of the Republican Age', in P. Bing and J. Bruss (eds.), *Brill's Companion to Hellenistic Epigram: Down to Philip* (Leiden: Brill), 521–41.

(2018) 'The Beginnings of Roman Epigram and Its Relationship with Hellenistic Poetry', in C. Henriksén (ed.), *A Companion to Ancient Epigram* (Hoboken, NJ: Wiley), 425–39.

Morello, R. (2018) 'Innovation and Cliché: The Letters of Caesar', in L. Grillo and C. B. Krebs (eds.), *The Cambridge Companion to the Writings of Julius Caesar* (Cambridge: Cambridge University Press), 223–34.

Morley, N. D. G. (2017) 'Resisting the Thucydides Trap', https://thesphinxblog.com/2017/03/31/resisting-the-thucydides-trap/.

Morley, N. D. G. and Harloe, K. (eds.) (2012) *Thucydides and the Modern World: Reception, Reinterpretation and Influence from the Renaissance to the Present* (Cambridge: Cambridge University Press).

Morrison, A. (2011) *Narrator in Archaic Greek and Hellenistic Poetry* (Cambridge: Cambridge University Press).

Morrissette, B. (1965) 'Narrative "You" in Contemporary Literature', *Comparative Literature Studies* 2, 1–24.

Morstein-Marx, R. (2007) 'Caesar's Alleged Fear of Prosecution and His *Ratio Absentis* in the Approach to the Civil War', *Historia* 56, 159–78.

(2009) 'Dignitas and res publica: Caesar and Republican Legitimacy', in K.-J. Hölkeskamp (ed.), *Eine politische Kultur (in) der Krise? Die 'letzte Generation' der römischen Republik* (Munich: Oldenbourg), 115–40.

Moyer, I. S. (2002) 'Herodotus and an Egyptian Mirage: The Genealogies of the Theban Priests', *JHS* 122, 70–90.

Muecke, F. (2005) 'Rome's First "Satirists": Themes and Genre in Ennius and Lucilius', in K. Freudenburg (ed.), *The Cambridge Companion to Roman Satire* (Cambridge: Cambridge University Press), 33–47.

Munson, R. V. (1991) 'The Madness of Cambyses (Herodotus 3.16–38)', *Arethusa* 24, 43–65.

(2001) *Telling Wonders: Ethnographic and Political Discourse in the Work of Herodotus* (Ann Arbor: University of Michigan Press).

(2012) 'Persians in Thucydides', in E. Foster and D. Lateiner (eds.), *Thucydides and Herodotus* (Oxford: Oxford University Press), 241–77.

(2013 [2009]) 'Who Are Herodotus' Persians?', in R. V. Munson (ed.), *Herodotus: Oxford Readings in Classical Studies*, vol. 2 (Oxford: Oxford University Press), 321–35.

(ed.) (2013) *Herodotus*, 2 vols. (Oxford: Oxford University Press).

(2017) 'Thucydides and Myth', in R. Balot, S. Forsdyke, and E. Foster (eds.), *The Oxford Handbook of Thucydides* (Oxford: Oxford University Press), 257–66.

Bibliography

(2019) 'Liberalizing Persia: The Shadow of a Greek Dream in Herodotus', in S. Fink and R. Rollinger (eds.), *Conceptualizing Past, Present, and Future: Proceedings of the Ninth Symposium of the Melammu Project in Helsinki/ Tartu, May 18–24, 2015* (Münster: Ugarit-Verlag), 495–507.

Murray, O. (1988) 'The Ionian Revolt', in J. Boardman, N. G. L. Hammond, D. M. Lewis, and M. Ostwald (eds.), *The Cambridge Ancient History,* vol. 4 *Persia, Greece and the Western Mediterranean c. 525 to 479 B.C.* (Cambridge: Cambridge University Press), 461–90.

(2001 [1987]) 'Herodotus and Oral History', in N. Luraghi (ed.), *The Historian's Craft in the Age of Herodotus* (Oxford: Oxford University Press), 16–44, originally in H. Sancisi-Weerdenburg and A. Kuhrt (eds.), *Achaemenid History,* vol. 2 *The Greek Sources* (Leiden: Nederlands Inst. voor het Nabije Oosten), 93–115.

(2018) *The Symposion: Drinking Greek Style. Essays on Greek Pleasure, 1983–2017,* ed. V. Cazzato (Oxford: Oxford University Press).

Musti, D. (2010) 'Un carattere fondamentale della storiografia polibiana: *Apodeiktikè historía'*, in T. Brüggemann, B. Meissner, and C. Mileta [et al.] (eds.), *Studia hellenistica et historiographica: Festschrift für Andreas Mehl* (Gutenberg: Computus), 203–10.

Mutschler, F.-H. (1975) *Erzählstil und Propaganda in Caesars Kommentarien* (Heidelberg: Winter).

Mynors, R. A. B. (1990) *Virgil: Georgics* (Oxford: Clarendon Press).

Mynott, J. (ed. and trans.) (2013) *Thucydides: The War of the Peloponnesians and the Athenians* (Cambridge: Cambridge University Press).

Naerebout, F. G. (2017) 'Moving in Unison: The Greek Chorus in Performance', in L. Gianvittorio (ed.), *Choreutika: Performing and Theorising Dance in Ancient Greece*, Biblioteca di *QUCC* 13 (Pisa: Serra), 39–66.

Nagy, G. (1990) *Pindar's Homer: The Lyric Possession of an Epic Past* (Baltimore, MD: Johns Hopkins University Press).

(1996) *Poetry as Performance: Homer and Beyond* (Cambridge: Cambridge University Press).

(2013) 'The Delian Maidens and Their Relevance to Choral Mimesis in Classical Drama', http://nrs.harvard.edu/urn-3:hlnc.essay:Nagy.The_ Delian_Maidens.2013.

Naiden, F. S. (1999) 'The Prospective Imperfect in Herodotus', *HSCP* 99, 135–49.

Neer, R. T and Kurke, L. (2014) 'Pindar Fr. 75 SM and the Politics of Athenian Space', *GRBS* 54, 527–79.

Nenci, G. (1990) 'L'Occidente *barbarico'*, in G. Nenci and O. Reverdin (eds.), *Hérodote et les peuples non grecs: neuf exposés suivis de discussions*, Entretiens sur l'Antiquité Classique, 35 (Vandoeuvres-Genève: Fondation Hardt), 301–21.

(1994) *Erodoto. Le Storie. Libro V: La rivolta della Ionia* (Milan: Fondazione Lorenzo Valla, Mondadori).

Newbold, R. F. (1976) 'The *Vulgus* in Tacitus', *RhM* 119, 85–92.

Bibliography

Newton, I. (1728) *The Chronology of Ancient Kingdoms Amended* (London: Printed for J. Tonson, and J. Osborn and T. Longman).

Nickau, K. (1990) 'Mythos und Logos bei Herodot', in W. Ax (ed.), *Memoria rerum veterum: Neue Beiträge zur antiken Historiographie und alten Geschichte. Festschrift für Carl Joachim Classen zum 60. Geburtstag* (Stuttgart: Steiner), 83–100.

Nicolai, R. (1995) 'Κτῆμα ἐς αἰεί: Aspetti della fortuna di Tucidide nel mondo antico', *RFIC* 123, 5–26.

(2001) 'Thucydides' Archaeology: Between Epic and Oral Traditions', in N. Luraghi (ed.), *The Historian's Craft in the Age of Herodotus* (Oxford: Oxford University Press), 263–85.

Nicolson, F. W. (1891) 'Greek and Roman Barbers', *HSCP* 2, 41–56.

Niles, J. D. (1999) Homo narrans: *The Poetics and Anthropology of Oral Literature* (Philadelphia: University of Pennsylvania Press).

Nolan, D. (2016) 'Caesar's *Exempla* and the Role of Centurions in Battle', in J. Armstrong (ed.), Circum mare: *Themes in Ancient Warfare* (Leiden: Brill), 34–64.

Nousek, D. L. (2018) 'Genres and Generic Contaminations: The *Commentarii*', in L. Grillo and C. B. Krebs (eds.), *The Cambridge Companion to the Writings of Julius Caesar* (Cambridge: Cambridge University Press), 97–109.

Nünning, V. (2012) 'Voicing Criticism in Eighteenth-Century Novels by Women: Narrative Attempts at Claiming Authority', *English Past and Present* 81–107.

Oakley, S. P. (1997) *A Commentary on Livy Books VI–X*, vol. 1 (Oxford: Clarendon Press).

Ober, J. (1998) *Political DisiIn Democratic Athens: Intellectual Critics of Popular Rule*, Martin Classical Lectures (Princeton, NJ: Princeton University Press).

Occhipinti, E. (2016) *The Hellenica Oxyrhynchia and Historiography: New Research Perspectives* (Leiden: Brill).

Ogilvie, R. M. (1965) *A Commentary on Livy Books 1–5* (Oxford: Clarendon Press).

O'Gorman, E. (2000) *Irony and Misreading in the Annals of Tacitus* (Cambridge: Cambridge University Press).

(2009) 'Intertextuality and Historiography', in A. Feldherr (ed.), *The Cambridge Companion to the Roman Historians* (Cambridge: Cambridge University Press), 231–41.

Olearius, G. (1709) ΤΑ ΤΩΝ ΦΙΛΟΣΤΡΑΤΩΝ ΛΕΙΠΟΜΕΝΑ ΠΑΝΤΑ. *Philostratorum quae supersunt omnia* (Leipzig: Apud Thomam Fritsch).

Olson, D. S. (2007) *Athenaeus: The Learned Banqueters,* vol. 1: *Books 1–3.106e,* Loeb Classical Library 204 (Cambridge, MA: Harvard University Press).

Oniga, R. (1990) *Il confine conteso: Lettura antropologica di un capitolo sallustiano,* Bellum Iugurthinum 79 (Bari: Edipuglia).

Ooms, S. and de Jonge, C.C. (2013) 'The semantics of ΕΝΑΓΩΝΙΟΣ in Greek literary criticism', *CP* 108, 95–110.

428 *Bibliography*

Ormerod, H. A. (1924) *Piracy in the Ancient World: An Essay in Mediterranean History* (Liverpool: Liverpool University Press).

Orwin, C. (1984) 'The Just and the Advantageous in Thucydides: The Case of the Mytilenaian Debate', *The American Political Science Review* 78, 485–94.

Osborne, R. and Rhodes, P. J (eds.) (2017) *Greek Historical Inscriptions: 478–404 BC* (Oxford: Oxford University Press).

Osgood, J. (2009) 'The Pen and the Sword: Writing and Conquest in Caesar's Gaul', *ClAnt* 28, 328–58.

Östenberg, I. (2009a) *Staging the World: Spoils, Captives, and Representations in the Roman Triumphal Procession* (Oxford: Oxford University Press).

   (2009b) '*Titulis oppida capta leget*: The Role of the Written Placards in the Roman Triumphal Procession', *MEFRA* 121, 463–72.

   (2013) '*Veni, vidi, vici* and Caesar's Triumph', *CQ* 63, 813–27.

Ostwald, M. (1979 [2009]) 'Diodotus, Son of Eucrates', *GRBS* 20, 5–13, reprinted as ch. 11 in M. Ostwald, *Language and History in Ancient Greek Culture* (Philadelphia: Pennsylvania State University Press, 2009).

   (1988) Ἀνάγκη *in Thucydides* (Atlanta: Scholars Press).

Otto, N. (2009) *Enargeia: Untersuchung zur Charakteristik alexandrinischer Dichtung*, *Hermes* Einzelschriften 102 (Stuttgart: Steiner).

Owen, G. E. L. (1983) 'Philosophical Invective', *Oxford Studies in Ancient Philosophy* 1, 1–25.

Page, R. E. (2006) *Literary and Linguistic Approaches to Feminist Narratology* (Basingstoke: Arts & Humanities Research Council; New York: Palgrave Macmillan).

Pani, M. (2001) *Le ragioni della storiografia in Grecia e a Roma: Una introduzione* (Bari: Edipuglia).

Panofsky, H. (1885) 'Quaestionum de historiae Herodoteae fontibus pars prima' (dissertation, Berlin).

Papadopoulos, J. K. (2003) *Ceramicus Redivivus: The Early Iron Age Potters' Field*, Hesperia Supplement 31 (Princeton, NJ: American School of Classical Studies at Athens).

Pape, W. (1981) 'Doppelgänger', *Enzyklopädie des Märchens* 3, 766–73.

Parker, V. (2004) 'Two Notes on Early Athenian History', *Tyche* 19, 131–48.

   (2011) 'Ephoros of Kyme (70)', in I. Worthington (ed.), *Brill's New Jacoby* (Leiden: Brill), online publication.

Parmeggiani, G. (1999) 'Mito e *spatium historicum* nelle *Storie* di Eforo di Cuma (Note a Eph. *FGrHist* 70 T8)', *RSA* 29, 107–25.

   (2011) *Eforo di Cuma: Studi di storiografia greca* (Bologna: Pàtron).

   (2014) 'On the Translation of Polybius 1.1.2', *Histos* 8, 180–8.

   (2018) 'How Sparta and Its Allies Went to War: Votes and Diplomacy in 432–1 B.C.', *Historia* 12, 244–55.

Parry, A. (1972a) 'Language and Characterization in Homer', *HSCP* 76, 1–22.

   (1972b [1989]) 'Thucydides' Historical Perspective', *YClS* 22, 47–61, reprinted in A. Parry (ed.), *The Language of Achilles and Other Papers* (Oxford: Clarendon Press), 286–300.

Bibliography

Paul, G. M. (1982) '*Vrbs Capta*', *Phoenix* 36, 144–55.

Pearson, L. (1987) *The Greek Historians of the West: Timaeus and His Predecessors* (Atlanta, GA: Scholars Press).

Pédech, P. (1964) *La méthode historique de Polybe* (Paris: Les Belles Lettres).

Pelikan Pittenger, M. R. (2008) *Contested Triumphs: Politics, Pageantry, and Performance in Livy's Republican Rome* (Berkeley: University of California Press).

Pelling, C. (1981) 'Caesar's Battle-Descriptions and the Defeat of Ariovistus', *Latomus* 40, 741–66.

   (1990 [2002]) 'Truth and Fiction in Plutarch's *Lives*', in D. A. Russell (ed.), *Antonine Literature* (Oxford: Clarendon Press), 19–52, reprinted in C. Pelling (ed.), *Plutarch and History: Eighteen Studies* (Swansea: Classical Press of Wales), 143–70.

   (1992 [2002]) 'Plutarch and Thucydides', in P. A. Stadter (ed.), *Plutarch and the Historical Tradition* (London: Routledge), 10–40, reprinted in C. Pelling (ed.), *Plutarch and History: Eighteen Studies* (Swansea: Classical Press of Wales), 117–42.

   (1997a) 'Biographical History? Cassius Dio on the Early Principate', in M. J. Edwards and S. Swain (eds.), *Portraits: Biographical Representation in the Greek and Latin Literature of the Roman Empire* (Oxford: Clarendon Press), 117–44.

   (1997b) 'East Is East and West Is West – Or Are They? National Stereotypes in Herodotus', *Histos* 1, 51–66.

   (2000) *Literary Texts and the Greek Historian* (London: Routledge).

   (2002a) 'Speech and Action: Herodotus' Debate on the Constitutions', *PCPhS* 48, 123–58.

   (2002b) *Plutarch and History: Eighteen Studies* (Swansea: Classical Press of Wales).

   (2006a) 'Breaking the Bounds: Writing about Caesar', in B. McGing and J. Mossman (eds.), *The Limits of Ancient Biography* (Swansea: Classical Press of Wales), 255–79.

   (2006b) 'Herodotus and Homer', in M. J. Clarke, B. G. F. Currie, and R. O. A. M. Lyne (eds.), *Epic Interactions: Perspectives on Homer, Virgil, and the Epic Tradition Presented to Jasper Griffin* (Oxford: Oxford University Press), 75–104.

   (2006c) 'Speech and Narrative', in C. Dewald and J. Marincola (eds.), *The Cambridge Companion to Herodotus* (Cambridge: Cambridge University Press), 103–21.

   (2007a) 'Aristagoras (5.49–55, 97)', in E. Irwin and E. Greenwood (eds.), *Reading Herodotus: A Study of the* logoi *in Book 5 of Herodotus'* Histories (Cambridge: Cambridge University Press), 179–201.

   (2007b) '*De malignitate Plutarchi*: Plutarch, Herodotus, and the Persian Wars', in E. Bridges, E. Hall, and P. J. Rhodes (eds.), *Cultural Responses to the Persian Wars: Antiquity to the Third Millennium* (Oxford: Oxford University Press), 145–64.

430 *Bibliography*

(2007c) 'Ion's *Epidemiai* and Plutarch's Ion', in V. Jennings and A. Katsaros (eds.), *The World of Ion of Chios* (Leiden: Brill), 75–109.

(2009a) 'Herodotus' Persian Stories: Narrative Shape and Historical Interpretation', *SyllClass* 27, 65–92.

(2009b) 'Tacitus' Personal Voice', in A. J. Woodman (ed.), *The Cambridge Companion to Tacitus* (Cambridge: Cambridge University Press), 147–67.

(2009c) 'Was There an Ancient Genre of "Autobiography"? Or Did Augustus Know What He Was Doing?', in C. Smith and A. Powell (eds.), *The Lost Memoirs of Augustus and the Development of Roman Autobiography* (Swansea: Classical Press of Wales), 41–64.

(2013) 'Xenophon's and Caesar's Third-Person Narratives – Or Are They?', in A. Marmodoro and J. Hill (eds.), *The Author's Voice in Classical and Late Antiquity* (Oxford: Oxford University Press), 39–75.

(2019) *Herodotus and the Question Why* (Austin: University of Texas Press).

(2022) *Thucydides: The Peloponnesian War. Book VI* (Cambridge: Cambridge University Press).

(2023) 'Plutarch and Biography', in A. Zadorojnyi and F. B. Titchener (eds.), *The Cambridge Companion to Plutarch* (Cambridge: Cambridge University Press), 11–28.

(forthcoming a) 'Literature as Evidence: The Case of Herodotus', in C. Carey, M. Edwards, and B. Griffith-Williams (eds.), *Evidence and Proof in Ancient Greece*.

(forthcoming b) 'Polybius' Self-Representation', in F. Maier and B. J. Gibson (eds.), *Brill's Companion to Polybius* (Leiden: Brill).

Peponi, A.-E. (2012) *Frontiers of Pleasure: Models of Aesthetic Response in Archaic and Classical Greek Thought* (Oxford: Oxford University Press).

Perrin, B. (ed.) (1914) *Lives*, Loeb Classical Library I (Cambridge, MA: Harvard University Press).

(ed.) (1916) *Lives*, Loeb Classical Library III (Cambridge, MA: Harvard University Press).

(ed.) (1918) *Lives*, Loeb Classical Library IV (Cambridge, MA: Harvard University Press).

(ed.) (1919) *Lives*, Loeb Classical Library VII (Cambridge, MA: Harvard University Press).

Peter, H. (1906) *Historicorum Romanorum Reliquiae*, vol. 2 (Leipzig: Teubner).

(1914) *Historicorum Romanorum Reliquiae²*, vol. 1 (Leipzig: Teubner).

Petzold, K. E. (1969) *Studien zur Methode des Polybios und zu ihrer historischen Auswertung* (Munich: Beck).

Pfeiffer, R. (1968) *History of Classical Scholarship: From the Beginning to the End of the Hellenistic Age* (Oxford: Clarendon Press).

Phelan, J. (1994) '*Self-Help* for Narratee and Narrative Audience: How "I" – And "You"? – Read "How"', *Style* 28, 350–65.

(1996) *Narrative as Rhetoric: Technique, Audiences, Ethics, Ideology* (Columbus: Ohio State University Press).

Bibliography

Piérart, M. (1995) 'Chios entre Athènes et Sparte. La contribution des exiles de Chios à l'effort de guerre lacédémonien pendant la Guerre du Péloponnèse. *IG* V 1, 1 + (*SEG* XXXIX 370)', *BCH* 119, 253–82.

Pigoń, J. (ed.) (2008) *The Children of Herodotus: Greek and Roman Historiography and Related Genres* (Newcastle-upon-Tyne: Cambridge Scholars Publisher).

Pinkster, H. (2015) *The Oxford Latin Syntax*, vol. 1 (Oxford: Oxford University Press).

Pitcher, L. (2018) 'Caesar and Greek Historians', in L. Grillo and C. B. Krebs (eds.), *The Cambridge Companion to the Writings of Julius Caesar* (Cambridge: Cambridge University Press), 237–48.

Plant, I. M. (1988) 'A Note on Thucydides 1,22,1', *Athenaeum* 66, 201–2.

Pohlenz, M. (1937) *Herodot: Der erste Geschichtschreiber des Abendlandes* (Leipzig: Teubner).

Porciani, L. (1999) 'Come si scrivono i discorsi: su Tucidide 1.22', *QS* 49, 103–35.

Potter, D. (1991) 'The Inscriptions on the Bronze Herakles from Mesene: Vologeses IV's War with Rome and the Date of Tacitus' *Annales*', *ZPE* 88, 277–90.

(2010) 'Caesar and the Helvetians', in G. G. Fagan and M. Trundle (eds.), *New Perspectives on Ancient Warfare* (Leiden: Brill), 305–29.

Power, T. (2011) 'Cyberchorus: Pindar's Κηληδόνες and the Aura of the Artificial', in L. Athanassaki and E. Bowie (eds.), *Archaic and Classical Choral Song: Performance, Politics and Dissemination* (Berlin: De Gruyter), 67–113.

Prince, G. (2008) 'Classical and/or Postclassical Narratology', *L'Esprit Créateur*, 115–23.

Pritchett, W. K. (1975) *Dionysius of Halicarnassus: On Thucydides* (Berkeley: University of California Press).

(1982) *Studies in Ancient Greek Topography: Part IV (Passes)* (Berkeley: University of California Press).

(1993) *The Liar School of Herodotos* (Amsterdam: J. C. Gieben).

Propp, V. J. (1928) *Morfologija skaski* (Leningrad: Academia).

Purcell, N. (1990) 'Mobility and the Polis', in O. Murray and S. Price (eds.), *The Greek City, from Homer to Alexander* (Oxford: Oxford University Press), 29–58.

(1995) 'On the Sacking of Carthage and Corinth', in D. Innes, H. Hine, and C. Pelling (eds.), *Ethics and Rhetoric: Classical Essays for Donald Russell on His Seventy-Fifth Birthday* (Oxford: Oxford University Press), 133–48.

Purves, A. C. (2010) *Space and Time in Ancient Greek Narrative* (Cambridge: Cambridge University Press).

(2013) 'Haptic Herodotus', in S. Butler and A.C. Purves (eds.), *Synaesthesia and the Ancient Senses* (Durham: Acumen), 35–50.

Quinton, A. M. (1954 [2015]) 'On Punishment', *Analysis* 14, 33–42, reprinted in G. Ezorsky (ed.), *Philosophical Perspectives on Punishment* (Albany: State University of New York Press), 6–15.

Bibliography

Raaflaub, K.A. (2002) 'Philosophy, Science, Politics: Herodotus and the Intellectual Trends of His Time', in E. J. Bakker, I. J. F. de Jong, and H. van Wees (eds.), *Brill's Companion to Herodotus* (Leiden: Brill), 149–86.

(2010) 'Ulterior Motives in Ancient Historiography: What Exactly, and Why?', in L. Foxhall, H.-J. Gehrke, and N. Luraghi (eds.), *Intentional History: Spinning Time in Ancient Greece* (Stuttgart: Steiner), 189–210.

(2013) '*Ktema es aiei*: Thucydides' Concept of "Learning through History" and Its Realization in His Work', in A. Tsakmakis and M. Tamiolaki (eds.), *Thucydides between History and Literature* (Berlin: De Gruyter), 3–21.

(2016) 'Die grosse Herausforderung. Herodot, Thukydides und die Erfindung einer neuen Form von Geschichtsschreibung', *Historische Zeitschrift* 302, 593–622.

(2017a) 'The *Civil War* as a Work of Propaganda', in K. Raaflaub (ed.), *The Landmark Julius Caesar* (New York: Pantheon), app. JJ: web essay at www.landmarkcaesar.com.

(ed.) (2017b) *The Landmark Julius Caesar* (New York: Pantheon).

(2018) 'Caesar, Literature, and Politics at the End of the Republic', in L. Grillo and C. B. Krebs (eds.), *The Cambridge Companion to the Writings of Julius Caesar* (Cambridge: Cambridge University Press), 13–28.

Race, W. H. (1987) '*P. OXY.* 2438 and the Order of Pindar's Works', *RhM* 130, 407–10.

(1997) *Nemean Odes – Isthmian Odes – Fragments*, Loeb Classical Library 485 (Cambridge, MA: Harvard University Press).

Radice, B. (1969) *Pliny. Letters and Panegyricus. II, Books VIII-X and the Panegyricus*. Loeb Classical Library. Cambridge, MA: Harvard University Press.

Rahe, P. (2002) 'Justice and Necessity: The Conduct of the Spartans and the Athenians in the Peloponnesian War', in M. Grimsley and C. J. Rogers (eds.), *Civilians in the Path of War* (Lincoln: University of Nebraska Press), 1–32.

Rainbird, J. (1986) 'The Fire Stations of Imperial Rome', *PBSR* 54, 147–69.

Ramage, E. S. (1983) 'Urban Problems in Ancient Rome', in R. T. Marchese (ed.), *Aspects of Graeco-Roman Urbanism*, BAR International Series 188 (Oxford: BAR International), 74–9.

Rambaud, M. (1966 [1953]) *L'art de la déformation historique dans les Commentaires de César* (Paris: Les Belles Lettres).

Raschke, W. J. (1979) 'The Chronology of the Early Books of Lucilius', *JRS* 69, 78–89.

Rasmussen, D. (1963) *Caesars* Commentarii: *Stil und Stilwandel am Beispiel der direkten Rede* (Göttingen: Vandenhoeck & Ruprecht).

Raubitschek, A. E. (1963) 'War Melos tributpflichtig?', *Historia* 12, 78–83.

Rawlings, H. R. (1858–60) 'KTEMA TE ES AIEI . . . AKOUEIN', *CP* 111, 107–16.

(2021) 'Thucydides' ἔργα', *Histos* 2021, 189–205.

Rawlinson, G. (1858–60) *The History of Herodotus*, 4 vols. (London: John Murray).

Bibliography

Rawson, E. (1994) *The Cambridge Ancient History*, vol. 9^2 (Cambridge: Cambridge University Press).

Reale, G. (2006) *I Presocratici. Prima traduzione intergrale con testi originali a fronte delle testimonianze e dei frammenti nella raccolta di Hermann Diels e Walther Kranz*, a cura di Giovanni Reale, con la collaborazione di Diego Fusaro, Maurizio Migliori, Ilaria Ramelli, Maria Timpanaro Cardini, Angelo Tonelli (Milan: Bompiani).

Redfield, J. (1985) 'Herodotus the Tourist', *CP* 80, 97–118.

Reed Doob, P. (1990) *The Idea of the Labyrinth from Classical Antiquity through the Middle Ages* (Ithaca, NY: Cornell University Press).

Rengakos, A. and Tsakmakis, A. (eds.) (2006) *Brill's Companion to Thucydides* (Leiden: Brill).

Rhodes, P. J. (1985) 'What Alcibiades Did or What Happened to Him', University of Durham Inaugural Lecture.

(1994) 'In Defence of the Greek Historians', *G&R* 41, 156–71.

Richardson, B. (1991) 'The Poetics and Politics of Second-Person Narrative', *Genre* 24, 309–30.

(2006) *Unnatural Voices: Extreme Narration in Modern and Contemporary Fiction* (Columbus: Ohio State University Press).

Richardson, J. (2000) *The Annals of London* (London: Cassell).

(2008) *The Language of Empire* (Cambridge: Cambridge University Press).

Richter, W. (1977) *Caesar als Darsteller seiner Taten. Eine Einführung* (Heidelberg: Winter).

Ricoeur, P. (2004) *Memory, History, Forgetting* (Chicago: University of Chicago Press).

Riggsby, A. M. (2006) *Caesar in Gaul and Rome: War in Words* (Austin: University of Texas Press).

(2018) 'The Politics of Geography', in L. Grillo and C. B. Krebs (eds.), *The Cambridge Companion to the Writings of Julius Caesar* (Cambridge: Cambridge University Press), 68–80.

(2019) *Mosaics of Knowledge: Representing Information in the Roman World* (Oxford: Oxford University Press).

Riginos, A. S. (1976) *Platonica: The Anecdotes Concerning the Life and Writings of Plato* (Leiden: Brill).

Rives, J. B. (1999) *Tacitus: Germania* (Oxford: Clarendon Press).

Robinson, E. (2017) 'Thucydides on the Causes and Outbreak of the Peloponnesian War', in R. Balot, S. Forsdyke, and E. Foster (eds.), *The Oxford Handbook of Thucydides* (Oxford: Oxford University Press), 115–24.

Robinson, O. (1977) 'Fire-Prevention at Rome', *Revue internationale des droits de l'antiquité* 24, 377–88.

Roche, P. (2016) 'Latin Prose Literature: Author and Authority in the Prefaces of Pliny and Quintilian', in A. Zissos (ed.), *A Companion to the Flavian Age of Imperial Rome* (Chichester: Wiley-Blackwell), 434–49.

Bibliography

Röhrich, L. (1949/50) 'Eine antike Grenzsage und ihre neuzeitlichen Parallelen', *WJA* 4, 339–69, reprinted in L. Röhrich, *Sage und Märchen: Erzählforschung heute* (Freiburg: Herder, 1976), 210–34.

Rölleke, H. (1977) 'Arnim, Achim von', *Enzykopädie des Märchens* 1, 815–20.

Roller, M. (2009) 'The Exemplary Past in Roman Historiography and Culture', in A. Feldherr (ed.), *The Cambridge Companion to the Roman Historians* (Cambridge: Cambridge University Press), 214–30.

Rollinger, R., Truschnegg, B., and Bichler, R. (eds.), (2011) *Herodot und das Perserreich* (Wiesbaden: Harrassowitz).

Rood, T. (1998) *Thucydides: Narrative and Explanation* (Oxford: Clarendon Press).

  (2006a) 'Herodotus and Foreign Lands', in C. Dewald and J. Marincola (eds.), *The Cambridge Companion to Herodotus* (Cambridge: Cambridge University Press), 290–305.

  (2006b) 'Objectivity and Authority: Thucydides' Historical Method', in A. Tsakmakis and A. Rengakos (eds.), *The Brill Companion to Thucydides* (Leiden: Brill), 225–49.

  (2010) 'Herodotus' Proem: Space, Time, and the Origins of International Relations', *Ariadne* 16, 43–74.

  (2012a) 'Herodotus', in I. J. F. de Jong (ed.), *Space in Ancient Literature: Studies in Ancient Greek Narrative* (Leiden: Brill), 121–40.

  (2012b) 'Polybius, Thucydides, and the First Punic War', in C. J. Smith and L. M. Yarrow (eds.), *Imperialism, Cultural Politics, and Polybius* (Oxford: Oxford University Press), 50–67.

  (2013) 'The Cylon Conspiracy: Thucydides and the Uses of the Past', in A. Tsakmakis and M. Tamiolaki (eds.), *Thucydides between History and Literature* (Berlin: De Gruyter), 119–38.

  (2018) 'Geographical and Historical Patterning in Diodorus Siculus', in A. Meeus (ed.), *Narrative in Hellenistic Historiography* (*Histos* Supplement 8; Newcastle-upon-Tyne), 23–68.

  (2019) 'Thucydides and Myth', in J. Baines, H. van der Blom, Y. S. Chen, and T. Rood (eds.), *Historical Consciousness and the Use of the Past in the Ancient World* (Sheffield: Equinox Publishing), 331–44.

Rosen, R. (2012) 'Satire in the Republic: From Lucilius to Horace', in S. Braund and J. Osgood (eds.), *A Companion to Persius and Juvenal* (Chichester: Wiley-Blackwell), 19–40.

Rosenstein, N. (2009) 'General and Imperialist', in M. Griffin (ed.), *A Companion to Julius Caesar* (Oxford: Wiley-Blackwell), 85–99.

Rosillo López, C. (2010) *La corruption à la fin de la République romaine (IIe-Ier s. av. J.-C.): Aspects politiques et financiers* (Stuttgart: Steiner).

Roskam, G. (2021) *Plutarch of Chaeronea* (Cambridge: Cambridge University Press.

Rösler, W. (1991) 'Die "Selbsthistorisierung" des Autors: Zur Stellung Herodots zwischen Mündlichkeit und Schriftlichkeit', *Philologus* 135, 215–20.

Bibliography

(2002) 'The *Histories* and Writing', in E. J. Bakker, I. J. F. de Jong, and H. van Wees (eds.), *Brill's Companion to Herodotus* (Leiden: Brill), 79–94.

Rossi, A. (2002) 'The Fall of Troy: Between Tradition and Genre', in D. S. Levene and D. P. Nelis (eds.), *Clio and the Poets: Augustan Poetry and the Traditions of Ancient Historiography* (Leiden: Brill), 231–51.

Rothe, S. (1989) *Kommentar zu ausgewählten Sophistenviten des Philostratos: Die Lehrstuhlinhaber in Athen und Rom* (Heidelberg: Groos).

Roveri, A. (1964) *Studi su Polibio* (Bologna: Zanichelli).

Rowe, G. O. (1967) 'Dramatic Structures in Caesar's *Bellum Civile*', *TAPA* 98, 399–414.

Rubincam, C. (2003) 'Numbers in Greek Poetry and Historiography: Quantifying Fehling', *CQ* 53, 448–63.

(2008) 'Herodotus and His Descendants: Numbers in Ancient and Modern Narratives of Xerxes' Campaign', *HSCP* 104, 93–138.

Ruffell, I. and Hau, L. I. (2017) 'Introduction', in I. Ruffell and L. I. Hau (eds.), *Truth and History in the Ancient World: Pluralising the Past* (New York : Routledge), 1–12.

Rüpke, J. (1992) 'Wer las Caesars *bella* als *Commentarii?*', *Gymnasium* 99, 201–26.

Russell, D. A. (ed.) (1964) *Longinus: On the Sublime* (Oxford: Clarendon Press).

(1993) 'Self-Disclosure in Plutarch and Horace', in G. Most, H. Petersmann, and A. Ritter (eds.), *Philanthropia kai eusebeia: Festschrift für Albrecht Dihle zum 70. Geburtstag* (Göttingen: Vandenhoeck & Ruprecht), 426–37.

Russell, D. A. and Winterbottom, M. (eds.) (1972) *Ancient Literary Criticism: The Principal Texts in New Translations* (Oxford: Oxford University Press).

Rusten, J. S. (ed.) (2009) *Thucydides: Oxford Readings in Classical Studies* (Oxford: Oxford University Press).

Rutherford, I. C. (2001) *Pindar's Paeans: A Reading of the Fragments with a Survey of the Genre* (Oxford: Oxford University Press).

Rutherford, R. B. (2012) *Greek Tragic Style: Form, Language and Interpretation* (Cambridge: Cambridge University Press).

(2013) *Homer*, 2nd ed., *Greece & Rome* New Surveys in the Classics 41; original edition 1996 (Cambridge: Cambridge University Press).

(2018) 'Herodotean Ironies', *Histos* 12, 1–48.

Ryan, M.-L. (2001) *Narrative as Virtual Reality: Immersion and Interactivity in Literature and Electronic Media* (Baltimore, MD: Johns Hopkins University Press).

Sablayrolles, R. (1996) *Libertinus miles: Les cohortes de vigiles*, CEFR 224 (Paris: De Boccard).

Saïd, S. (2002) 'Herodotus and Tragedy', in *Brill's Companion to Herodotus* (Leiden: Brill), 117–47.

Saller, R. (1980) 'Anecdotes as Historical Evidence for the Principate', *G&R* 27, 69–83.

436 Bibliography

Salmon, J. (2003) 'Cleisthenes (of Athens) and Corinth', in P. Derow and R. C. T. Parker (eds.), *Herodotus and His World: Essays from a Conference in Memory of George Forrest* (Oxford: Oxford University Press), 219–34.

Sanders, E. (2014) *Envy and Jealousy in Classical Athens. A Socio-Psychological Approach* (Oxford: Oxford University Press).

Sanford, A. J. and Emmott, C. (2012) *Mind, Brain and Narrative* (Cambridge: Cambridge University Press).

Saxonhouse, A. W. (2017) '*Kinēsis*, Navies, and the Power Trap in Thucydides', in R. Balot, S. Forsdyke, and E. Foster (eds.), *The Oxford Handbook of Thucydides* (Oxford: Oxford University Press), 339–53.

Sayce, A. H. (1883) *The Ancient Empires of the East: Herodotus I–III* (London: Macmillan).

Scaliger, J. J. (1583) *Opus nouum de emendatione temporum* (Paris).

(1598) *Opus nouum de emendatione temporum*, 2nd ed. (Leiden).

(1606a) *Animadversiones in Chronologica Eusebii*, in J. J. Scaliger, *Thesaurus temporum* (Leiden).

(1606b) *Isagogici chronologiae canones*, in J. J. Scaliger, *Thesaurus temporum* (Leiden).

(1607) *Elenchus utriusque orationis chronologicae D. Davidis Parei* (Leiden).

Scanlon, T. (1980) *The Influence of Thucydides on Sallust* (Heidelberg: Winter).

(2015) *Greek Historiography* (Chichester: Wiley-Blackwell).

Schadee, H. (2008) 'Caesar's Construction of Northern Europe: Inquiry, Contact, and Corruption in *De Bello Gallico*', *CQ* 58, 158–80.

(2017) 'Caesar as Ethnographer', in K. Raaflaub (ed.), *The Landmark Julius Caesar* (New York: Pantheon), app. FF: web essay at www.landmarkcaesar .com.

(2018) 'Writing War with Caesar: The *Commentarii*'s Afterlife in Military Memoirs', in L. Grillo and C. B. Krebs (eds.), *The Cambridge Companion to the Writings of Julius Caesar* (Cambridge: Cambridge University Press), 318–32.

Schauer, M. (2016) *Der Gallische Krieg: Geschichte und Täuschung in Caesars Meisterwerk* (Munich: Beck).

Scheller, P. (1911) 'De Hellenistica Historiae Conscribendae Arte' (dissertation, University of Leipzig).

Schepens, G. (1980) *L'autopsie' dans la méthode des historiens grecs du Ve siècle avant J.-C.* (Brussels: Paleis der Academiën [*Verhandelingen van de Koninklijke Academie voor Wetenschappen, Letteren en Schone Kunsten van België, Klasse der Letteren* Jaargang 42 No. 93]).

Schick, C. (1955) 'Studi sui primordi della prosa greca', *Archivio glottologico italiano* 40, 89–135.

Schieffer, R. (1972) 'Die Rede des Critognatus (*BG* VII 77) und Caesars Urteil über den Gallischen Krieg', *Gymnasium* 79, 477–94.

Schironi, F. (2018) *The Best of the grammarians: Aristarchus of Samothrace on the Iliad* (Ann Arbor: University of Michigan Press).

Bibliography

Schmitt, R. (2015) 'Herodotus as Practitioner of Iranian Anthroponomastics?', *Glotta* 91, 250–63.

Schmitz, T. A. (2009) 'Narrator and Audience in Philostratus' *Lives of the Sophists*', in E. L. Bowie and J. Elsner (eds.), *Philostratus* (Cambridge: Cambridge University Press), 49–68.

(2010) 'The Mytilene Debate in Thucydides', in D. Pausch (ed.), *Stimmen in der Geschichte. Funktionen von Reden in der antiken Historiographie*, Beiträge zur Altertumskunde 284 (Berlin: De Gruyter), 45–65.

Scholz, P. (2013) '*Philomathia* statt *philosophia*: Polybios, die Philosophie und die Idee der *paideia*', in V. Grieb and C. Koehn (eds.), *Polybios und seine Historien* (Stuttgart: Steiner), 285–300.

Scholz, P., Walter, U., and Winkle, C. (2013) *Fragmente römischer Memoiren* (Heidelberg: Verlag Antike).

Schwartz, E. (1897) 'Die Berichte über die Catilinarische Verschwörung', *Hermes* 32, 554–608.

(1929) *Das Geschichtswerk des Thukydides*, 2nd ed. (Bonn: Cohen).

Schweighäuser, J. (1822) *Lexicon Polybianum, ab Is. et Merico Casaubonis olim adumbratum; inde ab Jo. Aug. Ernesti elaboratum; nunc ab Joanne Schweighæusero passim emendatum plurimisque partibus auctum* (Oxford: W. Baxter).

Sciarrino, E. (2007) 'Roman Oratory before Cicero: The Elder Cato and Gaius Gracchus', in W. Dominik and J. Hall (eds.), *A Companion to Roman Rhetoric* (Oxford: Blackwell), 54–66.

(2011) *Cato the Censor and the Beginnings of Latin Prose: From Poetic Translation to Elite Transcription* (Columbus: Ohio State University Press).

Scott-Kilvert, I., and Pelling, C. (trans.) (2010) *Plutarch: Rome in Crisis* (London: Penguin Classics).

Scullion, S. (2006) 'Herodotus and Greek Religion', in C. Dewald and J. Marincola (eds.), *The Cambridge Companion to Herodotus* (Cambridge: Cambridge University Press), 192–208.

Seager, R. (2002) *Pompey the Great: A Political Biography*, 2nd ed. (Oxford: Blackwell).

(2003) 'Caesar and Gaul: Some Perspectives on the *Bellum Gallicum*', in F. Cairns and E. Fantham (eds.), *Caesar against Liberty: Perspectives on His Autocracy* (Cambridge: Cairns), 19–34.

Sealey, R. (1957) 'Thucydides, Herodotus, and the Causes of War', *CQ* 7, 1–12.

Seaman, M. G. (1997) 'The Athenian Expedition to Melos in 416 B.C.', *Historia* 46, 385–418.

Sedley, D. (2007) *Creationism and Its Critics in Antiquity* (Berkeley: University of California Press).

Shannon, K. E. (2012) 'Memory, Religion, and History in Nero's Great Fire: Tacitus *Annals* 15.41–47', *CQ* 62, 749–65.

Shannon-Henderson K. E. (2018) 'Women in Thucydides: Absence and Inferiority', in A. Tsakiropoulou-Summers and K. Kitsi-Mytakou (eds.),

Women and the Ideology of Political Exclusion: From Classical Antiquity to the Modern Era (London: Routledge), 89–103.

(2019) *Religion and Memory in Tacitus' Annals* (Oxford: Oxford University Press).

Shapiro, S. (1994) 'Learning through Suffering: Human Wisdom in Herodotus', *CJ* 89, 349–55.

Shaw, B. D. (2015) 'The Myth of the Neronian Persecution', *JRS* 105, 73–100.

Shear, J. (2011) *Polis and Revolution: Responding to Oligarchy in Classical Athens* (Cambridge: Cambridge University Press).

Sherk, R. K. (ed. and trans.) (1969) *Roman Documents from the Greek East* (Baltimore, MD: Johns Hopkins University Press).

Sigelman, A. C. (2016) *Pindar's Poetics of Immortality* (Cambridge: Cambridge University Press).

Simion, E. (1996) *The Return of the Author*, trans. J. W. Newcomb and L. Vianu (Evanston, IL: Northwestern University Press).

Simonton, M. (2017) *Classical Greek Oligarchy: A Political History* (Princeton, NJ: Princeton University Press).

Skinner, J. (2012) *The Invention of Greek Ethnography. Ethnography and History from Homer to Herodotus* (Oxford: Oxford University Press).

Skutsch, O. (1953) 'The Fall of the Capitol', *JRS* 43, 77–8.

(1978) 'The Fall of the Capitol Again', *JRS* 68, 93–4.

Slater, W. (1969) *A Lexicon to Pindar* (Berlin: De Gruyter).

Slings, S. (2002) 'Oral Strategies in the Language of Herodotus', in E. J. Bakker, I. J. F. de Jong, and H. van Wees (eds.), *Brill's Companion to Herodotus* (Leiden: Brill), 53–77.

Smith, C. (2009) 'Sulla's Memoirs', in C. Smith and A. Powell (eds.), *The Lost Memoirs of Augustus and the Development of Roman Autobiography* (Swansea: Classical Press of Wales), 65–85.

Smith, C. and Powell, A. (eds.) (2009) *The Lost Memoirs of Augustus and the Development of Roman Autobiography* (Swansea: Classical Press of Wales).

Smith, P.-B. (2014) 'Paul, Plutarch and the Problematic Practice of Self-Praise', *New Testament Studies* 60.3, 341–59.

Smyth, H. W. (1956) *Greek Grammar*, revised by Gorgon M. Messing (Cambridge, MA: Harvard University Press).

Snyder, H. A. (2015) *Jesus and Pocahontas: Gospel, Mission, and National Myth* (Eugene, OR: Cascade Books).

Sorabji, R. (1980) *Necessity, Cause and Blame: Perspectives on Aristotle's Theory* (London: Duckworth).

Soria, M. C. G. (1982) *Filóstrato el Ateniense, Vidas de los sofistas, introducción, traducción y notas de María Concepción Giner Soria*, Biblioteca clásica Gredos 55 (Madrid: Editorial Gredos).

Sourvinou-Inwood, C. (2003) *Tragedy and Athenian Religion* (Lanham, MD: Lexington Books).

Spelman, H. (2018) *Pindar and the Poetics of Permanence* (Oxford: Oxford University Press).

Stadter, P. A. (1965) *Plutarch's Historical Methods: An Analysis of the* Mulierum Virtutes (Cambridge, MA: Harvard University Press).

(1989) *A Commentary on Plutarch's* Pericles (Chapel Hill: North Carolina University Press).

Stahl, H.-P. (1975) 'Learning through Suffering? Croesus' Conversations in the History of Herodotus', *YClS* 24, 1–36.

(2003 [1966]) *Thucydides: Man's Place in History* (Swansea: Classical Press of Wales).

(2012) 'Herodotus and Thucydides on Blind Decisions Preceding Military Action', in E. Foster and D. Lateiner (eds.), *Thucydides and Herodotus* (Oxford: Oxford University Press), 125–53.

(2015) 'Herodotus and Thucydides on Not Learning from Mistakes', in C. Clark, E. Foster, and J. Hallet (eds.), *Kinesis: The Ancient Depiction of Gesture, Motion, and Emotion. Essays for Donald Lateiner* (Ann Arbor: University of Michigan Press), 74–85.

Ste. Croix, G. E. M. de (1972) *The Origins of the Peloponnesian War* (London: Duckworth; Ithaca, NY: Cornell University Press).

(1975 [1992]) 'Aristotle on History and Poetry (Poetics 9, 1451a36–b11)', in *The Ancient Historian and His Materials: Essays in Honour of C. E. Stevens* (Farnborough: Gregg International), 45–58, reprinted in A. O. Rorty (ed.), *Essays on Aristotle's* Poetics (Princeton, NJ: Princeton University Press), 23–32.

Stefec, R. S. (2016) *Flavii Philostrati Vitas sophistarum: Ad quas accedunt Polemonis Laodicensis Declamationes quae exstant duae* (Oxford: Clarendon Press).

Steiner, D. (2016) 'Harmonic Divergence: Pindar's Fr. 140b and Early Fifth-Century Choral Polemics', *JHS* 136, 132–51.

Stephanus, H. (1566) (ed.) *Herodoti Halicarnassei Historia* (Geneva).

Strasburger, H. (2013 [1955]) 'Herodotus and Periclean Athens', in R. V. Munson (ed.), *Herodotus: Oxford Readings in Classical Studies*, vol. 1 (Oxford: Oxford University Press), 295–320.

Strauch, G. (1699) *Breviarium chronologicum*, trans. G. Sault (London).

Strauss, R. and Krauss, C. (1942 [first performed]) *Capriccio: A Conversation Piece for Music* (Munich).

Strelan, R. (2013) *Luke the Priest: The Authority of the Author of the Third Gospel* (Aldershot: Ashgate).

Stronk, J. P. (2010) *Ctesias' Persian History, Part I: Introduction, Text, and Translation* (Düsseldorf: Wellem).

Stroup, S. C. (2010) *Catullus, Cicero, and a Society of Patrons: The Generation of the Text* (Cambridge: Cambridge University Press).

Suerbaum, W. (2002) *Die Archaische Literatur: Von den Anfängen bis Sullas Tod. Handbuch der Lateinischen Literatur der Antike 1* (Munich: Beck).

Sulimani, I. (2011) *Diodorus' Mythistory and the Pagan Mission: Historiography and Culture-Heroes in the First Pentad of the* Bibliotheke (Leiden: Brill).

Susini, G. (1984) 'Le lapis de Polla', *MAWBL* 46, 101–10.

440   *Bibliography*

Swain, S. (1991) 'The Reliability of Philostratus' *Lives of the Sophists*', *ClAnt* 10, 148–63.

(1996) *Hellenism and Empire: Language, Classicism, and Power in the Greek World, AD 50–250* (Oxford: Clarendon Press).

Syme, R. (1939) *The Roman Revolution* (Oxford: Clarendon Press).

(1964) *Sallust* (Berkeley: University of California Press).

Sze, C. P. (1977) 'Εἰκασία and πίστις in Plato's Cave Allegory', *CQ* 27, 127–38.

Tanner, R. G. (1970) 'Διάνοια and Plato's Cave', *CQ* 20, 81–91.

Tatum, J. (2011) 'The Late Republic: Autobiography and Memoirs in the Age of Civil Wars', in G. Marasco (ed.), *Political Autobiographies and Memoirs in Antiquity: A Brill Companion* (Leiden: Brill), 161–87.

Taylor, C. (2011) 'Graffiti and the Epigraphic Habit: Creating Communities and Writing Alternate Histories in Classical Attica', in J. A. Baird and C. Taylor (eds.), *Ancient Graffiti in Context* (London: Routledge), 90–109.

Thein, A. (2009) '*Felicitas* and the Memoirs of Sulla and Augustus', in C. Smith and A. Powell (eds.), *The Lost Memoirs of Augustus and the Development of Roman Autobiography* (Swansea: Classical Press of Wales), 87–109.

Thomas, D. (2009) 'Chronological Problems in the Continuation (1.1.1–2.3.10) of Xenophon's *Hellenika*', in J. Marincola, R. B. Strassler, and D. Thomas (eds.), *The Landmark Xenophon's* Hellenika*: A New Translation* (New York: Pantheon), 331–9.

Thomas, R. (1989) *Oral Tradition and Written Record in Classical Athens* (Cambridge: Cambridge University Press).

(1997) 'Ethnography, Proof and Argument in Herodotus' *Histories*,' *PCPhS* 43, 128–48.

(2000) *Herodotus in Context: Ethnography, Science and the Art of Persuasion* (Cambridge: Cambridge University Press).

(2001) 'Herodotus' *Histories* and the Floating Gap', in N. Luraghi (ed.), *The Historian's Craft in the Age of Herodotus* (Oxford: Oxford University Press), 198–210.

(2011) 'Herodotus' Persian Ethnography', in R. Rollinger, B. Truschnegg, and R. Bichler (eds.), *Herodot und das Persische Weltreich = Herodotus and the Persian Empire, Akten des 3. Internationalen Kolloquiums zum Thema Vorderasien im Spannungsfeld klassischer und altorientalischer Überlieferungen, Innsbruck, 24.–28. November 2008*, Classica et Orientalia 3 (Wiesbaden: Harrassowitz), 237–54.

(2012) 'Herodotus and Eastern Myths and *logoi*: Deioces the Mede and Pythius the Lydian', in E. Baragwanath and M. P. de Bakker (eds.), *Myth, Truth and Narrative in Herodotus* (Oxford: Oxford University Press), 233–53.

(2019) *Polis Histories, Collective Memories and the Greek World* (Cambridge: Cambridge University Press).

Thompson, S. (1946) *The Folktale* (New York: Holt, Rinehart and Winston).

(1955–58) *Motif-Index of Folk-Literature: A Classification of Narrative Elements in Folk-Tales, Ballads, Myths, Fables, Mediaeval Romances, Exempla, Fabliaux,*

Jest-Books, and Local Legends, revised and enlarged ed., 6 vols. (Copenhagen: Rosenkilde and Bagger).

Thornton, J. (2013) 'Polybius in Context: The Political Dimension of the *Histories*', in B. J. Gibson and T. Harrison (eds.), *Polybius and His World: Essays in Memory of F. W. Walbank* (Oxford: Oxford University Press), 213–29.

(2018) 'Un'intertestualità complessa: Paralleli tucididei (e non solo) alla giustificazione dell'intervento romano in Sicilia (Pol. 1.10.5-9)', in O. Devillers and B. Battistin Sebastiani (eds.), *Sources et modèles des historiens anciens* (Bordeaux: Ausonius), 99–109.

Throsby, C. (2016) 'Byron Burning', *Times Literary Supplement*, June 10.

Tinniswood, A. (2003) *By Permission of Heaven: The Story of the Great Fire of London* (London: Jonathan Cape).

Titchener, F. (1996) 'The Structure of Plutarch's *Nicias*', in J. Fernandez Delgado and F. Pordomingo Pardo (eds.), *Estudios sobre Plutarco. Aspectos formales. Actas del IV simposio español sobre Plutarco. Salamanca, 26 a 28 de mayo de 1994* (Salamanca: Universidad de Salamanca, Ediciones Clásicas), 351–7.

(2002) 'Plutarch and Roman(ized) Athens', in E. N. Ostenfeld, K. Blomqvist, and L. Nevett (eds.), *Greek Romans and Roman Greeks: Studies in Cultural Interaction*, Aarhus Studies in Mediterranean Antiquity 3 (Aarhus : Aarhus University Press), 136–41.

(2008) 'Is Plutarch's Nicias Devout, Superstitious, or Both?', in A. G. Nikolaidis (ed.), *The Unity of Plutarch's Work: 'Moralia' Themes in the 'Lives', Features of the 'Lives' in the 'Moralia'* (Berlin: De Gruyter), 277–84.

(2010) 'The Role of Reality in Plutarch's *Quaestiones Convivales*', in J. R. Ferreira, D. F. Leão, M. Tröster, and P. Barata Dias (eds.), *Symposion and Philanthropia in Plutarch*, Humanitas Supplementum 6 (Coimbra: Centro de Estudos Clássicos e Humanísticos), 395–401.

(2011) 'Plutarch's *Table talk*: Sampling a Rich Blend. A Survey of Scholarly Appraisal', in F. Klotz and K. Oikonomopoulou (eds.), *The Philosopher's Banquet: Plutarch's* Table Talk *in The Intellectual Culture of the Roman Empire* (Oxford: Oxford University Press), 35–48.

(2013) 'Plutarch the Architect: The Structure of Plutarch's *Nicias*', in G. Santamaría Heríquez (ed.), *Plutarco y Las Artes, XI Simposio Internacional de la Sociedad Española de Plutarquistas, 8–10 November 2012, Gran Canaria* (Madrid: Ediciones Clásicas), 249–54.

(2014) 'Fate and Fortune', in M. Beck (ed.), *A Companion to Plutarch* (Chichester: Wiley-Blackwell), 479–87.

Toher, M. (2017) *Nicolaus of Damascus: The Life of Augustus and the Autobiography* (Cambridge: Cambridge University Press).

Tolkien, J. R. R. (1964) *Tree and Leaf* (London: Allen and Unwin).

Tomlin, R. S. O. (2016) *Roman London's First Voices: Writing Tablets from the Bloomberg Excavations, 2010–2014*, MOLA Monograph 72 (London: Museum of London Archaeology).

442 *Bibliography*

Too, Y. L. (1998) *The Idea of Ancient Literary Criticism* (Oxford: Clarendon Press).

Török, L. (2014) *Herodotus in Nubia* (Leiden: Brill).

Trapp, M. (2004) 'Statesmanship in a Minor Key?', in L. de Blois, J. Bons, T. Kessels, and D. M. Schenkeveld (eds.), *The Statesman in Plutarch's Works: Proceedings of the Sixth International Conference of the International Plutarch Society, Nijmegen/Castle Hernen, May 1–5, 2002*, vol. 1: *Plutarch's Statesman and His Aftermath: Political, Philosophical, and Literary Aspects*. Mnemosyne Supplement 250/1 (Leiden: Brill), 189–200.

Treu, M. (1954) 'Athen und Melos und der Melierdialog des Thukydides', *Historia* 3, 253–73.

Trilling, L. (1972) *Sincerity and Authenticity* (London: Oxford University Press).

Trüdinger, K. (1918) *Studien zur Geschichte der griechisch-römischen Ethnographie* (Basel: E. Birkhäuser).

Tsakmakis, A. (1995) *Thukydides über die Vergangenheit*, Classica Monacensia 35 (Tübingen: Narr).

Tsakmakis, A. and Tamiolaki, M. (eds.) (2013) *Thucydides between History and Literature* (Berlin: De Gruyter).

Tucker, A. (2004) *Our Knowledge of the Past: A Philosophy of Historiography* (Cambridge: Cambridge University Press).

Tuplin, C. J. (1993) *The Failings of Empire: A Reading of Xenophon Hellenica 2.3.11–7.5.27*, Historia Einzelschriften 76 (Stuttgart: Steiner).

(2009) 'Revisiting Dareios' Scythian Expedition', in J. Nieling and E. Rehm (eds.), *The Achaemenid Impact in the Black Sea: Communication of Powers* (Aarhus: Aarhus University Press), 281–312.

(2013) 'Xenophon's *Cyropaedia*: Fictive History, Political Analysis and Thinking with Iranian Kings', in L. Mitchell and C. Melville (eds.), *Every Inch a King: Comparative Studies on Kings and Kingship in the Ancient and Medieval Worlds* (Leiden: Brill), 67–90.

Turner, J. W. (1979) 'The Kinds of Historical Fiction: An Essay in Definition and Methodology', *Genre* 12, 333–55.

Ullman, B. L. (1942) 'History and Tragedy', *TAPA* 73, 25–53.

Uther, H.-J. (2011) *The Types of International Folktales: A Classification and Bibliography*, Folklore Fellows Communications 284–6 (Helsinki: Suomalainen Tiedeakatemia).

(2013) *Handbuch zu den 'Kinder- und Hausmärchen' der Brüder Grimm*, 2nd ed. (Berlin: De Gruyter).

van den Berg, R. (2003) 'The Plight of the Poor Urban Tenant', *Revue Internationale des Droits de l'Antiquité* 50, 443–77.

van den Hout, M. P. J. (1988) *M. Cornelii Frontonis Epistulae* (Leipzig: Teubner).

(1999) *A Commentary on the Letters of M. Cornelius Fronto* (Leiden: Brill).

van der Blom, H. (2016) *Oratory and Political Career in the Late Roman Republic* (Cambridge: Cambridge University Press).

van Wees, H. (2017) 'Thucydides on Early Greek history', in R. Balot, S. Forsdyke, and E. Foster (eds.), *The Oxford Handbook of Thucydides* (Oxford: Oxford University Press), 39–62.

Bibliography

Vannicelli, P. (2001) 'Herodotus' Egypt and the Foundations of Universal History', in N. Luraghi (ed.), *The Historian's Craft in the Age of Herodotus* (Oxford: Oxford University Press), 211–40.

Vargish, T. (1985) *The Providential Aesthetic in Victorian Fiction* (Charlottesville: University Press of Virginia).

Vasaly, A. (2015) *Livy's Political Philosophy* (Cambridge: Cambridge University Press).

Vasunia, P. (2001) *The Gift of the Nile: Hellenizing Egypt from Aeschylus to Alexander* (Berkeley: University of California Press).

Veegens, D. J. (1839) *Disputatio literaria de Polycrate Samio* (Amsterdam: L. van Der Vinne).

Veith, G. (1967) 'Caesar als "Vater der Strategie"', in D. Rasmussen (ed.), *Caesar* (Darmstadt: Wissenschaftliche Buchgesellschaft), 372–8.

Vidal-Naquet, P. (1986) *The Black Hunter: Forms of Thought and Forms of Society in the Greek World*, trans. A. Szegedy-Maszak (Baltimore, MD: Johns Hopkins University Press).

Voigt, V. (2000) 'Propp. Vladimir Jakovlevič', *Enzyklopädie des Märchens* 10, 1435–42.

von Albrecht, M. (1997) *A History of Roman Literature: From Livius Andronicus to Boethius, with Special Regard to Its Influence on World Literature*, vol. 1, *Mnemosyne* Supplement 165 (Leiden: Brill).

von Fritz, K. (1957) 'Aristotle's Contribution to the Practice and Theory of Historiography', *University of California Publications in Philosophy* 28.3, 113–38.

von Scala, R. (1890) *Die Studien des Polybios I* (Stuttgart: Kohlhammer).

Waddell, P. (2013) 'Eloquent Collisions: The *Annales* of Tacitus, the Column of Trajan, and the Cinematic Quick-Cut', *Arethusa* 46, 471–97.

Walbank, F. W. (1957) *A Historical Commentary on Polybius*, vol. 1 (Oxford: Oxford University Press).

  (1960) 'History and Tragedy', *Historia* 9, 216–34.

  (1962 [1985]) 'Polemic in Polybius', *JRS* 52, 1–12, reprinted in F. W. Walbank (ed.), *Selected Papers: Studies in Greek and Roman History and Historiography* (Cambridge: Cambridge University Press), 262–79.

  (1965 [1985]) *Speeches in Greek Historians*, J. L. Myres Memorial Lectures, III (Oxford: Blackwell), reprinted in F. W. Walbank (ed.), *Selected Papers: Studies in Greek and Roman History and Historiography* (Cambridge: Cambridge University Press), 242–61.

  (1975) '*Symploke*: Its Role in Polybius' *Histories*', *YClS* 24, 197–212.

Walker, A. D. (1993) '*Enargeia* and the Spectator in Greek Historiography', *TAPA* 123, 353–77.

Wallace-Hadrill, A. (1983) *Suetonius: The Scholar and His Caesars* (London: Duckworth).

Wallinga, H. T. (2005) *Xerxes' Greek Adventure: The Naval Perspective* (Leiden: Brill).

444 *Bibliography*

Wallraff, M. (2012) 'Iulius Africanus and the Background of the Cesti', in M. Wallraff, C. Scardino, L. Mecella, and C. Guignard (eds.), *Iulius Africanus. Cesti. The Extant Fragments*, trans. W. Adler (Berlin: De Gruyter), xi–xvii.

Wallraff, M., Scardino, C., Mecella, L., and Guignard, C. (2012) *Iulius Africanus. Cesti. The Extant Fragments*, trans. W. Adler (Berlin: De Gruyter).

Walsh, J. J. (2019) *The Great Fire of Rome: Life and Death in the Ancient City* (Baltimore, MD: Johns Hopkins University Press).

Walter, U. (2003) '*Natam me consule Romam*: Historisch-politische Autobiographien in republikanischer Zeit: Ein Überblick', *AU* 46.2, 36–43.

(2004) *Memoria und res publica: Zur Geschichtskultur im republikanischen Rom* (Frankfurt am Main: Verlag Antike).

Wardle, D. (2014) *Suetonius: Life of Augustus* (Oxford: Oxford University Press).

Waters, M. (2014) *Ancient Persia: A Concise History of the Achaemenid Empire, 550–330 BCE* (Cambridge: Cambridge University Press).

(2017) *Ctesias' Persica and Its Near Eastern Context* (Madison: University of Wisconsin Press).

Weinstock, S. (1971) *Divus Julius* (Oxford: Clarendon Press).

Weissenborn, W. and Müller, H. J. (1908) *T. Livi Ab Vrbe Condita Libri*, 9th ed., vol. 1, Part 1 (Berlin: Weidmannsche Buchhandlung).

Welch, K. and Powell, A. (eds.) (1998) *Julius Caesar as Artful Reporter: The War Commentaries as Political Instruments* (London: Duckworth; Swansea: Classical Press of Wales).

Wellesley, K. (1972) *Cornelius Tacitus:* The Histories *Book III* (Sydney: Sydney University Press).

Wesseling, P. (1763) (ed.) *Herodoti Halicarnassei Historiarum libri IX, Musarum Nominibus Inscripti = Hērodotu Halikarnēssēos Historiōn Logoi* (Amsterdam: Schouten).

Wesselmann, K. (2011) *Mythische Erzählstrukturen in Herodots* Historien (Berlin: De Gruyter).

West, M. L. (2011) *The Making of the Iliad: Disquisition and Analytical Commentary* (Oxford: Oxford University Press).

West, S. (1985) 'Herodotus' Epigraphical Interests', *CQ* 35, 278–305.

(1991) 'Herodotus' Portrait of Hecataeus', *JHS* 111, 144–60.

(1992) 'Sesostris' Stelae (Herodotus 2.102–106)', *Historia* 41, 117–20.

(1999) 'Sophocles' *Antigone* and Herodotus' Book Three', in J. Griffin (ed.), *Sophocles Revisited: Essays Presented to Sir Hugh Lloyd-Jones* (Oxford: Oxford University Press), 109–36.

(2002) 'Scythia', in E. J. Bakker, I. J. F. de Jong, and H. van Wees (eds.), *Brill's Companion to Herodotus* (Leiden: Brill), 437–56.

(2004) 'Herodotus on Aristeas', in C. J. Tuplin (ed.), *Pontus and the Outside World: Studies in Black Sea History, Historiography, and Archaeology* (Leiden: Brill), 43–68.

(2011) 'Herodotus' Sources of Information on Persian Matters', in R. Rollinger, B. Truschnegg, and R. Bichler (eds.), *Herodot und das Persische Weltreich = Herodotus and the Persian Empire, Akten des 3. Internationalen*

Bibliography

Kolloquiums zum Thema Vorderasien im Spannungsfeld klassischer und altorientalischer Überlieferungen, *Innsbruck, 24.–28. November 2008*, Classica et Orientalia 3 (Wiesbaden: Harrassowitz), 256–72.

Wharton, D. (2009) 'On the Distribution of Adnominal Prepositional Phrases in Latin Prose', *CP* 104, 184–207.

White, H. (1912) *Appian's Roman History*, Loeb Classical Library 2–5 (Cambridge, MA: Harvard University Press).

 (1973) *Metahistory: The Historical Imagination in Nineteenth-Century Europe* (Baltimore, MD: Johns Hopkins University Press).

 (1978) *Tropics of Discourse: Essays in Cultural Criticism* (Baltimore, MD: Johns Hopkins University Press).

 (1980) 'The Value of Narrativity in the Representation of Reality', *Critical Inquiry* 7.1 (*On Narrative*), 5–27.

 (1987) *The Content of the Form: Narrative Discourse and Historical Representation* (Baltimore, MD: John Hopkins University Press).

Whitehead, D. (1979) 'Tacitus and the Loaded Alternative', *Latomus* 38, 474–95.

Whitmarsh, T. J. G. (2004) 'Philostratus', in I. J. F. de Jong, R. Nünlist, and A. M. Bowie (eds.), *Studies in Ancient Greek Narrative*, vol. 1: *Narrators, Narratees, and Narratives in Ancient Greek Literature*, Mnemosyne Supplement 257 (Leiden: Brill), 423–39.

Whitton, C. (2011) '*Dubitatio comparatiua*: A Misunderstood Idiom in Pliny (*Natural History* 7.150) and Tacitus (*Histories* 4.6) and Others', *CQ* 61, 267–77.

Wiater, N. (2016) 'Shifting Endings, Ambiguity and Deferred Closure in Polybius' *Histories*', in A. Lianeri (ed.), *Knowing Future Time in and through Greek Historiography* (Berlin: De Gruyter), 243–65.

 (2017) 'Expertise, "Character" and the "Authority Effect" in the "Early Roman History" of Dionysius of Halicarnassus', in J. König (ed.), *Authority and Expertise in Ancient Scientific Culture* (Cambridge: Cambridge University Press), 231–59.

Will, É. (1964) 'Deux livres sur les guerres médiques et leur temps', *Revue de Philologie, de Littérature et d'Histoire Anciennes* 38, 70–88.

Williams, B. (2002) *Truth and Truthfulness: An Essay in Genealogy* (Princeton, NJ: Princeton University Press).

Wills, J. (1996) *Repetition in Latin Poetry: Figures of Allusion* (Oxford: Clarendon Press).

Wilson, A. (2013) 'Hayden White's *Theory of the Historical Work*: A Re-examination', *Journal of the Philosophy of History* 7, 32–56.

 (2014) 'The Reflexive Test of Hayden White's *Metahistory*', *History and Theory* 53, 1–23.

Winnington-Ingram, R. P. (1965) 'Cleon and Diodotus', *BICS* 12, 70–82.

Winton, R. I. (1999) 'Thucydides, I.22.1', *Athenaeum* 87, 527–33.

Wiseman, A. and Wiseman, T. P. (trans.) (1980) *Julius Caesar: The Battle for Gaul* (Boston: David R. Godine).

Bibliography

Wiseman, T. P. (1993 [2011]) 'Lying Historians: Seven Types of Mendacity', in C. Gill and T. P. Wiseman (eds.), *Lies and Fiction in the Ancient World* (Austin: University of Texas Press; Exeter: University of Exeter Press), 122–46, reprinted in J. Marincola (ed.), *Greek and Roman Historiography* (Oxford: Oxford University Press), 314–36.

(1998) 'The Publication of *De Bello Gallico*', in K. Welch and A. Powell (eds.), *Julius Caesar as Artful Reporter: The War Commentaries as Political Instruments* (London: Duckworth; Swansea: Classical Press of Wales), 1–9.

(2002) 'History, Poetry, and *Annales*', in D. S. Levene and D. P. Nelis (eds.), *Clio and the Poets: Augustan Poetry and the Traditions of Ancient Historiography* (Leiden: Brill), 331–62.

(2015) *The Roman Audience: Classical Literature as Social History* (Oxford: Oxford University Press).

Wolpert, A. (2002) *Remembering Defeat: Civil War and Civic Memory in Ancient Athens* (Baltimore, MD: Johns Hopkins University Press).

Woodcock, E. C. (1959) *A New Latin Syntax* (London: Methuen).

Woodhead, A. G. (1960) 'Thucydides' Portrait of Cleon', *Mnemosyne* 13, 289–317.

Woodman, A. J. (1988) *Rhetoric in Classical Historiography: Four Studies* (London: CroomHelm).

(1998) *Tacitus Reviewed* (Oxford: Oxford University Press).

(2004) *Tacitus: The Annals* (Indianapolis, IN: Hackett).

(2006) 'Mutiny and Madness: Tacitus *Annals* 1.16–49', *Arethusa* 39, 303–29.

(2012) *From Poetry to History: Selected Papers* (Oxford: Oxford University Press).

(2017) *The Annals of Tacitus: Books 5 and 6* (Cambridge: Cambridge University Press).

(2018) *The Annals of Tacitus: Book 4* (Cambridge: Cambridge University Press).

Woodman, A. J. and Kraus, C. S. (2014) *Tacitus: Agricola* (Cambridge: Cambridge University Press).

Woodmansee, M. and Jaszi, P. (eds.) (1994) *The Construction of Authorship: Textual Appropriation in Law and Literature* (Durham, NC: Duke University Press).

Wright, W. C. (1921) *Philostratus and Eunapius: The Lives of the Sophists*, Loeb Classical Library 134 (Cambridge, MA: Harvard University Press).

Xenophontos, S. (2012) 'Plutarch's Compositional Technique in the *An Seni Respublica Gerenda Sit*: Clusters vs. Patterns', *AJPh* 133, 61–91.

Zali, V. (2015) *The Shape of Herodotean Rhetoric: A Study of the Speeches in Herodotus' Histories with Special Attention to Books 5–9* (Leiden: Brill).

Zambrini, A. (2006) 'Aspetti dell'etnografia in Jacoby', in C. Ampolo (ed.), *Aspetti dell'opera di Felix Jacoby* (Pisa: Edizioni della Normale), 189–200.

Bibliography

Ziolkowski, A. (1993) '*Vrbs direpta*, or How the Romans Sacked Cities', in J. Rich and G. Shipley (eds.), *War and Society in the Roman World* (London: Routledge), 69–91.

Ziolkowski, T. J. (2009) *Heidelberger Romantik: Mythos und Symbol* (Heidelberg: Winter).

Zuccarini, M. (2018) 'What's Love Got to Do with It? *Eros*, Democracy and Pericles' Rhetoric', *GRBS* 58, 473–89.

Zucchelli, B. (1985) 'Echi della Poetica di Aristotele in Polibio. A proposito di storiografia e tragedia', in V. E. Alfieri *et alii* (eds.), *Sapienza antica: Studi in onore di Domenico Pesce* (Milan: Franco Angeli Libri), 297–309.

Index Locorum

Literary sources

Ael.
NA
16.23, 51
Tact.
praef., 310
Aesch.
Ag.
219, 244
PV
135, 338
Aesop.
Prov.
2, 327
Alcm.
30 *PMGF*, 190
Andriscus
FGrHist
500 F 3, 323
Antioch. Hist.
FGrHist
555 F 13, 60
Ap. Rhod.
Argon
4.43, 338
App.
B Civ.
praef. 1.13/50, 343
praef. 15, 309
1.70–71, 349
1.120, 347
1.158–59, 347
2.91, 224
2.111/462–63, 339
2.112/469, 342
2.113/472, 342
2.116/488, 339
2.116/489, 339
2.117/493, 340
2.118/494–3.42/174, 343

2.118/496, 336
3.14/50–21/77, 344
3.23/87–89, 344
3.25/94, 343
3.28/105–08, 343–4
3.29/111–14, 344
3.29/112–30/115, 345
3.30/115–121, 344
3.30/117–119, 343, 345
3.31/120, 345, 349
3.31.120–23, 344
3.32/124–39/156, 345
3.32/124–56, 345
3.33/129, 341
3.40/164, 345
3.40/164–66, 336
3.41/167–42/174, 345
3.41/167–69, 345
3.42/170–74, 345, 350
4.12/45–51/223, 351
4.13/52, 337
4.44/185, 337
4.48/204–05, 337
4.49/210–14, 337
4.268, 347
Ill.
30.87, 384
Apul.
Apol.
9.6, 231
Ar.
Ach.
515–39, 36
1116, 109
Ec.
258, 331
Pl.
1003, 47
Arat.
1.1134 Martin, 331

Index Locorum

449

Arist.
  [*Ath. Pol.*]
    34–41, 38
    39, 38
    89b, 331
  De an.
    405a, 323
    429a, 323
    430a, 323
  Div. somn.
    463b, 319
  Eth. Nic.
    1094b.11–14, 380
    1173a, 323
  Gen. corr.
    335b, 319
  Hist. an.
    555^{b}18, 109
    555^{b}32, 109
    556^{a}8, 109
    638a, 323
  [*Mag. mor.*]
    2.7.3, 323
  Metaph.
    989b, 323
    1025a4, 25, 149
    1086b, 320
  Ph.
    195b31–198a13,
      149
    196b5–6, 149
    198b29, 149
    256b, 323
  Poet.
    1451a36–b11, 375
    1451b, 319
    1459a24–9, 152
  Pol.
    1274a, 331
    1285b4, 21, 73
    1309a, 323
  [*Pr.*]
    907a, 323
    929a, 323
    936b, 316
    957a, 319
  [*Rh. Al.*]
    31.3, 316
    36.16, 316
  Somn. vig.
    453b, 319
  Soph. el.
    184b, 323
  Spir.
    438b, 323
  Top.
    119a, 323
  fr.
    119 Rose, 323
    437 Rose, 323
    549 Rose, 55
Aristid.
  Or.
    36.41–63, 216
Aristox.
  Rhyth.
    (lib. 2) 22 Pighi, 332
Arr.
  Anab.
    1.12.5, 309
    5.6.5, 214
Artem.
    4.43, 75
Ath.
    1.15d, 194
    1.21e–22b, 184
    12.520c–d, 51
[Aur. Vict.]
  De vir. ill.
    47.7, 237

Caes.
  BAfr.
    86.2, 340
    88.6, 340
    92.4, 340
  BCiv.
    1.1.1, 275
    1.1–7, 287
    1.5.2, 288
    1.7–8, 281
    1.9.1–11.3, 281
    1.11.4–27, 289
    1.17, 287
    1.19–20, 287
    1.38, 287
    1.48–59, 284
    1.61, 287
    1.63–84, 288
    1.67, 287
    1.82–3, 287
    1.86–7, 287
    2.3.4, 277
    2.31–2, 282
    3.3–5, 287
    3.6.1, 288
    3.18, 287
    3.26.4–27.2, 288
    3.82.4, 278
    3.85.4, 282

Index Locorum

Caes. (cont.)
3.87, 278
3.96.1–2, 278
BGall.
1.1.1, 278
1.6.4, 288
1.7.8, 288
1.13–14, 287
1.15.5, 288
1.16–19, 288
1.26.2, 286
1.30–32, 281
1.31.9, 281
1.33.5, 286
1.34–6, 287
1.34–53, 286
1.35.4, 273
1.36.6, 286
1.42–5, 287
1.44.12, 275
1.46.4, 286
1.47.6, 286
1.47–51, 288
2.2.5, 288
2.19–27, 283
2.20.1, 284
2.27.3–5, 286
2.31.1, 278
2.35.1, 281
2.35.4, 274, 281
2.52.2, 278
3.1–6, 281
3.10.3–7, 277
3.14, 277
3.17–19, 285
4.7.2–5, 286
4.7–15, 286
4.9.3, 286
4.11.4, 286
4.13–53, 286
4.23–6, 283
4.38.5, 274
5.3–4, 288
5.7.3, 288
5.22.4–23.2, 275
5.26–37, 285
5.36.6–7, 285
5.38–52, 285
5.39–52, 283
5.41.7–8, 283
5.44, 284
5.46.4, 283
5.47.5, 285
5.52.4, 285
5.55–6, 288

6.11–28, 287
6.30.2, 288
6.32–42, 285
6.42, 288
7.1–5, 287
7.4, 288
7.8.4, 287
7.9.6, 287
7.14–28, 277
7.14–5, 287
7.20–1, 287
7.29–31, 287
7.37–9, 287
7.63–4, 287
7.66, 287
7.75–8, 287
7.77, 282
7.79–83, 288
7.80, 277
7.83, 287
7.84–8, 283
7.89.1–5, 287
7.90.8, 274
8 praef. 4, 276
8 praef. 5, 274,
   290
8 praef. 6, 272
8 praef. 7, 276
8.23.3–6, 281
8.24.3, 281
Cass. Dio
38.35, 275
43.15.1, 339
43.35.4, 339
44.1–3, 339
44.11, 339
44.12.3, 342
44.12–14.1, 339
44.18.4, 339
44.19.2, 341
45.3–9, 343
45.6.1–3, 345
45.11–13.1, 343
45.12.3–6, 346, 350
49.43.1, 365
53.19, 384
62.16.1, 369–70
62.16.2, 362
62.16.3, 367
62.16.6, 367
62.17.2, 364
62.18.1, 370
63.14.3, 359
64.17, 362
66.24, 355

Index Locorum

72[73].18.3–4, 384
72[73].21, 384
Cato
  FRHist
    5 F 87–93, 238
    5 F 88, 238
    5 F 93, 239
Cat.
  64.114, 365
Charon Hist.
  FGrHist
    262 T 1, 44–5, 60
    262 T 3a, 45
    262 T 3b, 45
    262 T 7, 45, 52, 56
    262 T 7a, 55, 60
    262 T 7b, 55
    262 T 9, 59
    262 T 10, 59
    262 T 12, 60
    262 T 17, 45, 52, 60
Chrysipp. Stoic.
  F 42 von Arnim, 323
  F 172 von Arnim, 323
  F 1103 von Arnim, 323
Cic.
  Arch.
    5, 231
  Att.
    1.19.10, 291
    1.20.6, 225
    2.1.1, 275, 278
    2.1.1–2, 225, 274, 291
    4.18.5, 275
    5.20, 275
    11.9.1, 85
    14.14.4, 343
    14.4.4, 348
    16.15.3, 346, 348
  Brut.
    42, 284
    132, 226, 231
    211, 229
    252–61, 272
    261, 272
    262, 272, 274, 290
  Cat.
    3.18–22, 154
  De or.
    2.53, 89
  Div.
    1.90, 281
    2.21, 154

Fam.
  15.1–2, 274
  15.4.2–10, 274
  5.12, 291
  5.12.8, 279
  12.25.3, 335
Fin.
  5.52, 276
Font.
  41, 88
Inv.
  1.23, 83
Leg.
  1.2.5–3.8, 277
Marc.
  29, 276
Nat. D.
  1.79, 231
Or.
  2.62–4, 290
Phil.
  1.3, 343
  2.35, 370
  2.88, 337
  2.91, 343
Pis.
  49–50, 273
Prov.
  8.19, 283
  11.27, 275
  12.30–14.34, 283
Rep.
  2.4, 87
S. Rosc.
  84, 370
Sen.
  42, 239
Tusc.
  5.7, 85
Ver.
  1.36–7, 227
  2.3.123, 230
  2.3.128, 230
  4.82, 88
  4.88, 88
Cl. Quadrigarius
  FRHist
    24 F 1–2, 356
    24 F 84, 355
Clearchus
  F 63 Wehrli, 331
Constantinus Porphyrogenitus
  De Virtutibus et Vitiis
    ii.103, 332

452   *Index Locorum*

Critodemus
  5.2.113, 323
  8.3.102, 323
Ctes.
  FGrHist
    688 T3, 25
    688 F 1b.(22.5), 25

Dem.
  24.80, 323
  60.9, 74
Demetr.
  Eloc.
    121, 293
Dicaearch. Hist.
  F 89 Wehrli,
    323
Diod. Sic.
  1.2.2, 73
  1.95.2, 171
  2.22.5, 25
  2.32.4, 25
  2.47.1, 73
  3.66.5, 73
  4.1.3, 73
  4.8.1, 73
  4.44.5, 73
  11.1.4, 152
  11.35, 154
  12.41.1, 34
  12.65.1–2, 31
  12.80.5, 32
  14.3–6, 38
  14.32–3, 38
  15.18.204, 53
  15.50.6, 73
  15.79.5, 73
  17.13.1, 367
  17.14.1, 360
  17.70.2, 367
  19.7.1, 367
  19.7.4, 367
  20.71.2, 367
  30.24, 238
  31.5, 238
  33.10.1, 73
Dion. Hal.
  Ant. Rom.
    1.2.2, 73
    1.39.1, 73
  Dem.
    14, 330
    24, 330
    44, 330
  Isoc.
    7.2, 330

    13, 330
Pomp.
    3.7, 45
Thuc.
    5, 45, 59, 61
    27, 330
    37–41, 24

Emp.
  DK
    31 B 59, 149
    31 B 59.2, 149
    31 B 61, 149
    31 B 85, 149
    31 B 98, 149
Ephipp.
  F 1 Meineke, 331
Ephorus
  FGrHist
    70 T 8,
      65
    70 F 186, 152
    70 F 31b, 316
Epicurus
  F 20.2 Arrighetti, 323
Erasistr.
  F 152 Garofalo, 323
  F 279 Garofalo, 323
Eratosth.
  [*Cat.*]
    1.22, 323
  FGrHist
    241 F 1c, 64
Eunap.
  VS
    ii.7, 248
Eur.
  Bacch.
    1136–8, 79
  IA
    449–50, 244
Euseb.
  Chron.
    2135, 249

Fabius Pictor
  FRHist
    F 4C/5P, 90
Fest.
  Gloss. Lat.
    p. 134, 85
Flor.
  2.13.94, 339
Front.
  Ep.
    2.118 Hout, 230

Index Locorum

453

Frontin.
Aq.
  1.18.2, 356

Gal.
Meth. Med.
  9.9, 293
Gell.
NA
  1.7.6, 236
  6.3, 238
  11.10.1, 236
  13.4.1, 88
  17.21.4, 153
  19.9, 231

Hecat.
FGrHist
  1 F 1, 302
  1 F 1a, 328
  1 F 169, 210
  1 F 301, 214
Hdt.
  1.1, 75, 124, 150, 381
  1.1–3, 158
  1.1–4, 381
  1.1–5, 62, 80
  1.1–1.5.2, 136
  1.1.2–4, 159
  1.2.1, 159
  1.4.1–4, 159–60
  1.5, 76
  1.5.2, 159
  1.5.3, 63, 135, 295
  1.5.4, 77
  1.7, 79
  1.10–12, 128
  1.11.4, 129
  1.19–20, 50
  1.27, 133
  1.29–33, 147
  1.30–3, 133
  1.32.9, 329
  1.37, 129
  1.38, 218
  1.46.1, 381
  1.52, 79
  1.53–56, 125
  1.56.2–3, 79
  1.57–8, 79
  1.59, 147
  1.59.6, 377
  1.60, 115
  1.60–1, 130
  1.60.4, 130

1.62.4, 146
1.67–8, 80
1.68, 150
1.68.3, 80
1.71.1–3, 161
1.71.4, 161
1.74, 161
1.76, 161
1.80, 50
1.82.1, 147
1.90–1, 125
1.91, 126
1.92.4, 129
1.93, 143
1.95.1, 76, 132, 308
1.118, 125
1.119, 125
1.122.3, 76
1.125, 163
1.125–6, 133
1.128–30, 162
1.128.7, 162
1.129, 131
1.130, 162
1.130.1, 162
1.131–4, 162
1.131.1, 102, 131, 164, 295
1.133.2, 160, 301
1.134.2, 165
1.135, 143, 165
1.136.2, 163
1.138.1, 128, 163
1.139, 147, 212
1.140.2, 295
1.141, 162
1.143.2, 80
1.152, 163
1.153.2, 163
1.153.3, 164
1.154, 164
1.155.4–156.1, 129
1.157–61, 59
1.163.2–4, 55
1.170, 147
1.170. 2–3, 75
1.170–1, 75
1.171.2, 78
1.171.2–6, 80
1.172, 79
1.173, 80
1.182, 144
1.190, 144
1.193.4, 295
1.196.1–3, 157
1.196.5, 157

Index Locorum

Hdt. (cont.)

1.199.1, 158
1.199.4, 213
1.200, 160
1.207, 162
1.207.6, 161
1.211–14, 162
2.1, 75, 143
2.2.5, 302
2.3–4, 112
2.3.2, 294
2.4.1, 124
2.5, 213
2.5.1, 104, 214
2.5.2, 213
2.11, 77
2.12.1, 214
2.13–14, 77
2.16.2, 218
2.19.3, 75
2.20.1, 302
2.23.1, 74
2.29, 216, 218
2.29.1, 75, 215, 218
2.31, 217
2.34.1, 75
2.37, 113
2.42–5, 79
2.45, 77
2.45.1, 74
2.47.2, 296
2.49, 144
2.49.2–3, 144
2.51, 144
2.51–2, 79
2.52.1, 79
2.53, 164
2.53.1–2, 102
2.56–7, 79
2.63, 80
2.73, 119
2.75, 109
2.75.1, 108
2.76.3, 109
2.77, 160
2.81, 144
2.91, 80, 145
2.91.1, 165
2.91.2–6, 165
2.91.3, 115
2.97.2, 210
2.98.2, 79
2.99, 110
2.99–142, 112
2.99.1, 75

2.100, 114
2.100–1, 110
2.101.1, 110, 116
2.102, 116
2.102–5, 145
2.102–42, 110
2.102.5, 116
2.104, 79, 144
2.106, 116
2.106.1, 116
2.109, 144
2.113–15, 159
2.113.1, 75
2.116.1, 75, 379
2.116–20, 79
2.120, 76–7, 159
2.120.1–2, 379
2.122–3, 115
2.123, 102, 144, 218
2.123.1, 123
2.123.3, 295
2.124–9, 115
2.124.5, 117
2.127.3, 117
2.134.1, 117
2.138.2, 301
2.142.1, 110, 116
2.143, 111–14
2.143.1–4, 111
2.143.4, 111
2.144, 80
2.145–6, 79
2.148, 218
2.149–50, 117
2.149.2, 117–18
2.152.4, 146
2.156.4–6, 80
2.158.5, 165
2.160, 173
2.160.1–4, 171
2.171, 144
2.171.1, 295
2.171.2, 80
2.171.3, 80
2.172, 135–6
2.182.1, 115
2.183, 119
3.3, 296
3.4, 145
3.4.1, 146
3.5.3, 80
3.9.2, 123
3.11, 106
3.12, 105, 214
3.12.1, 215

Index Locorum

3.12.3, 215
3.14, 131
3.14–6, 135
3.16, 135
3.21, 131
3.23–4, 132
3.27–9, 167
3.28–9, 140
3.30.2, 140
3.31–2, 131
3.33, 141
3.34.5, 131
3.36, 131
3.38, 176
3.38.1–2, 168
3.38.3, 168
3.39–43, 136
3.42.1, 146
3.47, 150
3.64, 140, 145
3.64.1, 141
3.64.3, 141, 167
3.72, 128
3.80, 23, 103
3.85–7, 128
3.91.1, 80
3.108.1, 149
3.108–9, 149
3.111.1, 80
3.115.2, 327
3.119, 131
3.122, 65, 71, 76
3.122.2, 62, 69, 379
3.127–8, 128
3.129, 146
3.130, 131
3.133–7, 131
3.138.4, 146
3.139, 146
3.139.2, 146
3.143.2, 130
3.154–8, 128
4.1, 143
4.1.3, 65
4.5.1, 115
4.5–12, 80
4.16.1, 218
4.16.2, 218
4.16–31.2, 218–19
4.18.1, 219
4.18.3, 219
4.19.1, 219
4.20.2, 219
4.21, 219
4.22, 219

4.23.2, 219
4.25.1, 210, 219
4.28.1, 219
4.28.2, 301
4.30.1, 308
4.32–5, 80
4.36.2, 302
4.42–43, 30
4.45, 80
4.76, 143
4.76–7, 166
4.76.2, 166
4.76.5, 166
4.76.6, 166
4.78, 166
4.78.3, 166
4.79.1, 166
4.79.1–2, 166
4.79.3, 166
4.80, 167
4.80.1–4, 167
4.80.5, 167
4.81, 117
4.82, 80
4.85.1, 80
4.93.1, 144
4.94–6, 144
4.126–32, 127
4.127.4, 80
4.134–6, 127
4.136–40, 127
4.141–3, 127
4.142, 127
4.145–9, 80
4.146–8, 145
4.150.1, 80
4.172, 109, 143
4.173, 123
4.179, 80
4.180, 144
4.189, 144
4.192.3, 75
4.195.2, 123
5.7, 80
5.9, 148
5.23–5, 128
5.32, 162
5.35, 147
5.36, 127
5.36.1, 147
5.43, 80
5.49, 220
5.51.1, 221
5.51.3, 221
5.52, 222

Index Locorum

Hdt. (cont.)
5.52.2, 221
5.52.2–3, 221
5.54.1, 222
5.54.2, 222
5.55.1, 376
5.57, 79
5.58, 79
5.58.3, 25
5.59–61, 80
5.62.2, 377
5.65.3–4, 80
5.66.2, 81
5.67.1, 142
5.67.3–4, 80
5.76, 79
5.80.1, 80
5.82.3, 81
5.86, 115
5.89, 81
5.91.1, 381
5.94.2, 80
5.97.3, 59
5.99–101, 168
5.100, 59
5.101.2, 164
6.21.1, 48
6.34–5, 46
6.35, 123
6.35.1, 80
6.37, 47
6.43, 23
6.47.1, 80
6.53–5, 80
6.54, 145
6.54.6, 377
6.57.5, 376
6.59, 378
6.61–4, 141
6.61–6, 146
6.61–70, 127
6.65–6, 123
6.66–71, 128
6.67.1, 142
6.69.1, 142
6.75.1, 141
6.75.3, 142
6.76, 142
6.80, 141–2
6.103–4, 123
6.105, 115
6.109–10, 132
6.111–17, 169
6.112.3, 301
6.121–4, 130, 378

6.123.2, 377
6.125, 378
6.125–131, 130
6.126–31, 378
6.129.4, 132
6.136, 123
6.137.1, 80, 123
6.137–8, 80
6.138.4, 80
7.3, 127, 146
7.6, 146
7.6.1, 169
7.8β, 169
7.8β.3, 169
7.8γ, 80
7.8γ1–3, 27
7.8γ, 169
7.9, 126, 174
7.9a–c, 278
7.9α, 169
7.10, 126
7.10β.1–2, 170
7.10η.1, 170
7.11, 80
7.11.2–3, 28
7.20, 160
7.20.2, 80
7.43.2, 81
7.49, 126
7.59.2, 80
7.61.3, 80
7.61–2, 145
7.62.1, 80
7.90, 80
7.91, 80
7.92, 80, 145
7.94, 80, 145
7.95.1, 80
7.101–5, 126
7.103.1–2, 173
7.134.1, 80
7.135, 126
7.137.2, 147
7.139.1, 294
7.150.2, 80
7.152, 102
7.152.3, 123
7.161, 80
7.166, 152
7.168, 150
7.170.2, 150
7.170–1, 80
7.184–187, 30
7.187, 125, 129
7.189.1–2, 80

Index Locorum

7.189.1–3, 123
7.190, 150
7.193.2, 80
7.197, 81
7.198.2, 81
7.204, 80
7.206, 174
7.208.1, 80
7.208.1–3, 158
7.209–10, 126
7.210–12, 170
7.211.3, 301
7.219–25, 170
7.221, 81
8.8.1, 379
8.15.1, 147, 152
8.26, 172
8.26.3, 158
8.35.2, 301
8.43, 80
8.44.2, 80
8.55, 81
8.57, 174
8.64.2, 81
8.68β, 173
8.69.2, 174
8.72, 174
8.79, 123
8.83–96, 170
8.91, 301
8.103, 126, 130
8.105–6, 151
8.106, 132
8.106.1, 151
8.106.4, 151
8.109.3, 138
8.111, 132
8.112.2–3, 175
8.117, 170
8.118–9, 133
8.119.1, 133
8.121.1, 81
8.125, 132
8.131.2, 80
8.132.2, 147
8.134.2, 80
8.141.2, 147
8.142.2, 125
9.16.4–5, 137
9.25.1, 130
9.27–8, 81
9.34, 80
9.41.2–3a, 174
9.41.4, 174
9.43, 79

9.51.2, 81
9.51.4, 81
9.53.2, 376
9.58–70, 170
9.63, 174
9.63–4, 125
9.73, 81
9.80.1, 278
9.82, 127, 131,
        160–1
9.82–3, 161
9.83, 150
9.84, 125
9.91.1, 154
9.91–2, 154
9.97–104, 170
9.100, 102
9.100–1, 152
9.101.1, 147
9.108–113, 126
9.113.2, 126
9.116.1–2, 81
9.120, 81
9.121, 170
9.122, 133
Heraclid. Pont.
    F 91 Wehrli, 323
Heraclit.
    DK
        12 A 16, 318
        12 B 129, 318
        12 B 40, 318
        12 B 89, 318
Hes.
    Op.
        345, 338
        427–8, 212
Hom.
    Il.
        9.593, 356
        16.644–55, 155
        21.12, 109
    Od.
        4.824, 214
Hor.
    Carm.
        2.1.1–9, 342
    Sat.
        2.1.30–34, 232
Hp.
    Aer.
        8.44, 214
        13.8, 214
        16.27, 214
        20.2, 214

458 Index Locorum

Hp. (cont.)
  20–2, 232
  24.29, 214
  24.32, 214
  24.47, 214
VM
  18, 214
  22, 214

Isoc.
  17.16, 323
Iust.
  43.3.4–11, 55

Jer.
  Chron.
    86a.16-7, 67
Joseph.
  BJ
    4.649, 362
Julius Africanus
  Cesti
    F 12, 11, 51
Juv.
  3.197–222, 356

Keil, *Gramm. Lat.*
  4.171.2–3, 86
  4.174.20–1, 86
  4.177.42–178.1, 86

Lampr. cat.
  124, 389
Liv.
  praef. 5, 95
  praef. 6, 94–5
  praef. 6–8, 82, 95
  praef. 7, 95
  praef. 8, 95
  praef. 9, 95
  praef. 9–10, 95
  praef. 9–10, 285
  1.1.1, 87
  1.1.1–6.2, 87
  1.1.1–7.3, 87
  1.1.8, 86
  1.4.1–2, 90, 95–6
  1.4.2, 91
  1.6.3, 87
  1.6.4, 87
  1.7.3, 85, 87, 90
  1.13, 88
  1.18.6, 86
  1.27, 88
  1.44.2, 91

1.59.9, 365
5.21.8–9, 96
5.39–55, 356
5.49, 362
5.53.9, 356
5.54.1, 362
5.55.4, 365
6.29.9, 88
7.28.9, 88
8.36.7, 86
9.36.2, 88
10.41.5, 88
21.1.1, 363
24.47.15, 356
26.27.1–3, 356
26.48.2, 86
30.26.5, 356
31.1.1–5, 385
38.39.1–2, 229
45.5.3, 238
45.20.4–25.4, 238
per.
  121, 342
[Longin.]
  Subl.
    26, 207
Lucil.
  fr. 656–7K = 671–2M, 232
Lucr.
  1.727, 93
  2.595, 93
  5.156–65, 93
  5.161, 93
  5.1306, 93
LXX
  *Ex.*10 4, 109
Lys.
  12, 38
  13, 38

Macr.
  Sat.
    2.4.11, 338
Mart.
  Spect.
    5.7, 355, 358
Menecl.
  FGrHist
    466 T 1, 75
Mosch.
  Ep. Bion.
    1.21, 338
Nep.
  Vit.
    proem, 389

Index Locorum

459

Nic. Dam.
FGrHist
90 T 13, 338
90 F 2, 341
90 F 61, 341
90 F 66.16–9, 341
90 F 130.20, 338
90 F 130.62–3, 340
90 F 130.59, 339
90 F 130.60, 340
90 F 130.61, 340
90 F 130.64, 340
90 F 130.67, 339
90 F 130.83–7, 338
90 F 130.95, 337
90 F 130.131, 343
90 F 132(2), 342
90 F 138, 342

Ov.
Met.
8.159–61, 365

Paus.
1.29.2, 202
3.25.2, 197
Philist.
FGrHist
556 F 53, 323
Philostr.
VS
1. praef. 479, 295
1. praef. 479–80, 309
1. praef. 480, 295
1. praef. 482, 301
1.2.562, 300
1.7.487, 307
1.13.497, 301
1.17.506, 304
1.19.511, 294
1.21.514, 294
1.21.514–5, 305
1.21.515, 294, 303
1.21.516, 303
1.21.520, 294, 303, 307
1.22.521–2, 300
1.22.523, 303
1.22.524, 304
1.24.528, 304
1.25.514, 296
1.25.533, 310
1.25.536, 303
1.25.537, 295, 303
1.25.538, 294, 296
1.25.540, 294
1.25.542–3, 305

1.25.543, 303
2.1.549, 202, 294, 296
2.1.550, 300, 302
2.1.552, 299
2.1.553, 302
2.1.559, 303
2.1.562–3, 296
2.1.564, 305
2.1.565, 293
2.1.605, 294
2.3.567, 299, 303
2.4.570, 307
2.5.570, 304
2.5.572, 308
2.5.574, 303
2.5.574–5, 303
2.5.575, 303
2.5.576, 301, 308
2.6, 295
2.6.576–7, 307
2.8.579, 299
2.8.580, 307
2.9, 298
2.9.582, 298
2.9.583, 298
2.9.584, 303, 308
2.9.585, 296, 301, 308
2.10, 298
2.10.585, 299
2.10.587, 299
2.15.595, 300
2.21.604, 297
2.21.609, 294
2.22.605, 308
2.23.605, 298
2.23.606, 298
2.24.607, 306
2.25.608, 293
2.25.612, 301
2.26.613, 303
2.26.615, 304
2.27.617, 297
2.30.623, 297
2.32.626, 297
2.33.628, 298
Phrynichus
Ecloge
praef., 310
Phylarch.
FGrHist
81 F 56, 323
Pind.
Isthm.
1.1–10, 187
2.47, 186

Index Locorum

Pind. (cont.)
Nem.
5.22, 200
9.7, 181
Ol.
3.2–10, 182
6.148a, 185
6.87–91, 185
13.18–19, 196
14.17, 196
14.18, 196
Pae.
2.96–103, 200
4.21–4, 189
6.15–18, 200
9.35–43, 191
12.1–8, 190
12.5–7, 196
Pyth.
1.1–4, 183
1.71–80, 152
4.299, 181
8.86, 192
9.1–3, 205
fr.
70b, 198, 200
75, 200
99, 197
107ab, 194,
196
140b, 192
141, 188
148, 197
156, 197
169.36, 338
schol.
Isthm.
1.6d, 187
Ol.
3.9b, 182
6.148a, 185
6.149a, 185
Pl.
Cra.
439c, 319
Euthd.
282c, 331
Grg.
467b, 301
Leg.
476c, 319
653e–654b, 200
731e, 322
800a, 319
803a, 323

915d, 323
Mx.
245d, 323
Phd.
81b–c, 316
81e, 316
83d, 316
86a, 316
273b, 316
Phdr.
247a, 181
Pol.
265e, 323
Prt.
320d–21b,
149
Resp.
438a, 331
476c, 319
476c *bis*, 319
514a–17a, 319
532d, 316
533b, 319
Tht.
158b, 319
158b *bis*, 319
184a, 331
Ti.
31b, 316
36d, 316
Plin.
HN
praef. 6, 276
7.92, 286
7.100, 237
7.153–64, 358
8.157, 51
17.5, 362
35.7, 88
36.107–8, 365
Plin.
Ep.
2.3.8, 97
4.7.2, 276
6.16, 357
6.20, 249, 357
6.20.5, 97
7.9.2, 97
10.33, 355
Plut.
Mor.
Amat.
749b, 249
An seni
792f, 246

Index Locorum

Bellone an pace
816d–e, 255
Cons. Uxor.
608b, 249, 251
De ad. et am.
48e, 249
De cur.
516a, 249
De def. or.
413a, 243
414a, 243
417f, 304
418d, 243
De E
387c, 249
387f, 248
391e, 248
De Herod.
854e–856d, 121
855b-856e, 389
858c, 130
867b, 132
De Is. et Os.
351c-384b, 249
De se laudando
541a, 244
542e–f, 288
542f, 243
De superst.
164e, 243
165b, 243
165c, 243
Prae. ger. reip.
800b, 257
801c, 256
806f, 258
806f–807b, 258
811b, 246
813e–f, 254
814a–c, 390
814c, 391
816b, 258
816d, 245
816d–e, 254
816e, 242
Regum apophthegmata
206e, 224
Quaest. conv.
629f, 249
635a, 249
660d, 249
687c, 249
704f–705a, 194
717c–d, 153
748bc, 195

Vit.
Aem.
1.1, 257
Ages.
19.10, 249
Alex.
1, 391
1.2, 374, 389
Ant.
5.9, 337
6.1–3, 339
13.3, 341
14.1, 336
16, 343
16.5, 345
Arist.
10.1, 247
18.3, 247
Artax.
8.1–2, 374
Brut.
8–10, 339
8.5–6, 341
11.1–3, 340
13, 339
17.6, 340
18.2–4, 341
C. Gracch.
13.2, 229
Caes.
4.3–4, 339
6.3, 339
11.6, 247
12, 272
46.1, 273
50.2, 224
57.2–3, 339
58.2, 339
62, 339
63.1, 339
66.1–3, 339
60.1, 339
66.12, 340
69.1, 339
Cat. Mai.
17.7, 239
29.5, 237
Comp. Nic. et Crass.
5.1, 243
Crass.
11, 245
Dem.
2.2, 249
Dion
24.1, 243

462 *Index Locorum*

Plut. (cont.)
  Fab.
    5.3, 247
  Flam.
    1.1, 249
  Lyc.
    18.2, 249
  Nic.
    1, 374, 389
    1.1, 246
    1.5, 389
    5.3, 244
    7.4–5, 245
    23.1–4, 243
    23.6, 243
  Pel.
    1.1, 389
  Per.
    1.3, 257
    6.2, 243
    7.4, 244
    30, 36
    35.2, 243
    36.5, 148
  Publ.
    8.2, 249
  Sert.
    1, 146
  Them.
    2.5–3.1, 244
    3.4, 247
    32.6, 249
  Thes.
    1, 389
  Tim.
    1.1, 257
Poll.
  Onom.
    praef. 1, 311
Polyaen.
  Strat.
    1.33, 154
    8.37, 55
Polyb.
  1.1.2, 315
  1.14.2, 321, 324
  1.14.5, 322, 325
  1.14.5–6, 321
  1.14.6, 322
  1.2.1, 320
  1.3.3–4, 316
  1.4, 382
  1.4.1–5, 320
  1.4.6, 318
  1.4.7, 318–19, 322

1.4.7–10, 316
1.4.7–11, 316
1.4.8, 319, 325, 327
1.4.11, 316
1.38.4, 325
2.12.2, 304
2.13.7, 329
2.56.2, 331
2.56.7–8, 10, 359
2.56.10, 367
2.58.13, 331
2.61.12, 331
2.62.2, 331
2.63.5, 331
3.4.1–8, 383
3.6.4, 328
4.20.5, 382
3.15.11, 330
3.21.1, 330
3.31.11–12, 321
3.32, 318
3.57–8, 329
3.58, 327
3.58–9, 333
3.59.1, 304
3.59.4, 326–7
4.39.11, 327
4.40, 327
4.40.3, 317
5.31.1, 304
5.33.2, 382
5.108.5, 319
6.11.8, 329
6.45.1, 382
7.7.6–7, 331
7.7.7, 332
9.1–2, 321
9.2.4, 329
9.35.7, 330
10.21.3, 329
10.27.7, 329
12.3.2–6, 324
12.4a.3–6, 382
12.10.9, 329
12.12b.1, 319
12.25b.4, 329
12.25f., 382
12.25i.5, 332
12.25i.7, 332–3
12.25i.9, 333
12.26d.2, 326
12.27.1, 317
12.27.2–6, 327
12.27.7, 382
12.27a.1–4, 326, 333

Index Locorum

12.27a.3–4, 327
12.28.10, 332
12.28.8–12, 382
15.34.1, 332
15.35.1, 332
16.11.5, 329
16.11.8, 330
16.14.1–8, 324
16.14.4, 329
16.17.9, 330
16.17.9–18.3, 324
16.18.2, 330
16.18.2–3, 330
18.15.13, 319
20.11.1, 329
21.44.1–3, 229
22.10.11, 330
22.18.11, 328
22.4.17, 330
23.1, 382
23.8, 382
24.10.7, 330
29.5.2, 329
30.3.4, 330
30.4, 238
30.21.9, 331
30.23.4, 330
33.21.1, 332
34.1.3, 382
36.9, 383
38.4, 322
38.4.1, 322
38.4.1–2, 322
38.4.5–8, 321
38.4.8, 322–3,
    325
Posidon.
  fr. 44E–K, 97
Prisc.
  Inst.
    ii p. 226, 239
Protag.
  DK
    80 B 4, 148
Ps.-Skyl.
  67, 46, 216
Ps.-Skym.
  698–703, 46

Quint.
  Inst.
    1.1.6, 229
    8.3.68, 367–8
    10.1.101–4, 290
    10.1.114, 272, 290

Rhet. Her.
  4.13, 92
  4.39, 367
Sall.
  Cat.
    3.3–4.2, 385
    8, 226
    8.5, 279
    43–2, 226
    54.3, 340
  Hist.
    1.8.M/1.2R,
      94
  Iug.
    4.3, 385
    5.1, 363
    79, 53
Sen.
  Con.
    2.1.11, 357
  De Ira
    2.23.4, 340
    2.34.2, 91
  Dial.
    12.16.6, 236
  Ep.
    91, 355
    91.1, 364
    91.2, 363
[Sen.]
  Oct.
    831, 362, 370
Serv.
  A.
    8.343, 85
Solin.
  40.16, 85
Soph.
  Aj.
    879, 327
Speusipp.
  F 81a Tarán, 323
Strab.
  1.2.6, 330
  7 fr. 51, 46
  10.5.2, 73
Suda
  ι 200, 511, 332
  λ 557, 32
Suet.
  Aug.
    7.2, 95
    10, 343
    10.1, 345

Index Locorum

Suet. (cont.)
  100.1, 154
Cl.
  25.2, 355
  41.2, 342
Dom.
  5, 355
Jul.
  7, 272
  30.4, 273
  30.5, 339
  37.2, 224
  55.1, 272
  56.4, 291
  56.6, 275
  76.1, 339
  80.3, 339
  81.4, 339
Nero
  9, 369
  21.1–2, 359
  22.1, 364
  38, 370
  38.1, 362–3, 365–6, 369
  38.2, 370
Tit.
  8, 355
  8.3, 356
Vesp.
  8.5, 356
Vit.
  8.2, 356
  15.3, 362
Tac.
Agr.
  1.2–3, 385
Ann.
  1.1.2, 386
  1.1.3, 386
  1.9.1, 154
  4.6.1, 87
  4.32, 374
  4.32.1, 356
  4.32–3, 386
  4.64.1, 356
  6.45.1, 356
  11.11.1, 386
  12.58, 356
  13.57.3, 355
  14.3.1, 369
  14.27.2, 369
  15.1.2, 355
  15.37.1, 371
  15.37.1–3, 360
  15.37.4, 360

15.38.1, 360, 362, 364, 369
15.38.3, 357
15.38.4–7, 366
15.38.6, 357
15.38.7, 369
15.38–9, 361
15.39.1–3, 368
15.40.1, 370
15.40.2, 362, 370
15.41.2, 362
15.42.1, 371
15.43.1, 357
15.67.2, 371
16.13.3, 355
Ger.
  2.3–4, 92
Hist.
  1.1, 385
  1.1.1–2, 386
  1.1.4, 387
  1.2, 386
  1.2.2, 357
  1.4.1, 367
  1.51.1, 367
  1.89.2, 372
  3.71, 357, 370
  3.71.4, 362
  4.32.1, 387
  4.32.2, 387
  4.33, 388
  4.34–5, 386
  5.2.1, 94
Theoc.
Id.
  10.19–20, 322
  24.36, 338
Theophr.
Caus. pl.
  6.8.5, 323
  6.17.1, 323
Ign.
  F 50, 323
Phys. op.
  12, 332
Sens.
  67, 323
  73, 323
  76, 323
fr.
  97.4 Wimmer, 323
Theopomp. Hist.
FGrHist
  115 T 20a, 328
Thgn.
  1.53–9, 163

Index Locorum 465

1.66–8, 163
1.82, 212
1.1109–14, 163
Thuc.
1.1.1, 25
1.1.3, 83
1.4, 379
1.9.1, 381
1.9.4, 323
1.10.3, 379
1.20–21, 376
1.20.2, 376
1.20.3, 376
1.21.1, 74, 89, 380
1.22, 23, 262–4, 267, 270, 285, 380
1.22–3, 320
1.22.3, 327
1.22.4, 74, 262, 321, 380
1.22.6, 303
1.23, 37, 381
1.23.3, 380
1.23.4–6, 288
1.23.5, 381
1.23.6, 37, 381
1.40.1, 295
1.68, 269
1.73–8, 265
1.75.2, 265
1.76.3, 265
1.87–88, 34
1.88, 37
1.88.1, 381
1.89, 376
1.90–2, 377
1.97.2, 44, 289
1.112.3, 31
1.118, 37
1.119, 34
1.125, 34
1.126–7, 377
1.128–38, 377
1.139, 34
1.145, 35
2.2.1, 289
2.9.4, 31
2.12, 36
2.40.2–3, 137
2.65.1, 381
2.65.7, 269
2.75–7, 277
2.77.4, 363
2.99.6, 47
3.36, 32

3.49.1, 36
3.53.1, 323
3.82.4, 278
3.91.1–3, 31
3.92.2, 278
3.113.6, 295
4.12.1, 278
4.18, 277
4.20, 277
4.27–29, 31
5.19.1, 289
5.20, 289
5.26.1, 289
5.32.1, 32
5.84.2, 31–2
5.84.3, 32
5.84–116, 31
5.89, 31
5.94, 31
5.98, 31
5.102, 33
5.103, 32
5.104, 33
5.105, 33
5.116, 32
6.17, 278
6.31.4, 381
6.54–9, 376
6.54.1, 376
6.54.2, 376
6.55.1, 295
6.59.2, 377
6.59.4, 376
6.98.2, 278
7.18.2, 35
7.28.3, 26
7.57.1, 381
7.69.2, 290
7.71, 277
7.77.3, 33
7.77.4, 33
Timaeus
566 F 60, 153
566 F 60, 328

Val. Max.
5.6 *ext.*4, 53
Vell. Pat.
2.11.1, 363
2.52.4–6, 340
2.58.2, 341
Verg.
A.
2, 356–7

Index Locorum

Verg. (cont.)
2.34, 362
2.596, 368
2.634–70, 368
5.144–5, 364
6.851–3, 283
7.661, 89
G.
3.103–4, 364
3.206, 85
Vitr.
De arch.
2.7.2, 355
2.9.6, 355
2.9.14, 355
2.9.16, 355

Xen.
An.
5.4.11–15, 287
5.4.27–34, 287
6.4.1–6, 287
Hell.
2.3.11–2.4.43, 38
2.4.38, 38
2.4.43, 39
7.5.26–7, 385
Mem.
4.2.19, 331
Xenocr.
F 225 Parente, 323
Xenoph.
DK
21 B 11–6, 164
21 B 14, 164
21 B 15, 165
21 B 16, 165

Epigraphical sources

Brosius (2000)
no. 35, 140
no. 47, 28

CIL
1.15, 233
1^2.2.4, 226
1^2.6–9, 234
1^2.14, 234
1^2.15, 233
6.1284–7, 234
6.1292, 234
6.1293, 233
6.30387a, 358
6.30387b, 358
6.30387c, 359
6.37039h, 234
6.37039i, 233
6.8.3, 226
CLE
10, 234
958, 233
II
3.1.272, 234
ILLRP
309–10, 234
315, 234
316, 233
454, 234
ILS
1–3, 234
6, 233
9, 234
4914, 358
Osborne – Rhodes, *GHI*
151, 31
153, 32
RDGE
43, 230
48C, 230
49, 230
SCPP
165–72, 229
174–6, 228
SEG
LXIII 66, 265
Tomlin 2016
WT44, 228

General Index

account
  day-by-day, 289
  first-person, 9
  third-person, 9
Achaean War, 322
Achaeans, 359
addressee. *See* second person
Aedui, 273
Aegina, 36
Aelianus Tacticus, 310
Aemilius Scaurus, M., 224–6, 240
aemulatio, 360
Aeolia, 162
Aeschylus, 185
Africa, 30, 271, 316
agency, 1, 237
akoē, 12, 118, 216–20, 307
akribeia, 263
Alcibiades, 378
Alcmaeonids, 130, 378
Alcman, 190, 205
Alesia, battle of, 277, 282, 286, 288
alētheia, 325
Alexander I of Macedon, 47
Alexander of Seleucia, 308
Alexander the Great, 29, 272
Aly, W., 43
Alyattes, 50, 143
Amasis, 136
ambiguity, 7–9, 102, 130, 132, 223
amigēs, 323, 325
Ammianus Marcellinus, 14, 375
Amphipolis, 47
anankē, 148, 294
anticipation, 367
Antiochus of Syracuse, 60
Antipater of Hierapolis, 297
Antium, 369
Antonius Gordianus, 12, 312
Antonius, Marcus, 335–7, 340, 343–9, 351–2
apeiroteros, 327

aphiloponos, 327, 334
Apollonius of Tyana, 304
Appian, 13, 309, 336–9, 343–9, 351–2
Archidamus, 36
Argos/Argives, 30, 142
Arion, 132
Ariovistus, 280–1, 286, 288
Aristagoras, 220–2
Aristides, 294, 296, 298, 301
Aristocles of Pergamum, 299
Aristophanes, 380
Aristotle, 8, 38, 149, 270, 319–20, 375
Aristoxenus, 332
Arrian, 214, 309
Artabanus, 27–8, 169–70, 175
Artabazus, 174–5
Artemisia, 8, 173–4
Artemisium, battle of, 30, 152, 175
Asinius Pollio, 336, 351–2
askepsia, 331, 334
Assyrians, 28
Astyages, 125, 131
Athenaeus, 45, 51, 183, 185, 195–6, 200
Athens/Athenians, 26, 30, 32–7, 169, 183, 201, 249, 255, 264–6, 277, 297, 303, 381
Atossa, 146
Atuatuci, 280
auctoritas, 3, 5, 239, 358, 366, 372
audience, 1–4, 7, 11, 15, 23–4, 27, 77, 126, 159, 162, 165, 169–70, 172, 179, 189–90, 196, 199, 204–5, 209, 212–13, 217, 235, 238, 255, 257, 279, 282, 354
  Greek, 103, 123, 132, 158, 167–8, 174, 176
  internal, 170
audio-spectacle, 180
Augustan era, 337, 349
Augustus, 13, 153, 336, 338, 341–52, 355
Aulus Gellius, 355
Aurelius, Marcus, 296, 298
authenticity, 229

General Index

author, 4–5, 10, 29, 47, 56, 58, 60, 73, 85, 94, 97,
121, 126, 136, 152, 155, 225, 242, 245, 258,
274, 279–82, 284, 290, 292, 308, 311, 319,
326, 330, 336, 338–9, 342, 349–50, 356,
370, 373–5, 378, 380, 385, 387, 389, 391
distinction from narrator, 7, 383
self-fashioning, 5
authority, 7, 11–12, 14–15, 192, 206, 210, 223, 258,
268, 311, 320, 353–5, 372, 385, 388, 391
bilateral, 15
creation of, 1
divine, 181
epic model of, 179
establishment of, 5, 9, 12, 206, 257, 315
historiographical, 371
interactive, 9
intersubjective, 7
of performers, 206
of the author, 266
of the historian, 15, 211
of the narrator, 223, 292
poetic, 9, 179
shared, 9
textual, 12, 211
autobiography, 224–5
autopsy, 7, 9, 101, 104, 106, 118, 214–16
Avaricum, siege of, 277
Avidius Cassius, C., 296
Axona, 280

Babylonia, 143
Bacchylides, 189, 194
barbarians, 158
speaking about Greeks, 158–76
barbarism, 282
basilikai diphtherai, 25
Bedriacum, 249
Behistun inscription, 25
Belgae, 280
Biahmu colossi, 117
biography, 10, 12, 14–15, 245, 257, 293,
389–90
blindness, 322
Bloomberg tablets, 227
Boeotia, 254–5
book, account, 10
Brixellum, 249
Brutus, M. Iunius, 335, 339–40, 350
Bysaltai, tribe of, 45–52
Byzantium, 162

Caecilius Metellus, L., 229
Caesar, C. Iulius, 9, 11–12, 70, 225, 247, 281,
335–45, 348–51, 373, 375
historical ambitions, 271–91

Caesarians, 344
Camarina, 264
Cambyses, 131, 140–1, 145, 148, 151,
167
Camillus, 362
Candaules, 128–9
Capitol, 345, 356, 370
Cappadocia, 161, 221
Caracalla, 297
Cardia, 45–52
Carthage, 153, 322, 356
Cassius Dio, 13, 307, 336, 339, 343, 346–50,
354, 362, 364, 367, 369–70, 383–4, 391
Cassius Longinus, C., 335, 339–40
catastrophe, 13
Cato, M. Porcius, the Elder, 235–40, 282
Catulus, Q. Lutatius, 224–6, 230–2, 235, 237
causality, 8, 11, 123, 141, 150–2, 287, 362, 382
causes, 1, 8, 34, 123, 149, 243, 282, 288, 290,
316, 328–9, 367, 381
Ceos, 186–7
Chaeronea, 248–9
Chambers, R., 2
charis, 187–92, 196
Charon of Lampsacus, 6, 43–60
Chersonesos, Thracian, 45
choices, aesthetic, 6
chronography, 45
chronology, 281
Cicero, M. Tullius, 9, 13, 83, 85, 88–9, 154,
225, 227, 230–1, 235, 237, 244, 272,
274–5, 277–8, 283, 285, 290–1, 335–7,
343–5, 347–8, 350–2
Cilicia, 221, 230
Cimbri, 240
civil war, 271, 278, 337, 340, 370
Claudius (emperor), 342, 355, 387
Claudius Quadrigarius, 355–6
Clazomenians, 46
Cleisthenes of Athens, 142
Cleisthenes of Sicyon, 142
clementia, 340
Cleomenes, 140, 142–3, 220–2
Cleon, 11, 245, 257, 265, 267–9, 380
cognitive approach, 209, 217, 222
cognitive science, 4, 208
coincidence, 7–8
Colonia Agrippinensis, 355
commentarius, 10–11, 15, 271–2, 274–5, 279,
284, 290–1, 373
Commodus, 311, 383–4
composition, authoritative, 179
connections, 8
conspiracy, 338–42, 351, 371
contingency, 11, 287

General Index

Corinth, 356
Cornelius Dolabella, P., 335
Cornelius Nepos, 229, 389
correspondence, 10
Crassus, M. Licinius, 229, 243, 273
Cremutius Cordus, A., 386, 388
Critias, 38
criticism, ancient, 222
Croesus, 129–30, 138, 147, 161–2, 378
Ctesias of Cnidus, 24–5
Cunaxa, battle of, 374
customs, 167, 286–7
    Greek, 8, 48, 144, 164, 166–8
Cylon, 377, 380
Cyrus, 50, 130–1, 133, 161–4, 175, 341
Cyzicus, 166

Darius, 25, 27, 126, 128, 146, 168
dative of reference, 210–11, 213, 216, 218, 222–3
debate, Mytilenean. *See* Thucydides
Decimus Brutus, 338
decree, Megarian, 36–7
dedicatee
    as co-author, 310–11
Delos, 185, 187
Delphi, 183, 242, 246, 248
Demaratus, 8, 128, 146, 172
Demosthenes, 74, 245
dialexis, 294
dialogue, 250
didacticism, 212
dignitas, 13, 311, 342, 350
digression, 11
Diodorus Siculus, 25, 31, 73
Diodotus, 10, 264–5, 267–9
Dionysia, 201
Dionysius of Halicarnassus, 24, 45, 59–60, 72–3
Dionysius of Miletus, 45, 299
diplomacy, 287
disaster, 13, 322, 354, 358, 360, 363–4, 367, 370–1
display, first-person, 10
dithyramb, 198
divine, 8, 90, 96, 148, 243
document, legal, 10, 226
Domitian, 307, 352, 358
Dorians, 211
Dorieus, 143
double-deixis, 208, 218, 222
doxography, 12, 293

East/West hostility, 158–60
Eburones, 284

Ecbatana, 140
Egypt/Egyptians, 70, 72, 74, 77–8, 105–8, 113, 119, 134, 141, 143–4, 146, 160, 165, 167, 170–2, 176, 212–15, 217, 222, 249, 271–2
ēkoun, 298–300
ekplēxis, 331
Elea/Eleans, 170–2
Elephantine, 207, 217
Eleusis, 39
eleutheria, 342
elogium, 233–5, 275
emotion, 267, 371
Empedocles, 148–9
empeirikē, 327
emperor, 228
Ephorus, 31, 382
epigram, 10
epitaphios, 269
Ethiopia, 220
ethnography, 157, 163, 277
    Herodotean, 164
    Persian, 128, 162
ethos
    of history, 324, 326, 328–30, 333
    of the historian, 324, 331
eulogy, 226
Eunapius, 248
exceptionality
    of events, 316
exoticism, 8
experience, virtual, 206, 208
explanation, 8, 120, 145, 148, 152, 275, 367, 369, 371. *See* causality
eyewitness, 7, 12, 214, 216, 218, 222, 311, 318–19, 354

Fabius Maximus, 247
Fabius Pictor, 91, 321–2, 324, 382
facts, 20
Fayûm, 117
Fehling, D., 7, 105, 108
fiction, 7, 11, 15, 20–1, 33, 282, 284
fictional device. *See* techniques, narrative
first person. *See* person
folklore studies, 41–3
folktale, 6
foreign practices. *See* ethnography
Fornara, C.W., 3
Fortuna, 288
forum, 237
Frontinus, 310
Fronto, 230–1

General Index

Gaius (emperor), 387
Galen, 293
Gallic sack, 356–7, 362, 365
gamechanger, 13, 373–5
Gaul/Gauls, 271, 273, 276, 279, 281, 286, 289, 346, 356, 365
Geneva, 288
geographers, 210, 213
geography, 47, 210, 212, 217–19, 277, 287, 289, 324
gesture, deictic, 221
glosses, narrative, 7
Golden House, 371
Gracchus, C., 235–6, 240
Gracchus, Ti., 235
Graces, 9, 181, 188, 196, 204
Greece/Greeks, 8, 30, 43, 47, 70, 129, 131, 134, 137, 144, 164–76, 238, 248–9, 254–5, 278, 303, 310, 316, 328, 345
  as Others, 176
Gaul/Gauls, 283
Gyges, 128–9

Hadrian, 388
Hadrianus of Tyre, 294, 296, 298
Halicarnassus, 173
Halys (river), 161
Hannibal, 247, 363
Harmodius and Aristogeiton, 376
Harpagus, 50, 125, 131
hearsay. *See akoē*
Hecataeus, 60, 63, 65–6, 74, 78, 111, 113, 115–16, 119, 210, 214, 302, 328, 375, 378
Heliodorus, 297
Hellanicus of Lesbos, 45
Hellenotamias, 264
Helvetii, 280, 288
Heraclitus, 317
hermēneuō, 293, 305
Herod the Great, 338, 342, 350–1
Herodes Atticus, 295–6, 299–300, 302, 304, 306, 310
Herodotus, 6–9, 13, 21–2, 26–30, 40, 43, 62–4, 71, 206–23, 262, 278, 286, 295–6, 309, 311, 320, 374–82, 385
  apodeixis, 115–16
  autopsy, 101–20
  coincidences and synchronisms, 140–56
  comparison with Charon of Lampsacus, 58–61
  Constitutional Debate, 23–4, 103
  glosses, 128
  irony, 124–8
  list of kings at Memphis, 110–15
  nature of time and language, 134–8

paradoxical or critical statements, 129–30
paratactic nature of narrative structure, 132–3
Polycrates and Minos, 76–8
skeletons of flying snakes at Bouto, 109
spatium mythicum and *spatium historicum*, 74–9
statues of Archpriests at Thebes, 110–15
style, 59–61
heteroglossia, 136
Himera, battle of, 152
Hipparchus. *See* Peisistratids
Hippias. *See* Peisistratids
Hippocrates, 293, 319
Hirtius, A., 271, 274, 281, 290
historian
  authoritative, 292
  deductive reasoning, 214
  narrative, 14, 353
historiography
  as ethical practice, 325
  canon of, 269
  digression, 12
  Greek, 9, 43, 59, 65–6, 277, 281, 283, 287, 326
  innovation, 12, 14
  of historiography, 328
  Republican, 386–7
  rhetorical school of, 15
  Roman, 247, 285
  Thucydidean, 11
history. *See spatium historicum*
  apodeiktikē, 315
  as a body, 316
  kata meros, 316–18, 320, 325, 331, 382
  moral, 324
  opposition with myth, 6, 62. *See* myth
  philosophy of, 12, 321, 323, 333
  tragic, 13, 358
  universal, 316, 321, 382
  uses of, 254
Homer, 123, 374, 379–80, 385
Horace, 232, 352
hyperbole, 359, 371
hypomnema, 291
hypotheseis stenas, 332

identity, authorial, 362
Ides of March, 13, 336, 350–1
Illyricum, 273
imitation, 142, 148, 354, 378
impartiality, 371
inconsistency, 8
indeterminacy, interpretive, 8
informant, 119, 122, 171, 217, 220, 285, 380
innovation, 14–15

General Index

instability, barbarian, 285
interaction, divine-human, 7
interests, antiquarian, 45
International Relations (theory), 266
intervention, authorial, 134
Ionia/Ionians, 127, 162, 211
Ionian Revolt, 147, 220
irony, 7, 9, 102–3
Iser, W., 2, 33–4
Isthmus, 186
Italy, 233, 249, 273, 281, 316

Jacoby, F., 6, 44–5, 65–70
Jerome, 68–9
Josephus, 341
judgement, suspension of, 8
Jugurtha, 363

kataskeuē, 330
krisis, 330
ktema es aiei, 265

Lacedaemonians. *See* Sparta/Spartans
Lampsacus, 52–3
landscape, virtual, 221
language, human, 8, 136–7
Laodicea ad Lycum, 303
laudatio, 226
Leonidas, 125
Lepidus, M. Aemilius, 336
letter, 229–30, 274–5, 279, 286, 295–6, 306, 311, 343, 348
lex Cornelia maiestatis, 273
lex Iulia repetundarum, 273
lexis, 330
libellum memoriale, 275
libertas, 342, 350
Libya, 144
Livy, 6, 82, 153, 285, 291, 351–2, 357, 362, 365, 385
  preface, 82–3
logographoi, 374
logoi, 143
Longinus, Ps.-, 207–9, 211, 215, 217, 223
Lucilius, C., 232, 240
Lucius Verus, 230
Lucretius, 93
Lugdunum, 355, 363
Lycurgus, 257
Lydia, 221

Macedonia, 249
Maeander (river), 216
Maiandrius, 130

Mantinea, battle of, 385
Mantineans, 359
map
  cartographic and hodological knowledge, 221
  mental, 221
  of Aristagoras, 220–1
Marathon, battle of, 27, 130, 168–9, 174, 247, 254–5
Marcus of Byzantium, 304
Mardonius, 27–8, 125, 137, 146, 161–2, 169–70, 174–6, 247, 278
Massagetae, 161
Massalia, 55
material, archival, 275
Media, 145, 148
Megara, 37
Melos/Melians, 31–3
memoirs, 224, 230, 279
  first person, 226
  in verse, 232
  Roman, 9, 225
memory, historical, 206
Memphis, 110–12
messenger, 169, 287
method, 22, 25, 29, 38, 43, 89, 279–80, 286, 289, 316, 320, 326
  Finnish. *See* method, historic-geographic
  historic-geographic, 42
  historiographical, 328
methodology, 6, 262, 290, 326, 328
methodology, historical, 328
Miletus/Milesians, 46–7, 220
Miltiades, 247
Miltiades the Elder, 46
mimesis, 220, 222
Mimnermus, 179
Minos, 63–4, 71
Mithradates VI, 272
Moeris, lake of, 117
mousikē, 180, 187, 191, 202
Muse(s), 1, 9, 179–83, 188–91, 199–200, 202, 204, 251, 385
Mycale, battle of, 170
myth, 15. *See spatium mythicum*
  opposition with history, 6, 62
mythical
  as temporality, 6
Mytilene/Mytilenaeans, 32, 266, 268, 277

Naris, 45–7
narratee, 9, 206–9, 211–13, 215–17, 219–20, 222–3
  extratextual, 208
  fictionalized, 218

472 *General Index*

narratee (cont.)
  intratextual, 208
  positionality of, 209
narrative, 213
  biographical, 232
  deformation of, 13
  depersonalized, 276, 279, 282
  first-person, 11, 222, 225, 235, 240
  justifying, 279
  logic, 281
  of a disaster, 354, 360, 370–1
  of a fire. *See* narrative, of a disaster
  oral, 43, 58
  second-person, 9, 208–9, 217
  self-contained, 280
  techniques. *See* techniques, narrative
  third-person, 11, 245, 280, 282
narrative device. *See* techniques, narrative
narratological topics. *See* techniques, narrative
narratology, 208–9, 222
  feminist, 4–5
  post-classical, 14
narrator, 206, 213, 215, 217–18, 220, 279–80
  authoritative, 12
  biographic, 294
  distinction from author, 383. *See* author
  first-person, 7, 211, 222
  historiographic, 294
  historiographical, 7
  impersonal, 211
  internal, 221
  intrusive, 12
  omniscient, 250
  self-representation, 206
Nero, 13, 248, 352, 354, 357, 360–6, 368–72, 387
Nerva, 310, 388
Nicetes of Smyrna, 299
Nicias, 31, 33, 243–4, 258
Nicolaus of Damascus, 13, 336–48, 350–1
Nicomedia, 355
Nile, 214, 216, 218
nobiles, 225
nomoi, 168
  Persian, 163, 211
Numidians, 363

objectivity, 11, 263, 297, 371
oida, 295, 298, 308
Olympia, 297, 304
Olympic Games, 170
omission, 11, 280
orality, 15, 210
  storytelling, 60

testimony, 24, 311
text, 210
order, Roman, 285
originality, 354
Ostia, 355
Other, the, 8, 158, 165, 167–8, 170

Pactyes, 164
pamphlet, 236
Papremis, battle of, 107–8
paradigm shift. *See* gamechanger
paradigms, causal, 8
paradosis, 323, 325
parasiōpaō, 329
paratext, 12, 309
Parian Marble, 69
Parion, 52–5
Pausanias, 122, 131, 161–2, 377
Peisistratids, 146, 153, 376
Peisistratus, 146, 377
Pelasgians, 144
Peloponnese, 175
Peloponnesian League, 34
Peloponnesian War, 34, 38, 269
Pelusium, 105–7, 214–15
Pentekontaetia, 376–7, 382
perceptions, cross-cultural, 175
performance
  divine, 197
  human, 199
Periander, 50
Pericles, 11, 34–7, 148, 243–4, 265, 269, 378, 380
Perseus, 145
Perseus of Macedon, 238
Persia/Persians, 25, 27–9, 44, 62, 102–3, 107, 126, 130–3, 136, 143, 145, 152, 158–65, 172–3, 175–6, 211, 214–15, 220, 222, 254, 278, 381
Persian Empire, 168
Persian Wars, 123, 137, 255, 376
person
  first, 215, 220, 224, 228, 230, 235, 237, 239–40, 280
  second, 15, 206, 208–9, 212, 214–15, 222–3
  third, 226, 231, 235, 279–80, 373
perspective
  of the narrator, 284
persuasion
  strategies of, 354
  top-down model of, 15
Pharsalus, battle of, 282
phasi, 300–4
Philinus of Akragas, 321–2, 324

General Index

Philistus, 374
philosopher, political, 10, 269
philosophy, political, 10–11, 15
Philostratus, 12, 292–312, 375
Phoenicians, 136, 159, 381
Phrygia, 221
Phylarchus, 331, 359, 382
Pindar, 9, 168, 179–205
  conception of authority, 179, 200, 202, 205
  divine model of authority, 181
Plataea
  battle of, 30, 125, 131, 137, 147, 152, 162, 170, 174, 247
  Theban attack on, 36, 277
Plato, 200, 202, 319, 322
Pliny, 97, 249, 386
Plutarch, 10, 14, 36, 55, 121, 195, 200, 288, 336–7, 339, 341, 346, 374, 389–91
  On the Malice of Herodotus, 121–4, 132, 137–8
  self-praise and self-presentation, 241–58
poeticae fabulae, 6
poets, choral
  as *chorodidaskaloi*, 186
Pohlenz, M., 65, 69
point of view
  non-Greek, 158, 160, 162, 167–8, 170–1, 175–6
  non-Roman, 285, 290
  of the writer, 279
point-of-view, manipulation of, 9
Polemo, 294–5, 299, 305, 309
Polus of Agrigentum, 301
Polybius, 5, 12, 14, 229, 278, 280, 315–34, 359, 367, 374, 382–5, 391
  as historical theorist, 328
  historiographical neologisms, 12, 315
  self-positioning, 14
Polycrates, 63–4, 71, 130, 139, 141, 379
polyphony, 7
Pompey, 229, 271–3, 281–2, 287–8
Posidonius, 374
Potidaea, 36
power, discursive, 15
Pratinas, 194
prejudices, 175
Presocratics, 8, 148
priests, Egyptian, 78, 159, 212
princeps, 388
probability, use of, 282, 284
Proclus of Naucratis, 297
Protagoras, 148
Ps.-Skylax, 46
Ps.-Skymnos, 46
Psammetichus, 131, 146

pseudos, 326
psychological approach, 209
ptōcheuontes pragmatōn, 332
Ptolemy of Naucratis, 300
Puteoli, 355
Pydna, battle of, 238
pyramids, 117–18
Pythagoras, 144

Quintilian, 290, 367

Ravenna, 249
reader, 9, 206–7, 209–10, 212, 215, 217–18, 221–3, 253, 279, 287
  as symmetrical collaborator, 7
reception, 11, 214, 217
references, intratextual, 7
religious practices
  Egyptian, 167
Remi, 280
report, 11, 74, 80, 119, 121, 216–17, 220, 272, 274–6, 280, 284–5, 287, 289, 299, 323, 345
rerum gestarum monumenta, 6
Res gestae, 275
res publica, 13, 283, 342, 350, 389
Rhine, 271, 287
Rhodians, 237–9
Roman Empire, 228, 248, 254
Romanness, 286
Rome/Romans, 6, 11–12, 14, 26, 85–7, 89–90, 93, 153, 224, 226, 229, 231–2, 238, 240, 249, 251, 254–5, 272, 274–6, 278–9, 285–6, 289–91, 310, 316, 335, 337–8, 344–7, 349, 352, 354–6, 360, 362, 364–5, 367, 369, 371, 373, 375, 382–3, 391
  fire in AD 64, 13
Romulus, 6, 87, 90–1, 95–6, 257
rostra, 226
Royal Road, 221
Rutherford, R.B., 124–8
Rutilius Rufus, P., 224–5

Salamis, battle of, 30, 130, 132, 152, 170, 173
Sallust, 53, 94, 226, 277, 281, 291, 363, 385
Samos/Samians, 130, 144, 146
Sardis, 59, 63, 164, 168, 220
satire, 10, 226, 232, 234–5
Scaliger, J.J., 6, 69–72
Scione, 32
Scipio Hispanus, Cn. Cornelius, 233
Scopelianus, 293–4, 303, 305, 307
Scyles (Scythian king), 166–7
Scythia/Scythians, 116, 127, 143, 166–8, 176, 210, 218–20

General Index

second person. *See* person
selection, 94, 280, 333
selectivity, 11, 21
self-address, 208, 212
self-authorization, 5
self-expression, 233, 240
self-portrait, 285
self-praise, 10, 288
self-presentation, 10, 225, 238, 390
  epigraphical, 226
Senate, 228–30, 237–9, 273–4, 279, 281, 286,
  335–8, 343–4, 349
senatus consultum, 228
Seneca the Elder, 357
Seneca the Younger, 91, 363–4
Sennacherib, 27
sententiae, 239
Sesostris, 116–17, 145
Sextus Empiricus, 318
Sextus Pompeius, 336
Sicilian expedition, 33
Sicily, 227–9, 233, 242
Sicyon, 341
Simonides, 189, 194
Smerdis the Magus, 140
Solon, 133, 147, 179, 257
sōmatoeidēs. See history as a body
sophists, 295–6
  second-century, 302, 311
Sophocles, 327
source
  oral, 7, 218, 220, 222
  written, 295–6, 299, 301
Spain, 228, 288, 336
Sparta/Spartans, 30–2, 35–7, 125, 162, 169,
  220–1, 242, 247, 256, 265, 277, 381
spatium historicum, 6, 62–72, 74–5, 78–9
spatium mythicum, 6, 62–9, 72, 74–5, 78–9
speaker, authoritative, 240
speech, 10, 226, 236–7, 277, 282, 287
  direct, 11, 282
  indirect, 11, 282
  invention of, 5
  second person, 9
sphragis, 10
statement(s)
  first-person, 15, 205
  of autopsy, 7
  on methodology, 290
  paradoxical, 7
  self-referential, 189–90
storytelling, 6, 58
Strabo, 46, 60
strategies
  rhetorical, 12

Strymon, 47
style, 8, 12, 43, 210–11, 230–2, 235, 239–40,
  272, 275–6, 278, 282, 304–7, 329–30,
  360, 377–8, 383–4, 391
  first-person, 227, 230
subscriptio, 228, 308
Suessiones, 280
Suetonius, 13, 154, 336, 343, 346–7, 349, 354,
  362, 364–5, 367, 369–70, 374
Sulla, 224–5, 282, 350
superstition, 242–3
Susa, 220
Sybaris, 48–52
symplokē, 316
Syracuse, 33, 277
Syria, 140

ta deonta, 263, 268
Tacitus, 13, 92, 94, 153, 354–5, 373, 375,
  385–9
Talthybius, 147
technique, rhetorical, 210
techniques, narrative, 20, 22–3, 279
  chronology, 6, 38–40
  gaps and omissions, 6, 33–8
  irony, 101
  motivation, attribution of, 6
Tencteri, 286
terateia, 331
Thebes/Thebans, 35–6, 183, 187
Themistocles, 122, 132, 138, 175, 244, 247,
  257–8, 377
Theocritus, 231, 322
Theodotus, 308
Theognis, 163–4, 175, 179
Theopompus, 328
Theramenes, 38
Thermopylae, battle of, 30, 125, 152, 170–4
Theseus, 257
third person. *See* person
Third Punic War, 323
Thirty Tyrants, 39
Thirty Years' Peace, 34–5
Thrace, 148
Thrasybulus, 38, 50
Thucydides, 10–11, 13, 21–3, 25–6, 30–9, 47,
  64, 74, 83, 89, 162, 246, 277–8, 280–1,
  285–8, 290, 296, 303, 309, 311, 320, 363,
  373–4, 382, 389, 391
  Archaeology, 14, 73, 378–9
  in opposition to Herodotus, 375–82
  Mytilenean Debate, 261–70
Tiberius, 387
Timaeus, 326, 328, 332, 374, 382
time, 8, 11, 62–79, 134, 137, 148, 207, 288–9

General Index

475

Timoleon, 242
to katholou, 320
tour guide, 101, 104, 217
tradition, 13–14, 60, 71, 73, 116, 142, 154, 172,
    293, 300–3, 315, 325, 359, 369, 371,
    374–5, 380, 382, 389, 391
  historical, 13, 70, 72–3, 372
  historiographical, 3, 12, 14–15, 65, 328, 331,
    333–4, 336–7, 342, 344, 351
  intellectual, 8
  local, 58, 79, 205
  musical, 189
  oral, 6–7, 9, 26, 43, 91, 110
  poetic, 77, 79, 368, 372
  textual, 12
Trajan, 310, 354, 388
travel, virtual, 9, 214, 217
Trojan War, 67, 75, 159–60
trustworthiness, 101, 109, 114, 117, 119,
    164
truth, 2, 6, 10, 19–23, 32, 39–40, 66, 77, 125–6,
    128, 132–3, 136, 138, 140, 149, 163, 168,
    170, 174, 213, 290, 304, 316–17, 319,
    321–2, 324–5, 333, 376, 380–1
  historical, 10, 352
  rhetoric of, 5
  theory of, 15
truthfulness, 114
tryphē, 48
tychē, 148
tyrannicide, 14, 339, 341–2

urbs capta, 356, 367
Usipetes, 286

Varro, 6, 64–5, 69–74
Varus of Perge, 307
Vedius Damianus, 298
Veii, 362
Vercingetorix, 271, 286–7
Verres, 227–8
Vindolanda tablets, 227
Virgil, 85, 357, 364, 368
virtus, 286
Vitruvius, 355
von Leyden, W., 63–6

White, H., 20
Wiseman, T.P., 2, 21
Woodman, A.J., 2, 20
writings
  autobiographical, 10, 232
  chronological, 74
  geographic, 210

Xenophanes, 165, 175
Xenophon, 21, 23, 38–40, 231, 275, 280, 282,
    286–8, 374–5, 384
Xerxes, 27–30, 129, 131–2, 146, 159, 161–2,
    169, 171–6
xympasa gnomē, 264, 268

zētēsis, 262